# The Ultimate Guide to Bowhunting Skills, Tactics, and Techniques

# The Ultimate Guide to Bowhunting Skills, Tactics, and Techniques

*edited by* **Jay Cassell**

Skyhorse Publishing

Skyhorse Publishing books may be purchased in bulk at special discounts for sales promotion, corporate gifts, fund-raising, or educational purposes. Special editions can also be created to specifications. For details, contact the Special Sales Department, Skyhorse Publishing, 307 West 36th Street, 11th Floor, New York, NY 10018 or info@skyhorsepublishing.com.



Visit our website at www.skyhorsepublishing.com.

10 9 8 7 6 5 4 3 2 1

Library of Congress Cataloging-in-Publication Data is available on file.

Cover design by Owen Corrigan

ISBN: 978-1-62914-398-9
Ebook ISBN: 978-1-63220-794-4

Printed in Canada

# Contents

# Part 1

# *Bowhunting*

# Introduction

With more advanced equipment, more land opening up to bowhunters (especially in suburban areas), and with deer numbers skyrocketing past the 30 million mark nationwide, it's no wonder that the number of bowhunters has also increased—to almost five million at last count, out of an estimated 40 million hunters nationwide. At its core, bowhunting is a challenging sport, requiring constant practice and careful studying of the quarry. For a hunter to succeed, he needs to be at the top of his game. Everything must be right. The hunter must be downwind of his quarry; his scent must be kept to a minimum; his camo must blend with the surroundings and the foliage (or lack thereof); he must be able to get within bow range of the deer, which in most cases in around 30 yards; if hunting from a stand, his stand must be situated in a likely area for a buck or doe to travel—perhaps just off an intersection of trails, or in a funnel area between two knobs in the woods, or near trail that leads to feeding or bedding areas. Not only that, but the hunter must know his equipment. Even today, when compound bows and crossbows promote greater accuracy, the fact is that you must practice, and practice quite a bit, before the season. Shoot your bow from all angles—from your roof, uphill, downhill, sitting, standing, you name it. For when that moment comes and a big bucks suddenly materializes within bow range, you want to be efficient, and make a perfect shot. Yes, wounds can occur, but you want to cut back on the chances of that happening as much as possible. And when you finally do make that perfect shot, and you take the animal you've been envisioning all off-season, well, there is no feeling of accomplishment quite like it. Then, of course, later, when you sit down to eat a venison roast or chop or steak, you'll know that this is something you made happen. Only you.

In this, *The Ultimate Guide to Bowhunting Skills, Tactics, and Techniques*, I've pulled together a variety of bowhunting experts, including the likes of Peter Fiduccia, Steve Bartylla, John Trout, and Todd Kuhn. The expertise they bring to the table, the tips, tactics, and techniques they reveal, can only help but make you a better bowhunter, no matter what your current skill level may be. And that, in turn, will help you take more deer and, hopefully, share your improved bowhunting skills with others. And it doesn't get any better than that.

—Jay Cassell

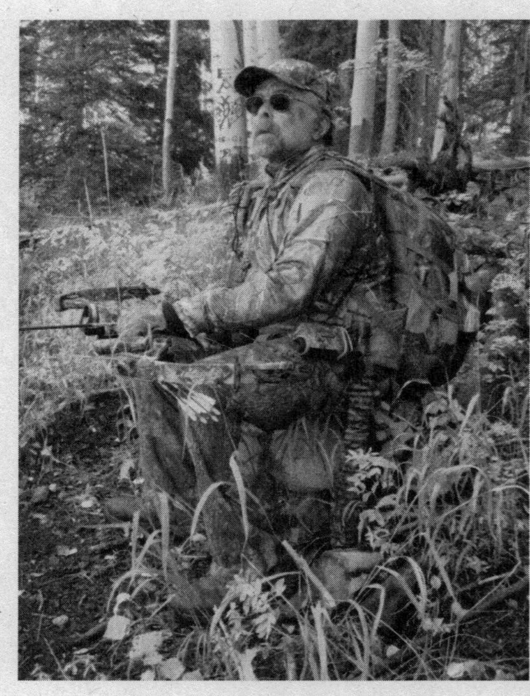

# Pursuit of the Perfect Arrow

My first "bow," hand-fashioned from a heavy willow branch, was as crooked as a dog's leg. It was strung with cotton cord spooled on a wooden spindle that had been bought from a dusty mercantile in upstate New York. The cord was destined for my grandmothers clothes line.

My grandfather, an outdoorsman, squirreled away the remnant twine on a hand-hewed header in a tool shed he'd built in the early 1920s. Its roof pitched and yawed, having grown temperamental, afflicted from decades of heavy snows and legume growth that enshrined the ancient structure. Teetering on its floor joists, its once firm stance had succumbed to the roots of a neighboring balsam fir.

To a four-year-old, that shed held a unique fascination for a vivid imagination and a spirit for adventure. Rusty tin-lidded jars of milky glass held untold treasures: snelled hooks, brass buttons, curtain rings, and a pocketknife that was bequeathed to me when I turned old enough to handle it with respect and care.

On the front step of this shed, my grandfather spun dramatic tales of his adolescence and fascination with the bow. Once he finished, I'd run off with that stick and twine in hand, searching for rabid grizzlies and other foe worthy of attention from my finely-crafted weapon.

My first real bow was a Fred Bear. I remember it vividly. I stood tall in the backyard of our house in central Florida, my lemonwood Ranger a thing of beauty in the eyes of a youthful beholder. It had its share of nicks and scratches—all badges of courage etched by mighty warriors from distant lands who too stood tall behind this bow. Mighty men of stern resolve who'd fought hand-to-hand against overwhelming odds. They'd been bloodied in battles, but had emerged victorious. The spoils of victory were theirs.

Author on an early morning South Dakota turkey hunt.

My knobby knees rattled as I strained to bend those limbs and stretch the frayed string. I longed to be a warrior, too. Years later, my mom told me the bow's patina wasn't earned in battle but from bouncing from one garage sale to the next. Nonetheless, for one scrawny kid, the seed was sown and the dream was born.

**Fast Forward**

Those who haven't been exposed to archery often ask me why I shoot. For me, (and hundreds of thousands of other archery fanatics), the answer is relatively simple: I love it. For us, the bow and arrow are somehow addictive, casting a spell of intrigue and romance over those who shoulder it.

I consider myself an atypical archer, shooting around sixty arrows a day on weekdays, close to double that on weekends. For anyone who drops by my house, it's immediately obvious that I'm an addict. For starters, there's a hundred-yard range in my backyard. Well-worn bag targets hang on pressure treated 4x4s, arranged incrementally and staggered at twenty, forty, sixty, eighty, a hundred yards. The ragged target faces are testament of the hundreds, if not thousands, of arrows they've been pounded with over time.

Now that I live north of the Mason-Dixon line, there are occasions when the weather turns persnickety. When it does, I move indoors to my twenty-yard range in my basement. While my wife isn't overly thrilled with the idea of arrows zinging around in the basement, I've yet to hit anything down there of real or sentimental value.

Archery has since morphed into a lifetime pursuit of perfection—perfection in the sense of the human machine (that of muscle, tendon, and bone) mastering the mechanical machine (the bow's components).

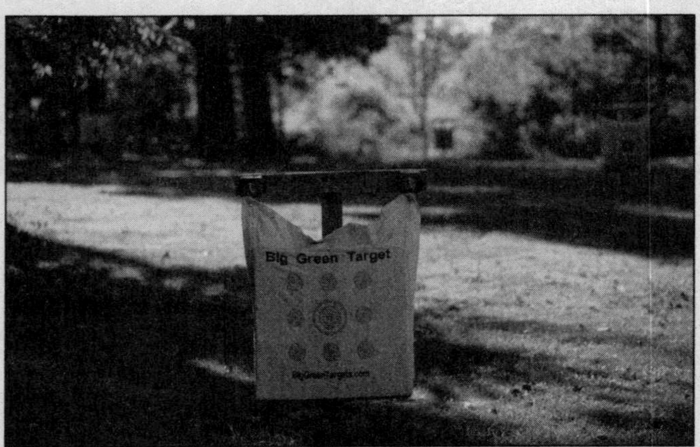


Cause for Intrigue: 100-yard backyard range.

Archery is a sport of solitude, not one given to crowds.

As I mentioned, I have a hundred-yard range. A bag target hanging 100-yards away is a daunting sight. For most visitors, it holds such intrigue. Those uninitiated to the archery game immediately assume they've stumbled on a neighborhood gun range. Once I explain the function of my range, visitors are stupefied. The first question out of everyone's mouth is "How far is it to that target down there," there being the farthest target. And so begins my sermon on the virtues of archery.

You see, archery is an odd sport—one of solitude. Not unlike that of the long distance runner. It's a sport of seclusion and relative recluse for those who choose to participate. There are no referees, no umpires, or line judges. There's no clock to run out other than when daylight recedes into night on a day's hunt. There's no overtime—no mulligan, handicaps, or cheering crowds. For team members, the uniform is a favorite brand of camouflage.

Archery is a sport requiring discipline of the hand, head, and heart. You see, to excel you must train the hand through much repetition and discipline the head through mental calisthenics. And to *really* excel, you must possess a heart whose desire is to achieve.

In engineering terms, a compound bow is a simple machine. It's so simple, you'll be hard pressed to name more than five or so components that actually move. In contrast, an automobile has more than 20,000 moving parts. But how could this mechanical contrivance, one of such rudimentary intent—that of casting arrows downrange—possess such a degree of intrigue for countless generations of archery enthusiasts?

When the compound was first introduced, it was much maligned by traditionalists. It was, after all, like shooting a gun, right? Well, not so much. The modern compound, with its array of accessories, is at best only as accurate as the human machine throttling it.

A bowhunter's team uniform is his favorite camo brand.

While the act of drawing the bow isn't too difficult, it is extremely challenging to do it with a complete concert of an amalgam of muscles. When working in perfect concert, the mind and body achieves flawless form and the perfect shot. While most believe that is defined as a "pie-plate sized group at twenty yards," that is far from "perfection attained."

Achieving the perfect arrow with a compound is rare. No matter how good you get (or think you are), you can still improve. No archer can consistently hit the mark. In fact, it is for that reason we keep coming back to the sport. It's what draws newbies and challenges the most ardent of archers to continue improving. It is, in its purest form, a lifetime pursuit of the perfect arrow.

## Making a Case for Compounds and Bowhunting

Bowhunting has experienced unparalleled growth as a sport. A sport of meager beginnings, the first "compound" was kludged together by Holless Wilbur Allen in the mid-1960s. Allen's contraption was a longbow with the limb tips cut off. He then lashed crude pulleys to the limbs and configured a makeshift string and cable system. Crude at best, the first "compound" cobbled together would be the predecessor of all that is "compound" today.

Today's modern compound is an astounding feat of mechanical engineering and materials science. From its meager beginnings in a tinkerer's crowded Missouri garage, the compound has morphed into a stealthy, powerful machine capable of clustering arrows into tight target groups at exaggerated distances.

### Weird Science

With the whirlwind of advances that we witness each year, it seems these machines are only

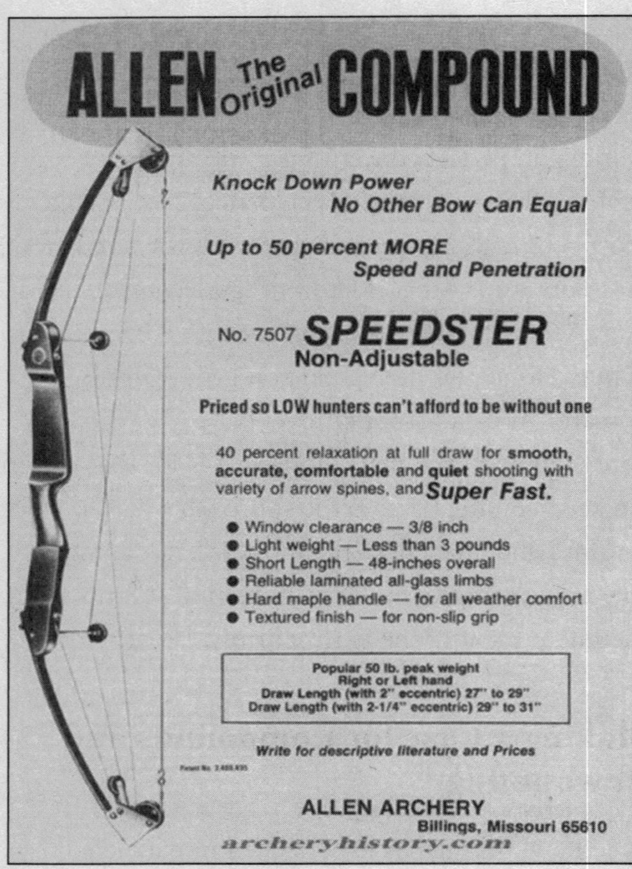


The original Wilbur Allen compound bow advertisement.

physically limited by the imagination of those who use them. Advances in materials science continue, offering compound designers more options. Solid fiberglass limbs have been replaced by limbs reinforced and lightened with space-age carbon fibers. Carbon nanotube technology will be available in compound limbs within the next year or so, offering even more stout and resilient materials from which to design and build archery components.

New copolymers blend resins with long-strand carbon fibers, and other proprietary fillers are incorporated into designs with improved performance. This slurry is molded into parts and assemblies that rival machined aircraft quality aluminum for structural integrity and are physically lighter.

Scientific advancements in coatings have contributed to the rapid advancements in compounds. Progress in fluoropolymers, aluminum surfacing science, and elastomeric coatings have led to reduced friction on bow component surfaces, as well as resistance to wear. All of these have led to more mechanically efficient bows.

Cam systems are modeled using complex computer aided design (CAD) programs that plot their efficiencies and match them perfectly to the compound's limbs, riser, string, and cable systems. These programs can actually simulate drawing and firing the compound; enabling design engineers to predict where structural inefficiencies may manifest prior to cutting the first prototyping part. These efficiencies make a more rugged bow with higher mechanical efficiencies, tighter tolerances, and top-end performance while lowering the overall mass weight.

### Technology Rules

As compounds have evolved, so has the sport of bowhunting. Modern compounds are capable of harvesting animals at dizzying distances. Consequently, the evolution of accessories and hunting tactics has accelerated to keep pace with the quantum leaps in bow performance.

Early bowhunters carried compounds into the field that were capable "of astounding performance" (as one was advertised) comparable to lobbing arrows at 180 feet-per-second with a whopping 30-some foot pounds of kinetic energy. These modern-day compound predecessors limited the bowhunter to shoot distances of 20 yards or less. In stark comparison, today's compounds are capable of shooting arrows more than 360 feet-per-second and carry over 100 foot pounds of kinetic energy. Today, a bowhunter's effective range is limited only by his or her physical ability, not by his or her equipment.

Beyond the bow itself, modern archery equipment has evolved, keeping pace with the advances in compound technologies. Sights, arrows, arrow rests, stabilizers, quivers, and other ancillary equipment have made the bow more efficient while increasing the enjoyment of shooting.

Even with a bow's impressive performance, it's still a primitive weapon. So why bowhunt? Well, the answer is quite rudimentary. For me, bowhunting presents challenges unparalleled by other forms of hunting, and the up-close-and-personal style of bowhunting adds to the challenge. Having to slip within a short physical distance from the animal for a shot also adds to the excitement. Narrowing this distance also requires the hunter to be more skilled, both in woodsmanship and in the skill required to make an ethical kill shot. Neither of these are easy nor are they learned anywhere other than in the woods or afield.

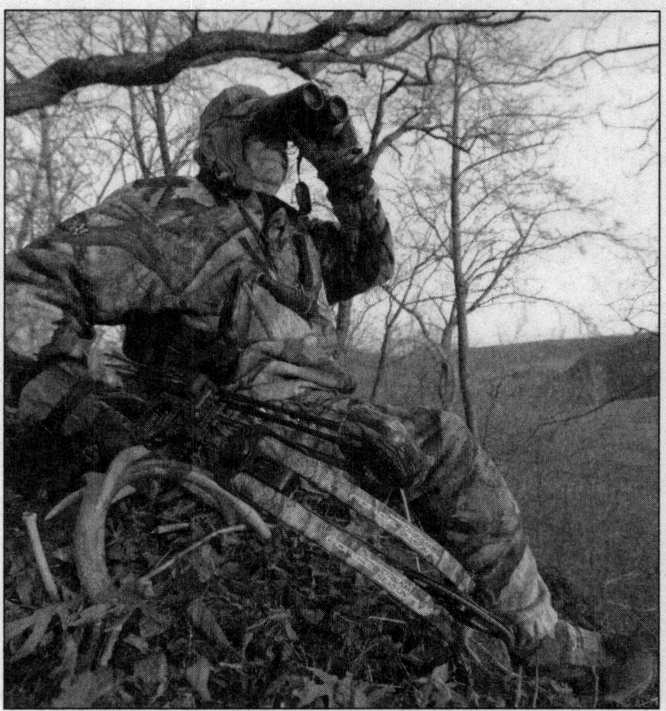

Bowhunter glassing field from the confines of a ground blind fashioned from native prunings.

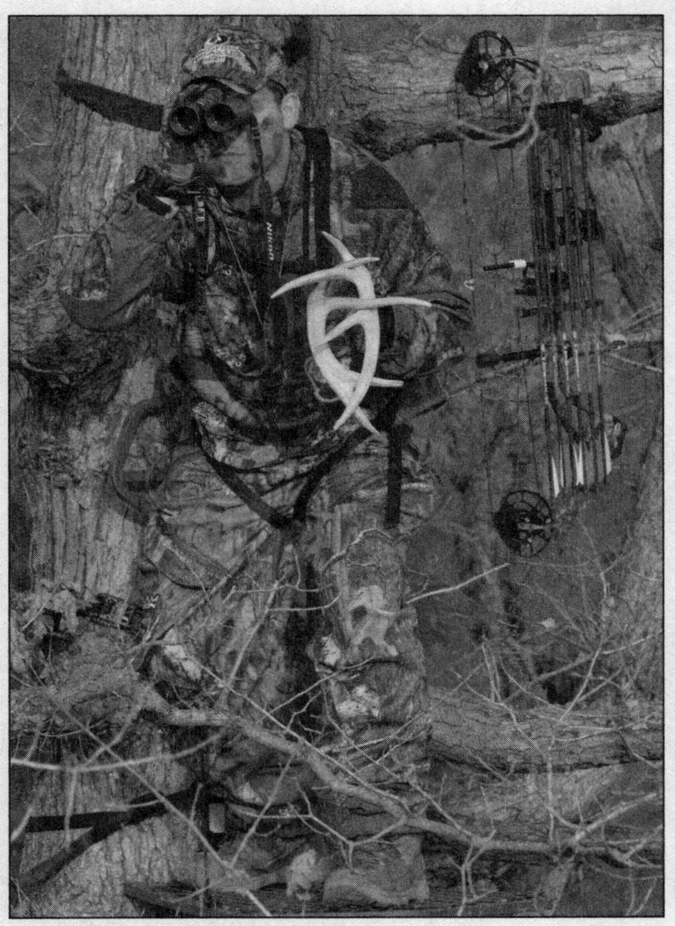

A bowhunter glasses from his elevated perch.

Contrast this with hunting using high-powered rifles. Please understand first and foremost that I hold no prejudice or malice toward rifle hunters. I have hunted with a rifle and loved every minute of it. However, I prefer bowhunting. That being said, rifle hunting removes some (not all) of the woodsmanship factors—those skills requiring the hunter to negotiate close to his or her target animal.

**Spot-and-Stalk, Treestands, and Ground Blinds.**

The need to get close presents significant challenges, depending on your method of hunting—spot-and-stalking, tree standing, or ground blinding.

Getting close using a tree stand or ground blind requires hours of scouting and surveillance. Each observation is used to paint a tactical picture of what a particular deer is doing.

Once this is decided, the bowhunter can formulate a hunting strategy. But it doesn't end once you're committed to a specific tree or ground blind position—the game has typically just begun. Rarely does a new tree stand or ground blind position pay off with an animal. As you hunt and observe the movement of the animals, the strategy changes and so the hunter must evolve and adapt.

The same rigors apply to spot-and-stalking. However, for me, spot-and-stalking is the most challenging (and rewarding) bowhunting technique. It demands incredible bowmanship, that of being capable of executing the most difficult of nontraditional shots. Nontraditional as in kneeling, seated, crouched, angled, leaning, and so on.

Adding to the difficulty is the need to be physically capable of closing the distance between the animal and yourself. This may include literally hours of crawling, slipping, jogging, and anything in between. All require the bowhunter to be in top physical shape.

Spot-and-stalking requires an archer be able to execute shots from a number of positions.

The challenge is not all physical, however. You must also consider the mental chess match you enter into with the animal and the environment. Every move made to negotiate closer to the animal is predicated on past experiences, those that educate the bowhunter on what can be done tactically and those that cannot be done tactically but are still successful. In most cases, sadly, the animal and the environment win the chess match. Whether the animal sees you or the wind changes, tipping the animal of your approach—you lose. That's what makes it challenging.

### An Economy of Scale

One of the last reasons folks are flocking to bow-hunting (both compounds and crossbows) is there simply isn't enough contiguous ground on which to rifle hunt. Larger tracts of farmlands have been split, segmented, and subdivided throughout the past few decades. The family farms of yesteryear simply don't appear with the frequency they once did. Challenging economic times have led to family farms being sold off in small plots.

So a depressed economy has led to an economy of space for hunters. These plots, sometimes as small as a few acres and once a large aggregate of property, were hunted with high-powered rifles. Now, they no longer offer a safe opportunity to gun hunt. However, in contrast, these small tracts offer ample bowhunting space. In fact, my largest deer to date was taken on a postage stamp-sized tract of land in a neighborhood that was adjacent to a farm. These small tracts often times offer protected sanctuary for mammoth whitetails.

### An Abridged History of Archery

Early historical facts surrounding the bow and its development are sketchy at best. As a weapon, it

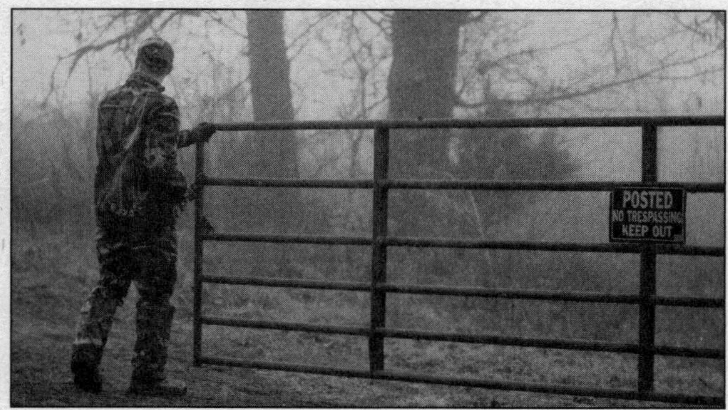


Large expansive tracts of land are shrinking at an accelerated pace.

dates back a few millenniums As such, much of what is surmised about early archers has been discovered through archeological digs. To date, the oldest archery relics were unearthed in Africa. Arrowheads discovered in the area date back to approximately 25000 BC.

More than 5,000 miles south of Africa, scientists discovered a burial tomb in Italy containing a skeleton with a fragmented flint arrowhead lodged in the pelvis. Through carbon dating, scientists estimate that the flint dates back to 11000 BC. Ancient Egyptian drawings dating from 7500 to 5000 BC depict humans using early bows for hunting food and for warfare.

Scientists estimate that around 2800 BC, the first composite bow (built from two separate materials glued together) was made of wood, tipped with animal horn, and lashed together with animal sinew and some type of ancient glue. The bowstring was made of sheep intestines, which launched very light arrows.

In battles, early Egyptian armies utilized archers on chariots to outflank the enemy on the battlefield. The chariots and skilled archers proved too much for opposing foot soldiers and their handheld weaponry. Literature found in ancient China dated between 1500 and 1027 BC included the first description of crossbows built and used in China.

Somewhere around 250 BC, the Parthian civilization (now modern Iran and Afghanistan) mounted expert archers on horseback. These archers developed an odd but highly effective battle technique. The archers would pretend to flee the battlefied, and the enemy would give chase. Once their opponents were in bow range, they would turn around on their horses and launch arrows back at the advancing army. Historians venture that this is where the term "parting shot" came from.

Qin Shihuang, the first emperor of China, was buried with six-thousand life-sized terracotta figures, some of which modeled carrying primitive crossbows. In Rome, a fellow named Sebastian was the commander of the Praetorian Guards for the Roman Emperor. He was shot to death with arrows when his deep Christian faith was discovered in 228 AD. Oddly enough, after being shot repeatedly and assumed dead, he was found alive and nursed back to health by family friends.

Once he was again healthy, Sebastian announced his Christian faith on the steps of the Emperor's palace. The guards were ordered to beat him to death with their clubs. After he was pummeled to death, his body was recovered by friends (probably the same ones that found him the first time) and was secretly buried in the catacombs under Rome. Sebastian became known as the Patron Saint of Archers.

Infamous Mongol warrior Genghis Khan was documented as utilizing composite bows of seventy pounds of draw weight and thumb ring releases to unleash the bowstring in 1208 AD. These bows were far superior to those used by other armies. These same Mongol soldiers would wrap silk cloth under their clothing as an arrow shield. When struck by an enemy's arrow, the silk fabric wrapped around the enemy's arrowhead, impeding penetration.

In 1307 AD, the legendary William Tell refused to bow (in a display of indentured servitude) to the imperial power and was thus ordered to shoot an apple off his son's head. Legend has it that Tell had another arrow hidden just in case he injured or killed his son. If he had, he was going to kill the government official who had ordered him to shoot at his son. Naturally, as the story goes, he successfully shot the apple off his sons head, sparing the official's life, too.

In 1346 AD, the French army included crossbowequipped soldiers. Their crossbows were powerful because they were drawn via hand crank. During the Battle of Crécy, Edward III of England led his army into battle against the French. The French were defeated handily when rain moistened their bowstrings the night before the battle, causing them to stretch. The waterlogged strings misfired and broke during the battle. The French, knowing the rain would compromise their strings, had placed them under their helmets during the rainstorm. The dry strings proved deadly.

Both crossbows and compound bows were considered the most effective battle weapons throughout what is modern day now modern day Europe and Asia until the early 1500s when the musket was invented. The year 1588 AD marked the last time bows were used in warfare when 10,000 soldiers from the English fleet, armed with muskets, defeated the Spanish Armada which was armed with bows. In the latter half of the 1600s, contests of archery skill became vogue in England.

In 1545, *Toxophilus,* a book about longbow archery by Roger Ascham, was published in London. Dedicated to King Henry VIII, it was the first book on archery written in English. According to legend, Ascham was a keen archer and scholar, lecturing at St John's College, Cambridge. The premise of the book was his defense of archery as a sport fitting of the educated.

The beginning of modern archery arguably dates back to 1879 when inventor Ephraim Morton of Plymouth, Massachusetts, was granted a United States patent for his wood handled bow equipped with steel rod limbs.

Archery gained international exposure as a sport when it was included in the Olympic Games in 1904, 1908, and 1920. It was discontinued for a while, and then reinstated during the 1972 Olympics. Meanwhile, in 1934, the first bowhunting season opened in Wisconsin, and in 1937, the

The patent Ephraim Morton of Plymouth received for a bow equipped with steel rod limbs marked the beginning of modern archery.

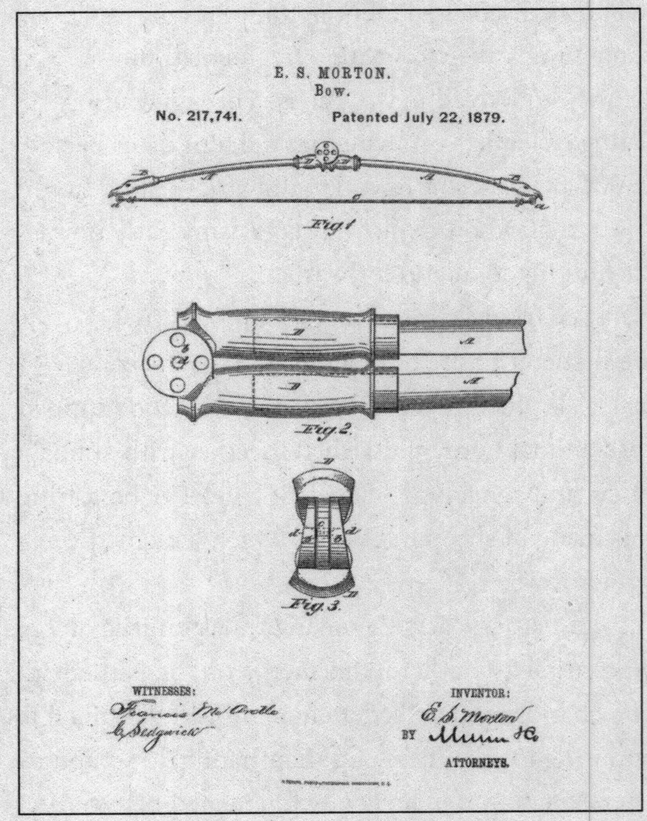

first modern sights were used in target archery competitions.

In 1939, James Easton began tinkering with manufacturing arrows out of aluminum instead of the traditional wood. By 1941, Larry Hughes won the American National Championship using Easton's aluminum arrows. Easton, of course, went on to found Easton Technical Products, which continues to be a leader in the archery industry. Easton produced its first trademarked aluminum arrows, the 24 SRT-X, in 1946.

In 1942, Earl Hoyt, Jr. founded Hoyt Archery, Co. In the decades to follow, Hoyt's company would go on to become one of the largest and most successful archery companies in the world. In 1951, Max Hamilton introduced the first plastic fletching, the Plastifletch, which marked the start of today's arrow vane industry.

James Easton, inventor of the aluminum arrow.

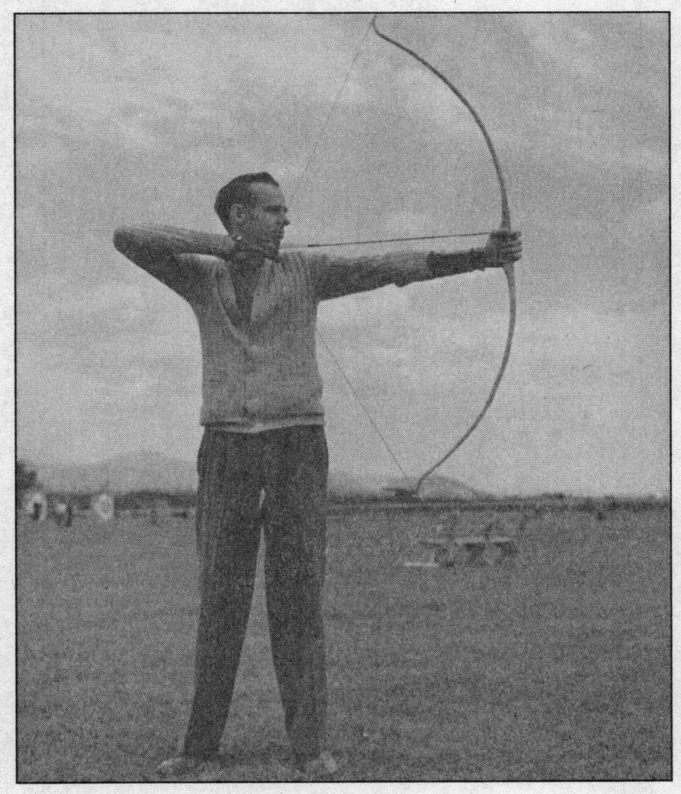

Earl Hoyt, founder of the company that bears his name.

Meanwhile, Fred Bear of Bear Archery introduced the first recurve bow in 1953. Previous bows were longbows, that is, bows with straight limbs. Bear's recurve had oddly shaped limbs that were purported to improve accuracy and increase speed.

By 1956, Earl Hoyt developed the first pistol grip bow handle, and Easton introduced his new XX75 aluminum arrow shaft in 1958. In 1966, Easton continued innovating arrows, extruding their X7 aluminum shaft. However, the largest advancement in modern archery is attributed to a Missourian.

Holless Wilbur Allen was born on July 12, 1909. Allen was a tinkerer and avid archer. Legend has it that Allen had grown tired of the drawbacks of traditional bows and longed for something faster and a bit easier to shoot.

So one day in his garage, Allen decided to cut the limb tips off his recurve and added two pulleys to decrease the amount of effort it took to draw the bow. With that, he had unknowingly launched the modern archery industry. His new prototype performed considerably better than his recurve, though it was very, very crude.

On June 23, 1966, Allen applied for a patent titled "Archery Bow with Draw-Force Multiplying

Archery icon Fred Bear in his shop.

Attachments." In December of 1969, the US Patent and Trademark Office issued Allen his patent (patent number 3,486,495). Allen joined forces with Tom Jennings, a revered traditional bowyer, to begin manufacturing of the first compound bows. Tragically, Allen was killed in a two-car collision on June 28, 1979.

In 1970, the compound bow and release aid made their national debut at the United States National Archery Competition. In 1971, Andy Simo, founder of New Archery Products (NAP), invented the first flipper-style rest, increasing archery accuracy ten-fold over shooting off a padded bow shelf. Simo's NAP would grow into one of the largest archery accessory companies, offering a wide variety of over-the-top engineered shooting components. That same year, archery legend Pete Shepley founded Precision Shooting Equipment (PSE) in Illinois. Shepley, an engineer by education, worked for Magnavox as a product engineer. Shepley's love for shooting led him to tinker with different designs. The company he

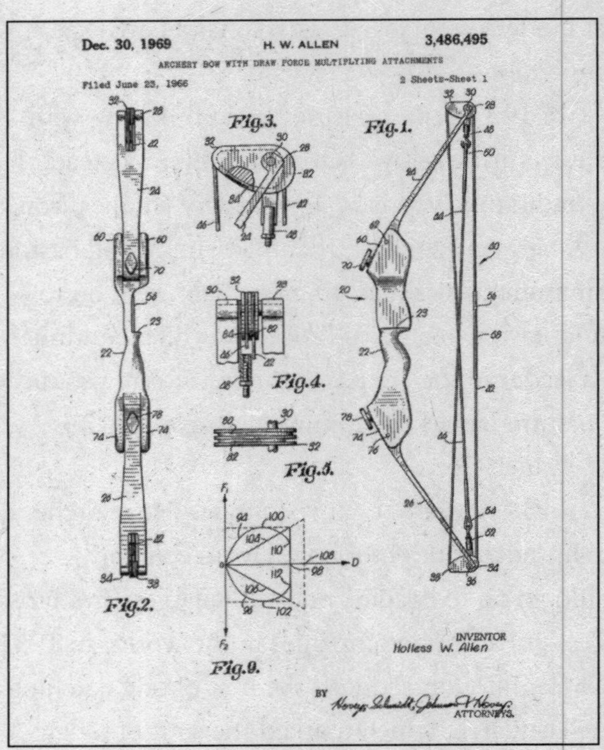


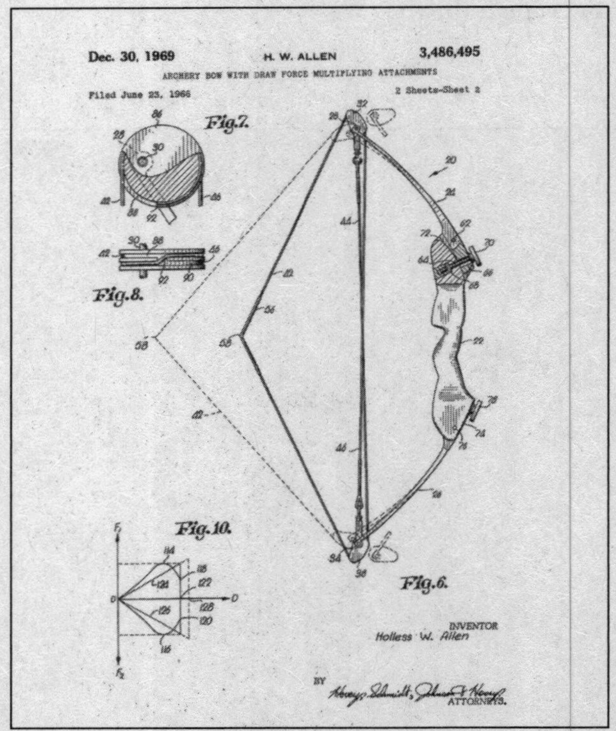


Holless Allen's original compound patent USPTO Patent 3,486,495 Archery Bow with Draw Force Multiplying Attachments

founded continues to lead the archery industry in innovative engineering today.

In 1974, archery legend Freddie Troncoso invented the first dual prong arrow rest, elevating archery accuracy even further over Simo's flipper-style rest. The year 1982 marked the first time compounds with actual lobe-shaped cams were introduced (previous compounds featured round wheels). The following year, Easton introduced the first carbon arrow shaft. From here on out, the timeline of improvements begin to blur as innovations are developed seemingly overnight and more archers and hunters become archery inventors and manufacturers.

**The Arch of Innovation**

Archery companies are pressured to one-up their products each year. Throughout the late 1960s and early 1970s, improvements in compound design were happening on an almost daily basis. The compound design was in its adolescence, and improvements came quickly and easily. These quantum leaps in technological advances continued through the eighties and nineties. The new millennium saw technological advances slow as the fundamental design of the compound had matured.

As is the case with any industry, the bowhunting industry evolved in cycles and

Andy Simo, founder of New Archery Products.

Precision Shooting Equipment's founder Pete Shepley, today and circa 1969.

eventually matured. The improvements that followed became incrementally smaller. For instance, solar power was harnessed and collected in the late 1 760s. Swiss scientist Horace de Saussure was credited with building the world's first solar collector in 1 767. Yet some 245 years later, our government still pitches "new" solar power green initiatives as though this idea is something new.

As a student of the game of archery, I watch each year for new and innovative improvements, yet they have appeared less frequently in the past twenty years. Admittedly, small tweaks in design are made by manufacturers and then advertised as earth-shattering new designs. In reality, these are simple twists on current designs polished with marketing hype.

For example, about ten years ago, one bow company espoused at length about their new and innovative cam system. Ads screamed of this breakthrough technology; cutting-edge science, engineering, and manufacturing melded together to form the ultimate power propulsion system for compounds. Well, truth be told, the design had been patented some twenty years earlier and never really marketed with zeal. So much for the latest and greatest innovation!

When asked where I see the industry going in the next decade, I hesitate to provide a definitive answer. This is because, barring any new discoveries in materials science, the industry and their compounds have squeezed almost every pound of power out of the compound machine.

Despite its limitations, the archery game continues to intrigue many. I'm hoping you'll find something to your liking in this book—something that will enlighten or stir your interest in bowhunting.

## Up Close and Personal

Humidity drapes on you like a warm, wet bed sheet. You struggle against gravity and impending sunrise, inching your climber ever higher. Your lungs offer their objection, burning as you quietly gasp to draw your next breath of this air you wear.

Once you've reached hunting height, you settle into the pre-dawn darkness—one so dark you need a flashlight to find your pocket. Your heart pounds uncontrollably and your temples throb with each rustle of leaves and snap of a twig. The anticipation of what the first fingers of sunlight will reveal on the forest floor some thirty feet below is deafening.

The acrid smell of repellent fills your nose and stings your eyes as it shoulders itself against the airborne horde that clouds around your head and hands. The early light stretches through nature's mossy hardwood window shades, and you stare cross-eyed as a salty bead of sweat trickles down the bridge of your nose.

Resolute to remain motionless, you battle the urge to brush it aside. Finally, it drips onto the standing platform with a gentle, yet discernible "tink." Welcome to the archery opener and early season bowhunting!

This precious time is what the fraternal brotherhood of bowhunters yearns for. To the uninitiated, this ritual is remotely odd and seemingly painful. To those of the order, those with unwavering resolve, it's what defines our being. Adrenaline is our drug of choice. We are, proudly and passionately, after all, bowhunters. I invite you to join the ranks. Here's why.

### Learn to Be a Better Hunter

I'm not going to beat around the bush or sugarcoat this for any number of reasons;

bowhunters are the best hunters in the woods. Don't get mad at me; it is what it is. Consider the following.

Close your eyes and picture the first days of the war in Iraq. Remote images of sorties dropping smart bombs filled our living rooms and dens. We cheered as bombs dropped several miles away found their way to the intended targets.

Gun hunting, to me, is much the same. There you sit in a shooting house, covering a 100-acre agricultural field with a high-powered rifle. In stark contrast, a bowhunter has an effective range on a good day in the south of about forty yards. With this diminutive affective range, a bowhunter must get into a deer's comfort zone, into their living room if you will, to deliver a lethal arrow.

**Scent Control**

Being a good bowhunter means being a master woodsman. As such, many individual facets must be considered and contemplated. Scent control is exponentially more important to a bowhunter than someone hunting with a gun. Make a mistake here with the wind and it's over. Much has been written on the subject, so we won't be laver the point.

**Stand Management and Etiquette**

Stand management is another consideration that's critical. Several factors require forethought including shooting lanes, animal travel direction, sunrise and sunset, predominant wind direction, hunting height, stand orientation, and more.

Stand etiquette is also of paramount importance. There are two distinct entities here: 1) management of yourself and 2) equipment management. Managing "yourself" refers to the ability to cloak yourself from an animal's eyes and ears. This is not an easy skill to learn. Curbing or minimizing movement takes practice.

Equipment management takes time to perfect as well. This affects your ability to setup your hunting platform (stand) in the most ergonomically and efficient manner. You must know how to place your essentials about the stand to make you as comfortable negotiating them as you are driving your automobile.

**Early Season Pattern ability**

A distinct advantage early season bowhunters have is that deer are very predictable now. While many hunters center their season's hopes, dreams, and much-coveted vacation time around the rut,

Author and his Texas Axis deer.

Author with his Wyoming antelope.

rutting bucks wander willy-nilly in search of breedable does. This search may take them miles from their core area. Conversely, during early season, whitetails fall into a predictable pattern, one that puts grounding one in your favor.

Early season deer are driven by the need to feed and rehydrate themselves. When the temperature rises, a deer's metabolism goes into overdrive. As whitetail binge on readily available nutrition, their need for water increases. This need for water makes them susceptible. Locate their water and food source and you'll find success.

**Go Where No One Has Gone Before**

As urban sprawl continues to cast its shadow across the landscape, whitetails are being pinched out of their natural habitat. No matter if you agree with urban expanse, more whitetails are forced to live within the confines of this urbanscape.

Hardwoods, swamps, and other intimate places of refuge are diminishing. Whitetails are squeezed like frosting through a batter bag into backyards, small woodlots, and neighborhoods. The family farm and its corn fields and CRP succumb to suburbia, concrete, condos, and corporate America.

Author with an Illinois buck shot with a muzzleloader, although he prefers archery equipment.

Author with a rare white deer—not an albino, but a completely white whitetail deer.

Significantly more opportunities to hunt pristine areas where no other hunters have been before now exist. Moreover, we're able to hunt very small tracks of lands where guns are considered off-limits. Along these same lines, the owners of these small tracts are much more likely to allow bowhunting than that of high-powered rifle hunting. In many cases, the animals are unpressured and relatively tolerant of humans and their presence.

**It's Just Fun!**

Admittedly, shooting a gun has its distinct appeal. The smell of gunpowder and seeing a quarter-size group at 100 yards is satisfying. However, the thrill of attaining a shaft-to-shaft arrow group at thirty yards eclipses high-powered, magnification-assisted groupings.

Archery and bowhunting can be addictive. It's a sport that can be done year-round in most cases and is one the entire family can enjoy together. There's an archery setup for any age, gender and skill level. It's also relatively inexpensive to get into. Complete combination (i.e., bow, sight, arrow rest, arrows, and quiver) kits retail for as little as $199.

# Speaking "Bow"

Merriam Webster's definition of compound is "to put together (parts) so as to form a whole: combine." In its simplest form, a compound bow is a combination of various components that, when assembled into a complete mechanical machine, produces a vehicle capable of sending arrows downrange at speeds that exceed those of a traditional bow.

Anyone who has spent time around the archery game has probably learned to speak the "language of compounds." For the archery insider, the jargon and odd nomenclature of those in the know comes easily.

Typically weighing around four odd pounds, compound bows are capable of shooting arrows at amazing speeds. But to fully understand these incredible machines, it is important to understand the vernacular of the sport. Such oddities as "brace height," "idler," "eccentrics," "tiller," "cam lean," "hysteresis," "draw force curve" and so on can leave the head swimming in short order.

Here's an introduction to the compound and what you'll need to know to fit in.

## The Fundamentals

Compounds all share common components—those parts that make a compound tick.

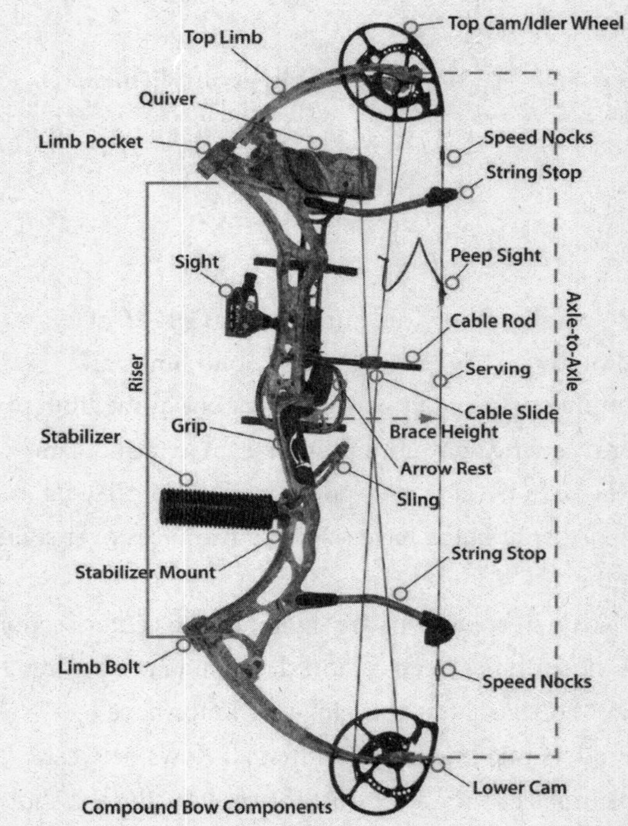


Compound components.

### Limbs

For a bow to propel an arrow, it must generate and store energy. Pulling the bow string generates this energy and the bow limbs store the energy. When this energy is unleashed and applied to the arrow, it is propelled downrange.

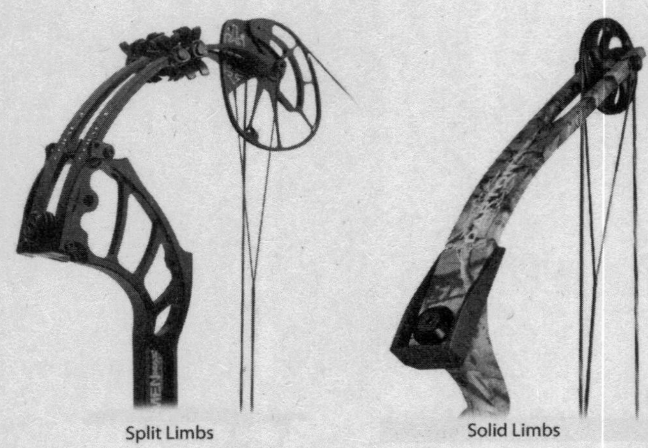


Split limbs versus solid limbs. Makers of split limbs claim advantages over solid limbs while solid limb manufacturers tout their limbs advantages.

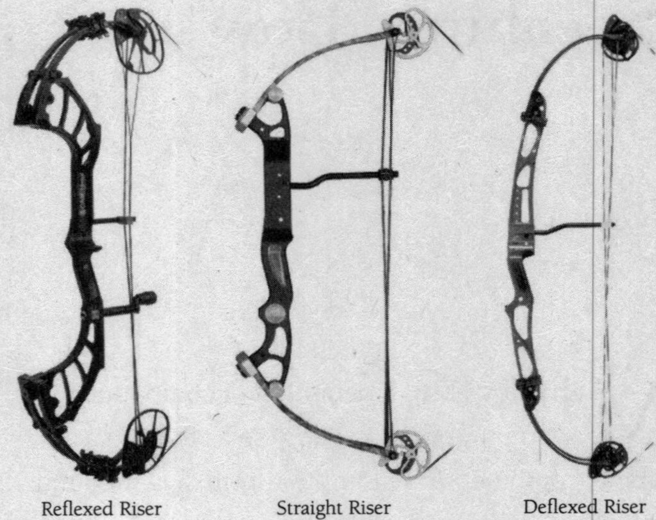


Riser configurations vary from one model and manufacturer to the next.

Limbs come in a number of styles. Most commonly, they are *solid limbs*. Solid limbs are simply one-piece units with a slot cut in the limb tip for receiving and mounting the cam axle and cam. *Split limbs* became very popular in the late 1990s. In theory, split limbs have several advantages over solid limbs.

First, split limbs are lighter as the center section of the limb has been removed. Some manufacturers have gone as far as to claim split limbs have less aerodynamic drag, arguing that air flows between the limbs as they are thrust forward during the shot. They further postulate this makes the limbs "faster reacting" and thus the bow faster. For me, this is a stretch.

Split limbs have a disadvantage as each is manufactured independently of others. As such, each limb exhibits its own flexure (the way they bend) characteristics. The problem lies in attempting to match a pair of limbs on the top and bottom of the bow. Independently flexing limbs can cause cam lean *(see Cam Lean)*.

**Riser**

The functional purpose of a bow's riser is to anchor the two limbs and offer a place for the archer to grip the bow. Risers come in a myriad of styles and shapes. However, there are three general geometries. They are: 1) deflexed, 2) reflexed, and 3) straight.

When discussing riser geometry, one must consider the relationship of the shooter's bow hand to the string.

Each riser geometry offers both advantages and disadvantages. A *reflexed riser* positions the handle back toward the shooter. By moving the bow's handle back further, the bow's *brace height* (the measure in inches from a resting string to the bow's grip at the farthest point) is decreased. As brace height is decreased, the bow's *power stroke* is increased as the string must travel further before releasing the arrow.

By increasing the distance the string has to travel, it also increases the distance the bow can accelerate the arrow (hence its power stroke). Thus, a shorter brace height generates more arrow speed. However, there are trade-offs for this added speed. By shortening the bow's brace height, the length of the lever arm between the string at rest (referred to as *equilibrium*) and the handle is decreased. By decreasing this lever, it multiplies, or compounds, any shooter-induced errors.

If the shooter torques the bow to the left during the shot, the effect of that error is multiplied downrange. Additionally, a shorter brace height and longer power stroke increases the time the arrow is physically on the string. By increasing the shot's time, the shooter has more time to make slight errors in shooting technique. This, in turn, leads to errant arrow flight and delivery to the target.

A *deflexed riser* is the polar opposite of a reflexed riser. Instead of the riser bending inward, the riser geometry flexes outward, away from the shooter. This increases the bow's brace height, shortening the power stroke and slowing the bow's top speed. However, while speed suffers, accuracy is increased as the riser's length of the lever arm between the string at rest (remember equilibrium) and the handle is increased. By increasing this lever length, shooter errors are minimized. Additionally, with a shortened power stroke, the effect of shooter errors is diminished as the arrow is on the string a shorter amount of time. Traditionally, deflexed risers are typically found on target-style bows.

Bows with *straight risers* are a compromise between reflexed and deflexed risers. Straight risers have a neutral geometry, that is, they are neither reflexed nor deflexed. Straight risers are a compromise for archers who want speed and accuracy but are unwilling to settle for the compromises of the reflexed and deflexed riser designs.

## Riser Manufacturing Processes

High-end compounds typically have risers manufactured using a CNC (computer numerical control) machine. The CNC utilizes a complex computer program to automatically or robotically cut the intricate riser profile. Either solid aluminum billets are used or extruded aluminum blanks serve as the base material. Risers milled in this fashion are referred to as a *machined riser.* Machined risers are the most precise risers and demand the highest dollar in the bow market.

*Cast magnesium alloy risers* are produced using conventional casting methods. These include sand castings, permanent and semi permanent mold and shell castings, investment castings, and die-castings. Production is fast and less precise than machined risers. As such, cast risers are found on lower-priced compounds in general.

*Forged risers* utilize a manufacturing process that shapes metal with localized compressive forces. Depending on the manufacturer, forging can be performed "cold," "warm," or "hot." The type of forging used is dependent on temperature. Forging produces a part that is stronger than an equivalent cast or machined part. Due to the complexity of equipment required to produce forged risers, few manufacturers opt to manufacture them.

### Cam System

The basic cam system on a compound bow is made up of a string, one or two *eccentrics* (cams), and one or two harnesses or cables. According to Robert Norton and his *Design of Machinery,* "In mechanical engineering, an eccentric is a circular disk solidly fixed to a rotating axle with its center offset from that of the axle" (hence the word "eccentric," off center).

## Bowstring and Cables

The bowstring on a compound launches the arrow. Most modern bowstrings are made of advanced, man-made materials that do not stretch. In the past, compound bowstrings had a problem of stretching after being installed. When the bowstring stretches, it changes the timing and tune of the bow. As the string stretches non-uniformly, the cams rotate in an unsymmetrical manner, and one rotates out of sync with the other.

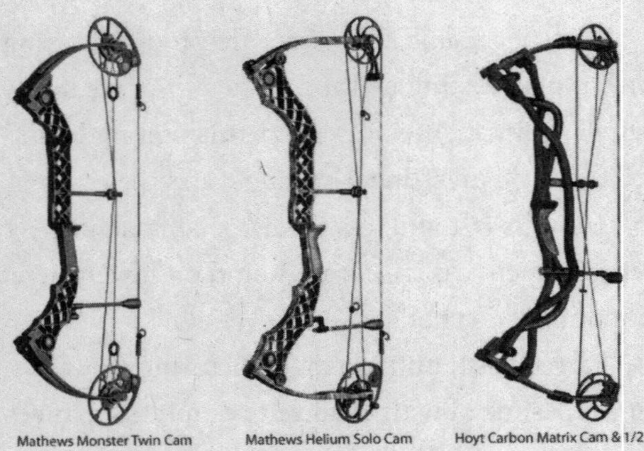


Various cam configurations exist. Each cam system offers distinct advantages. No one stand-alone cam system is perfect or offers the best of all worlds.

Most compound bow manufacturers now use pre-stretched strings that do not stretch. Common bowstring materials include Dacron B50 (stretch equals 2.6 percent), Spectra (a composite ultra-high molecular weight polyethylene), Dyneema (high modulus polyethylene), Fast Flight S4 (high modulus polyethylene; stretch equals 1 percent), polyester, Kevlar (paraaramid synthetic fiber; stretch equals 0.8 percent), and Vectran (a spun fiber of liquid crystal polymer).

### Bowstring Serving

The point where the arrow nocks (mounts) to the bowstring would wear very quickly, leading to failure, if not "served" with an additional wrap of *serving* material. Serving materials are typically made of nylon.

### Cables

Compound bows utilize pulleys, wheels, or cams to load the limbs with energy. These are physically lashed together cables.

### Grip

When we discussed the compound riser, we mentioned the grip. A bow's grip is just that, a place where the archer physically holds the bow. Bow grips come in an array of shapes, styles, and construction materials. They range from very large to very demur. Grip style and shape is a matter of shooter preference.

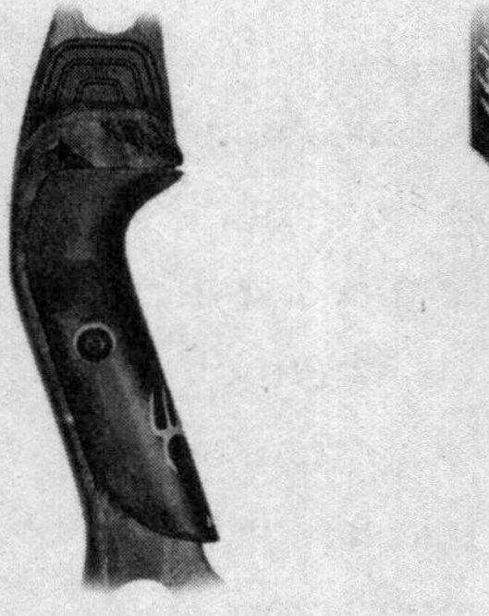
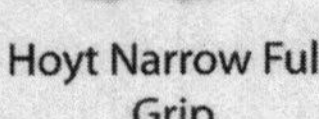

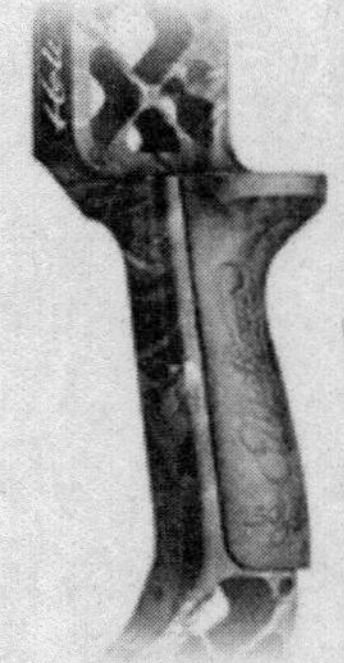

Various grips range from the diminutive to the bulbous, each designed for individual tastes and preferences.

### Arrow Shelf

Modern compounds have a horizontal shelf manufactured into the riser that contains the arrow and allows for the mounting of an *arrow rest*. Early compounds did not have an arrow shelf, and archers were often injured when a broadhead-equipped arrow would drop off early arrow rests and onto the archer's hand.

**Axle-to-axle Measurement**

The axle-to-axle measurement of a bow is from the top cam axle (or *idler wheel*) to the bottom cam axle. Axle-to-axle measurements provide the archery consumer with a general idea of the overall physical size of the compound. Keep in mind that this measure does not take into account the eccentrics (i.e., cams and/or idler wheel).

**Berger Hole**

In an effort to standardize certain compound features so the mounting of archery accessories can be standardized (i.e., sights, stabilizers, and arrow rests), manufacturers drill and tap a Berger hole just above the arrow shelf. The hole is named after Victor Berger, who invented the "Berger Button," an early plunger-style arrow rest. Most bow technicians center the arrow horizontally on this hole.

**Bow Sling**

This bow accessory mounts on the front of the bow's riser to the *stabilizer mounting hole*. Because the compound bow lurches forward following the shot, slings serve to keep the bow contained or lashed to the shooter's hand.

**Brace Height**

The *brace height* is the measurement, in inches, from the crotch (or throat) of the grip to the bowstring when the compound is at rest or equilibrium. In general, the brace height of a bow is indicative of how "forgiving" the bow will shoot.

In most cases, a brace height of less than seven inches indicates the manufacturer is attempting to achieve fast arrow speeds. Brace heights over seven inches are indicative of more a forgiving bow (one more tolerant of shooter error). The distance between the string at rest and the throat of the grip determines the lever arm distance of a bow.

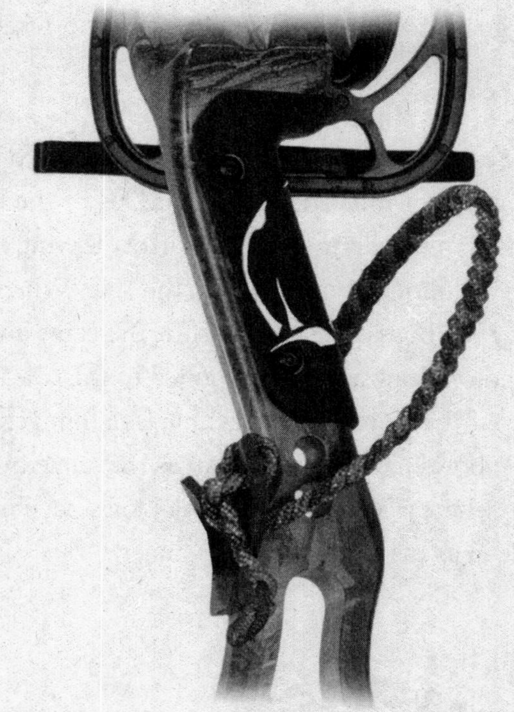

A bow sling provides confidence when shooting.

**Cable Guard**

Compound bows utilize pulleys, wheels, or cams to load the limbs with energy. These are physically lashed together with cables. The cable guard is a perpendicular rod that holds the cables off-center of the riser's mid-line so they do not interfere with the bow's string. Cable guards come in various sizes and configurations. Some are as simple as a rod with a slide. Others are machined parts with dual bearing equipped rollers that the cables track in.

**Cable Slide**

When a cable guard rod is utilized to manage the cables, many manufacturers use a plastic slide (or some type of thermoplastic) in which the cables are mounted. This allows the cables to slide along the cable guard rod via the slide almost friction-free.

**Cam Lean**

The buss cables are connected directly to the cable guard or rod. The cable guard keeps the buss cables from interfering with the arrow leaving the bow by pulling the cables off to the side. When pulling the buss cables to the side, the cams are affected on draw as they are pulled to the side. The result is what is referred to as *cam lean*. Longer axle-to-axle bows have less cam lean as the angle is not as acute, whereas shorter axle-toaxle bows have more cam lean as the angle is more acute.

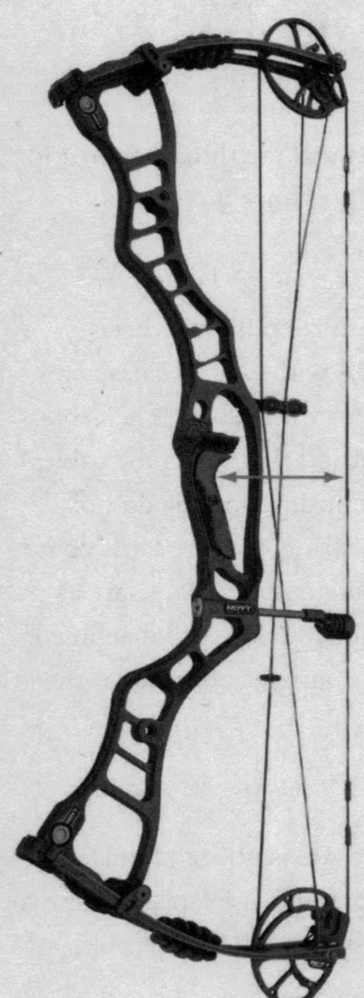

Brace height measure determines how forgiving of shooter-induced error a bow will be.

Cam lean is a relatively simple phenomenon. Cams are mounted on cam axles. As the bow is drawn, the cams are rotated and forces are placed on the cams, axles, and limb tips. As these forces are not equal, the cam is forced to lean to one side or another on the axle.

No bow is void of cam lean. Some will argue that cam lean is bad; others relish it. While both arguments have merit, there is not, in my opinion, a definitive argument for one side or the other. I personally know a few top-level professional 3-D archers who introduce severe cam lean into their rigs to get perfect arrow flight.

If you talk to a few other top-level 3-D professionals, they'll tell you cam lean is the work of the devil. I'll leave it up to you to decide for yourself as experience will be your best teacher. The one thing I can say without hesitation is this: Solid limb bows have less cam lean than split limb bows. This is due to the torsional strength and rigidity of the limbs at the tips. Split limb bows have less torsional rigidity and thus flex more and result in more cam lean.

**D-Loop**

When using a mechanical release attached directly to the bowstring, repetitive shots can cause wear and abrasion to the bowstring. In many cases, this can lead to breakage. Most archers attach a short length of looped cord to their bowstring. This looped cord, or D-Loop, allows attachment of the mechanical release to the loop, eliminating bowstring wear and subsequent breakage.

**Draw Weight**

The *draw weight* is the amount of force required to draw a compound bow. This is measured in pounds.

**Feet-Per-Second (FPS)**

This is the numerical measure of how fast a projectile is moving. In archery, it typically refers to arrow speed. Feet-per-second can be converted to miles-perhour by multiplying fps x 0.682 = mph.

**Grains**

This is a unit of mass measurement nominally based on the mass of a single seed of wheat . This method of measuring dates back to the Bronze Age.

**IBO Speed**

The International Bowhunting Organization, or IBO, established a standard for measuring a compound bows speed in feet-per-second (FPS).

IBO Speed is equal to 350-total-grain-weight arrow (shaft, fletchings, nock, and point) shot from a bow with 30-inch draw length and the draw weight set at 70 pounds

**Idler Wheel**

On solo-cam bows, or bows with one cam, the top wheel is referred to as the idler wheel.

**Let-Off**

An advantage of the compound bow is its ability to load the bow limbs with energy and then reduce the weight at the conclusion of the draw to a manageable weight. This reduction in draw weight at full draw is referred to as *let-off*. Let-off is articulated in a percentage. If a bow has an 80 percent let-off, at a draw weight of seventy pounds, the shooter will be holding the equivalent of fourteen pounds at full draw.

**Mechanical Release**

This is a device capable of securing the bowstring during draw, which gives the archer a mechanical advantage over drawing the bow using his fingers. Multiple designs exist, however. Generally speaking, mechanical releases contain a set of jaws to grip the bowstring or D-Loop, a trigger, and some sort of wrist strap or grip.

**Nock**

A nock is the plastic (some may be manufactured of aluminum) appendage on the rear of an arrow that the bowstring slides into.

**Nocking Point**

The point or position on a bowstring that the archer positions his or her arrow prior to drawing and releasing it is known as the *nocking point*.

**Peep Sight**

Compound bows are typically aimed using a *sight* (refer to sight on the next page). Sights are mounted to the bow and are positioned at arm's length when the bow is drawn. Peep sights are installed into the bowstring. This hollow, donut-shaped device allows the shooter to look through the hole at full draw and align his sight pins on the target. The peep sight operates much like a rear sight on a rifle.

**Quiver**

Dating back to ancient times, the quiver is a receptacle for arrows. Usually mounting on the bow's riser, the quiver holds one to nine arrows. Quivers come in an array of sizes and shapes. Most are detachable from the compound bow. Quivers hold broadheadequipped arrows safely, shielding the razor edges from the shooter.

**Sight**

The archery *sight* is a relatively crude aiming device that is mounted on the bow's riser. Three types of sights are available: 1) pins, 2) crosshairs, and 3) laser dot.

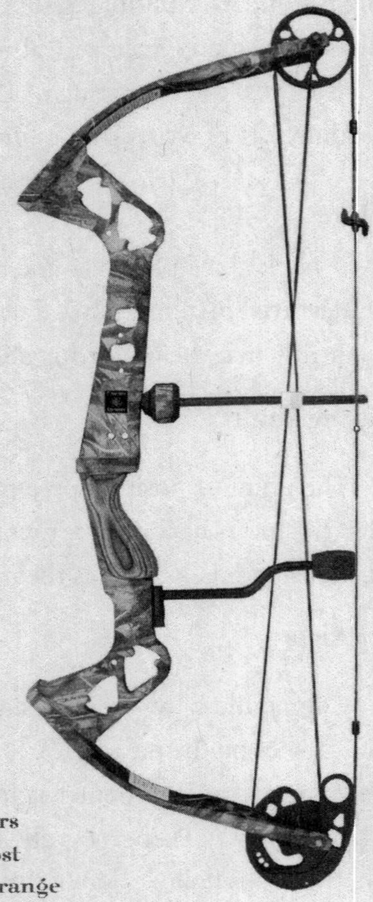

This concept bow offers 99 percent let-off. Most compounds are in the range of 60 to 85 percent let-off.

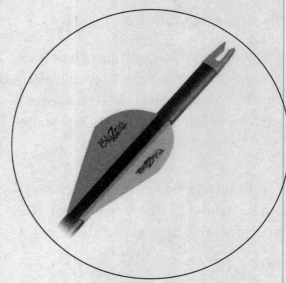

Arrow nock serves as the physical connection between the string and the arrow shaft.

Peep sights allows for precision aiming.

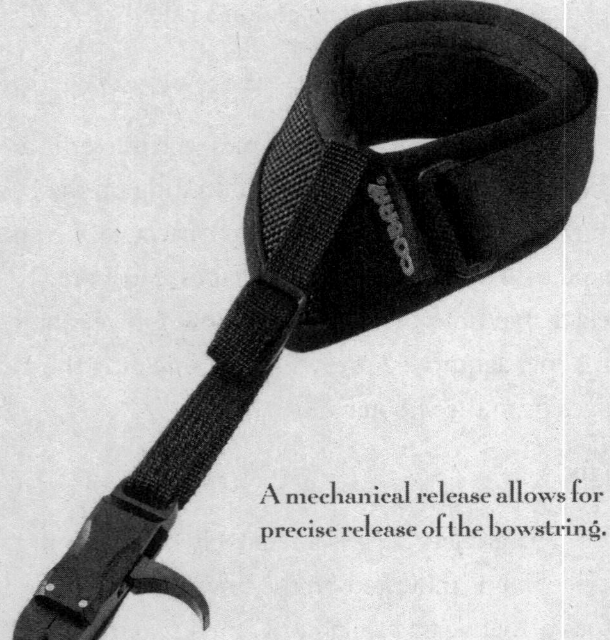


A mechanical release allows for precise release of the bowstring.

A hooded peep sight shades the sun on bright days.

Quivers provide safe and easy arrow access.

Modern sights are marvels of engineering. A quality sight makes accurate arrows easy.

**Silencers**

These are typically rubber appendages that either glue-on, stick-on, or mechanically attach to the compound bow in any number of positions along the bows framework. These appendages do little to quiet a bow's shot noise or minimize vibration as they only add mass to the compound bow.

**Stabilizer**

The stabilizer is an accessory that mounts to the compound's riser. A plethora of designs are currently available. Originally designed to counter-balance a bow's mass for target shooters, modern stabilizers are now marketed as "vibration and noise eliminating devices." While their value as a counterweight is undeniable, their ability to reduce vibration or noise is highly suspect.

**Tiller**

The tiller measurement is the measurement from the point where the limb meets the riser and the string in a perpendicular line. Each bow will have two tiller measurements and generally should be the same.

## Weird Science: Building the 400+ FPS Compound

Like some strange spring ritual, archers annually migrate to local pro shops to pour over the newest of industry offerings. Undoubtedly when fondling the recent arrivals, the first words the faithful will utter are "how fast is it?" Like candy apple red muscle cars, no bow can be "too fast." If it'll peel the paint off the house with blistering speed, folks will flock in droves to it.

The modern compound had its meager beginnings in the one-car garage of Missouri's

Holless Allen in the early 1960s. It's hard to imagine that the anemic and frail recurve that Allen lashed with pulleys would morph into today's compound powerplants.

In the fifty-some odd years since, evolutions in co-polymers, metallurgy, and man-made fibers have been mindboggling. Synergistically, these scientific and engineering advancements have pushed the speed envelope right up against a brick wall.

Even with these technological achievements, compounds still haven't reached the holy grail of speed: the magical 400 feet-per-second benchmark.

**What the Desaguliers?**

France's John Theophilus Desaguliers first described the phenomenon of friction in the 1600s. Friction, in an engineering sense, is the force that opposes the relative motion or tendency of such motion of two surfaces in contact. Okay, simple enough—stuff rubbing against stuff keeps it from moving freely.

Friction, as it relates to bows, is the primary reason why compounds haven't attained 400 feet-per-second. You see, it's this friction that limits the efficiency of the simple machine we call a bow. Friction in machines produces unwanted side effects—those of heat, noise, and vibration. Admittedly, other factors contribute to energy losses, but we'll not focus on these.

Theoretically, if we could eliminate friction, or significantly reduce it, we could improve a bow's efficiency and exceed the 400-feet-per-second barrier. So it's this friction, or hysteresis, that we'll minimize in our new theoretical 400-plus feet per second mega ground pounder bow.

**Bio-Kinetic Limbs**

Bow limbs are under two distinct physical forces when they are flexed. The face (i.e., the portion of the limb facing the shooter) is under *compression* (i.e., withstanding axially directed pushing forces), and the back (i.e., the portion of the limb facing the target) is under *tension* (a force that stretches or elongates a material).

Human bones have complex internal and external structures, making them lightweight, yet exceptionally strong. One of the types of tissue that makes up bone is the mineralized osseous tissue, also called bone tissue. Osseous tissue gives bone its rigidity and honeycomb-like three-dimensional internal structure.

To minimize friction and weight, our bio-kinetic limbs are molded using a carbon-to-carbon molecularly bonded matrix. Our artificial matrix mimics bone tissue's honeycomb-like structure with a synthetic mineral component. Our new limbs are stiff in compression while offering little friction in the tension mode. *Net Speed Gain: +13 fps*

**Tri-Cam System**

The centerpiece of eccentrics will be a double pulley system mounted on our near-parallel bio-kinetic limbs. Our new cam system will provide a 5:1 ratio of movement between the bio-kinetic limbs and the arrow.

To accomplish this, our cams (pulleys) will not rotate as complete disks, but as narrow rings sliding on a highly polished hollow cylinder only slightly dimensionally smaller than the cams. A single-cam will be centrally placed near the handle to reduce mass on the bio-kinetic limb tips. Raised micro-grooves will be machined into the cam groove surfaces. These grooves minimize string and cable friction by reducing surface area. *Net Speed Gain: +8 fps*

**Cable Guard and Pulley Bio-Cylinders**

Traditional pulleys have significant mass that has to start rotating, which uses up energy and adds to the weight at the end of the limb that has to

**Off-Season Tune-Up and Storage**

Winter's chill sets in, and the season has closed. Now's a great time to drop off your rig for an annual check-up. Off-season service is both fast and inexpensive. It's also an opportunity to avoid the crowds that jam shops prior to the next opener.

Your local tech will put your bow in a press and remove the string. Once removed, they'll check for wear, as well as check the axles, cam bearings, or bushings.

Keep in mind that an inevitable wet weather outing can negatively affect the performance of these, so an annual checkup is prudent. Depending on your particular make and model, it's a good idea to have them lubricate axles, bushings, or cam bearings as deemed appropriate.

Prior to mothballing your bow, apply a generous amount of bowstring wax to the string and cables. Additionally, store your bow in a climate controlled space where it won't be exposed to extreme temperature swings.

When storing your bow, consider a quality hard case to keep it nestled in safety. It's also a good idea to remove broadheads from arrows. Store these prickly critters somewhere other than with your bow. For some reason, their honed edges have a propensity for finding strings and cables.

**Taping Speed**

The International Bowhunting Organization (IBO) developed a standard formula for measuring arrow speeds. Arrow speed is tested using an arrow with a mass weight of 350-grains, a thirty-inch draw length, and seventy-pound draw weight. By using this formula, bow manufacturers rate the speed of their bows in a uniform manner. This apples-to-apples rating system allows consumers to compare relative bow speeds.

The Archery Manufacturers and Merchants Organization (AMO) now known as the Archery Trade Association (ATA) developed a standard for measuring arrow speed. A bow must have a maximum draw weight of sixty pounds. The arrow must weigh 540-grains with a draw length set at thirty inches.

accelerate as the arrow is released. In our bow, the conventional pulley or cam is reduced to a thin ring that rotates on a hollow axle shaft, about an inch in diameter, anchored to the limb.

The outside of the ring is grooved to guide the string or cable, and it rotates on the axle on a film of synthetic lubricating fluid similar to the synovial fluid in your joints, reducing both inertia and friction. *Net Gain: +2 fps*

**Nano-Tech String/Cable System**

Our string and cable system will take advantage of cylindrical carbon nanotubes woven into "rope." Using nanotubes will exponentially decrease the string, cable diameters, and surface area.

Reducing the surface area decreases surface friction and increases the string's velocity. An anti-wear coating is bonded onto the surface of the cylindrical carbon weave nanotube strings and cables, which offers substantial protection. *Net Gain: +8 fps*

**Uni-Lite Aeros**

Arrow shafts will be considerably smaller in diameter and lighter than their traditional carbon counterparts (thus minimizing aerodynamic drag). Our shafts and their components (i.e., field points, vanes, and nocks) will be molded of one-piece thin-walled, radially woven composite. Field points and broadheads are molded into the shaft and of the same composite, eliminating the weight of the ferrule.

Uni-composite components reduce arrow shaft weights and increase arrow speeds while minimizing the criticality of arrow spine. Vanes are replaced with integrally molded ultra low-profile airfoil equipped fins that high-speed spin-stabilize our low mass Uni-Lite Aeros. A pulverized magnetic dust is added to the radial complex to enhance arrow rest performance. *Net Gain: +18 fps*

**Magna-Force Arrow Rest**

A powerful magnetic field will levitate our Uni-Lite Aeros without any rest-to-shaft contact. Floating in this field, the arrow will leave the bow in a friction-free state. Pulverized magnetic dust in the arrow shaft provides the repulsion force. *Net Gain: +8 fps*

**Zero-Resist Release**

Much like our arrow rest, the centerpiece of our mechanical release will be a powerful magnet that holds our Nano-Tech string during the draw cycle. As the trigger is engaged, the magnetic field releases the string effortlessly, increasing string velocity and ultimately arrow speed. *Net Speed Gain: +2 fps*

**Post-Hunt Checklist**

You labored from dawn-to-dusk on your stand, struggling to remain motionless while aloft in your whitetail haunt. Or conversely, you scratched and clawed your way up, negotiating nauseating miles of altitude challenging terrain, in pursuit of your trophy.

At day's end, the dirt under your nails, melded with the sweat and blood soaked soil that's been ground into the cracks of your palms, usher credit to your resolve to "just get it done."

Busted, broken, and exhausted, you return to camp. Your thoughts now focus on anything other than hunting. Before grabbing that steamy cup of Joe, perform these tasks to ensure your next hunt doesn't result in a costly equipment meltdown.

1. "Pluck" the bowstring to check for any loose components. The vibration induced from the bowstring will ferret out any nuts, bolts, or screws in need of tightening.
2. Check the knock loop for any obvious signs of fraying or wear. Rest assured that worn knock loops only break when attempting to draw on that animal of a lifetime.
3. Check your bowstring, peep sight serving, and string serving for any wear. Sticks, limbs, and rocks can make quick work of these. Reserve and re-wax as deemed appropriate.
4. Visually check limbs for any signs of fatigue. These may include chips, splinters, or cracks. Oddly enough, limbs are susceptible to failure as they are under tremendous stress. Once you've completed your visual inspection, gently run your fingers over the limbs to tactically check for defects.
5. Check arrow nocks to ensure that they are aligned correctly. A misaligned nock, one quickly knocked and released during the heat of battle, results in horrific flight. This

is not an option when attempting to harvest prized game.

6. Broadheads have a strange capacity to loosen up. Check these to make sure they are both tight and sharp. Bees wax (string wax) applied to the threads can help ensure they remain tight no matter how tough the going gets.
7. Fiber-optics revolutionized the archery sight game. However, these extrusions are also fragile and prone to breakage. Visually check these for damage. In addition, if you have a battery-operated sight light, fire it up to ensure the battery is up to snuff.
8. Arrows can get damaged during transit in vehicles, on four-wheelers hauling them up a hillside, or at the end of a pull-up rope. Flex each shaft to check for damage. If defects are found, cull these from your quiver. Additionally, check vanes for damage.
9. Cams are the powerplants central to your arrow launcher. Give them a visual for any foreign debris that might have inadvertently become lodged there.
10. By all means, if possible, shoot a few arrows to make sure that your bow is still sighted in.
11. Draw your bow and check peep alignment. Peeps have an ugly tendency to creep and move. Drawing on an animal is not the time to discover yours has gone south.
12. Limb pockets are wonders of modern engineering; most archers have no idea how integral these are to bow performance. Typically, manufacturers heavily lubricate these. As such, they are prone to attracting dust and dirt. Check for these and clean as necessary.
13. Exercise your release several times to ensure it's working properly. Hook it to the string and gently put some tension on it. *(Note: Don't pull your string back any further than half an inch.)*

**Where to Buy? That is the Question.**

So you're in the market for a new bow. You've essentially got three options. It's either big retailer, discount catalog, or the local mom-and-pop shop.

Both meglo-mart retailers and discount catalog houses offer great pricing. Granted, both deal in enormous volume. However, while they shine on price, they lose this luster in a lack of archery knowledge.

Consider this: Local archery pro shops have hardcore archery nuts that can whip your new setup into shape without blinking. The downside is this—you're going to pay a bit more for your dream rig (typically about $50–75 on a complete rig).

An extra $75 may sound like a lot, but consider this: When ordering your dream setup, you are left to make all the decisions. That includes bow, arrow rest, sight, release, arrows, silencers, loop, quiver, field points, broadheads, sling, etc.

So do you consider yourself enough of an archery expert to gather all these components together? One capable of planting carbon shafts in the bull's eye at fifty and beyond?

# Part 2

# *Gear*

# Introduction

Let's face it, bowhunters are gear heads. We all love new stuff—we like to test it, shoot it, practice with it, take it afield, all in the name of being at the top of our game. Come on, how many of you are shooting a bow that's at least ten years old? Not many, I would guess, as every year bowmakers come out with faster and more efficient bows. Go onto any of their websites—Bow Tech, Martin, Mathews, PSE, you name it—and you'll find new and better bows than last year. The only question is, is now the year your fork over your hard-earned pay for a new bow? Or, do you wait for next year? A new bow sometimes can wait, unless your current bow has been damaged. But you will need new arrows on a regular basis, as well as field tips and broadheads. You're probably good with your current quiver and sights. As for releases, it's always good to have a backup, especially if you're taking a road trip.

Then there is the ancillary gear. Treestands, blinds, decoys—and what about new camo clothing, boots, gloves, backpacks, and more? You can get carried away with all this—but that's half the fun.

In this chapter, we dwell on the essential gear—the bow, the arrow, the broadhead. You get this far, you'll be able to figure out the rest—either by going to bow shops, going online, or perhaps buying a copy of Todd Kuhn's book, *Shooter's Bible Guide to Bowhunting*, published by Skyhorse. We're publishing a few of Todd' s chapters in this book, but his guide covers everything. Hey, what's another $19.95 when you're already into a bow for $800, sights for $125, broadheads (three for $35), and much more?

—Jay Cassell

# The Compound Bow

Today, most bowhunters shoot compound bows. Indeed, we tend to think of ourselves as "normal." This has not always been the case, though. Even now, thousands of bowhunters still enjoy the "hunting the hard way" challenge with traditional bows.

## LET-OFF

There is no difference between a compound bow and a longbow . . . at least at the simplest level of design. They are both springs built to propel an object forward through the air.

Otherwise, the difference between compounds and all other bows is pronounced. A compound bow uses cams and cables to reduce the effort required to pull the string to full draw and hold it there while you sight at your target. This reduced effort is let-off. It allows you to draw and hold a compound much longer than you could hold a longbow or a recurve, which have no let-off.

Let-off is the key to understanding how a compound bow works and why this kind of bow is so popular. The cams near the limb tips of a compound bow act like pulleys. They allow you to hold a compound at full draw using less force than the bow's rated draw weight.

Begin with an average 65-pound draw weight bow, with a cam system that advertises 75percent let-off. You need to pull back the full 65 pounds of weight, but when you do, the cam or cams roll over and you are left holding only 25 percent of 65 pounds or 16 ¼ pounds at full draw. Most adults can hold that amount of weight for some time while they steady their breathing, select the proper sight pin and slowly squeeze the trigger of their release aid. Of course, you must still pull through the peak weight of 65 pounds, and that can be prolonged on some high-energy speed bows, but it nevertheless takes only a few moments before you reach full draw and peak let-off.

By comparison, to pull and hold your 65-pound recurve at full draw takes a continuous 65-pound effort. Neither recurves nor longbows have let-off, and holding one of them at 65 pounds for any length of time without shaking, and while maintaining a steady sight picture, is a difficult task, even for a strong person. Traditional bowhunters typically release the string almost immediately upon reaching full draw.

Cam design determines the reduction in draw force. In the early 2000s, 33 percent let-off was standard and 50 percent was thought to be the limit at which a bow would provide quality performance. Indeed, 50 percent let-off seemed high in its day.

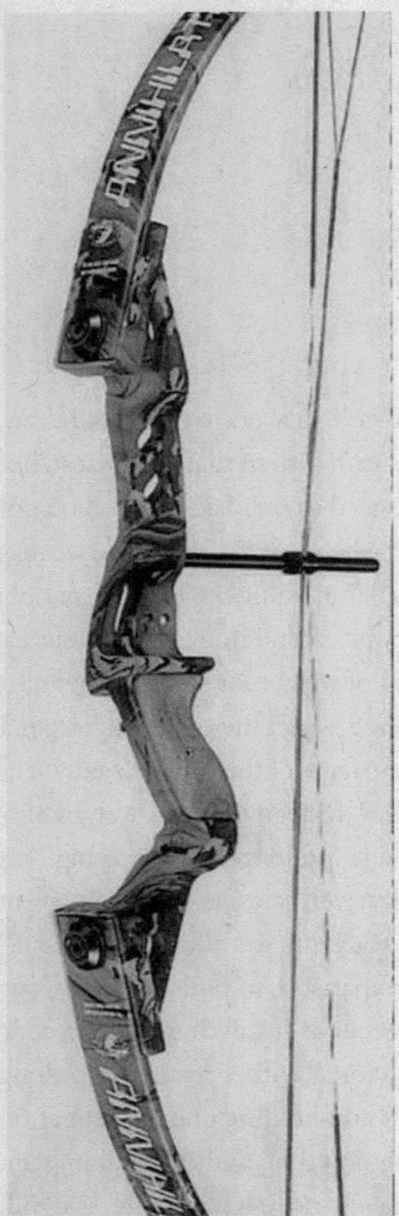

Over the years, several companies have promoted an angled grip styling on the theory that when you naturally extend your arm and hand (with nothing in it), you realize that your hand and grip are not vertical. A right-hander will naturally have a clockwise tilt and a left-hander will have a counterclockwise tilt. Several bow manufacturers have introduced machined risers with arrow shelf cut-outs or offsets based on this concept, calling it a natural or ergonomic grip. The bow pictured is an older style McPherson Annihilator. (This mimics the "cant" or tilt of a longbow, where the arrow lays not on the horizontal shelf, but more in the "V" between the shelf and the riser. Shooting with feathers rather than plastic vanes minimizes deflection of your arrow off the bow riser.)

Designs and materials have improved since then. Now, bows with let-off as high as 80 and 85 percent are common and, in the right hands, can achieve consistent, high-quality shooting performance. Compound bows with high let-off sell better than bows with low let-off, perhaps four-to-one. Today, the average bow is sold with 75 percent let-off, and manufacturers make optional modules for 65 and even 85 percent let-off. Some manufacturers include them with a bow purchase and others sell them as optional accessories.

When you are considering the purchase of a compound bow, you should be aware that some states, lobbied by advocates in the traditional archery camp, have adopted limits to let-off in the same manner that they have occasionally limited electronic shooting and hunting aids.

The Carbon G3 from Hoyt Archery is a good example of the trend to lower holding weights. Just 31.5 inches axle-to-axle with a 6.75-inch brace height, this 332 fps (ATA rated) speed bow is sold with their RKT Cam & 1/2 that gives about 80 percent letoff. You can buy a Carbon G3 in eight color and camo options.

Once you reach full draw, a bow with a lower holding weight is easier to aim and shoot effectively. That is conventional wisdom and it is true to a point, but high let-off bows are under such stress that they tend to be finicky with sharp draw-force curves. This means that if you allow the string to creep forward only slightly, your cams will want to snap over and let the arrow go immediately!

With a low let-off bow, say 50 or 65 percent, it is relatively easy to let down, not shoot an arrow after you come to full draw. You will feel the cams snap over and the bow will give your arm a jerk, but the strain is manageable. Let down a high let-off bow, however, and you should be prepared for a couple of difficult moments wrestling with the string. Hold the string securely with your fingers and consciously move your finger or thumb away from your release trigger or you could dry fire your bow. If you dry fire, you could damage it beyond repair and void your warranty.

Just like the precise grain weight of individual broadheads in a pack of three, let-off will not be an exact figure on most compound bows. It will vary slightly depending upon the modular arrangement of a bow's cam (or cams), your draw weight and draw length and the amount of string and cable stretch. Let-off may vary as much as seven percent above or below the advertised rating. So if you test your Bowtech Insanity CPXL on an accurate bow scale and find that your expected holding weight varies by half a pound or so when you ramp it up from 60 to 70 pounds, remember that this is essentially a normal condition of compounds.

## ONE-CAM, TWO-CAM

For perhaps 25 years, from the moment Holless W. Allen applied for his patent in the late 1960s, bows with top and bottom cams were "normal." These wheels or irregularly shaped cams were machined or molded as mirror images of one another. Beginning in the 1990s, this twin-cam design fell out of popularity.

In about 1990, Matt McPherson's one-cam bow revolution gained momentum. His one-cam bows had a single, eccentrically shaped, machined cam on the bottom limb and a perfectly round, balance wheel, called an idler, on the top limb. This revolution was so complete that all manufacturers have produced one-cam bow designs. For a few years recently, it was difficult to find a high-performance twin-cam bow. Around 2005, at companies like Hoyt and PSE, twin-cam ("cam and a half") designs are quietly beginning to again dominate the line-up.

Although the one-cam revolution made most twin-cam bows seem obsolete, they were not without performance kinks. One-cam bows were slower than twin-cam bows and nock travel was inconsistent. Upon release, the nock and bowstring should thrust an arrow forward in a straight line. It took archery engineers several years to work through these difficulties, but today, one-cam shooting systems have "arrived" in both speed and consistency of performance.

Why did many bowhunters believe the one-cam bow was better than the twin-cam bow? With twin-cam bows, cams must turn synchronously to prevent the nock point locator, against which your arrow clips, from moving forward in an uneven manner. Synchronous cam movement is called "timing." On out-of-time twin-cam bows, the nock point locator moves forward through the power stroke with a wave motion, up and down. This provides less than excellent propulsion to your arrow, which flies erratically and takes longer to stabilize in flight.

In the early '90s, timing problems on were exacerbated on twin-cam bows as all-synthetic strings and cables replaced Dacron bowstrings and plastic-coated steel cables. Using materials like the early versions of FastFlight, all-synthetic systems may indeed have been "stronger than steel," but steel does not stretch. These new synthetic materials did stretch, and that compounded the difficulty of achieving straight-line nock travel.

One-cam bows eliminated these timing problems. If there was only one cam on the lower limb and a round idler on the top limb, obviously there could not be a problem synchronizing roll-over. By definition, a one-cam bow cannot go out of time with itself. (The wheel or idler on the top limb of a one-cam bow does not just provide a rolling surface with minimal friction, although that is important. It helps insure balanced limb action and straight-line nock and arrow travel.)

Today, many bowhunters have concluded that the nock-point-travel controversy was exaggerated. It may have been significant among competition archers, where the difference between winning and losing can be the breadth of a hair at 35 yards, and "line cutters" or fat shafts are often preferred to thinner arrows for that reason. This kind of shooting precision is impossible to achieve in the field and is not necessary in actual hunting conditions.

Why then do you visit a mass merchant and find two-cam bows in boxes on their shelves, when you and most friends bought one-cam bows from a sporting goods store? Mass merchants deliver a huge volume of goods effectively, but at lower prices because they provide no service, support or advice that is trustworthy beyond the simplest concepts. As demand for twin-cam bows declined, the price that manufacturers could command for them fell. Enter the useful mass merchant.

Traditionally, there have been three wheel or cam styles for twin-cam bows. In the early '80s, manufacturers built bows with precisely round wheels and simply offset the axle holes from the center to imitate lobed cams and give you let-off. In the mid to late 1980s, wheels were largely supplanted–except on entry-level compounds–by more powerful oblong cams which often had dramatic lobes and cutouts, and which delivered greater arrow speed. Because the rim of a cam has two tracks–one for your bowstring and the other for your cable–you could describe a bow as having soft, medium or hard cams, depending on their shape and expected performance, and you would be understood on shooting ranges and in pro shops across the continent.

**SOFT CAMS:** These cams are often called energy wheels. They have a round lobe over which the bowstring travels in its groove, and a smooth but irregularly shaped lobe for the cable in its groove. On energy wheels, the rounded string lobe is what gives you the smooth, easy pull. The oval cable lobe lets you wring more speed from your bow than a fully rounded lobe. According to archery engineering expert Norb Mullaney, soft cams store about one foot-pound (ft-lb) of energy for each pound of draw weight. This means a 70-pound bow stores about 70 ft-lb of kinetic energy. That is enough to win 3-D competitions and to hunt big game.

**MEDIUM CAMS:** Both string and cable sides of these cams have oval lobes. These cams are more dynamic, but they still allow a relatively smooth draw. Medium cams allow more energy storage and more speed than energy wheels. As a general rule, Mullaney says, medium cams store approximately 1 ¼ ft-lb of energy for each pound of peak weight. Consequently, your 70-pound bow stores around 87.5 ft-lb of energy.

**HARD CAMS:** Think of hard cams as hatchet cams because they have a severely elliptical shape or lobe on both the bowstring and cable sides. Archery engineer Mullaney says these cams can potentially store as much as 1 1/2 ft-lb of energy per pound of draw weight, if properly tuned. With hatchet cams, your 70-pound bow can potentially store more than 100 ft-lb of energy. Twin-cam bows built with two hatchet cams can be very fast. They can also be very difficult to shoot well, and so they are not recommended for beginners.

## UNDERSTANDING A DRAW FORCE CURVE

An engineering drawing called a draw force curve represents the total stored energy in a compound bow from its rest position to full draw … and even beyond. It also represents the increasing muscle strength you need as you pull to full draw; how far you must pull at peak draw weight; and how rapidly the bow lets-off and by how much.

On the horizontal X-axis, a draw force curve plots inches of draw length, while on the vertical Y-axis it shows pounds of draw weight. The area beneath the resulting curve (and you can construct a draw force curve for any bow) is the total stored energy or foot-pounds (ft-lbs) that could possibly be sunk into your arrow when you shoot. No bow actually imparts 100 percent of its stored energy to an arrow, but the more efficient your set-up is, the greater the percentage of energy transferred and the greater your broadhead's impact power.

The effort required to draw a bow with energy wheels or soft cams builds gradually, peaks sharply and then slides gradually into the "valley," the point where the holding weight is least and let-off is maximized. Acclaimed archery entertainer and trick-shot artist Bob Markworth shoots a bow with this style soft cam at a low draw weight because it is easy for him to manage as he shoots balloons out of his assistant's hand!

You can draw any compound bow beyond its valley, but it is not recommended. Pulling up the back of the valley, or against "the wall" as it is called, causes the bow to shoot inefficiently as thrust against your arrow increases, then decreases, and at last increases again before it leaves the string. This herky-jerky motion does not promote smooth arrow flight.

With hard cams, your drawing effort will increase sharply, last perhaps for 10 inches at peak weight, and then drop rapidly into a short, steep valley. Unlike a bow with soft cams that drop you smoothly into the valley, if you are unused to shooting a hard cam, you will feel a distinct and unpleasant jerk when a hard cam drops into its valley.

What this means is that bows with hard cams require greater and more prolonged effort to pull to full draw or to draw through the draw force cycle. Bows equipped with medium cams, fall somewhere between the two twin-cam extremes of soft, round cam, and hard cam.

Hard cams typically give you greater arrow speed than soft cams, but for the reasons mentioned above, many bowhunters find them less pleasant and more difficult to shoot accurately, especially if trophy deer cause even the slightest buck fever. A hard cam's short valley, a couple inches or so, demands that you hold the bow at full draw with discipline. The slightest bit of let-down or anticipation can either cause you to release prematurely or else change the arrow's impact point by several inches, even at short range. Beyond a short-range shot, that is enough to miss completely.

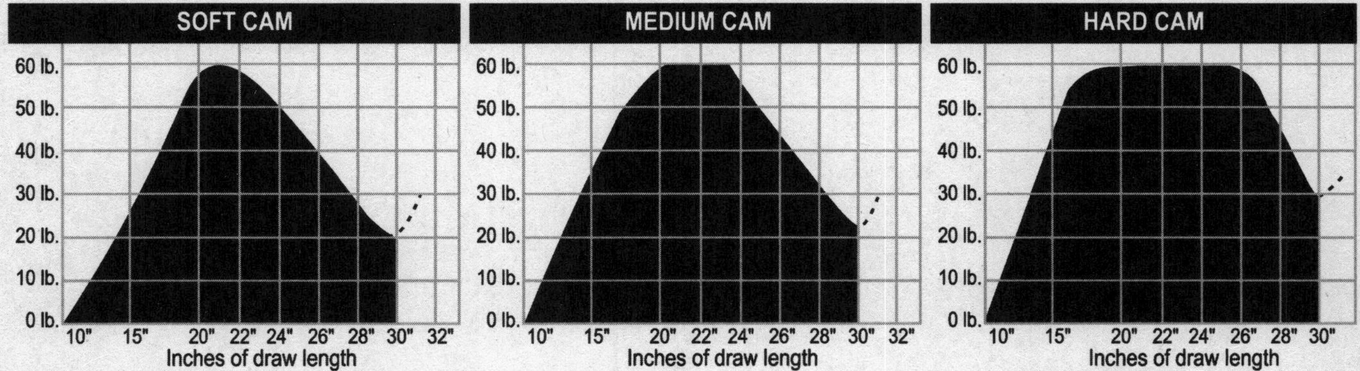


Force draw (or draw force) curves tell us a number of things about our bows. They give us a pictorial representation of the energy our bow stores at full draw, the point at which our cam reaches peak draw, at which it begins the let-off and the valley at our given draw length. The above diagrams represent hypothetical bows.

Increased speed causes quite a few problems. Fast bows are more temperamental than slower ones. Slight flaws in your release are exaggerated by the manner in which your arrow absorbs energy. In other words, "columnar loading" (the mechanics of applying an energy vector only to the base of an arrow shaft rather than unevenly throughout its length) initially makes the nock end of your arrow want to fly faster than your broadhead end!

Finally, without attention to dampening the noise of a shot, a well-tuned hard-cam bow will be noisier than a soft-cam bow. Why? Hard, angular cams transmit a greater amount of energy to your arrow . . . but also to the bow. This causes vibration, noisy vibration, and what is known as "riser buzz" and "tennis elbow."

Because it is a high-energy system and leaves some of that energy within your arm and the bow after a shot, a fast, radical, hard-cam bow built with a single-cam or twin-cams requires continuous maintenance and tuning. So, if spending time paper-tuning your equipment and checking it regularly at your work bench is not a problem for you, a hard-cam bow may be just right. For long shots at unknown distances, the increased arrow speed and flatter trajectory of hard-cam bows certainly offer advantages. Again, expect that the trade-off is more time spent tuning your set-up.

The average bowhunter who limits himself or herself to 20 or 30 yard shots will probably be more successful and perhaps happier, too, with a soft- or a medium-cam bow. Although they will launch arrows slower, they are quieter, smoother-shooting and easier to keep tuned.

# Straight Arrow

In the jungle of Papua New Guinea, Bob Markworth's hunting friend, Kapara, learned that a bow and well-developed hunting skills are practically useless without a good arrow. The arrow drives home your point; it delivers your message.

Although Kapara might disagree, for us, an arrow is an assembled shaft plus the required components, such as a broadhead and steering feathers. Except for some bowfishing shafts, which may be solid and very heavy, are tied to the bow via a string and are typically shot a short distance, hunting shafts are hollow and lightweight.

Obviously, a shaft has two ends. On the front, you mount a point, sometimes directly onto the shaft and sometimes via an insert. Toward the rear, you mount stabilizing fletching, and on the very butt end, a notched "nock" that holds the shaft on your bowstring.

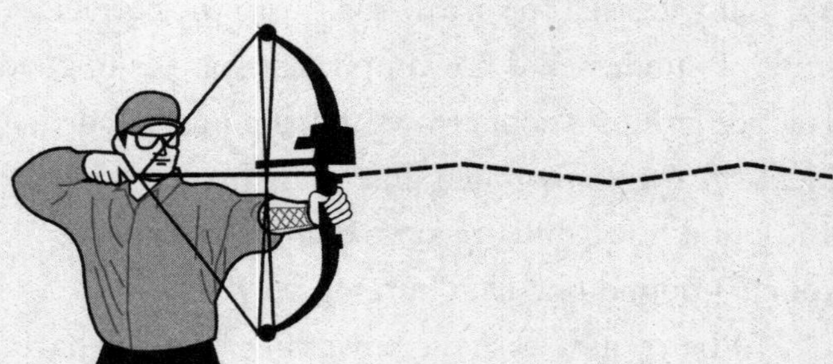

Your arrow immediately responds to the manner of your release. A finger release (top) causes your arrow to swing around your moving fingers as the string bursts forward, and this imparts a side-to-side effect to your arrow in the horizontal plane, called "wallowing." Shoot with a mechanical release aid and your arrow is given its forward motion in part by the nock set–hence the emphasis on straight-line nock travel–and this causes "porpoising," or up-and-down movement in the vertical plane.

## UNDERSTANDING YOUR ARROW

Arrow shafts are measured and graded by their "spine" or stiffness. This is an important term to understand because manufacturers build arrows in many different spines. For perfect arrow flight, you must match the right arrow size and spine to your bow.

According to the Archery Trade Association, spine is the amount of bend in an arrow shaft caused by a specific weight placed at its center while the shaft is supported at the ends. In addition, the recovery characteristics of an arrow permit it to bend and then return to its original shape while in flight. This definition fits any type of arrow: wood, aluminum, carbon or composite.

An arrow shaft bends as it leaves the bowstring, recovering to its original straight shape several yards down range. This is called "archer's paradox." Its spine is a measure of how much it bends. All arrows from every kind of bow bend when they are shot (with the possible exception of those from Kapara's bow). Some bend more than others. Your job is to minimize that bending so your arrow rapidly achieves stability. If bending occurs at the right frequency before the arrow straightens, its path can be true; otherwise, it will fly poorly.

Shafts released by a mechanical release aid flex in a vertical plane, parallel to the long axis of the bow, while those released with fingers flex in a horizontal plane, perpendicular to the long axis of the bow. A shaft that is correctly spined for your bow set-up will flex less and recover more quickly than one of improper spine. As you are tuning for hunting season, this is an important factor.

For best arrow flight with your hunting set-up, you will need the arrow shaft with the correct spine. To understand how important spine is to good practice groups, shoot arrows that are mismatched. Identical arrows fly much differently from your 45-pound bowfishing recurve than they do from your 70-pound one-cam hunting bow.

When you release the bowstring, you still have power over the bow, but the arrow is gone and out of your control. Like words hastily spoken, you cannot recall the arrow. Therefore, it is critical to find the arrow that flies best from your set-up. This is why arrow-shaft manufacturers offer a fairly bewildering array of sizes and instructions for determining the proper spine.

Each arrow-shaft manufacturer publishes an arrow-shaft selection chart. These are designed to help you match a specific spine (or perhaps as many as three) with the finished arrow's length, the point weight you use, your draw length, the draw weight you are shooting and the type of wheel or cam the bow has, if any: round, hard twin cam, one-cam or recurve. If your arrows are not grouping well, consult the arrow chart for the brand you are shooting. Your shafts may be spined incorrectly for your draw weight. Manufacturers who develop new arrows and stay abreast of emerging bow technology routinely update their arrow charts. Check with a pro shop for current information.

Although one will be most highly recommended, several arrow sizes will normally fly smoothly from your bow. If you are fortunate enough to have a full-line archery dealer in your neighborhood, you may be able to test several size shafts to learn which flies best.

An arrow's spine rating is determined by its wall thickness, diameter, length and the weight of the head, but diameter has the greatest influence.

Usually, the larger the diameter and thicker the walls, the greater the spine. However, a larger diameter arrow with a thin wall can be made stiffer (and lighter) than a smaller diameter arrow with a thick wall.

Shorter shafts will be stiffer than longer shafts. Obviously, a 32-inch 2213 shaft will flex much more than a 26-inch 2213 shaft.

Heavy heads reduce an arrow's spine. A 32-inch 2213 aluminum arrow with a 125-gr. broadhead will flex more than an identical arrow with a 100-gr. head.

Many other variables also affect spine and can change the way your arrow behaves when it is shot. Large fletching, for example, stiffens an arrow in flight. An arrow rest's spring tension setting can affect arrow flight enough to effectively change spine value. And, of course, the way you release the arrow can affect its spine; arrows released with fingers bend more than those shot with a release.

Consider a 30-inch aluminum shaft with a manufacturer's spine rating of 2315. That number, 2315, is printed on the arrow. The first two numbers indicate the shaft's diameter in 64ths of an inch. This arrow is 23/64 inches in diameter, about a third of an inch. The second two numbers tell you its wall thickness in thousandths of an inch, in this case 15/1,000-inch. The manufacturer says this shaft weighs 350 gr. By contrast, a 30-inch 2413 aluminum shaft with a diameter of 24/64-inch and wall thickness of 13/1,000-inch from the same manufacturer weighs 312 gr. Although these shafts have comparable spine, one outweighs the other by 11 percent, and that is significant from a point of view of energy the arrow absorbs when you release the string.

Typically, any given carbon shaft will work over a wider range of spine sizes than will aluminum shafts. This means it is easier to choose the correct spine for a carbon shaft than for an aluminum shaft.

## SHAFT SIZE AND WEIGHT

After you make a spine selection, your next consideration is weight. All things being equal, for speed, your best selection will be a lightweight arrow, probably built on a carbon shaft. Lightweight carbon arrows fly faster and with a flatter trajectory than comparably spined aluminum arrows. That is the good news, but that is not every consideration.

No arrow ever absorbs all of a bow's stored energy and lightweight arrows absorb less than heavy arrows, which may absorb as much as 80 percent of a bow's deliverable energy. This means lightweight arrows leave more energy behind in vibration, shock and noise, so you feel a shot much more in your hand and your arm, your bow set-up must be checked more frequently to be sure it does not fall apart, and your shot is noisier. The noise of a 300 fps arrow needs to be dampened and a variety of accessories are designed to help: string silencers, limb pads, extra padding or "socks" in the bow's limb pockets, shock-absorbing stabilizers and so on.

It is an arguable point, but because they absorb less energy, lightweight shafts may not penetrate as well as heavier shafts. This complicates your selection of broadheads. Penetration is not a factor for a competitor shooting at a foam target or a Spartana grass matt, but for a bowhunter aiming at flesh and bone, it is crucial to a generous blood trail.

Light aluminum shafts have thinner walls, and are not as durable as heavier shafts. Although several very good arrow straighteners exist, once the shaft has taken a crease, it is impossible to remove it completely. Never use it again for bowhunting.

A final consideration is that ultralight, high-speed arrows tipped with broadheads are more temperamental than heavier and slower, but more stable arrows. Unless your shot is perfect, very light arrows are likely to react instantly to any variation other than ideal shooting conditions.

The old rule recommended nine gr. of arrow weight for every pound of draw weight. For a 60-pound bow, you shot a 540-gr. arrow. Given modern bow and arrow construction and today's emphasis on a light, fast arrow, modern bowhunters have discarded the old rule. Nevertheless, using draw weight to determine arrow weight is still appropriate. Today, six grains of arrow weight per pound of draw weight is acceptable.

## MEASURING ARROW SPEED

We measure arrow speed and rate a bow's performance two ways. Understand the two systems and you will have a standard against which you can tune your own shooting system. Keep in mind that published bow speed is usually the peak arrow speed a company's can achieve. Do not imagine that you can shoot the bow at this speed without a lot of effort.

"Bow speed" is the speed of a properly spined arrow shot from that bow and it is measured in feet per second (fps). A bow shooting 300 fps has become the standard for manufacturers and bowhunters. 300 fps is fast. We usually do not relate it to miles per hour (mph)–in the same way we do not measure the family car in feet per second–but an arrow traveling that fast is moving 1,080,000 feet per hour. That is an awfully big number, but if you were traveling 300 fps–204.55 mph–in the family car, your children would be bug-eyed in terror.

The original speed rating was called "AMO" and it has always been the lesser of the two measures. AMO stands for the Archery Manufacturer's and Merchants Organization (now known as the Archery Trade Association, and some manufacturers are now designating speed as ATA), and it oversees equipment standardization and lobbies in support of bowhunting. The AMO rating is the speed the normal archer will attain with minimum effort. A bow is AMO rated at 30-inch draw length, 60-pound draw weight and a 540-gr. arrow (nine grains of arrow weight per pound of draw weight).

The newer and faster "IBO" speed rating is named after the International Bowhunting Organization, which sponsors 3-D tournaments. Think of the IBO rating as the maximum speed your bow can produce under ideal conditions when the set-up, including the arrow, is perfect. IBO speeds are determined with a 30-inch draw length, a draw weight of 70- pounds and a lightweight, 350-gr. arrow (five grains of arrow weight per pound of draw weight).

Lighter arrows (five grains, not nine) at heavier draw weights (70 pounds, not 60) fly faster. A typical high-end hunting bow will shoot 223 fps AMO. The same bow tested on the IBO scale shoots 300 fps. It will take a significant amount of tuning, tinkering and proper equipment selection to make your arrows fly at that speed.

## THE CHRONOGRAPH

You measure arrow speed with a chronograph. Most pro shops and many clubs have one. 3-D tournaments will have one available to ensure that competitors shoot to standard. (Both ASA and IBO limit arrow speed to 280 fps.) Chronographs are not expensive and they are accurate, especially with a three-shot average.

A chronograph clocks how long it takes your arrow to pass over a photoelectric circuit actuated when the arrow interrupts a beam of light. This chronograph style can be adjusted to the length of an arrow and it automatically resets. The ProChrono Digital from Competition Electronics is powered by a single nine-volt battery and will give readings from 22 to 7,000 fps in temperatures from 33 to 100 degrees. It is lightweight, easy to set up and has an error of plus or minus a couple of percentage points.

The Shooting Chrony works on the same principle, measuring with a 99.5 percent accuracy. The Master Chrony uses a 16-foot phone cord to connect it to a digital display unit and optional printer. The value of a separate readout and printer is that you can move the display away from the actual shooting.

The Arrowspeed RadarChron by Sports Sensors is a small Doppler radar that uses microwave technology (high frequency, short wavelength 5.8-gigahertz energy) to measure arrow speed. Unlike optical chronographs, the short-range microwave operation of the Arrowspeed cannot be affected by background light or shadows. The Arrowspeed is 2.5 inches by 3.69 inches and weighs 2.7 ounces. It is powered by a three-volt camera battery and has a plus-or-minus two percent error range between 150 and 450 fps.

## MEASURING KINETIC ENERGY

Arguably, kinetic energy (KE) is an important concept in bowhunting because it is one of our few relative measures of penetration. Without penetrating ability, you simply have no hunting ability. Penetration with a broadhead-tipped arrow means slicing and bleeding, because that is how an arrow kills a game animal. With clean shots to the vitals, good penetration means a good blood trail and a dead game animal within minutes.

It is no longer arguable whether you want a broadhead to pass completely through an animal or to remain inside it. When pre-historic bowhunters shot big game, their flint arrowheads certainly remained inside the animal, but these hunters often used poison because their arrows did not pack enough KE to kill a deer or a giraffe quickly by hemorrhaging alone. Bow and arrow dynamics are different today. The idea that a broadhead should remain inside an animal and continue to cut its insides as it runs is discredited.

The penetration standard today is an arrow tipped with a super-sharp broadhead that passes cleanly and quickly through an animal. This gives you an entry hole and an exit hole, both leaking blood. Because most deer and bears are shot from treestands, it is important to have that lower exit hole for blood to drain as the heart pumps.

Eland are the largest of the African antelope and bulls can weigh up to 2,000 pounds. To take one of these trophies requires an arrow that delivers greater kinetic energy than is needed to take a 150-pound whitetail buck. Hunting consultant and "journeyman bowhunter" Rick Valdez has successfully taken most of the world's big-game animals and many small ones as well. He harvested his African eland in July 2001 while hunting with Nico Lourens Safaris and shooting carbon arrows and mechanical broadheads.

How much kinetic energy is enough? There is no standard, but the larger the game animal, the greater the KE required for a quick, clean kill. For a 100-pound deer, 40 to 50 foot-pounds is sufficient; less is acceptable with precise arrow placement. For larger, heavier animals like elk or caribou, you should step up your on-target energy delivery. A dramatic increase in KE is required for Cape buffalo or brown bear.

The formula for calculating kinetic energy in foot-pounds is speed (in fps) squared, multiplied by total arrow weight (in grains, including your broadhead), divided by 450,240. A foot-pound is the energy required to raise one pound, one foot against gravity. Under laboratory conditions, you would think that an arrow with 50 foot-pounds of KE should penetrate twice as far as an arrow with 25 foot-pounds. Penetration is a complex result of many factors however, and it is not that simple.

Studying the formula, many bowhunters assume that a fast light arrow will give them greater KE, but the formula is deceptive in several respects. A light arrow absorbs less energy than a heavy arrow and, depending on the size, number and orientation of your broadhead blades and type of broadhead, it may retain its energy longer in flight!

Here is an example. Let us say you are shooting 250 fps with a 500-grain Easton aluminum shaft, which includes a 100-grain broadhead and the insert. What happens if you switch to a 400-grain Carbon Force arrow with a 75-grain head? You pick up about ten fps, but the heavier projectile delivers 69.4 foot-pounds of KE while the lighter (but faster!) arrow gives you 60.0 foot-pounds. The lighter projectile has 16 percent less energy at chronograph or point-blank range than the heavier projectile!

At close range, say ten to 20 yards, this should not make a difference, but what about longer distances? Again, conventional wisdom suggests that the heavier arrow will retain more energy at 30 or 40 yards.

In his book Idiot Proof Archery, archery coach and bowhunter Bernie Pellerite argues that this is not so because the larger, heavier arrow is subject to greater resistance or drag than the smaller, lighter arrow. A smaller, lighter shaft with a mechanical head in his experiments retains greater energy at 40 yards because it encounters less resistance than an arrow with fixed blades.

Conventional wisdom also says that another way to increase KE is to increase your draw weight. Increase just five pounds and you can pick up about 10 percent in energy and gain speed and a flatter trajectory.

We also know that stiffer, straight-flying arrows out-penetrate wobbly arrows. For deepest penetration, your arrow's energy must be directed down the centerline of the shaft, because when a flexing arrow hits game—unless it is flying perfectly and hits perfectly straight-on—the shaft whips to one side. This diminishes the energy available to drive the shaft through your quarry. In perfect flight, all energy is centered behind the broadhead.

Walking or running animals cause arrows to lurch sideways on impact. The broadhead enters, the shaft whips to one side, and penetration suffers. For best penetration, never shoot at a running animal. Unless your bow is extra-heavy, you will probably fail to shoot completely through it.

Unfortunately, there is no formula for determining what game animals can (or should) be hunted with any particular bow set-up. In the field, too many conditions interfere with precise measurements. Nevertheless, Easton has published the following recommendations which, they note, are intended only to be a guide. If you have any doubt about your own set-up, err on the high side and remember that while heavier arrows absorb more KE, resistance slows those heavier set-ups and reduces the KE available to drive your shaft completely through an animal. Undoubtedly, the ideal size and weight arrow is the one that you can put successfully on target within your own shooting range.

| KE (FT/LB) OF YOUR SET-UP | SUITABLE FOR HUNTING |
|---|---|
| Less than 25 | Small game: rabbit and squirrel |
| 26–41 | Medium game: pronghorn and deer |
| 42–65 | Large game: black bear, elk, and wild boar |
| 66 and higher | Big Game: African plains game, grizzly, and brown bears |

## SHOULD YOU SHOOT ALUMINUM OR CARBON ARROWS?

Aluminum or carbon? Each type shaft has its proponents and detractors. "Carbon has unquestionably grown in popularity," says Deb Adamson at Easton, which manufactures Easton aluminum and Beman carbon shafts. "Carbon shafts are excellent and the price has fallen in the last few years, but assuming they come from the manufacturer straight (a carbon shaft cannot be straightened) it is going to be hard to beat a carbon shaft for speed, accuracy and durability. An arrow shaft is what delivers your broadhead on target, so we do not believe you should economize there. Buy quality and that means an exacting level of straightness with tight-fitting components."

Aluminum arrow shafts have been the standard for years, only recently being overtaken by the carbon revolution. Aluminum arrows are consistent in size and weight, thanks to precise manufacturing tolerances. They are formed by drawing aluminum tubes across a mandrel until they meet exact specifications for diameter, wall thickness and weight. The shafts are then straightened to tolerances as fine as .0015 inch.

The straighter they are, the more they cost, but how straight is straight enough? Usually, competitors want supreme, ultra-straight grades. For bowhunting, medium grades are fine.

Aluminum shafts are available in more than 50 sizes, with diameters ranging from 14/64 to 26/64 inch, and wall thickness from .011 to .19 inch. Within this range, everyone who shoots a bow can find a good shaft, one with the correct combination of spine and weight, from ultra-light for speed to ultra-heavy for maximum launch energy.

Any aluminum arrow can bend and break and the thinner the wall, the more susceptible it is to damage. Aluminum arrows with thick walls, however, hold up well under hunting conditions. Within a limited range, aluminum shafts can be straightened and reused for practice, not for hunting.

A standard feature of aluminum shafts is the use of head and nock inserts made of aluminum, plastic or carbon. Aluminum inserts are anchored with hot-melt glue. Carbon inserts, which weigh 10 to 15 gr. less than aluminum, may be installed with epoxy . . . or are of the press-fit style that can be used without glue because they fit so tightly inside the tubes.

Aluminum arrows come in a multitude of camouflage designs and colors to fit every bowhunter's taste. They are also less expensive than carbon shafts.

Carbon arrows may be all-carbon or composite or even aluminum covered by multiple wraps of woven carbon matt. These shafts are characterized by relatively small diameter and light weight; even at their maximum length and stiffness, they are lighter than aluminum. Carbon allows you to keep kinetic energy delivery high and gives you a speed advantage, too.

Carbon shafts bend, but do not stay bent, so you will never need to straighten them, and they can break if they hit a hard object. The biggest problem for carbon may come from being struck by another arrow at a target butt. Unlike aluminum, a carbon shaft that is chipped or creased is unusable and should be discarded, because splinters of carbon are extremely sharp and even a small shred of ingested carbon, if an arrow were to fracture in a game animal, could be deadly.

Arrow penetration tests using different types of foam targets give carbon arrows the edge over aluminum arrows with comparable spine, due primarily to carbon's smaller diameter. Larger-diameter shafts drift a little more in a crosswind, too.

Although dot and 3-D shooters prefer larger aluminum shafts called "line cutters," many bowhunters argue that slender carbon shafts, offering less surface resistance, do penetrate better. Others say the hole made by a broadhead is so much larger than the shaft diameter that penetration is unlikely to be affected by shaft size.

Carbon's small diameter has caused rest-clearance problems on older style shoot-through rests. With a larger diameter shaft, a rest's launcher arms can be spread apart, allowing lots of room for fletching to clear. With carbon shafts, support arm tips must be placed close together. Fletching must line up perfectly to slip between the arms.

In the early 1990s, carbon shaft design was in its infancy. Heads and nocks were occasionally attached with outserts, which slipped over the end of the shafts. That technology has been refined and today's inserts help with consistent arrow flight and ease of changing heads.

Initial thinking behind carbon arrows was that they were tough, flexible and would help bowhunters pick up arrow speed. In recent years, even many traditional archers have switched to carbon arrows. One reason for such a strong movement to carbon is their stiff spine in relation to weight. Traditional archers prefer wood shafts, but a recurve shooter with a long draw often has difficulty buying adequately spined cedar shafts. Plus wood arrows are expensive and difficult to find with good, straight grain. With carbon, you get plenty of spine at any arrow length.

A second reason for the move to carbon is the small diameter of carbon arrows. Unlike compound bows, not all recurves and longbows are cut past center. This makes carbon attractive, because a small-diameter shaft lays closer to the bow's centerline than a larger diameter wood or aluminum shaft.

Early carbon arrows were almost prohibitively expensive. The development of new grades of carbon, however, and new manufacturing methods have put low-end carbon shafts in a price range comparable to the best grades of aluminum.

Cedar arrows have a strong following among ardent stick bow shooters and some archers believe wood is a superior arrow material because it has flexing qualities similar to carbon that make arrows forgiving. Nevertheless, solid wood arrows do not perform as consistently as aluminum or carbon because they are heavy, the direction of grain must be consistent and they are hard to re-straighten if they bend.

Even hand-selected cedar varies greatly in density and weight, and cedar shafts must be methodically matched for spine. Well-matched cedar shafts can be shot accurately from stick bows and they can be painted and fletched handsomely.

Although, quality wood arrows cost more than any other shaft material, they have a brittle reputation and their durability is less than desirable, even when completely waterproofed. In addition, they can absorb water and warp in wet weather.

## CARBON SHAFT SAFETY

Carbon shafts are suitable for any hunting application. If carbon arrows are abused, hit by other arrows or slapped against hard objects, however, damage to the carbon fibers can occur. Carbon arrows should always be gently flexed and twisted end-to-end as well as visually inspected for delamination or splitting before shooting. A damaged shaft could fail on release and hurt you or others.

When you set up a bow to shoot carbon, be sure to check your rest settings, specifically prong spacing to insure your arrows will not fall through. Be aware also of your arrow's position during the draw to avoid having it fall off the rest, as it could become jammed between the rest and riser. An arrow jammed between the rest and riser or between the prongs of the rest will fail.

Carbon hunting arrows could break or delaminate after being shot into an animal, resulting in sharp splinter-like fragments left inside its body. A break may occur inside an animal and not be immediately obvious after you recover it. These fragments will be harmful if ingested, so use extreme caution when field dressing game. In the past, manufacturers have recommended that you remove flesh in the immediate area of the wound, clean the area surrounding the wound, and dispose of any meat that might contain carbon splinters.

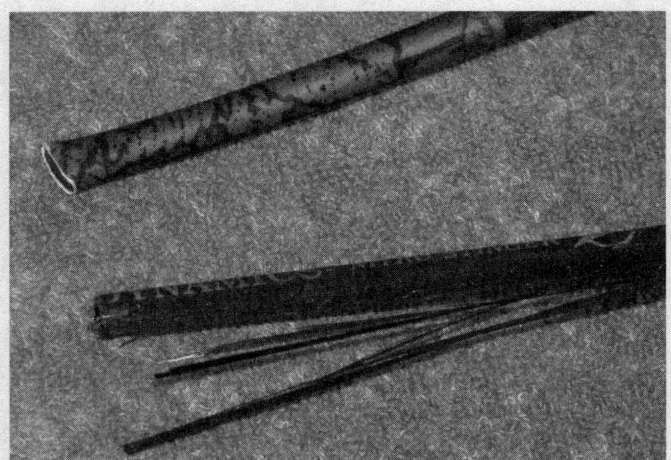

Factors that differentiate aluminum from carbon/graphite arrows are how they bend, how they break, and the potential results. All shafts bend slightly as they leave your bowstring, even wood. An aluminum arrow will bend and can be repaired–some–but the result of hitting a rock will most likely be a broken shaft, and a broadhead and insert driven down into the fore-end as much as an inch. Bowhunters occasionally find broken aluminum shafts when they field dress a game animal. Stepping on a shaft or hitting a tree may give it a permanent crease, too. In either case, the arrow should be discarded. A carbon shaft, on the other hand, will bend a great deal and still recover fully. If a carbon arrow shatters as it passes through a big-game animal, and this is exceptionally rare, harmful carbon splinters can remain inside the body cavity. Unless they are removed before the meat is packaged and prepared for the table, these splinters can be deadly. While carbon shafts resist the dings and dents you find in oft-used aluminum arrows, they should also be discarded if damaged.

## SHAFT ACCESSORIES

Once you have chosen between carbon or aluminum and made a properly spined shaft selection for your draw weight and style of bow, you must attach things to that shaft: fletching to steer it, a nock to hold it on the bowstring and some type of arrow point and insert. Every shaft type has its own set of options, and your archery club or pro shop can guide you through the selection and set-up process until it becomes second nature.

Whatever you choose, unless you have the pro shop set everything up or you buy ready-made arrows, your new arrow shaft will be useless. Wood arrows must be tapered, and there are special tools for both ends. Carbon and aluminum shafts must have lightweight threaded inserts installed for standard practice points or broadheads. The inserts should fit tightly and should press absolutely straight into the shaft; rotate them to be sure that any glue used completely encircles the insert; finally, press them onto a flat surface to be sure they are fully seated. Unless you buy the correct size insert for your arrow, all bets are off, and if you glue the insert in crooked, your chance of hitting what you are shooting at dramatically decreases. With the increasing popularity of carbon, there has been a major push to standardize. Around 2005, main-line carbon shafts use carbon inserts of the same style as aluminum shafts, but the two are not interchangeable because of the differing shaft sizes.

The beauty of the broadhead insert is that it allows you to screw in and then remove arrow points as often as you desire. On the back end, you can experiment with different types of arrow nocks or even use one of the relatively new, stick-on tunable nocks that rotate to give you the best fletching-arrow rest orientation.

The arrow nock is critical to shooting performance. Nocks attach to the rear of your arrow shaft to hold it on the bowstring. They should snap on the string snugly, but not so tight that they hinder arrow flight when you release. Bowhunters who shoot release-aids often say they prefer nocks to be a little tighter than finger shooters. This keeps arrows from falling off the string after contact with the jaws of a release.

Consistency is crucial for successful bowhunting. Your arrows should fit the string identically and release with equal force. Once you find a nock that fits your bowstring and snaps on and off perfectly, use the same brand and size on all arrows.

Two types of nocks are preferred, but the one-piece nock that is glued directly onto a swaged shaft is being replaced for both aluminum and carbon shafts by press-in nocks that are easy to rotate for fletching clearance over your rest. To rotate a glue-on nock, you must melt it with heat and then cut it off.

You must put the nock on the shaft straight. A crooked nock pushes arrows slightly sideways when you release, causing your arrow to fly erratically. If one arrow consistently hits wide or high, immediately check the nock for straightness. In the field, you can cradle the arrow on a smooth surface like the "V" between your pinched together fingernails and blow on the fletching to spin the arrow. If there is any wobble in the nock, replace it. Inexpensive arrow spinners are available from Apple Archery to help you check nock and broadhead straightness. This simple step can significantly improve your accuracy.

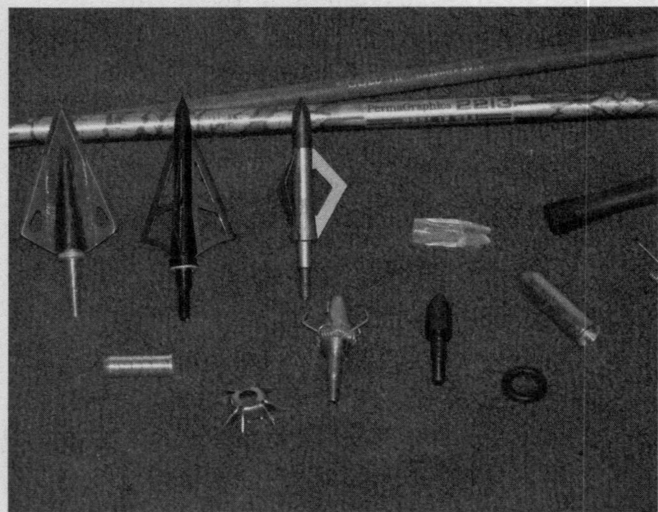

Arrows are sized by stiffness or spine, to help you decide which shaft will fly best with your set-up. Unless the shaft is wood, the manufacturer's spine index is roll printed on it. The Easton 2213 aluminum shaft has a diameter of 22/64 inches and a wall thickness of 13/1,000 inch. These shafts are drawn from 7075-T9 aluminum and have a weight tolerance of + 1% and a straightness of + .002 inches. The Gold Tip graphite XT Hunter has a weight tolerance of + 2 gr. per dozen and a straightness tolerance of + .003 inch per shaft. This arrow weighs 8.2 gr./inch with a .400-inch spine, an outside diameter of .295 inches and an inside diameter of .246 inches. You must add components to a bare shaft to make it a useful arrow, but every component you add will change its performance. It is a conundrum. This means that for ideal flight and broadhead delivery, you must take exceptional care building and maintaining your arrows: inserts and nocks must be applied in a straight line and broadheads must spin true, indicating that the force applied comes in a single direction with no torqued side vectors.

## FLETCHING

An arrow's feathers or vanes give your shaft stability in flight. Ideally, it should begin to rotate,

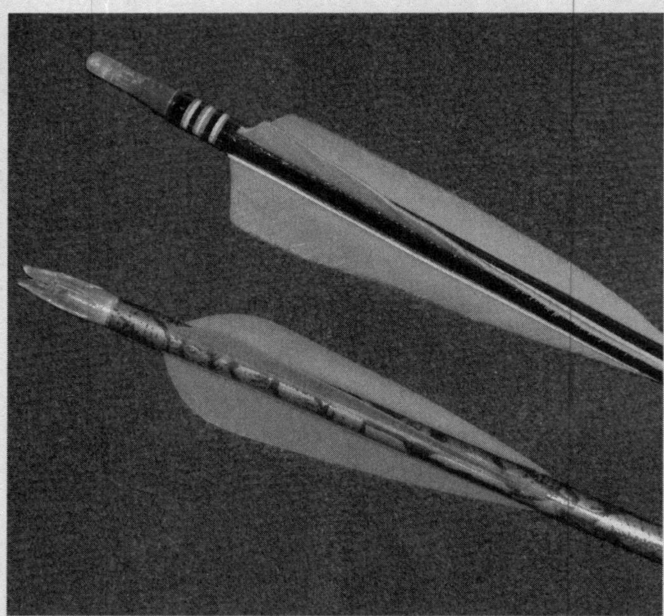

Among the other choices you make in developing your individual bowhunting set-up is whether to shoot arrows fletched with vanes or feathers. Plastic vanes made from urethane, vinyl or Mylar, are more durable and quieter than feathers. Feathers, taken from the wings of white pen-raised turkeys and dyed, are more forgiving of shooting-form errors and incidental contact with your arrow rest or a branch. They also weigh less than vanes; hence, arrows fletched with feathers are a few feet per second faster than arrows fletched with comparably sized vanes.

like a bullet fired from a rifled barrel with twisting internal lands and grooves, as soon as it clears the riser.

Man has used bird feathers to stabilize arrows since he began shooting the bow. Feathers are not as popular now as they were just a dozen years ago because we rely so heavily on plastic vanes. Some archery pro-shop owners believe that 90 percent of all arrows shot today use plastic vanes.

## SPEED

Arrow speed is a big issue. Even small, custom bow manufacturers say prospective buyers ask what speed their bows can attain. Many people do not know that, among all the other variables, arrow fletching makes a difference in speed and feathers weigh less than plastic vanes. Bob Link at Trueflight says, "If you use feathers, there is less mass to accelerate and less wasted energy. Feathers save as much as 40 grains weight over full-length plastic vanes, and if they hit your arrow rest or bow riser they less interference. This also contributes to higher arrow speed."

Finally, feathers provide superior guidance, which helps prevent yawing and fishtailing–erratic oscillations that add drag and slow an arrow down.

"On typical equipment," Link says, "independent tests confirm a five-feet-per-second gain as the arrow leaves the bow."

And how about down range? Velocity testing by archery engineer Norb Mullaney has shown that comparable feather-fletched arrows are still traveling four feet per second faster than plastic at 29 yards. Therefore, at usual bowhunting ranges, feather-fletched arrows travel faster and have flatter trajectories than plastic-fletched arrows.

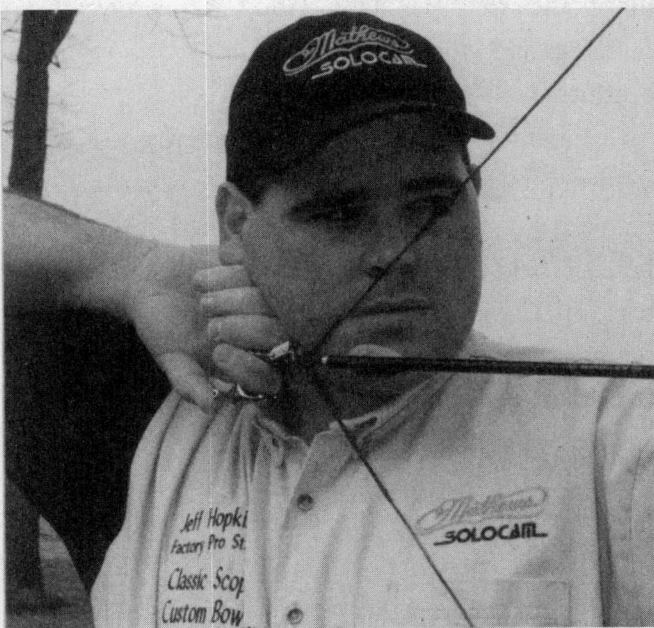


These two photos on the previous page compare typical anchor positions of a finger shooter and a release shooter. The amount of string contact with the release agent–fingers or mechanical release–is apparent and this helps understand archer's paradox or the bending of an arrow in the horizontal plane around the bow riser when released with fingers. When released with a mechanical release, the arrow flexes vertically from the columnar loading applied to your shaft. Finger shooter Gene Goldacker, a bowhunter and NFAA competitor, anchors with the knuckle of his thumb at the point of his jaw, rather than a more typical anchor with the tip of the index or middle finger at the corner of the mouth. For true alignment, his kisser button is pre-set to touch the tip of his nose and the string comes back to touch his lips also. This gives him multiple checks on his anchor in addition to the peep sight. Release shooter Jeff Hopkins, a bowhunter and world class 3-D champion, anchors behind his jaw. Jeff draws the string to the exact position each time by bringing it back to touch his nose and the corner of his mouth. Jeff also uses a peep sight.

## STABILITY

Feathers stabilize arrows better and faster than vanes. A feather's surface has a regular, rippling roughness that causes a periodic disturbance in airflow over it. Trueflight calls this "grip." When an arrow "yaws" or flexes to the side, grip helps realign it faster than a smooth plastic vane.

The weight savings with feathers also helps stability. Any weight added to the rear of the arrow makes the arrow less stable. Add too much weight on its rear and the arrow will try to fly down range butt first.

Finally, as fletching crosses the arrow rest following release, you will experience occasional incidental contact even on a well-tuned bow. Feathers fold down out of the way, and then pop back up. Plastic vanes, because they are more rigid, bounce the rear of the arrow out of alignment. This deflection causes substantial arrow swing and is aggravated by a plastic vane's weight and lack of grip.

## YAWING

"Yaw" or "porpoising" is caused by columnar loading of the shaft and thrust applied in the vertical plane. For a microsecond, the end wants to go faster than the middle and the heavy head is least responsive to movement in any direction. The result is yawing or vertical flexing, sometimes called porpoising.

While the arrow is yawed, aerodynamic forces push it away from where you aimed it. Due to the more sluggish straightening ability of plastic vanes, the arrow oscillates from one yawed condition to another and this flexing costs speed, range and accuracy. While the condition gradually decreases, feather faithful believe feathers decrease it faster than vanes. What's more, the penetration of a yawed arrow is lower than a straight arrow. Yawing dissipates energy away from straight-line penetration.

## THE FEATHER RECORD

A feather's ability to fold down if it hits something eliminates the large initial reaction after contact. A feather's light weight and "grip" adds to an arrow's stability and brings it into straight flight quickly. The combination of all these advantages means good arrow flight is more readily achievable with feathers. Thus, a feather-fletched arrow tolerates a range of bow variables and some errors in shooting form. Feathers also make tuning easier.

Feathers fly well even with variations in spine, bow weight and form of release. In the field, not many variables are controllable. Small variations in form are normal. Time, terrain, obstacles, cross winds . . . all these things add variation. A feather-fletched arrow simply tolerates variations better than vanes.

Because most of them shoot off a solid and unforgiving arrow shelf, traditional archers overwhelmingly shoot feathers. A minority of recurve shooters use a flipper-style rest and cushion plunger. This minority uses low-profile vanes, but their shafts are quite small and they tend to be expert in shooting form with a flawless release.

Feathers give traditional bowhunters control. Their feathers certainly hit the bow's riser at the shelf area before lying down flat, thereby causing remarkably little arrow flight interference. Feather adherents argue that the same thing happens when a shot hits or passes close to a branch.

According to Gateway Feather, bowhunters who consider using feathers rather than vanes often ask, "What orientation feathers should I use, left-wing or right-wing?" and "I shoot right handed. Should I use right-wing feathers?" Feathers from a turkey's left wing and right wing grow in mirrored curves and archers concerned with eliminating any possible source of error are interested. By all accounts, whether you use left- or right-wing feathers is not an issue that makes any measurable difference, because arrows do not being to spin until they are clear of the bow.

"Right-wing feathers, those with the little edge we call a 'catch lip,' have the lip on the left and rotate the shaft clockwise," Link says. "Left-wing feathers, with the 'catch lip' on the right side of the base, rotate counter-clockwise as seen by the shooter."

The big knocks on feathers are that they soak up moisture and are noisy. A rain-soaked feather changes your shooting dynamic because the weight is greater and a wet feather will not respond as quickly as a vane or a dry feather. However, several waterproofing agents are available to prevent their soaking up moisture.

Vanes shoot quieter than feathers. In a quiet wood, you can hear the flight of a feathered shaft, notes Roger Grundman of Flex-Fletch. Today, because bowhunters are doing everything possible to silence their shot, this is an issue. Vanes have very little "whistle" or flutter. On the other hand, the soft s-s-s-s-s sound of an arrow might only be a bird in flight or the wind rustling through leaves.

## VANES

Bowhunters who want the latest gear and greatest arrow speed typically switch to vanes, but Link wonders if this is their best choice. "High-performance set-ups mean more energy and lower flight times," he says. "Stability and solid guidance are even more important. Any errors in form or equipment imperfections will be magnified. Less time is available for your guidance system to work."

While it is less of a problem today, plastic's flexibility and stiffness can change with variations in temperature. Plastic becomes more rigid in cold weather and more flexible in hot weather. This affects arrow flight and bow tuning.

Ultra-slow motion film shows that when an arrow is shot, plastic vanes ripple and flap as if the shooter were shaking a towel. This begins immediately due to the low strength-to-weight ratio of plastic, and it continues as the arrow plunges down range. The same film shows feathers quickly regaining an upright and stabilizing posture, even at high speed.

Plastic vanes cost less than feathers and are easier to mass-produce. Feathers grow on white birds and are plucked and cut by hand; the bases are ground and the feather is dyed. These manual operations cause feathers to cost more than plastic.

## FLETCHING PARTICULARS

You want the smallest fletching that will keep your arrow's weight and friction profile at a minimum. Larger fletching stabilizes better, but at some point, the large vanes develop too much drag and cause, rather than cure, a problem with arrow stabilization.

"In general," Link has written, "a five-inch, three-fletch or four-inch, four-fletch will give excellent results on hunting arrows. High-speed bows shooting wide, heavy heads may require something in the 5 3/4-inch length." This may no longer be true.

These days, bowhunters with fast bows are shooting a stiff arrow. The arrow is tipped with a lightweight head, perhaps even a mechanical head with very little profile, not a "wide, heavy" broadhead. A four-inch, three-fletch configuration is standard, and plastic vanes are the public's overwhelming choice because they are bright, cheap and easy to work with. It is rare to find a bowhunter shooting four-fletch arrows.

Bowhunters argue about everything, including the best fletching shape, especially at its rear end. Conventional wisdom says for just the right amount of drag to steady your flying arrow, an offset (glued on straight, but at a slight angle to the centerline of the shaft) or helical (curved slightly around the shaft) mount works best to add gyroscopic stabilizing and help the shaft rotate. Helical and offset fletching produces more rotation and stability than straight-mounted vanes.

Whether you shoot low-profile parabolic fletching (round back), shield-cut (a chopped back end) or some magnum style, this is a matter of personal style and is not important for flight.

With fletching, the final word may be that whatever size, style or orientation you choose, make your arrows uniform so you can test and tune for best arrow flight.

## ROTATION

At the speed an arrow rotates with correctly positioned fletching (beginning an inch to an inch and a half forward of the base of the shaft), the speed of rotation is from 1,200 to 2,500 revolutions per minute.

Trueflight commissioned a test with typical hunting arrows fletched using feathers in a strongly helical Bitzenburger clamp. After the initial "spinup" period, the arrow rotated at 2,850 rpm, or about one turn every five feet!

A note about consistency: Not only must arrow shafts be matched to a given bow, but they must also be matched to each other. Small variations in length, diameter, head weight and fletching style can make it impossible to achieve consistent arrow flight and tight groups. Your finished arrows should be identical in weight. Even with identical spine values, arrows with weight variations as small as five grains can have differing impact points at various ranges, especially shooting broadheads.

# Pressing Your Point Home: Your Broadhead

## STAY SHARP!

Floyd "Sonny" Templeton owns a septic tank cleaning business in Lincoln, Montana, a mile-high mountain town of 1,000 residents 14 miles west of the Continental Divide. It is hard work, but the area is stunningly beautiful, rich in big game and he is his own boss.

Templeton sets his own hours and he turns down jobs if they conflict with his hunting. Typically, he begins work as the snow melts sometime in April and, except for emergencies, he is finished for the year by mid-November when the ground begins to freeze again. It is this freedom, this very American self-indulgent entrepreneurial attitude, that nearly got him killed.

On the 22nd of September, 1997, Templeton stared into the cold, impassionate eyes of a man-killer and the experience was one that sends chills up his spine to this very day. That he lived to tell his story is a testament to years of experience in the outdoors, to keeping a cool head under extreme circumstances and to making the perfect shot when the pressure was on.

Ask about Floyd Templeton in Lincoln and people will shake their heads. Everyone knows him as "Sonny," a family man with grown-up kids. He laughs in a congenial and self-conscious manner and says he's "more or less a homebody."

Templeton may seem average, but get him on the subject of bowhunting and this homebody demonstrates a superior grasp of environmental concepts, biological issues and hunting tactics. Templeton truly "lives to hunt."

Templeton's brothers-in-law taught him to hunt "back east" in Bucks County, Pennsylvania. By 1968, though, he had gotten tired of the "rat race" and so moved his family to Montana. He says they would never, ever consider moving "back east."

Despite his laid-back attitude toward business, Templeton is not a sleepy, stay-at-home guy. He is thoughtful and well-traveled, an instructor for the International Bowhunter Education Program and a former Director of the Montana Bowhunter's Association. Bowhunting since he was 15 years old, the 50-ish outdoorsman has 17 animals listed in the Pope & Young record book: whitetails, pronghorns, elk and mountain lions.

"I haven't hunted with a gun in years, now," he says.

Standing five-feet-ten-inches tall, with a salt-and-pepper beard and a wide-open, Big Sky kind of smile, he's every inch a friendly, robust mountain man. When he fits an arrow on the string of his compound bow, however, he is anything but laid back. "Concentrated" comes to mind, for Templeton shoots instinctively, without sights. He "looks" his arrow into its target, a difficult shooting technique to master.

Sonny Templeton is an informed and dedicated bowhunter who understands environmental issues and is involved in the rough-and-tumble politics needed to ensure a future for those who want to hunt in a state with such rich and diverse resources as Montana. Sonny is proud of a string of bowhunting trophies that include his 70 6/8 P&Y antelope.

On Templeton's special day that September in 1997, he was elk hunting alone, even though it is not elk but whitetails that are his particular passion. Long, cool shadows were flooding down the slopes and reaching out across the floor of the high mountain meadows.

His enthusiasm to hunt, which he admits is boundless some days, over-whelmed the practicalities of his situation. He could hunt. Therefore, he did.

Templeton did not give a lot of thought to what he would he do if he actually killed an elk. How would he manage, faced with the deep, starry darkness of the high Rockies, the certain possibility of predators, including grizzlies, a long hike to his pick-up truck and 800 pounds of meat and antlers on the forest floor? Knowing Templeton, he would have managed . . . somehow.

On the 22nd, Templeton was hunting at almost two miles above sea level. Elk were visible in a distant meadow and it stood to reason that he would find a good bull or perhaps two, shadowing the herd of cows, calves and immature males. He made his way in their direction and bugled loudly. It was a melodious and echoing, multi-note screech that ended in a diminishing series of grunts and chuckles. Perfect.

Laying his bow at his feet, the right hander next chirped vigorously, making the high-pitched twittering sound of a cow talking to her calf. The elk were relaxed, as if they had never been stalked by man or beast.

Templeton had not passed another truck for miles on the rugged, unpaved US Forest Service logging road. He was very much alone and he liked his hunting that way: silent, lonely, deadly.

"Something," Templeton says, made him turn his head to the right. It could have been a deer or a bear, or even a trophy bull skulking through the timber, searching for the interloper who was squealing challenges down into the mountain basin. A bull with antlers surpassing his most recent trophy would cause his heart to pound with excitement, but any elk up close is exciting.

Templeton was not afraid of hunting alone, except for the possibility of getting lost in the Lewis & Clark Range. That would mean spending the night on a cold mountain and hours of fumbling around until he cut a road. It was not Montana's most difficult real estate, but it was tough enough if one became disoriented without a map or compass.

Templeton had seen occasional lions and bears, and his stepson, Chris, had an uncomfortably close encounter with a lion once. Other hunters told stories about the rangy, quarrelsome cats ... predators which rely primarily on sight and sound rather than smell ... walking right under their treestands, unaware of the human competitor. Had the lions detected them, the hunters would have known immediately, because cats are inquisitive, superb climbers and very fast.

Sonny Templeton was already an experienced bowhunter when the mountain lion stalked him in September 1997. A few years earlier, in December 1993, he took a lion that weighed 170 pounds and scored 14 11/16 P&Y.

"Doggone that elk scent!"

The bowhunter had, in fact, killed a big "book lion" just four years earlier. It weighed 170 pounds and lived on as a crouching, snarling wall mount to remind Templeton of his high altitude chase through the snow.

Templeton was not concerned about lions. He figured he knew lions. He had killed a big one already.

Or perhaps Templeton just thought he knew lions, because the rustling in the willows nearby was not a deer or a squirrel; it was a stalking lion and it was well aware of Templeton's presence. The hunter had become the hunted.

Templeton's first emotion was irritation. His sublime, human cocoon of superiority was not immediately threatened. He might have to yell at it to scare it away and there would go a perfectly good elk set up.

Templeton's time had come. Too bad about the elk hunt. He hollered at the lion, which slipped out of the brush a scant 15 yards away. The lion dropped into a crouch and crept toward him, legs tensed, ears laid back. Perfectly silent on four splayed, padded paws.

Templeton yelled again and still, "It just kept coming."

Adopting a tactic that wildlife management professionals suggest may work in some situations, Templeton opened his camo jacket as wide as possible to appear larger than life. All the while, he kept yelling.

In its totality, the incident only lasted a minute, but to Templeton it seems, in the recounting, to have taken far longer.

Templeton and the cat never took their eyes off each other. Each sized up the other for a weakness.

Templeton was mystified by the unrelenting gaze of the carnivore, the glassy-eyed stare of the cat's oversize watery pupils.

The lion was telling him, "Don't take offense. This isn't personal." Templeton, of course, knew otherwise. It was rapidly becoming very personal.

The big cat crept closer and finally, in exasperation, Templeton did what any hiker or hunter would do: He reached down and picked up several rocks. Throwing them at the stalking lion, Templeton believes he would have done anything to break the cat's concentration.

Templeton's first throw missed high, but the second whacked the animal squarely on the shoulder. Hard. The cat was undeterred. Less than ten yards away, its long tail twitched and its belly scraped the ground. Crouched. Tense.

In a single leap, big cats can cover 40 feet, six times their body length. Had it chosen to spring, it would have been on top of the bowhunter in an instant. But this cat just stared and bared its yellow teeth as it advanced, perhaps allowing the hot closeness of the hunter's anxious scent to center it mentally for one death-dealing charge.

"After the rock hit and it didn't run away, I thought, 'I'm in trouble.' I don't know why it didn't occur to me earlier, but at that point I began to get scared." At that point, Templeton decided his only salvation lay in self-defense.

He knew that if he ran, the lion would kill him. His death would be swift, a few seconds. Compared to a healthy, middle-aged man, a lion is far stronger and lightning fast. A killing machine, its teeth and hinged jaw are designed for separating vertebrae and crushing the victim's windpipe while its two-inch claws slash deep for a bloody hold as its victim staggers in terror.

Unlike the old saying, Templeton would know what hit him. Even though it would be over quickly, the last moments of his life would not be pleasant. Roughly equal in size, there was a chance that he could have fought off the attack . . . an outside chance.

Templeton's bow lay at his feet. Without taking his eyes off the advancing cat, he picked it up and nocked an arrow. The lion edged closer, never blinking, never stopping.

Compared to his 170-pound trophy, this animal seemed huge, but on that earlier day in 1993, Templeton had been the hunter, not the quarry. This lion moved toward him in absolute silence, never once blinking. As its soft paws filed inexorably forward, the beauty of great strength showed in the thick muscles of its back and shoulders, sending a shiver up Templeton's spine.

Literally in the lion's face, the bowhunter was out of time. He did not want to think about his training, especially how the bow is an effective killing instrument, but not a "stopper." A 165-grain ballistic tip bullet from a high-power rifle traveling 2,800 feet per second with a force of 2,873 foot pounds of kinetic energy . . . now that's a stopper. But a 60- or 70-foot pound bow was all Templeton had.

Ears laid back, head up, the lion was a mere eight yards away now. Its long, tawny body hung low to the ground, tail twitching from side to side, when Templeton drew, sighted instinctively and released his arrow. One shot. It had to be good. At this close range, it had to stop the big carnivore. Templeton's life depended on it.

Traveling at 200 miles per hour, the 600-grain broadhead-tipped arrow slammed into the lion's skull just beneath its left eye. With the cat making directly for him, there was no option other than a head-on shot.

If Templeton missed or only slightly wounded it, the cat could still have caught and killed him,

In September 1997, bowhunter Sonny Templeton of Lincoln, Montana, remained cool under extreme pressure and buried his three-blade broadhead in the skull of a mountain lion at about six to eight yards as it methodically stalked him.

sinking its narrow, wickedly curving canines deep between two neck vertebrae or disemboweling him with powerful claws on whirling, muscular rear legs.

But this day, Templeton did not miss. The stunned animal screamed in surprise and whirled, writhing in pain as it tore at the aluminum shaft. With supreme presence of mind, Templeton shot again, this time taking the lion squarely through its chest.

The scrambling, eerily whining cat disappeared; it was dead or dying. Templeton was certain the second arrow had delivered the fatal blow.

He was angry that this encounter had taken place. It seemed to be a terrible waste. As Templeton wrestled with adrenaline-tremors, the anger for having his day's hunt ruined ebbed. He had lived an adventure, one he would tell his kids about. Perhaps his grand-kids, too, but he hated to shoot the lion. He wished it had run away when he hit it with the rock. It was a beautiful creature and the mountains belonged to it and its prey. Templeton knew he had just been in the wrong place at the wrong time, so he headed toward his pick-up.

Overarched by looming pines and shrouded by dark green firs, the dirt road gradually disappeared beneath his feet. The lion was nowhere to be seen or heard. That could be a good thing or it could be bad, depending. The elk, of course, were long gone.

It was eerily quiet now and Templeton was suddenly conscious of being alone. His footsteps echoed in his ears as he listened to night sounds and the swishing throb of blood in his ears. A scurry in the bushes. A hooting owl. The distant, yipping howl of a coyote. But there was no soft pant or moonlight glint off yellow fangs.

The hike out took forever. When Templeton's body fully responded with a burst of chemical emotion, he shook with anger at the waste of the cat's life and, at last, the fear of "what could have been," as well. The shaking left him with a touch of nausea and the classic self-doubt of adrenaline withdrawal.

Still, his outdoor training and a cool head guided him, because as he walked he hung blaze-orange ribbons to guide him and Montana game warden Jeff Campbell back to the spot of the encounter the next day. Never once did Templeton stop moving, though, not to tie a boot lace or pee in the bush or drink from his canteen.

When he reached the safety of his truck, Templeton rolled up the windows, locked the doors and turned on the lights. Then he made the decision that separates him from many others. He decided to notify the game warden.

"I was afraid they wouldn't believe me and that they would fine me or I would lose my hunting license," Templeton says, but he called Campbell anyway. He could as easily have remained silent and no one, barring some freak happenstance, would ever have been the wiser.

Returning to the mountain the next day, Templeton and the warden found the lion just 25 yards from the spot Templeton was standing when it first approached. It had died within a minute of the second shot. The first arrow split the bone at the base of the left eye and would eventually have killed it, but the arrow through the chest spelled the cat's doom.

Examining the scuff marks and the dried blood, the game warden determined that Templeton waited to shoot until the lion was only six yards away. Campbell agreed that Templeton shot in self-defense. Laboratory analysis found no evidence that the lion was diseased, injured in any way or somehow pathologically predisposed to attack.

"He told me I did everything right," Templeton says. "He said he wouldn't have let it get that close! One leap and it would have been on top of me."

Today, Templeton thinks of his lion encounter as an isolated incident. "In the back of my mind, though, it's always there," he reflects. "I carry pepper spray now, but you know, until that happened with that lion, I never hesitated a minute about going off to hunt. I'd just go. I'm much more careful about that . . ."

## THE CUTTING EDGE

No arrow is complete without a specialized point. Shooting an arrow without a proper point at any target is a sure way to destroy the arrow and

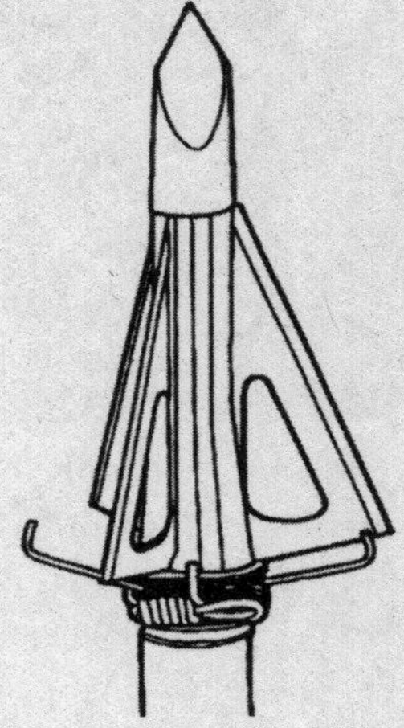

The original Judo Point (second from left) and some of the more recent imitations. Judo-style blunt heads retard penetration because the wire arms make the flying arrow flip upward rather than bury itself under the grass, so your arrow is easier to find after a shot on the range or in the field. Combined with a field point, springy-arms are extremely effective on small game and, with a broadhead, the sturdier Adder (second from right) or a set of Muzzy Grasshoppers (to the right) is great for preventing pass-through shots on wild turkeys.

miss the target, as well. Without a sharp, sturdy broadhead on his arrow, Templeton would certainly have died on the mountain that day in 1997.

There are four categories of arrow point, depending on how you intend to use them. For practice or recreational shooting, you might choose field, bullet or blunt points. For bowfishing, heads are designed with barbs to stab and hold fish. For elite national and international competition, there are points manufactured to precision tolerances that the average bowhunter will never use or need. Finally, and most important to the 3,000,000 bowhunters in the US and Canada, there is a wide variety of hunting broadheads.

## GET THE RIGHT PRACTICE

The average bowhunter purchases a handful of field or bullet points when they buy a new bow or even new arrows. A couple will go in their pocket, a few in the fanny pack, several in the archery tackle box and not less than a couple will end up rattling around on the floor of the pick-up or in the glove compartment. You never know when you might need to warm up.

For bowhunters, practice points help you perform the initial zeroing before you begin practice with broadheads. Whether you choose bullet points or field points or a hybrid head, the styling of these practice points makes them fly precisely and pull relatively easily out of any type target–foam, layered fiber or compressed hay bales.

The standard for hunting accuracy for many years has been hitting an eight-inch paper plate consistently at 20 yards. That general size approximates the vital area of a big-game animal. Public shooting ranges are littered with shredded paper plates that have been fastened to hay bales with twisted sections of coat hanger.

Before our 21st century "accuracy environment," however, such technicalities as matching the grain weight of your practice points to the grain weight of your broadhead were not considered to be important, given all of the other factors involved in making a clean shot. Even the engineers at some archery companies said that matching the weight of practice points with actual hunting heads was frivolous and unnecessary. Usually, however, they were not bowhunters.

Today, the bar of accuracy is raised. Even novice bowhunters understand the need to shoot tight groups. Practice points are now available in multiple sizes to match the weight of your hunting head and to help you understand the flight characteristics and impact points possible to your draw weight and arrow spine with differing weight heads.

Practice points are measured in two ways: diameter in .064-thousandths inch (to match the diameter of your arrow shaft) and weight in grains. Typically, these machined steel points screw into a lightweight, threaded aluminum or plastic adapter. If you shoot a traditional set-up, glue-on field points are available for practice with wooden shafts.

One very popular style of practice head that can also be used successfully for small-game hunting or a warm-up during the day (called "stump shooting") is the "Judo Point." Practice outdoors has usually meant that arrows with bullet or field points that miss their target or shoot through it would slide under the grass and then be hard to locate, especially with camouflaged shafts. If you were shooting a broadhead, this can be very dangerous as a vertical blade can cause serious injury if stepped on.

The Judo Point was designed with a blunt tip and extended, springy wires to slow down the arrow's forward momentum and catch or hang-up in grass and weeds. Zwickey advertises it as the "unloseable miracle point."

Similar points or variations on the classic Judo concept are available from several manufacturers. Each is designed to hit with a powerful punch and then snag with their exposed wire arms. Every bowhunter will want to have a few Judo Points or similar wire-arm-equipped arrowheads in their fanny pack for a practice shot or some opportunistic shot at small game.

An acceptable option for small-game hunting is a rubber blunt, because you should not shoot at small game with bare field points. Field points will certainly kill squirrels and rabbits, but their tendency is to pass completely through and continue flying. A small animal would certainly die from the hit, but it may climb a tree or run into a hole before it expires and your arrow could fly 100 dangerous yards from its original point of impact.

## MEET YOUR BROADHEAD

If there is one item every bowhunter is opinionated about, it is his broadhead. Bowhunters will argue the pros and cons of broadheads even when they cannot recall the model bow they are using. When they have to study the fabric for a camo name, they will know the width of their broad-head's blades. Fortunately, there are practically as many broadhead brands, styles and weights as there are bowhunters, so there is much to choose from … and to argue endlessly about!

Arrowheads for hunting and warfare may date back 30,000 years or even more, well into the Paleolithic or "Stone Age," and before the art of metalworking was widely understood. Once metal became available as refined copper and bronze, it quickly supplanted stone as the material of choice for arrowheads. Frontier reports exist of Native American warriors taking the iron rims off wagon wheels and wooden barrels, then hammering and cutting that supremely tough metal into arrowheads.

Metal supplanted stone because it could be mass-produced to specifications for an army of warriors, not necessarily because it was individually a better killing head. In the beginning, copper and bronze were not harder or necessarily more durable than a finely flaked stone head. With some touch-up to the edges, though, metal heads could be used repeatedly, just like stone.

It is true that stone heads, especially those made of superbly fine-grained materials like obsidian (a rare volcanic glass), could be made as surgically sharp as any metal head–many would argue, sharper. But they were brittle, and delicate stone heads could eat up daylight, manufacturing them one at a time. Whether metal was superior to stone for an arrowhead may ultimately have been more a question of the availability of finely layered materials, such as high-grade flint, that lent themselves to "napping" or flaking to create small pointed heads. In a world of truly infinite possibilities, it could simply have been a matter of fashion, too; the bowhunter's endless argument about the best broadhead.

Regarding broadheads, practical and philosophical arguments abound. Now, with the rise in popularity of mechanical or open-on-impact heads and super-fast arrows, those arguments have intensified.

There are three rules to keep in mind when you are making a broadhead selection. First, the more blades and the thicker the point and ferrule, the more difficult it becomes for the broadhead to achieve maximum potential speed, penetrate deeply and punch entirely through a thick-bodied big-game animal. Second, the more streamlined a broadhead is, the fewer and smaller its blades, the less friction it generates during flight and the more penetration it can

The Nitron by New Archery Products is a good example of styling in replaceable-blade broadheads. The three-blade, 100- gr. broadhead has a 1 1/16-inch cutting diameter. Its ferrule and point are a single-piece, made from steel and nickel-plated. Short and tough, the broadhead comes fully assembled. Each blade is held in place in slots in the ferrule with small screws.

achieve at distance. Third, because live, water-saturated flesh does not react like dry, rigid foam, the size of an arrow shaft behind your broadhead affects resistance in flight, but has little or no effect on penetration.

## REPLACEABLE-BLADE BROADHEAD

Dozens of companies make replaceable-blade broadheads. Most of them are excellent. This style hunting head essentially became the bowhunting standard in the late '70s. A quality, slim-line replaceable-blade head will fly true, cut easily and penetrate rapidly. Blades lock securely in slots machined in the central shaft, called a "ferrule," which is usually structural aluminum, although various composite materials are also used. You must have a head that will not lose its blades if it hits heavy bone in elk, or even in deer. (There are many stories about bowhunters unexpectedly finding a loose or broken blade with a bare hand, usually from their own arrow, while field dressing a downed game animal. The result can be deadly from bleeding or infection.)

Replaceable blade heads come in a three- or four-blade configuration. Blades are commonly vented; that means sections are cut out of their flat surface. Most bowhunters believe the vented design helps minimize wind-planing, and manufacturers claim that heads are designed so that the columnar loss of steel does not weaken a head's integrity or striking power. (On the other hand, some manufacturers of mechanical heads suggest that these vented sections create additional opportunities for wind interference and friction in flight. If it is true, the vents slow down your arrow.)

The number of blades in a broadhead, the thickness of those blades, whether they are vented or not, the shape of the ferrule and the style of tip on the head (chisel, cut-to-tip or conical) are far less important than obtaining good arrow flight and being able to put your broadhead precisely into the vitals of game animals. Nevertheless, a three-blade style is the most common replaceable blade head in the deer woods. A fourth blade on a head–and remember, this is the leading, guiding edge of your arrow–may require that you increase the number or size of the fletching for good stabilization or rotation in flight. A good rule of thumb is to match the number of feathers or vanes to the number of blades you are shooting and as your head size increases, increase the size of the fletching.

When arrow speed became a factor in purchasing equipment in the early 1990s, most bowhunters began experimenting with carbon shafts tipped with smaller, lighter heads with low-profile (narrower) blades from their compound bows. Lighter heads and shorter, lighter arrows helped boost top arrow speeds above 300 fps— about 200 mph when measured within a few feet of the bow—but complete, pass-through penetration became an issue and it remains an issue to this day.

Speed, in itself, did nothing to promote desirable arrow flight or accuracy. A fast, inaccurate or uncontrollable arrow was worse than a total miss. With fast arrows, it was not possible to assume that broadheads were mounted correctly if they simply remained intact on the ferrule after a shot.

Properly mounting a broadhead of any kind means its tip is in line with the center of the arrow shaft. Upon release, your bowstring thrusts the arrow forward. You want that thrust to load the column of the arrow, thereby delivering the bow's stored energy to your shaft without angled force vectors to torque the arrow in any direction.

After you have grouped arrows using field points, you have to shoot broadheads. Broadhead practice is "a must" before you shoot at live game. The recommended target is one of the several varieties of durable foam or layered material sold through sporting goods stores. With care, broadheads pull out relatively easily and the design of many foam targets replicates the size and appearance of big game. (Shooting broadheads into these targets will eventually destroy them, but repair kits and replaceable "kill zones" are available from many manufacturers.)

The only certain way to fine-tune arrow flight for accuracy and consistency is to practice with the arrows and broadheads you will use for hunting. If you cannot shoot tight groups with your preferred broadhead, or if it comes apart or the tip bends after shooting, you should immediately try another brand or style. It is much less expensive to experiment with a number of broadheads than it is to miss or wound a game animal.

## MECHANICAL BROADHEADS

Blades that open when a head hits its target define a class of broadheads collectively referred to as expandable, mechanical or open-on-impact. Theoretically, these heads fly like a practice point, penetrate like a fixed-blade head and cut like a sharp replaceable-blade head. Open-on-impact is a wonderful idea. For a generation, bowhunters have worked seriously on the design, studying concepts such as "rotational momentum" and "gyroscopic stabilization" that mean little to the average hunter.

Regardless of their engineering and design, mechanical broadheads remained somewhat controversial until recently. Now, many of the practical difficulties have been engineered almost to perfection. In theory, they are wonderful, but the practical difficulties are great.

These are the bowhunting benefits of open-on-impact heads:

They fly like field points. This means your practice and set-up time is shorter because the time needed to tune your heads for excellent flight declines. In a mordantly time-conscious society, this is an important advantage.

Because they offer less resistance to the wind, arrows tipped with expandable heads wind-plane less than any other type head. This means if you shoot inside your effective range, you will have fewer misses, less wounded game.

Tipped with expandable broadheads on arrows that fly straighter to their target, hit with greater efficiency and penetrate as well as any other fine head, bowhunters are making the most sensible and best ethical decision when they shoot mechanicals.

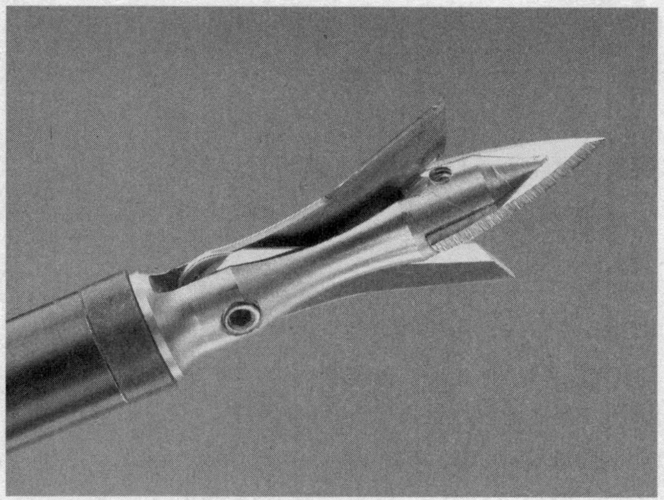

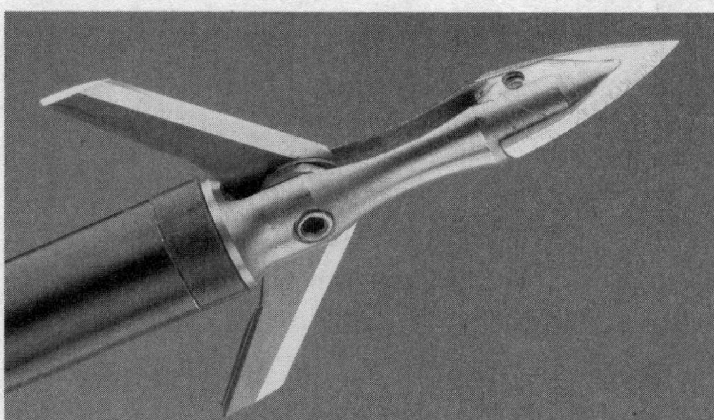

Call them expandable, mechanical or open-on-impact broadheads, but this new generation of hunting heads is designed to fly like a dart and cut like a machete. The 100-gr. Ironhead XP, for example, came pre-assembled and features a one-piece stainless steel body and two .030-inch stainless blades. Wide open, the Ironhead XP has a 11/8-inch cutting diameter. This head features relatively new expandable styling, with very small, resharpenable or replaceable cut-on-contact blades set at a 90-degree angle to the main blades, and positioned at the tip of the ferrule.

The arguments against mechanicals are that bowhunting is a privilege that requires practice, patience, and dedication. While they may fly like field points, unless they hit and deliver their energy in the perpendicular plane, they may or may not penetrate and cut through as advertised.

Bowhunters who do not like expandable heads claim they occasionally fail to work properly and that they are responsible for more wounded and un-recovered game animals than non-mechanical heads. They argue that bowhunters shooting open-on-impact heads should consider drawing heavier weight bows to insure that impact energy and penetration are adequate.

Although it cannot be proven, anti-mechanical hunters say that because open-on-impact heads fly like field points, bowhunters are tempted to shoot beyond their limitations. Individuals who are comfortable shooting inside 30 yards will try 40- or 50-yard shots. At those ranges, the arrow has less energy for penetration and the margin of error is greater.

The argument that mechanical heads do not cause a significant blood trail because they usually fail to cut completely through a game animal is questionable, because many thousands of the largest big game have been taken with open-on-impact heads. Most mechanicals are designed to cut big holes on impact and when they are fully deployed inside an animal, but an exit hole is definitely desirable. Otherwise, blood will only seep out of the entry hole, which is higher on the body than the exit hole and tracking is harder. Probably, the energy required to push a mechanical completely through big game needs to be greater than with other heads, as the blades are often much wider than fixed-blade or one-piece heads.

What worries many bowhunters is that if expandable heads fly like field points, and set-up and tuning is fast compared to conventional heads, bowhunters will not be spending enough time practicing and becoming familiar with their gear. In this scenario, the short-term benefits are outweighed by the lack of long-term interest and understanding.

Whether any of the above objections are credible across-the-board is uncertain; probably not. What is certainly true is that bowhunters have embraced open-on-impact heads. Estimates vary, but one hears that as many as half or more of all bowhunters now shoot mechanicals. Some established companies refuse to manufacture any expandable head, but others have accepted the open-on-impact concept and placed their faith in superior engineering.

Nevertheless, common-sense archery rules apply. If you choose to shoot an open-on-impact head, you must experiment before taking them to the field. Shoot into foam targets to test the type and weight head that works best from your set-up. Wait for quality broadside shots. Shoot within your effective range. Think of the animal at all times and remember that the objective is always a quick, clean kill.

Measure open-on-impact broadheads with the same qualities as traditional heads: size, weight, cutting diameter, number of blades, width and thickness of blades, type of point (cut-on-contact or punch-cut), and locking style. In addition, however, these heads have significant mechanical characteristics, such as how the blades are attached to the ferrule; how they swing or spring open; and even whether the blades swing forward or backward on impact.

If you choose an expandable blade head, you will want to be sure the Kinetic Energy (foot-pounds) delivered by your arrow will be sufficient to penetrate, fully deploy the head and then cut a long, wide blood channel. Archery engineers who are also bowhunters recommend shooting no less than 50 ft-lbs for moderate game like deer, and up to 65 ft-lbs or even more for larger game, such as elk.

The most fashionable trend in broadheads is developing a mechanical head with a small, fixed head forward, thereby allowing the cut-on-contact front tip to open an immediate wound channel for the opening mechanical blades. Properly developed, this is a terrific combination of technologies that indeed combines the best worlds of penetration and low-resistance arrow flight.

## FIXED-BLADE BROADHEADS

What could be easier than gluing a broadhead on your wood arrow shaft or screwing one into an adapter in your shaft? If it becomes dull, you sharpen it with a file, a ceramic stick or a sheet of fine-grit sandpaper. If the tip hits a rock and the blade bends, you straighten it or throw it away. The only tricky part is your responsibility to keep these heads sharp and flying true, because no head less than surgically sharp should be shot at a game animal.

Single-piece heads are simple, nothing-can-go-wrong arrowheads. Nothing moves, and there is nothing to replace. In practically any thickness–.040 inches is standard for the main blade while the insert or "bleeder blade," if any, may measure only .015 inches–they are suitable for taking any big-game animal. With a heavy bow and arrow combination, this judgment includes elephant and Cape buffalo, as Howard Hill, Fred Bear and Bob Swinehart proved hunting Africa in the 1950s and 1960s with fixed, single-piece heads. Nevertheless, these days a minority of bowhunters uses single-piece broadheads.

Those who shoot traditionally with recurves and longbows gravitate to single-piece broadheads. Traditional bowhunters shooting recurves and longbows derive much of their enjoyment from simplifying their gear and even their methods of shooting and hunting. Single-piece, fixed-blade heads with or without inserts represent less than 10 percent of the total broadhead market.

"Traditional archers shoot more than people using compounds because they have more fun," says Bob Mayo, who manufactures Ace broadheads.

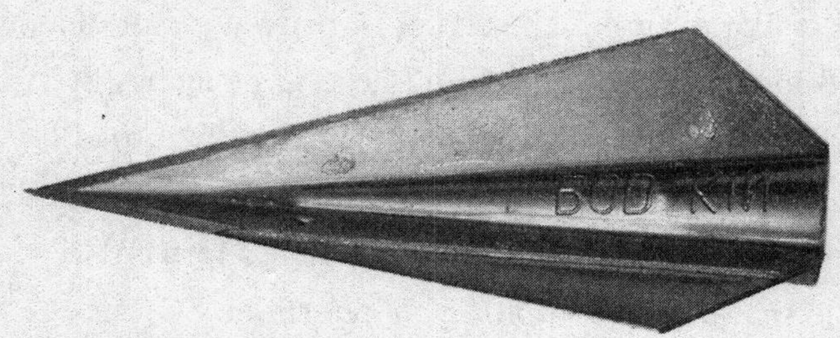

The Whiffen Bodkin is an old-style fixed-blade broadhead. The Bodkin was designed by Milwaukee's Larry Whiffen. Senior–now a member of the Archery Hall of Fame–in 1946, field tested by Fred Bear and brought to market three years later. Sharpening a Bodkin is easy as the straight blades are made from soft steel.

"Since we traditional-style hunters usually glue heads onto wood arrow shafts, when we can find good wood shafts, we use one-piece heads because they are tougher and last longer. We don't lose blades or tips when we practice shooting into 3-D targets or hay bales."

A fixed-blade head may look simple to bowhunters who are accustomed to complex mechanical heads with moving parts or heads with replaceable blades, the construction of a good traditional head is a precision business.

Traditional heads may be sharpened with sandpaper, a file or on a stone. Mayo glues his 165-gr. Ace Express onto a wood arrow shaft. Then, holding his file stationary, he draws the head toward him, base to tip. When he is using a sharpening stone, he recommends beginning with coarse grit and working toward fine. A few drops of honing oil will increase the effectiveness of this procedure. Finally, he smoothes the cutting edge of his heads with a ceramic stick.

Three-blade Whiffen Bodkins and other styles with edges that lie flat are designed to be sharpened on a sheet of fine-grained sandpaper lying on a tabletop. Use the same butt-to-tip sharpening method Mayo uses with his Arkansas stones. The steel of a Bodkin is soft, so it is easy to sharpen. That also means it quickly loses its edge and must be touched-up often.

The orientation of broadheads on an arrow shaft is a much-debated topic, especially with large, flat heads like the 160-gr., 1 1/2-inch Magnus, the 130-gr. Zwickey Black Diamond Delta or the massive, 210-gr., .048-inch Steel Force Premium from Ballistic Archery. Many bowhunters believe this is irrelevant, but these large blades definitely play a part in steering and stabilizing the arrow in flight.

Mayo says he, like many traditional hunters– and he mentioned famous traditional trick-shot artist Byron Ferguson, for example—mount blades vertically. This is a reasonable accommodation given the normal wallowing of an arrow as it leaves a bowstring released by one's fingers.

Speaking of proper blade orientation, several popular styles are designed with offset blades so that they will spin or rotate independent of the arrow shaft. The 100-gr. Razorbak 100 from New Archery Products, for example, features a .039-inch thick cut-on-contact main blade, a .020-inch bleeder blade and a 1 1/8-inch cutting diameter. Set in a tough composite sleeve, this sleeve with its vented blades actually rotates around the ferrule during flight.

Traditional heads are larger in both size and weight than replaceable-blade or mechanical heads. The super-heavyweight 200-grain Ace Super Express is one of the largest ever produced and sold commercially. Mayo says, "At the distances we traditional archers take game animals, 25-yards or less, these heavy heads don't substantially affect arrow flight, and heavier arrows at short range definitely penetrate better."

## FORWARD-OF-CENTER

A technical question about arrow balance with a mounted broadhead has generated considerable discussion. Most bowhunters shooting within their comfort zone can ignore this controversy, but anyone who is obsessed with pinpoint shooting or is experiencing erratic or unbalanced arrow flight should study "forward-of-center."

Forward-of-center or FOC balancing is one of many things that affect arrow flight. It can be critical for speed bows with high let-off and high draw weight. Unlike many technical issues, FOC is easy to determine. First, measure your arrow from the throat of the nock to the tip of your installed broadhead. Next, mark the arrow at the center or halfway point. Place the arrow on the side of your finger or on some other thin balancing point, and also mark that point. Finally, measure the distance from the center of your arrow to the balance mark and divide that number by the total length of the arrow.

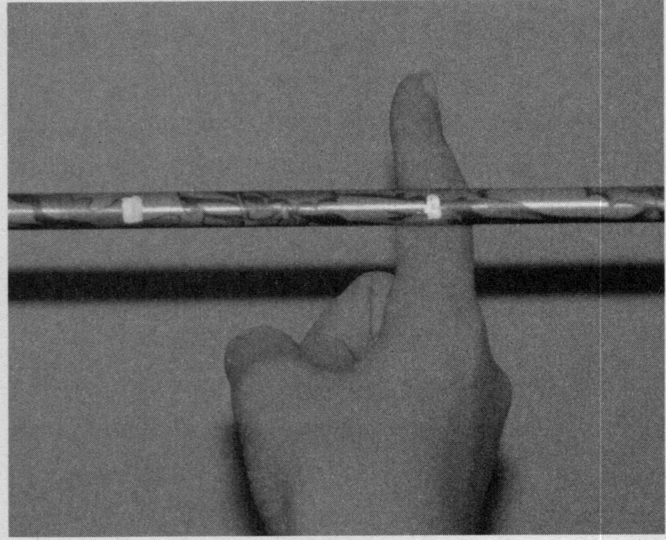

With a nock and broadhead, the author's arrow measured 35 1/4-inches long. The center of the arrow was therefore 17 5/8-inches from either end. The forward-of-center balance was 2 5/8-inches forward and FOC was 7.45 percent. This would be considered low for a carbon shaft and possibly require a heavier broadhead. For the Easton XX75 2213 Superlight aluminum pictured, however, realizing that the author shoots with fingers and that his arrows fly at only moderate speeds (around 240 fps), this is not too low for consistency.

For example, the center or halfway point of a 28-inch shaft with nock and head is 14 inches. It will balance forward-of-center because the broadhead is heavier than the fletching and nock on the rear. If the arrow balances three inches forward of the shaft's halfway point, you determine FOC as three divided by 28, or 10.7 percent.

Archery technicians suggest that an FOC of 10 to 12 percent is about right for balanced, accurate arrow flight. Some even recommend a higher FOC, 12 to 15 percent, for carbon shafts and lower FOC, 8 to 10 percent, for aluminum shafts.

In the same example, if you shoot a heavy head and the balance point was four inches forward of the halfway point, the FOC would be 14.28 percent and you could predict marginal arrow flight. To stabilize the flight of your arrow, you would want to try some combination of a lighter broadhead or heavier fletching or even a longer arrow.

Nevertheless, FOC is only one of many indicators that help us shoot a fast, accurate arrow that delivers all of its energy in-line through its tip when it hits.

## ALL ABOUT GRAIN WEIGHT

Broadheads are sold at specific grain weights. Bowhunters need to understand that advertised grain weights are only approximations. If you weigh any given broadhead on a digital scale, you will probably find that it varies from five to ten percent heavier or lighter than advertised. Although competition archers fret about matching total shaft weights precisely, this amount of variation is not significant for bowhunting. On the other hand, if you can alter your heads or forward balance to make all heads weigh precisely the same without changing flight dynamics, why not do so.

Although we are not too familiar with weights expressed in grains outside our broadheads and bullets, the "grain" is the basic British unit of weight and hence our inherited system. This system evolved over more than 3,000 years. Historically, the grain was based on the weight of one grain of English barley.

Today, the "pound avoirdupois" is what we typically refer to as a pound when we check a bow's draw weight. Our pound equals 7,000 grains, abbreviated gr. An ounce, therefore—and there are 16 ounces in one pound avoirdupois—equals 437.5 gr.

Why do we still measure broadheads with such an old-fashioned weight as grains? The development of mass-produced, commercially available broadheads may be a 20th-century phenomenon, but bullets were manufactured and sold by grain weight in the 19th century. Ours may be a compact phenomenon, but what are the options? You could measure heads in tenths or hundredths of an ounce, but with 16, not 10, ounces in a pound, this may be really confusing. Or we could switch, with the rest of the world, to the metric scale, and that move is probably on the horizon as more and more packaging contains grams and millimeters and other detritus of that number-ten-based system.

## BROADHEAD COLLECTING

There is a serious collector's interest in broadheads. Greg Schwehr, membership chairman of the American Broadhead Collectors Club (ABCC), says the group is a worldwide organization of men and women who enjoy collecting archery and bowhunting memorabilia, including gear catalogs, books, leather goods, bows, equipment, autographed arrows and, of course, broadheads. All of these can be traded for in the club.

In their quarterly newsletter, Broadhead, Schwehr says members find information about old and new broadheads and the manufacturers. One primary function of the club and publication is for members to trade heads. At an annual meeting each summer, usually at one of the large archery shoots in the Midwest, collectors get together to do "some serious trading."

The ABCC has published five books on identifying broadheads: four volumes of Best of Broadhead and one volume of old broadhead

Collecting old archery memorabilia is a lifetime sport in its own right, and thousands of archers and collectors participate. The items most in demand are uncommon recurves, longbows and broadheads: The designs are curious, each has an interesting history and many of them are exceptionally rare. A 12-pack (only six show) of 1960-vintage, glue-on Fred Bear Razorheads in their original packaging cost $4.95 in the mid-'50s. Today, this pack could sell for more than $100.

advertisements. A list of members is available for trading and networking. A master list of broadheads has been compiled during the past quarter century, listing every head known to have been manufactured and sold, including sizes, weights, date and manufacturer information.

Schwehr says the club designates a member to buy a small number of all new heads. "This individual then makes heads available to other members at a low cost, eliminating the need for every collector to buy complete packages."

ABCC membership is $20 for one year. If you are interested, please contact: American Broadhead Collectors Club, Greg Schwehr, Membership Chairman, 9717 W. Reichert Place, Milwaukee, WI 53225.

# Part 3

# *Whitetail Tactics*

# Introduction

This is justifiably the largest section of this book. Why justifiably? Because there are almost infinite ways to hunt whitetails. You have to factor in what part of the country you hunt, the terrain, the weather, the size of the herd, the timing of the rut, the moon phase, plus your preferred method of hunting. If you're a bowhunter, chances are you hunt from a treestand or, perhaps, a blind. So, where do you set up your stand? Is there an ideal approach route to it? How often should you hunt in a season? Every day? Once a week? Once a month or even a season? And when you do hunt it, do you take the same path to it every time? A different path? In mornings only? Evenings? And when you're in your stand, how long do you stay? All day? Only mornings? Only late afternoons until dark? And if you're in your stand and not seeing anything, should you stay in it, figuring a buck is going to come waltzing down the trail any moment? Or, do you climb down and try that other stand you set up by the swamp?

This section pretty covers it all, with detailed chapters on tracking, calling, rattling, using cover and attractor scents, setting up treestands in prime locations, hunting the various stages of the rut, plus expert tips on how to pattern bucks, use the wind to your advantage, consistently take bucks on public land, and much more. Plus there's a bonus section, highlighting the taking of six trophy bucks by bowhunters in six states.

Read this section carefully, refer to it often, and you will become a better bowhunter, guaranteed!

—Jay Cassell

# TRACKING
## Defining Tracking

As with most of the other tactics in this book, the art, or more precisely, the ability, to follow the tracks left by a deer until you actually catch sight of the animal is a crucial tool in becoming a more skillful hunter.

There are two types of tracking to define, however. The first is an absolute necessity for any dedicated, ethical, deer hunter. This is the ability to track a wounded animal by either the blood trail left by the inflicted wound, or by the "sign" left on the forest ground, grass, branches, vegetation, and even rocks along its escape route. This type of tracking ends when the hunter either finds the dead deer or is able to spot it and finish it off.

This is a tracking skill that every hunter must learn in order to lessen the odds of losing a deer that he has wounded. The odds are (whether you are a seasoned veteran or a novice) sometime during your hunting life, you will indeed wound a deer and have to follow its blood trail in order to recover it. That is a fact no long-time hunter escapes. Despite what your friends or anyone else says, the wounding of one, and sometimes even a few, deer over a lifetime of hunting is inevitable. Wounded game has been part of the "hunt" since our cave man ancestors hurled spears and released arrows. As hunters, each and every one of us is morally responsible to know how to make every effort to recover a wounded deer. The recovery begins by understanding how to effectively follow the tracks, blood, and other signs from a wounded deer.

We all dream about following the tracks of a buck like this until we catch up with him in his bed or he stops to check his back trail to find out what is "dogging" him.

To become proficient at this type of tracking takes a lot of practice, persistence, and patience.

With this type of tracking, the more trails of wounded deer you follow, the better you become at finding wounded game. Each and every blood trail is totally unique. But, in the end, the same general information will be garnered each and every time you're afield so that you can log (in your memory or on paper) and refer to it time and again. It will teach those who pay attention something new and different every single time. For this reason, long before you ever have the "call" of having to find a deer you have wounded, learn through firsthand experience when you can.

Anytime you are hunting with a friend who wounds a deer, volunteer to help him trail it. Keep a low profile, especially if the hunter you are assisting is experienced in trailing wounded deer, but stay alert to what is happening. It is important not to feel embarrassed about asking an experienced tracker questions regarding the sign left behind. Take the time to join in on tracking, even when it means giving up some of your valuable hunting time. The experience you gain will make you a more proficient hunter: a hunter other deerstalkers and non-hunters alike will respect and admire. I cover this type of tracking further along in the book in much more detail. It is important information for all hunters, both skilled and beginner, to read carefully.

The second type of tracking is more romantic. It conjures up a spark of adventure lying deep in every hunter. To find a track of a deer and follow it until you are able to get a clean shot at the deer, especially a mature buck, is to most hunters, the ultimate deer hunting experience. It is one of the most exhilarating and captivating aspects of deer hunting. To be skilled enough to trail a buck by following his tracks and finally tagging him on his turf, while playing by his rules, is the underlying desire for almost all deer hunters. For most of us, it generates a feeling of satisfaction like no other deer-hunting tactic can.

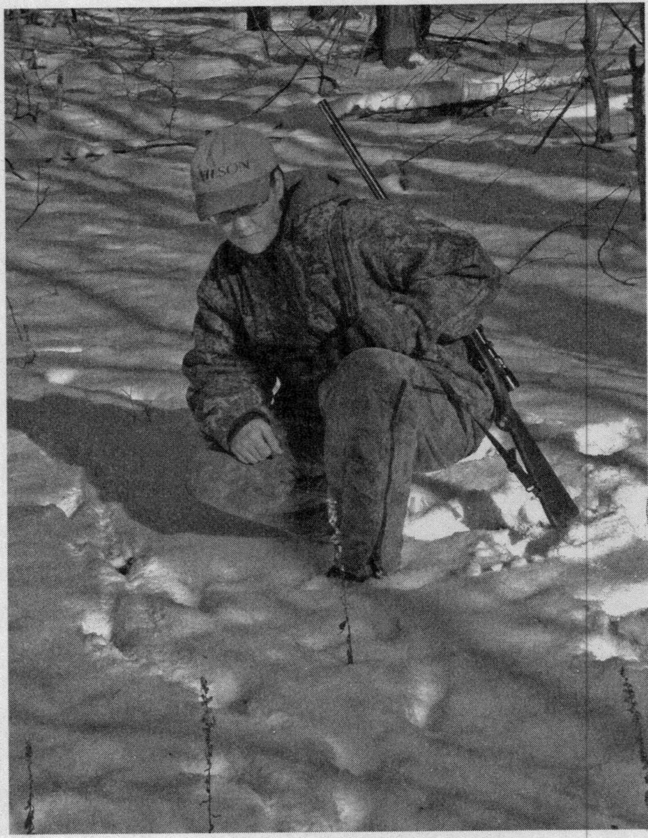

Following the tracks of a wounded deer even in the snow takes patience and skill only learned after you have tracked several bucks.

Through most of my deer-hunting life, when I daydream about taking a wise, old buck with a heavy, wide set of antlers, a long drop tine and a few gnarly kickers, I imagine that I cross his track while I'm slowly still-hunting through the woods after a fresh snow fall. The track is, of course, wide, long, and set deep in the snow. The distance between each hoof print is unusually long. And, there is always some defect in the hoof to set the track apart from other bucks—least I confuse it as I set out to walk him down. My daydream takes me over mountains, through swamps, into thickets, cedar forests, and eventually, back the other way as the buck inevitably tries to circle behind me. Just before legal shooting light comes to an end, I spot him as he stops to check his back trail. Without the buck ever seeing me, I send a brush-cutting bullet whistling over the blow-downs—and before the big buck can react to the report of the rifle, the bullet finds its mark and the buck crumbles instantly and quietly into the fresh snow. I have had this daydream many times during my hunting life, and I'll bet most of you have had some version of the same fantasy, too.

While most of us romanticize about duplicating the efforts of well-known trackers of Maine and Vermont, like Hal Blood, the Benoits, and Berniers (I often quip that perhaps to be a famous tracker from New England, your last name must begin with the letter "B"), the reality about tracking, however, is that it is a tactic that requires a heavy dose of reality and common sense.

The most overlooked truth about tracking for most buck hunters across the nation, especially those in heavily hunted areas, is to acknowledge that in order to become the next Blood, Benoit, or Bernier, a hunter must have un-pressured hunting space and plenty of it. This is the key element for tracking down bucks as consistently as the trackers mentioned above. A successful tracker must also know how to quickly interpret track signs left by deer. It also requires one to hone his skill of orienteering. And, when tracking bucks in big woods, it demands that the tracker be in above-average physical condition. I often compare it to bighorn sheep hunting, because following a buck up and down ridges, over blow-downs, through thickets, swamps, and bogs can quickly sap the strength of even the most athletic hunter, especially in the legs. Most of all, successful tracking of a buck in the wild backcountry of Maine, or in the remote regions of Vermont, New Hampshire, or the Adirondacks of New York State, requires a lot of patience, more patience than most hunters have. But in the end, it demands diligent persistence. Without this skill, you are better off never taking after the track of a buck in big woods country–period. Therein may be the most overlooked element of a successful big woods tracker.

But those elements are not only what it takes to be a skilled tracker. Equally as important, a hunter must know when to give up on the track. I know you have all read that some trackers follow the prints overnight and into the next morning. While that makes good reading, and is very romantic, it is impractical and never really a tactic used by anyone. The fact is, in most states, such activity is illegal. Even without a firearm and gun, following a buck during the night can be considered "harassment of wildlife" by most state game departments. Chasing after a buck at night, by the mere definition of pursuit, is hunting. As far as I know, hunting at night is prohibited in every state. An ethical sportsman should understand that he has lost the battle of the chase for the day if by legal sun set the hunter has not caught up with the buck and killed it. It doesn't mean that by legal sunset you hand someone else

Hal Blood, Master Maine Guide, is recognized as one of the leading trackers in North America. He has the endurance and strength necessary to track a buck for long hours in deep snow over mountains, swamps, and lowlands. This buck scored 1661 8 B&C points. Credit: Debbie Blood.

your firearm and continue to harass the buck, with flashlight in hand, through the night–as far-fetched as that might be.

Anything less presses against the ethical edges of hunting and fair chase. Again, a hunter would be wise to remember that in many states, dogging a buck overnight carrying a firearm and packing a flashlight (even one that is stowed away in your backpack) will test the patience of almost any game warden. The nonsense of some hunters tracking a buck overnight and staying with the track until shooting light the next morning is, in my mind's eye, a vast exaggeration of the truth and of the ethics of hunting as well. It is also not sporting to the deer, despite the glamour it evokes. It also taxes my patience. Staying with the deer through the dead of night over hill and dale and running him ragged until you spot him the next morning, then shooting him, and then still being in good enough shape to drag out this 300-pound buck–is just down right hooey! It is meant to sell magazines and to make other trackers feel less of themselves. That crawls under my skin. Anyone can track a deer at night. There's no magic involved, as the deer is less spooky of what's on his back trail.

To prove this point, I know we have all walked out of the woods after leaving our stand once legal shooting hours are over. During the egress, many of us have bumped into a buck or doe. Inevitably, instead of snorting and immediately running away, many times, these deer will remain frozen in their tracks, trying to "make you out." I have even had mature bucks walk

within feet of me trying to identify what I was. Even though this may be hard to believe, I am sure there are many hunters who can collaborate. I have even had deer stand there with the wind blowing my scent directly to them. Darkness just seems to make deer less afraid of human scent and/or human outlines than during daylight. So, dogging a buck at night isn't "the ultimate challenge" it has been hyped-up to be.

The fact is, the longer you track a buck, the greater the chances become that another hunter will shoot him. I can't tell you how many times I have taken up the trail of a buck in the snow, in country that is under-hunted, only to hear the inevitable report of a firearm coming from the direction the track was heading. In most cases, I have followed the track until it leads me to the dead buck and the hunter who shot him. In my conversation with the successful hunter, he usually winds up telling me he shot the buck as it was "checking its back-trail." Sad

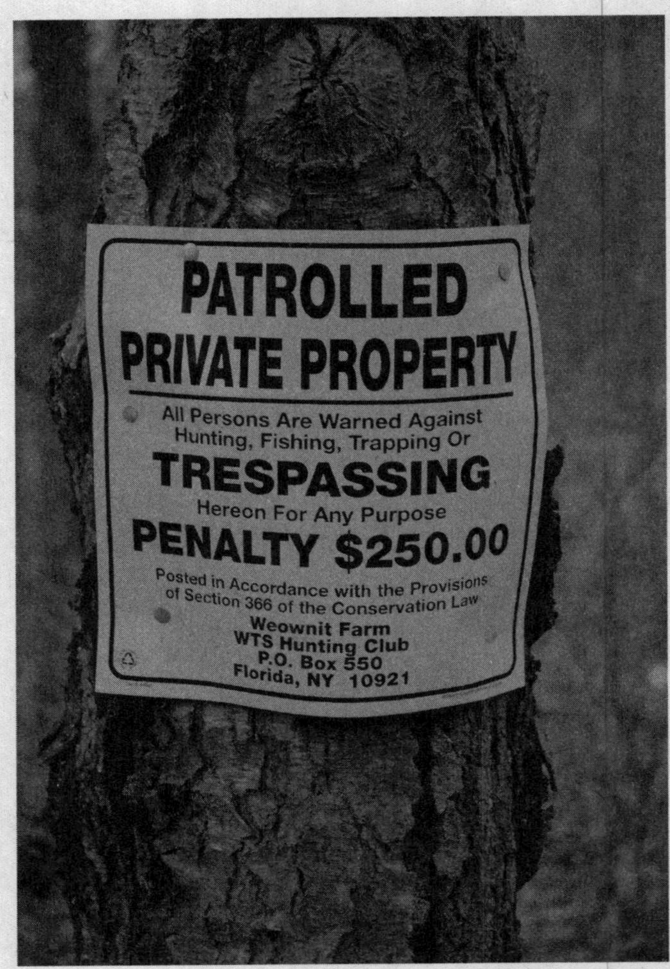


Posted signs are a reality check that means the chase has come to an end in places other than big woods

as it is, undressing the mystique of tracking leaves the bare facts—tracking isn't always what it's cracked up to be!

I share these negatives not to discourage you from becoming a tracker, but rather to give you confidence and to share some common sense about the tactic.

## Know Your Terrain

If you have ever hunted deer in Maine, you have learned a few things about just how wild that state can be. For the most part, western Maine is a maze of thick wilderness. Even its system of logging roads can be confusing to the first-time hunter. Let me share a story with you of just how confusing the logging roads can be. This is a story that is embarrassing for me to tell, but it is the truth, and as such has its value in sharing with you, no matter how foolish it makes me feel.

Several years ago while bear hunting in Maine, I drove my truck into the hunting area by following my outfitter who was driving ahead of me. Once we reached the area, he directed me to my stand and told me "just reverse the directions to find your way out without any trouble." Having a great sense of direction, I didn't think twice about it and headed to my stand. I made sure I noted each turn on the many logging roads we took on a tape recorder as we traveled. Just before the outfitter left, he asked, "Do you think you'll be able to find your way back?" I smiled with confidence and said, "Of course."

By now you surmise that when I tried to drive out in the pitch dark, all the logging roads looked the same. It was hard to differentiate the landmarks I logged during daylight on my way in. Each turn left me feeling like I made a mistake. I couldn't recognize anything—nothing looked familiar in the dark. You guessed it. I became hopelessly lost. So lost that after four hours of trying in vein to find my way back to the main road, I had to radio for help. Not that I wasn't calling in earlier—I was. But I couldn't raise the base camp. Finally, I got to a high point on a small knoll where the radio worked and I reached the lodge. When I told them what had happened, I heard the howls of laughter of the other hunters in camp, including my guest—former baseball great, Wade Boggs. Over the radio, the outfitter told me, "Stop where you are and don't move again. When you see my lights, beep your horn and call me on the radio." It took him (and several other hunters who came along for the ride to see the hunter who was lost in his truck) over an hour to locate me! When they did, I wasn't embarrassed or ashamed of getting lost.

The fact is, this is big—very big—country that all looks exactly the same. And unless a person is very familiar with traveling the systems of logging roads in the back-country, getting lost even in daylight, never mind the dead of night, is a reality. The same holds true when hunting through the big woods of Maine or any other state or area that is new to you. The fact is, before you set out on a track of a deer in strange country, you'd better think twice—no, make that three times. You must have years of experience with the land you hunt before attempting to track a buck (or in my case drive a truck), for miles and miles. Actually, that's good advice anytime you're thinking of picking up a buck track in wilderness country.

If you are tracking a buck in the snow and you think you can retrace your footsteps to get out, this still can be problematic. Moreover, an unsuspecting snow storm or heavy rain can eliminate all your foot prints. There goes your back trail, making it impossible to follow your steps back out of the woods.

I learned that lesson early in my deer-hunting career. When I was 17 (back in the '60s), I was on my first hunt in the Adirondack Mountains in New York. This is a vast wilderness that, in places, compares to anything Maine offers. I was hunting in the town of Childwold on a 50,000-acre tree farm owned by International Paper. It was the fourth day of the hunt. That afternoon, on the way to my stand, which was about 500 yards from a logging road and about 1,000 yards from where I parked my truck, I cut a big track in the fresh snow (in those days, there was usually snow on the ground by mid-October).

Thinking I could follow my back trail out, because I thought I had learned enough about the area to do so, I took off after the deer. It was 2:30 p.m. when I began tracking. That was my first mistake. I slowly walked off to the side of the deer track—cutting back to it every so often to check that it was the same print. After an hour or so, I spotted the buck. I remember his rack even to this day. I probably recall it bigger than it actually was, but he was the first buck I had ever tracked in the "big" woods.

As I slowly raised my rifle, he casually disappeared into a stand of heavy pine trees. I followed him in. The stand of evergreens was immense and the buck lead me on a wild goose chase as he constantly circled around me. I spotted

When a wounded deer finds its way into standing corn like this, keep a keen eye out, not only for the blood on the stalks and ground, but also for him possibly being bedded ahead of you.

him two more times—each time only for a moment. The last time I saw him, I realized how dark it was getting. I could hardly see him in the scope. I glanced at my watch and it was only 4 pm Fear instantly over took me. That was my next mistake.

I instinctively knew I had to immediately abandon the track and try to get back to my truck. I never found my way out that day. Even following my back trail became hard as the light faded. I spent the most harrowing night of my young life hopelessly lost in the big woods of the Adirondacks. I walked and walked (I didn't know better back then that I should have remained where I was), and called and called for help. No one answered. I shot most of my shells, keeping only a few in case I met up with a bear who was in a foul mood.

At dawn I was tired, scared, hungry, wet, disoriented and about to freak out when I heard voices. I ran toward them and to my joy and shock, I emerged on a trail that boy scouts—little boy scouts—were happily walking along. The scoutmaster quickly scolded me for carrying a firearm on the Boy Scout's property. It didn't take him long, after sizing me up, to realize my story was true. In the end, I had walked miles from my truck overnight–many miles. The scout leader took me to camp, warmed me up, fed me, calmed me down, and drove me back to my truck. I won't tell you how far. My lesson and the lesson any one who wants to track deer should take from this is to know your hunting area.

With all that said, tracking down a buck and bagging him can be the most challenging and satisfying of all deer hunting tactics. It takes a conditioned hunter, with experience in several areas of survival and hunting skills to become a seasoned, consistently successful deerstalker. Once accomplished, however, the art of stalking a buck can help you bag your deer when other hunters can't seem to tag out.

# Tracking on Farmlands and in Small Woods

The best strategy for successful tracking in heavily pressured areas (or for that matter in wilderness areas) is to know the travel routes of the deer. Know what to expect from a wise old buck that has you dogging his trail. Know what he'll do under that type of pressure. What are his favorite escape trails? Where will he head when he's nervous about being followed? How will he react to your pressure? If you know these things in advance, you can plan a tracking tactic that will work.

Even the best tracker will cut a trail and then stop to lay out a plan. In some cases, he calls for reinforcements. Once a track is found, a call over the radio brings a few other ardent trackers together. The stalker with the most stamina is elected to take up the track. Before he does, where legal, the other two or three hunters plan to take up stands—sometimes a long distance away from the track, far enough away as to require the stalker to wait an hour or so before starting after the buck. Once in place, they signal each other and the tracking begins. As the primary stalker gets on the track, he stays with it until he either jumps the buck and shoots it himself or until he pressures the buck enough that it becomes so worried about its back trail that it begins to forget to pay as much attention to what is ahead of him. Often, the buck winds up walking into one of the hunters who has taken a stand on a known escape route or on a logging road that crosses from one section of property to another.

Talkabout 2-Way Radios can be used to call hunting companions, to help track a wounded deer, drag one from the woods, or for emergencies and other needed conversations during the hunt. They should not be used for idol chatter while hunting, however.

This is, in fact, how most trackers get their bucks. It is a rewarding hunt, filled with skill and challenges. This strategy is not for the unskilled or those who lack the ability to be patient and persistent. It is especially not for those who cannot keep the ethics of hunting upper-most in their minds and know enough to call off the stalk in fairness to both the sport and the game—if and when that time does arrive.

During my several decades of hunting, I have tracked elk, moose, mule deer, white-tailed deer and even a few bear. Aside from whitetails, I have only successfully tracked and shot two bull elk. But when it comes to tracking whitetails, I have had much better success. I have tried to get the drop on 75 whitetails by following their tracks. Now that may not seem like a lot of deer tracking, but I suggest, for my type of hunting, and for the areas I hunt, it is. Remember, some hunt bucks, like the famous trackers of New England, almost exclusively by tracking them. In real-world deer hunting, a majority of deer hunters track deer only incidentally to a more usual type of hunt. They pick up what appears to be a big, fresh, buck track in the snow while on their way to their stand, or on a deer drive, or as they slowly still-hunt through the woods, hoping to spot or jump a deer from cover. That is the hard-core truth. It is how I generally decide to follow a deer track anyway. It is rare that I leave the camp with the absolute intention of riding along a logging road or walking down a trail looking for a buck track. It is very rare for me to pass up what looks like a good track to continue to search for an ever larger track, like so many of the more famous trackers say they do. So, I guess when compared to some, I'm a casual tracker or perhaps an incidental one. I track, but only when the spirit or sign moves me. For my type of hunting, it works perfectly for me.

I shot this mule deer after tracking him in soft sand and dirt. His tracks were easy to follow not only because they were left in soft earth, but also because one hoof was chipped.

Even though I have taken up the track of 75 deer, I can count the number of successful hunts (where following the trail ended up with me actually killing a buck) on one hand.

One was shot as I caught him feeding off-guard on the branch of a cedar tree. Another buck met his fate when I noticed his prints were getting closer together in the snow, suggesting he was slowing down. I shot him as he tried to sneak away as he slowly walked up a small creek. I shot another tracked buck as I spotted him trying to circle downwind to see what was dogging him. I quickly, but quietly, got to a spot where I thought I could cut him off—which I did. An interesting note here is that all bucks were tracked in snow that was at least three inches and not more than eight inches deep.

Each and every tracking experience taught me something and helped me become a better tracker in the heavily-hunted areas and type of terrain that I track deer in. I learned more from the numerous deer I tracked that eventually gave me the slip, than I did from the bucks I outsmarted.

## Lesson Passed On

A couple of years ago, I was hunting on my farm in the southern tier of New York. I was hunting with my long-time hunting companions, my wife Kate and twin cousins Leo and Ralph Somma. Opening day dawned with about 18 inches of fallen snow and more was still falling. It was not too much later, when my cousin Ralph called on the radio and asked me to meet him by his stand. When I got there, he told me he shot a nice eight-point buck and wanted some help tracking it. So, I brought along his

I took this 12-point buck after tracking him on a mountain in Warwick, New York. I wait until the pressure drives bucks to this hard-to-get-to area on the backside of a steep mountain where the chance of seeing another is slim.

Ralph Somma shot this buck the first season on our farm. We had to track the buck for over a mile before Ralph made the finishing shot. It was bedded down with a doe!

brother Leo and my son Cody (who was 14 at the time). After discussing our strategy, Ralph suggested that since we did not know the land well enough yet (it was our first season hunting the land), he would take a stand where we suspected the buck might circle back to. I was going to slowly pick up the buck's track and blood trail and follow after the deer.

I brought my son along with me to give him a first-hand experience of tracking a wounded deer. We weren't on the track more than 100 yards when I turned and said to Cody, "Judging by the tracks and the blood in the snow, this buck is slowing down. He should be close by." Those words barely left my mouth when the buck jumped up from behind a deadfall not ten yards to my left. In the surprise and excitement of the moment, I fired and missed. The buck ran off in a different direction.

Again, we picked up the track. This time, there was much less blood to help us. I could see from the hoof prints that the buck was about to bed down ahead of us. I told Cody to keep a sharp eye out. Fifty yards later, Cody spotted the buck sneaking off to our left through some heavy pines. The buck didn't offer a shot, but he was, in fact, heading in a direction that would soon put him in Ralph's path. Each time we jumped the buck, the possibility of him being shot by another hunter on adjoining property became more and more realistic, especially since it was opening day. With this in mind, we slowed our pace and hoped that the buck would slow his pace, too. Just then, a single, muffled report from Ralph's 12-gauge Browning Deer Stalker rang out not 100 yards from us. I took a moment to share with Cody that with a little patience, knowledge to not pressure the buck, and good planning skills, we put together a good tracking effort to get this buck.

Remember what I said earlier about "real-world" tracking. Well, that's what I do. I don't get the chance to track deer in remote, wilderness areas like Maine or the Adirondacks on a regular basis. In fact, when I'm hunting with an outfitter while taping a television segment for our TV show, *Woods 'N' Water*, no matter how remote the area, we don't track a mature buck with me, the guide, and a cameraman. It cuts the odds of bagging a buck down to a percentage neither the guide nor I can accept. I have a limited amount of time to produce the show and we stand a better chance of scoring if I take a stand, rattle, or call.

All the bucks that I have tracked and shot were in areas where other hunters were. In my view, that is just as much of an achievement as picking up a track of a wilderness buck and taking it to the final confrontation. In my mind, it requires more hunting and tracking skills than wilderness tracking. But in the end, both are challenging and require specialized hunting skills, equipment, and tactics to be successful.

## Play the Odds

In the numerous times that I have cut a track and followed it, I managed to see the buck I was following about 70 percent of the time. This is a testament to how successful tracking can be under the right circumstances. About 30 percent of the bucks were never spotted, nor was I able to tell if anyone else shot at or killed them. I simply never caught up with the elusive phantoms. Each beguiled all my attempts at running them down and won the match by giving me—and everyone else around them—the slip.

Even though a majority of the bucks I have tracked and killed lived on lands that could be hunted by others, the one element that remained constant is that they were taken in hard-to-reach places. Most bucks were taken in mountainous areas that I consider to be under-hunted ground—lands that I like to call "tough terrain" where most hunters don't like to go. They are lands that are high and steep and once a hunter gets that high and that far back in, there is usually very little other hunting pressure to contend with. Only one of the bucks was taken in "big woods wilderness country." In fact, several other bucks were shot within 50 miles of Manhattan, New York in southern Orange County! I attribute my success in catching up with all of these bucks, however, almost solely to the element of low hunting pressure. Don't let anyone

Kate is examining tracks left by a big deer on our farm. She followed the track but never caught up to the deer. The snow was perfect: soft, fresh, and not too deep.

ever tell you anything different about tracking. Consistent successful tracking goes hand-and-hand with unpressured big woods hunting grounds. You can take that statement to the deer hunting bank—period. These types of areas can be found anywhere you hunt, no matter how populated the area is. There is always some type of terrain that other hunters just won't hunt in (swamps, steep mountains and the like). Find such areas and the chances of catching up to a buck whose tracks you are following increases ten-fold.

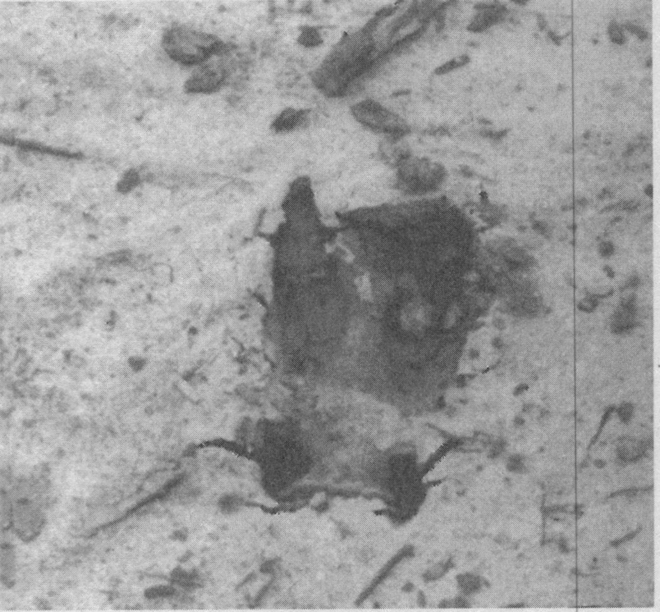

The splayed hoof, deep dewclaws and over length of this print suggest its maker was most likely a buck. The savvy tracker checks other available sign to confirm this.

## Hoof Tracks

There are, of course, other elements that help make a tracker more successful. First and foremost, understand an overwhelming majority of successful tracking is done in fresh, soft, snow that isn't too deep. Next, make it your business to learn all you can about a deer's hoof prints. For instance, is the length of a track of significant importance? It isn't to me. Is the width of a track what really determines a big track? From my experience it is. If it is 3 to 3½ inches wide, I have learned that I am following a mature deer. Learn what the significance is of how deep a track is that is left in mud, snow, or sand. A mature buck puts most of his weight on his front quarters when walking. It's obvious then that his front feet will sink deeper into the ground than his rear feet. If the track you're following has prints that indicate the front feet are deeper than the rear feet, you're most likely on a mature buck track. Mature bucks swagger as they walk, too. This means there will be a stagger effect between their front right and front left legs—another indication you're following an older buck. Smaller does and bucks leave tracks that are much closer together. Learn the importance of determining if the buck is walking, trotting, or running by knowing how far apart the tracks will be when a deer is in a walking stride or in a trotting or running gait.

Learn to detect what other factors indicate whether the track you are looking at actually belongs to a buck and not a mature, heavy doe. Remember a mature buck is a totally different animal than even a mature doe. He acts differently, instinctively thinks differently, eats differently, and walks differently. Bucks walk in a random way often stopping to make or freshen a rub or scrape. In snow cover, you will see where he has urinated between his tracks. You'll also discover that does, even mature does, usually leave almost perfect heart-shaped tracks. They also walk in a straight line.

A crucial element to tracking is to learn to identify the track as soon as you have picked it up. Know what makes the track you're following unique from other deer tracks around it. Burn its image in your mind quickly. If the deer joins up with other deer, identifying and singling out its track from the other tracks will keep you on the correct trail.

## Is It a Fresh Track?

Keep in mind that if you are on a track during a snow-fall and then the snow suddenly stops, and you find tracks that the snow hasn't filled yet, your buck probably isn't very far ahead of you. In fact, depending on what the buck is doing, he may only be 15 to 30 minutes in front of you! A fresh track is always more defined, too, especially around the edges. Older tracks begin to crumble and are less definable. One very important element in this learning process is to understand what tracks are fresh enough to set out after, and what aren't. Only experience will help you here. It took me a long time to learn this part of tracking. I eventually learned to place my boot print next to the buck track and compare the two. If the deer track looked a lot less definable than my track, I guessed it was too old to follow. If it is somewhat less sharp than the boot print, but reasonably close, it usually is worth stalking. Of course, if it is as sharp as your boot print, then get on it quickly.

## Know the Escape Routes

It bears repeating that you have to know your hunting area. Even more important, know where deer escape routes are. This is especially true for the real-world type of tracking most of us will do. Knowing an escape route of a wilderness buck is somewhat less important, simply because the buck has so many choices available to it when covering a lot of ground in big woods. This is not true, however, when it comes to hunting bucks with a lot less territory available to them. They are more inclined to quickly head toward an escape route than their big woods cousins. This simply means that a hunter who knows where these escape routes are, increases his chances tremendously when tracking bucks in heavily hunted areas.

Learn where deer head when they are being pressured by something on their back trail. Know as many escape routes as possible. Learn to anticipate what a buck being followed by a predator will do and what he might not do, or where he will head in good weather or in bad weather, on wet ground or in snow. Bucks have a sixth sense about snow. They instinctively know they are easier to follow in snow and will react differently when pursued in it.

## Perseverance

Next come the elements that separate the really good trackers from the casual ones. These are the elements of the mind and body. A truly good tracker has character. He or she is able to muster the spirit to go on when the body and mind wants nothing

Master tracker Hal Blood with a buck he tracked and killed. Once Hal is on a buck's track, the buck might as well make out his will. Credit: Hal Blood.

more than to quit. This person has the ability to stay totally focused on the job at hand and is able to dig deep when everything else tells him to turn back. A good tracker has the competitive spirit. He or she wants to succeed—he has to have a will to win. The buck has almost the same determination to put as much distance between it and whatever is on its back trail. It has an intense will to survive.

One of the most impressive trackers in big-woods country I know has all of the above qualifications: Hal Blood. In his book, "*Hunting Big Woods Bucks*," Blood emphasizes his dogged approach to following a track. In several of his stories about taking up the chase in big, wild country, Blood makes it clear that his tenacity for outlasting bitter cold temperatures, deep snow, mountainous terrain, wind, and even rain, overcomes any desire his body sends to his mind to quit the trail. For anyone who intends to track mature bucks in big woods, he must first commit to being a determined tracker like Hal Blood.

Another example of a single-minded tracker who hunts in heavily pressured areas, is my long-time hunting companion, Ralph Somma. His ability to focus on nothing else other than staying on the track and sign is second-to-none. In the many years I have hunted with him, I have seen other hunters quit a trail, only to have Ralph pick it up, follow the track, and find the animal. This type of concentration is absolutely important when you're trailing a buck in heavily hunted areas. It is absolutely crucial when trailing the tracks and blood trail in areas where there are numerous other hunters.

## Keep Your Pace

One of the most critical points to becoming a consistently good tracker is knowing how to effectively follow a track. There are times when you want to pick up the pace and move fast. Other times it is much better to slow down and move at a snail's pace, almost like you're in slow motion. By watching a buck's tracks closely, you will know what he is doing and how you should proceed.

If you make the wrong decision, one of two conditions will develop. You will either see a flash of brown or glimpse at the glare of an antler as it drifts into a patch of cover as the buck escapes. Don't expect a mature buck to flag as it sneaks away. A wise old buck has learned to tuck his tail between his legs, especially when he has a predator on his back trail. That's what a tracker is to a buck–nothing more than a predator. I mention this because it is a little-known fact that mature male game animals—like whitetail, mule bucks, bull elk, and moose—that are predated upon learn to live secretive lives. They instinctively avoid being caught with a group or herd of their kin. They are lon ers and live within the boundaries of being stalked by predators. They have evolved with an intense instinct to out-maneuver their pursuer rather than blindly run from danger in their attempt to get away. The older the animal, the more ingrained this behavior is in his psyche.

Therefore, the wise or seasoned tracker rarely expects to see a flagging, running buck as he tracks his prey. He knows that he is more inclined to see a buck sneaking off ahead of him. On the other hand, if you track too slowly, you will never see the deer at all.

But, if tracking is done correctly, the reward will be getting a shot at your trophy. For instance, if the buck's tracks have a longer stride than what you have been following, he has picked up speed. Once you determine this has happened, you have to increase your speed, too. If his tracks begin to wander, or pace around nervously in a very small area, or begin to circle, he's on to you and is preparing to give you the slip. Now is the time to slow down to fine tune your pursuit by keeping all your senses at full alert and moving with one cautious step at a time. Keep your eyes scanning the surrounding terrain. Proceed with extreme caution—he most likely is not far away. Learning when to do what, will help make you a better tracker. Again, experience will help you.

Also remember to concentrate at looking at what is in front of you—but not directly in front of you. Most bucks that are being tracked have a habit—a natural instinct—to move off their track and watch for their pursuer's approach from one side or the other. Another problem is that too many first-time trackers, and even some who have been at it awhile, often become over-involved with studying the tracks. This is one of the most common and costly mistakes a tracker can make. Surprisingly, bucks who are being trailed for a long time will often slow up and hide to check out what is after them. This is why hunters who track sometimes see the deer several times during a stalk. This is what makes tracking a fascinating hunting strategy.

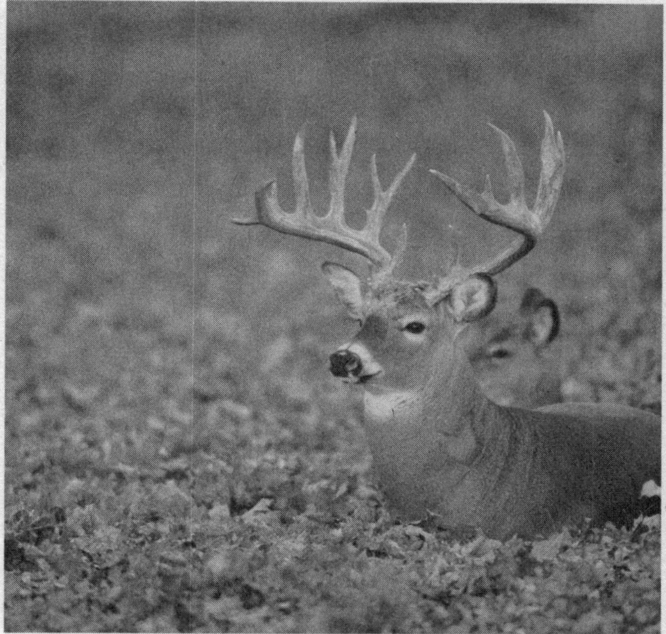

Bedded bucks will use the slightest rise on the ground to get a better view. When tracking, keep a keen eye out for small rises in the terrain. Credit: Ted Rose.

## Looking Down On You

Bucks prefer to get higher than the pursuers on their back trail—even if it is only slightly higher. While I was hunting whitetails in Montana, we were following a track through a clear-cut. The terrain was flat, but there were several piles of blowdowns made up of tree tops as well as piles of brush. The clear-cut twisted and turned for over a mile in front of us. Each time we rounded a bend into a new clearing, I expected to see a buck sneaking off from behind a blowdown or pile of brush. Halfway through the clear-cut, I noticed the buck's tracks were getting much closer together and were milling about before moving off again. I realized he couldn't be too far off and I slowed my pace. As I scanned the blowdowns, a movement caught my attention. As I looked over, I saw the buck staring at me as he stood on the only bare ground rise in the entire clear cut. It was not more than two feet high and five feet wide. It offered him, however, what the blow downs could not–a clear unobstructed view of the predator on his back trail. Before I could react, he was gone. I logged the incident in my mind and have never forgotten it. Many times since, I have seen mature bucks use this tactic to help escape their pursuer.

If you are tracking a buck even in the flattest of terrain and you come to a knoll or even the slightest increase in elevation in the topography, pay particular attention to it. If you do, you'll never get caught with your pants down. It is crucial to keep a keen eye on the natural cover off to the side and ahead of you. Glance from side to side, look for an antler, an eye, a nose, or even the entire deer. I know you have read that it is better to look for parts of deer when still-hunting. But, when you're tracking a deer, be ready for anything. Many times I have been surprised and even shocked to come around a bend or enter a stand of pines to see the buck standing there looking back over his shoulder at me. Sometimes, I have come up on them while they were facing their back trail. This usually happens after they have been dogged for a longer period than they want to tolerate. Seasoned trackers always know to be alert to what's ahead of them when they're following a set of tracks.

## One-of-a-Kind Track

Several years ago, just after a snow had stopped late in the day, around 3 p.m., I immediately went hunting on a ridge behind my old house. I found an unusual track with a very defined chip in the left hoof. It led me to a ravine that I knew well. Most times, only young bucks occupied it. (I firmly believe that certain grounds attract young bucks and other parts of the terrain attract mature bucks.) Even though the track was indicative of an older deer, I wasn't convinced since I rarely saw big bucks in this area. As I approached the ledge, a huge-racked buck sprung up from beneath me. Before I could get my Knight blackpowder rifle up, he was gone. By that time, it was already late and I decided not to give chase in hopes he would return to this spot over the next few days.

The following day it snowed again. When the snow finally stopped, at about 10 in the morning, I left to go hunting. Once again, I picked up the chipped hoof tracks heading in the same direction. I approached with extreme caution. As I got to the deep ravine, I glanced at the tracks and saw that they meandered down between the rocks on the ledge toward the spot he had jumped up from the day before. I was looking for the buck when out of the corner of my eye, I saw him just slightly above me and to my right! He went down the ledge, then doubled back up and bedded at the highest spot just off to the right. In this spot he could watch anything that came up from the valley below. Pretty cagey, huh? Again, he was gone before I had a chance to react. This time, I had plenty of time to follow his tracks. Over the next several hours, I saw him twice. I was tired, however, and my reaction time was much slower than his. Again, the buck had won the match. I figured he had out-played me and that the chances of him returning to this location would be slim to none. I did plan on getting some rest and hoped I could cut his very unusual track again in the same area.

The following day, I left at the break of daylight. I took a new route to where I had stopped the hunt the day before. But as I began to climb the mountain, I again cut the fresh tracks of the buck I was hunting. The tracks were coming from the cornfields

I followed this buck's fresh tracks in snow and was able to get a shot at him two hours later. I had its tooth aged and the results said he was 10.5 years old, which may be why his antlers dropped earlier than usual. To age your deer accurately visit www.deerage.com.

across the road. He, too, was heading up the mountain. Taking a good guess as to where he was heading, I quickly walked and trotted to the spot where I had jumped him twice before. I'd hoped the buck was taking his time, meandering, and stopping to browse on his way up the mountain. As I reached the area, I set up my deer-tail decoy for insurance. If I was successful in cutting the buck off, I intended to distract him by twitching the deer tail as I made my shot. I no sooner hung the tail from a branch and settled into my ground blind when I saw the buck walking parallel to my back trail!

For some reason, he decided to take his usual route to the ravine and ledge where he bedded down at the top of the mountain. Before reaching the area where he started to travel down the ledge, he made a sharp turn and started down the ravine. I moved up to the edge and peaked down. The buck moved off so suddenly because a hot doe was 50 yards below. He chased after her and they went up the other side. I watched as another buck with a slightly smaller rack chased my buck down the other side of the ridge and ran off with the doe.

The chase was on again. I followed his track for exactly three hours back and forth over several ridges. Luckily, I leased the 500 acres I was hunting and it bordered 1,000 acres of land no one had permission to hunt on. His tracks eventually lead me back to the spot where I had previously jumped him twice. Just as I crested the top of the ridge, I noticed his tracks stopped on the side of the ridge. The tracks appeared to indicate that he had paced around and then headed toward the flat on top of the ridge. I circled off to the side and approached the knoll slowly, carefully scanning back and forth for him. Then, I saw him looking over the ridge away from my direction and down into the ravine—almost like he expected me to be coming up any minute. The .50 caliber echoed through the valley as the 200 grain Sabot hit its mark. The big buck never lifted his head. He died in his bed looking over the ledge for his pursuer. If I hadn't noticed how his tracks paused and then headed away, I would have never known to slow up and cut off to the side.

One point to note. I also knew when to quit the track as darkness settled in the first day. I knew I didn't have the strength nor the focus to stay on the track the second day and I knew I had him when I was able to read what his tracks meant the third day of this amazing hunt.

The buck had 12 points. His antlers were heavy and palmated. His body was bone-thin though and when I went to drag him out, one of his antlers pulled off. I guessed he was an old buck that had seen better days. I confirmed this when I sent a tooth to a lab and they aged it at an incredible ten years and four months old! No wonder he was hanging out in an area where younger bucks frequented. He was probably run out of his old haunts by other mature bucks that were just too strong for him any more. In any case, being able to read sign from his track enabled me to take this handsome and savvy buck.

# Tracking Strategies

Now that I have covered the fundamentals of tracking, I would like to get to the "real meat" of stalking after a buck's prints—the tips and strategies that will put a buck you are trailing in your crosshairs. I'm sure many of you have heard and read that some hunters can absolutely tell the difference between a buck and a doe track. Some, especially biologists, steadfastly agree that it is impossible to absolutely tell the difference between a buck and a doe track. I agree with this but only in a general sense.

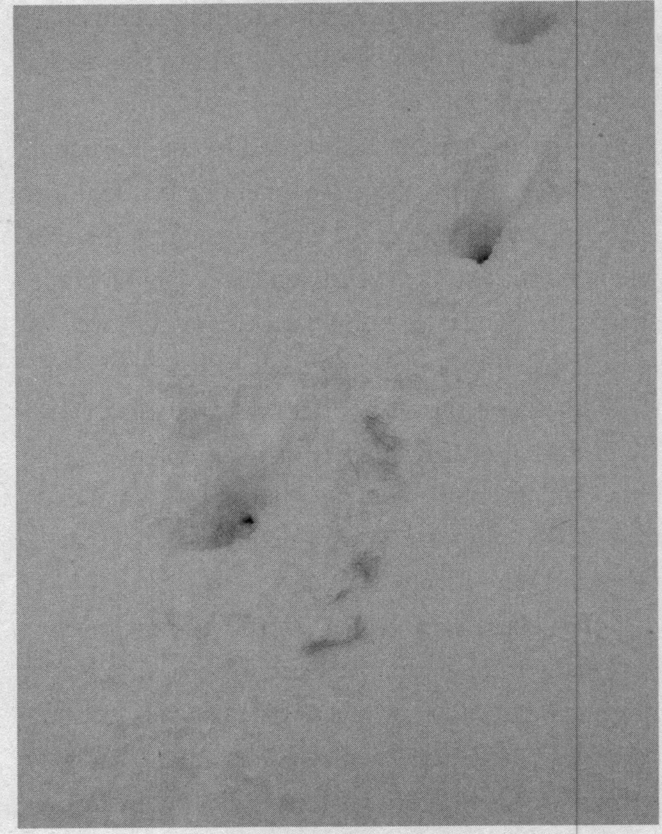

These splayed tracks were accompanied by drag marks and deer hair. A savvy tracker keeps one eye out for any changes in the tracks or drag marks while using his other eye to spot a buck before *it* sees him!

## Doe Versus Buck

There are indicators to help you separate a buck's track from a doe's track. These indicators all have to do with the size, width, splay, and depth of the print.

Hunters often overlook other indicators that will help differentiate between a buck and doe track and can tip the odds in your favor. If you elevate your detective work to visualize not only the track itself more but also the sign that surrounds it, you will, more often than not, be able to tell a buck track from a doe track.

## What Size is the Track?

The first thing a tracker should look at is the size of the hoof print. No matter how big a doe may get, it is a rare thing that she will achieve the body weight of a big buck. Therefore, her track will rarely be as large as a big buck's track—but it can be confused with a medium-sized buck's track. Occasionally, an old doe that has made it through eight or more seasons may actually be big enough to

Dewclaw marks left deep in soil or snow suggest the deer that left it may be a heavy mature buck or it could be from an old matriarchal doe. Credit: Ted Rose.

have a track that is comparable to that of a mature whitetail buck.

## Dewclaws

Another factor to consider when identifying a buck or doe track is the depth of the snow. If there is less than two or three inches of snow, a doe walking at a normal pace usually doesn't leave tracks with the dewclaw marks. This is not so with a mature buck. He always leaves tracks with his dewclaw imprints, despite the snow's depth. I have noticed that the heavier the buck is, the deeper the dewclaw's imprints will be in the snow. Keep in mind that the dewclaw imprints will always be present if the deer was running in the snow no matter if they are left by a buck or doe. Again, a good tracking detective will soon discover that a buck's dewclaws—even when running—are larger in size than a doe's dewclaws. They also leave marks in the snow that exceed the width of the buck print it.

## Distance Between Prints

Another good indicator of whether or not you are following a mature buck or just an average one is the distance between the left print and the right print. If it's eight inches, it's a good-sized buck. Ten inches and you know you are following a really good-sized animal. Twelve inches or more and you're on the trail of a trophy-class whitetail.

You can know this because as a buck matures, several physical characteristics stand out and help determine or estimate his age. At 3½ years old, a buck's chest appears deeper than the hindquarters, giving the appearance of a well-conditioned racehorse. At 4½ years old, his fully muscled neck blends into the shoulders and his waistline is as deep as his chest. At 5½ and 6½ years old, a buck's neck blends completely into its shoulders and the front of its body appears to be one large mass. A buck older than this is a conundrum and can be misleading. Once a buck is older than 6½ years, its tracks are often mistaken for a younger buck's tracks due to the lack of muscularity in the older buck's shoulders.

The difference in distance between tracks, therefore, develops as the buck matures. His chest gets deeper which puts more weight on his fore legs and often causes him to have a flat-footed, long stride.

Another indication of an older buck is drag marks. If a buck is dragging his hoofs when he is walking, even in a very light snowfall, it's a good bet that he is an older buck. Older deer, 4½ years and older, will have a tendency to drag their feet more than younger bucks.

When the snow is more than a few inches deep, all deer appear to drag their feet. Bucks will still drag their feet more than does. But it is hard to identify buck from doe tracks in several inches of snow.

I also see this sign when hunting in Texas on dry, dusty sundaroes. There is always a top layer of loose soil where a buck's prints are sharp and identifiable. Older bucks, even on this type of terrain, still tend to drag their hooves.

Whenever a buck urinates, he drips urine on the soil or snow. When tracking a buck, look for drops of urine for several feet after a spot of urine is found. It will be a very good indication that you're trailing a buck. Credit: Ted Rose.

The deep chest, thick neck, girth, big belly and the body weight of this buck show that he is a mature buck that is at least 40 years old and maybe older. Credit: Ted Rose.

A buck tends to swagger when he walks. The greater the swag, the bigger the buck. Unlike a doe that will travel through and under brush, a big buck is more likely to go around such vegetation to avoid tangling his antlers, rather than go through or under it. This is especially true for wide-racked bucks. Some bucks are too lazy, however, to go around an obstacle and will push their way through it. In this instance, it is important to see how a buck moves through the brush. Usually, one hoof will be off to one side as he steps to work his rack through the tangles. A good tracking detective deciphers small clues like this to help interpret the track he is following.

## Urine

An additional way to help identify whether or not a track belongs to a buck is to look for urine. A buck urinates as he walks. There will be dribble marks in the snow. I often laugh to myself when I see this, because it reminds me of any guy who is over

50 and has any kind of prostate problem. Dribbling becomes part of everyday life for older males—bucks and men alike.

The reason a buck urinates like this is because he is marking his scent as he travels through areas. We have all seen how a dog marks each and every tree or hydrant on his morning walk. A buck is doing the same thing. These dribbled urine marks can sometimes go as far as three to five feet. A doe, on the other hand, will almost always squat and urinate in one place. Even when a buck is urinating to relieve himself, the urine leaves a different pattern than that of a doe. A doe's urine will be concentrated in a small area and in a relatively small spot. The urine mark will show up behind or centered on her tracks. A buck's urine appears in front of his tracks. As any male knows, the penis is not as stationary as we would sometimes like it to be. Therefore, the hanging appendage will wobble around much like a fire hose that the fireman does not have control of, causing urine to be scattered over a large area in the snow. While what I have said may seem like the urine is spread over quite a distance, it's only a matter of several inches.

Use your nose when following a large track–especially during the rut. A big, mature whitetail's urine exudes a strong, musky odor. It is unmistakable once you have learned to identify it. Over the years, while hunting with friends, I have stopped in my tracks and taken a long deep sniff of the air. When I do this, in almost every case, I have been able to find either a marking of urine in the snow or in a scrape. At the time, the odor is so powerful and potent it can be tasted in the molecules of the air. This may seem hard to believe, but I promise you that once you have learned to identify this scent, you, too, will have the same reaction.

The ability to pick up this scent is a learned skill, which will pay off big dividends to those who pay attention to it. It can direct you to a hot primary scrape, a trail of a buck following a doe, into a buck's core area, and many times, to his mid-day bed. The tactic works on bare ground and in snow.

## Other Sign

Many times a buck will leave sign that is not as obvious as his tracks or scat. This type of sign is harder to see especially for the novice tracker and, therefore, often goes unnoticed. This is unfortunate because this sign provides as much information about the direction the buck is heading, what size his antlers might be, if he's after a doe and much more. To discover this type of information, a tracker needs to be more of a detective than he or she is when simply following a buck's hoof prints.

## Antler Tip Marks in Snow

For instance, I once tracked a set of hoof prints that were wide, set deep in the snow, and had splayed toes. This indicated to me that the track probably belonged to a mature buck. At that time, as long as a buck had points on his rack, he was fair game as far as I was concerned. So, I set out after the prints in earnest. After a few hours walking all over the mountain, I was about to give up. The weather was getting colder and I only had a couple hours of light left. Just then, I looked more closely at the track which was at the base of a log where the buck had been nibbling some fungus.

I clearly saw his nose print in the snow. As I examined it more closely, I noticed that the tips of his antlers were imprinted in the snow on either side of his nose print. This really caught my attention because most often, the tips from the main beams don't leave imprints in the snow. It's usually the second, third, and fourth tines that leave their mark.

As a buck lowers his head to sniff or feed, especially in snow, the tips of his antlers will often make an imprint in the snow or soft earth. Credit: Ted Rose.

I had to look twice at the width between the points. I pulled out my tiny tape measure (which is always in my pack) and discovered that the points were 22 inches from tip to tip. I also saw several other marks in the snow that were obviously from other tines on his rack. To quit following his trail now was absolutely out of the question.

As it turned out, I jumped the buck on his trail just an hour later. Unfortunately, this was one of those occasions where the thrill of the chase ended with the buck escaping. My mind was briefly diverted by studying his track too hard and I never saw the buck jump from behind a blow down and run off before I could get a clean shot.

The point is, there are a lot of other clues that a buck leaves behind for a tracker to decipher other than his hoof prints. I mention this because many of us become so mesmerized by the hoof prints when we are on the track of a buck, that we often overlook other equally important messages that we should pick up.

For instance, I have learned that antler imprints in the snow can suggest how many points are on the buck's rack. As mentioned above, the imprints in snow are usually left by the second, third, and fourth tines and not the brow tines nor tips of the main beams. Therefore, if you see three points on each side, the buck you are trailing is most likely a ten-pointer.

## Buck Antlers in Bed

Bucks that lie in their beds will most often leave an imprint of one side of their antler in the snow. Seasoned hunters and some biologists say that this will usually be from the left side of the buck's head, as most bucks will lay out and put the left side of their head down to sleep. Not that this makes any difference here—I just thought I'd mention this particular behavior.

## Back Print in the Front

New trackers are often confused as to exactly what they are looking at. They are often confused as to whether they are looking at the front hoof or the back hoof. You are always looking at the back hoof. The reason is simple; a deer (buck or doe) will always put its back foot in the same spot its front hoof just made. Therefore, the front track is always covered by the back hoof track. Remember that the back hoof of a deer is always smaller than the front.

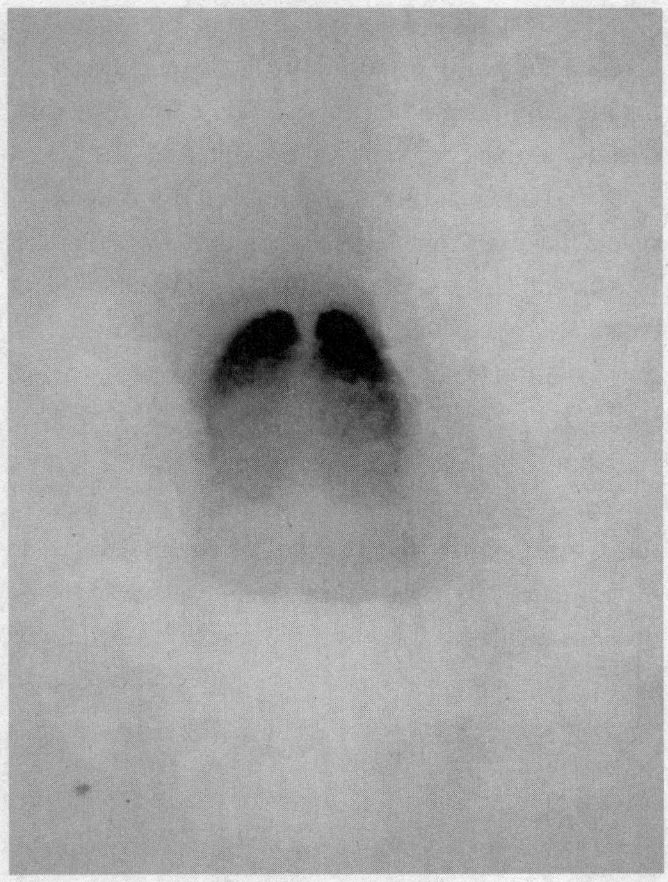

No matter what deer track you are following the front track will always be covered by the deer's back hooves. A deer's back hoof is always smaller than the front hoof, too.

This is a good point to know for two reasons. One: you will learn to look for unique markings of a hoof such as chips, splits, shape, size, etc., to help you identify one buck's tracks from others as you continue on the trail. Two: if you are not sure about the track you are following, stay with it long enough until you come to a spot where the buck stops or mills about. As soon as this happens, the buck will leave a front hoof print that you can size up to help determine how big of an animal he might be. Once you have determined that the track you are on is a buck track and it is the size that you want to follow, you can once again take up your search on its trail.

## Is That Track Fresh?

Once of the most-often asked questions from hunters who are interested in tracking deer is, "How can you determine whether a track is fresh or not?" The only way to determine if a track has been made "only moments ago"—is if you see the buck standing in the tracks!

Basically, there are many variables when it comes to aging a track in the snow or on bare ground. A wet snow will help keep the track sharp for a longer period than a dry snow. Sometimes this can be problematic when the tracker believes the track is fresher than it actually is. In a dry snow, a track will often have crystals of ice forming in it. So, if you know how long the snow has been on the ground, it will help you gauge the age of the track more reliably.

Tracks that are constantly blown over with new snow are most difficult to age. Under these conditions, any tracker will have a hard time locating a good set of tracks and aging them correctly.

Finally, trying to identify tracks in snow that has been affected by a warmer temperature—or even rain—can be alluding. Under these conditions, the tracks will look older and in some instances, appear larger than they really are because of melting conditions.

## Tracks and Droppings

This is where you separate the men trackers from the boy trackers. This tactic requires one to feel and smell deer droppings. Sometimes I squeeze the droppings between my fingers and break them apart to look for the type of forage the deer has been eating. By doing this, you can get a good idea of how close the buck is in front of you. On a cold day, droppings freeze quicker than normal. The easier

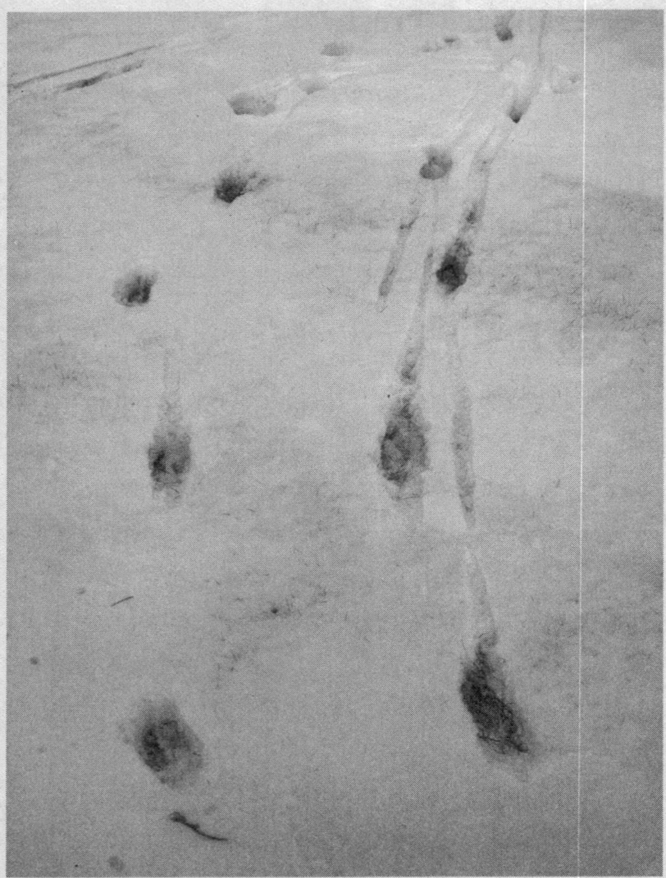

Foul weather (ice, snow, and rain) distort deer tracks making it difficult to tell how long ago they were made.

the scat squashes and the wetter it is, the fresher the scat. When it has a mucous texture on the outside and has a fresh odor, drop the crap, and scan for the buck with your eyes. He may be really close!

I know many trackers who swear they can tell the difference between a buck dropping and a doe dropping. Other seasoned trackers are absolutely adamant that there is no difference between dung that is stuck together in clumps as opposed to individual pellets.

I fall squarely in the middle of these two camps. As with anything else with tracking, clumpy scat and single pellet droppings are once again only indicators. Nothing about tracking sign is absolutely written in stone. Droppings change from season to season and from what the animals are currently feeding on.

For instance, in the summer when foliage is greener, the dropping will more likely be clumped together. But herein lies the quandary. Some say that because of that, you can't tell the difference between buck and doe scat. But I have noticed that a buck's scat is like everything else about a buck, whether it is his track, his chest, his stride, his neck, whatever—it is usually larger than a doe's. In the case of his poop, may I delicately suggest—here, too, he has a heavier load.

But this doesn't necessarily mean that he will leave a large, elongated clump of dung. I learned this when I started keeping stats on my Deer Diary Stat cards in 1975. Each time I field dressed a decent-sized buck, I noticed the scat in his colon

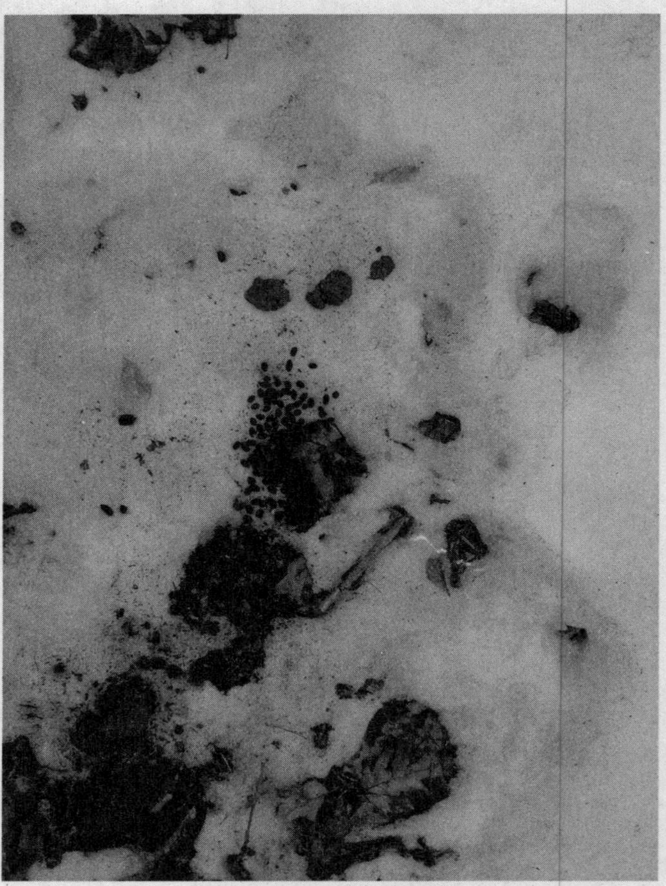

Although there isn't a steadfast way to identify the sex of a deer by its scat, there are indicators that suggest if it was left by a buck or doe.

was usually comprised of individual pellets. I got so curious about this that I decided to do some research on my own. Over the remaining part of the year, I field dressed several fresh road-killed bucks to see if this phenomenon was different than during the hunting season. It wasn't. Each buck had single pellets in its colon. As the years passed, the stat cards clearly indicated a pattern that demonstrated that most of the time, most of the bucks had single pellets in their colons. However, there were times when this did not hold true, but not enough times to change the overall findings.

I noticed that buck scat was larger than the pellets from does (in areas I hunt). That may be different in wilderness areas, but I would not know since I do most of my tracking in farmlands or in the suburbs.

It bears repeating here that unlike my tracker colleagues who trail bucks in wilderness areas, I'm following bucks that more than likely will run into other hunters or enter private land. And so will you, if you find yourself tracking in the real-world conditions in which most of us hunt.

I mention this because when I find a track I want to follow, I have other elements to consider than the trackers who live in Maine and Vermont. Time is against me and with them. The longer I'm on a trail, the less likely the tracking will end in the taking of the buck. That may be depressing to hear, but if you're tracking on a limited number of acres, it is reality. And if you want to be a tracker, you have to own up to that fact early on. Once you do, you will become a better tracker in pressured hunting country and a very good tracker in wilderness areas.

Let me give you a comparison. For the sake of this example, I will refer to big woods or wilderness trackers as BWTs (big woods trackers) and other trackers as PWTs (pressured woods trackers), as that is mostly how this type of tactic divides itself. When a BWT takes up after a buck, he has time to follow the quarry without a lot of pressure. PWTs don't have that benefit. The BWT can dog his prey for many hours without much care that he will run it into another hunter. Not so in the areas where a PWT hunts. Big Woods Trackers can even react to sign differently than their PWT comrades.

Let's say either a BWT or PWT picks up a buck track early in the morning. They both can assume the buck is most likely bedded down. The BWT can now make a plan and head off on the trail. The PWT has to first take into account whether or not the buck is bedded down on land he can track on, or if the buck is bedded on his neighbor's posted property. If the BWT gets close to his buck and he notices that the buck is picking up his tempo, the BWT can, without much thought, pick up his pace as well. A PWT can't do that. He has to stop and think about where the buck is heading. If it is circling, he has a chance to continue to follow it even at a quick pace. If, on the other hand, the PWT determines that the buck is headed in a beeline toward another property, he has to slow the chase and give the buck time to settle down and hope that the buck circles back or remains within his hunting area—or the hunt has ended. In fact, so I don't boggle your mind with this comparison, there are a lot of tactical tracking differences between the big woods tracker and the tracker who follows hoof prints within smaller plots of land.

I mention this because I don't want you to become depressed when you lose a buck that moves out of your area when you are tracking him. I also don't want you to feel like you are not a good tracker if you don't score on the first several trails you follow. Wilderness trackers have a way of making a lot of other would-be, real-world trackers feel incompetent. I'm sure they don't mean to, but they

I followed this buck's tracks along a sandy embankment on a 5,300-acre ranch in Wyoming. I didn't have to worry that I would push him onto other private land.

do. Don't expect to shoot even a majority of bucks that you track in heavily lived in or hunted places.

In big woods country, you should be able to increase your success to one in ten tracks you take up. The fact is, no matter what the success ratio is in big woods or heavily pressured areas, killing a buck you have tracked is the ultimate deer hunting experience—one that invokes all our primordial feelings.

As trackers, we become one with our surroundings and with our quarry. We are the hunter and they are the prey. We have stalked them fair and square on their home turf and under their rules and we have come away better for it. Tracking teaches us to be much more patient, observant, diligent, and unrelenting hunters. Like our cavemen ancestors, we become the efficient predators all hunters strive to be.

Most of us do not hunt huge tracts of big woods. Therefore hunters tracking deer in suburbia, farmlands or small tracts of property have to be concerned about forcing the deer to move off their property and onto posted land.
Credit: Ted Rose.

# CALLING AND RATTLING
## Matching the Calls to the Season

Whitetail hunters are fortunate to have three distinct periods during which they can attempt to lure deer with calling, rattling, or decoying. Calling, in particular, is extremely period-sensitive. The pre-rut hunter should definitely use different calling strategies than one who calls during the post-rut period. And the peak-of-the-rut hunter might easily have better luck using completely different tactics altogether.

### CALLING DURING THE PRE-RUT

The pre-rut period is many archers' favorite hunting time, simply because animals are more predictable than they will be later in the season. Undisturbed deer move about fairly freely. Almost a year has passed since they have heard calls or smelled bottled scents. Hunters have not been busting them from their beds or flinging arrows or bullets their way, so resident whitetails have gradually lowered their guard. This is why the pre-rut, or preseason, is a superb time to practice deer calling. Undisturbed deer are less likely to be suspicious. Someone using calls now has an excellent chance of having numerous deer respond. Poor calling skills are less likely to prove negative now than later, when whitetails have become so wily they will respond only to the most realistic-sounding calls—if they respond at all. The pre-rut period provides hunters with a learning curve. Even if hunters screw up, which they probably will, they'll still learn something and call in deer while they're at it.

Calling during the pre-rut nets deer that are less likely to be suspicious. Credit: Mark Drury.

Deer are more susceptible to calling during the pre-rut not only because they have been left alone for almost a year but because does are still actively with fawns. Does that gave birth in the late spring may even be accompanied by suckling fawns. As we've learned, does are extremely social animals for much of the year. Most feed, bed, and travel in family groups. These maternal groups consist of a doe matriarch, her off spring, and the fawns of her offspring. If fawns are still suckling, button bucks and sometimes even spikes or forked-horns are also included in the group. Some groups include individuals from other generations, too. That's why in some areas it's not uncommon to see eight, nine, or even ten does feeding together. Spikes and forked-horns are banished at around eighteen months of age, probably to prevent inbreeding with siblings and mothers. An estrous doe will leave her maternal group only until she has been bred. She will then return.

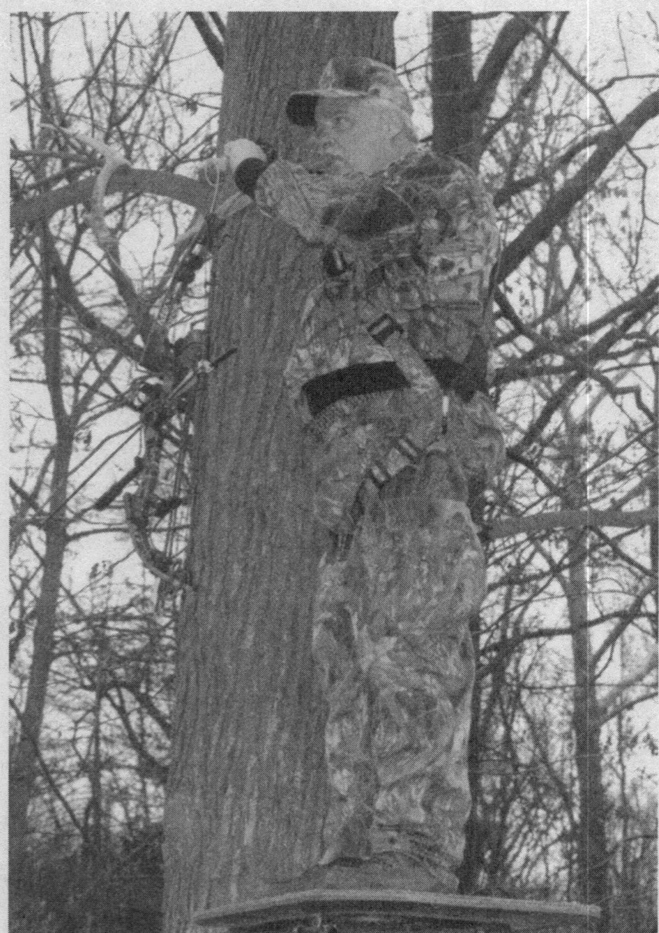

A whitetail hunter should use different calling strategies during the post-rut period than during the pre-rut period. Credit: Jim Holdenried.

An intact maternal group will be attracted to the sound of a bleat or a blat, particularly if one or two of its members have wandered away for the time being. Cohesive doe grunts can also work wonders, as can dominant doe grunts. Fawn distress calls or fawn bleats will work well, too, especially in areas where archery seasons open in September. In most areas, even as hormones are beginning their slow, steady rise in whitetail bloodstreams, deer will remain, for the time being, in maternal and bachelor groups. Doe vocalizations can be used to attract other does, fawns, and bucks from both groups of animals. Bucks are not quite ready to go searching for does yet, but should they hear a nearby doe bleat or blat, they will sometimes become so curious they will respond to find out who made it and why.

Should you see a group of does feeding, try your technique on them. Stick with one particular call instead of throwing everything at them at once—or at least stick with one call at a time until you thoroughly understand what each of your calls is saying. Bleat or blat to them—*baa-baaaa! baa-baaaaa!* If one or more of the animals raises its head and peers in your direction, you have succeeded in getting their attention. Do not call again unless the deer lose interest. When you do call again, call just enough to pique their interest. Don't overdo it. The object is to engage their curiosity enough so that they will feel compelled to check things out. A doe bleat or blat used toward the end of the pre-rut period serves another purpose, too: Any doe enticed to within shooting range might be accompanied by a buck nosing about before the rut begins in earnest.

An intact maternal doe group will be attracted to the sound of a bleat or a blat if one of its members has wandered away. Credit: Kathy Etling.

For a foolproof method of attracting one or more does, turn to the fawn bleat or fawn distress call. Hunters and bowhunters intent on getting a head start on their winter meat supply often rely solely on these two calls during the early weeks of hunting season. Venison from deer that have not yet run for long periods or been chased all over the countryside may taste less gamey than meat from stressed deer. If population ratios are heavily skewed in favor of does, the fawn bleat or fawn distress call

Matching his calling techniques to the period of the rut helps Peter Fiduccia consistently take trophy whitetails.

Especially in early season, fawn bleats can draw in almost any deer in the woods. Credit: Knight & Hale Game Calls.

provides an incredibly effective solution for hunters seeking to lower doe numbers. It's not unheard of for one or more bucks to respond to these calls, either. Doe bleats, doe blats, fawn bleats, and fawn distress calls make excellent sense during the earliest pre season because they will attract almost any deer in the woods.

"I've brought in does with bleat calls and with fawn distress calls, but that fawn distress call is going to get every deer's attention and bring them to high alert," said M.R. James in a word of warning to those who are thinking of relying solely on a fawn distress call. James, a world-renowned bowhunter from Montana, is the founder and editor emeritus of *Bowhunter Magazine*.

The most overlooked stage of the whitetail's cycle, as it relates to hunting, is the pre-rut period, according to noted whitetail authority Peter Fiduccia. But Fiduccia also believes the pre-rut is the least likely hunting period to be exploited. In his opinion, the day you start discovering fresh scrapes in many locations is the day on which the pre-rut is finally in full swing. This correlates roughly to early October in most parts of the country. Bleats, blats, fawn bleats and fawn distress calls will work as well as they did earlier in the preseason, but as the rut nears, it's time to increase both the number and the variety of the whitetail calls you use.

"I get extremely vocal," said Brad Harris of Outland Sports. "I rely on both bleating and contact grunts." A short *burp*, whether imitating a doe's

Calling is the first tactic Brad Harris will use during the pre-rut period. Credit: Brad Harris.

softer, higher-pitched grunt or a buck's deeper grunt, will appeal to whitetail bucks. "The buck hearing such a grunt knows something is going on," Harris said. "His only unanswered question is whether he should come over to investigate. If he thinks it's a doe, well, he's not sure whether she's looking for the company of a buck. Yet the buck is nearing the stage where he's downright eager for doe company, in hope of breeding yet to come. Should the buck think the grunt has been made by another buck, his aggressive nature might compel him to seek out the source of the call. This is true whether he's already alone or just ready to depart his bachelor group. If a doe responds, I don't mind either, because she may pull in a trailing buck with her.

"For the past ten years I've kept a hunting diary," Harris continued. "Each day I've hunted I've jotted down the events that took place that day. My entries confirm that I've taken a higher percentage of good bucks during the pre-rut period than at any other time. I believe a good part of my success can be attributed to it being easier at this time to pattern or link a big buck to a particular scrape-line, rubline, or core area. Whenever I hunt the pre-rut, calling is

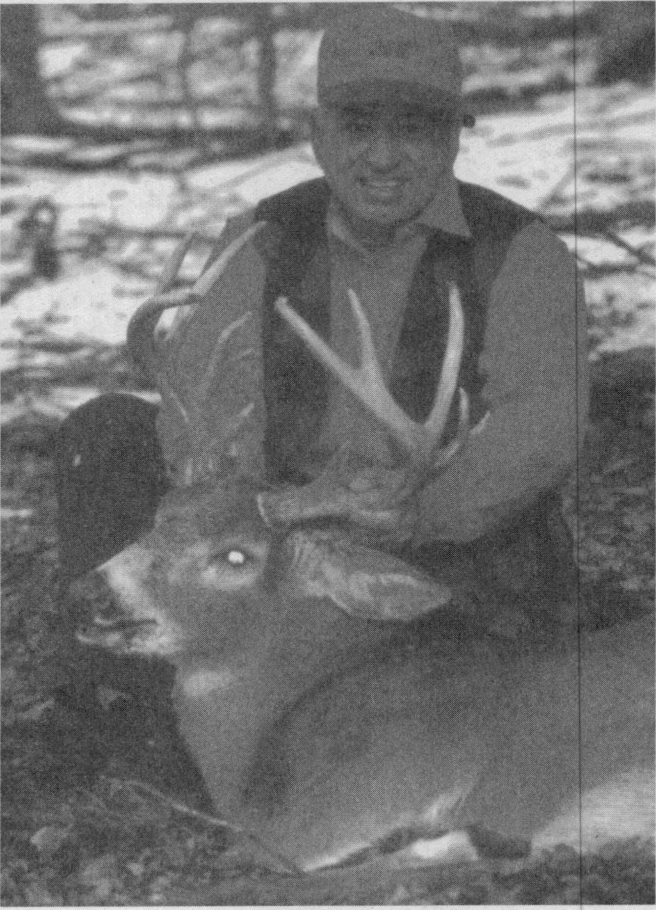

Call softly and don't call too often are the two rules Peter Fiduccia follows when hunting wary whitetail trophies. Credit: Fiduccia Enterprises.

the very first tactic I'll use. It is the pre-rut's number one tactic, in my opinion, if your objective is to attract a nice buck to within bow range."

Legions of whitetail addicts are hooked on pre-rut calling, including one of the country's finest outdoor editors, Jay Cassell. Cassell, who's been hunting whitetails for more than two decades, swears by the fawn bleat in the early season. "As the season progresses, I'll switch to the estrous doe blat," he said. "As for my favorite brand, it doesn't seem to matter. They all work well enough to call in deer. But to be perfectly honest, I use my mouth and vocal cords more than any store-bought call. I just make a *baa—aaaaa!* sound with my mouth, quavering the sound somewhat in the middle tonal range, and that seems to work as well as anything else. The best thing about relying on my voice is never having to dig around in my pockets when a deer appears, or worry about a call or lanyard hanging up at an inopportune time."

"My very favorite time of year to call deer is during the pre-rut," said M.R. James. "I'm especially enamored of the two weeks prior to the primary rut, before bucks go crazy chasing does and mostly ignore calls and rattling in favor of the real thing. I prefer one of those cold, quiet mornings when sound carries well and you can hear a buck coming from a long way away. I'll use a doe bleat, but I will also use a grunt call if I jump a buck out of his bed. If I do, I'll drop to one knee, stay real still until the buck relaxes, if I can see him, and then grunt. You can actually tell if the buck hears you. He will often turn around and come back, searching for the grunt he heard. As unbelievable as it may sound, I was even able to shoot with my bow at one such buck, even though I was on the ground and he was looking for me."

Bob Zaiglin, in his capacity as manager and wildlife biologist for literally hundreds of thousands of huntable Texas acres, spends most of each fall and winter guiding hunters and hunting himself. Zaiglin is one of the country's finest trophy whitetail hunters. He spends an inordinate amount of time trying to think like a whitetail so he can become a better hunter and biologist. Through the years he's come up with some excellent tactics and interesting twists that have enabled his hunters to take more and better whitetails.

"During the pre-rut period I usually rely on short grunts," Zaiglin said. "I don't grunt a lot. What I'll do is slip close to a food plot or stock tank [pond] using the wind to my advantage. As I'm slipping into position, I'll be making a few grunts. I then position myself on any nearby mound, slight elevation, or brush pile where I have a good view of the food plot or stock tank. Surprisingly, I don't blow many deer out of the country when I'm slipping along, making an occasional grunt. Deer seem to give me some slack because I'm grunting; maybe they think I'm another deer.

"The pre-rut is a sensitive time, especially here in Texas," Zaiglin continued. "Deer are well fed. They don't have to move very much. Since our weather is extremely warm, that cuts down on deer movements, too. And while I use the grunt call to calm down deer as I'm moving into position during the pre-rut, and may even have called a number of bucks in, the pre-rut is when I'm setting the stage for my favorite hunting period, the primary rut."

Calling has helped Peter Fiduccia take big bucks at different times of the season for more than thirty years. No wonder he has so much good advice to share. "I've found that one of the best grunt calls to make during the pre-rut is the trailing grunt," Fiduccia said. "The trailing grunt is simply a series of soft, short, burp-like sounds a buck makes as he searches for a doe. The buck may make only the occasional grunt as he's traveling. His nose may or may not be locked onto the ground. He may zigzag back and forth so he doesn't lose the scent, but could also be traveling in a straight line, as though being pulled by a string. During the pre-rut, it is unlikely that every buck with its nose to the ground is on the scent of an estrous doe. Instead, the buck is probably excited about a scent that reveals that a particular doe may be nearing her estrous cycle. Bucks seem to possess a sixth sense that cues them early on into low-level pursuit. They may never exceed a no-nonsense walk. But they seem to sense that if they can catch up with the doe, they can stay with her until she comes into estrus."

To make the trailing or "burp" grunt, simply blow on your grunt tube at middle to low pitch and volume—*burp, burp, burp, burp, burp, burp*. Fiduccia has dubbed this call the "burp-o-matic" and, indeed, that is exactly what it sounds like. The buck may emit a constant stream of quiet grunts, or he may grunt only when he takes each step. Some trailing bucks may make a grunt only every ten seconds, others only every thirty seconds, and others may emit only an occasional grunt a minute or more apart. Remember that each buck is an individual. It is unlikely that any two will sound exactly alike.

That provides you with a lot of latitude for mistakes and experimentation. There's no telling what will work from one day to the next, or from one set of weather conditions to another. Keep the volume low, follow each burp with a second or two of silence, and try not to sound too aggressive. Make a series of low burps, or a trailing grunt series, then wait thirty minutes before repeating the series. "I do this every thirty minutes, like clockwork, until I leave the woods," Fiduccia said. "Should I see a deer respond, I'll stop calling. Not only do I watch for interested deer, though; I'll also listen for them. The wise hunter keeps his ears as well as his eyes attuned to his surroundings. Sometimes you may hear a deer grunting in response. Should this be the case, remain at high alert. The deer is probably coming in to see what's going on."

Trial and error will teach you how much to call, as well as how loudly or softly. Credit: Kathy Etling.

Larry D. Jones grunted in this big Colorado whitetail and arrowed him from a tree stand overlooking a well-traveled trail. Credit: M.R. James.

Hunters who consider calling vital to their success are quite specific about when the tactic works best. "If it's windy, I won't use a grunt call," Zaiglin said. "Even if you blow loudly, the sound just doesn't carry very well."

"I find that calling works best in the pre-rut if there's a slight breeze," Harris noted. "I'll get excited on a cool, sunny morning with a five-mile-per-hour breeze. Should a deer respond, the breeze will stir leaves and brush just enough to conceal my movements. Sound will still carry extremely well. Dead calm days are all right, but in my experience deer are much spookier then. Obviously, success improves dramatically right after a storm or cold front has moved through an area, or after extended periods of bad weather, no matter if it's wind, rain, or cold. I try never to miss going out on such occasions."

## CALLING DURING THE PEAK OF THE RUT

The flurry of excitement that occurs during the whitetail's primary rut affects hunters as in no other season. The actual dates may vary somewhat depending upon a number of variables: latitude, the state in which you're hunting, the subspecies of deer you're hunting, and even, to a limited extent, the weather. In some places, transplanted whitetails rut at a different time than native varieties, really gumming up rut forecasts. But in most areas of the continent the whitetail rut occurs sometime between the last week in October and the first or second week in February, with rutting deer in all parts of their ranges wearing themselves down in their quest to breed and perpetuate both their species and their own lineage. On some not-yet-totally-understood biological cue, does enter their estrous cycles. In well-balanced whitetail populations—those with buck-to-doe ratios of 1:1 or 1:2—it's amazing how does will enter estrus at nearly the same time. With hot does racing everywhere, bucks lose all caution. If they aren't chasing hot does, they're trailing them. And if they're not trailing does, they're out trolling the woods for them. That's the very best time to be out hunting.

In 1996, for instance, on the Thursday before that year's first shotgun season, Dale Carter, of Carter's Hunting Lodge in Pike County, Illinois, was feeling under the weather. He'd almost decided not to go hunting that afternoon, but changed his mind at the last minute. He decided to try a new stand, one he'd just recently hung. To reach this stand, Carter had to walk down a long ridge and well back into a stand of thick timber. He climbed into the stand and waited, wondering if he'd made a mistake going out when he was feeling so ill.

Here are just a few of the big bucks taken by bowhunters at Carter's Hunting Lodge near Pittsburg in Pike County, Illinois. Credit: Bob Etling.

At about 4:00 pm a buck entered the hollow about 150 yards from where Carter was waiting. The deer stepped down into a ditch that sliced through the hollow, then stepped back out and headed toward him. "I hadn't yet taken my bow down," Carter said. "I'd forgotten my binoculars, so I was unsure whether the buck was a 'shooter.'" By the time the buck had closed the distance to fifty yards, Carter had seen all he needed to see. He removed his bow from its hanger while the deer kept coming. The buck walked into a shooting lane, and Carter blew his grunt call. The buck stopped, quartering away, and presented the archer with a perfect shot.

That buck, a big 10-point, grossed 162 Boone and Crockett points. When Carter got his hands on those antlers, he quickly forgot he'd ever been sick.

Dale Carter hunts some of the best whitetail locations in the coun try. Lush vegetation covers the hills and bluffs that stand at the edges of fertile crop fields. Slow, meandering streams flow through the area. Pike County, in fact, is part of Illinois's "Golden Triangle," a northern delta of sorts, where the Illinois River and weathering glaciers have, through the eons, piled up the mineral-rich silt and loess responsible for the many spectacular antlers taken in this region.

Bob Zaiglin believes, based on deer movements, that the whitetail's actual breeding activity peaks well before the peak of the rut. Credit: Bob Zaiglin.

Carter, who is a guide and outfitter as well as hunter, uses deer calls not only to stop bucks where he can get a clear shot, but also to bring deer within archery range. Although Carter's Hunting Lodge once catered to both firearms hunters and bowhunters, the Carters eventually switched to an all-archery operation. One reason for the change was to keep whitetails reason ably undisturbed and thus moving about more freely for a longer period of time. Anyone who runs such an outfit relies a great deal on the magic of deer calling.

So does Bob Zaiglin. "I prefer not calling until deer are moving extremely well during the rut," he stated. "We know fairly well when each year's rut will begin. And by the rut, I mean when deer *appear* to be most active, not necessarily when most breeding occurs. Personally, I believe actual breeding activity peaks well before what we hunters call the peak of the rut, based on deer movement. But it's deer movement that gets hunters excited. An abrupt change in temperature from warm to cold or a big storm usually stimulates the whitetail activity that we call the peak of the rut. Calls can be very effective now, but seldom do I rely on just a call. I prefer, instead, to both grunt and rattle. If I'm rattling and a buck comes in, I'll use the grunt call to hold him there. The grunt call adds an incredible touch of authenticity to the combat scene. Bucks will look and look, maybe even leave completely, and then return to see who's grunting. That's critical when you're hunting in the brush. Usually when you rattle alone [without calling], a buck will bust in through the brush and give everyone an adrenaline rush, but it's not an effective way to hunt on its own. When you use the grunt, though, the animal may pause, may even turn and give the hunter a chance to look him over and decide whether to shoot."

While Carter opted to use the grunt to make a buck stop, Zaiglin prefers including the call as part of his rattling sequence. Rattling is highly effective when hunters spice it up with grunts, snorts, and hoof-stomping. Zaiglin, through years of trial and error, has experimented with the grunts he produces to determine what type works best. What he's discovered is important enough to be included in this section: "When I'm done with a particular rattling sequence, I'll end up by making some very lengthy, really guttural grunts. A buck, like a person, moans when it's hurt, sometimes producing a tremendous amount of noise. This moaning sound seems to be extremely attractive to bucks. Bucks are incredibly curious. If they hear the sounds of battle, they can't help themselves. Like people who race or run to the sounds of a car crash, a buck will run in to see what is going on and who is involved. Simple curiosity leads to more hunter-taken bucks than any other factor."

Ohio bowhunter Mike Beatty used a doe bleat canister on November 8, 2000, while he was hunting a mix of corn fields and woodlots in Greene County. The corn was still standing and Beatty was almost as wet as the surrounding countryside due to a steady, drizzling rain. The bowhunter figured that the rut's peak was just kicking in, so he set out three containers of estrous doe scent in a triangular pattern around his tree stand. Beatty had positioned his stand eighteen feet up in a pin oak, about ten yards from the edge of the corn.

A slight breeze was blowing toward the tree stand. After an hour of not seeing or hearing any deer, Beatty used the bleat canister to make three bleats, with a pause after each. Five minutes later, he detected an 8-point buck moving through the woods, about 150 yards out. He thought he'd seen this buck while scouting during the summer with his son Andrew. As luck would have it, there was a shooting lane cleared in the buck's direction. Nerves did the rest. Even though Beatty managed to turn around very quietly, he started shaking so badly that he feared he would not be able to get off a clean shot. But then the big buck solved Beatty's problem by simply turning around and walking away in the same direction he'd come from. Beatty assumed that since the deer had been behind him—and the wind was blowing in Beatty's face—that the buck had winded him.

Still shaken, Beatty pulled out his grunt tube. He made a few calls and added some light rattling sounds to the mix. A short while later, he made three plaintive bleats with the doe bleat canister. When he checked behind himself a few minutes later, he saw another deer coming from the same spot the 8-pointer had just vacated. He stood up and grabbed his bow. This time, he didn't worry about trying to sneak or hide his movements. It was quickly getting dark, and he knew this would be his last opportunity of the day.

"I could see that it was a different deer," Beatty said. "I put the tree I was standing in between me and the deer's head so I couldn't see his rack and get nervous. I followed his rump around until he reached a thorn tree that was my fifteen-yard marker."

Buckmasters' Russell Thornberry awards Mike Beatty the prestigious Golden Laurel citation for his tremendous Ohio buck that scored 286 4/8 BTR system. Courtesy Buckmasters.

The buck quartered toward Beatty, who hit his release as the animal ducked under the thorn tree. The buck immediately spun around and raced away.

Although Beatty spent a long, nervous night wondering if the steady rain that had begun falling would obscure any blood trail after failing to find the buck right after his shot, all turned out well. The following morning, Beatty and Andrew returned to the search before the boy had to be at school. "It was about the break of day and still overcast," Beatty said. "We went across a cattle pasture to where I'd lost the trail the night before."

Halfway across the pasture, Andrew tugged on Beatty's shirttail. "Dad! There he is!" The deer was only thirty yards from where Beatty had stopped looking the night before.

Beatty's huge buck is perhaps the largest whitetail ever to be taken with the aid of deer calls. With 286 4/8 inches of antler mass using the Buckmasters Trophy Record (BTR) scoring system, the Beatty buck unseated Dale Larson's 1998 Kansas white-tail as the No. 1 Irregular in BTR's compound bow category. Although the letoff of Beatty's bow will probably prevent it from being listed in the Pope and Young Club's record book, it will undoubtedly score well up in the Boone and Crockett Club's record book and rank as the world record taken by archery tackle. Not bad for one night's work with a few deer calls in a drizzling rain.

Jim Holdenried, who has called in nearly all of his trophy whitetails—including two Boone and Crockett bucks—said he's grunted in hundreds of deer through the years. "That doesn't include the ones that walked by that could have been attracted to my grunt," he said. "If I see a smaller buck, one that I'm not interested in bagging, I won't grunt. I already know how well this tactic works. I don't want to educate the little guys. That way, maybe they'll be more willing to come to a call after they've grown to trophy size."

Holdenried generally hunts whitetails in several states each fall. He's a good observer, too. He pays close attention to details that might escape other hunters. "This past season in Kansas I was hunting from a tree stand when I saw a buck that probably would have scored about 115 heading into a dense thicket," Holdenried said. "I didn't grunt to him because I didn't want to educate him, nor did I want him to come in. I thought I'd wait and see what happened. Many times if you see one buck, another, better one may be lurking nearby.

"About twenty minutes later, a good buck appeared in the same area where the smaller one had been," Holdenried continued. "I grunted to get his attention, but while he looked my way, he never made a move toward me. I grunted again. This time, I pulled him in at an angle.

"The buck started walking along the thicket's edge toward me. As he did so I knew I'd get a thirty-five-yard shot. But then, instead of continuing straight in my direction, he went into the thicket for about ten or fifteen yards. I could barely make him out as he put down some scrapes, made a few rubs, rubbed his suborbital glands over brush, and licked branches. Almost every whitetail behavior he could think of, it seemed like this buck was doing. All the while, I kept grunting constantly. I varied the mix to keep it interesting. First, I'd make some aggressive power grunts. I'd wait a while, then make some soft ones. Instead of coming out where I might get a shot, the buck went farther into the thicket. When I lost sight of him completely, I pulled out a different brand of grunt call and hit it loud three or four times. I stopped, and then blew on the first grunt tube for a while.

Suddenly, I heard something pop. I looked straight ahead, and there was the buck, moving purposefully out of the thicket and coming straight for me, downwind of my position. He never grunted in reply. When he left the thicket he was thirty-five yards distant. I knew he would probably spook as he circled downwind of my position, but I kept grunting anyway. I don't know how I got away with it, but that buck came in directly downwind of my position and I shot him as he stood right under my tree stand! When he was standing beneath me, he picked up his head and sniffed the air to try to scent the other 'buck.' I'd picked up my bow when he was thirty or thirty-five yards away, but I just knew I'd never get a shot. So when he was under my tree, he'd lifted his head, put it back down, then looked behind him to the left. When he did that, I wondered if he saw another, bigger buck behind him. I looked, just to be sure there wasn't, and then I shot him. This is one buck I don't think I would have bagged had it not been for using those dueling grunt tubes."

Holdenried's Kansas buck's rack eventually netted in the mid-140s in the Boone and Crockett scoring system.

Holdenried has seen this type of big buck behavior before. "Many times when bucks are tending does, they'll go into a thicket and just stand in there with the doe," he said. "I've watched them hanging around in thickets for an hour and more. The doe will just be standing there, so the buck stands there, too, watching her every move. When she moves, he will, too. In my opinion, if he's acting interested in the doe—tending but not chasing—you may be able to lure him out of there if you set up properly and convince him there's something he needs to be aware of not too far away."

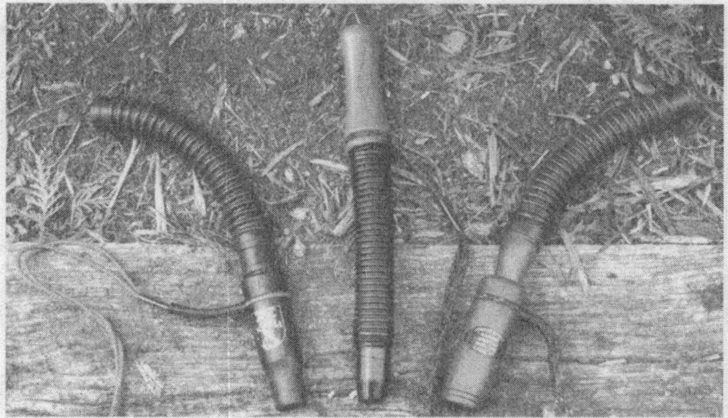

Jim Holdenried packs three brands of buck grunter so that he's sure he has the perfect-sounding grunt call for every occasion. Credit: Jim Holdenried.

Holdenried has tried many deer vocalizations, but the grunt remains his favorite. Why? "I have faith in it," he said. "It's like a fisherman tying on his favorite lure. During my worst season out of the past ten, I called in perhaps ten or twelve bucks. Think about that. I called in that many and that wasn't a good year! During an average season I'll call in anywhere from twenty-four to thirty-six bucks. Over the years, I have called in hundreds and hundreds of deer. I knew they were coming in, too, because these were all deer I watched coming in to the grunt, not deer that I *think* were responding to the call.

"I use the tending grunt most of the time," Holdenried continued. "If a buck is chasing a doe on a hard chase, I'll use an aggressive grunt along with a soft grunt. The loud, aggressive grunts are indicative of a big buck chasing a doe on a hard run. She'll be running hard and he may lose sight of her, so he'll be grunting loudly so she doesn't forget he's on her trail.

On a day when bucks are running does hard, I might be able to grunt in four or five bucks."

Here, in Jim Holdenried's own words, is how he makes grunt tube music for a big buck's ears: "First, I'll make three or four soft grunts—maybe as many as six or seven soft grunts, but never any more than that. I'll wait a second or two. Then I'll softly grunt twice more. I'll wait three or four seconds, then grunt another three times. Now, I'll wait ten or fifteen minutes, just to see if the first grunt sequence will pull in any nearby bucks. If no bucks respond, then I may do one of two things. I may do another soft sequence just like the first one. Or, I may do the entire sequence using loud, aggressive grunts. When I'm through, I'll again wait quietly for ten or fifteen minutes to see what shows up, if anything. This is my favorite tactic for use during the hard rut. This works especially well when you've seen a big buck chasing a doe, but he hasn't come close enough for a shot."

Unlike some advocates of rattling, Holdenried doesn't normally switch calling locations. "My theory is simple: Let the deer come to me."

Surprisingly, Holdenried has had tremendous luck hunting from tree stands positioned not far off the forest floor. "I had a great deer season last year [2001]," he said. "I took a Missouri buck that scored in the mid-140s with my bow, a Kansas buck with my bow that scored in the upper 140s, and a Boone and Crockett Illinois buck with my shotgun. Two of those bucks—including the Boone and Crockett—were taken from tree stands positioned only three feet above the ground. The other buck was taken from a stand eight feet above the ground. As I've gotten older, I've gotten wiser. You don't have to get nosebleeds from the altitude to take good deer from tree stands."

Nosebleeds are definitely not an option when you're hunting the way I was during the past season. I've sometimes gone several years without taking a whitetail from our Missouri farm. I'm after big bucks or no bucks. I don't have a problem with this philosophy, either. My husband, daughter, and her husband all hunt there with me. If we're to maintain any semblance of a good buck-to-doe ratio that means someone will have to refrain from shooting smaller bucks. Those someones are usually Bob and me, since Julie and Rick both work full-time and can often only get away to hunt on weekends. This past November, I'd already been rifle hunting from dawn until dark for the first eight days of the season. I'd seen lots of bucks, including two that, in hindsight, I probably should have taken. But I hadn't shot, and buck sightings had tapered way off as deer became more nocturnal in their habits.

Bob had told me about his favorite spot, but I had my own honey holes that I preferred to hunt. After sightings declined, though, I thought that going to Bob's out-of-the-way ground blind might make sense. I arrived early in the morning, when it was still dark. I settled in so that a small tree was at my back. The spot was in a thick grove of small pines. To my left was an overgrown cedar glade. Mature pine-oak forest surrounded me on other sides. The rolling terrain dumped into a gulch in front of me, while a ridgetop crested gently to my rear.

Early on, I saw no deer. But it was cold and quite still so my hopes remained high. I'm an inveterate user of binoculars, so when it appeared as though nothing was moving, I decided to start poking through the brush to see what I could see. I scanned slowly, left to right, looking for anything that might suggest a whitetail. Imagine my surprise when I inadvertently detected a doe that I'd had no idea was there, standing like a statue only about a hundred yards away. She was staring back over her left shoulder. I couldn't make out much of her body, but I could see her head and ears clearly.

Since she was watching behind her so intently, I knew there was a chance that a buck was with her. As my eyes tired, I lowered the binoculars. I kept watching, though, and when I saw movement, I immediately raised them again. The doe was gone! I kept the binoculars trained on the spot where she'd been standing, but no other deer appeared. I began scanning the rest of the area. Nothing. Finally, about five minutes later, a spike buck with one long horn popped out where the doe had been standing. He stood there, testing the air with his nose, stretching out his neck first forward, then upward. The small buck seemed unsure of himself. He stood there for a long time before he, too, moved out of sight and up the hill.

The woods were extremely thick, and I could see very little through the brush where the spike had gone. But I kept looking, and eventually I caught glimpses of something moving about through the trees. Then that movement died down, too. Fifteen minutes elapsed before I heard a slight noise directly behind me. Since I was sitting on the ground, I moved my head slightly to try to see what it might be. Not six feet from me stood the doe! She didn't have a clue that I was there, either. Again, she was peering intently over her right shoulder. I carefully twisted around a little more and almost came unglued when I saw a big buck only about two feet behind her. There was nothing I could do! My gun was on my lap.

As I watched, the doe twitched her tail and loped off. The buck put his nose to the ground briefly, then loped off behind her. As the deer put distance between us, I remembered the grunt call hanging around my neck. I quickly blew several series of grunts. I blew fairly loudly because I knew the deer would be making quite a bit of noise as they ran through the understory. The grunts didn't seem to make a difference, and both deer soon vanished from my sight.

I waited there, dejected, for five minutes before I noticed movement out of the corner of my eye. I moved slightly in the direction of the movement. The big buck had reappeared. His head was high, and he was looking toward me. He began walking, head erect, eyes bright, and with a stiff-legged gait. The path he was on was very indistinct, but I knew it angled up the hill toward me. Closer and closer he came. I could see flashes of antlers between the trees. He was thirty yards away, then twenty, then ten. He paused only a moment before turning and heading right for where I sat on the ground. When his head went behind a tree, I raised my rifle. His antlers were at least as large as one of the earlier bucks I had regretted not shooting. He emerged from behind the tree and seemed to tower over me from where I was sitting on the ground. Five yards, then three, and it was almost a self-defense situation. He still had not seen me when I fired the .300 Weatherby. The 8-pointer lunged to his right, then fell to his knees and toppled to the ground. Although not record-book class, his rack was high, nineteen inches wide, and fairly heavy. But I didn't care how big he was, to

Grunting in this nice Missouri buck was the author's most thrilling calling experience to date. Credit: Bob Etling.

be honest! It was unquestionably the most exciting experience I'd ever had when calling deer!

Brad Harris loves to call deer, but he doesn't just amble out into the woods and begin calling. "During the peak of the rut I'm always looking for good places to set up," he said. "I think choosing the place from which you plan to call is an important part of the equation. Look for heavily used travel routes, particularly any close to definite big buck sign. I certainly like to see big rubs and, if distinguishable, large tracks. In the rocky Ozarks, seeing tracks isn't always easy. What makes the peak of the rut exciting for me is simply knowing there will be more opportunities to see—and pos sibly take—bucks during daylight hours. This is the time to start using doe bleats. Mix in a few loud, aggressive-sounding grunts, too. Any buck hearing these sounds will assume that some unknown buck is behaving agonistically toward another buck, and it very well might be over a doe. If an area's dominant buck hears the commotion, he may be fooled into thinking his territory has been invaded and a fight or breeding is going on right on his home turf. Some bucks won't tolerate this and will come in readily. Others may take their time, but will eventually come in. During the rut's peak I rely on my calls to a tremendous degree. Bucks are actively engaged with does. They're already trailing or tending or chasing them, and they are less dependent on rublines or scrapelines, at least for the time being. This is when it pays to increase the volume, frequency, and aggressive nature of calls.

"I love hunting the rut," Harris concluded. "This is the time when even the mon ster bucks will make an occasional mistake. That's what you're always hoping for. The largest deer I've ever seen killed was one my son took a few years ago. That buck grossed 195 Boone and Crock-ett points. The buck had been hot after a doe. We grunted to stop him, but for all we know he and the doe had been attracted to our earlier grunting sequences. Anyway, the buck stopped and that was that. In all my years of hunting, I've taken my biggest bucks during the

Brad Harris likes to call near heavily used travel routes, especially if they are close to big buck sign. Credit: Brad Harris.

Use the tending grunt with some doe bleats, or rattle with passion to fool a dominant buck into believing its territory has been invaded by an outsider.

Brad Harris grunted this buck to a standstill after it chased a doe past his son's tree stand during the peak of Missouri's rut period. Credit: Brad Harris.

rut when I've either caught them alone or they were between does and spoiling for a fight."

"About three years ago, I was in a tree stand about a mile from my home in New York," recalled Jay Cassell. "It was the peak of the rut, and I could hear a buck grunting from the swamp behind my stand. I first attempted to call him in with grunt calls. He'd answer me, but he wouldn't come in. So I decided to try the estrous doe blat. As soon as I made a few blats, the 6-pointer I'd heard grunting came in close enough—about twenty-five yards—so that I was able to swivel around in my stand and shoot him with my bow. He wasn't a monster deer, but I didn't really care. It's just so exciting when you can call them in like that."

To make the estrous doe blat, Cassell simply blows a short blat on his doe bleater two or three times. "If you listen carefully when does are walking past your stand, you might hear them making this noise," Cassell said. "When you see a buck chasing a doe, tune out his grunting and try to concentrate on the noises *she's* making. That's an estrous doe blat."

Mel Dutton, another hunter who's sold on calling, has been hunting South Dakota whitetails for longer than he cares to remember. Dutton, who owns a large ranch that his family operates, is responsible for reviving the practice of decoying white-tailed deer and pronghorn antelope. His packable, mobile decoys can be used by themselves, or a bowhunter can crouch behind one until an animal gets close enough for a shot. Since the animal, be it antelope or whitetail, actually thinks it's seeing another one of its kind, it's expecting movement. If the archer rises from behind the decoy and shoots in one fluid motion, the animal should remain still for as long as it takes to get off a good shot.

Dutton is also sold on deer calling. "I use doe bleats during the rut," he said. "I'll bleat very softly, perhaps three or four times, then wait for about four or five minutes. I'll use either a commercial call or one of those bleat canisters."

Dutton also uses doe bleats during rut. "I bleat very softly, maybe three or four bleats in a row. Then I wait about four or five minutes. But I personally feel the buck grunt works better for me."

As for which brand of call works best, Dutton is unmoved by advertising claims. "I think any call will work," he said. "If you've got four grunt calls, I think each will get about the same results. I can't see one having any big advantage over another."

If it's the peak of the rut, 90 percent of the time Dutton will use the buck grunt. "I blow on it two or three times in a row, then pause if I don't see a deer," he said. "It's wide-open country here in South Dakota. If you're set up in a good location, you can see several drainages that feed some of the tributaries to the river. I'll get back into one of the little wooded pockets where most of the deer in a given area spend a lot of time and call. Then I'll just start grunting. Sometimes I'll grunt quite a lot."

Dutton has had many successes hunting like this. "Last November I grunted in one good buck that came all the way in, and then I decided not to take him. I was in a tree stand near a heavy use area where deer were feeding. The cottonwoods in this particular drainage were spaced out fairly dramatically, and the rest of the terrain was open. I noticed this buck about two hundred yards away. I tried rattling, but he'd just turn his head and look. He didn't seem the least bit interested. So I grunted, and that got his attention. I continued to grunt, probably about twenty times in all. The buck started trotting toward me and didn't stop until he was twenty yards away. He looked around as though trying to locate the other deer, then he circled my tree. There was a slight breeze blowing, but he never caught my scent. This was a pretty respectable buck, too. He probably would have scored about 120. Grunting is just a real effective tactic. If you aren't using it, it's about time you try it for yourself."

All breeding bucks are stressed by the rigors of the primary rut. Bucks put on fat all summer while in their bachelor groups. As the pre-rut period approaches, they break away from each other to become loners. At this point, the bucks are sole ly interested in finding hot does to breed. This is their biological imperative, and they will literally wear themselves out to accomplish it. They rub the bark off saplings and small trees, an intense exercise that strengthens neck, shoulders, and back; they lose interest in food and rarely feed; and they'll often move all day and all night, particularly when they can detect no hunters in the woods. In the early stages of whitetail courtship, bucks often race several hundred yards after non-receptive does before losing interest, and they may do so several times each day. Later in the season, when does start their estrous cycles, bucks still chase them, but eventually the does will stand to be bred. The estrous period for each doe lasts about twenty-four hours and, when possible, a buck will usually stay with a doe for that entire time.

After tending one doe, the buck is soon looking for another. If a smaller buck is tending a doe and is intercepted by a larger buck, the smaller animal will usually have to leave or fight to keep his doe. With so much going on in the deer woods during the rut period, it's no wonder so many mature bucks wear themselves out.

The rigors of whitetail breeding are so intense, according to research conducted at Texas A&I University by wildlife researcher Charles DeYoung, that about 25 percent of all bucks will die each year even when no hunting is allowed. We don't notice a lot of dead and dying deer in the woods once the season has ended simply because hunters take so many bucks that would have died anyway, regardless of the legality of hunting. This study provides another excellent reason that hunting whitetails simply makes good biological sense.

## CALLING DURING THE POST-RUT PERIOD

Every now and then, the north wind gusted so hard it made my eyes water, my nose numb, and my teeth chatter. If it hadn't been for the sun's pale rays burning fee bly through my coveralls that mid-December morning, I don't know how long I would have lasted out on stand. I'd seen deer, and was glad I had, because if I hadn't seen them I might already have made a beeline back to the house. But so far, all I'd spotted were a few feeding does.

During one of the wind's lulls, however, I heard a familiar sound. A buck was grunting somewhere behind my tree stand. There was a rustling of leaves that soon got louder and louder, and then I saw two deer running right beneath my stand. The second one, a buck, was trailing so closely behind the doe that his antlers seemed to be slapping her flanks with each stride. The two animals streaked past so quickly that I didn't even have time to draw my bow, much less shoot. They were moving so rapidly that

I wouldn't have attempted a shot anyway. When they finally topped the next ridge—the buck still glued to the doe's heels—I knew I was witnessing the whitetail rut the second time around.

When both the pre-rut and the rut are just fond memories, you have to take your hunting up a notch for the second rut, sometimes called the second season. Many hunters give up when the primary rut draws to a close. They know the late season's bad rap, and many believe that rap is well deserved. Whitetails aren't stupid. Pressure them even slightly and some bucks become almost totally nocturnal. Because of this, you'll almost always see more animals during the primary rut than during the second rut. But don't count the second rut out too soon. Bucks—including big ones—will be up and moving then. Hardy hunters who force themselves to leave their warm beds and get out in the field will have a good chance of success the second time around.

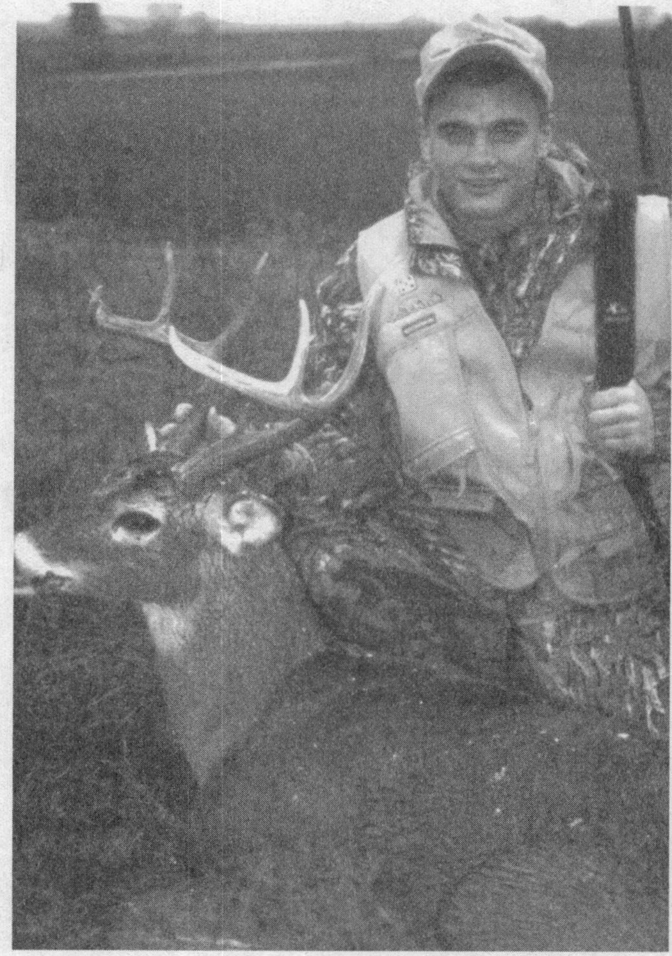
The post-rut provides deer callers with a second or third chance to take a deer. Credit: John Phillips.

Even if only one or two does in your area begin their estrous cycles and initiate a second rut, it will be well worth your while to go hunting. Everywhere that hot doe travels, she'll leave her own hot doe scent upon the ground. Whenever a buck cross es her trail, he'll immediately be interested, especially if few other does are cycling at the time. One hot doe can lead a lot of bucks past your stand, even if you never actually see her yourself. If she passed by in the dark, well before you even got to your stand, you could still reap the benefits hours later. How often have you seen a buck, nose to the ground like a bloodhound, intently following a trail where no other deer have gone? Smart money says that buck is tracking a doe that traveled there before you ever arrived on stand.

Peter Fiduccia believes that deer are especially edgy in the late season. They have been heavily pressured and have probably been called to repeatedly. Because of this, he recommends using a short series of calls to lure out deer that may be holed up in brush or thick cover. "Give them time to listen and look for a while before making up their minds," he said. "Deer are curious. They want to find out what's going on. But after the main firearms hunting seasons have closed, they will be much more cautious than just a few weeks earlier.

During the post-rut, does that have not yet been successfully bred will again come into estrus. Late-born fawns from the preceding spring may also experience their first estrous cycle in the early weeks of winter. Grunting can be effective in various areas even well into January and February, especially if there is a visible resurgence in deer activity. Does may be seen urinating while rubbing their hocks together in a dead-on imitation of a buck freshening a scrape. They may be heard emitting soft grunts, too. These cohesive or contact grunts are made for the purpose of attracting a nearby buck. This is a good time to use such a grunt in the hopes of doing the same.

Does also make a dominant-subordinate grunt to reprimand fawns and yearlings as well as to warn off young bucks or does from other subdominant family groups. A dominant doe will even use the dominant-subordinate grunt to threaten dominant bucks, particularly when these animals have cast their antlers. Researchers have made note of a wide array of doe grunts, ranging from high-pitched squeaks to deep, throaty grunts quite similar to those of bucks. A post-rut doe grunt, though, is a more demanding vocalization. The doe expects a buck to answer, and if a buck isn't forth coming, she actively attempts to seek one out. Alert hunters may discern her steady grunts as she wanders through the woods. Although such doe grunts are usually higher-pitched than those of bucks, this isn't always true. To imitate the late-season estrous doe grunt, simply make two or three long, drawn-out, middle-tonal-range burps in a row: *buuurp . . . buuurp . . . buuurp*. Wait fifteen or twenty seconds and repeat. Then wait several minutes before repeating the sequence. The call is insistent, but not loud. If made properly, it should sound like a soft cry for attention.

The post-rut buck grunt is as excited a sound as you're likely to hear in the woods. The buck that gets on the trail of one of the few remaining hot does seems to realize that this may be his last time to breed this season. He is vocal in his desires. But this is the time when younger bucks, animals that have not yet been worn out by the rigors of fighting, running does, and mating, can pull off a big upset by whipping a more dominant animal and claiming a hot doe's favors for himself. The post-rut buck grunt isn't so much a *burp* as an *eeerp*. Draw out each syllable of this grunt, while making it slightly louder and higher pitched than the buck grunt you made just one month earlier. Make three long, high-pitched grunts, pause a few seconds, and repeat. Wait several minutes before making another series of grunts. Should this not work, make an extended series of excited post-rut grunts. This is one time you might want to throw caution to the winds. Don't worry about calling too much. Try moving your head as you grunt, or cup your hand over your call to vary the sounds, as though the buck is moving through brush and behind trees. Continue grunting for one, two, or even three minutes. When you stop, pay close attention to nearby terrain for even the slightest indication of a curious whitetail.

The post-rut period is ideal for using both buck and doe grunts. You can grunt slightly more during this time than any other period of the whitetail rut. You can experiment a little more freely during this time by grunting louder, too. Sounding excited during the post-rut is a good thing.

Many successful hunters rely a great deal on this second season. It provides them with a second or third chance to take a deer. "Evidence of the second rut is never as distinct as that from the first," explains Missouri's Mark Drury, founder of M.A.D. Calls, a division of Outland Sports. "One reason is that the number of does entering a second estrous cycle may vary from year to year." Drury, together with his brother Terry, nevertheless agrees that it's still an excellent time to kill a big buck.

When Mark hunts the second rut period, he heads back to those places where he keyed in on deer earlier in the season. "I'm looking for core areas with lots of rubs and scrapes, or thick, brushy, bedding grounds. I believe thicker cover attracts and holds bucks not harvested during the firearms season. Bucks hide in areas they know best. I call these areas their "comfort zones." Whenever I hunt comfort zones, I'm extremely careful of buck feeding or bedding areas. Since bucks have recently been subjected to intense hunting pressure, they're much spookier now than at any other time of the year."

During the late season, Mark reexamines old, untended scrapes. "During the late season a buck will often re-open scrapes you'd earlier written off as being totally unproductive," he said.

"I took a nice buck on December 7 one year," Mark continued. "To zero in on a feeding area, I'd placed my stand in a triangular patch of timber alongside a river. That timber served as a funnel for deer using a nearby crop field. I saw some awesome behavior that year, including a good 9-point buck that was grunting after and chasing seven does all over the place. He eventually came close enough for a shot. His rack gross scored 128 Pope and Young points."

According to Mark, rattling and calling will both work during the second rut. "Both tactics will work well in the early season, but may fall off somewhat during the rut," he said. "But I've found that they will both come on strong again later in the season. Since fewer does are in estrus during the late season, competition is intense among remaining bucks for those does that are. This intense competition makes rattling and calling pay off. The tending grunt, doe bleat, and doe grunt will all produce now."

"I believe that short, continuous grunts are just as effective during the late season as rattling is during the rut," added Bob Zaiglin. "These grunts don't have to be as loud, or as long, or as intimidating as the grunts you made just a month or so previous ly. All you want a listening buck to know is that he may be missing some action. And if the grunts attract does, so much the better. A buck might trail a doe right into where you've set up."

Zaiglin continues to rattle and grunt even during the post-rut period. "I carry on some of the darnedest ruckuses with rattling horns and grunt calls you've ever heard. I do so despite the great 1:1.2 buck-to-doe ratio that exists on our ranches. But even with this great ratio, some does will recycle. When they do, you'll see bucks schooling around them. It's not uncommon to see six, eight, or even ten bucks hovering around one hot doe. When that happens, confrontations are bound to take place. If one does, the sound of that confrontation will be very attractive to other bucks. Even bucks that aren't fluttering around a hot doe are looking for some action. Whenever the sounds of a fight reach their ears, they'll come in looking for the hot doe that's probably at the bottom of the ruckus."

After Zaiglin rattles, he'll grunt and stomp his feet on the ground for several minutes. "I'm

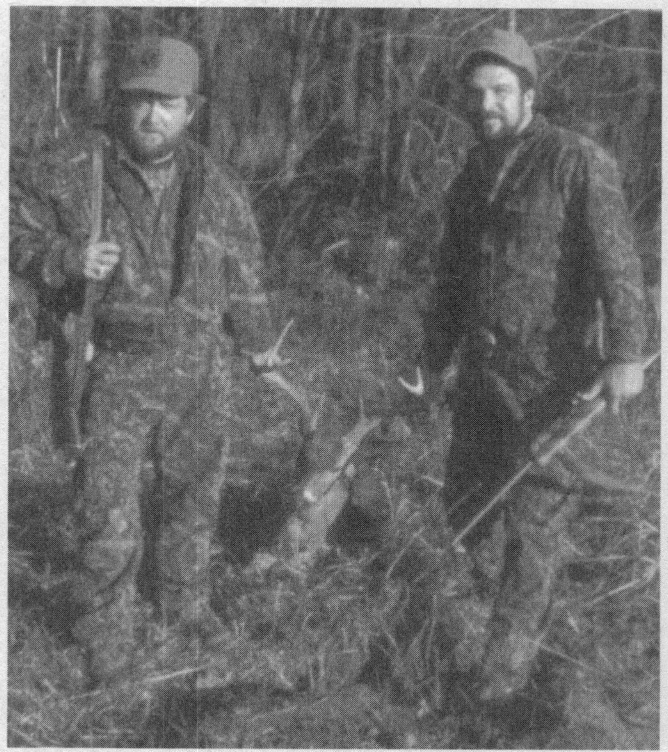

"It's sheer accident if a hunter ever kills a good Alabama buck before January," according to noted guide Billy Macoy. Credit: Billy Macoy.

trying to create an illusion of a buck hazing a doe after an altercation with another buck," he said. "Those sounds seem to attract bucks, particularly if they're schooling around a doe. The sound might not be nearly as appealing to bucks that have worn themselves out during the rut and are trying to regain their strength. Such bucks will remain near food plots, trying to regain their strength. After the rut's peak, some bucks have had it with fighting, at least for the time being. What I do is grunt and stomp for several minutes, like I'm a buck hazing a doe after the rattling. That seems to be very attractive to a buck, particularly when they're schooling."

In some areas of the Deep South, hunters aren't even able to take advantage of the second whitetail rut. "It's a sheer accident here in Alabama if a hunter ever kills a good buck before January," claimed Billy Macoy of Lineville. "I guide deer hunters at Southern Sportsman Lodge in Hayneville, and our deer just don't start moving in their rutting patterns until January at the earliest. Our season ends on January 31, and I know good bucks are killed in auto/deer accidents well into February. That makes me think our second rut occurs after our hunting season is over."

Dennis Smith of Alabama, host of *Outdoors South,* hunts the Alabama hills about an hour west of Atlanta. "Where I hunt I'll see scrapes everywhere during the first week of December," he said. "Bucks will be chasing does all over the woods. During the last week of January and well into February, bucks go wild again. I found fresh scrapes everywhere late last season. This doesn't actually seem to correspond with a second rut, as I understand it, since so much time has elapsed between those two observable rut periods. That leads me to think that in some areas, two distinct rut periods occur because these areas may be populated by two different whitetail subspecies."

Smith could be right. Many areas in the United States lost most of their native deer populations back in the late 1800s or early 1900s, for a variety of reasons, so wildlife managers stocked these depleted areas with deer from other areas that still had strong populations. For that reason, for example, descendants of northern whitetails now roam Georgia and rut at a different time than their southern cousins. Some hunters who think they are hunting a second rut might actually be hunting a second *primary* rut with a completely different cast of whitetail characters.

Peter Fiduccia had a tremendous 2001. "I shot a big buck in New York state," he said. "After that my wife, Kate, and I traveled to Saskatchewan, where it was bitterly cold and windy. I didn't even see a deer for several days. Then, everything broke loose in the span of a couple of days. On this occasion, I'd set up near a field. I soon noticed a doe that would run out to the edge of the same field I was hunting, race into the middle of that field, and then run back to the field edge. I thought this was strange behavior, but then I realized that she was probably flirting with a buck in the woodlot at the field's edge.

"The preceding day, I'd scared a nice buck in the 150 to 165 Boone and Crockett class," Fiduccia continued. "I'd thought I'd be safe grunting to a buck that big, but I wasn't. Perhaps he'd been beaten up by bigger bucks. Who knows? In any event, the buck ran off, so I wasn't about to try grunting now, not after spooking the buck the day before. I decided to try the doe blat on her. I blatted, and she became very interested in the sound. She started moving my way, coming within forty or fifty yards of my stand.

"As she came closer, I watched the surroundings carefully. I noticed that two bucks in a nearby woodlot paralleled the doe's course as she made her way toward me. The first buck was an extremely heavy-beamed 10-pointer. His rack was symmetrical, and I thought he would probably score in the 155-point range. I kept my eyes on him, while he kept his eyes on the doe. As I watched, the second buck appeared from behind the 150-class animal. He, too, stood there looking at the doe in front of me. Had I not used the blat call, I doubt whether I would have seen this buck at all.

"I blatted again," Fiduccia said. "The doe stared up at my tree stand, then trotted behind my stand and through an open pasture. I can only guess she was trying to get a better look at what was making the sound, or she was trying to get downwind of me. As the doe moved away, the larger of the two bucks must have become concerned that the doe was leaving. He broke out of the woodlot and entered the pasture only about forty yards from where I was waiting. I steadied the Leupold Vari-X III®'s crosshairs upon the buck's vitals and pulled the trigger. The Thompson Center 30/06 roared, and the buck fell to the ground."

Fiduccia had scored on one of Saskatchewan's regal non-typical whitetails. The buck's massive rack grossed 207⅜ using the Boone and Crockett system. It is a hunt that neither Fiduccia nor his videographer wife, Kate, is ever likely to forget. Would it have been possible without the judicious use of the proper deer call? No one real ly knows. But can you really afford not to learn all you can about this superior whitetail hunting tactic, no matter what the season may be?

Whether you choose to hunt the pre-rut, the peak of the rut, or the post-rut periods, you can't go wrong with calling. Credit: Brad Harris.

Whenever you choose to hunt—pre-rut, primary rut, second rut, or all three—you can't go wrong with calling. As you've learned from the anecdotes related here, each season features its own brand of calling excitement. But no matter what the sea son, the more time you invest in learning how to call whitetails, the greater your chances of hanging a trophy on your wall while filling your freezer with venison.

# Advanced Deer Calling

Many hunters rely on deer calling no matter when or where they hunt. Old, reliable calls remain their bread-and-butter choices, but they can also see the wisdom in expanding their calling repertoire to include calls most other hunters can't imagine using no matter what the circumstances.

One such hunter is Peter Fiduccia of New York State. Unlike many big buck hunters, Fiduccia is eager to share the keys to his calling success. If you are interested in becoming a more well-rounded deer caller with tricks you can pull out of your hat no matter what the situation, learning about these calls is worth your while, too.

EZ Grunter Xtreme is excellent in close ranges. Credit: Knight & Hale Game Calls.

Fiduccia truly believes in the power of deer calling. For that reason, he feels it's imperative that anyone who uses deer calls get a firm grounding in what deer vocalizations sound like. Whether you learn by watching a TV show such as Fiduccia's *Woods 'N' Water,* buy a hunting DVD, or go onto a website such as Knightandhale.com or Primos.com and listen to what the experts have to say, learning how deer really sound will give you confidence in your own calling ability. "Confidence is the secret to calling success," Fiduccia said. "Knowing your calls sound authentic, and then believing that they are going to work, is critical to your eventual success."

## ONE HUNTER'S CALLING STRATEGY

Fiduccia is a confident caller because he's used the method to score on whitetails for nearly forty years. He prefers blowing calls softly most of the time. Only occasionally will he resort to a louder, more aggressive tone. "I'm convinced that you will often chase off smaller, less dominant animals," he said. "Even if they'd already started to respond to your calls."

Fiduccia has other calling tips, too:

- Don't call too much. After all, you've put the ball in the buck's court, at least in a figurative sense. Most deer don't call excessively. Why mimic an abnormal deer behavior that could rouse a whitetail's suspicion?
- Don't call when you can see or hear that a buck has responded and is making his way to you. This is the time to make the buck's curiosity work for you rather than against you.

Fiduccia joins the ranks of hunters like Bob Zaiglin and Brad Harris, both of whom are fearless when it comes to using a snort call. "The snort is the

When whitetails race off snorting in alarm, try snorting to them to calm them down and call them back. Credit: Kathy Etling.

most misunderstood call of all," Fiduccia explained. "It doesn't only signify flight and alarm. A deer will use various snorts, either alone or in combination with other vocalizations, to spice up its vocabulary. Any hunter who wants to become a proficient deer caller must be able to reproduce these sounds because they can pay big dividends for those fearless enough—and wise enough—to use them when the right opportunity arises."

## THE ALARM SNORT

This is probably the snort a deer will make when a hunter on his way to a deer stand inadvertently spooks the animal. If you feel certain that the deer has not winded you, wait until it snorts a second time. Then imitate the snorts the frightened whitetail has just made: *whew . . . whew!* Blow hard a single time either on your snort call or with your mouth. Wait for about two seconds. Blow again. Should the deer respond by snorting again, answer it with the same kinds of snorts and in the same cadence. Keep doing this as long as the deer is snorting.

Many times the deer will be circling back to where you are standing. If conditions are perfect, you might even get a shot.

"I snorted at one buck fifty-seven times," Fiduccia recalled. "Each time I'd snort, the buck would answer me. I was positive I was communicating with a wary old patriarch. Instead, a small 6-point emerged from a nearby stand of pines." Still, snorting a frightened deer back is a thrill every hunter should get to experience at least once in life.

Fiduccia's wife, Kate, has also successfully snorted in deer. Kate had been still-hunting through a climax forest when she inadvertently stepped on a dead branch. The branch cracked loudly, spooking a nearby buck. The animal ran off, snorting. Kate snorted in reply. This cat and mouse game went on for several minutes before the spike finally stepped out from behind a copse of cedars and Kate was able to down it with one shot.

Peter Fiduccia is one of the country's most inventive deer callers. Although I've never hunted with him, I've been using a snort call for years, usually in conjunction with antler-rattling. Fiduccia, though, actively looks for deer on which he can use

Hands Free Soft Grunter helps you minimize movement. Credit: Knight & Hale Game Calls.

the alarm snort, particularly when he's bowhunting. "I'll walk through heavy cover with the wind in my face, occasionally snapping twigs or kicking leaves," Fiduccia said. "If all goes as planned, I'll alarm a buck into jumping up from its bed. If the buck responds with an alarm snort, I know there's a fairly good chance I'll be able to call him back. I'll alarm snort in return, making sure that before I do I'm well hidden in heavy brush or pines. The buck will usually walk past me in search of the other deer. I've shot several nice bucks at ranges less than ten yards while using this tactic. As the buck gets closer to you, blow the call more softly and in the opposite direction of his approach. This makes it seem as though the 'other deer' is walking away."

## THE ALARM-DISTRESS SNORT

The alarm-distress snort can be a dynamite call when used by a hunter who's aware of its potential. "Of the four recognizable cadences of snort, the alarm- distress snort is my favorite," said Fiduccia. As someone who is also always seek ing to learn more about whitetails—and how to put that knowledge to good use while I'm hunting—I'm impressed with the many ways in which Fiduccia has made this call pay off. "One of most effective is to use the alarm-distress snort to aggressively roust a bedded buck from heavy cover," Fiduccia continued. "I use it when I'm hunting thick cedar swamps, laurel thickets, and standing corn. I've had my best luck when I've been able to climb above large areas of thick cover—like onto a rock shelf or other vantage point. Once I'm in such a position, I'll blow my alarm-distress snort—*whew . . . whew . . . whew-whew-whew!* When a whitetail makes this snort, the volume trails off as the deer runs away. Okay, so let's say I'm on a ledge looking down into a tangle of laurels below. The first thing I'll do is drip about four or five drops of commercial interdigital scent, so that it's exposed briefly to the air. I'll start stomping my foot, and then I'll begin to blow or snort. Rather than convincing whitetails to lie low, this display seems to have the opposite effect. I can't begin to tell you how often a buck has picked up its head from some thicket to stare in my direction. Or he might start sneaking away, and you'll be able to nail him. Once you blow that call, instinct takes over. From the second the buck was born, his doe instilled in him that this sound means real trouble—leave the area now! The buck doesn't wait to find out why it should leave the area. Its gut instinct is to get up and then get out. I used the alarm-distress snort to successively take a 14-point buck in Montana that grossed 168 Boone and Crockett points. I use the interdigital scent simply to make the entire scenario seem more realistic."

Fiduccia has given this topic plenty of thought. "Another good way to use the alarm-distress snort is to locate thick cover where whitetails are sure to be holed up, like a cedar patch or swamp, and then post hunters along deer escape routes. Hunters should set up on the outermost fringes of the cover. Once they're on stand, wait about half an hour for things to settle down, then walk into the middle of the thickest cover. Don't even try to be quiet. Once you get into a place that looks like it would be a good bedding area, follow the steps listed above. Start with the interdigital gland scent. Stomp your feet. Then make the alarm-dis tress snort: *whew . . . whew . . . whew . . . whew, whew, whew, whew!* Hesitate for a second or so between each of the first three snorts, then finish by making the next four in rapid succession. If deer are hid ing, they should make a beeline for escape routes."

Use an alarm-distress snort to aggressively roust a bedded buck from heavy cover, then shoot it as it sneaks out or pauses to look back

Fiduccia told of another good use for the alarm-distress snort. "I'll use it to roust deer from cattails, out from under ledges, from brush piles or small woodlots, and from crops still standing in fields," he said. Fiduccia knows how often nice bucks bed down in the safety of standing corn. To nail such a buck, Fiduccia will pick a corner of the field where the last two rows in each direction converge. "Hunker down in any nearby cover so that the wind is blowing toward you," he advised. "Put out several drops of interdigital scent, then follow with foot-stomps and alarm-distress snorts. Sometimes, after making the first call, you'll hear deer slipping around in the corn looking for a safe exit. When they find what they think might be a good escape route they may poke their heads out of the corn to look both ways before heading to the nearest cover. This is when you'll usually get your best opportunity for a shot."

## THE GRUNT-SNORT-WHEEZE

Jerry Shively, an outfitter from Thompson Falls, Montana, is a big advocate of combination grunt, snort, and wheeze calls. "These are phenomenal calls, especially if you know you're in an area being frequented by a big buck. They can be used any number of ways, too. They're great buck grunters, number one. But if you see a good one coming in—or know he's in the area—use them as a grunt-snort-wheeze, the most dominant of all buck vocalizations. I guarantee: If he can hear you, any dominant buck will be coming in. If you can see the deer, so much the better. You'll be able to see him get all agitated as he tries to peg where the sound is coming from. It won't be long and he'll be on his way. If you don't see him, just rely on your gut feeling. It's amazing how often some sixth sense will tell you how much to call and when. But if you see just a mediocre buck, don't give him the full treatment. A wheeze will probably scare him off."

Anything goes when deer calling. It's reconciling yourself to the fact that any call—a grunt, snort, blat, or bleat—when used at the right time can result in the most spectacular whitetail hunting action you've ever known.

# Getting Started Rattling

Does rattling sound like a hunting tactic you'd like to try, yet you're not quite sure then saw off its antlers? Perhaps you have a set of antlers from a deer you took last season then saw off its antlers? Perhaps you have a set of antlers from a deer you took last season or before. Or, perhaps you can prevail upon someone you know for his or her next set of antlers. Should you wait until spring when you can go hunting for a nice, fresh set of matched sheds? And what's wrong with synthetics, anyway? Do they work as well as the real McCoy? Do sheds work as well or sound as realistic as fresh antlers? What about rattling devices? Surely whitetails must suspect that any "rattling" created by store-bought devices is phony, right?

Through the years I've interviewed many whitetail experts for the express purpose of learning what each believed was the most foolproof way of rattling in whitetails. While each expert's methods are amazingly similar to those of the others, and while even their preferred rattling sequences bear more than a passing resemblance to those of the other experts, and while the parameters they look for when they are preparing to set up are not that much different, it's clear that each of our experts has definite opinions about what another hunter should do and use to create the most realistic-sounding mock buck battles possible.

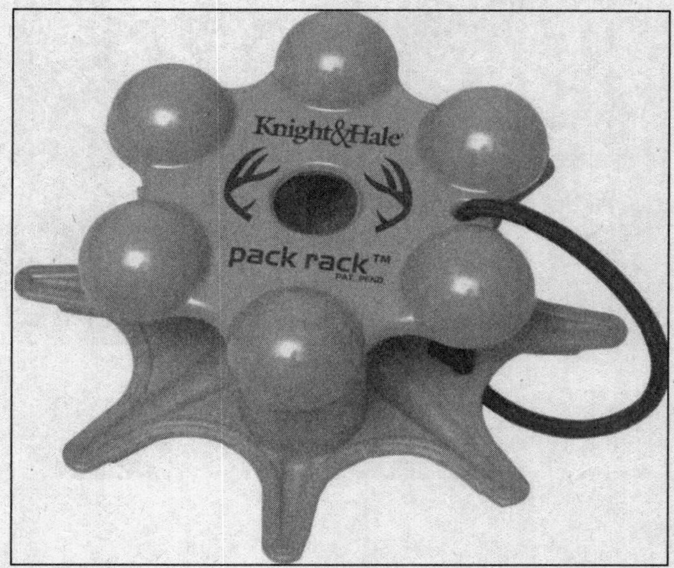

Synthetic Antlers. Credit: Knight & Hale Game Calls.

## Synthetic, Real, or Something Else?

I've used both synthetic antlers and real antlers, and I honestly have never been able to tell much difference between the two. I've rattled in deer using both types. If I were asked to put my feelings about the two antler types into words, I suppose I would say that real antlers sound more solid when clashed together. The synthetics I used seemed to be slightly higher-pitched, and they seemed to reverberate a bit more. I can't truthfully say this reverberation is a negative, though. The sound from the synthetic

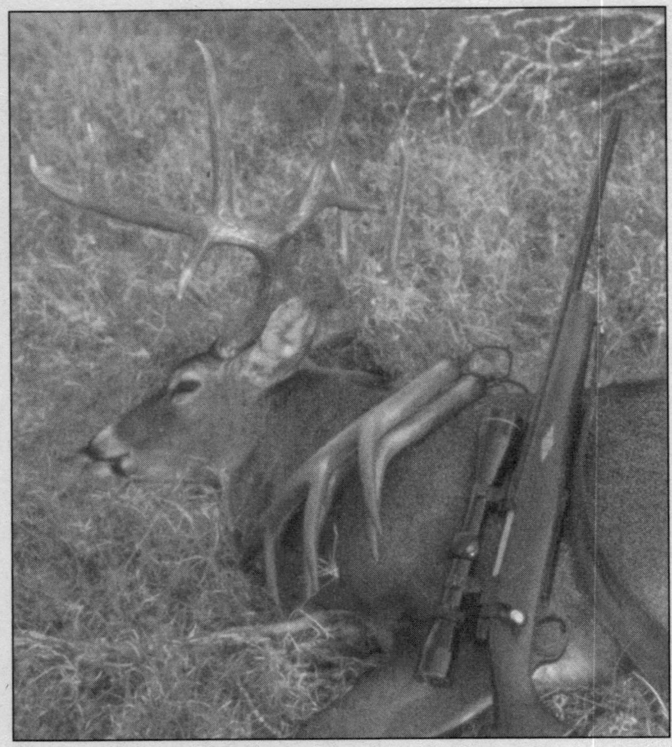

Although Bob Zaiglin prefers to use fresh sheds to rattle in bucks, he has done quite well with synthetics, too, as evidenced by the buck in this photo. Credit: Bob Zaiglin.

antlers might actually have carried farther because of it than the sound from my real rattling horns. Were I to go rattling at this very moment, whether I would grab the synthetics or authentics would be a moot point. In fact, I'm so impressed with a few of the rattling devices I've recently seen that I just might use them instead. But more about them later.

Some hunters swear that nothing sounds like a fresh set of rattling horns. But if you bring antlers inside at the end of each day and rarely expose them to the elements, even a twenty-year-old set will sound identical to a set removed from a buck's head today. To get that so-called "fresh" sound, some hunters soak their sheds in water, no matter how new they may be, for several hours. Others rub their sheds down with petroleum jelly to seal in freshness Still other experts prefer oiling or waxing their sheds with a scent-free product to preserve that "just-off-the-buck" degree of freshness.

Bob Zaiglin uses a large set of real antlers for his rattling horns. Mickey Hellickson looks for the heaviest, freshest pair of shed antlers he can find. "I've been using some massive horns lately," Hellickson said. "I cut off the brow tines and then shaved the surrounding area smooth to the beam so they're easy to grip. A large set of horns produces the greatest volume. My study revealed that volume is more important than any other factor to rattling success. The higher the volume, the greater the distance over which it will be heard. The greater the distance, the more bucks that will hear it. And if more bucks hear your rattling, more bucks are bound to respond."

Proponents of using real antlers include other successful hunters, too, experts like Peter Fiduccia, Jay Cassell, and Jim Holdenried. "Using smaller antlers won't discourage smaller bucks from investigating," Fiduccia pointed out. "And

Although he usually prefers synthetics, Jerry Shively used real antlers to lure this fine Montana buck in for Mark Easterling. Credit: Jerry Shively.

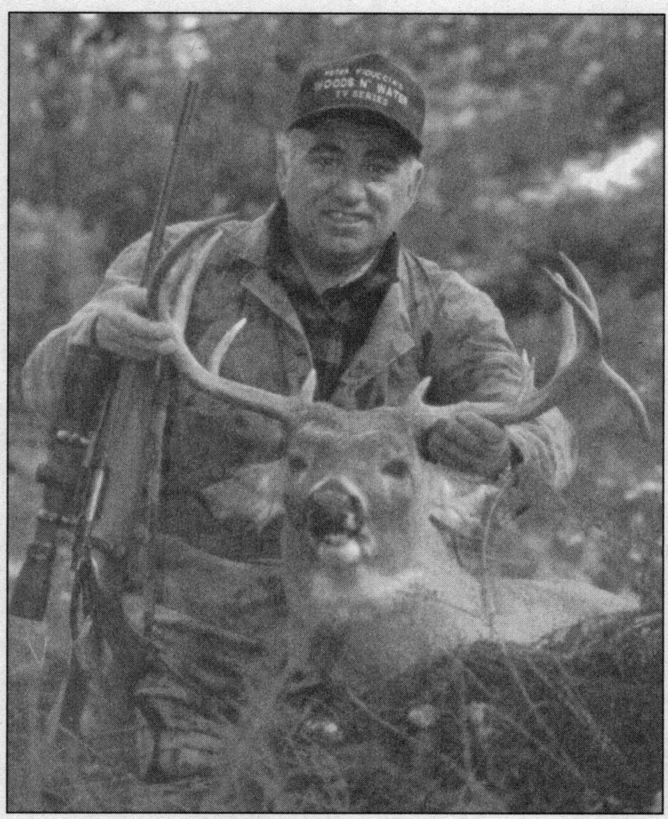


According to Peter Fiduccia, not only will smaller antlers rattle in bucks of all sizes, they're easier to pack around. Credit: Fiduccia Enterprises.

Modify real antlers before using them to rattle by cutting off the ends of tines; otherwise you could be seriously injured—or worse—if you fell on them while walking or climbing into a stand. Credit: Kathy Etling.

smaller antlers are far easier to pack around." Cassell agrees. "I want to imitate the sound of smaller bucks fighting," he said. "By doing so, I hope to lure in a larger buck who's hoping to whip both their [smaller bucks'] butts."

Fiduccia noted that synthetic antlers usually don't have to be modified for safety's sake, but that if you don't modify real antlers you could be hurt in an accident while pulling them into your stand, climbing hills, or negotiating bluffs. "Always be cautious when using real antlers in a public hunting area," he warned. Fiduccia modified his set of smaller antlers by trimming off sharp tines and drilling a hole through each base where he threaded a lanyard.

"I use real antlers for the most part," said Jim Holdenried. "I prefer a set of sheds the would score about 125 Pope and Young points. Smaller rattling horns don't do it for me, particularly not for more intense, 'hard' rattling sequences." Holdenried also removes sharp tines to keep them from cutting or jabbing his hands. "I've used a rattling bag, but I have better luck with real antlers," he concluded.

"I've used real antlers, synthetic antlers, and rattling bags," noted M.R. James. "I like actual antlers, real and synthetic, because of the sounds produced when I tickle the tines together or really grind the beams. Artificial antlers don't sound as true to me, but the deer don't seem to mind or notice. My

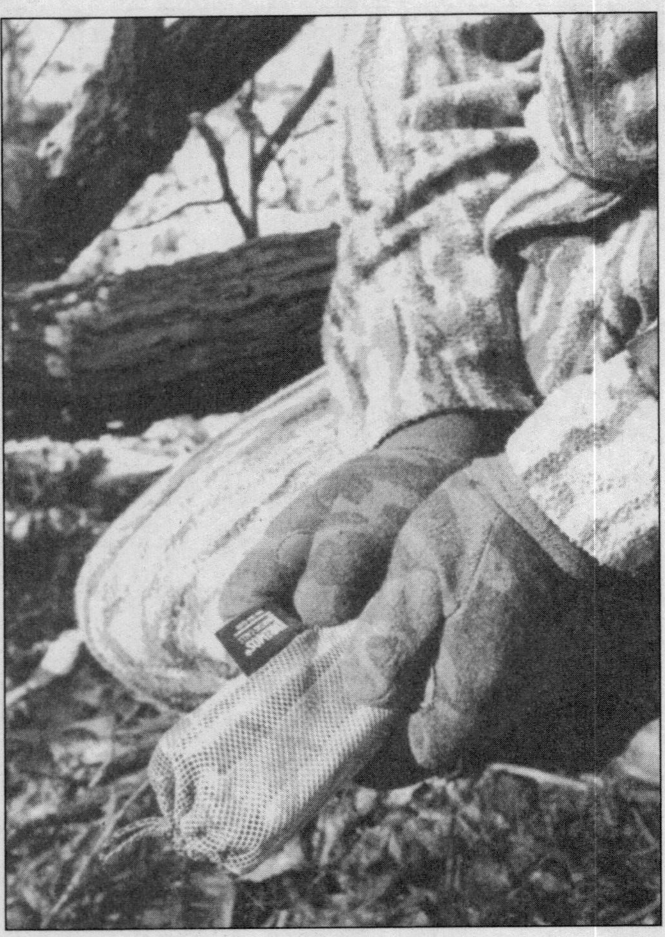

A nylon mesh rattle bag containing ceramic dowels is both easier and safer to carry than antlers and sounds authentic enough to fool rutting bucks. Credit: M.R. James.

favorite set of horns is a pair of sheds I found that score about 135 Pope and Young points."

For ease when packing into a hunting area and climbing into tree stands, James says it's hard to beat a rattle bag. "Rattle bags may have their drawbacks, but they're sure handy to tote," he said. "I prefer rattling bags full of ceramic dowels rather than wooden dowels. Ceramic just seems to work better, especially in wet weather when wood may swell and lose its crisp tones."

"I've heard it all, and the best sounds are produced by real antlers or good quality synthetics," said Gary Roberson of Burnham Brothers Game Calls in Menard, Texas.

## Other Rattling "Tricks"

Somewhat in the same vein, M.R. James will sometimes tie a rope to his rattling horns, then tie the rope to a bush or tree below his stand. He then lowers the antlers on this "haul" line so that they are resting in the bush or next to the sapling. When he jerks on the line, the antlers thrash about in the brush where they might attract a nearby deer.

One thing all of these hunters have in common is a high degree of originality and an ability to take tricks they've learned about and make them their own. "Some hunters will fasten a string to a sapling, then pull on it from their stand, high above, to create the illusion of a buck rubbing the sapling," Peter Fiduccia said. Fiduccia sometimes fills a third of a plastic zipper lock bag with fish tank gravel. He places the gravel-laden bag inside another plastic bag. He then makes a small hole through each bag,

Mick Hellickson uses the largest set of real antlers he can find to produce the loud rattling that attracts big bucks like this one. Credit: Mickey Hellickson.

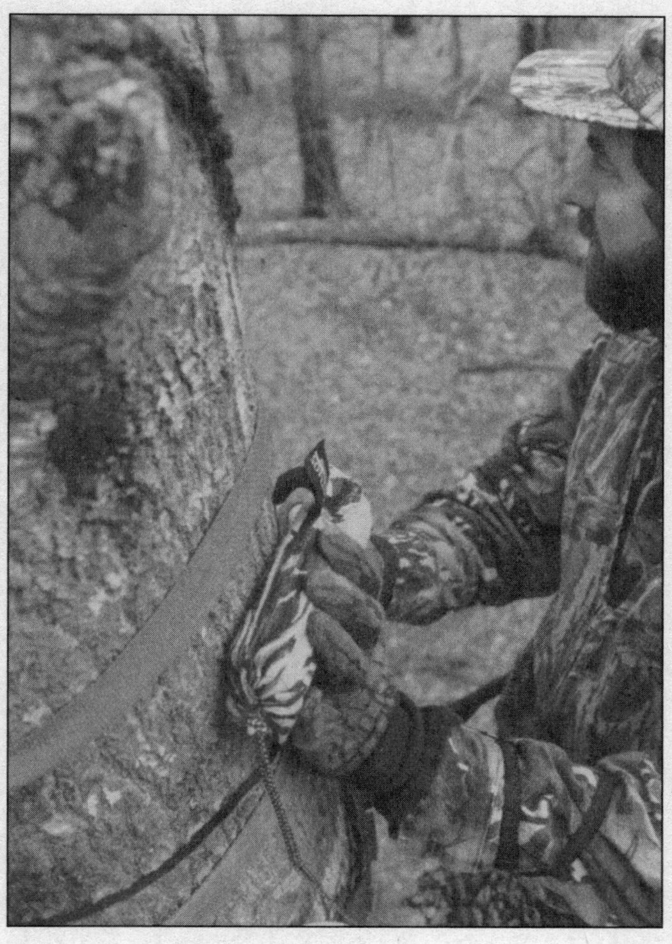

A rattle bag can be rolled against a tree trunk—or your leg—to create the sound of sparring bucks with a minimum amount of movement, as Wilbur Primos demonstrates. Credit: M.R. James.

runs a long string through both, and attaches the bags to his ankle. In this manner he's able to rattle with his foot, with a minimum of movement, while he's waiting in his tree stand. As he rattles, he moves his foot back and forth to drag the bag over the undergrowth and forest litter beneath his stand. "This is just another way of setting the stage so that any buck listening will think a battle is going on," he said. "It provides a realistic sound, right down to the 'hooves' moving back and forth across the forest floor."

## Rattling from Ground Blinds

The argument about whether tree stands or ground blinds are better continues to rage among rattling experts. "I prefer ground blinds," said Fiduccia. "Ground blinds work better for breaking up your profile or as something easy to hide behind. I've often made my ground blinds from stacks of cedar trees."

In agricultural areas, many hunters who rely on rattling report excellent success when set up behind a blind made of straw bales. The advantage here is that the blind is fairly stable, even during high winds, and it provides a great screen for hiding hunter movement. Being able to mask movement is vitally important to trophy bowhunters like Judy Kovar of Illinois.

## Scouting for Sparring Circles

"What I'm looking for is an open spot that's surrounded by fairly heavy cover," said Jerry Shively. "The places that seem to work the best are those where I've watched bucks fighting over the years. Bucks seem to have very definite locales where they prefer to fight. You can identify one of these spots by the sparring circle evident on the ground. I've hunted this one piece of property for more than twenty years and I know all the bucks' favorite places to fight." As its name suggests, a sparring circle is a large, round area where you can tell animals were trampling the ground beneath their hooves. Grass may be flattened within this circle, or the earth may be mostly bare because bucks have fought there for many years. Brush and undergrowth may be battered and beaten, too. The ground may also reveal paw marks and antler gouges. The more such sign you discover in a particular location, the better your chances will be of rattling in a buck there.

"I don't really return to certain rattling locations per se," Bob Zaiglin said. "But I get these vibrations about a spot. I know, everybody laughs, but as I'm walking through the brush I really start feeling like This is an area that I'd be in if I were a buck. Or, man, this looks really deery. Look at all those fresh scrapes. So, I move on to step two of my process: looking for a good place to station both my hunter and myself. I want to be in a spot where I can see in both directions. I really believe I rattle up more deer due to confidence than technique. I'm so confident when I think I've found a good spot that I'm almost positive that's why I've had such fantastic success." Zaiglin has rattled up whitetails everywhere he's hunted, even back home in Pennsylvania. In Texas, he's rattled up several hundred deer that have been taken by his hunters and hundreds more that his hunters have passed up.

## One Rattler, Two hunters

Shively's favorite rattling tactic, when guiding hunters, is to position two hunters on stands two or three hundred yards apart. He then splits the distance between them and rattles. "My hunters usually see deer, but I won't," he said. "Since they're elevated they have a better view of the terrain. Since hundreds of yards separate them, one may see one buck while the other sees a different buck. I once had two hunters shoot at two different bucks at the same exact moment. None of us were aware of it until we got together afterward. 'I shot,' said the one. 'No, I shot,' said the other. My head started spinning, but then I found out they'd both scored on really nice whitetails."

## Rattling from Tree Stands

If you decide to do your solo rattling from a tree stand, choose a tree with a trunk that is large enough to hide you, should the need arise. "It's a good idea to always rattle from the side of the tree where you do not expect the buck to appear," Peter Fiduccia said. "Natural cover to break up your outline is a must. It's particularly helpful beneath your feet so that any deer looking upward will be unable to make out your human silhouette." Deer

A tree with a thick trunk and plentiful foliage will break up your silhouette and prevent the deer from spotting you. Credit: Randy Templeton.

A rattle bag can be rolled against a tree trunk—or your leg—to create the sound of sparring bucks with a minimum amount of movement, as Wilbur Primos demonstrates. Credit: M.R. James.

peering upward are a fact of life when rattling or calling emanates from the treetops rather than from down on the ground. You can sometimes mitigate that effect by rattling from the sides of steep hollows where the sound appears to be coming from farther up the hillside, even if you are in a tree stand. The risk in this maneuver is that a deer may come in higher up on the hillside, be on the same level as you, and be able to see you in the tree stand. "Another good ploy is to position yourself where you can whack your rattling horns against a leafy limb," Fiduccia said. "This simulates the sounds of a buck thrashing its rack in a bush or sapling. Don't be afraid to thwack the rattling horns against the tree's trunk, either. Doing so provides an even greater degree of realism."

Don Kisky likes to play with a big buck's mind by making him think that the rattling—the "fight"—they hear is going on just over the hill. Credit: Don and Kandi Kisky.

"I find it hard to get deer to commit to coming in when I'm waiting in a tree stand in an area where deer can see quite well," Don Kisky said. "One of my favorite tricks is to make them think that the rattling is going on just over the hill. Whenever deer can see well, they become extremely cautious. That's why I like rattling from the edge of a bluff or creek where it's difficult for them to circle downwind of me."

## Rattling Sequences

"I'll always make a snort-wheeze before I start rattling," Kisky continued. "If I see two bucks in the distance, I'll use the snort-wheeze, too. When I rattle, I really go at it. I think it's impossible to make too much noise when you rattle during the rut. Of course, when you're busy flailing around rattling, it's easy for a buck to spot you. That's one reason I keep my sequences loud, but short. My normal sequence lasts just ten seconds. If you rattle too long, bucks may sneak in and spot you and you'll never even know they were there." Kisky has used rattling to take many of his biggest deer. These include bucks that were gross-scored at 197, 181, 179, 177, 171, 167, and 161, among others. To say that Kisky knows what he's doing with a set of rattling horns in his hand would be a major understatement.

"I do all my hard rattling from mid- to late October," Jim Holdenried said. "Prime time for me is from the eighteenth to the thirty-first and perhaps during early November, particularly if the action is somewhat dead. Those are the days when you

Don Kisky keeps his rattling sequences loud but short to pull in trophy bucks like this to within bow range. Credit: Don and Kandy Kisky.

might not be ready and suddenly, here they come at a dead run!"

"One thing you have to know about antler-rattling is that it's as much about what you're feeling as anything else," added Bob Zaiglin. "Say a buck is two hundred yards away—or maybe you only think he is. If you have the feeling that you are close to the buck of a lifetime and you want to bring him in, try just tickling the antlers at first. This is a great tactic to use during the cold, early morning hours following a warm spell. Some people like to clash those antlers together as hard as they can, but I can't help but think that this type of noise might inhibit deer from coming in. It's only on the second or third time I grind those antlers together that I begin to get louder and enhance my sequence so that it appears to any buck that may be listening that the ground and the brush are being torn apart by those 'two battling whitetails.' And that's what I want him to think."

"I'll start rattling right before the rut begins, around the first of November," Jerry Shively said. "We'll start with some light rattling and some get-acquainted grunts, nothing dominant or too loud. Our deer aren't yet fighting at this time. They aren't acting really aggressive. When you see them sparring, they're still just tickling their horns. I rattle just enough to work on their curiosity."

Kandi Kisky has taken deer as large as some of husband Don's, including this massive 170+ whitetail shot with a muzzleloader. Credit: Don and Kandi Kisky.

Shively doesn't get serious about his rattling and grunting until about a week before the rut starts on November 15. "You can make a tremendous amount of noise out there if you're trying to mimic two deer seriously going at it," he said. "There is no way a single hunter can make enough noise to accurately duplicate it."

M.R. James begins his rattling sequences with buck grunts, and then starts raking a tree trunk with his antlers. "I start off slow, as if the 'bucks' are merely sparring," he said. "I'll mesh the antlers for several periods of ten to fifteen seconds with soundless intervals between the sequences. I let the action build in intensity as the 'fight' progresses, with prolonged grinding of the beams and clicking of the tines, but with occasional pauses. I seldom rattle for more than 90 to 120 seconds per sequence. I conclude by 'tickling the tines' one final time, then finishing off with three or four aggressive buck grunts." As a bowhunter, James will seldom move on to a different stand site. Instead, he may rattle from the same stand site six to eight times during a four-hour period to attract any bucks that may be traveling through his hunting area.

"Do I vary my rattling sequences?" asked Brad Harris, rhetorically. "Yes, quite a bit. The way in which I vary my sequences intrigues hunters. I tell them that you have to get in tune with your surroundings. I rattle the way I feel, the way the weather makes me feel. On some days, it just seems like deer should be more responsive, so I'll rattle or call more often. On doldrum days, I'm more laid back, quieter, and I don't rattle as much."

One of Harris's typical rattling sequences will begin with one loud aggressive grunt in every direction. "That should get the buck's head up," Harris said. "He's now listening, so I pause a few seconds, then start rattling as though one buck has just confronted another, and then the battle begins. I rattle five to thirty seconds, just swiping the antlers together, and then I'll pause, listen, and wait, because you never know if a buck is just over the next ridge. I'll rattle, then pause, then rattle perhaps two times more while pausing and listening. I'll rattle, wait, and then maybe grunt. Even after I've quit rattling, I'll probably make a grunt every now and then in case the buck is coming but I'm unable to see him."

If it's windy, Harris will rattle loudly and more often. "You have to adjust to conditions," he said. "If I'm in an area where I'm able to see long distances, then I'll probably rattle less. Cold, clear conditions usually mean rattling will be more productive than on warm or hot days."

Peter Fiduccia explained every detail he puts into his rattling sequences. "First, I find a good spot where I can set up," he said. "I'll start by dribbling some buck urine around the area. I then do my best to create the illusion I'm after. This means stomping my feet, stepping hard upon leaves and twigs, adding some aggressive grunts, hitting my horns against tree limbs, and then slamming the antlers against the ground or tree trunks. I'll do this for fifteen seconds, thirty seconds, forty-five seconds, or even an entire minute. I'll then pause to look and listen in all directions. You must stay alert. If you think it might work, shake a nearby sapling or stomp on the ground to entice any nearby whitetails into showing themselves."

Fiduccia then waits between fifteen and twenty minutes before rattling again. "The next time I'll wait thirty minutes," he said. "Some people move to a new area, but I prefer to stay put. Should a buck appear, try always to be positioned in a place where you're able to shake a sapling or grunt or do both. If you are unable to do this, then try to have a rattling buddy along who can. This simple motion or call may be the last nail in that buck's coffin. What you do is provide him with one final motive to rush in and see what's going on."

Fiduccia warns hunters who are new to the rattling game to remain at high alert for any sign of a nearby buck, including the sound of a snort or grunt, the slight movement of legs beneath nearby brush, sunlight glinting off an antler tine, a silhouette where you don't remember seeing one before. "Deer are shifty critters," he said. "Now you see them, now you don't."

## The Best Times to Rattle?

Although all of our experts would rattle all day long, their consensus "best time" was early morning, particularly one that was frosty cold and windstill. Bob Zaiglin qualified his choice when he said, "I've rattled all day long, for many years. It doesn't matter where you might be rattling from—if it's not close to a deer you'd like to take, it will be for naught. Sunup is my favorite time to rattle, but you must be woods-wise enough to figure out where the buck you want is hiding, then decide how best to try to rattle him in. If you can get to within five hundred yards of where that is without disturbing him, your rattling and calling techniques will be perhaps 60 percent effective. If you can close that distance to two hundred yards, those techniques may increase in effectiveness to as much as 90 percent."

"I learned one time-management lesson the hard way," added M.R. James. "I owned this one place in the Indiana suburbs that had some great whitetail hunting. One morning I went in early and climbed up into my stand. It was still dark when I began rattling. I heard something, looked down, and saw a buck. It walked right under my stand. The only problem was it was still dark. I could see antlers, but it wasn't legal shooting time yet. I learned the hard way not to rattle too early or too late. It's difficult passing up a nice buck that you rattled in fair and square because you couldn't wait until it was time to shoot."

"Without a doubt, the first ten minutes of light and the last ten minutes are the very best times to rattle," said Don Kisky.

Jerry Shively reports having better rattling luck in the afternoons and evenings. Even so, he admitted, "There are days when I can't do anything wrong—but there are just as many days when I can't do anything right."

## From Which Direction Will Bucks Come?

Mickey Hellickson's Texas research study confirmed that bucks are more likely to approach a rattler's position from the downwind side. Surprisingly, mature bucks were no more likely to approach from downwind than younger animals were. A few bucks from all age classes broke precedent to come in from directions other than downwind. "I've rattled bucks in from all directions," said Bob Zaiglin. "They don't always come in from downwind. What will happen, though, is that the buck will usually circumvent the rattler to come in from the downwind side. That's why rattling with a team works so well.

"Say you have a north wind," he said, to illustrate his point. "One person is in a stand in a mesquite tree that's south of where the other person is rattling from the ground. The person in the stand to the south of the rattler will always see far more deer than the one who is rattling."

"I've rarely had bucks come rushing in except in Texas," M.R. James said. "The bucks I rattle in in other places usually approach my position slowly, their ears back, hair standing up on the backs of their necks, walking stiff-legged, and posturing. I've watched plenty of these bucks raking trees or brush with their antlers as they came closer to my stand. I've arrowed several that swaggered in and stopped directly beneath my tree. I really believe deer can pinpoint the exact location of any 'buck fight' they hear. It's a big thrill for me to rattle or grunt a good buck close enough to shoot at with a bow."

To which, I'm sure, the rest of our experts would add a fervent "Amen."

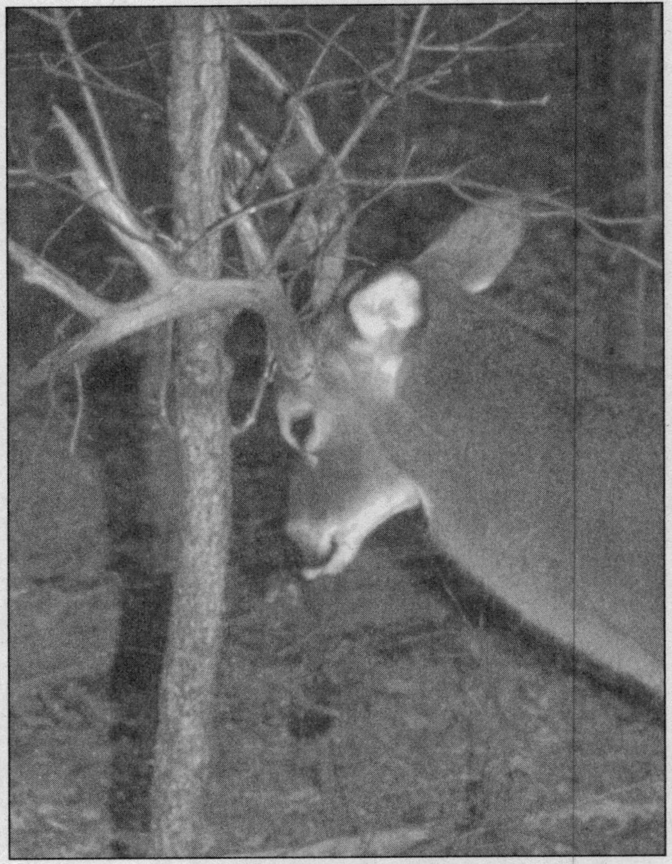

When rattling or calling, stay alert to any buck that might walk in stiff-legged and posturing, just waiting to work over a sapling with its antlers. Credit: Bob Etling.

# Rattling: What to Expect

Okay, you're out in the field. You've started rattling. What should you expect to happen, and when?

To begin, remember that deer don't *only* vocalize. Nor do they merely tickle, mesh, or clash their antlers together in the sounds of battle, mock or authentic. Deer will also stomp their hooves to communicate with each other. Whether the stomping emanates from a doe that's trying to warn her youngsters or a buck reluctant to continue on the path it is taking, foot-stomping provides not only an aural warning via other deer's ears, but also a visual warning during periods of high winds. In the latter case, nearby deer may be able to see an agitated animal better than they can hear it.

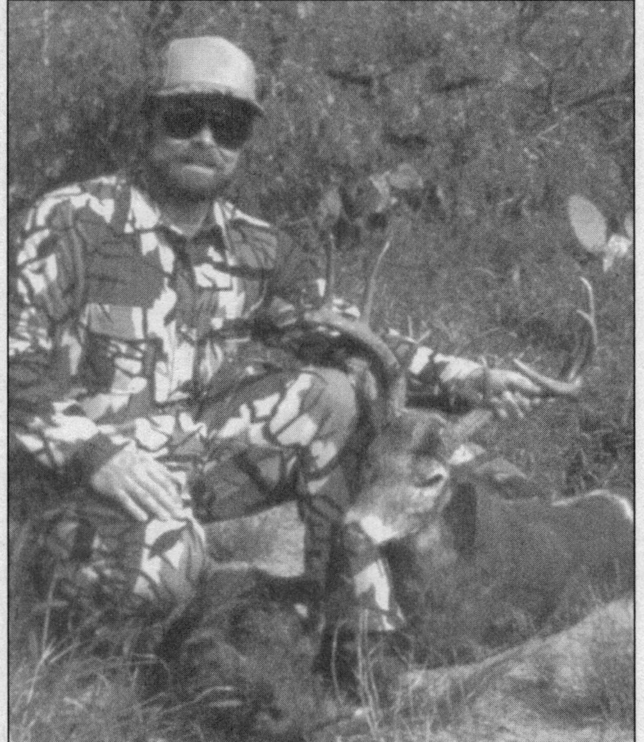

Jay Cassell with a buck he rattled out of some heavy mesquite brush on a ranch near San Antonio, Texas. Credit: Jay Cassell.

Foot-stomping imparts a chemical message as well. A deer's hooves emit a pheromone—a chemical message—from the *interdigital gland,* a scent gland between the two parts of the deer's cloven hoof. A white-tail stomping on a trail, for example, is providing an olfactory warning to any deer that may follow that something wasn't quite right here. Whether it was the scent of a human hunter carried from afar or something along the trail that seemed out of place and, therefore, potentially dangerous, the interdigital gland does its work subtly and swiftly. Many hunters sweeten mock scrapes and mock rubs with commercial interdigital gland scent or with hooves frozen and preserved from previous seasons. Should a deer you decline to shoot discover your rattling setup and start stomping its foot because it suspects a human is nearby, your best recourse is to relocate. Any other deer that comes by will immediately be alert to the presence of danger. Move, but do so carefully. Don't stand up, believing that you haven't rattled in a buck, and then be startled to see a white tail bobbing off into the distance.

If an agitated buck races in looking for another buck, his pawing and stomping of the ground will not leave a negative olfactory warning for other deer. Although his hoof-stomping provides an auditory signal, if an olfactory threat or agonistic signal is

Create the total illusion when rattling from the ground by using your antlers to rake trees, leaves, and brush and to thump the ground like a buck's hooves. Credit: M.R. James

communicated as well, biologists, at least as far as I know, are unaware of it. Should a buck race in and stomp prior to a "fight" that never materializes—and you miss your chance to take him—no olfactory warning will be given unless the buck realizes that a human is there. If it fails to do so, you might even be able to rattle him in again. Should he run off unaware that a human was nearby, there's no reason for you to leave.

Moving your rattling location may work wonders, especially if there's a lot of great hunting ground and few other hunters, as in much of Texas and the West. Such a strategy may prove less lucrative in the East, Midwest, and South, where hunter densities are much higher. In states as scattered as Michigan, Missouri, Pennsylvania, and Georgia, staying in one place—even all day—is preferable unless you are hunting a large tract of

Avoid moving your rattling setup too frequently, because thick undergrowth can work to a whitetail's advantage and you might not see a deer approaching. Credit: Don and Kandi Kisky

private land with few other hunters. One reason to avoid moving your rattling setup too often is that thick undergrowth can work to a whitetail's advantage by camouflaging its presence until the last possible moment. If you move and reveal your position, you're aiding the whitetail's cause. Stay put. Let *him* make the mistakes.

For every buck that bursts onto the scene in response to your rattling sequences, probably four or five others choose to take a wait-and-see attitude and remain hidden. These deer may be subdominants, their native caution holding them back to see what will transpire next. Or perhaps a dominant buck is biding his time, waiting for the best moment to charge into view. It's always possible that no buck has heard your rattling, but a buck is heading your way as you prepare to give up for the day. Should you leave the stand and risk spooking a possibly responsive buck? Granted, there are no guarantees that this theoretical "buck" will ever make its appearance. But it might also be the buck you bag.

## A Rattler's Most Important Quality

Should you decide to give calling, rattling, and decoying a go, you must also work on the one quality that will help you succeed more than any other when using these techniques: patience. The more you rattle from any given stand, the more likely a buck will eventually investigate. Perhaps his curiosity finally maxes out. Perhaps he just traveled into hearing range. Perhaps he's finally bred the doe he was following, and he's looking for another. When he hears the sound of antlers clashing, he might think the "fight" is being waged over another hot doe and come storming in. Or maybe you've finally agitated him beyond all reckoning and he stampedes in to find out what in tarnation is going on. In any event, patience is a crucial part of the art of deceiving whitetails.

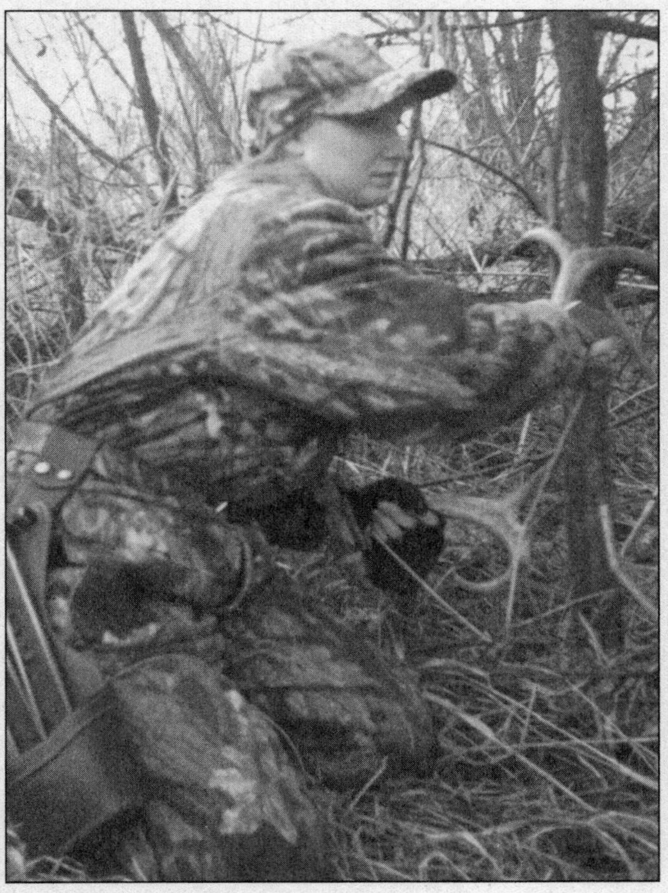

In most states, rattling from one place all day is preferable to moving, as archer Holly Fuller demonstrates. Credit: Holly Fuller.

## Where to Rattle?

If conditions are right, whitetail bucks—unlike turkey gobblers—will come in to almost any location. Bucks responding to rattling will race up hills and down, may storm across creeks, and will

Successful rattlers like Iowa's Don Kisky agree that the one quality that will most help you succeed is patience. Credit: Don and Kandi Kisky.

even race across bare fields, so great is their desire to view or participate in the "fight" now underway.

"I've experienced some of my best November rattling in eastern Colorado, along the Arkansas River," M.R. James said. "At this one ranch you could see deer at such a great distance you could actually watch as bucks ran across pastures or hopped fences to reach the rattling. That was some of the most exciting rattling I've ever experienced."

Don't be reluctant to set up anywhere you feel there's a halfway decent chance of rattling in a buck. Just be sure there is a good place for you to hide until you or your hunting partner is able to make the shot.

Early in the season, rattle in areas where you have seen bucks moving about in their bachelor groups. Look for core areas where early rubs have been made on small, insignificant saplings and where platter-sized scrapes roughly mark the animal's semi-territorial boundaries.

Bob Zaiglin team-rattles by setting up in a thicket that will disguise his movement well upwind of where his hunter is positioned in a tree stand. Credit: Bob Zaiglin.

As the primary rut approaches, remember that bucks will be traveling. They may return to core areas regularly, but they are more likely to check in only occasionally. No matter what size a buck's normal home range may be, once the rut commences, all home range bets are off. While some bucks may remain true to their annual home range, others may look for estrous does elsewhere. Some radio-collared bucks have been tracked thirty miles away from their annual home ranges, although this is the exception, not the rule. Don't waste your time targeting a particular buck that may no longer be in the area. Instead, set up close to an area frequented by one or more doe family groups. Whenever does are in estrus, bucks won't be far away.

## Stay Alert

Once when M.R. James was hunting in Illinois he set up his stand in a point of woods where three trails converged. "I climbed into my stand and began rattling," he said. "Now, I could see for a long way in every direction. I mustn't have been looking in the right place, because all of a sudden I saw something move out of the corner of my eye. This buck must have run all the way across the corn field in front of me without me seeing it. When I did, the buck was only fifty yards away. He walked in, licking his nose, and I shot him."

## Can You Rattle Too Much?

Too much of a good thing can sometimes work against you. That may be as true of rattling as it is of partaking of too many boilermakers on a Saturday night. Don Kisky believes too much rattling during past hunting seasons has worked against him more recently. "I've rattled so much in the past that I honestly think the five- and six-year-old bucks on

M.R. James's whitetail hunting tools: rattling antlers, a rattle bag, and deer calls. He won't leave home without 'em. Credit M.R. James.

our farm have become conditioned to the sound. Older bucks don't respond as readily as they once did. Yet I can hunt a farm where deer aren't used to the sound and rattle one right in. I've rattled in most of my larger bucks, but now, when they get to within seventy or eighty yards, I'll rely on grunting to bring them the rest of the way in. Three of my five largest whitetails have been grunted or rattled in."

# Advanced Antler-Rattling

Wham! I hit the shed antlers together as hard as I could and then quickly pulled them apart. Again, I slammed the antlers together with all of my force. This time I kept the antlers entwined and twisted the tines and beams against each other for several seconds. I repeated this several times. Two minutes into the rattling sequence I noticed movement and a flash of gray out in front of me.

The deer stopped out of sight behind a thick clump of mesquite trees. I continued to rattle, but tried to shield all of my movements from the deer. After sev eral anxious moments, the deer stepped into view. His rack was huge. The main beams were over twenty inches apart and carried eleven typical points. The tines were also very tall and symmetrical. The only flaw, if there was one, was his lack of mass.

The buck had been sighted and photographed earlier, during the fall deer survey, by ranch owner Stuart Stedman. Based on these photographs and my sighting, we estimated the buck's gross Boone and Crockett Club score to be in the 160s. The only reason this buck was still alive was because of his age—he was only 4½ years old!

The buck, #180, was one of 130 bucks that we had captured and equipped with radio-transmitting collars since my research started in 1992. We captured this buck in October of that same year. At that time, Dr. Charles DeYoung of Texas A&M University-Kingsville had estimated the buck's age at 2½ years. DeYoung, who has aged literally thousands of live deer, aged every buck we captured each fall based on the amount of lower jaw tooth wear. In 1992, this buck's rack tallied up a gross Boone and Crockett score of 89, with seven points and no brow tines.

It was now mid-November. I was collecting data for an ongoing study on buck responses to antler-rattling. Dr. Larry Marchinton, from the University of Georgia, DeYoung, and I had been studying this aspect of breeding whitetail behavior

Wearing a camo headnet or face mask and gloves when you rattle will help hide your moving parts from sharpeyed—and suspicious—bucks. Credit: M.R. James.

Mickey Hellickson's first antler-rattling study proved that the post-rut and the pre-rut periods were the best times to rattle in mature, trophy-caliber bucks. Credit: Mickey Hellickson.

for three years. This project would satisfy part of my doctoral requirements at the University of Georgia.

The first part of this study was conducted at the Rob and Bessie Welder Wildlife Refuge, north of Sinton, Texas. Our primary goal was to determine which type of rattling sequence attracted the highest number of bucks. The results of this three-year study were reported in an issue of *The Journal of the Texas Trophy Hunters*.

## Recap of Earlier Results

In a previous publication, we tested four rattling sequences on whitetails. These sequences varied by length as well as rattling volume. We rattled a total of 171 times during the three periods of the whitetail breeding season. Our rattling attracted a total of 111 bucks. We found that loud rattling attracted nearly three times as many bucks as quiet rattling, and that the length of the rattling sequence was not important. We discovered that the post-rut and pre-rut periods were the best times to rattle in mature, trophy-caliber bucks. The rut's peak was tops if the objective was to rattle in large numbers of bucks. Rattling sessions that took place between 7:30 and 10:30 am attracted more bucks than sessions conducted either at midday or in the afternoon. Cloudy days with little wind and mild temperatures represented the most productive weather conditions for rattling.

## A Second Antler-Rattling Study

The goal of this, the second part of our antler-rattling study, would be to rattle to specific radio-collared bucks, and then measure each animal's responses. Each of the 130 collared bucks was outfitted with a transmitter attached to a neck collar that produced a unique radio signal. We tracked each buck using telemetry for an entire year. We located each buck's position a minimum of one or two times each day.

To track the bucks, we used a radio receiver connected to a large antenna. We dialed the frequency of the buck we wished to locate into the receiver and then drove the ranch roads, stopping every quarter mile to search for the animal. At each stop, the antenna would be swung 360 degrees in an

Hellickson's study also revealed that cloudy days with little wind and mild temperatures were the most productive when rattling for whitetails. Credit: Mickey Hellickson.

attempt to detect the buck's signal. Once we picked up the correct signal, we determined the direction from which the signal was strongest. A compass was used to plot a bearing in that direction. We then stopped two more times at locations farther down the road, where we repeated the process. When we had three bearings to use for triangulation, we drew each on a map. The intersection of these three lines represented the buck's approximate location.

Forty-three of the 130 bucks that we had captured and radio-collared had been equipped with special activity-sensing transmitters. These transmitters told us whether each buck was bedded or active whenever we located him, even though we were usually not able to see him. Each buck's collar produced a radio signal at a rate of one pulse per second if the buck was not moving and the collar around its neck was stationary. Whenever the buck moved, the collar would also move, which would increase the radio signal to two or more pulses per second. Therefore, whenever we located one of these bucks, we could tell if he was not moving and bedded; or active, simply by the radio pulse rate.

One day I used radiotelemetry to map Buck #180's position. On this particular occasion I drove downwind of the buck and parked the truck. I eased in toward him quietly until I believed I'd closed the gap between us to no more than two to three hundred yards. At that point, I turned on the receiver and zeroed it in on the buck. In this manner I was able to detect his responses as I rattled to him by the pulse rate of his signal. I started the rattling sequence related at the beginning of this article.

Buck #180's radio signal became active almost immediately. As I continued to rattle, the pulse rate quickened even more, while the signal became louder. Based on this information, I knew not only that the buck was active, but that he was moving toward me. One minute into the sequence the signal had become so loud that I knew the buck would appear at any moment!

The buck stepped into the opening and almost immediately turned and disappeared back into the brush. I gathered up the telemetry equipment and returned to the truck. After I'd reached the truck, I waited thirty minutes and relocated the buck with three new bearings. I was thus able to determine how far and in what direction he had traveled after responding to my rattling.

Through the use of this cutting-edge technology, we were able to measure the individual responses of many whitetail bucks both during and after we rattled to them. We could tell whether or not each buck responded to our rattling, even if the animal did not move close enough for us to see him. Finally, rattling response rates were determined based on the gross Boone and Crockett scores of each buck as well as its age, which had been determined by patterns of tooth wear.

## The Results

The results of the second part of our study were extremely interesting. With research assistants Fred

Steubing and Justin McCoy aiding us, each autumn from 1994 to 1996 we located the same eighteen bucks. We'd previously collared them with the activity-sensing radio transmitters described above. During this phase of the study we located each buck, walked quietly to within two or three hundred yards of him, then created a long, loud rattling sequence. In all, we rattled 33 times near these 18 bucks. Five of the bucks were located and rattled to during the pre-rut period, 14 during the rut's peak, and 14 others during the post-rut.

During 24 of the 33 sessions (73 percent), bucks responded by becoming active and moving closer to the source of the rattling. In other words, *nearly three out every four bucks responded to rattling if they were upwind and within hearing range.* I doubt whether most hunters could have predicted that bucks would respond at such an incredible rate. Before I conducted this study, I personally believed that fewer than 25 percent of the bucks within hearing range would respond to our rattling.

During our 33 rattling sessions, the horn rattler succeeded only 11 times in spotting the collared buck that was the object of our rattling. Rattling during this second study was performed by one person situated at ground level. We realize that not having a second observer nearby in a 30-foot-tall tower significantly reduced the number of bucks sighted. And yet the 33 percent sighting rate during the second part of the study compared favorably with results from our first Welder Refuge study. During that study, the person rattling from the ground spotted only 48 of the 111 bucks (43 percent) seen by the observer in the tower.

This illustrates how critical it is for a hunter to be waiting in an elevated position.

Rattling with a partner is probably the most efficient way to consistently see and take whitetail bucks. While the shooter climbs into a tripod or some other type of elevated stand, another person should rattle from the ground. Stand sites should be selected upwind of open areas to even further increase the number of bucks seen, since the majority of bucks respond from downwind.

Fewer bucks responded to rattling during the pre-rut than during the rut's peak and post-rut periods. During the pre-rut, 2 of 5 (40 percent) rattling sessions culminated in the buck becoming active and moving closer to the rattling. During the rut's peak, 11 of 14 (79 percent) bucks became active and moved closer, while 11 of 14 bucks (79 percent) became active and moved closer during the post-rut period. The rut's peak response rate was slightly lower than what had been observed during the study's initial Welder Refuge phase, while the response rate during the post-rut period was higher.

Buck response rates were highest during morning rattling sessions. Midday and afternoon sessions elicited identical response rates that were

During thirty-three research study sessions, the horn rattler spotted the buck targeted by the rattling only eleven times. Hence the need for a rattling team.
Credit: Mickey Hellickson.

When this old Montana buck responded to rattling during the rut period, M.R. James arrowed him at fifteen yards. Credit: M.R. James.

slightly lower than those registered after morning sessions. Eight radio-collared bucks responded to 9 morning rattling sessions (89 percent response rate). Six bucks responded to the 9 midday sessions (67 percent), while 10 bucks responded to 15 afternoon sessions (67 percent response rate). Midday buck response rates during this second phase of the study were higher than those attained during the study's first phase at Welder Refuge.

During nine sessions, bucks either did not respond at all or they became active but moved away from the person rattling. The average age of bucks that responded to our rattling was 5.8 years, while the average for bucks that did not respond was 7.4 years. This seems to indicate that older bucks may be less susceptible to antler-rattling.

Thirty minutes after responding to the rattling, a buck would move an average of almost a third of a mile. Two bucks traveled nearly three quarters of a mile. Two other bucks moved very little. We were able to relocate them in their original positions. After responding to our rattling, most of the bucks (73 percent) moved to an area upwind of where they had been originally, even though we had rattled from a downwind location. In other words, a buck typically first moved downwind toward the rattling. After responding in this manner, each buck then usually moved back upwind beyond the place where we'd originally located him. Buck movements away from our rattling site were highest during the post-rut and lowest during the pre-rut periods.

We rattled more than once to 11 bucks to determine if bucks learned to avoid rattling. In every case but four, bucks responded during either the second, third, or fourth rattling session in the same way that they had responded during the first. The four exceptions failed to respond during the initial rattling session, but responded during the second. We rattled to Buck #1940, a 6.5-year-old during the

M.R. James rattled in this rutting buck less than 150 yards from his Montana home. Credit: M.R. James.

study's first year, four times. Each time he responded by becoming active and moving closer. Our results seem to indicate that bucks will continue to respond in a positive manner to rattling, even if they have already responded to a previous rattling session.

When the data were analyzed based upon each buck's known gross Boone and Crockett score, the results were surprising. Most hunters probably believe that trophy bucks are less likely than other bucks to respond to rattling. In this study, we found that the opposite was true. The bucks were separated into two groups. One group, which we called the "cull" group, included every buck with antlers that scored less than 130 Boone and Crockett points. All bucks with gross antler scores that exceeded 130 Boone and Crockett points were placed in the "trophy" group. Sixty-seven percent of the trophy bucks responded to our rattling compared to only 50 percent of the cull bucks. In addition, bucks in the cull group moved, on average, nearly two and one-half times farther between pre- and post-rattling locations than did those bucks in the trophy group.

## Our Results Should Improve Hunting Success

Our hope is that hunters will use our research results to increase their chances of success during upcoming seasons. Antler rattling is perhaps the most exciting deer hunting technique there is. Little compares to the sight of a mature buck with an immense rack rushing into view in response to rattling—that much we know.

We thank the many individuals who assisted with our antler-rattling and data collection. Rob, Fred, Bronson, Brent, Don, Justin, Scott, George, and William happily volunteered their time to work on this project. We also owe a debt of gratitude to the Rob and Bessie Welder Wildlife Foundation and its staff, the Neva and Wesley West Foundation and ranch owner Stuart Stedman, the University of Georgia, Texas A&M University-Kingsville, and the Caesar Kleberg Wildlife Research Institute for financial support of this research. See results on the following page.

***Table 1. Radio-collared buck response rates to antler-rattling by time of day and period of the breeding season (number in parentheses is number of bucks that responded divided by the number of bucks that were tested).***

| Period Of Breeding Season | Number Of Bucks Tested | Time Of Day | | | |
|---|---|---|---|---|---|
| | | 0730–1030 | 1030–1330 | 1330–1630 | TOTAL |
| Pre-rut | 5 | No Sessions Performed | 50% (1/2) | 33% (1/3) | 40% (2/5) |
| Rut peak | 14 | 100% (5/5) | 67% (2/3) | 67% (4/6) | 79% (11/14) |
| Post-rut | 14 | 75% (3/4) | 75% (3/4) | 83% (5/6) | 79% (11/14) |
| Total | 33 | 89% (8/9) | 67% (6/9) | 67% (1OT5) | 73% (24/33) |

***Table 2. Age and type of response (Y = yes, buck did respond; N = no, buck did not respond) of eleven radio-collared bucks that were rattled to on more than one occasion.***

| Buck Identification Number | Age | Rattling Session | | | |
|---|---|---|---|---|---|
| | | 1 | 2 | 3 | 4 |
| 180 | 4.5 | Y | Y | | |
| 602 | 4.5 | N | Y | | |
| 1540 | 4.5 | N | Y | Y | |
| 1721 | 4.5 | Y | Y | | |
| 1300 | 5.5 | Y | Y | | |
| 1462 | 5.5 | N | Y | | |
| 924 | 6.5 | Y | Y | | |
| 1940 | 6.5 | Y | Y | Y | Y |
| 1326 | 7.5 | Y | Y | | |
| 980 | 9.5 | N | N | | |
| 1561 | 9.5 | N | Y | | |

# Closing the Deal

In the good old days, when I'd catch a glimpse of a nice buck slinking along just out of range, I had four options at my disposal: I could wring my hands; clench my teeth; hold my breath; or try striking a deal with the Almighty ("Lord, steer that buck my way, and I'll be home for Christmas."). The grunt call and modern rattling tactics have added a couple more arrows to my quiver of tricks, but I'm still dealing with too many shoulda, coulda, woulda hunts. Rattling, in particular, unnerves me. No other hunting tactic produces as many close shaves that start out rosy and end up dismally.

Take the buck I once rattled within three paces of my treestand (seems like yesterday). He circled directly behind me, and I didn't know he was there until I heard him grunt. A tree limb obstructed a good view of his rack—not to mention a clean alley to his chest—so all I could do was hold my bow at half-mast and wait. Would that I drew right away! His massive 10-point rack, bobbing up and down m the brush as he trotted away, would have easily put him into the Boone and Crockett record books! But it was too late to get the draw, let alone aim for a killing shot. Another close shave.

If I had it to do over, I'd certainly do some things a bit differently. It's all about closing the deal, a subject I've become intimately familiar with of late. Subtle refinements to the game of calling and rattling deer can close the books on many accounts.

## Grunt Gumption

Although a few hunters and some Indian tribes have been calling deer for more than a century, the so-called grunt call era blossomed m the 1980s. Larry Richardson's paper, "Acoustics of White-tailed Deer," published in the Journal of Mammology in 1983, sparked much of the fire. Richardson documented seven different sounds after recording them with sensitive microphones and analyzing their "sonograms" with a sophisticated instrument, the Spectograph. In 1988, Tom Atkinson with the University of Georgia published his findings on the subject in the American Midland Naturalist; at least 12 different vocalizations were reported. From a pure hunting perspective, the grunt—particularly

David Hale (left) and Harold Knight (right) have helped pioneer the commercial grunt tube. Larry Richardson started it all with his paper, "Acoustics of White-tailed Deer," published in 1983.

the "tending grunt"—emerged as the call with the greatest in-the-woods potential.

We've come a long way since verifying that this call is worth taking along on every deer hunt, and in spite of its overuse hunters continue to score on bucks that would have otherwise escaped untouched. Still, I believe we can tweak the grunt call's overall effectiveness, especially for luring bucks those few extra critical steps. The starting point is picking a call with the proper pitch.

The first generation of grunt calls all sounded pretty much alike and were improvisations of reed-type duck calls (a plastic reed vibrating against a hollow chamber when blown gently). Eventually manufacturers learned better ways to mimic the pig-like grunt of a buck tending a receptive doe. Some designs proved to be better than others.

Producing the Moonbeams video series taught me this valuable lesson a few years ago. It all crystallized for me in the wee hours of a marathon editing session when I was trying to "sweeten" the sound of a distant grunting buck. (With mixers and software programs it's often possible to modify the audio track to make subtle sounds more distinct.) It took about a dozen passes to get it right, and that's when it struck me: The typical buck grunt in the wild isn't nearly as guttural as many commercial models make it out to be. In fact, a real grunt is comparatively sharp and piercing—like running a finger across the teeth of a large comb, only a little deeper.

I couldn't wait to test a raft of makes and models with my production company's sophisticated audio equipment to see which ones compared most favorably to the buck on film. After-hours sessions turned up a fistful of calls that my ears liked the best; however, my sound technician wasn't convinced, and he brought up a good point. "I think you're hearing what you want to hear," he said. "I can't tell that much of difference, and I'll bet the deer can't either." He might have been right about my ears, but it would boil down to how well deer can hear.

The sound frequency of whitetails is only 500–12,000 Hz, but by pointing each ear in a different direction, a deer can measure the difference in time it takes for approaching sound waves to reach each lobe. This allows them to pinpoint specific sounds with surprising accuracy.

## An Earful of Advice

Research indicates that a whitetail's brainstem response to pitch (sound frequency) is only 500-12,000 Hz, while a human's range is closer to 20-20,000 Hz. But deer have learned to make up for their less sensitive auditory system. The net result actually gives them the edge in hearing perception. I got a graphic illustration of this during an encounter with a Northwoods buck that looked as big as a moose.

A light ram had dampened my spirits that day, as my waterproof-breathable raingear was proving to be more breathable than waterproof. Just 15 more minutes, I thought to myself as I watched the intersection of two trails below my treestand in a towering white pine. Suddenly I got one of those sixth-sense sensations that told me to check my backside. I slowly turned my neck like a snowy owl as I kept my body statue-still. Sure enough, there, behind a big blowdown, stood a barrel-chested buck with a thick, chocolate-brown rack. For the longest time he didn't twitch a muscle, and I thought I might be hallucinating. But my heart began to race when I noticed his breath in the cool, damp air.

He was only two paces from a clear shot, but that's a huge distance when a buck decides to hold his ground until he's good and ready. Would you believe that, over the next 30 minutes, neither one of us didn't move an inch? What a sinking feeling it was to climb down my treestand in pitch dark, wondering what happened to the buck. To make matters worse, to this day a hitch in my neck reminds me of that painful incident.

But the lesson was a valuable one. I firmly believe that that buck was relying on listening skills. In fact, he never raised his nose to test the air. Perhaps his instincts told him that the steady rain would restrict the movement of odor molecules that evening, or that odors wouldn't carry as they normally would. Whatever the reason, the buck seemed to know that his ears were a better front-line defense than his nose.

Make no mistake, deer can hear. If you could swivel your ears like a whitetail, you could make a comfortable living with Barnum & Bailey, as deer ears can pivot 270 degrees. They function like sonar. By pointing each ear in a different direction, a deer can measure the difference in time it takes for approaching sound waves to reach each lobe. This, in turn, allows him to locate the source of specific sounds with surprising accuracy.

Armed with this knowledge and a fannypack stuffed with an assortment of grunt calls, I experimented on every deer I saw over a four-month stretch. While most calls produced intermittent results and none were foolproof, a handful of models proved more effective than their competitors. Because specific models come and go, depending

Always grunt louder if a buck appears to ignore you and grunt softer the closer the buck gets.

on sales and not necessarily on productiveness, I'll share the manufacturers: Hunter's Specialties, Primos Hunting Calls, M.A.D.). Calls, and Knight & Hale Game Calls. Again, to a casual observer most commercial grunt calls sound alike, save for loudness (more below). But I'm glad I took the time to compare apples with apples to avoid a few lemons. The main point is, if deer are consistently hanging up just out of range, your grunt call might sound more like a mallard than a whitetail. Find a better one.

Once you get your hands on an authentic-sounding call that produces the sharp treble (not muffled bass) we're looking for, learn how to use it wisely Let's rehearse a few do's and don'ts:

- Do call if the buck is losing ground and losing interest.
- Do call LOUDER if the buck appears to ignore first attempts.
- Do call SOFTER the closer the buck gets.
- Don't call if the buck is looking your way
- Don't call if the buck is gaining ground or appears interested.
- Don't call the same way (tone, duration, intensity) every time.
- Don't call when in doubt.

Keep in mind two additional pointers. First, no grunt call is worth a hoot if bucks can't hear it. That's why I always carry a "magnum" model with an extra-large sound chamber. It may sound a little "quacky" up close, but it really reverberates in the woods and gives me the extra carrying distance (up to 75 yards) I need to turn a distant buck. It's more of an attention-getter call (what the heck was that?) than a true lure call (where's that buck?). If you don't have time to switch from the former to the latter, be sure to muffle the sound with your fingers for up close coaxing.

Second, the tending grunt that simulates bucks in hot pursuit of does isn't the only call worth buying; two other calls also merit strong consideration. The so-called snort-wheeze is a sound that rutting bucks make when they're unusually aggressive. This doesn't happen very often, so don't overuse this "lure of last resort." M.A.D.)., by the way, makes an excellent one. And the so-called aggravated grunt, that ranges from a "bellow" to an elongated ticking sound, should also be part of your repertoire. An economical option is one of the new "variable" models that allow for adjustments to the call's pitch during operation. Some even produce a tonal range high enough for bleats.

Several game call manufacturers suggest that whitetails converse in a language as complex as humans, necessitating a myriad of calls to handle a myriad of hunting situations. While whitetails do "talk," I believe it's misleading to say they engage in dialogue. The calls discussed above should suffice for most hunting applications, with the possible exception of the doe bleat. This is an excellent long-distance attention-grabber for bucks, because its exceptionally high pitch pierces the woods particularly well. But a bleat's not going to transform you into the Pied Piper of Whitetaildom. And neither will a grunt call; nothing's magic and nothing always works. Still, if you blow the wrong call or make the wrong sound, you could blow—not close—the deal.

## Rattling: Quality Counts

Hunters must first put themselves in the Red Zone if they expect to score, meaning rattling can be a waste of time if you don't do your homework. For starters, always hunt balanced deer herds. We've noted that the lower the doe-to-buck ratio, the more competition among bucks, and the more "differences of opinion" will end up escalating into head-to-head combat.

Southern deer herds are notoriously unbalanced, with does typically outnumbering bucks by as much as 10:1 or more. At first glance, this is not the best place to rattle in a record-book buck. According to the Pope and Young Club, Florida ranked 46th on the list of record entries with only six. South Carolina placed 43rd with 17 typical Pope and Young entries. Discounting Texas' 10th place (449), and the in-between "midriff states of Kentucky (13th; 307) and Virginia (21st; 151), we're left pondering: Arkansas (24th; 110), Mississippi (25th; 101), Georgia (26th; 100), Tennessee (29th; 70), Alabama (30th; 68), and North Carolina (33rd; 59).

But statistics can be misleading. Times are changing. Thanks to educational efforts of the Quality Deer Management Association (QDMA), headquartered in Watkinsville, Georgia, many southern states have adopted regulatory changes that are beginning to alter the antler landscape. Consider that "harvestable" bucks must now have: At least eight antler points or be at least 15 inches wide in a six-county area in Georgia; in Mississippi, at least four antler points; in Arkansas, at least three antler points on one side. Further, in Tennessee the buck limit was reduced from 11 to three. And new regs in a tri-parish area in Louisiana implemented a six-point antler minimum while liberalizing antlerless deer harvest options.

So hunting's getting better in the South. A few falls ago, I found my thrill on a hill in South Carolina. The folks at Wildhaven enrolled 2,000 acres of prime whitetail habitat into a stepped-up deer-management program. The Shannon boys, Billy and Rusty, are smashing the notion that all whitetail bucks below the Mason-Dixon line are stunted and runt-racked. The key to growing braggin' bucks down South is elementary, they insist: Keep does in check, whittle down the buck population of 8-pointers, and let the 10-or-betters dominate the gene pool. Based on a quick week of bowhunting, I'd have to say the boys are doing just fine. For more information, contact Wildhaven, Rt. 3, Box 425-B, St. Mathews, SC 29135; 800/239-9951.

Billy (left) and Rusty (right) with sheds proving it's possible to grow big bucks down South.

This fine South Carolina buck I took during my stay at Wildhaven debunks the theory that you can't rattle effectively below the Mason-Dixon line. You just need balanced deer herds and rattle-able real estate.

Meanwhile, good rattling ground in the Midwest, where the Borealix and Dakotensis subspecies are known for producing impressive racks, is getting harder to find. To begin with, hunting pressure on public lands has escalated as private land access has dwindled in recent times. A chief contributor is the environmental movement. Nature-loving non-hunters relocating to rural areas have been deceived into thinking they can "preserve" wildlife; they post their lands and wall off hunters. Meanwhile, numerous "coalitions" funded by left-of-center foundations, such as the Pew Charitable Trust and the Turner Foundation, have effectively stifled rural economies: Logging, agriculture, dairy farming, mining, and ranching have especially been targeted. Most of these landowners used to welcome hunters but now many depend on "trespass fees" to make ends meet.

Then there's a serious access issue spawned by the "wilderness society" crowd. Numerous NGOs (non-governmental organizations) are working behind the scenes to "unmanage" forested tracts by designating multiple-purpose areas as permanent wildernesses. A key component of this movement is closing off roads and trails, such as the Clinton Administration's roadless campaign affecting 60 million acres of federal land. An unfortunate side-effect is increased hunting pressure; limiting access concentrates, rather than spreads out, where hunters can go.

One solution for dealing with this trend is the Hunting Club. Enterprising hunters pooling their resources can lease ground managed primarily for hunting and secondarily for other activities such as farming, logging, and ranching. What does this have to do with rattling? Everything. Rattling in quality whitetails in a quality habitat is but a pipe dream if you don't critically analyze every potential hotspot, whether or not you pay for hunting rights.

## Rattle-able Real Estate

As I strive to refine my hunting techniques over the years, one thing I've learned the hard way is that not all hunting ground is created equal. It's a cruel joke that two seemingly identical parcels can produce disparate results. While they may both host the same number of deer, including mature bucks, one will usually be more rattle-able than the other. You need to know what to look for before you leap, and it doesn't matter if you're dealing with Scottland County, Missouri; Pike County, Illinois; Buffalo County Wisconsin; or Dooley County, Georgia.

For example, in spite of rattling's considerable carrying distance—up to several hundred yards—it's pointless to rattle where bucks can't hear you. It should go without saying that you need to pick a spot where bucks are likely to hang out during hunting hours. But this flies right over the head of many hunters. Stated simply, there are only three places you can rattle—where deer feed, where they bed, and travel corridors connecting the two. Which type of habitat should you be concentrating on?

The best place to rattle is a travel corridor. Why? Because confining serious rattling sessions to where bucks are likely to be on their feet will bring more dingers to the bell. The Full Moon tactic of rattling the cage of bedded bucks is often necessary because of the number of "C" days (bedding areas) the Moon Guide predicts in a given lunar month of 28 days. But if you get a chance to rattle on a "B" or "A" day, you'll be dealing with more daytime buck movement. Here's the secret: For some reason bucks on their feet are more responsive to rattling than those that are bedded down. It seems that once a buck curls up for the day he gets into a bunker mentality and survival dominates his thinking. You might be able to tease him within hearing distance, but coaxing him those critical extra yards will be tough.

Next, narrow down travel corridors where natural funnels and terrain features constrict deer traffic. It's a familiar tune, no doubt, but I've seen a lot of hunters make two critical mistakes. Either they waste time over "hot" buck sign that's typically associated with a buck's bedding area, or they try to set up where the terrain is relatively featureless. Hunters should spend the extra time looking for a spot where bucks are likely to be coming and going rather than settling for low-percentage areas.

A shortcut might be the "corner-cutter." Regardless of the time of year, bucks will take the quickest route connecting their destination and point of origin. Start by determining where bucks and does are bedding—they never bed together with the exception of a buck tending an estrus doe—and slip m between. Exactly where depends on the topography. Conspicuous terrain features always shape the way a buck is likely to travel. It may be a steep bluff or a river bend; the head of a deep hollow or a ridge point; a saddle on a knoll; or the edge of a swamp. Sooner or later a buck skirting one of these features will show up on his way to a hot date. Less-distinct features can be equally effective: ditch crossings, dips in a field, beaver dams, and the like.

The corner-cutter becomes my top priority when "rut economics" comes into play. When the demand for does exceeds the supply, you can count on accelerated buck movement. It's a wonderful time to plop down at a key spot and let the bucks come to you.

An interesting exception is deliberately setting up shop near traditional doe bedding areas when the Rut Guide predicts that the prerut is about to unfold. "Doe bedding areas are taylor-made for the prerut," says Mike Weaver. "Bucks get tired of waiting for does to come into estrus, especially when only one or two have cycled in a local herd. Bucks hate to miss out, so they scent-check each doe bedding area in their territory to see who's hot and who's not. Sometimes a buck will even kick does out of their beds to get a better whiff. If you've got stands placed in the right spots, you could see action any time of the day during this stage [of the] rut."

I've successfully rattled in bucks on opening day, during the rut, and just after the rut when a blanket of snow covered the landscape. While timing is important, the better the spot, the better the rattling. When evaluating prospective hunting areas, make a list of these key components to rate their true potential.

## Rattling Basics and Beyond

Now that you're m position to score, it's time to call the right play. Before we get to rattling's best-kept secret, here are the ground rules.

Always rattle:

- Regardless of the calendar period, not just the during the rut.
- Aggressively during the rut, particularly during the prerut and the post-rut "trolling" stage when competition for breeding rights is keen.
- Conservatively if you find yourself dealing with a lot of adolescent bucks; one of these juveniles could peg you and blow your cover.

Never rattle:

- For "the heck of it" (expect results and be prepared to shoot at the drop of a hat).
- At a buck facing your direction.
- At a buck that's traveling toward you.

How skilled does one have to be to effectively counterfeit a pair of bucks butting heads? In my opinion, technique is over-rated with two glaring exceptions.

An incident that occurred while hunting with J & S Trophy Hunts in southern Iowa proved to me that technique isn't everything. I'd timed the rut just right and managed to score on a nice 10-pointer in spite of unusually hot weather that severely restricted daytime whitetail movement. One evening in camp a hunter complained about "another guy setting up too close" who was "rattling too often." I had a hard time swallowing the notion that my friend, Steve Shoop, would compromise any hunter's chances (Shoop has earned my respect as the best in the business). So I jumped into the conversation.

"Are you sure it was a hunter rattling and not real bucks fighting?" I asked.

"Damn sure," snapped the hunter. "The guy was using [a set] of those cheap imitation gizmos—ya know, made out of plastic."

"How could you tell?" I persisted.

"It was easy," he insisted. "They sounded hollow and tinny Besides, [the guy] carried on all morning long. Bucks don't do that."

Well, that hunter was dead wrong. I spared his ego by not telling him I was the closest hunter to him and that I'd glassed a pair of bucks fighting off and on from dawn to nearly noon that morning. So the question begs, if this guy can't discern the real thing, how can he reproduce it?

This anecdote raises another point that costs hunters opportunities for closing the deal: When the rut's on, they don't rattle enough! Scrap the conventional "wisdom" that says too much rattling will "give your position away." Rattling is a natural sound during the breeding season, and deer know it. Besides, bucks are incapable of reasoning, "Hey, there's too much fighting going on around here; must be hunters trying to fool us." If you're going to rattle, RATTLE.

If you're going to rattle, RATTLE. And be READY.

On the other hand, there's a lot more to rattling than smacking a pair of main beams together. In fact, when I rattle, I mostly grind. Surely you've heard stories of bucks "locking up" for extended periods (each year bucks fight to their deaths because they couldn't unlock). Fact is, when bucks go head to head, they mostly push and shove and shake their heads. This is precisely the sound we want to imitate most, not merely the initial crack of antlers making contact at the beginning of a heated contest. So make sure GRINDING is the main goal; twist those antlers against each other instead of banging away.

In spite of all of these precautions, chances are you'll still end up rattling m a buck that circles in the thick stuff or hangs up short. This is especially common for bowhunters, with their limited effective range. After mulling this over for nearly two decades, I've concluded that the cause and the cure are one and the same. According to Pope and Young statistics, about 80 percent of all record-book bucks are taken from treestands. While it's hard to argue with the benefits of an elevated position—unequalled visibility, superior scent control, improved carrying distance for calling—this tactic hurts rattling as much as it helps.

Here's why rattling from a treestand is often a good-beginning, bad-ending proposition. When a buck picks up on the racket, either he closes ground quickly or circles cautiously. But many times your position above the ground prevents the buck from pinpointing your location. So he pulls up short a "comfortable distance" away as he evaluates what he thought he heard while waiting for additional clues. Sure, a timely grunt call might help, as alluded to earlier, but what the buck really wants to hear is the fighting sound of rivals squaring off.

Let's make sure we know this is fact and not supposition. Three reasons explain why the sound of cracking and grinding antlers consistently attract bucks like no other in nature: 1) During the rut,

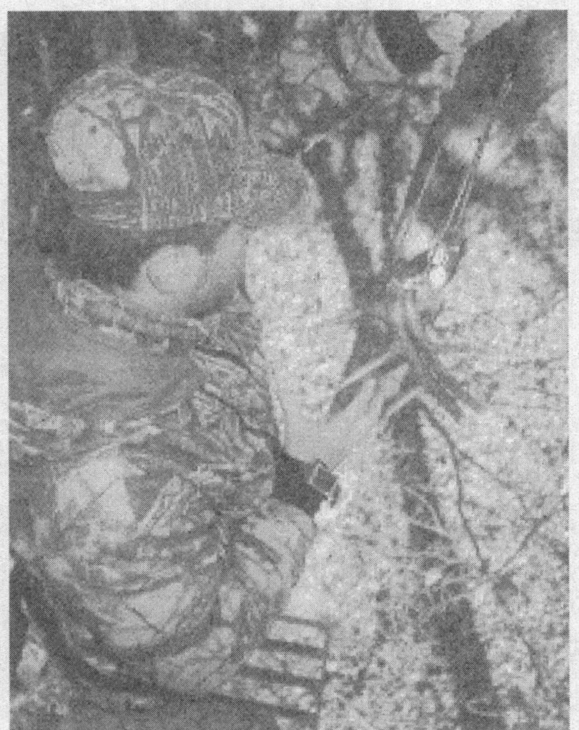

My slick trick of jangling from a treestand is sure to close the deal more often than not.

bucks instinctively know hot does are often part of a fight scene; 2) early m the fall, before hunting pressure puts bucks on the defensive, curiosity is a natural response; 3) about a month after the primary rut, bucks contend aggressively for a limited number of "second estrus" does. Add it all up, and it all adds up: When stuck in neutral, all a buck wants to hear is MORE RATTLING.

But this is impossible, you say, as any movement will surely tip off the buck. Not necessarily. You've made a good pitch, and now it's time to close the deal. The solution, however, requires a willingness to stake the outcome on a novel rattling technique that seems risky at best. I call it "jangling." Specifically, I'm talking about aggressively clanging together a pair of antlers suspended from a rope below your treestand. I first heard about it from Mike Weaver, who perfected the technique from years of experimenting on mature bucks. "Without jangling," he confided, "four [of my] Pope and Young bucks would have certainly gotten away. They were on a half-trot when they did a complete 180 and ended right in my lap." Indeed, when you pull a Mr. Bow jangles impersonation, it gives a buck something to zero in on, and he often bolts on a dead run straight for your treestand.

Naturally, considerable caution and forethought are necessary for handling standoffish bucks. For example, I've learned the hard way that I better stow my antlers at the base of my tree rather than hanging them on a tree limb at arm's reach. By tying a rope to my treestand so the antlers dangle at ground level, I can reach over unnoticed and give them a timely yank without suffering detection. And timing is always critical. Just as the best time to grunt at a sighted buck is when he swings his head, you want to jangle just as the buck is about to head out.

An Illinois bruiser fell for this tactic recently. The symmetrical 10-pointer tiptoed cautiously toward me about 15 minutes after I'd rattled hard for a minute or so. In fact, I was considering a second session when I first laid eyes on him. Predictably; he froze about 75 yards out, so I tried a seductive grunt when he wasn't looking. No interest. I waited until he took his next step before I grunted a second time. Again no interest. But when he turned to leave, I yanked on the rope and jangled as hard as I could. Whamo! A few leaps and bounds put the buck right below me facing my direction. After a brief standoff, the buck hopped into a thicket that was, well, too thick to shoot through. Though it was another close shave, I squeezed two extra chances out of the encounter. That buck was lucky . . .

When you're trying to drum up some buck business, always start each session from above. But when you're done, always return the antlers to the ground rather than the other way around. In fact, I typically conclude each rattling session by letting the antlers free-fall with a crash landing. I can't prove this triggers more bucks, but I know I've rattled in a lot of them since I adopted this ritual.

In addition, it's a good idea to add the sound of rustling leaves to the sounds of clangin' 'n' bangin'. Gently bounce the antlers against the forest floor, rolling them over dried leaves, sticks, and grass. Another ploy is unleashing more rope and casting the antlers 15 feet or so off to one side. Then drag them back before more jangling. These extra sounds tossed into the mix can really make a difference at times. Simply put, they're what a buck expects to hear when he thinks rivals are squaring off in the distance.

Grunting and rattling are the most effective aggressive tactics available to modern hunters. While they aren't complicated or difficult to master, they're easy to use incorrectly. But these new wrinkles will help even the score and close more deals.

**JURY-RIGGED FOR RATTLING**

This seven-step program is a sure cure for Post-Rattling Depression:

1. Start with a medium-sized pair of main beams: a rack that would score about 120 Pope and Young inches is about right (any smaller and the sound won't carry far. any larger and the sound might be too intimidating to other deer).
2. Saw off the brow tines. They'll only get in the way and could cause injury. Likewise, remove unessential non-typical points. and file down the burrs at the base of the main beams to prevent chafing.
3. Drill a quarter-men hole, just above the pedicle. through both main beams.
4. Cut a heavy-duty polyester cord about three feet long and thread it through both holes. Tie a pair of double-knots at each end to prevent slippage.
5. Tie a loop in the middle of the cord with a simple overhand knot (the loop should be about one inch in diameter).
6. Cut a rope to lengtn-at least 10 feet longer than necessary to reach the ground from the height of your treestand. Secure one end to the above loop with a pair of half-hitches and cinch the other end to the seat of your treestand; knot it up where you can reach it without looking down.
7. Always start each ratting session from above and stow the antlers at ground level between sessions.

# SCENTS

## Behind the Labels: Basic Types of Scent Reduction Products

Here is the thing: dogs can be trained to find an explosive material, sealed in plastic, buried in the ground, and untouched for years. They do it routinely in war-torn areas where land mines have been used indiscriminately. For that matter, I'm still impressed when my brittany goes dashing at full speed 15 or 20 yards past a small clump of cover, only to slam on the brakes, do a 180, and lock up on point. A single bobwhite quail might be in that clump of cover—a lone, non-smoking, non-perspiring little bird that did not wash with scented shampoo that morning, or eat garlic at dinner or bacon for breakfast, or stop to pump gas on his way to the field, or—well, you get the point. Everything produces some odor, and dogs, along with most of the animals we hunt, have incredible olfactory abilities. I will refrain from enumerating all the possible sources of odor on the human body. Are you skeptical that it is possible for a hunter to truly eliminate his scent, even for a short while? I am.

The real question, I believe, is not whether it is possible to entirely eliminate odor. The real question for bowhunters is whether or not it is possible to reduce odor sufficiently to give hunters an edge they would not otherwise have. Would you wash with unscented soap every time you went hunting if it meant that on one occasion you might slip within 35 yards of a bedded mule deer buck, instead of getting picked off at 55 yards? Would you wear an odor eliminating outfit including hat and headnet day after day if it meant that sometime in the next three years a 160-class whitetail buck might stop for 3 seconds at 25 yards before running off, as opposed to turning and running without a pause when it got to 30 yards? Realistically, chances are you will never know for sure if the bear you just arrowed would have turned and run before offering a shot had you not sprinkled baking soda in your boots or used non-scented detergent to wash your parka.

It is difficult to be certain about the degree of effectiveness of these and other products in a given situation for several reasons. Little truly independent research has been done on the subject. Scent, as we have seen, is a matter of volatile (gaseous) molecules being carried through the air to the sensory organs, in this case nasal passages, of an animal. While the technology and methodology may exist to determine the concentration of these molecules in a given controlled area, few independent labs with the necessary resources have to date had sufficient motivation to conduct the kind of research that would provide useful information to hunters. Further complicating things, hunters are dealing with biology and uncontrolled conditions, not machines in a lab. A machine may indicate the concentration of various molecules in an enclosed space, but that does not tell us how those molecules behave in a forest or on a prairie. It also doesn't tell us at what level of concentration a given species under given circumstances can detect those molecules, or how it will react to various concentrations of them.

What hunters have mostly relied upon, then, is common sense and anecdotal evidence accumulated by hunters in the field. I'll confess a bias: I'm highly skeptical of common sense. For thousands of years common sense told us the earth is flat and the sun circles it. Science came along to tell us the earth is round and it circles the sun, and I'm inclined to go with science. Having said, that I would nonetheless point out that I am sure I will smell my hunting partner more quickly, from further away, and with a more noticeable reaction, after a week in elk camp than was the case on the first day of the hunt. Is it unreasonable to suspect that the same is true for most game animals? Anecdotal hunting evidence is far from perfect, but it is evidence and should not be ignored, especially in the absence of other evidence. And anecdotal evidence suggests that scent reduction can make a difference. Virtually every consistently successful bowhunter I know makes some effort to reduce or control scent in some way.

Not all the anecdotal evidence available on the subject comes from hunters. Among the more convincing sources of evidence are trappers. Though I've done very little trapping personally, as a hunter I've long been fascinated by it. If hunters are concerned about odor control and the use of scent, successful trappers seem to be obsessed with it. Evidence from trappers strikes me as particularly convincing for the reason that trapping by nature tends to reduce or eliminate many of the variables involved in hunting. For instance, if I'm hunting an elk wallow, a bull approaches, stops momentarily, then retreats into the brush, any number of things might explain the behavior. Did he catch my scent in the air? Did he come across scent I left on the ground as I approached the wallow? Did he see me? Hear me? Did another animal scare him off or warn him of my presence? I will probably never know. In the case of trapping, most of these variables would not apply. Some trappers run trap lines daily through the season, and almost all of them over the years experiment with a variety of locations and trap sets. Further, much as most of them enjoy trapping, trapping is hard work, and many trappers are looking for supplemental income. They tend to do what works, with as little wasted time and effort as possible. The fact that almost all of them are convinced careful scent control is a major factor in their success is telling.

Somewhere out there, perhaps, is a consistently successful bowhunter who pays no attention to scent control. I just haven't met him. Imperfect though the evidence may be, thousands upon thousands of hunters have logged countless hours in the field and have come to the conclusion that taking some measures to reduce scent while hunting is worth the effort and the expense.

## Sources of Odor

When hunters talk about controlling odor, they are talking about two things. One involves the odors with which they or their clothing and gear may be contaminated, including soaps and shampoos, shaving creams, lotions, ointments, smoke, gas fumes, oils, mothballs, foods and beverages, cooking odors, and any other substance that hunters or their gear may come in contact with. For that matter, the clothing or gear may itself emit odor. The sources of most of these odors are clear enough. They are in our kitchens, our bathrooms, our garages, basements, and even storage sheds. When we leave home, they may be in our cars and trucks, in the diners we stop in for breakfast, in the gas stations where we stop for gas. Sometimes, they are just plain in the air around us.

Another type of odor is the one produced continuously by hunters' bodies and their breath, or more specifically by various secretions and the action of bacteria on these secretions. Most perspiration is produced by eccrine glands that cover the entire body, and has little if any odor, consisting primarily of water and a few salts. Apocrine glands, however, produce perspiration that is much higher in fats and proteins. These fats and proteins, along with hair, dead skin, and other detritus form a rich medium for bacteria, and it is the action of these bacteria on the fats and other ingredients of perspiration that causes most body odor. In effect, apocrine glands are human scent glands. Most are located in the armpits and the pubic areas. (Interestingly, some of us have more apocrine glands than do others. Asian populations, for instance, have far fewer apocrine glands, and in some cases none at all. In Japan, body odor is considered a medical condition.) It is no accident, of course, that the areas of the body containing apocrine glands tend to be covered in hair. Hair contributes to an environment favorable for the formation of odor-causing bacteria, and holds odor. Laugh if you like at those hard-core trophy hunters out there who shave their underarms during hunting season—I know I do—but they may be on to something. I haven't yet got up the nerve to ask them if they shave their groin areas, also.

We can speculate about whether body odors or contaminant scents are more important, and which of these odors animals may or may not associate with humans or with danger, but the simplest and safest course of action for any hunter concerned about scent control is to try and keep all odors to an absolute minimum. Knowing how best to do this requires a basic understanding of how various scent reduction products work. Though manufacturers like to imply that their products will reduce or eliminate any form of scent, the fact is that some are better suited to reducing body odors at its source, while others are better suited for applying to clothing and other gear. At the time of this writing, scent control is a rapidly growing part of the hunting industry and new technology, much of it borrowed from medical and other applications, is developing so rapidly that it is difficult to stay abreast of it. Much of what follows is to some extent a sort of snapshot of the industry as it exists today.

## Start Clean, Stay Clean

There is no scent reduction product that cannot be overwhelmed at some point. Scent control

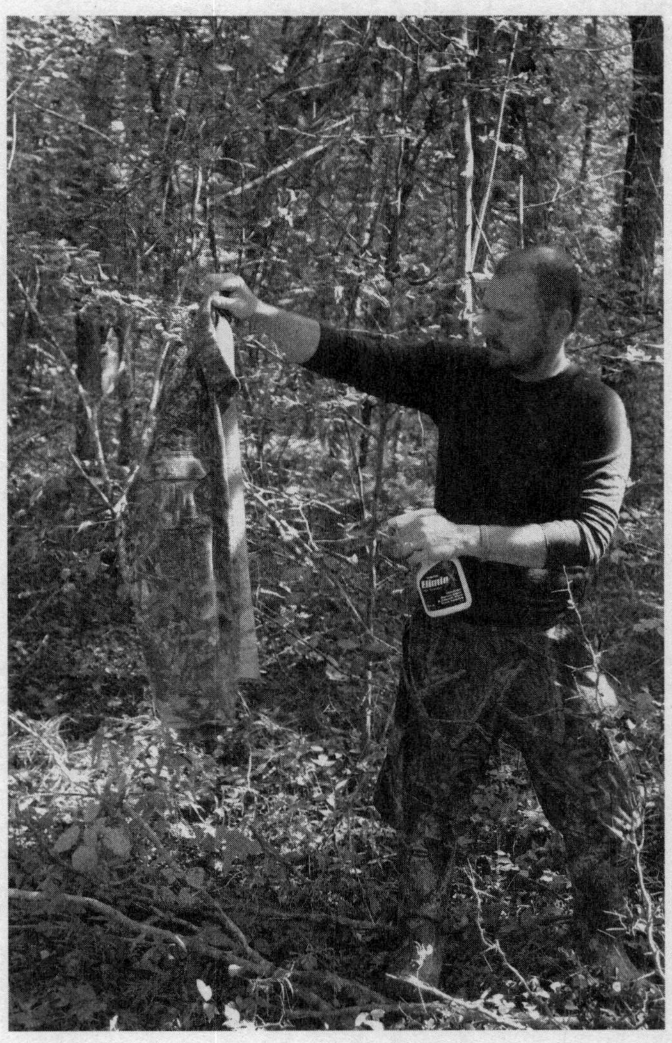

Whenever possible, keep hunting clothes in sealed containers until it's time to hunt. Apply scent reducers right before hunting.

begins with getting clean and staying as clean as possible, and it only stands to reason that the cleaner the hunter, the less chance for any scent control product to fail. In fact, the scent-control regimen of some very successful hunters is as simple as washing themselves and their clothing thoroughly in scent-free soaps or detergents. Starting clean is easy enough, but staying clean is more challenging. What often happens is that hunters work up a sweat getting to their stand (or into their stand). Leaving off the parka or jacket until getting settled into a stand can alleviate that problem. Increasing numbers of bowhunters prefer ladder stands and ground blinds, partly because we bowhunters are an aging population. In the process, they are discovering that not only are ladder stands and ground blinds easier and safer, but getting into them is also quicker and quieter, and does not require working up a sweat, especially compared to climbers.

## The Chemistry Behind the Products

Essentially, there are three types of commercially produced products intended to reduce odors. These are 1) antimicrobials, designed to prevent the formation of certain odors by killing or inhibiting the growth of bacteria that cause these odors, or by neutralizing acidity 2) products designed to prevent the formation of the gas molecules that form odors, or which create a chemical reaction such as oxidation, to destroy odors, and 3) products with materials such as activated carbon that adsorb odors. Some products combine two of these types of scent control, and by using various layers of clothing or different types of scent control products, many hunters simultaneously employ all three.

Sodium bicarbonate—more commonly referred to as baking soda—is famous for its ability to control odors by neutralizing acids, including the acids present in perspiration. It has some antimicrobial properties in that its presence creates a less inviting habitat for many types of bacteria, and it absorbs moisture, which creates an environment in which bacteria can thrive. It is the active ingredient in a number of the scent control products being marketed to hunters. If the product suggests you can gargle with it, there is a good chance its active ingredient is baking soda. The best way to use many of these products is to apply them directly to the skin after showering. Apply them everywhere, if you like, but pay special attention to the areas that perspire the most. Plain baking soda can be useful, either as a deodorant (mix it with a little corn starch to keep it from clumping), as a toothpaste, or a mouth rinse. For hunters who cannot (or prefer not) to line-dry clothes, a few tablespoons of baking soda in the dryer can reduce odors present in the dryer.

Most common deodorants are antimicrobials, including the unscented products marketed to hunters. Antiperspirants differ from deodorants in that they clog the pores to prevent perspiration, as opposed to acting on the perspiration. Though they might contain zinc or aluminum or other ingredients that have an antimicrobial effect, they prevent body odor primarily by preventing the perspiration on which bacteria thrive.

A number of herbs, minerals, and other substances are claimed to have deodorant effects, in some cases by acting as antimicrobials. Many people are interested in these because of allergies to ingredients often found in commercial deodorants, or because the commercial products cause irritation, or because they have concerns about the long-term health effects of deodorants. Determining the validity of claims made on behalf of "natural" deodorants is difficult if not impossible, and most of the evidence is purely anecdotal. The lack of scientific evidence supporting many of the claims may simply be an indication that there are no organizations sufficiently motivated to spend time and money researching the effectiveness of, for instance, coconut oil, as a deodorant. Coconut oil is among the substances sometimes touted as a deodorant, along with chlorophyll, sesame seed oil, aloe, and various "crystals" and minerals, often containing bauxite, alum, or zinc. Chlorophyll and zinc in particular have long been touted as natural deodorants.

Another antimicrobial is silver, which is increasingly being used in clothing. The U.S. army has for some time issued to infantrymen socks with silver in the fabric to control the growth of bacteria that give rise to a number of foot ailments. In more recent years, several makers of hunting garments offer socks and undergarments incorporating silver. The idea, again, is to prevent the growth of the bacteria that cause body odors.

Stopping odors by controlling the conditions that create them is one approach; another approach entails a chemical interaction with substances to prevent volatility, or destroying odors as quickly as they form through oxidation. As we have seen, odors are formed when substances release molecules into the atmosphere. Some substances are not volatile. Steel, for instance, is not volatile and normally has no odor. A chemical reaction that controls volatility—that is, one that stops the release of molecules into the air—prevents odors. Many of the scent reduction products that are sprayed onto the skin, clothing, or gear, operate by reducing volatility or creating other chemical changes that prevent the formation of odors.

Finally, there are the products that adsorb or absorb odors. Manufacturers like to point up the differences, but from the hunter's perspective it matters little. Technically, adsorption refers to a process in which molecules cling to the surface of other molecules. Absorption, on the other hand, refers to a process in which molecules are actually drawn into or contained within other molecules. Doubtless the best known of these products (in the hunting industry) exists in the form of carbon-impregnated clothing. Any bowhunter who has looked at an ad for these garments probably has a basic understanding of how they are supposed to work. Tiny carbon granules trap and hold odor molecules, preventing their release into the air. Eventually the granules are full up, and can contain no more odor molecules. An application of heat releases some, if not all of these molecules, freeing the carbon granules to trap odors again. The use of activated carbon has long had industrial and military applications, usually for controlling or neutralizing toxic substances of various kinds. The military often issues carbon clothing to personnel in areas where there is the threat of chemical weapons. It works.

The use of carbon clothing for odor control is more controversial. In industrial applications, carbon that has adsorbed its capacity and will be re-used is heated at temperatures that would destroy any garments. In military applications, carbon clothing is issued in airtight containers, and is intended to be used once, then discarded. The argument is often made that the temperatures to which carbon clothing is exposed in clothes dryer are insufficient to achieve the desired results. The case made by the manufacturers of these garments is that heat at these temperatures, while it may not entirely eliminate the scent molecules trapped by the carbon, will eliminate enough of them to enable the garment to work as intended. In addition, to some extent time may be substituted for temperature. By exposing carbon clothing to moderate temperatures for longer periods of time, we can achieve the same results as if we exposed it to higher temperatures for a short period of time.

Critics also suggest that to be effective, carbon must have scent molecules forced through it under pressure, or the scent molecules will simply find their way around the carbon molecules. Put an air filter in the middle of a room, as one argument goes, and it will have little if any effect. Put it in ducts or vents where air is forced through it, and it can work. This does not explain how carbon clothing protects military personnel from toxic chemicals, though it may be a simple matter of the concentration of carbon used. (That is, if the carbon particles are sufficiently concentrated that molecules cannot get around them, they can be effective.) The arguments about carbon clothing go back and forth. In recent years, lawsuits have been filed against the makers of carbon hunting clothing, and in at least one case, a ruling has been made. It was the kind of ruling that enables both sides to claim partial victory. In plain English, it seemed to suggest that some of the ads on the part of the carbon clothing companies had to be toned down. The implication is that the product may be useful, but claims of 100% effectiveness (as in "Forget the wind, just hunt") were excessive.

## Cyclodextrins

Harnessing technology to control odors is a relatively recent phenomenon in the hunting community, but major industries ranging from the medical industry to companies involved in food, sanitation, household cleaners and detergents, and others have long experimented with technical means of reducing or eliminating odor. One fairly recent development along these lines has been the increasing use of cyclodextrins for odor control. (Probably the best known product currently using cyclodextrins is Proctor and Gamble's Febreze, a popular household odor eliminator.) In addition to reducing or eliminating odor, cyclodextrins can actually store and deliver odor (such as perfumes), and have also been used to release and store medications gradually into the body over time.

In layman's terms, here is how they work. Cyclodextrins are complex molecules, similar to sugars, and are shaped much like a doughnut. They tend to join together in strings that form tubes or hollowed out cones. The exterior is hydrophobic (repels water), while the interior is hydrophilic (attracts water). In addition, they can be ionically charged to create an electrostatic attraction with other molecules. The effect is that they attract and absorb other molecules (including the volatile molecules that are the source of odors), storing them in their hollow cavities. Eventually, of course, all the cyclodextrins are full of molecules. When this happens, additional cyclodextrins must be applied to the source of odor, at least in the case of sprays such as Febreze. In the case of clothing that contains cyclodextrins in the fabric, the odor molecules can be removed simply by washing and drying the garment.

Sound too good to be true? The scent control industry is highly competitive, and every product has its critics, many of whom make other products, or are on the payroll of those who do. There is a great deal of protective secrecy, rumors fly everywhere, and lawyers make a lot of money initiating or defending suits. Getting solid, unbiased information is difficult, and manufacturers often start to sound like politicians: "I'm sorry, but I can't discuss that while it's in litigation."

So far, the criticism sometimes heard regarding cyclodextrins is that they are good at containing certain odor molecules, not so good at containing others. So, for instance, cyclodextrins may be good at containing body odor, but may not eliminate odors of frying bacon. Or they might be good at eliminating the odor from the dog that rubbed against your leg on your way out the door, but not at eliminating campfire smoke. Dan River, the company that makes No-Trace hunting clothing, insists that the cyclodextrins in their clothing will effectively reduce body odor as well as external contaminants that may contaminate hunting clothes. Who is correct? It is true that a given cyclodextrin may attract and hold certain odor molecules, and not others. It is also true, however, that to some extent cyclodextrins can be tailored to work for a variety of molecules. It may be possible to make use of a variety of cyclodextrins to operate on a variety of odors. As a case in point, Proctor and Gamble claims that Febreze is effective on a wide range of household odors, from pet odors to cooking odors to cigarette smoke.

Just how much odor can cyclodextrins absorb? As of this writing, No Trace is the only brand of hunting garments making use of cyclodextrins. "If you sit for awhile in a truck that just smells strongly of gas fumes," concedes No Trace's Dewey Knight, "you could end up out in the woods hunting before the No Trace has an opportunity to absorb all the odor." Normally though, continues Knight, you can hunt up to a week before you'll need to wash the clothing to reactivate its scent reducing properties. "Of course that is under typical hunting conditions," Knight explains. "If you're very active and the weather is warm and you're sweating a lot, that time might be reduced." In any case, the same things can be said for most any odor reduction process on the market. All can be overwhelmed with very heavy odors, and the performance of all of them can be affected by activity levels, temperature, humidity, and other factors.

The fact that cylcodextrins have been used for some time, and continue to be used, in the medical and pharmaceutical industry as well as in other industries, suggests that they have some legitimacy. In fact, cyclodextrins have been tested by the scientific community, including specifically the use of cyclodextrins in clothing. Two tests I'm familiar with were conducted at the University of North Carolina, and by the Journal of Inclusion Phenomena and Macrocylic Chemistry. The limitation of these studies, and others like them, is that they examined the ability of cyclodextrins to increase the effectiveness of flame retardants, and to hold for release various kinds of perfumes or antimicrobials. Specific tests of their abilities to absorb odors were not to my knowledge conducted, although the tests that were conducted yielded positive results and could be construed to indicate that cyclodextrins in clothing are—or at least have the potential to be—effective odor reducers.

As always, hunters will doubtless conduct their own tests on these products, and will arrive at their own conclusions about whether or not this technology works. The tests will be less than scientific. On the other hand, they will be conducted in the only arena that truly matters to the hunter, which is out in the woods in the presence of game. And, scientific as any more formal tests might be, it is probable that the only way to know for certain if such a product can defeat the super sensitive noses of game animals is to wear them in the presence of game animals and observe their responses. For sure, what we can say at a minimum about cyclodextrins at this point is that they represent a promising technology for helping hunters with the most challenging aspect of big game hunting

## Blinds

Blinds haven't traditionally been thought of as scent reduction products, so I've given them their own category. When I say "traditionally," I mean that few hunters would associate blinds with reductions in scent—but that's not to say the thought has never occurred to any hunters. In recent years, with the growing popularity of commercially produced, fully enclosed blinds, a number of hunters have suggested that these blinds could help contain scent. Use of such ground blinds is increasing in popularity, but they have not been commonly used long enough to accumulate the kind of anecdotal evidence that has built up around other scent reducing products.

Still, it doesn't seem inconceivable that blinds could afford some degree of scent control, if only because they block the wind, thereby preventing it from carrying at least some scent downwind. More recently, some blind makers have been offering in blinds the same carbon-impregnated fabrics that are offered in hunting garments. Short of that, hunters are well-advised to avoid contaminating blinds with foreign odors to the extent possible. Hunters generally prefer to set up blinds at least a few days prior to hunting from them, mostly to allow game to become accustomed to seeing them in the environment. It could be, though, that allowing the blinds to de-odorize, or the game to become accustomed to their odor, is at least as important as visual considerations. Many hunters also pile dirt, leaves, sticks, and other debris around the base of the blind, to aid in preventing the escape of odor from inside the blind. Whether blinds are designed with scent reduction in mind or not, it only makes sense for bowhunters using ground blinds to keep scent considerations in mind.

## What Does Science Say?

Many readers aren't old enough to recall the controversy in the 1960s and '70s surrounding the health effects of smoking cigarettes. Suffice it to say that there was no shortage of scientists and even medical professionals willing to state for the record that there was no evidence supporting the notion that cigarettes increased the likelihood of contracting cancer. Sadly, many of them continued to maintain that position in the face of mountains of evidence to the contrary. Much of the public didn't know what to believe. That issue has been resolved by time, of course. Maybe a better comparison is the more current controversy surrounding global warming. Unless you happen to be a climatologist, you are more or less in the position of having to choose which scientists you believe. The science of scent reduction—at least as it pertains to its practical applications in hunting situations—is still in its infancy. There are arguments and counter-arguments, with experts testifying for and against the efficacy of different scent reducing products.

In the only truly independent scientific study of scent control I have found—at least as it might have some relevance to a hunting situation—Dr. John Shivik of the National Wildlife Research Center extensively tested the ability of seven search dogs to find people wearing carbon-impregnated clothing, compared to their ability to locate people not wearing such clothing. The people were placed in blinds, the dogs were allowed to sniff a piece of fabric previously handled by the people in the blinds, and dogs and handlers were then given specified amounts of time in which to locate the subjects. In all but one of 42 trials, dogs found all the test subjects within the allotted time. Dr. Shivik found that persons not wearing carbon suits were detected from slightly greater distances, but did not find the differences in distance to be statistically significant. While noting that he believed it possible for individuals to put on sealed carbon suits in such a way as to remain undetectable to dogs, his overall conclusion was that for practical purposes, carbon suits are ineffective.

If you think that settles the issue once and for all, you are not a scientific thinker.

In fairness, if we are going to be truly scientific in our approach, we have to concede that the results of one test are never conclusive. It will be interesting to see if other researchers can duplicate these results, or if they arrive at different conclusions. As a side note, it is significant (though not surprising) that Shivik did observe significant differences in the time it took dogs to find subjects, and these differences were related to barometric pressure, humidity, and the variability of the wind. Shivik also speculated that one probable source of contamination of the suits was that wearers handled them in putting them on. Bowhunters using these suits might want to consider wearing rubber gloves when donning them.

Scent-Lok's Glenn Sesselman also makes an interesting point in regard to this study. Search dogs, he points out, are trained to detect a faint odor, then follow that odor as it grows stronger until they reach the source. A wild animal is not seeking the source of the odor, and if it is faint will not seek the source of it (assuming it isn't food or a female in heat). In most cases the animal will simply not react at all to a very faint odor.

Scent-Lok has funded several studies of their product, including at least one study in which it was compared to another product and found to be superior. The study was conducted by professors at the University of North Carolina, which is internationally renowned for its college of textiles. Laboratory testing indicated that Scent-Lok fabric was very efficient at adsorbing a wide range of odors and, perhaps most significantly, that it could in fact be regenerated sufficiently in an ordinary clothes dryer to remain effective for repeated use. The public has every right to be skeptical of studies that are not independently funded and conducted. In fairness, though, it should be pointed out that the academics conducting these studies are more than credible scientists, and that when they present their findings they put their reputations on the lines. Further, such studies are expensive. Few outside the industry are likely to invest the time, money, and human resources necessary to conduct a truly scientific study of this issue.

The criticism may be raised also that a study conducted in a lab is not necessarily a predictor of results outdoors. Fair enough, but this really only points to the limitations of science. A very large part of what defines scientific methodology is control of variables so that valid comparisons can be made. Laboratories offer a great deal of control. Operating in the outdoors makes control of variables such as temperature, wind velocity and direction, and humidity (to name only a few), extremely difficult or impossible.

In time, we may accumulate sufficient evidence to convince any rational, educated hunter that a given type of scent reduction product does or does not work. In the meantime, it would behoove hunters to keep an open mind on the subject. The more serious and consistently successful hunters I know tend to employ at least some of these scent-reduction products, and some use them all. They wash with unscented soaps, apply unscented deodorants, wear scent-reducing clothing of one type or another, or use scent reducing powders or sprays. None that I know totally ignore wind direction, and most take it seriously.

My own experiences, which I present here as neither less nor more valid than those of any other experienced hunter, are inconclusive. I am convinced that reducing scent is possible and that it makes a difference. How much of a difference is not clear. Depending on circumstances, I use some or all of these products. I have been detected by game when following a rigid scent control regimen. I have also had game downwind of me for extended periods of time, and remained undetected. In addition I have observed, as have many hunters, that game animals at times appear to detect an odor, but not to a degree that causes them to bolt. The head comes up, perhaps, and they appear to change from a relaxed state to a tense state. They look around, as if looking for the source of a faint odor. It could be that they detect an odor, but think it is at some distance, or are simply unable to locate the source of it. I've even had deer snort, or jump and run a short distance, only to stop. On more than one occasion I've had the opportunity to arrow animals that I'm sure were aware of my presence, but couldn't locate me. It is not unreasonable to speculate in these situations that keeping scent to a minimum is the difference between an animal that becomes alert to possible danger and remains in the area long enough to provide a shooting opportunity, and one that bolts instantly.

Based on all this, I am inclined to continue using scent reducing strategies unless and until more extensive scientific studies convince me they are ineffective. My feeling, which appears to be in accord with the thoughts of many experienced hunters, is that getting within bow range of mature big game animals is sufficiently difficult that I want any edge I can get.

# Cover Scents

Behavioral scientists have observed that white-tailed deer can distinguish between as many as twenty different scents simultaneously, and it seems reasonable to assume that most of the species we hunt have similar capabilities. There is reason to wonder if it is even possible to fool a game animal's nose by attempting to cover one scent with another. Before you give up on the idea of cover scents, though, you might want to consider this question: Why do most dogs seem to delight in rolling in the foulest, rottenest, most disgusting carcasses or other sources of odors they can find? Biologists tell us this behavior is common to wild as well as domesticated canines, and many theorize that the behavior is an attempt to mask scent, as an aid in stalking prey. Along similar lines, why do canines, felines, and other critters often kick dirt over their droppings, if not to reduce or mask scent?

If it is true that animals engage in these behaviors to cover their scent, then thousands upon thousands of years of evolution would seem to support the notion that it is indeed possible to mask scent to a degree that will make a hunter less easily detected by his prey. While it seems unlikely that scent can be entirely eliminated in this manner, perhaps it can be reduced to such a degree that it cannot be detected for as great a distance, or as quickly, by a prey species. Or perhaps the mixture of aromas causes a momentary hesitation, giving the predator a few extra seconds that can make the difference.

Native Americans were known to sometimes apply cover scents of one sort or another. Some tribes routinely sat in the smoke from campfires, convinced this cover scent gave them an edge when stalking into bow range of their quarry. They may not have understood scientific methodology, but they hunted almost daily all their lives, and for generation after generation depended on successful hunts for their very survival.

On a recent South African hunt, Wilhelm Greeff of Zingelani Safaris strongly urged me to burn cattle or zebra dung near my blind as a cover scent, insisting that it made a difference. Jim Litmer of Third Hand Archery products was in camp.

"We kept dung burning on and off all day outside our blind near a waterhole," Jim told me one night over dinner. "When the dung was burning, game came in. When the dung wasn't burning, no game came to the waterhole. At one point three rhinos came in and decided to stay awhile. They hung around until the dung burned up, and soon after that they spooked and ran off." My own experience was not quite so conclusive, but I can report that numerous species of game came to the waterhole I was watching while the dung was burning, including zebras, waterbuck, kudu, and numerous warthogs.

Did a cover scent encourage this bear to come into bow range? It's impossible to be certain, but positive results are hard to argue with.

## What Kind of Cover Scent to Use?

This is a more complicated question than it might at first appear to be. Typically, cover scents attempt to produce a strong smell that is common in the environment. Earth scent, pine scent, and the urine of common creatures such as foxes and raccoons are probably the most popular cover scents. Usually, earth and pine scents are sprayed on or attached to an item of clothing in the form of wafers or patches, while urines are usually applied a few drops at a time to boot soles before entering the woods, to prevent deer from readily discerning the trail. As in the case of food scents, some hunters feel it's important to use cover scents that are common to the area. Dirt would seem to be a common element, but, would a generic dirt scent closely resemble everything from the red clay of Georgia, to the sand of the South Carolina Low Country, to the fertile loam of the Midwest?

What about the use of urine from predators such as foxes? While some studies indicate that animals may react negatively to the urine of predators, even more studies suggest otherwise. Then too, although the urine of various species may have different odors depending on what they have eaten, urine does tend to break down quickly to the point at which, according to biologists, all mammal urine soon smells basically the same. More than a few successful deer hunters routinely apply fox urine to their boots before entering the woods.

Still other hunters scoff at the notion that an animal is put on the alert by, for instance, the scent of pines in an area where there are no pine trees. My own take on this is that since it is easy to use a scent that is common to the area being hunted, why not do it, just in case. Here is another consideration: If half the hunters in the woods are using earth scent (or pine scent, or fox urine), might not a deer learn to associate that scent with hunters? In the West, many hunters, especially elk hunters, hunt from spike camps, where they usually spend at least some time sitting around campfires. Like their Native American predecessors, some successful modern hunters are of the opinion that the smell of smoke acts as an effective cover scent. Most of us have heard stories about hunters who smoke cigarettes on deer stands, putting a smoking butt in the fork of a tree just long enough to shoot an approaching deer, then finishing the smoke before climbing down to take up the trail. Happily, I quit smoking years ago, but I can confirm the truthfulness of those stories, having done that very thing myself. Could cigarette smoke be a cover scent?

Assuming cover scents can work, whether or not smoke (or any other scent) can act as a cover would probably depend upon whether or not deer have learned to associate the smoke, or other scents, with humans, and more specifically with danger. It seems unlikely that animals in more-or-less remote areas would make that connection—although if they experience pain or a threat from one smoking hunter, the association could be made quickly. At the same time, deer that often come into contact with people, whether in heavily populated suburban areas, farm country, or areas where they are subject to heavy hunting pressure, would be quite likely to associate the smell of smoke with humans.

## Cover Scents vs. Scent Reducers

I have spoken with one manufacturer that specifically recommends against using cover scents in conjunction with scent reducers. Most don't address the issue, while others insist that it makes perfect sense to do so. Many scent reducers work by absorbing scent, adsorbing scent, or chemically interacting with substances to prevent odors from forming. All these products have a capacity. Products that absorb or adsorb odor molecules at some point are filled up, and become ineffective until they are cleaned or reactivated in some manner, and products that oxidize or in some similar chemical reaction neutralize scent are in effect "used up" in the process. It would seem to make no sense to invest in, for instance, a Scent-Lok suit, then spray pine scent all over it. The Scent-Lok will absorb the pine scent, counteracting its effectiveness. What's worse, the carbon particles in the Scent-Lok will reach capacity and then fail to adsorb any additional odors. In the case of some spray-on products, it is possible to reapply them frequently. Still, it would not seem logical to use a cover scent, then use a product that will attempt to neutralize that scent. If the scent reducer succeeds, the cover is not working. If the cover scent succeeds, the scent reducer is not working.

Some scent reducers, such as most soaps, detergents, and deodorants, work primarily as antimicrobials, preventing the formation of bacteria that cause body odor. In that case, the two products might be used in conjunction, since the cover scent would not prevent the scent reducer from killing bacteria and in this way preventing body odor. Another way to use cover scents involves placing them slightly downwind, where they can provide cover without fighting scent-reducing products.

# Attractant Scents

The 140-class whitetail was more than 100 yards out when Kentuckian Jason Strunk first spotted it crossing a bean field. Though it was far-off and moving in the wrong direction when he lost sight of it, Jason cautiously stood up, lifted his bow from its holder, and turned in his tree stand. When the buck came around a bend in the logging road about two minutes later, Jason waited for the right moment, tooted on his hands-free grunt tube to stop the buck in a shooting lane, and loosed a perfectly aimed arrow. Not ten seconds later, he watched it drop. How did Strunk know that buck was headed his way? He had laid down a scent trail with a drag rag on his way into the stand less than an hour before, starting at the far edge of the bean field and circling carefully to his stand. When he saw the buck cross the field with its nose to the ground, he knew it was following his scent trail.

There are scents on the market designed to attract not only whitetailed deer, but mulies, sitkas, blacktail deer, elk, bear, wild hogs, moose, all the North American wild canines, bobcats, cougars, and even small game and furbearers such as rabbits, raccoons, and skunks. There is no question that game can be lured into shooting position with scents. What is equally clear is that scent doesn't always work. And when it does work, just why is a controversial issue.

Realistic hunters aren't really expecting to find something that always works. They're looking for something that gives them an edge—something that makes the odds against scoring on any given day a little lower. How many times would you use scent for one opportunity at a good buck?

The issues for hunters are what kind of scents work, when do they work, and when (and why) do they often not work? Attractant scents can be divided into several categories, though there may be some overlap. These are food scents, sex scents, and curiosity scents. Urine can also be a category of its own. Though it is often considered a sex scent, and might also be considered a curiosity scent, we'll explain why we list it as a category of its own when we get to it. Why do I say there may be some overlap among these categories? Until we can get inside an animal's head, we really have no way of knowing for certain what motivates it. Was it hungry and fooled by that bottled apple scent, or was it curious about a strange new smell it had never encountered before? Was that rutting elk fooled by the cow-in-heat scent, or was it curious about something that vaguely resembled the scent of a cow-in-heat but wasn't? Some would argue that any time animals respond to a bottled or synthesized scent, they are responding mostly from curiosity. And of course some hunters would say, "Who cares why they come in, just so they come in?" Manufacturers themselves recognize the overlap. Many refer to their scents as lures. The ingredients are something they prefer to keep secret, but they often indicate that the lure contains a mixture of ingredients designed to appeal to hunger or curiosity or both.

## Food Scents

First let's distinguish between "food" and "food scents." In states such as Texas, where baiting deer is perfectly legal, hunters may put corn, apples, beets, or similar foods out as bait, and it seems reasonable to assume deer that encounter the bait for the first time are responding to smell. Bears, too, are hunted over bait in some states and Canadian provinces.

That is not what we are talking about, however. By "food scents," we are referring to bottled scents made from concentrates or synthetic odors, or solid mixtures that are volatile enough to produce food scents that can be detected from some distance, or various products that are heated or even boiled to produce scents intended to resemble foods. An interesting issue related to food scents is the oft heard caution about using the scents of foods that do not occur naturally in a given area. The idea is that a deer that suddenly detects the scent of, say, apples, in an area where there are no apple trees, will react with suspicion, or will sense in some way that something is not right and will avoid the area.

As in the case of similar concerns about cover scents, many biologists, and some hunters, scoff at that idea. In their opinion, the idea that a deer catches a whiff of corn in an area where there is no cornfield and is suddenly on the alert or suspicious that something is fishy, is just ridiculous. Deer are very wary, or so goes the reasoning, but they're not that complicated. They don't think that way. If it smells like something good to eat and they're hungry, they'll check it out. If the smell is unfamiliar but not threatening, they may or may not react with curiosity.

We can speculate about why animals respond to certain foods at certain times, and others at other times, but ultimately it's something only the animals themselves know for certain. It's probably often associated with seasonal factors, or the amount of sugar, protein, or other nutrients present in a given food source at a given stage of ripeness. The bottom line for many hunters, though, is that putting out a food scent is unlikely to do any harm, and can sometimes be the ticket to success.

## Curiosity Scents

Most animals, especially deer, are curious to some degree, which is the idea behind curiosity scents. Animals investigate their environment, and one of their chief instruments of investigation is the nose. Whitetails have been referred to as one-hundred-pound noses that run around smelling everything in the woods. Given their curiosity and their reliance on their noses, it's not surprising that deer will, on occasion, approach the source of a strong, unusual, or unknown aroma to check it out.

What exactly are curiosity scents? In the case of commercially produced scents, that is a difficult question, since manufacturers are highly secretive about the formulas they have developed, if their ads are to be believed, after years of research. In a University of Georgia study involving the use of motion-activated cameras placed over a variety of scents, the numbers of deer attracted to car polish rivaled the numbers attracted to several kinds of urine and food scents. (Of course, who is to say the deer were not reacting to urine and food scents out of curiosity?)

## Sexual Attractants

Sexual attractants don't just get game animals excited,they get hunters excited. No mystery there—when you consider that close to and during the rut is the one time, for many species, when even the most cautious, trophy-class animals allow their obsession with estrous females to make them vulnerable, it's not surprising that hunters would seek to take advantage of that vulnerability. Probably the most commonly used sexual attractant is doe-in-heat urine, which may be placed on the ground, used to saturate a rag or a wick and hung from a tree, or even sprayed into the air. Hunters also frequently use doe urine to lay down scent trails, saturating a rag that can be dragged, or a pad that can be worn on a boot sole.

Dominant buck urine, too, is popular. The idea is that bucks detecting the scent of another buck in their area will feel challenged and will seek out the buck to chase it off. Still others theorize that dominant buck urine can attract and hold does in a given area. It has been demonstrated that does can determine the difference between subordinate and dominant bucks simply by smelling their urine. Though we tend to think of the bucks as seeking the does, does will frequent areas containing dominant bucks, and especially in those areas where the buck to doe ratio is in good balance, does may travel outside their home ranges to find dominant bucks.

Among the better trophy hunters I know are several who begin placing dominant buck scents in various forms throughout their hunting area, usually late in the summer, though sometimes earlier, and in one case year-round. The theory is that this brings more does in the area, and keeps them there, and in turn more bucks are drawn into that area as the rut approaches.

Earlier we suggested that urine could be considered a category in itself. Here is why: ungulates, including deer, tend to be fascinated by urine of any kind. It seems to be a means of communication within the species, but may also tell deer about other species, including predators, in the area. There is some controversy regarding how deer react to the urine of predators, but regardless of how they react, they do seem drawn to check out urine. Ordinary doe urine is a commonly used scent. Many hunters believe that it doesn't make sense to use doe-in-heat scent before any does are likely to be in heat, but there are some other reasons not to use it. One reason is that it tends to repel does. The hunter looking primarily to cull does from a local herd or put venison in the freezer probably doesn't want to repel does. Beyond that, some hunters theorize that does attract bucks, so why drive away does?

The whole issue of how deer react to human urine has generated the widest possible response from hunters. At one extreme are the hunters who use bottles or other devices to avoid contaminating their hunting location with the smell of human urine. At the other extreme are hunters who intentionally "contaminate" their stand sites with human urine, deposit human urine in scrapes, and even create mock scrapes with human urine, in the belief that it attracts deer. A number of more-or-less scientific studies in recent years have examined deer response to a variety of scents. The studies aren't always conclusive, but they do tend to point in a couple of interesting directions. One of these is that deer herds confined in pens don't always react to smells the same way wild deer do. The other is that neither penned nor freeranging deer appear to have strong aversions to human urine, and may exhibit some curiosity about it. The bottom line is: Human urine may or may not attract deer to some degree, but it doesn't seem to repel them. Leave the urine

More than one whitetail buck has followed a hot scent straight into the lap of a waiting bowhunter.

bottles at home and let fly from your tree stand if you want.

Urine is not the only way deer convey sexual messages to one another—various glandular secretions, such as those deposited by bucks on rubs, may serve a similar function, along with the tarsal glands. A buck in rut can be smelled, even by the inferior noses of humans, for some distance under the right conditions, and any hunter who has picked a buck up by the hind legs to lift him into a pick-up truck, or who has ridden in an SUV with a buck behind the seat, is intimately acquainted with that aroma. Various commercial producers have attempted to bottle or mimic tarsal gland scent, and more than a few hunters like to trim off the tarsal glands of a tagged buck, to use as a lure. Many hunters freeze them in plastic bags for repeated use.

## Pheromones

We can't address the issue of sexual scents without taking a look at pheromones. Pheromones are organic chemical substances used by various species to communicate with one another, or to produce any of a number of instinctive responses. Many insects, in particular, are known to use pheromones heavily. Pheromones may enable an ant to tell its community the location of a food source, for instance, or allow a colony of bees to coordinate an exodus from a hive to establish a new colony elsewhere. They also stimulate sexual activity. Insects aren't the only species that make use of pheromones. Mammals do, also.

Hunters became very excited about pheromones, more specifically the volatile substances produced by females in heat to produce sexual responses in males. A buck or a bull detecting these pheromones will instinctively react to them—every time. Hunters who first learned about pheromones thought that they had hit on the holy grail of deer hunting: A scent that would invariably cause any buck to come to the source of the pheromones. Their hopes were dashed, however, by another incontrovertible fact: After they're released by the deer, these pheromones last for anywhere from 15 seconds to, at most, six minutes. They work for animals in heat because animals in heat produce fresh pheromones continuously.

Does this mean that, as a practical matter, there is no such thing as doe-in-heat scent? Some experts would argue that that is indeed the case. Consider, though, that scientists have identified at least 93 substances in the urine of a doe in heat. It seems entirely possible that a buck can tell a doe is in heat even without the pheromones. Will a buck respond to a doe even if the pheromones aren't present? We can't say with any certainty, but experiences like those of Jason Strunk suggest that a buck will, at least sometimes, follow a trail of doe-in-heat scent, regardless of what the ingredients may be and regardless of whether or not it contains pheromones.

## Timing

When is a good time to use scents? In the case of curiosity scents, arguably any time, since curiosity is not seasonal. It seems unlikely, though, that a buck eagerly seeking a hot doe—or a doe being pursued by a randy buck—would stray far from its route to check a smell out of curiosity. It also seems unlikely that a deer heading for a dinner of alfalfa, corn, or clover would delay getting dinner to check out a strange aroma. Nonetheless, any hunter who has spent time in the woods knows that deer aren't always chasing or being chased by other deer, nor are they always making a beeline for the nearest preferred food. Deer take their sweet time, most of the time, and tend to amble along slowly, browsing and grazing as they go.

When it comes to using food scents, timing raises some interesting and complex issues. As a general rule, most hunters, and even some manufacturers, recommend using food scents early in the season, pre-rut, and late in the season, post-rut. Why? Because the periods immediately before the rut, and during the peak of the rut, are the prime times for doe-in-heat scents or dominant buck scents.

To my knowledge, no one has done any sort of scientific (or, for that matter, unscientific) study to determine if doe-in-heat or dominant buck scents outperform food scents during the rut. Most manufacturers have little incentive to pursue such an inquiry; the status quo is that hunters use food scents on some hunts, sexual attractants on others. Why limit sales to one or the other?

How often have you heard that the best way to hunt bucks during the rut is to hunt where the does are? If that's sound advice, wouldn't it make perfect sense to attract does to your stand with food scents? Perhaps in some updated edition of this book, we'll have an answer to that question.

But the issue of when to use a given food scent is much more complicated than whether or not food scents are or are not more effective than sexual attractants at various times in the season. While it's true that deer like a variety of foods, it's also well documented that at any given time, deer have a preferred food and will often pass up other foods to get to it. Further, their priorities change, sometimes from one day to the next. Deer may pass up any food source available to get at alfalfa in late summer or early autumn. Later they might switch to soybeans, passing up alfalfa to get the beans. When the acorns fall, deer will abandon every other food source to get to them. Though they readily eat the acorns from red oaks, they seem to prefer the less bitter white oak acorn. Why these changing preferences? Availability has something to do with it, but in many cases, it's a matter of what is ripe. And some plants—especially broadleaf green plants such as the brassicas that are so popular these days in food plots—become sweeter after a frost or two. They may literally be ignored one day, and sought after to the exclusion of nearly everything else the next day.

What does all this have to do with food scents? Neither corn scents nor apple scents are likely to be at their most effective if acorns are dropping in the woods. And while all this might seem to suggest that acorn scents should be effective any time, there is the fact that deer seem to prefer foods with varying amounts of protein or sugars depending on the time of the year and whether they are bulking up with protein or seeking high-energy foods with more sugars.

Timing as it pertains to the use of sexual scents would seem to be a more straightforward matter. Though there is some evidence that the scents released by bucks can actually stimulate does to come into heat, the timing of the rut is fairly predictable. A doe, as every deer hunter knows, will run from a buck until she is good and ready to stand still for him. At the same time, it is unlikely that a buck would respond to a doe in heat if not for the increased level of testosterone that courses through his veins as the rut kicks in. That would suggest that the best time to use dominant buck or doe-in-heat scent would be the period leading up to, and during, the time that the rut takes place, beginning when bucks begin frequently scraping, rubbing, and cruising for does, and very late in the season when testosterone levels have dropped.

## Proper Use

Many bowhunters use an attraction scent in the hope that wandering deer will hit the scent stream and follow it to the source, where they are waiting to loose a well-aimed arrow. Others, though they would welcome such an occurrence, have more limited expectations. Their hope is that a deer passing by will stop to sniff or lick the source of the scent, pausing long enough and in a correct position to give them a perfect shot. In either case, it only makes sense to put the source of the scent in a spot that is comfortably within bow range, in the open, and likely to position the deer for a broadside shot.

It also makes sense to use the wind very carefully. It's a tricky situation—on the one hand, you want to position the scent source upwind of areas you expect deer to move through, while on the other hand you don't want them to get your scent. Obviously this is a situation in which scent control (reduction of the hunter's scent) is extremely important. In other circumstances, it is possible the target will be passing by upwind, but in the case of using attractant scents, game will be in a more-or-less downwind position. The trick here, aside from maximum personal scent control, is to position the scent source neither directly upwind nor downwind from the hunter, but crosswind. Ideally, game will hit the scent stream prior to being directly downwind of the hunter and follow it in without ever hitting the hunter's scent stream.

Hunters use a variety of media for conveying scent, including various wicks, drag rags, boot pads, liquids, gels, and homemade devices or concoctions. Which is the most effective may depend to some extent on current conditions. One consideration, according to Jamis Gamache of HeatWave Scents, is weather. "The use of liquid-based scent when it is raining or if temperatures are extremely cold is minimized greatly," explains Jamis, "because the scent is diluted with the rain or the liquid freezes. A better type [of] device would be a scentimpregnated wafer in which the scent is built into the device."

When conditions are favorable, Jamis believes aerosol sprays can disperse scent better than can a liquid on a wick. A few years ago, Jamis became sufficiently sold on heated scents that he formed his own company, HeatWave Scents. It's no secret that heat increases the volatility of most substances, which means, in effect, that it makes odors stronger. Not that you have to be a chemist to understand that fact.

"Think of it this way," says Jamis. "After a long day of hunting, you walk into the house and there is a hot pot of chili on the stove. You know right away when you walk in that something smells great. The next day you walk in and the leftover chili is still on the stove but is not heated. You practically need to stumble over it before you realize it is there. The same holds true for game scents. By heating or atomizing the scent, it produces a much stronger aroma, which is more apt to attract game to your hunting area."

At the beginning of this chapter, I made reference to laying down a scent trail with drag rags. Usually this is a rut-hunting strategy, and the attractant is doe-in-heat urine. I know at least one hunter who makes it a point to always step in deer droppings when he comes across them on his way to his stand, and claims to have taken a nice buck that followed that scent to his stand. Would food scents work? I know of no one who has tried it. I'd be inclined to think it could be very effective for bear hunters, but I, for one, would be leery of putting a food scent on any part of my body in bear country. One technique that I see increasing numbers of deer hunters using involves soaking a drag rag with liquid scent, putting it on the end of a stick, and by that means laying down a trail that is not directly in their own footsteps. It can't hurt, and some hunters are convinced that it makes bucks less likely to detect the hunter's scent.

Earlier I made reference to some serious trophy hunters who begin making mock scrapes and putting out dominant buck scent in the summer, and sometimes year-round, in the belief that it attracts and holds does and bucks in an area.

## Natural vs. Synthetic Scents

On a hunt in the mountains of Virginia several years ago, I stepped out of a pickup truck, said good luck to my hunting companions in the backseat, and watched momentarily as the guide drove off down the logging road, leaving me in the predawn stillness of a crisp fall morning. It was the end of October and the perfect time, it seemed to me, to lay down a scent line to my stand using a drag rag with a little doe-in-heat scent. I removed the bottle of scent from my daypack and, in the darkness, attempted to squirt a little onto my drag rag. Nothing came out. I shook it a few times and squeezed again with my fingers. Still nothing. Finally, I squeezed with my whole hand. The entire top of the bottle burst open and doe-inheat scent sprayed all over me. I gathered my gear and began walking toward my stand, and soon heard something walking in the dry leaves behind me. I stopped and it stopped. I began walking and again I heard it, unmistakably following me. Eventually I was able to make out a forkhorn buck, following about 40 or 50 yards behind me. It left when I climbed into my stand, but later came back and hung around all morning. It ran off when I climbed down at lunchtime to make my way back to the logging road for the ride back to the lodge. The

Most camo is effective. Some patterns excel in one specific habitat while others, like the pattern above, are more all-purpose.

truck came along, with several other hunters inside, and stopped. I climbed in. The truck went about ten yards and stopped, the door flew open, and I flew out. I had to ride back to the lodge in the bed of the truck.

Being the scientific type that I am, I deduced several things from this experience. First, that the forkhorn buck sure was interested in something about me, and my best guess is that the doe-in-heat shower I took by the logging road had a lot to do with it. Second, you want to avoid contaminating yourself or your gear with that stuff if at all possible, but sometimes it is not possible.

I bring this up because it represents one of the arguments in favor of synthetic, as opposed to natural, scents. The near certainty of occasional contamination is definitely on the con side for natural scents, and on the pro side for synthetics, which tend to be easier to handle and less offensive, at least to humans.

Scents of nearly any kind can be synthesized in laboratories. Are these inferior or superior to natural scents? Contamination and convenience of handling aside, there are other issues to consider. On the pro side for synthetics, the argument is that certain natural substances, particularly urine, break down into other compounds, including ammonia. The ammonia smell is perfectly natural, and hence, arguably, a good thing. Soon after it is bottled, though, bacteria begin breaking urine down into unnatural compounds—unless special measures, including the use of preservatives, are used to prevent this. And preservatives, or so goes the argument, have their own unnatural scent. Synthetic scents, on the other hand, won't break down. And they're easier to use, since hunters needn't worry about when they were produced, or how they are stored, or how long they will be effective after the package is opened.

On the negative side for synthetic scents, some question whether or not it is possible to produce a synthetic scent that will fool an animal's nose. An animal will not have the same reaction, according to this line of reasoning, to a synthetic as opposed to a naturally produced scent. Animals that respond to a synthetic scent, according to this position, are reacting out of curiosity, and not because they are genuinely fooled.

Here is another controversial issue concerning the use of natural urines: Some products contain not deer, elk, or moose urine, but the urine of cattle or sheep. In fact, some cow- or doe-in-heat products actually contain the urine of cattle or sheep in heat. Hunters were scandalized to make that discovery, but it's not all that clear they should have been—for one simple reason: Target animals respond to them, and no scientific evidence to date proves that the urine from real does is more effective than the urine of other ungulates in heat. To further cloud the argument, recent studies indicate that the pheromones that get bucks and bulls (not to mention hunters) so excited are not present in urine, but in vaginal secretions. In a University of Georgia study, white-tailed bucks, when given a choice between vaginal secretions of estrous does and the urine of estrous does, ignored the urine and went in the direction of the secretions virtually every time.

Once again, we get into the motives of animals. Certainly the argument can be made that whether or not we truly fool an animal's nose, or whether it is reacting to a sexual stimulus or simply out of curiosity, doesn't matter. All that matters is, does it respond? To my knowledge, no scientific studies have been completed regarding how animals react to natural versus synthetic scents, or fresh urine deposited by animals in the wild as compared to urine bottled on a farm and used weeks or months later.

Be sure to tie the knot so there's enough space for the antlers to jangle together when suspended from a rope.

# Take a Stand

Stand-hunting in the north woods can be very effective. But to be successful, you must master the arts of sitting and being patient, and you must find a good place to put your tree stand or ground blind. It takes a certain mindset to keep yourself in one spot, especially if you're not seeing deer. I say this as someone who hasn't mastered the art of either sitting or patience, but I don't intend to worry about them until the day comes when I can't get over the next ridge. I do respect people who *can* sit, though, and I've guided many over the years.

## WHERE TO LOCATE YOUR STAND

### Scouting on Paper

Where you put your stand is obviously an important consideration. Let's assume you're heading to the north woods for the first time. Buy some topographical (topo) maps of the area and study them before you go. This will save you some scouting time if you know what kinds of features to look for on the map. Look for ridges—especially long, steep ridges—with saddles through them. Look for wet areas, including lakes, streams, and bogs. Even if you're hunting in relatively flat country, study the higher ground, since that's probably where the hardwoods—and most of the deers' food—will be. Look for ravines or finger ridges that connect the two ravines. Once you've marked these features, find roads or trails that will take you near them.

Now that you've scouted on paper, you're ready to hit the road for some real scouting. Before you take to the woods on foot, drive through the area in your vehicle and check to see if any new roads have been built for logging since the date on the map. Many topo maps were last updated in the late eighties, and some haven't been updated since the seventies. Update your map by drawing in new roads and features such as clear-cuts that aren't shown on the map.

**SUCCESSFUL SCOUTING WITH A TOPO MAP**

When I wanted to change my hunting area in the mid-eighties, the only topo maps available were from the 1920s. A whole forest could have been logged and regrown in that time! I looked over the maps and found an area I liked. It had a mountain ridge about three miles long with a lake on one side. I had only one day to scout at the site—in early October. I drove in on each side of the mountain as far as I could and then walked farther on overgrown logging roads. The area looked and felt right. It had some big hardwood ridges with green growth up high, and I was encouraged to see a few tracks in the leaves. That fall and the following one, I shot nice bucks on that mountain. My topo map scout ing had been a success.

**Scouting on Site**

When you head into the woods to scout, check out the streams first. Streams and other wet areas are good places to find deer signpost rubs as this is where brown ash, a favorite of deer, usually grows. Look for wet deer runs crossing streams at shallow spots or places where the stream banks are low. These are good stand locations because the deer tend to use these runs repeatedly. If there are signposts at a crossing, it's probably an especially good place for a stand.

After you've scouted the streams, work your way up the ridges, checking spring seeps for signposts. If you find a run paralleling the ridge, follow it—there's a good chance it will lead to a passage through the ridge. Also check hardwood ridges for feeding sign (evidence of pawing for ferns or vegetation nipped), especially if you discover fresh droppings. Does usually spend time in places like this, so consider placing your stand near one during the rut. Does in the big woods don't have specific bedding areas. They wander about feeding and then bed at a good vantage point to detect danger. Several bucks may pass through such an area once they start looking for does.

Early May is a good time to scout. The snow has just melted, and the leaves haven't come out yet. The woods look just as they did in late fall. Trails will still be beaten down, and scrapes will be easy to spot, even at a distance. Rubs will be fairly bright, and strings of bark will still be hanging from them. If you can't scout in May, you might as well wait until late fall after the leaves are off the trees. During the summer, it's hard to see much with the foliage out, and rubs will have turned gray and started to heal, making them difficult to spot. Personally, I do my scouting about a week before deer-hunting season. The leaves have been down for a week or two, giving the deer time make some tracks. (Scouting in early October is discouraging—as the leaves come raining down, they cover tracks as fast as the deer make them. You might be walking through good deer country and swear there isn't a deer around!)

**Don't Be Afraid to Cover Some Ground When Scouting**

When you're scouting for a stand location, don't be afraid to cover a lot of ground. I've seen

The buck that sparred with this beech sapling must have long tines to twist it up this way. (Note the well-worn trail that continues on.)

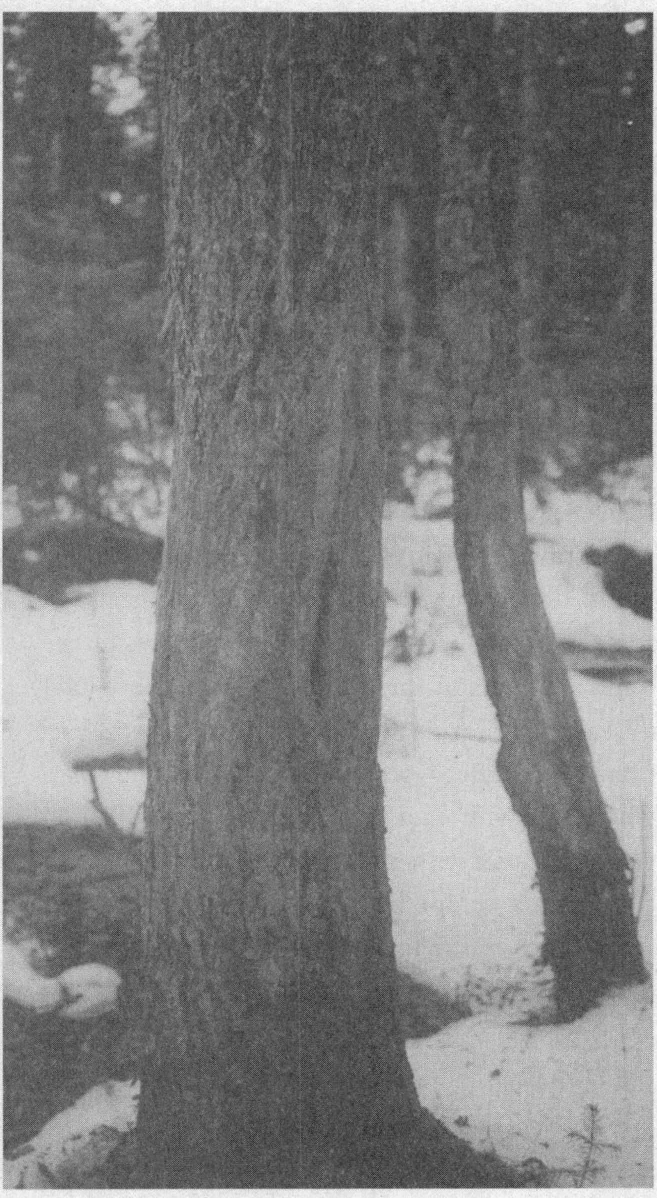
A typical area where brown ash grows—a wet run through the thick green growth.

hunters go into the woods a quarter mile or so and look around a little bit. If they don't see much sign, they give up and go somewhere else. If you go far enough into the woods and check the streams and ridges, you *will* find buck sign. You may also find a better way to get to a stand location you're considering.

**A SHORT DRAG**

Once I was scouting a new area a week before the season, and I had some hunters coming in who wanted to stand-hunt. After going up and down some big hardwood ridges for a couple of miles, I found a spot where bucks had been traveling down from a softwood bluff into the hard woods. I built a ground blind there, realizing that in my travels I had made my way to within half a mile of an old truck road that I could drive to. When I left that spot to work my way out, I hit a deer run. It was going my way, so I followed it.

I came to a place where the trees were torn up with fresh rubs, so I went uphill about fifty yards and built another ground blind. After hiking another hundred yards down the ridge,

One of the Massachusetts boys with his high-racked seven-pointer taken out of a ground blind overlooking a rub line.

I came out at the road. What luck—a nice rub line close to a road!

The first day the hunters were there, I walked each one to a blind, but all they saw were a couple of does. The next day they swapped blinds, so I walked them both in again. Only half an hour after I dropped the hunter at the blind closer to the road, he started shooting. I hurried over and found him standing over a beautiful, high-racked sevenpointer. We had a good chuckle about the short drag—we could see the truck from where he shot the deer!

### Scouting During Hunting Season

I do more scouting during hunting season than at any other time. As I still-hunt and when I'm tracking bucks, I frequently learn more in one day about the locations of buck travel corridors, rubs, and other signposts than I do in a week of pre-season scouting. I sometimes end up in areas that are new to me, which I call connecting the dots, because I sometimes learn where competing bucks' ranges overlap. These overlap areas are great places for stands, because you have a chance to see two bucks instead of just one.

### The Best Stand Locations

Try to put your stand in one of these three types of locations:

**Doe feeding areas:** These are best once the rut kicks in and the bucks change their travel patterns to check on the does.

**Travel corridors**: Look for corridors that funnel deer through natural terrain features like shallow stream beds. These are great places for a stand any time during the season, and you're likely to see many deer near them. Place your stand back from the corridor—where it's easier to watch the whole area without a buck slipping around behind you—in a spot with good wind advantage.

**Near a scrape line or a rub line:** Stands near scrape lines or rub lines work well any time during the season, and if you can find an inter section of

This hunter is prepared to stay on stand as long as it takes to get his chance at a buck.

Travel corridors are often found where a steep ridge levels out.

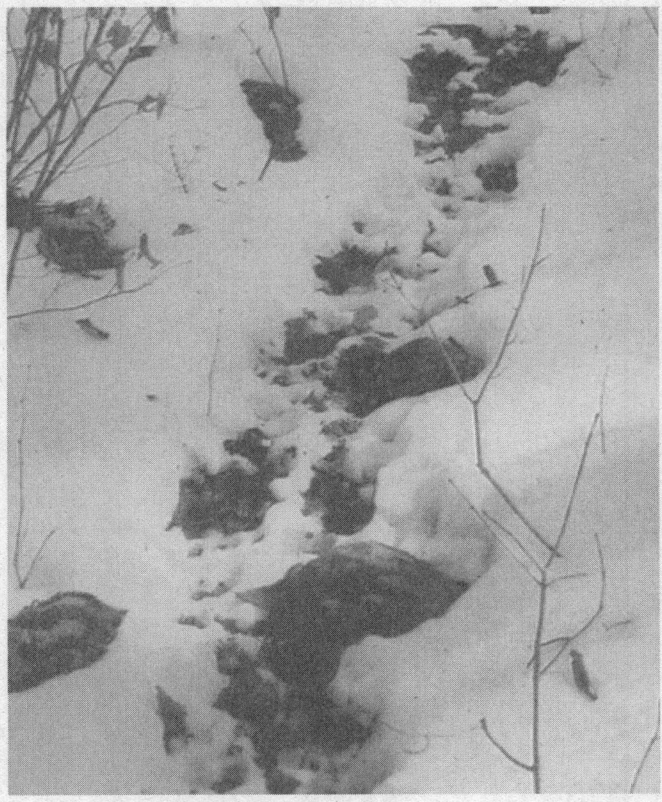

A well-worn trail dropping down from a saddle. An ideal stand location.

two lines, you'll have even better luck. Early in the season, the bucks will be establishing lines. Later, they'll be checking their scrapes and rubs as they make rounds to see if other bucks are horning in on their territory.

**A SUCCESSFUL BLIND NEAR A CORRIDOR**

A travel corridor was about a quarter mile from the tents at one of our remote camps, and deer used it almost daily. The corridor came from a mountain down a finger ridge, crossed a logging road, and then split into smaller trails in a softwood bottom with a stream running through it. One evening I had just returned to camp when one of the hunters—who had already filled his tag—said he had seen a buck and two does come through the corridor. I ran up to check the tracks and confirmed it was a good buck. It was the peak of the rut, so I figured he'd still be hanging around the does in the morning. The does' tracks led down into the low ground, so I planned to have the two other hunters, Bob and Bill, there the next day.

Bill with his 225-pound buck. He took this buck while posted up on a trail that a doe had already gone down. The buck was an eight-pointer, but had broken most of his points off while fighting.

When we got to the corridor in the morning, we saw that the three deer had come back across the trail in the night, and the buck had made a scrape in the trail. A little more trail-checking showed us that the does had recently gone back down to the low ground, but the buck hadn't. I told the hunters I thought the buck would be back, and sent Bob down to the rock blind while had Bill post to cover the crossing. I followed the buck's tracks up the mountain, thinking that if he had bedded up there and I jumped him, he'd come back down. I got up a little way and jumped a buck, but it wasn't the one I was looking for, so I continued on. After a while, I saw that my buck had turned and was heading back toward

Bill, following the does' tracks. Just then, I heard shooting down below. I hurried along, following the tracks, and soon I could see Bill standing in the trail ahead. When I got down to him, he told me the buck had come right down the ridge and stopped about seventy-five yards from him, so he put the crosshairs on him and fired. The buck took off and cleared the trail as if he hadn't been hit. Bill fired again, and the buck disappeared into the green growth, although Bill didn't think he could have missed. I saw no blood as I followed the running track into the softwood, but after about a hundred yards, there lay Bill's buck, stretched out on top of a blowdown he couldn't make it across. He was a battle-scarred old buck and weighed 225 pounds. He was an eight-pointer, but his antlers had broken off to points flush at the beam from fighting.

**ON STAND NEAR A SCRAPE**

One year it had been quite warm prior to hunting season, and buck activity was fairly low. As I scouted during the week before the season started, I could not find any good scrapes in the area where I wanted to hunt. I did find where a good buck had been sparring with a few trees on a rub line and knew there were other bucks in the area, even though the sign didn't indicate it.

Eddie, my hunter that week, had hunted in Maine for three years and had never even seen a buck. This was his first hunt with me, so when he came in on Sunday, I explained that the conditions were not the best, but we were going to make the most of them. He said he didn't care what size buck he shot, he just wanted a Maine buck. Well, Eddie got his first Maine buck on his second day on stand. A nice five-pointer came right down the rub line, checking the big boy's work.

Eddy's first Maine buck, taken while watching a well-used scrape line.

Would Eddie have killed the big boy if he had passed up the five-point? Who knows. To him, the five-pointer was a trophy he had waited four years for. When you're on stand, you never know which buck will show up first. But one thing's for sure—if you scout your stand location well, you'll have a better chance of scoring on a buck than if you just pick any old stump to sit on.

**Tree Stand or Ground Blind?**

Once you've found the perfect place for your stand, you have to consider how to spend a week or

A simple ground blind can be made from dead limbs and small spruce or fir trees.

so there comfortably and still have a good chance of scoring a buck. Tree stands are the most popular way to hunt in most of the whitetail's range. They have advantages, but they also have drawbacks. They are great around grown-up clear-cuts, where you need to see over the new growth, and they're also good around swales and bogs where the tall grass can hide a deer, or in green growth where visibility is low and you might need to see behind you.

This beech rub was done by a big-racked buck. Note how the limb is mangled and twisted. Courtesy: Susan C. Morse.

But tree stands are not so great if you've picked a spot farther out than you want to carry a stand, or if you're likely to get antsy sitting in a very limited amount of space for a very long period of time. It's hard to sit for eight or nine hours without stretching or moving around. It can also be extremely cold when the wind is blowing and you're up in a tree with no shelter.

I prefer ground blinds in most situations. I've found very few situations where they don't work. You might think deer smelling your scent would be problem, but it doesn't seem to be, since the wind rarely blows in one direction long enough to carry the scent far. If you use a good cover scent and deer scent, you'll have no problem. I also like ground blinds because I can carry an axe or saw when I scout and make blinds as I find good locations. Also, in a well-made ground blind, you'll stay warmer than in a tree stand, because you'll be able to move around, stretch, and be sheltered from the wind.

**Building a Ground Blind**

I find a spot on a ridge looking downhill or with enough thick cover in back of me that a buck can't sneak around behind the blind. I use what's available in the woods. I might start with an uprooted tree or a log. Then I make a frame with small dead logs about as high as my neck will be when I'm sitting down. Next I try to find some spruce boughs to block off the wind and break up the outline of the blind to make it less visible to deer. Then I remove dead twigs and leaves from the floor of the blind so I won't make noise as I move around.

I can sit in a place like this for hours. If I need to move around, it's no problem—I can even make a little fire right inside if necessary. You'll be surprised how close deer will come to a ground blind without ever knowing you're there.

**A GROUND BLIND NEAR A SCRAPE AND A RUB**

A few years ago, I built a ground blind in a tangle of spruce blowdowns with a thick stand of spruce behind it. It looked so natural that I did very little to camouflage it. Thirty yards in front of it was a good scrape on a rub line leading into a swamp. The first day I put Sean in the blind. He said a six-pointer came to the scrape but never stopped in the opening, so he didn't shoot. I told him that in that mess I doubted whether bucks could *stop* in an opening—he'd have to shoot when they *crossed* an opening. He went back the next day and a spike horn showed up, but since he wanted the six-pointer he'd seen the day before, he just watched the spike. Pretty soon, the spike walked right up to the edge of the blind and tried to look in. Sean sat perfectly still, and after a while the spike went to check out the scrape. It stayed around so long that Sean changed his mind and shot it—his first Maine buck.

**Summing Up**

Stand-hunting is a very effective way to hunt bucks *if* you develop a mindset that keeps you on stand no matter what the weather or what you see (or don't see!). I tell my hunters that it takes only a second for that once-in-a-lifetime buck to show up. If you're prepared for the elements and you've picked an appropriate spot for your blind, you'll have a good chance of a buck showing up while you're there.

This is the Dueling Buck where he fell after being grunted back to me while I was tracking him.

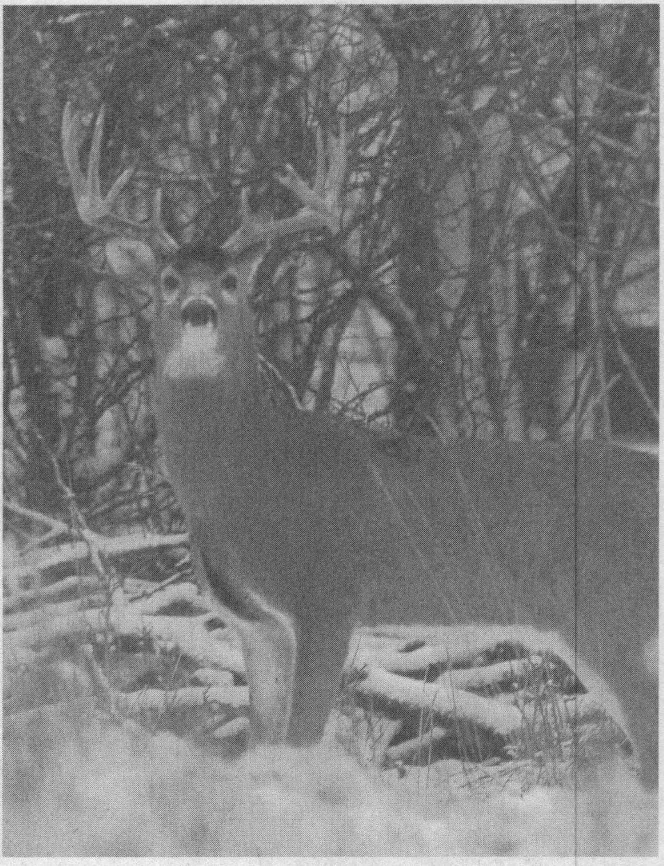

Being able to surprise a mature buck takes skill and patience. Hunters must be prepared to react quickly to a scene like this when stalking or tracking big bucks.

# Choosing the Best Stand Location for Success

Stand-hunting is a very successful way to hunt in the big woods. It allows a hunter who may not be able to walk the distances necessary to track and still-hunt the opportunity to hunt in the big woods. It also gives the hunter another option when the conditions are poor for tracking or still-hunting.

Stand-hunting in the big woods is far different from hunting in agricultural areas, for a variety of reasons. The number one reason is that there is so much territory for a buck to travel in that he could be anywhere on any given day. This requires stand hunters to have the patience to stay in their stands day after day, all day, no matter what the conditions.

Unlike other areas, where standhunting is a morning and evening event, in the big woods you are just as likely to shoot a buck in the middle of the day. The stand-hunter is also going to have to do the proper scouting to ensure a good stand location. From my experience, a big woods buck spends most of his time traveling through 10 percent of his territory. In this chapter, I'm going to help you figure out where that 10 percent is. We'll also explore ways to capitalize on those areas no matter what time of the season you hunt.

There are several types of stands locations that are effective in the big woods. There are certain times that one specific stand location may be better than another, and they can vary from year to year. By having stands in several different locations, you will be able to maximize your odds of seeing a buck. Too many hunters pick a stand location just because it looks like a good area, or because they have good visibility there. In the big woods, there are a lot

This buck was taken from a ground blind while watching a scrape.

of good-looking places that deer have not passed through in years. Stand-hunting in some of these areas will become an exercise in futility, and the odds of shooting a buck are somewhere between slim and none. In my first book, I talked mostly about pre-rut and rut stands. I am going to expand on those types of stands by breaking them down into four basic locations. They are: pre-rut, rut, all-season, and migration trail stands.

## Pre-rut Stands

In the pre-rut period, bucks mostly are just getting ready for the rut. They've had all summer to fatten up, and now they know the chance to spread their genes will arrive soon. The bucks are laying down scrapes and rubs throughout their territories. They are crossing paths with other bucks and making a point to announce their presence by marking signpost rubs with their scents.

I believe sitting over a signpost rub, especially if more than one buck is using it, is the most effective pre-rut stand. Since most of the signposts are made in obscure, out-of-the-way places, a buck is more likely to show up there during the day. If there is a breeding scrape near a signpost, it makes the stand location that much better, because there are most likely does in the area. Keep in mind that a mature buck has a huge territory and is not going to pass through the same area every day.

I passed along a signpost area I found to Matt Whitegiver, one of the guides working for me, so he could put up a stand there. I wasn't hunting that area anymore because it had grown up too thick to be very good for still-hunting. There were plenty of deer around and I knew a stand-hunter would have a good chance at tak ing a buck there.

This particular place was at the back corner of a hardwood chop ping. The chopping had grown up with raspberry bushes and saplings. Bordering the chopping on two sides was an old grown up softwood clear-cut and cedar bogs. Just inside the softwoods, at the corner of the chopping, were several signpost rubs. I also found a couple of scrapes in the corner of the chopping.

Matt put up a ground blind with the intention of having a hunter there for the first week of the season. The hunter who was going to hunt this spot had brought a tree stand and wanted to use it instead of the ground blind. Matt carried the tree stand in the first morning, and the hunter climbed up in it to sit for the day. When the hunter came out of the woods at the end of the day, he told Matt that he had seen thirteen does. Matt told the hunter that he had seen more deer in one day than most people see in a week.

The next day, the hunter didn't see a single deer from his tree stand and told Matt he wasn't going to go back there. Even I could n't convince the guy to stay in that stand. Talk about trusting your guide! The next day, Matt moved the hunter to another stand. The hunter's tree stand was still at the first place, so at about noontime Matt decided that he might as well go in and bring the stand out. As he was heading in he spotted a deer walking down by the stand. He stopped and waited to see what it was. It turned out to be a nice eight-point buck and it walked right under the tree stand. I guess sometimes lessons have to be learned the hard way.

I've learned that there is a different dynamic to stand-hunting in the big woods of northern Canada. This area is a mostly a coniferous forest that contains very little feed for deer, with the exception of some isolated cedar bogs. In fact, most of these areas didn't contain any deer until they were logged. Most of the logging has been by clear-cutting and has created a vast amount of feed for deer by letting in sunlight so new plants can grow. The logging has allowed deer to expand into new areas.

Even though it is big woods, the habits of the deer around clear-cuts are more like that of farm-country deer. You have to view the clear-cuts almost as you would agricultural fields, and not like most big woods areas, where there is feed almost anywhere. The only other places that contain much feed for the deer around these coniferous forests are near the swale bogs where sunlight has allowed the feed to grow. Unlike the big woods bucks of the east, bucks in these areas tend to travel the same trails as the does do.

In areas with a lot of these clear-cuts, the best stand locations are in cuts that are not visible from a road. This might be the back of a cut that is hidden from the road by a knoll or that has no drivable road to it. Lee Libby found one such place on a cold, rainy morning in Ontario.

Lee was sick with a cold that morning, so when the other guys got out of the truck to hunt, they told him that he should sit in the vehicle until the rain stopped. Lee, being Lee, couldn't stand to be in the truck, so he decided to hunt his way to the back of a clear-cut that was grown up with head-high jack pines. He worked his way down the old road leading into the cut. When the road ended, he couldn't see twenty yards, so he walked up onto a ledge to look for a better view of the cut. From the ledge he could see several hundred yards down into a ravine that ran to the back of the clear-cut. Lee hadn't been standing there very long when he spotted a good buck standing on the other side of the cut, about 200 yards away. At the sound of Lee's muzzle-loader going off, the buck dropped in his tracks. When Lee got over to the buck, he discovered that he had shot a beautiful fourteen-pointer.

Later in the season, Mike Featherstone's friend Dave shot anoth er buck in the exact same spot. What made this a good stand location was that, at the back of the clear-cut, there was a buffer strip of woods that dropped down a steep ridge into a lake. That made it difficult for the deer to go around the cut. Those two bucks had been using that hidden ravine to cross the clear-cut as they traveled along the lake.

Some clear-cuts are used heavily by deer and others are not. You will have to check for feeding sign while scouting. Quite often these clear-cuts border a swale. These grassy swales are created when the beavers flood an area and kill all the trees. When the clear-cuts bor der a swale, there is usually a strip of woods between the cut and the swale called a buffer strip. By walking the back of the clear-cuts, you can usually see if there is a swale behind it.

Swales have good stand locations around them. They can run for miles, so deer have to cross them at some point. Quite often, the cross ings will be at a narrow point in the swale. Deer also like to cross where there is a corner in the swale. It is easy to spot these crossings in the swale grass by walking along the edge of it and looking for the bent-over grass. If there are rubs or scrapes at these trail crossings, you've found an excellent location for a stand.

## Rut Stands

Once the rut begins, the only thing a mature buck has on his mind is breeding. This makes it impossible to predict when and where he may be at any time. The best chance of seeing a buck from a stand all this time now is by hunting around the does. If you have a stand by a signpost rub with a breeding scrape near it, the odds of seeing a buck there are very good. However, some of the obscure signposts in a buck's territory may not get visited once the rut starts. I've checked on some signposts during the rut while looking for a buck track to

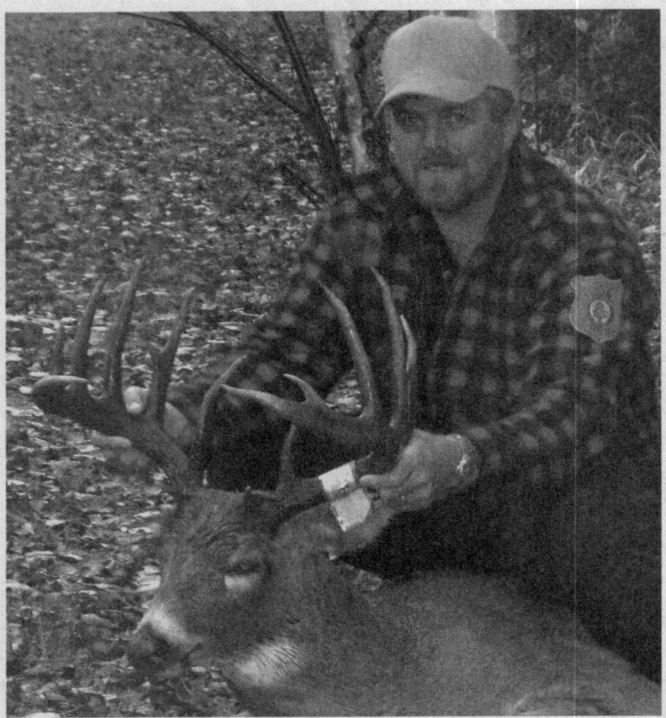

Guide Lee Libby with his 245-pound fourteen-pointer taken while watching a travel corridor in the back of a clear-cut in Ontario.

follow without seeing a track on week-old snow. That's not to say that a buck won't pass a signpost, but the ones they do pass prob ably will be between the areas where there are does.

Gene Nygaard shot this 205-pound eight-pointer while stand-hunting a doe area at a Cedar Ridge remote camp.

I feel the best stand locations during the rut are near does, and the does in any area may move from year to year depending on the food source. This means that you have to find the hardwood ridges or chop pings that the does are using. The more does in an area the better, because the odds of one being in estrus at any given time are greater. Every buck within miles will be checking on the does that they know are there, and you should be able to find a breeding scrape in an area where there are does. This scrape should be the prime loca tion for your stand. Pick a good vantage point where the wind will be in your favor.

This is a great time to use some doe-in-estrus scent. One way to use this scent is to put it on scent pads for your feet and use them when you walk to your stand. There is a chance that a buck might cross your trail and follow the scent right to you. If you don't have any scent pads, attach a small piece of rag to a string and tie it around your ankle so it drags on the ground behind you. Another way to use estrus scent is to hang a dispenser or spray it on a limb downwind of your stand. Make sure you have a clear shooting lane to the scent, because a buck most likely will stop there to smell it.

## All-Season Stands

Certain stand locations are effective any time of the season. These locations usually are associated with natural travel corridors, such as ridge saddles, stream crossings, or other terrain fea tures. The best way to find a potential stand location is to study a topo map of the area. Look for steep ridges that have saddles through them. The longer and steeper the ridge is, the better, because it will funnel more deer through the saddle.

Deer travel for the most part by taking the path of least resistance and following the natural flow of the terrain. They also tend to cross streams where the water is shallow. Shallow water moves faster and creates a riffle, which is less likely to freeze in cold weather. One day late in the season, I was tracking a buck along a ridge above a small stream. I knew a doe had been staying near the end of the ridge, and when I got there, I could see buck tracks were everywhere. I cir cled the area and found four different buck tracks leaving it, all going in the same direction. All of the buck tracks had been made the night before, and they all had checked on the doe. When the bucks dropped down into a flat along the stream, they converged on the same point to cross the stream. The stream was frozen except for about ten feet of fast-moving water where the bucks crossed, and the stream bank was cut back from years of deer crossing there. The combina tion of the flat along the stream and the shallow water made this a nat ural place for deer to cross and a great place for a stand.

Finding good stand locations is helpful for the still-hunter or tracker. You can use them for stopping points when still-hunting or as a place to look for a buck track to follow. One year, I was scouting an area that I had found the previous year. I found the area while track ing a buck through it, and there was enough good sign to warrant going back. I was fortunate enough to have a little snow on the ground when I went back to do some scouting. I cut a good buck track that was a couple of days old coming down out of a saddle. The track turned along a steep hardwood ridge and intersected another buck track that was going in the opposite direction. As I looked down the other track, I could see a scrape. Twenty yards away from it, there was another scrape. I could see that this ridge was funneling the bucks around it and thought it would be a good place for a stand.

I continued on the tracks until they came to the end of the ridge, and I realized that it was the spot where the buck I tracked the year before had gone. It was an intersection of two buck trails, so I thought that this could be a real hotspot for a stand. A lit tle shelf that stuck out from the ridge would make a good ambush point. I decided this was going to be one of my taking-a-break or sandwich spots when I was in the area.

I didn't get back into that spot until the third week of the season that year. There was a dusting of snow on the ground, and I was track ing a buck with a client. We had picked the track up about a mile away and followed it off the end of the ridge to the trail intersection. The buck then went down in the low ground where there was no snow. It was getting to be sandwich time, so we went up to the little shelf to take a break. We spent an hour there and then continued on our hunt.

The next week, I was hunting for myself with a cameraman named Rob Wing, and I decided to try that area again. I picked up an aver age-sized buck track that morning on crusty snow. I followed the buck around a swamp as he checked on some does. The buck finally headed up a ridge and started following the track of a monster buck that had been there the day before. Both bucks were headed back along the ridge toward the swamp. I decided to hunt toward the little shelf, which was about a half mile away, in hopes of finding a better track to follow. I was thinking that a buck might have come out of the saddle in the steep ridge, but no such luck.

Once again, I decided to take a sandwich break on the shelf. Rob and I went up on the shelf and kicked out a place to sit where we could watch both trails. Once I sat down, I realized I couldn't see down into the hardwood ravine. I thought about moving over, but fig ured anything coming through the saddle would come around the shelf. Boy, did I call that one wrong.

We had been sitting there about half an hour and I was just get ting my cookies out when Rob said he could here crust breaking in the ravine. I got up on one knee and spotted a deer walking along about 100 yards away. I took out my binoculars and got them focused just in time to see a tall-tined buck pass between two trees. I brought my gun up but couldn't get a shot, because now all I could see were flicks of brown as the buck disappeared into the green growth. Had I only followed my instincts and moved over to where I could see in the ravine, I would have seen the buck coming from more than 100 yards away. The buck had come down out of the saddle, right where we had just checked for tracks. Oh well, that's the way it goes. But at least it proved to be a good stand, and I know I'll be there again.

Sometimes a good stand location requires a long walk to get to it. Other times you might find a good location close to or where a buck crosses a gravel road or winter road. Bucks tend to avoid roads with a lot of activity, especially during the day, but in some areas there are just too many logging roads to avoid them. Usually, these road crossings are in travel corridors between terrain features where bucks have always traveled. There is a place like this in one of my remote camp areas.

When they logged the area about ten years ago, they built a road between a steep ridge and a swale bog. The road ended in line with the end of the bog and just beyond where the ridge ended. A brushy ravine crossed the road and had ledges on the backside of it and a flat area about seventy-five yards long between the ravine and the end of the steep ridge. It was a natural travel corridor. Over the years, we tracked plenty of bucks across the road at that spot. The second week of the season one year, Mike Featherstone had some hunters who wanted to stand-hunt. He told one of them to put his tree stand up where he could watch this crossing. Mike drove off, and the hunter put his stand up and climbed into it just as it started to snow. Fifteen min utes later, the hunter spotted a buck making his way up to the road. He said the buck looked both ways and stepped into the road. One quick shot and that hunter had himself the big woods buck of his dreams. Being in the right place at the right time is everything!

## Migration-Trail Stands

Deer use migration trails to get to their wintering areas. These trails can be miles long, and the closer to the yard they get, the more deer use them. When the snow begins to get deep and temperatures drop to near zero degrees for an extended period, the deer will start moving toward their yarding area by following these age-worn trails. Usually this migration takes place in early December, but occasion ally begins in late November. When it does, these trails are great places for stand-hunters to set up. Does and fawns are typically the first to go to the yards, but mature bucks that may not otherwise go to a yard will follow a doe in estrus to it.

Migration trails sometimes are the most productive stands of all. They are easy to find and identify, once they start being used. All but an occasional track in the migration trail will be going in the same direction. Usually a track going in the opposite direction is a buck searching the trail for a doe or going back to where he came from.

The easiest way to find a migration trail is by driving logging roads. Once you locate a crossing, check your map for another road in the direction the deer are coming from. Try to find the largest area of woods that the deer are coming from so there is less of a chance another hunter is set up on the same trail. Another good place to look for migration trails is along streams and around lakes or ponds. These are natural places for them, because there usually is softwood cover that keeps the snow depth down.

You may find a migration trail while hunting on bare ground with out realizing what it is. If you find a well-worn trail in the woods that doesn't appear like it's being used very much, there's a good chance that it's a migration trail. Hundreds of deer use these trails every year to get to and from the yard, causing the trails to get worn into the ground. Other than that, these trails see very little use. I've checked migration trails week after week during the season without ever see ing a track. Then, once the migration starts, I will find new tracks on them every day. You may not be able to use a migration-trail stand every year, but the years you can could be productive ones.

## Up Your Odds

Stand-hunting is also a good time to try calling deer. Calling can increase your chances of seeing a buck, because you may lure one that is passing out of sight back toward your stand. Obviously, calling is not going to work every time, but I've seen it work enough to know it helps tip the odds in your favor. It also helps to pass the time when you're spending a long day on stand.

Rattling is most effective during the pre-rut period. It is well suit ed to hunting in the big woods by virtue of the sound carrying the far thest of any calls. When deer densities are low, the farther the sound carries, the more likely a buck will hear it. One year at Cedar Ridge, three of the hunters in camp rattled in good bucks in one week. Two of the bucks were put on the pole and the third buck was missed. I wasn't very far away from one of the hunters, so I got a first-hand account of what happened.

Lee Libby and I had been guiding our clients in the same area. Lee had a father and son, both named Gary, and I was guiding one of my regular clients, Sue Morse. Gary Tiso (senior) had missed the buck he rattled in from his tree stand on Tuesday. Thursday morning was clear and cold with about an inch of snow on the ground. Lee set up Gary junior against the root ball of a blown-down tree, where he could watch a logging road. There had been a good buck crossing the road quite frequently near two grown-up clear-cuts, so Lee figured this spot would be a good bet. Sue and I decided to sit for a while that morning in a ravine where we had found some good buck activity the day before. We hadn't been sitting there long when a shot rang out in the distance. About five minutes later, two more shots echoed through the cold, still air. The shots had come from Gary junior's direction, so I decided to go check on him.

I walked the half mile back to the truck and drove toward Gary, not knowing at the time exactly where he was sitting, but just driving along and looking for footprints going into the woods. I spotted him standing beside the root ball, thirty yards off

Gary Tiso rattled in this 205-pound eight-pointer in the pre-rut at a Cedar Ridge remote camp.

the road. He said he'd shot a buck and pointed at the ground behind him. When I asked him if he had called Lee on the radio, he told me that in his excitement, he had dropped the radio in the water and it wasn't working. I got my radio out and called Lee to tell him Gary had shot a buck. While we were waiting for Lee to get there, Gary told me his story.

He said Lee put him in a chair against the root ball for cover, with a good view of where the buck had been crossing the road. As soon as Lee left to put his father on stand, Gary did a rattling sequence and settled in for the wait. He said about fifteen minutes later, he heard a stick snap behind him. He knew it must be a deer, so he turned his head to peek through the roots.

Gary said he couldn't believe his eyes when he saw a nice eight-point buck walking right toward him through the whips. He eased his gun up over the roots just as the buck stopped about thirty feet away. Gary said all he could see was the buck's head above the whips—and at the shot, the buck dropped dead in his tracks. That buck had pin pointed the rattling, and it didn't take him long to get there.

Buck grunting as well as doe bleating also can be effective when sitting on stand. There are so many different calls on the market today that trying to pick the right one can be overwhelming. Not all deer sound alike, so not all calls have to sound alike. Using a call proper ly is far more important than the brand of call you use. To be effec tive at calling, you have to learn what sounds to make in certain situations. I don't consider myself an expert deer caller, because I don't sit on stand to practice it enough. Most of the calling I do is to tip the odds in my favor while tracking and still-hunting. I still rely on my trusty old Alaskan deer call, but they are not made anymore. If you want to learn how to call deer effectively, I suggest you contact Peter Fiduccia, at Woods 'N' Water, Inc. Peter, who has been calling deer for more than forty years and is the foremost authority on the subject, says that to call deer effectively you have to "create the illusion." His books and DVDs will help you to learn the proper calls for every situation.

## Quick Stands

Sometimes a stand made quickly or at the spur of the moment can pay off in places where circumstances tell you to take a stand there. It might be some hot doe activity you stumbled across or some new buck sign that piques your interest. A stand doesn't have to be elaborate; it could be some boughs thrown down on the ground so you can sit against a tree. Don't be afraid to take a chance on a hunch, because sometimes hunches can change your luck.

One of my guides, Tom Hamilton, had his hunters sit in an area that I had been moose hunting in that fall. I told Tom that I'd found where a couple of different bucks were hanging around some new choppings.

Tom decided to scout around in that area the next day and found a good scrape line through one of the choppings. He brushed up a quick ground blind with the intention of putting a hunter in it the fol lowing day. It snowed in the night, and Tom took a hunter into that stand shortly after daylight the next morning. Not long after, a nice eight-point buck came along, opening up his scrapes again. That was the last trip that buck made through his territory.

There are many different types of stands a hunter can use, includ ing commercially made ladder stands as well as portable climbing and hang-on stands. There are also pop-up-tent type blinds that are good for blocking the wind and keeping your scent from dispersing.

The type of woods and terrain you're hunting will dictate which stand or blind is the best choice for the area. The type of stand you use also will depend on how far back in the woods your stand loca tion is. If it is a good walk in, you may prefer to go with a blind made from natural materials around the area. Ground blinds can be made as simple or as elaborate as you choose.

But no matter what type of stand you decide to sit in, the proper location for it is far more important than the stand itself.

A ladder stand is quick and easy to get into and it gives a hunter the advantage.

This buck is scent checking (flehmening) for any does that might be coming intro estrus. Credit: Sue Morse.

# Stand Placement: 7 Steps to Staying in Bucks All Season

As beneficial as learning how to combat odor has been in delivering shot opportunities, developing a strategy for stand placement during the various phases of the season has been every bit as critical for putting me in the right position. I feel so strongly about this that half of my first book, *Advanced Stand Hunting Strategies*, is dedicated to nothing else.

When you really break it down, a mature buck and his habitat go through many changes over the course of a season. It should come as no surprise to students of trophy bucks that changing testosterone levels trigger many of the significant behaviors and processes these animals endure. In chronological order, the testosterone's rise and eventual fall prompts velvet shedding and increased aggression, serves as a priming mechanism for rubbing and scraping, becomes a factor in increased daylight movement, and, ultimately, causes the eventual shedding of the antlers. Of course, one must also factor the estrous cycles of does and the presence of fawns into the equation. All of that results in some serious changes in a buck's life.

The deer's habitat goes through many changes as well, transforming from a relatively lush bounty that provides protective cover to a setting that is comparatively barren. Food sources are also undergoing massive changes in both desirability and availability.

Once one begins grasping all of the changes that occur over a hunting season, it becomes easy to understand that a buck's wants, needs and desires also change. Not coincidentally, his general patterns shift with these changes. Because of that, it only makes sense to change our hunting strategies to mirror these facts.

Effectively doing this really boils down to answering what drives bucks during the season. From that, we can see seven distinct phases of season: early season, the October lull, peak scrape phase, chase phase, breeding phase, second rut and post rut. With that understanding, we can devise precise strategies for each phase that maximize the hunter's odds by focusing on what bucks want and need.

## EARLY-SEASON SUCCESS

To begin the season, bucks are living a pretty good life. Food sources and cover are plentiful. Depending on the date of the opener, bucks are either experiencing the tail end of their bachelor grouping days or have just recently disbanded. Either way, though a loose pecking order has already been established, the all-out battles for position within the buck hierarchy and breeding rights are still to come. All in all, it's a pretty good time to be a mature buck.

Buck patterns change with the phases of season. To keep yourself in mature bucks all season long, you must change with them.

During this phase of season, consisting of approximately the first two weeks after the opener, food, water, safety and comfort are the bucks' top priorities. Because they haven't had to worry about man much yet, many still feel relatively safe moving during late-afternoon hours. All of this makes targeting a mature buck's food and water sources a good choice.

Obviously, a critical component in pulling that off is finding at least one mature buck to target. Early-season success is all about nailing a buck's route between bedding and food and water. Unlike during the rut, bucks won't be covering much ground. If you aren't keyed into their patterns, the odds of success plummet. Observations and scouting cameras performing surveillance on selected foods and water sources are tremendous aids.

When employing either, you have three goals. Obviously, the first is to make sure a shooter is present. Next, pinpointing his trail is key. All too often, one close call is all a hunter can hope for. Blowing it by guessing and setting up on a trail upwind of the buck's entrance route almost always equals failure for hunters who don't take odor control to the extreme. Last, finding and documenting his track can be extremely beneficial. It's important to mention scouting now so you can begin to understand how tracks can be put to productive use.

Though nailing the early-season patterns of one buck is a good start, it's always best to have backups. My goal each season is to have the patterns of three separate bucks nailed for early season. I've found that having three allows me to shift between them enough to keep each buck off guard and my stands fresh. Along with that, it provides a safety blanket for when something unexpected ruins the best-laid plans on one or two of these bucks.

At this point, I'm sure many readers are thinking that it's impossible for them to pattern three mature bucks. I also wouldn't be surprised if some believe the only reason I can is because I'm a spoiled writer with sole access to endless acres of prime hunting lands. As much as I wish this were the case, I can honestly say that it isn't. I'm blessed to work as a consultant for some of the top outfitters, and I do receive the right to hunt as partial payment. However, their clients always come first.

I begin the hunting season in my home state of Wisconsin each year, with every intention of filling that buck tag before moving on to other states. I'm extremely lucky to work with Tom Indrebo who, along with his wife, Laurie, owns and operates Bluff Country Outfitters in trophy rich Buffalo County. One of the three bucks I strive to pattern does come from their lands.

The other two are almost always on Wisconsin's heavily hunted public lands. It shouldn't come as a surprise that most hunters don't believe mature bucks exist in such areas. I'm here to tell you that they do in more cases than not. I also have firsthand knowledge that it's the same for public lands in Minnesota, Michigan, Iowa, Illinois, Kansas, Missouri and Alberta, Canada.

Particularly around bedding areas, stand sites should be prepared well before season begins.

Though I haven't hunted public lands in other regions of the white-tail's range, I do know hunters who have unearthed mature bucks on public lands in most states and provinces. In other words, if you're willing to put in the work and some miles on the truck, I feel confident that the majority of readers are capable of patterning three mature bucks. However, just like me, most will also have to compete with other hunters on public lands to accomplish that.

Another consideration is that I want to be done patterning these bucks and have stands prepared a full week before season begins, which provides a little time for the woods to settle down. However, concluding your observations and stand prep much before that time increases the risk that the buck's patterns may naturally change before season begins.

When determining stand sites, a balance must be struck between getting within bow range and staying undetected. So long as the buck doesn't bust the hunter, the battle continues. Once busted, the war is almost always over. Because of that, I take an outside approach, focusing my hunting on the fringes of a buck's core area and only moving in when necessary.

Even when focusing on the outside, one should only hunt stands that offer the best access and lowest odds of disturbing the buck. Obviously, for most hunters, that includes only hunting stands with the right wind. Because of the low impact they typically provide, sitting stands on food and water sources qualifies as a productive way of hunting from the outside.

The risk of using these stands is that the hunter had better be prepared to stay pinned in the tree until after dark. Crawling down before, a sea of eyes will effectively blow the deal, even if Mr. Big isn't amongst them.

A stand placed just off of the food source, back in the woods where the trail splits or is intersected by a crossing trail, is another good choice. Being 20–50 yards back in is often enough to catch bucks during the last few minutes of legal hours. The price is that the hunter loses the possibility of selecting the wrong trail, but still having a monarch feed its way into range.

The choice should ultimately be made according to which placement is least intrusive and still provides maximum odds of a daylight encounter. With all of that in place, early season can be a great time to arrow a mature buck!

## BEATING THE OCTOBER LULL

Unfortunately, in most areas receiving pressure, daylight sightings on the food and water sources dry up after the first couple weeks of season, In many areas, this is also about the same time that leaves begin dropping. The combination of hunting pressure and the sudden nakedness of the woods drives many mature bucks toward a more nocturnal lifestyle.

I believe the approaching breeding phase further inspires this. Between fighting, chasing does and breeding, bucks burn more energy during that phase than in any other. At the same time, feeding activity is often dramatically reduced. The net result is the need to build a thick layer of fat to serve as energy reserves for the approaching breeding phase. Reducing movement by spending the daylight hours lounging in bed and gorging themselves during the dark hours is the avenue many mature bucks use to build the impressive fat layers they will soon rely on.

Because of all this, it's often necessary to get close to a buck's bedding area to realize daylight movement. The mission is to set up along the buck's path to food, as close to his bed as is reasonably possible, without him knowing you're there.

A big part of that is getting in and out unnoticed. Remember, if all plays out the way we hope, the buck will be in that bed when we slip in for our afternoon hunt. If he catches us, the jig is up.

There really isn't a cut-and-dried answer to how close we can get. Many factors, such as wind direction, topography, the buck's ability to see approaching danger, the noise made entering the stand and the hunter's own skill at slipping undetected through the woods, all work together to decide what this distance is.

Complicating matters is that we want to get it right the first time. Bucks are very in tune to the territory close to their bedding areas. Even when we keep trimming activities and other disturbances to a minimum, chances are it's asking too much to get away with adjusting stand locations around the buck's bedding area. Ideally, the stand should be prepped. before season and left alone.

Ultimately, the precise placement becomes a balance between being close enough to realize daylight movement, the amount of noise that will be made getting in, the buck's ability to see from his bed, and each hunter's ability to remain undetected. As with many things in hunting, allow common sense and woodsmanship to be your guides. Do that, and the October lull can be beaten!

## SCRAPING UP BUCKS

As challenging as the lull can be, it also serves as the doorway to the peak scraping phase. Now is when things start getting to be really fun for those who have done their homework.

At this point, building testosterone levels are really starting to show their effect. With breeding time approaching, bucks want to firmly establish their position in the hierarchy and advertise their presence. Because of that, fresh scrapes and rubs are now appearing daily.

Scrapes are now great places to hunt, but there are hurdles to doing so effectively. One of them is that a mature buck can make over 200 scrapes during a season. Of these, he tends a relatively low percentage on a consistent basis. Furthermore, though his daylight movements are now on the rise, most of his scraping activities will still occur at night. Ultimately, successful scrape-hunting techniques boil down to proper timing, targeting scrapes that are consistently used by mature bucks during daylight hours, and keeping bucks ignorant of the fact that they're being hunted.

By the beginning of the peak scraping phase, bucks are really starting to feel the effects of their rising testosterone levels.

The timing factor is important because if hot scrapes are hunted too early, chances are good that the bucks working them are still predominately nocturnal. Under those conditions, the most likely outcome is that the bucks will be educated and abandon the scrapes before the hunter has a fighting chance. On the flip side, once the chase phase begins, mature bucks are way too focused on finding does to worry about regularly tending even their hottest scrapes.

I've found hunting scrapes to be the best during the 12-day period before the chase phase begins. In most of the upper Midwest, that translates to the last five days of October and the first seven days of November. In other areas, backing up from the peak breeding date by three weeks is a good starting point.

Next, one must find the right scrapes to target. The best route to uncovering consistently worked scrapes comes through spring scouting. Because scrapes are whitetails' equivalent of billboards, it only makes sense that the most effective advertising will be located in areas where deer activities are concentrated. Provided that drastic changes don't occur in deer patterns or habitat, those locations remain the same year after year, and so do the sites of the most productive scrapes.

Finding scrapes in the spring provides the opportunity to gauge the level of use they received. Simply put, scrapes with a deep bowled-out shape or overly exaggerated ovals of dirt accurately reveal that they were worked the most consistently last fall. Because of the likelihood that they will be used heavily again, it's a very good bet that they will be hot scrapes again during the coming season.

If spring scouting simply isn't an option, the task becomes harder, but certainly not impossible. Mid-October scouting trips reveal many scrapes. The trick is determining which ones are being used most heavily. Performing these in-season scouts during mid-day hours helps minimize disturbances.

Once the area's consistently worked scrapes have been found, one must then target the scrapes most likely to be used during daylight. Though field-edge scrapes often look impressive, scrapes located back in the woods or in secluded openings are better choices. The feeling of safety these areas provide can be enough to entice a buck to visit during daylight. Scrapes located near a buck's bedding area also provide better odds of intercepting him during daylight, as he slips into his bedroom after a late night or decides to get up a little earlier in the afternoon. Finally, scrapes positioned on the downwind sides of doe-bedding areas are good choices.

Stand location is an important consideration. Because many mature bucks check scrapes by skirting them on the downwind side, a lot of stands that cover scrapes allow many bucks to slip through outside of bow range.

Personally, I've always had the best luck by placing stands about 20 yards away on the prevailing wind's downwind side of the scrape. Doing this not only allows me to cover the scrape, but also to cover the bucks that are slipping by as much as 50 yards downwind. I have found that such positioning produces more shot opportunities than any other. Following those guidelines can produce fantastic results.

## BEATING THE CHASE

As the scrape phase draws to a close, the insanity begins. With a handful of early does already bred and more does being on the cusp of readiness, mature bucks now seem to lose their composure. It's almost as if they can't resist checking every doe they can find. If she is close, you can bet they'll chase her all around the woods. Heck, they'll often even dog does that are over a week or more away from being ready to breed.

For as much fun as the bucks seem to have, does that are not ready for breeding appear not to want to have anything to do with their games. They often head for the thickest cover they can find and run circles through it, trying to lose their pursuers. Often, the chase doesn't end until either she loses the bucks in the cover or they tire of her and go off to find another doe and repeat the process.

Two stand placements work very well during this phase. The first is stands placed in funnels separating doe concentrations. Because bucks are going from doe concentration to doe concentration, their travels will likely involve using these funnels.

The next effective placement is slapping stands in the thickest cover the area provides. In this case, it's best to pick trees that are on the downwind edge of the cover and that offer the best concealment. Because the doe is likely to run all over the cover, providing shot opportunities in unpredictable locations, I've found that going undetected is a better strategy than setting up where the most sign can be covered. Chances are every bit as good she'll lead them by there as anywhere else.

Another consideration is that in this situation, numerous shooting lanes are a must. When trying to arrow a buck chasing a doe, the chances of things occurring in an orderly fashion are almost nonexistent.

Balancing your need for numerous shooting lanes with your ability to refrain from clear-cutting the cover will tilt the odds toward the buck eventually stopping in an opening. Setting up on the edge of the thicket means half of the stand-coverage area will require less trimming to create shooting lanes. Still, because of the overall level of trimming required, it's best to prepare these stand sites well before season begins. When in the right place at the right time, this brief, five-day or so phase can result in literally having a parade of bucks pass the stand.

## BRINGING ORDER TO THE BREEDING CHAOS

Obviously, the chase phase signals that breeding time has nearly arrived. I've always found it rather ironic that so many hunters are convinced that the breeding phase offers their best chance of arrowing Mr. Big. Frankly, I've long believed that this is the phase that requires more luck than any other.

The idea of patterning a specific buck now has been thrown out the window. During the breeding phase, most mature bucks dramatically expand their home ranges, with a percentage abandoning them altogether. Simply put, they are putting on the miles in search of hot does. Once she's found, he will try to corral her off in an area where he can have her all to himself. If she resists his lead, he will follow her anywhere she wants to go. In other words, his patterns have been thrown out the window.

Understanding what a buck wants and how he gets it is the key to bringing order to this chaos. Mature bucks want to find a steady supply of hot does. To accomplish this, they must check the locations where does concentrate. Additionally, bucks need to do that in ways that expend the least amount of effort and provide the greatest safety.

Strategically positioned topographical funnels help them save energy and feel safe, offering the easiest route through otherwise challenging terrain.

For example, if there's a saddle in a steep ridge, it gives bucks that want to cross over the ridge an energy-saving option. By choosing to cross at the low spot, they're able to save gas for their doe-finding road trip. The steeper the ridge and lower the saddle, the more inviting that route becomes to the bucks. When a saddle separates two doe concentrations or food sources and doe-bedding areas, it can be a great setup.

Habitat funnels most often address the safety factor. To illustrate this, picture two square blocks of timber surrounded by open farm fields. Now, add a brush-choked fence line connecting them. After checking the does in one block, the buck can make a death run across the open field or travel the fence line's cover to the other timber. Unless previously educated by brushes with hunters in the funnel, the route with cover will appear much safer.

The best funnels are those that seem to be the easiest and safest routes to where bucks want to go. During the rut, funnels separating deer concentrations often result in the best stands available.

Another tactic that plays to rutting bucks' weaknesses is hunting doe-bedding areas. These are great places for bucks to find receptive does. That makes them great places for hunters to score.

Bucks commonly rely on the wind to help them scent-check does. The bucks' ability to determine the occupants" readiness by skirting the downwind side of a bedding area allows the hunter to effectively predict how most bucks will travel.

Setting stands 20 to 40 yards out from the downwind sides of doe-bedding areas is a good bet. However, when hunting large bedding areas, it's helpful to narrow movement down further. If a natural pinch point isn't present, the next best option is a stand placement that also covers the bedroom s main entrance and exit routes.

The final touch is a creative scent strategy: Because bucks are already cruising these bedding areas for does, estrus scents can be very effective at bringing them in for the shot. Estrus-drenched scent wicks can be placed on both sides of the stand to cut off bucks before they hit the hunter's odor stream. If a buck takes a route farther downwind than anticipated, he'll hit one of the two wicks' odor stream before encountering the hunter's scent.

Though one can never remove the element of luck from hunting the breeding phase, hunters certainly can stack the odds in their favor. Hunting funnels and doe-bedding areas are two ways of doing just that.

## GEARING UP FOR LATE-SEASON SUCCESS

Once breeding winds down, bucks' priorities shift drastically. Regardless of whether we're talking northern or southern regions, the stresses of the rut commonly cause mature bucks to lose 25 to 30 percent of their body weight.

At this point, a buck's primary interest no longer lies in cementing his standing in the buck hierarchy or in finding receptive does. Certainly, he is still more than happy to take advantage of breeding opportunities, but his primary focus is on surviving winter.

With food sources now at a seasonal low point, deer concentrate at the best options still available.

In farm country, a standing row crop can draw them from over 10 miles away. In the big woods, fresh new growth after logging can be a deer magnet. In northern regions, traditional yarding areas are capable of pulling deer from incredible distances. All of these activities are aimed toward increasing their odds of survival.

As in early season, finding Mr. Big and nailing his food source is critical Furthermore, when the temps dip below the seasonal average for your hunting area, the same early-season stand-placement strategies can work well.

However, the key to that placement strategy working is most often the temperature. When the temps drop significantly below normal, as opposed to feeding during the late-night hours, deer have survival incentive to shift their feeding activities to the comparatively warmer late afternoon hours. When that occurs, the amount of daylight feeding can be significant.

Unfortunately, when temps are in the normal to warm range, many bucks hardly move during daylight. For that reason, the same tactics used during the lull phase must be implemented.

As a side note, hunting close to buck-bedding areas is the tactic of choice during any conditions that lead bucks toward more nocturnal activities.

Regardless of which approach is used, one must understand that these deer are now more hypersensitive to disturbances than at any other point in season. They have survived the war of firearms and most of bow season by knowing the importance of avoiding humans.

That makes it even more critical to keep disturbances to a minimum and get it right the first time. If a stand is positioned on the wrong trail, the hunter gets winded or the access route in or out spooks deer, the chances of success go down dramatically. Even more than during any other phase of bow season, late-season hunters don't get many second chances.

During the second rut, decoys can be effectively used to pull bucks to your location. Though buck decoys are the author's choice during most of season, during the breeding and second-rut phases, he prefers to use either just a doe decoy or a buck-and-doe combination.

With all that said, late season may be the best-kept secret of hunting. Many of my very best hunts have occurred under the most miserable conditions that late season can throw at a hunter.

## CAPITALIZING ON THE SECOND RUT

When it comes to the second rut, my entire strategy revolves around finding where the family groups are feeding. Find that and you will almost always find the bucks, regardless of the abundance or complete lack of buck sign. The second rut is very hit-and-miss. Unlike the first go around, the breeding window isn't nearly as tight and nowhere near as many females are available.

Frankly, the second rut can happen any day of late season and will most often occur in several little bursts. In most of the whitetail's upper Midwest and northern range, I believe that determining the second rut by adding 28 days to peak breeding is a myth. That date is when does that missed the first go around will come back into estrus. Though I don't dispute the estrous cycle, I simply don't believe that enough does are missed the first time they come into estrus to be a factor. Instead, I believe that fawns coming into estrus for the first time make up the majority of the second-rut breeding opportunities in these regions. Down south, I credit the late breeding of does to the breeding phase being spread out over a much longer period of time. In either case, I believe that predicting when these breeding opportunities will occur is impossible.

Though bucks rarely will go wandering in search of second-rut breeding opportunities, they certainly won't them pass up. Because there aren't many breeding opportunities left, we can use this to our advantage.

Mature bucks can still respond very positively to estrous scents. Often, because they aren't already with a doe, bucks will actually respond better than they did during the first rut. Because of that, it only makes sense to use strategically placed scent wicks to draw bucks to our stand. That's particularly beneficial when hunting stands that guard broader areas, such as food sources.

Estrous scents are even more effective when paired with doe decoys. With the exception of late season and the breeding phase, I most commonly use buck decoys. Not only do I believe they are more effective during most of season, but they also work to keep does away. Frankly, when does spend much time near a decoy, it almost always ends with a snorting-and-foot-stomping fest. However, during the breeding and second-rut phases, I feel decoys draw bucks much better when used as a doe.

Decoys work most effectively during late season when stands can't be placed in the thick of the action. Often, because of the sheer numbers of deer that prime late-season food sources draw, it can be impossible to place stands downwind of all the deer. In such cases, it's best to place stands in areas less desirable, but safer to hunt. The risk of does hanging around the decoy will be minimized. At the same time, the combination of a quality estrous scent, decoy and a few estrous calls can be just the ticket to drawing a buck across a food source.

As I'm sure you gathered from what I wrote earlier in this section, I don't really believe that you can separate the second rut from late season. To me, they both consist of the same time period, and which one is dominant on any given day will be decided by the doe-fawn's readiness.

Still, I break the late season and second rut into separate phases because of the hunting techniques used for both. As far as choosing which one to use on a given day, I begin hunting late-season strategies for the first few weeks after the breeding phase concludes. After that, I'll switch between late-season and second-rut strategies fairly regularly, allowing the weather to decide which I'll use most often. If it's nasty cold, I'm hunting the food sources. If it's mild, I'm back by the bed. To switch things up occasionally, I'll pull out the scents and decoys. Of course, if I see breeding signs, I'll focus more heavily on second-rut strategies for a while. At the very least, routinely changing things keeps the deer off balance and the stands fresher.

## CONCLUSION

With the number of changes that occur to the habitat and food sources, as well as those the bucks endure, it's no wonder that pitifully few stand locations are good from opening day to the close of season. Staying in bucks the entire season requires that stand sites be shifted to take advantage of what drives bucks during each phase. Doing that is the ticket to making hunting each phase of season as productive as it can be.

Spring is the best time to find hot scrapes to hunt during the upcoming season, but they can still be uncovered during season. However, one must be careful not to educate deer with careless scouting trips.

# THE RUT
## The Rut's Golden Rules

For just a moment, think about the number of times I've mentioned that it doesn't take a lot of skill to kill a trophy whitetail during the primary rut. All you need is a little luck. If there's a big one in the area, he could walk by you or some other hunter leaning against a tree two hundred yards away. However, things can still go terribly wrong for folks like you and I who work so hard to shoot a mature buck.

Some hunters stick to one favorite ambush location where they were successful in the past. Keep an open mind, scout continuously and keep an eye on the does.

Most serious deer hunters spend countless hours reading about rut-hunting tactics that can be applied during the hunting season. Let's face it. In the past decade, there has been no shortage of articles on the subject. Some tell you how to hunt big bucks during all portions of the archery season, and there are stories that suggest proven drills—from luring bucks into range with a call, to hunting food sources, rub lines, scrapes and trails. You've already read about these topics, however there's much more to the story.

Don't get me wrong. Articles that focus on tactics to fool rutting trophy bucks deserve the full attention of any serious trophy whitetail hunter. I

If you pattern the does during the primary rut, you will soon know if a big buck is in the area during the primary rut. However, be realistic and aware that quality private lands and remote public areas are the places where big bucks prefer to roam in search of does.

read them with interest and I always keep an open mind. However, in most of these stories, at least six ingredients are commonly overlooked. In fact, regardless of the tactics you use, you must consider the following advanced common-sense topics if you hope to tag a trophy.

## 1. Pattern the Does

Despite our desire to hunt the same stomping grounds year after year, we must be sure that a trophy buck exists before deciding on a location. For instance, I have "favorite" areas that I know as well as the inside of my hunting closet (my wife disagrees). It's fun to hunt these areas because of past experiences and successes, but they are not necessarily the places to be during the rut. Simply said, a mature whitetail buck must roam this territory if I am to have a chance at intercepting him.

Getting stuck on an old spot can be detrimental to tagging a big buck. It's true that some favorite spots are almost always good places to be, and there are often good reasons why certain ambush locations consistently produce big bucks. Nonetheless, I would suggest keep one eye and ear open. Returning to a spot where you once took a trophy buck does not mean that lightning will strike twice in the same place.

Since "seeing is believing," many veteran bowhunters spend several hours watching food sources before the season. Take my good friend Tim Hillsmeyer, who has tagged several Pope and Young caliber bucks. Near dusk, Hillsmeyer often drives the roads in agricultural areas to locate big bucks, because the deer are visiting food sources in daylight hours. He also sets up near food sources with his binoculars handy, making certain that his presence is not detected while watching a particular field.

We discussed this tactic in the pre-rut section, but I mention it again to remind you that it's the existence of does that will attract bucks during primary rut. For this reason, you must know where the does will be. My point is, never limit your scouting to the pre-rut only. It's necessary to know exactly where a big buck is feeding and bedding if you want to pattern and kill him during pre-rut, and the same is true during the primary rut. It's necessary to know exactly where the does are feeding and bedding if you want to pattern and kill that same big buck you didn't shoot during the pre-rut.

## 2. Build Landowner Relations

It pays to have a good relationship with a landowner to tag a mature buck. It's no big secret; most successful trophy hunters pursue bucks on private lands that have little pressure. However, always consider gaining access to remote public ground that borders private land. Topographic maps are essential tools because many public-land bucks that survive year after year take refuge on or near adjoining private lands or hard-to-reach public ground when they feel pressured.

One item that will be helpful is an *Atlas and Gazetteer* by DeLorme, which provide topo maps of entire states in book format and are available at many sporting goods stores and bookstores. Finally, consider visiting the assessor's office in the county you hunt and purchasing a plat book to learn names of landowners.

## 3. Avoid Temptation

If you really want to tag a trophy buck, common sense dictates that you must overlook bucks that have not yet reached their full potential. If you want to take only a buck that makes it into the record books, you must be able to judge antlers quickly and effectively in the field—on short notice. Of course, your idea of a trophy may differ from that of another hunter.

If the area you hunt offers numerous tags, it can be more difficult to pass a smaller buck that offers a shot. You could simply take the lesser buck and continue hunting for a wall-hanger. Unfortunately, though, bad news accompanies that practice.

First, consider that shooting any deer may disqualify the area as a potential trophy-producing site. When you shoot a deer in a particular region, you are sure to create a disturbance and leave behind scent—a situation that can become critical if you must track the deer for a long distance.

It is also possible that shooting the smaller buck will cause the does, which would have brought in the wall-hanger, to vacate the area. For this reason alone, many dedicated trophy hunters refuse to harvest a smaller buck just because they carry an "extra" tag. I don't have a problem with shooting does and small bucks when tags are available. I'm just saying that serious trophy hunters know where their priorities lie, and will wait until the time is right before shooting just any deer.

If you have more than one tag, you might hold off on shooting a lesser buck until you kill a trophy. Shooting just any buck can quickly spoil a hunting area for days to come.

## 4. Error! Error!

Hillsmeyer claims that the most serious error a trophy hunter can make is scouting too often in the wrong places. He added that once a mature buck knows he is being hunted, the hunt might be over.

"Flush a buck out of hiding a time or two, and you can bet he's going somewhere else," said Hillsmeyer. "It's imperative that you do your scouting wisely, and then get in and out of an area without the buck knowing you are there."

I discussed this error in the pre-rut section, but I want to emphasize that a big buck will not appreciate getting bumped, even during the primary rut. If there are lots of does in the area, he might have spent several days there, even if it's unfamiliar territory. If you spook him, he'll probably take his chances looking for does elsewhere. Unlike subordinate bucks, mature bucks seldom "forgive and forget."

Since second shots at big bucks are rare, most trophy hunters never take chances when it comes to wind direction. In fact, hunting where the wind blows toward the area you expect the deer to come from is one way to insure you never see the buck you are waiting for. Thus, if the wind is wrong for your best ambush location, choose another even if it doesn't look as promising. It's better to sit in a bad location and not see any deer than to sit in a good location and spook one.

You should also pay close attention to air currents as you approach an ambush location, since they may differ from the actual wind direction. This can be accomplished easily by using scentless wind testing powder.

## 5. Hit it Hard

I'm proud of several bucks I've taken that now hang on my living room wall, and I can honestly say that most of them did not come easy. It seems I always have to walk so many miles, hang so many stands, lose so much sleep and see so many other deer before my shooting opportunity comes. It's like having a quota that must be filled, except there still are no guarantees that I will enjoy success even when the quota is met. Many readers have probably had the same experiences.

The one thing I must always do is hunt hard. I make it a point to be out there every chance I get. In other words, "Never put off till tomorrow what you can do today." Sure, you could get lucky and have a wall-hanger walk past you any time, but when the primary rut is in high gear, "Tomorrow may never come." The odds are more in your favor for getting one "tomorrow" if you're out there today.

Tim Hillsmeyer points out that you must hunt hard, even during the primary rut, if you hope to get a chance at a trophy whitetail. He claims that even if you don't get him today, you'll learn something that will help you tomorrow.

Hillsmeyer hit the nail on the head. "You can think of a thousand excuses why you shouldn't hunt, but the buck you are after is the one good reason to be there."

The best point Hillsmeyer makes about hunting often, though, is that you learn something each time you are there. You might not see the right buck today, but the experience could teach you something that will help you next time.

Logically speaking, we can safely assume that the whitetail's habits change considerably from week to week. They might not, but if they do and you are not aware of it, you'll be a day late when you head for the woods. Food sources change, as does hunting pressure. Each plays an important part in the whitetail's habits, and the hunter who is there at every opportunity may stay one step ahead of the bucks. Actually, change that to "does," the most

Don't think for a moment that hunting from the perch is the only way to kill a trophy buck. The primary rut is one of the best times to choose a ground ambush location and to still-hunt.

important word in the rut dictionary when you are trying to kill a big buck.

## 6. Choose Versatile Ambush Locations

It does help to stay on the move when it comes to ambush locations. I mentioned this in part I, but it's also valuable during the primary rut. Never limit yourself to hunting only from a tree stand when the breeding is underway.

Bowhunters are the world's worst about getting into a tree-stand rut, and some archers refuse to hunt from a ground site even when they switch to hunting with a firearm. Most assume they have no chance of killing a mature buck from the ground. I used to feel that way many years ago, but that was before I had taken several whitetails from a ground ambush.

Don't get me wrong. I'd rather be in a tree. I feel my best chance of intercepting a trophy buck is when I'm elevated in any portion of the hunting season. But when bucks are going crazy during the rut, why limit yourself to hunting from a tree? The rut is prime time to take a big buck from the ground, which means you can set up quickly in remote locations that have not been touched by others.

Then there's the still-hunting side of killing trophy bucks. Hillsmeyer, who usually hunts from a tree stand, has taken several bucks on the ground. He prefers a stiff wind and a quiet floor for still-hunting during the primary rut, when the foliage is thin, but he hunts on the ground during all phases of the rut.

You could say that hunting for a trophy buck is like baking a cake. You need to use the right methods and ingredients if you hope to get a topnotch finished product. In the case of hunting trophy whitetails during the primary rut, the scrapes, rubs, trails, and food sources of the does are the methods. The six previously mentioned topics are the ingredients. On the other hand, you might just try tempting a buck.

# Buck Foolery

You already know that the rut is the best time to take advantage of a mature buck. His survival instincts hit rock bottom, and a rutting buck's vulnerability is the key to luring him into bow or gun range. Easier said than done, but an effective tactic that many hunters overlook because they are so engrossed in rubs, scrapes, and trails.

Previous failure is probably the main reason hunters don't seriously attempt to lure in bucks. If it didn't work once, they assume it's a waste of time. Now don't get me wrong. There is no fool-proof lure tactic. However, I know of at least three methods that can bring rutting bucks into range. And one of them comes real close to being perfect, if conditions are right.

## The Grunt Phenomenon

I'm going to get the good news over first: Grunting to a mature buck during primary rut is the most reliable buck foolery method mentioned in this chapter. For a bowhunter, it should be considered the next best thing to a surefire tactic. In my opinion, grunting succeeds almost as often as it fails, providing conditions are favorable.

Consider the huge eight-pointer I harvested just a few months before writing this chapter. I had spotted a small buck earlier that morning. Wouldn't you know it: He walked within fifteen yards of my tree stand. I saw the big buck I wanted later, walking a ridge eighty yards to the west. I could tell immediately he wasn't likely to come in my direction.

The peak rut was only days away. This buck was alone. He was also out trooping around two hours after dawn. The wind was blowing from south to north, and my grunt call was handy. The stage was set to try calling this buck in closer.

My first grunt went unheard. The second grunt stopped him. The third prompted him to start walking toward me, and my heart pounded harder with each step he took. He came so rapidly that I wasn't sure there was enough time to prepare

The author shot this buck just days before the breeding began after luring him in with a grunt call. Credit: Vikki L. Trout.

for a shooting opportunity. And that's the way it often works. He never stopped coming, and within seconds he was walking by only ten yards away. I released as he passed through an opening just before hitting a thicket that would stop a Mack truck, much less my swiftly moving arrow. I won't go into the tracking details that followed, but I will say that eight hours later, my wife, and friend were helping me drag him out.

What's ironic is that just days before taking that buck, I had written a magazine article about grunting to rutting bucks. In that piece, I talked about another buck that was fooled by a grunt call. The conditions were remarkably similar to those that allowed me to take the huge eight-pointer I just mentioned earlier.

Veteran hunters know that whitetails are not vocal animals. Unlike turkeys that converse with other turkeys constantly, and elk that communicate regularly with other elk, deer seldom have much to say. However, they do talk under certain conditions.

Timing is of the essence when calling to a buck. You must call when the bucks are likely to respond, and the rut is the perfect time.

I carry a grunt tube with me throughout the hunting season. That includes the pre-rut and post-rut periods, and the time between. But I know that grunting too early in the season often fails to get a buck's attention, and may even arouse suspicion. Early in the pre-rut period, mature bucks are busy leaving rubs and scrapes but seldom spend any time pursuing does. Small bucks may check out a doe and even try chasing one, but the big boys know the right time is still days or weeks away.

Bucks commonly grunt when they pursue a doe, either while trailing one that passed by a few hours before or when in immediate pursuit of a hot doe. The grunt is triggered by the buck's excitement, so when he hears the grunt of another buck, he may find it necessary to investigate the source.

Not all bucks will respond to a grunt, but the possibility exists that they will when they are not in pursuit of a hot doe. There is little any hunter can do to lure a buck away from a breeding doe, or one that is about to breed.

Random calling is optional. In other words, you can try grunting at various times on stand when you do not see deer. I know some hunters who use a grunt tube every thirty minutes, hoping to attract a customer that is within hearing range. Unfortunately, random calling may hurt more than it helps.

We know a lot about call-shy turkeys, but we still are in the learning stages when it comes to luring in bucks with a grunt tube. Too much calling makes deer suspicious. I agree with that theory, for the most part. Look at it this way: Calling randomly will seldom produce results, and it will alert deer that something is not on the up-and-up. The idea is to grunt to a buck that would not otherwise offer a shooting opportunity. Why risk spoiling an opportunity with random calling?

Many grunts are not heard at a considerable distance. Today, many companies manufacture grunt calls capable of plenty of volume.

## Volume Counts

I can't tell you how many times I have called to a buck, only to have it continue on its merry way because it did not hear my grunts. A gentle breeze, noisy leaves, and calling too softly will cause this. Several years ago, I could not find a grunt tube that provided the volume necessary to attract most of the bucks I saw. Today, there are many that will produce the louder sounds.

It's hard to say just how far away a buck can hear your grunts, but I believe they can easily hear loud grunts more than one hundred yards off when favorable winds exist. By the way, I said "loud" and "favorable." Favorable conditions could mean a buck that is standing still, with no wind and no leaves falling.

But too much volume can hurt when a buck is close in open woods. I seldom grunt to a buck that is only forty to fifty yards away, unless I'm in a dense area. Bucks can hone in on a grunt that they hear loud and clear, and often, if they don't see other deer, they will not come closer.

When calling to a buck, grunt loud enough to get his attention. If he continues onward, you can assume he didn't hear you. Even if a mature buck doesn't want to respond to your call, you can bet he will stop and look toward you. I usually grunt again to help the buck pinpoint the sound, and to make certain he is convinced he did indeed hear a grunt.

Personally, I would much rather carry a loud grunt call. You can always tone it down if necessary, but you can't make a gentle call sound louder.

## Do and Don't Grunt When . . .

First, never grunt to a downwind buck. He will scent and the game will be over. Normally, when a buck is interested in your grunt, he will come straight at you. Never have I seen one circle and come to a grunt with its nose in the wind. However, if there is any chance that he can wind you, he probably will.

If you have a small buck in the area and spot a big buck at a distance, you have the perfect live decoy to accompany a grunt call.

I've already mentioned not grunting to a buck that is in pursuit of a doe. However, having another

This buck is trailing another deer. He could be following a doe, or another buck. However, at this moment he's most vulnerable to grunts and will probably respond.

deer around can be the perfect opportunity to grunt. The other deer becomes a living decoy that creates a perfect scenario.

Several years ago, I watched a mature buck chase a doe for thirty minutes. Never did the pair pass by in bow range. However, when a button buck walked in and began feeding on acorns nearby, I took advantage of the situation. The bigger buck lost the doe's trail and returned with his nose on the ground. He was about fifty yards from me and close enough to hear my grunt. When he spotted the young buck, he came without hesitation, ears slicked back, ready to kick his rival's you know what. Wow! Did he ever get a surprise when he hit the twenty-yard mark!

Another excellent time to grunt is when you see the right buck trailing another deer. First, consider that you don't know whether he's following a doe, or another buck. Bucks love to follow other bucks during primary rut, almost as much as they love following the trail of a doe.

One of the biggest bucks I ever lured into bow range with a grunt call came to me only after I distracted his attention from the trail of another deer. Unfortunately, I missed that 150-inch buck at twenty-three yards because I rushed the shot. My arrow sailed over his back.

In summarizing the use of grunts calls, let's just say that conditions constitute ninety percent of your success, or failure. You must grunt when everything is right or forget it. Grunt calls work, plain and simple. It's no big deal to pack one along, but it can become a big deal when other tactics fail. Or you could try something else in conjunction with grunts—some of the time.

## Decoying a Buck

More than likely, you haven't heard much about using decoys to bring "trophy" bucks into range. However, that's not because it's a new tactic that will soon blow all other strategies to the moon and back. Nope. It's just not really a great tactic to depend on. Decoys certainly attract attention, but too many things go wrong, as more and more hunters find out each season.

The primary rut is a great time to decoy bucks, and it's true that decoys today look real convincing. I own a couple of Flambeau decoys that will make you feel *good* if you were to see them from your ambush location. Of course, it's the real deer, particularly the big bucks, we're trying to fool.

Apart from looking real, there's a little more good news about decoys. They can sometimes work wonders and keep a buck from laying low. You know how it is: A buck gets to a field and skirts the edge, sees another deer, or decoy, and just might walk into the middle of an open arena. So much for "safety in numbers."

Another bit of good news is that you can use grunts in conjunction with buck decoys, a tactic that is often quite effective.

Many hunters have wondered which is best—a buck or a doe decoy. However, you can bet that when a mature buck spots a buck decoy and hears a grunt, he probably will want to get in the last word.

It's hard to say which are better, buck or doe decoys, but I'll go with buck decoys during the primary rut. Veteran decoyers might argue the point, but there's nothing carved in stone just yet. I'm fond of buck decoys because I believe they appeal to mature bucks, while little bucks are likely to respond to *any* decoy. Trophy whitetails seldom walk up to every doe they see. They can tell if a doe is breeding, or close to it, and they don't waste their time on just any doe, or decoy. A decoy with small antlers, though, is another story. They just can't ignore another buck during the rut, even if he's small.

The major problem with decoys is those doggoned does. They can't stand to see another deer that doesn't move. Your decoy will drive the does nuts. Even if you use decoys with moveable tails, does may not fall for it. They are curious animals when it comes to strangers in the area. They're also quite inhospitable toward other deer that just stand around and don't do anything.

It's almost inevitable that a doe will see your decoy before a big buck, and when she spots a decoy, she will investigate. Ninety-nine times out of a hundred, that will spoil your chance at a big buck if one happens to be around. Does will stomp, snort, and anything else a deer can do at a decoy to make sure you wasted your day's hunt.

Here are a few suggestions that will increase your chances of success: Wear rubber gloves when handling decoys. Sometimes a doe will walk up and smell a decoy, and you don't want to leave human scent all over the decoy or the surrounding area for that matter. A bowhunter should keep his decoy within range, even if it's on top of him. I would also suggest you take advantage of the first killing opportunity. With a decoy, everything could go wrong without warning. Last but not least, you can use scents to entice a buck to your decoy.

## Fooling Bucks with Scent

Decoying big bucks is a whole lot newer than using scents to attract them. Still, there's a lot we don't know about using scents, such as which ones work best, and exactly how to use them in ways that are most likely to attract a trophy buck.

I might as well let the cat out of the bag: I'm not a consistent scent user. They do work sometimes, but in my book they rank only one tactic higher up than decoys. I've seen occasional results that have shown me there's a good reason why we have hundreds of scent companies, but that's not to say all scent companies offer proven products.

For best results when it comes to using scent products, you have to understand the different types of scents available. There are commercially manufactured scents and naturals. Some companies have their own deer. Urine is gathered from both bucks and doe, and then bottled and packaged. Sometimes the urine comes from estrus does and becomes one of the company's most "pushed" products.

I don't much favor using cover scents—not even those that smell exactly like the various parts of the environment. They have nothing to do with hunting the different phases of the rut.

That's not to say such manufactured scents are duds. On the contrary, many veteran hunters will attest that they have lured mature bucks into range with synthetics and proudly purchase them as often as they buy genuine scents.

A product's age and packaging might determine if the scent will lure in a big buck, or sanitary conditions could spoil the scent before it's ever packaged. There's a lot we don't know about scents.

From watching captive whitetails hour after hour, I do know that urine is probably the best scent to use. I consistently see bucks lip curl whenever they scent a spot where a doe has urinated. And to be quite honest, it doesn't really matter if that doe is in estrus. If it's early autumn long before the breeding or late winter after the breeding is over, the bucks will usually lip curl.

Just how often a buck will trail the doe that left the scent is questionable. That's hard to determine with captive deer, and impossible in the wild.

Let's assume though, that the sex scent (synthetic, urine or another) is fresh and one hundred percent unspoiled. Whether or not it's going to work for you depends on how you use it, and the mood of the buck that intercepts the scent.

I do know that hot trails are necessary to lure a buck into range. Whenever I make scent trails, I wear boot pads and consistently soak them as I walk. It's expensive, but more effective than soaking the pads once and walking to your ambush location. By soaking them repeatedly, I know the trail gets hotter coming to me. If I soak the pads only once, the trail gets colder with each step taken. Any buck can tell a hot trail from a cold one.

Another method of using scents, and probably one of the best, is to place scent stations around an ambush location. This is most effective for a bowhunter hoping to get a buck to stop, or to force him to come a little closer.

You can use scent pads or cotton containers to make scent stations. Soak each of the stations, hang them about five feet off the ground, sit back, and wait. However, don't expect the bucks to take numbers to see who can get to you first. Scent stations won't draw bucks in from a long distance. As I've discovered enough times, bucks have to be close to the scent to smell it, even when a perfect gentle breeze delivers the smell. Thus, I believe scent stations are most effective once a buck appears.

## Mock Scrapes

A scent station could become a mock scrape—if you want it to. I've made several over the years, and I've seen several mock scrapes turn into the real thing, worked by passing bucks on a regular basis. I have never killed a monster buck over a mock scrape, however.

To make a scrape work, you must first place it in the right location. Some hunters claim that a real scrape or scrapes in the area make a good starting point. However, if there are genuine scrapes, why in the world would you want to take a chance on spoiling them? "Hello!"

That brings us to the starting gate. Always wear rubber boots and rubber gloves when you make a mock scrape. Avoid brushing against debris and continue these practices even when checking mock scrapes in the days ahead.

You'll want to choose a site where there is an overhanging limb. Moreover, you'll want to find a spot where a buck will probably pass by, and

Mock scrapes can work, but keep in mind they should be placed in the best possible location to attract a mature buck in daylight hours.

Scent drippers will keep your mock scrape smelling strong. However, don't handle these devices without using rubber gloves.

that he might come to in daylight hours. This isn't necessarily a well-used trail. Actually, you should already know where the does are spending time, that is where you want your scrape. Also, avoid open areas and place the scrape where it might become a scrape line. In other words, a fenceline, wooded draw or other natural travel corridor might work perfectly.

Scrape lines are much more valuable to the hunter than the biggest, active scrape in the area. Keep that in mind when making a mock scrape. You can make more than one and try to establish a scrape line, or you can make one and hope a buck, or bucks, take care of the others.

Think about your ambush location when preparing a mock scrape. Wind direction and your ability to move in and out of the area without getting too close to the scrape are top priorities.

After selecting a site, use a stick to clear a spot on the ground about three feet in diameter. Don't lay the stick down on the ground and forget it. Carry it with you and stuff into a logjam or something similar, so it won't be found.

Apply scent to the scrape, and don't be shy about turning the bottle upside down. The ground soaks up scent quickly, not to mention rain or even a morning dew day after day. The more scent, the longer it lasts. On the other hand, you might consider using a scent-dripping device—a good way to disperse scent slowly over a long period.

I do believe that a rub nearby might not hurt your chances of a scrape being hit. However, that doesn't necessarily mean it will increase your chances. Choose a tree that a buck will like, such as a maple or pine, remove some bark and step away. You can also apply a tarsal scent to the tree if you really want to be creative.

Hunters use tarsal scent to make a buck think another has moved in. Some hunters claim they are more effective than the hottest sex scents—but the truth is, we'll never know all there is to know about fooling bucks with scents.

In moving on, let me say that I don't believe grunt calls, decoys, and scents are the answer to most problems that haunt the deer hunter. Grunt calls are closest and they can be your ace in the hole, but even they won't substitute for good hunting skills. That's exactly why you should consider these and every other possible method for taking a trophy whitetail when the rutting mechanism dial is turned up all the way.

# Eye-Level Bucks

Many deer hunters, both archers and gunners, have fallen into a trend. They simply have to hunt from a tree stand. Unfortunately, these individuals are missing fabulous opportunities to get eye-level with a buck. During the primary rut, when vulnerable bucks might cover ground at all hours of the day, the stage is set for taking a trophy whitetail from a ground ambush location, or by still-hunting.

It's been many years since I first nestled into a ground blind. I still remember feeling vulnerable to the sharp eyes of a wary whitetail that approached slowly. However, as the deer walked up to within twenty-five yards, I realized my ground blind had provided the necessary concealment.

At the time, the six-point buck that fell to my charge of black powder was only the second deer I had taken by way of a ground blind. But it did build my confidence, opening the door to many more opportunities. Now don't get me wrong. For four decades of hunting whitetails, I have relied on tree stand tactics to fill many of my tags. Nevertheless, I have learned it is advantageous to be versatile, particularly during the primary rut.

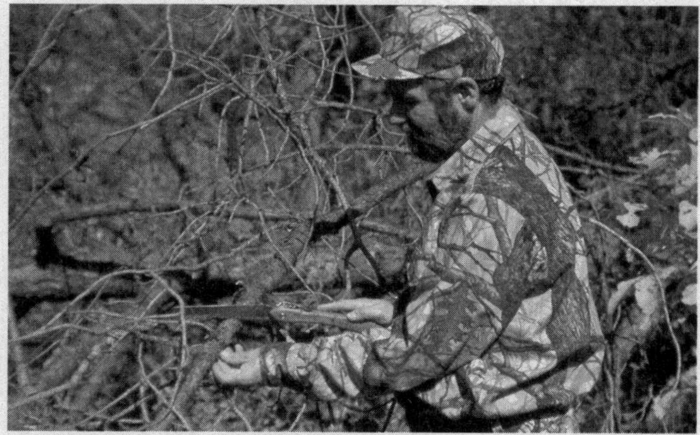

When ground hunting, don't rely on lots of visibility. The thickest locations are usually best and close encounters are what eye-level contact with a buck is all about. Credit: Vikki L. Trout.

Since then, I have taken several whitetails from the ground, including the best buck I've harvested to date. I love the challenge, but even better, I know it increases my chances of success when favorable conditions exist. The conditions I speak of are the ongoing primary rut, and a hunter being in the right place to make it count.

First, consider that nearly every bowhunter and many firearm hunters prefer using tree stands. It has been this way now for eons; if trees are available, most hunters will choose to hunt by way of the perch.

Unfortunately, though, the continued use of tree stands, particularly on lands where intensive hunting pressure occurs, has made the whitetails a bit wiser. No deer walks around consistently looking up, but many whitetails have sharpened their survival instincts by expecting danger from above.

This is the primary reason why many hunters now find it necessary to climb high each time they use tree stands. I can remember using hand-constructed permanent stands years ago and never climbing above twelve feet. I can also remember surprising many deer. But as the years passed and the whitetail became wiser, I found it necessary to climb much higher, and this trend continues today.

Now let's examine those areas that, in order to hunt effectively, require you to stay eye level with the deer. These are prime locations where the dense cover hides the trees. Yet many hunters often sacrifice hunting these great sites simply because they cannot use a tree stand.

There are also times when the hunter is very exposed while hunting from an elevated position. Light camouflage may help you blend against a sky background, but you cannot hide your movements. You can also assume that a deer may see your silhouette.

Once the leaves have fallen, which is usually the case during the primary rut, I find it much easier to remain hidden by getting eye level with the bucks. If done correctly, a ground blind can totally conceal me from the sharp eyes of the wariest doe and the trophy buck that might accompany her.

Now for the big reason why you should consider staying eye level with the bucks during the primary rut: You can hunt most anywhere, and you can make things happen. You are never stuck in a lull zone. Moving to new ambush locations, or still-hunting when favorable conditions exist, are proven and dependable tactics for killing a big buck. But you need to know how to do it right.

## Choosing the Ambush Site

To begin, whether you're a bow or a gun hunters, don't choose a location where visibility allows you to see for a considerable distance and shoot farther. A ground blind located smack-dab in the middle of a thicket, where visibility is poor, can often be a better choice.

Keep in mind, mature bucks often prefer the thickest cover to travel in daylight hours. The good news, though, is that you are better hidden in these locations, too. Thus, when choosing your ambush location, disregard visibility. Have faith that the deer will soon show up where you want them, and be assured that if they do, you will get a shot within easy range. Just because I use a firearm, for example, I do not mind setting up in an area of poor visibility where I can see only thirty to forty yards to the right trail, scrape or food source. And when bowhunting on the ground, I often find myself selecting an ambush site only twenty yards from where the deer will soon be.

## Hiding Out

With modern camouflage, it is not difficult to blend in with any surroundings. In fact it's probably easier when hunting on the ground than from a tree.

The author has taken a number of whitetails while hunting from the ground, and relying upon natural foliage for concealment. Credit: Vikki L. Trout.

Today's commercial blinds have opened the door to lots of opportunities, but the ground hunting tactics herein are focused on natural setups—using the terrain and foliage for concealment. Commercial ground blinds are effective, par- ticularly those that are placed ahead of time so deer get used to them. However, many times you must select a ground location immediately, and nothing beats a natural look to keep you hidden.

I almost always avoid setting up on top of hills, where a thick background does not come easily. Instead, I will select the side of a hill where there is no daylight behind me. When hunting in flat country, I rely totally on my constructed ground blind itself to conceal me.

I prefer to pile up natural foliage behind me—limbs and vegetation, and/or trees when available. However, I do not limit the construction of the blind to my backside. I will place the debris on both sides to help me remain hidden in case a deer approaches from an unexpected direction.

As for the front side, where the shot is likely to occur, I have found that having a tree—or trees—to hide behind works best. Only recently, I cashed in on a whitetail while bowhunting on the ground by getting behind a fairly small pine tree. My background had enough natural foliage to help me blend effectively. Finally, I also attribute my success to hunting on a suitable day when the wind direction was stable.

A tree-stand hunter will sometimes go undetected by an approaching deer, even when an air current shifts directions briefly in favor of the whitetail. The ground hunter, though, is rarely forgiven. The wrong wind direction will most certainly give the hunter away without warning, and his or her hunt will end in disaster. For this reason, I suggest that you never take chances and settle into the ambush location only when you know the wind is favorable for you.

## Make the First Shot Count

When hunting an eye-level buck, you might be tempted to take your shot before the deer has become broadside or quartered away. However, it is vitally important, particularly for the bowhunter, that you wait for the best shooting opportunity. The firearm hunter can also discover quickly that a quartering- into shot is unwarranted.

You should always carry along pruning shears or a small hand saw to open shooting lanes. This is as helpful for the gun hunter as it is for the bowhunter. When clearing is necessary, and it usually is if you have selected the best and thickest location, do it first with your eyes from the shooting angle. Trim only what is necessary, and then return

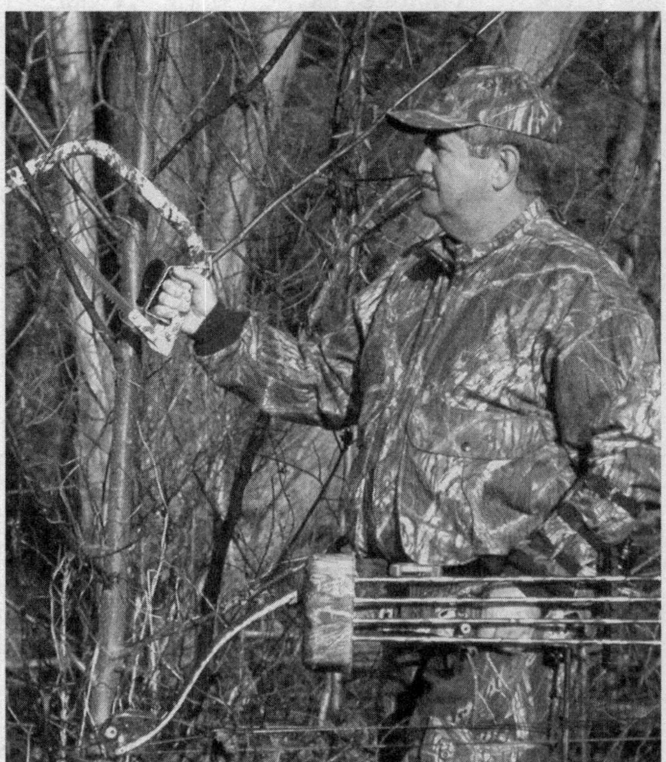

When clearing shooting lanes for hunting on the ground, it's better to clear too little than too much.

to the blind and look for other limbs before clearing more, since it's always better not to remove too much. Believe me, if there's one thing a whitetail will spot quickly, it is a thick area that has suddenly opened up.

Finally, use a small stool to keep yourself lower to the ground and better hidden when the time comes to raise your bow or gun. One exception is when you choose a spur-of-the-moment setup behind a clump of thick trees. Then you will probably blend better if you stand.

Sitting keeps me more comfortable for longer periods and helps me avoid unnecessary moving. Also, most of us can shoot more accurately when sitting. When bowhunting, it's much easier to master shooting from a seat than it is to try getting off the ground and onto your knees.

If you've never tried hunting from a ground blind, the primary rut is a good time to begin. It's yesterday's technique, and something that can fool a trophy buck when he's most vulnerable. But that's not all. It makes still-hunting an option when favorable conditions exist.

## Introduction to Still-Hunting

I've mentioned Tim Hillsmeyer and some of his hunting tactics previously in this book, and for good reason. He has certainly tagged his share of mature bucks with bow and gun. However, there's more to his story. He started bowhunting in the late 1960s, and in those early years, he never climbed into a tree stand. He relied solely on still-hunting to outsmart a few of the bucks that roamed the countryside near his southern Indiana home.

Eventually, Hillsmeyer did begin hunting by way of the tree stand, but only after years of experience hunting on the ground. He learned that the still-hunter must wait for the best days. He also learned that some days are just made for the stalker. That's exactly why he still hunts on the ground occasionally.

Tim Hillsmeyer shot this 125-inch buck at a distance of only three yards while still-hunting.

Hillsmeyer's closest shot from the ground occurred in 1985, when he shot a 125-inch buck at only three yards. Success did not come easy, however, and he refers to his early years of still-hunting as the "School of Hard Knocks." It was simply trial and error until he gained the necessary confidence to be a successful still-hunter.

## Why Still-Hunt?

"If you limit yourself to only one style of hunting, you're going to be limited on the number of opportunities you will get to be successful," explained Hillsmeyer. "I would never go fishing with only one lure, nor would I want to hunt by using only one tactic. On some days you may need to still-hunt to see deer."

Still-hunting can sharpen your overall woodsmanship skills. It may be that you will learn more about patterning bucks simply because you must meet them on their terms. Hillsmeyer still-hunts during all phases of the rut and relies much on what he learns that way to pattern big bucks. Remember, during the primary rut you can often count on bucks to move, which increases your chances of succeeding.

Hillsmeyer compares stalking bucks to squirrel hunting. Most squirrel hunters see deer up close, but often refuse to try hunting on the ground when the deer season opens. Squirrel hunting forces you to slow down, one of the necessary skills for being a successful stalker. Hillsmeyer recalled reading an article many years ago in which a bowhunter stated, "If you think you're moving too slow, then slow down." This statement has helped Hillsmeyer considerably. In other words, it's not how much ground you cover, it's how cover it.

Still-hunting is more in your favor after a rain and/or when conditions are breezy. However, it's how you go about it that will determine your chance of success when stalking a mature buck.

## Still-Hunting Tactics

The hunter must know the area to still-hunt it effectively. However, Hillsmeyer said that you are sure to learn the terrain better after still-hunting any area a few times. Practice makes perfect.

You will move from one type of terrain to the other when still-hunting, starting in a wooded area, perhaps, and moving into a thicket or grown-up field. A universal camo will help you blend with a variety of terrain.

A quality binocular is essential, but it must not hinder you when it comes time to shoot. Hillsmeyer puts the strap over his right shoulder and places the binocular under his left arm to keep it out of his way.

Hillsmeyer also recommends dressing lighter than normal in colder temperatures. Too many clothes, he claims, will usually hurt more than they help. Sweating comes all too quickly when you still-hunt, and you must be able to shoot comfortably without your clothing interfering with your equipment.

Veteran still-hunters prefer to do it after a rain, when they can move quietly. Hillsmeyer also likes stalking under these conditions, but he stays on the ground other times, too. A breezy day sets up another opportunity. Even a gentle wind will help to deaden the sounds of a moving hunter, but be warned: The stalker must watch every step.

"I always look ahead whenever I stop to see where I should place my feet," noted Hillsmeyer. "You have to avoid any debris that will create a disturbance. If you can do this, you don't have to wait for a wet and windy day to still-hunt."

When the primary rut begins, Hillsmeyer said that the bucks begin moving on alternate routes looking for does. Once a doe in the area has come into estrus, it may cause the trophy bucks to make mistakes. These bucks will cover more ground, giving the stalker a chance to intercept them.

Although most stalkers might prefer walking with the wind in their faces, Hillsmeyer often moves into a crosswind when trying to locate a big buck.

"I have seldom seen big bucks walking with the wind at their tail," he says. "They just don't make these kinds of mistakes often."

By walking into a crosswind, Hillsmeyer can often spot the bucks doing the same. And if his human scent goes undetected, it all boils down to seeing the buck before it sees you. That's the key to shifting the hunt more in favor of the hunter.

According to Hillsmeyer, every hunter has a sixth sense that can become an accurate, reliable tool. It tells you when you should stop and when you should move. Also, look for vantage points whenever you stop, simply because you never know when a shot opportunity will come. The stalker must always believe that a buck may be close anytime and place.

As Hillsmeyer puts it, "Ground hunting is an exciting opportunity to play the game in the whitetail's field." He's right. You're in their element and you must pass a difficult test to be successful. When you do, you will experience the thrill of winning against the odds.

Keep in mind, many of the tactics mentioned in this chapter, cannot be relied upon when hunting pressure intensifies. And let's face it; at some point during the primary rut, pressure will turn any hot area into a dead-zone without warning.

# High-Anxiety Bucks

At some point during the primary rut the bucks in your area will undoubtedly become severely stressed due to hunting pressure, compliments of you and me. It comes without warning and it's an annual event that can't be escaped.

Hunting pressure affects does, fawns, and subordinate bucks just as it does mature bucks, so how will it your hunting during the primary rut? For starters, you already know that your best chance of ambushing a trophy deer is to be where the does are hanging out. If the does are there, the bucks will come. The kicker is, if the does are no longer visiting the same food sources and bedding areas they once did, you can forget about the bucks showing up. Of course, there's a little more to the story, as we've already discussed, but you get the point. More than likely the hunting pressure had already led to high-anxiety bucks in your area before the does were affected.

Hunting pressure affects the does just as it does the bucks. Their food sources and bedding areas will change without warning.

Just how long it takes for the bucks to feel pressure and change their habits depends upon the size of the area and how many hunters are there. Even a two hundred-acre area can change overnight, as I've experienced on more than one occasion. The smaller the area, the fewer hunters it takes to send a message that immediately causes deer to change their movements. In fact, just one hunter can change it all.

It's not only firearm hunters that send bucks into a nervous frenzy. I know of one wildlife refuge that allows bowhunting by random draw only. Even during the primary rut, the place goes sour in just a couple of days once a handful of archers are turned loose.

The changing habits of a buck will vary, but two facts stand out: Even a little hunting pressure will cause a buck to change bedding areas, and the more pressure he endures, the more nocturnal he becomes.

I won't say much about nocturnal bucks in this chapter, except that I don't believe any buck ever becomes totally nocturnal. It might seem like he has, but chances are he's just not where you thought he should be. Also, during the primary rut, the bucks maintain a breeding instinct. Although their survival instincts might outweigh their breeding instincts, the urge to breed is still a factor. However, by the post-rut period and any time scars of the previous hunting pressure are very pronounced, a mature buck might move less in daylight hours than he ever did before. You'll get to read about so-called nocturnal bucks in Part III.

## Remain Confident

Enough said about the difficulty of hunting pressured bucks. I don't want to completely shake your confidence for hunting the rut once the pressure sets in. Confidence provides hope for tagging a pressured trophy whitetail.

We often hear a lot of shooting on opening morning, and our gut feeling is that the buck we are hunting has surely fallen to someone else. That's always a possibility, but it's equally likely he's still out there. Consider that many hunters will be happy enough to take any legal buck or doe, and a lot of the shooting could be from meat hunters. It's important for you to believe that the trophy buck on which you've pinned your hopes is still a candidate for your attention.

Even though hunting pressure might cause a mature buck to move less in daylight hours, he will still maintain breeding instincts.

It's no big secret that most deer are harvested during the first two or three days of the firearm season, if not on opening day. Knowing this, hunters are eager to get out there sooner rather than later—recognizing that once bucks get pressured, they will start disappearing, and the biggest, oldest, wisest bucks are the first to take cover.

It's also true that during the breeding season, a doe might help you by leading the right buck past your stand. But overall, a buck's survival instincts suddenly become more powerful than his urge to breed. They do remain killable, though, because they don't actually crawl into a hole and disappear.

Confidence will keep you in the woods, and staying there is absolutely necessary to kill a pressured buck. You won't see as many deer as you do at other times, but keep in mind the big bucks are more prone to making mistakes. You only need to know where they will be to take advantage of their errors.

## No-Man's Land

Big bucks head for no-man's land once the hunting pressure intensifies. However, allow me to set the record straight. You might think no-man's land is some place miles from anywhere, perhaps someplace that you can only get in to using your luckiest parachute. Nope. No-man's land is probably close to your hunting area, and could be smack-dab in the middle of it.

Granted, you do have to get away from the crowds. You see, no matter how well you go about reducing your scent and taking all the other precautions necessary to keep your presence unknown, some other hunter could be screwing up the area as soon as you walk to or from your

Be prepared to change to a new ambush location at a moment's notice. In many areas, including some private lands, hunting pressure will force bucks into different habits only twenty-four to forty-eight hours after the firearm season debuts.

ambush location. This is precisely why I have a problem hunting with certain outfitters, who try to run through too many hunters, allowing the area to be spoiled. When hunting big bucks, I must be in control; when I'm not in control, who's to say what's going on? I can hunt a great ambush location, but the outfitter might send in Crazy Joe, who decides he's going to hike around the area for twenty minutes. So much for that hotspot.

Typically, no-man's land is an area where man doesn't venture. It could be a square tract of no more than one hundred yards, or a narrow strip thirty yards wide and two hundred yards long. And it could be anywhere, including in your own backyard.

## Hideaways

Common sense tells us that bucks seek security in out-of-the-way places. In my early days of hunting, I considered these areas to be places where the devil himself wouldn't go. As the years passed, though, and I remained persistent, always looking for pressured bucks, it became obvious the bucks were right under my nose.

Bucks like it thick, and any dense area appears attractive to them when they're pressured. Bucks look for various types of hideaways, including pine thickets, stands of bramble bushes, cutover areas, honeysuckle and saplings. If the area looks to you like it would be difficult to get in and out of, it is probably an ideal place for a pressured buck.

Of course, not every area has an appropriate thicket. Be aware that a mature buck, and particularly does and fawns, will not leave an area and travel miles to get away from pressure. They stick around and hide in whatever is available.

Now that I told you about dense areas appealing to big bucks, you should know there's a flip-side to everything. Surprisingly, overgrown weed fields usually attract high-anxiety bucks, yet most hunters overlook them and seek denser areas. This is precisely why a buck will not hesitate to seek out a bedding area in nothing more than a grown-up field.

Many landowners take advantage of set-aside programs, leaving their fields to grow. By late autumn, at the onset of the hunting pressure, these fields are often waist-deep and very attractive to a nervous whitetail.

Then there are wetlands. A friend of mine set up a stand in a swamp after being drawn for a special hunt. He assumed most hunters would not penetrate the marsh, and instead would stick to the timber and thickets surrounding the wetland. On the second day of his hunt, after seeing several deer, he cashed in on a huge buck. Although most hunters participating in the hunt claimed they saw nothing but other hunters, the successful hunter said he did not see anyone.

Although bucks will bed in lightly flooded areas, they do not bed down in deep standing water. However, they go into these places because they know hunters don't. The bucks utilize the water as a safe haven, and seek out dry land in the middle of the wetlands.

I know of one hunting group that leases land in a low area. Each year, about the time the primary rut is in full swing and the hunting pressure is intensifying, the area usually floods. The deer head for a ridge in the middle of the flooded terrain and stay there, enjoying security at its finest. There are usually an ample supply of acorns on the ridge to keep the deer fed. Hunters have been quite successful taking a boat into the area and setting up along the perimeter of the ridge.

When the wisest old bucks move to escape hunting pressure, you must also move. Try setting up on the perimeters of areas such as grown-up fields, standing corn, cutover areas, and swampy ground.

Standing corn is another option. True, there is little chance of finding standing corn by the time the rut arrives, but it's not impossible. Sometimes, a farmer harvests everything except a small patch of corn, and even that small area can become a haven for a spooky buck.

## Narrowing the Field

You must locate the best possible hideaway or hideaways in your area. That's not easy on any day, but it's even more difficult when the bucks are pressured and you have to start scouting all over again.

I suggest you walk the perimeters of areas that might attract a pressured buck and look for rubs and scrapes. Despite a big buck's desire to hide out, something in his old head keeps him thinking about pretty little does. Thus, the first thing he will want to do when he exits his hideaway is leave sign. For him, it's probably a territorial factor to mark the new area with scent.

You should also look for trails with fresh sign and droppings. Don't look for wide, gouged trails; any trails you locate have probably not been used long. In some cases, you might only find tracks. The key is to hone in on anything that points to a possible hideaway.

## Stake 'Em Out

Once you have located a promising hideout, you are one step closer to filling a tag. Now you have to decide how to hunt the hideaway, and the better you know the area, the easier it will be to select the right ambush locations.

When choosing an ambush location, you must avoid penetrating the hideaway. This is a buck's sacred ground. He's already been pushed there, and even if it took a sound dose of hunting pressure to do it, it will take only a little more of the same to sound the alarm and push him to another hideout.

During the firearm season, I rely on bowhunting methods, and I don't worry about visibility, even when hunting grown-up fields and marshes. I look at it this way: A buck selects a hideout because it makes him feel protected. Once he moves, he will probably head wherever there's cover to keep him secluded. Thus, the best setup is probably on the fringe of the hideout, near the thickest cover that borders it.

Consider that any encounter with a hiding buck will probably be a close encounter. A mature buck is cautious and not as likely to make the same mistake he might have made on opening day of the firearm season. You can bet your luckiest tree stand that he will not move with the wind at his south end. In other words, if the wind is out of the north and you set up on the south end of a thicket because your scent blows directly away from the buck's hideaway, you probably won't see much.

Then again, a cautious buck in hiding will travel crosswind, or with the wind in his face. You can't set up with the wind blowing directly into the buck's nose, but you can plan your ambush for a crosswind.

Selecting several ambush sites will keep you versatile and keep the bucks guessing. Tree-stand hunters can never rely on only one ambush location, since the wind will not be right all the time. However, don't allow yourself to slip back in time and start hunting well-used trails that once attracted the does.

Each year there are hunters who bring their bucks out of the woods late in the breeding season simply because they did *something right.* Most of them understood the options and remained confident. They knew ahead of time where a pressured buck would hang out, and that any area could be considered a safe haven year after year. Thus, if you find a reliable area one season and you don't get your buck before the pressure accelerates, remember it for next time.

I'm not going to kid you. It's tough killing a pressured buck even during the rut, and no matter how much you know about their changing habits, you might as well be ready for a challenge. Here's the way it works: Within twenty-four hours, you can go from the easiest conditions for ambushing a mature buck to the most difficult.

# Tracking a Rutting Buck

Waiting for the right buck to come along is what trophy hunting is all about. Sometimes it takes weeks—sometimes it takes years. When the perfect shot opportunity finally arrives, though, the last thing you want is to blow it by hitting the deer poorly. Nevertheless, tracking a wounded animal is as common as tree stands in the deer woods. Anyone who hunts often is going to find himself tracking his own deer, or helping someone else track one.

But tracking a buck in the primary rut is not the same as tracking a buck during the pre-rut and post-rut periods. It's a completely different game, and knowing the differences could help you recover the trophy of a lifetime.

In my book *Finding Wounded Deer,* I briefly discussed tracking a wounded buck during the rut. Of course, it will only be necessary if you don't hit him perfectly. We can start there.

Assuming you already have an understanding of shot placement, you already know that a buck hit in both lungs won't run far. A broadhead or projectile will get the job done effectively and promptly when it passes through the vital organs. However, less than perfect hits will result in a tracking experience you may never forget. None of us knows all there is to know about tracking a wounded deer. But you should have a complete understanding of the key facts, including the common habits of a wounded buck during the rut, before circumstances lead you to the task of tracking a rutting one.

## Colors of Blood

Some blood is bright red and some is dark. Both shades tell different stories, and either could

Before assuming what a wounded rutting buck might do next, you must first know what type of wound you are dealing with. Credit: Vikki L. Trout.

mean a long tracking situation. Lung shots result in bright red blood—sometimes pink. Heart and artery shots produce crimson blood, but it's never dark. These wounds result in a downed deer fairly quickly and a short tracking job. Little or no experience is usually necessary.

However, bright blood can also indicate a muscle wound, and dark blood means a wound to the paunch. Either way, you face the possibility of a long tracking situation.

Many veteran hunters can recognize the difference in the colors of blood at first glance. It's easier to do when the blood is wet, since dried blood tends to look dark. Blood color is also easiest to determine when there is lots of it. Keep in mind, though, you might find both bright and dark blood when you shoot at a deer that quarters into or away. For instance, a projectile could enter in the paunch and exit through the hip if the animal was quartering into when you shot. Quartering-into shots are not recommended, but I say this to point out how easily you can be fooled if your broadhead or bullet angles through the animal.

## What's Next?

I would suggest you never begin tracking a deer unless you know the type of wound you are dealing with, since some require waiting—and some don't. Normally, I base it upon the color of blood alone, but if dark blood prevails, I know the wound is to the liver, stomach and/or intestines, and it's best to wait. If I find bright blood, I pursue the animal quickly and quietly.

Many muscle wounds are superficial. However, some of these deer are recovered when pushed slowly and quietly to keep them bleeding. A paunch shot deer, on the other hand, should be left alone for several hours. I usually allow four to six hours to begin tracking, and sometimes I wait overnight if I shoot the deer in the evening. Most gut-shot deer will bed down quickly (that includes big bucks during rut). Because of a sparse blood trail, it's best to let the animal alone. Time is then on your side. Always remember the golden rule that applies to tracking a wounded deer anytime: The less distance you have to track the animal, the better your chance of a recovery.

## Reading a Blood Trail

You can learn a lot by following a blood trail. For instance, if drops of blood are shaped like teardrops, you can assume the deer is running. The splatter marks are usually found only at the top of the droplet, pointing out which way the deer is traveling.

A standing or walking deer will leave round drops of blood. Usually, there are splatter marks completely encircling the droplet. If the deer is walking, the blood droplets may be spaced a few inches or more apart, but if the deer stands in one place, the blood will accumulate in small areas and might appear as pools.

That brings us to another important fact: Never assume a deer is about to go down just because you find lots of blood. True, artery wounds will usually result in a large quantity of blood and a deer succumbing in seconds, and internal bleeding kills far more deer than external bleeding. But external bleeding can fool you. Consider that a deer must lose one-third of its blood to bleed to death. Now consider how much just one cup of blood would spread over an area, though it isn't even close to one-third of the volume of blood in an adult deer's body.

Two blood trails usually tell you that a deer is bleeding on both sides, and that there are both entry and exit holes. That's good news because more

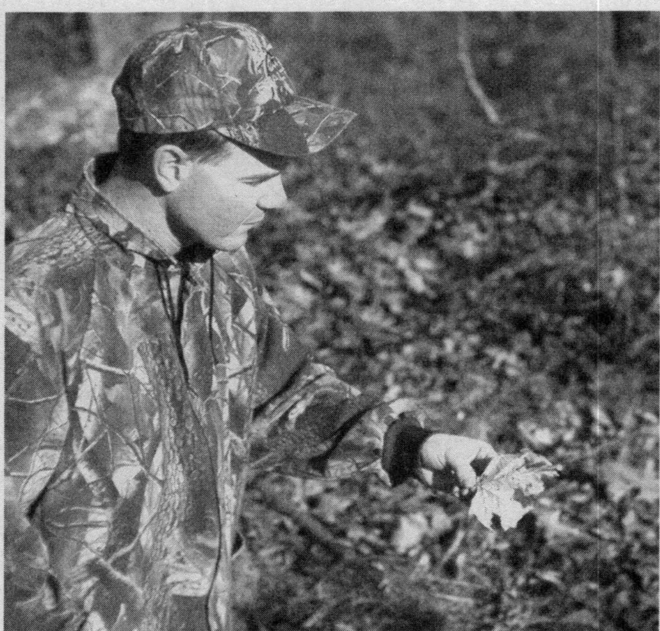

The author's son, John, attempts to decipher the wound he is dealing with. The better you can read a blood trail, the better understanding you will have about how to track a rutting buck.

penetration is always better, and it results in more blood getting to the ground.

Gut-shot deer seldom bleed a lot externally. Typically, stomach and intestinal matter will often clog the departure and sometimes the entry hole, particularly once a deer travels a distance of fifty to one hundred yards. Blood might get to the ground at first, but it will quickly dissipate. By the way, you should know that any wound to the paunch will result in a dead deer, usually within a few hours. Deer with intestinal wounds often go farther and don't succumb as quickly as those with liver and stomach wounds.

Muscle wounds often bleed profusely, but many of them will often clot after the animal travels one hundred to two hundred yards. Shoulder and back wounds typically clot faster than neck, leg, and hip wounds. Hip wounds seldom clot totally, which allows the hunter to stay on the trail of the animal, and most hunters recover a hip-shot deer if they pursue it slowly and quietly.

## Big Buck Endurance

The distance you must track a deer in order to recover it depends upon several factors, a few of which I've already mentioned. However, when it comes to bucks in the primary rut, some of the "golden rules" change.

For instance, most double-lung shot deer will run no more than eighty to one hundred yards before going down, if they don't drop immediately. Big bucks seem to travel farther. I know of one that didn't go down until he surpassed the 175-yard marker—a mature buck that field dressed over 250 pounds. Not all, but many other big bucks I've observed and heard about, showed similar stamina on their final run.

For many years, I kept statistics on the distances deer ran with different types of wounds. These records included bucks, does, and fawns. In nearly every situation, mature bucks ran greater distances than does and young bucks. Not surprisingly, fawns usually succumbed faster than bucks and does: Most adult deer hit through both lungs traveled eighty to one hundred yards before dropping. Most fawns traveled less than sixty yards.

I can still recall a buck I shot one morning during the primary rut. The liver was hit, and in most cases this results in a dead deer within two to three hours. Not this time. I started tracking the huge eleven-pointer at noon, several hours after shooting him. A couple of hours later I lost the blood trail, and at 3 p.m., jumped the buck from his bed. I marked the spot and left the deer alone.

The following morning I returned with Vikki and Tim Hillsmeyer. After about two hours, we located the buck. He had covered a distance of several hundred yards from where I shot him. Stomach tissue had clogged both the entry and departure holes made by my arrow, which prevented blood from getting to the ground. Upon field dressing the deer, I found a perfect slice in the liver where the broadhead had passed through. Based upon the time I shot him and the time I jumped him, the buck had positively survived the liver wound for at least nine hours. The actual time he survived could have been much longer.

None of this means too much as far as a recovery is concerned. A perfect hit is a downed animal. Even the big bucks that travel a few extra yards usually leave easy-to-follow blood trails when hit well. What's important, though, is that in the case of a less-than-perfect shot, a buck can travel farther than most deer would with a similar wound.

## Home Range of Rutting Bucks

Previously in this book, I discussed home ranges and distances a buck might travel in the rut. Not all mature bucks will travel long distances during the primary rut, but many do, and almost all will go beyond the home range where they spent most of their time during the pre-rut period.

It's normal for wounded deer to circle if they don't succumb quickly. Deer with muscle wounds, as well as most paunch-shot deer, might travel for a short distance, but after one hundred to two hundred yards, most will make a gradual turn and start angling. They do not move in straight lines.

The exception is a big buck during the primary rut. I've noticed they travel a near straight line, and you can usually figure that's what they'll do when pushed. I speculate that this is because, when wounded, they prefer the sense of security they had in their home range, perhaps the familiarity of their old bedding grounds. There is no concrete evidence to explain why most wounded rutting bucks travel farther than most wounded does, or farther than bucks do during pre-rut and post-rut. However, you can bet they will—providing they don't die before given the opportunity.

Most wounded deer tend to circle after traveling a few hundred yards. During the primary rut, many bucks tend to travel straight for long distances.

Earlier in this chapter, I discussed paunch-shot deer bedding down. I don't believe that a gut-shot buck will want to travel too far before bedding down just because he happens to be outside his home range. Whether it's the primary rut or the pre-rut, bucks with abdominal wounds seem to bed down just as soon as they feel safe. The difference I've seen is when a buck receives a muscle or abdominal wound, and is pushed. I've pushed both bucks and does during pre-rut and post-rut, and they typically circle and do not travel straight for any considerable distance. But during the primary rut, the bucks will cover more ground and stay on a straighter course.

The distances I have tracked wounded bucks during the rut have varied, and I have followed bucks just as far in the pre-rut as in the post-rut, but they didn't really end up anywhere different. In other words, during the primary rut they traveled nearly a straight line and ended up in strange territory a mile or more from where they were shot. Early and late in the season, when I suspect bucks are in their home range, I have also tracked them for a mile, but they

During the primary rut, bucks often travel a considerable distance from their home range. Could it be they will attempt to head for their familiar stomping grounds when wounded?

did not end up more than a quarter- or half-mile from where they were shot.

For more detailed tracking facts, you should find yourself a reliable tracking book. Remember: If you have to track a wounded mature buck during the primary rut, expect a few surprises. As for tracking post-rut bucks, it's back to the same old stuff—well almost. Please read on.

# Does the Moon Trigger the Rut?

If questions seem to be falling like raindrops into a sea of shallow answers, it's because the rut needs to be wired into Moon strategies. First I'll sort out the rut phases so you won't be fazed by the ever-changing whitetail behavior in the fall. Next—are you ready for this?—I'll explain how a Michigan bowhunter uses the New Moon to plan the best hunting trip of his life. Last, I'll examine a technique ripe for trophy rutting whitetails during a key lunar period.

Gary Smalley, best-selling author and family counselor, articulates the main distinction between the sexes: Males are essentially in a constant state of sexual readiness, whereas females generally need something to get them ready. "Men have a sexual thought, on average, about every 20 seconds," he quips. If this is the case with humans, what about deer? During the rut, novice and veteran hunters alike can't help notice some bucks behaving like teenaged boys. Though much has been written about the advantages of hunting during the breeding season, most deer hunters I come in contact with still don't seem to get it . . .

## The Rut Phase Craze

Contrary to popular belief, there are two distinct ruts in the whitetail world. The first ensures the propagation of the species; the second all but guarantees that deer hunters will return home scratching their heads instead of showing off some trophy headgear.

The first rut, of course, is the annual breeding season of deer. The second involves the many ill-conceived, fatally flawed strategies hunters have concocted over the years to take advantage of the only significant weakness of a slippery whitetail buck—his mating urge. I say hunters are stuck in a rut because they commit the same basic miscues at key times when deer behavior is actually quite predictable.

The key to bagging a whitetail will never change: Be in the right place at the right time. As I've said many times throughout this book, we need to know what deer are doing now, not last month, last week or even yesterday. So here's a phase-by-phase blow on each stage of the rut. Time references reflect Midwest latitudes where the rutting season commences earlier than in Southern states (e.g. peak rut is generally mid-November in the Midwest; December or January in the South and Southeast).

## Phase 1: Sparring

Technically speaking, the rut begins when does go into heat. Then and only then will the ladies "stand" to be bred by a buck. Obviously, bucks interested in mating are vulnerable to lucky hunters—research shows that does become hyperactive within their core areas, and breeding bucks frequently venture far and wide of theirs—but this isn't the only time deer make mistakes. The early phase has its share of opportunities, even though it hasn't gotten the ink it deserves.

Around mid-September, so-called bachelor groups of two or more bucks are often seen feeding or bedding in close proximity to one another. A common misconception is that bucks are capable of breeding well before does enter estrus, so standard rut tactics (sex lures, mock scrapes, aggressive grunt calls and so on) should work. To the contrary, bucks are more interested m other bucks than does at this time. A hunter invading a buck fraternity expecting to arouse a sexual response is wasting his time. There are better options.

This initial phase is a special time of the year when the dominance hierarchy of bucks is sorted out by sparring: A pair of bucks square off in a pushing contest, with the stronger individual usually establishing his dominance. It's quite simple. Yet misunderstandings abound.

For one, don't confuse sparring with the ballyhooed technique of rattling. The former is more like a shoving match; the later is intended to mimic a down-and-dirty fight (which won't occur until later on). And by the way don't let convincing stories of raging bucks battling to the bitter end mislead you. (Such fights are actually quite rare.)

Also, don't underestimate the sparring season. Sparring is a formality that bucks engage in everywhere. Clear winners and losers emerge, and the pecking order becomes well established before does enter estrus. Bucks older than 3½ years don't spar as much as younger bucks that are less sure of their position in the hierarchy; they may spar among themselves long after dominant breeding bucks have ceased (turning their attention to the does).

With this in mind, why not take advantage of the sparring ritual? Antler tickling—not rattling—has drawn m many a buck that would have otherwise

During the sparring phase of the rut, bucks are more concerned about their pecking order than does.

I watched this doe lead the trailing buck around for about an hour before he finally bedded down about 75 yards away.

passed by out of range. There's nothing mysterious or complicated about the technique. Simply tickle a pair of antlers together periodically then wait for a response. Keep in mind that a buck isn't likely to approach without any reservations; he wants to size up the competition before rushing into a match, so you must be on red alert at all times. My friend Wyatt Bream, a construction worker transplanted from Texas to the Upper Midwest, relates an example of what can go wrong, if you don't keep a grip on yourself.

"In South Texas, hunters rattle a lot but it never seems to work up here," he told me. "Then I tried 'tickling.' The very first time I touched a pair of antlers together, two bucks appeared—one to my right, the other to my left. Before I could draw my bow, they were pushing and shoving like a couple of sixth-graders at a school playground." Bream became so engrossed in the mock battle that when the bucks suddenly separated without warning, he reacted in slow motion; the bucks trotted away gracefully as the five-thumbed bowhunter fumbled to draw.

Antler tickling can be effective, because it arouses the natural curiosity of whitetail bucks when they're most curious. Try it later on, however, and all you'll probably see are spikes and forkhorns—dominant bucks won't respond because they've already earned their right to a share of does.

Where to tickle? Briefly, bucks in the sparring phase of the rut stick pretty much to a well-defined home range centered around a specific food source, Bucks eat more at this time of year than any other, and this is the key to intercepting them. In agricultural lands, you can't beat bean fields. In the south, "greenfields" planted with clover or ryegrass are favored. Just remember the Moon: inch back toward cover as the Moon peaks during increasing periods of daylight.

## Phase 2: The Pseudo-Stage

This phase isn't included in any wildlife journal. But it's out there. As bachelor groups begin to disperse, bucks filter into predictable staging areas: downwind from social doe groups. The bucks are simply waiting for the first does to cycle. After all, they don't want to miss any action. By spending most of their time downwind from traditional doe bedding areas, dominant bucks can keep sub-dominant bucks at bay, too.

We've already discussed the significance of early-season rubs. You can find them without even looking for them—if you know how to identify the does' daytime bedding areas. "They're strategically situated for all sectors of wind, and they have plenty of shade from the sun and shelter from adverse winds," Myles says." When you find a main bedding area, you'll know it by all the sign. The beds will always seem fresh. If you're in doubt, walk downwind about 100 yards or so. You'll see the rubs."

This stage isn't real productive, so you're better off laying back, playing the waiting game. Remember Myles' buck pictured on page 75 for which he waited till everything was right? That's the essence of trophy hunting. Use the Moon and your knowledge of how the rut changes deer behavior, then move in for the kill.

## Phase 3: The Courtship

The staging game usually lasts about a week and bleeds into subsequent breeding cycles. A gradual rise m male hormone production and a marked change in the scent of does triggers this next phase. The real fun starts when, all of a sudden, bucks begin hunting for and harassing does. The courtship phase is a good time to be in the woods if you're the kind of person who wins lotteries: A buck's pattern breaks down now, and he could end up most anywhere a hot doe takes him.

Deer courtship is a strange phenomenon that many hunters misinterpret. They see does being trailed by adolescent bucks, noses to the ground like bloodhounds, even though most does are at least several days away from estrus. Experienced breeding bucks know this, of course, and about all you'll see early in this phase are teenagers that don't quite know how to handle their hormones.

Standard rut tactics apply at this time such as discriminant use of estrous deer lures (for those who believe in such products), tending-grunt calls, primary-scrape and rub-line monitoring and so on. You know this. But do you know how to read does?

Bucks aren't interested in blind dates during the tending stage of the rut: rather, bucks lead does out of the mainstream of deer travel, forcing you to hunt in some oddball places.

If you know how to interpret a doe's body language, you could nail a good buck by hardly trying. In a word, a hot doe is nervous. She's not quite ready to accept the aggressive advances of an infatuated buck, so she tolerates him only at a distance—well behind her, not alongside her. Studies indicate trailing distances vary from 150 feet to a quarter-mile. If the buck gets too close, the doe scampers off nervously

How does this affect practical hunting strategy? First and foremost, hunt where the majority of does are feeding and bedding—doe sign, not buck sign, is paramount now. Second, keep up with the does' reproduction cycle, and be ready when a buck comes a courtin'.

Suppose you notice a fidgety doe tiptoeing past your treestand. Her tail's cocked, and she's plumb antsy. If she prances by out of range, I say you've got a sure bet if you hurry... Get down from your treestand and get on her trail pronto! A buck could be close behind, nose to nose with the woods floor. He won't notice you hunched beside a tree or bush.

Besides reading each doe's body language, glass her tarsal gland (located on the inside joint of both hind legs). As she comes into season, this gland turns from tan-brown to matted black. If her tail stands erect, cocked to the side, she's available and definitely looking. Which leads to the next rutting phase.

## Phase 4: Tending (Breeding)

Many are the colorful (usually embellished) stories of bucks and does pairing off during the peak of the rut. I'm afraid I do not share the euphoric outlook of most writers concerning this time of the deer season. This is when luck, not game plans drawn from studious research and copious field notes, plays the biggest role. Though I've experienced plenty of luck in the past, it's never been the right kind. But if you've got the confidence of a home-run hitter when he gets on a 3-0 count and his third-base coach flashes the green light, here's what you're probably doing:

• Monitoring does around the clock, setting up in pockets where bucks steer does away from the main deer traffic. This is hard to do, but I've forced myself on at least two occasions in which it paid off during a time when I would have drawn blanks. Regarding productive areas, I know where they're not.

"It isn't where just about every seasoned bowhunter hangs a treestand," says popular video producer and game call manufacturer Mark Drury. "I leave those mesmerizing rubs and scrapes alone—because so will the bucks—and try to figure out where a buck could take a hot date an not be pestered by rivals. This is one of the few instances in which deer seem to act almost human-like." So, forget about traditional prerut courtship areas; bucks are busy tending does and aren't interested in blind dates.

• Situating yourself ***between*** doe social groups. Each family seems to stake out a little core area that it frequents on a regular basis. Set up between several, and you could catch a two-timing buck.

• While monitoring does, you're watching for weather conditions that could dictate wholesale diet changes; where you'll find the kitchen, you'll find the ladies.

## Phase 5: Post-Rut & Recovery

As a general rule, between 60 and 80 percent of the does are bred during the first major estrous cycle. A doe remains in heat for about 24 hours, and if she isn't bred during this period, she'll likely cycle again approximately 25 to 29 days later in most areas of the country, Experienced breeding bucks know all good things must come to an end, but it takes them a few days to figure it out. Even then, they're eager for one more fling... When the demand of anxious bucks begins to exceed the supply of willing does, a special time unfolds.

After this, bucks begin to conserve energy, moving mostly to stretch or water for the next three days to a week. The recovery phase also takes hunters awhile to figure out what's going on. It seems that one day deer are popping up across the countryside like targets on a shooting gallery, and the next day only a fawn or two turns up. During this phase, breeding bucks are more difficult to kill than at any other time; they've come to their senses and are back in their comfort and safety mode. It's back to the bedroom for savvy hunters—even during early and late Moon times.

Fortunately, recuperation is short-lived. When the buck's up and taking nourishment, you want to see the Man in the Moon peaking overhead or underfoot early and late in the day. Depending on the area of the country, this could be the first half of December or as late as mid-January Once again, key on food sources close to a buck's bedroom where he can make efficient beelines to and from his sleeping quarters.

By the time the buck's strength returns, another round of does enters estrus, and the mating ritual repeats itself. If you adopt a game plan that corresponds to the buck's ***current*** phase of behavior, you won't be fazed by seemingly contradictory events.

## Does The New Moon Set The Ret?

Too cold. Too hot. Not enough rain. Too wet. Not enough bucks. Too many antlerless permits. Must have been last week. Too bad I have to work next week.

If the rut is such a big deal, why all the excuses for not scoring during this can't-miss time? Trouble is, the rut's so dang fickle. One year it seems to peak early, the next year, it's two weeks late. Or it hits like lightning for a couple of days (when you are working) or barely trickles along with little or no fanfare; then, just when you concluded the rut is a memory, a buddy exclaims, "By George, you shoulda seen all the bucks!"

Wouldn't it be nice if hunters didn't need clairvoyant powers to know exactly when rut activity peaks? Then timing each rut phase—especially courtship flurries—would be a dream come true. All we'd have to do is plug in the deer's lunar cycle and we could plan rut-hunts months, even years, in advance.

Forget the power of the Dark Side. And forget about Star Wars' hooded Emperor, with his eerie opaque eyes and grotesque face declaring, "It is all happening as I have foreseen." Veteran Michigan bowhunter Bob Scriver says anyone can predict the rut—he claims to have done so eight years in a row—with a simple New Moon formula. With it, he can gauge the timing, intensity and duration of the rut as well as predict the kind of subsequent rut(s) hunters will likely face.

"I've been bowhunting for over 20 years, and ever since I can remember I've kept a log on the Moon and related rutting activity," he said. "I'm absolutely convinced that the New Moon is the key to the rut."

Before we get into the details, let's review a few basic facts about the whitetail reproductive cycle. First, does coming into estrus determine peak breeding activity "But there's often a substantial difference between 'peak of the rut' and 'peak breeding,'" says Bob Zaiglin. "The first is when the average hunter thinks deer are hyperactive, and the second is when the majority of does are actually being bred. The 'peak of the rut' occurs when bucks aggressively search for does, typically just before most of them come into estrus or just after estrus has been terminated. 'Peak breeding,' on the other hand, may actually be a relatively benign period as far as hunting excitement goes. We examine embryos in the spring here *in* South Texas to back-date for dates of conception, and they don't always line up with when we've seen the most bucks the previous fall."

Second, photoperiodism—the diminishing ratio of daylight to darkness—triggers the onset of the reproductive cycle. Just like when a buck's headgear begins to form, when longer days signal its pituitary gland to release testosterone, a doe undergoes a similar transformation in the fall—as the days become shorter, her pineal gland releases melatonin, a substance influencing the release of sex hormones from the pituitary. The pineal gland acts as a translator of photoperiod clues, and this is where the New Moon comes in.

"I see a cycle that's tied to periods of light and dark that just happens to coincide with the lunar cycle," Scriver said. "Is it any coincidence that the female cycle and the lunar cycle are [approximately] 28 days?" As previously noted, the Moon's face-to-face cycle is 29.5 days and its siderial cycle is 27.3 days; thus the average is 28.4 days. Studies on does showed spans of 28 and 29 days between successive heats in New York; 21 to 27 days in Upper Michigan; and 25 to 30 clays in Minnesota.

Still, the variability begs explanation, as do hunter reports on inconsistent "rut dates" from fall to fall. "The New Moon is the answer," Scriver says. "A doe's pineal gland doesn't just measure waning sunlight, but it responds to all light, including that of the Moon. So it shouldn't come as a surprise that when a New Moon arrives earlier than a traditional rutting date for a given [genetic and geographic] deer population, the peak rut is skewed ahead of schedule.

"The doe's pineal gland tells [its pituitary gland] that the light is less, so 'the day must be shorter.' Estrogen levels then increase, and she cycles in heat. Poultry farmers have artificially manipulated light levels to enhance egg production for years. So has the Michigan DNR for boosting pheasant production. It's no big deal."

The "optimum length of day" is always the starting point for deter- mining traditional rutting dates. For example, in higher latitudes the rut begins earlier—daylight is shorter—with local exceptions of heavy snowfall (fawns must be birthed during favorable spring conditions). Next factor moonlight, which can make the day seem longer or shorter,

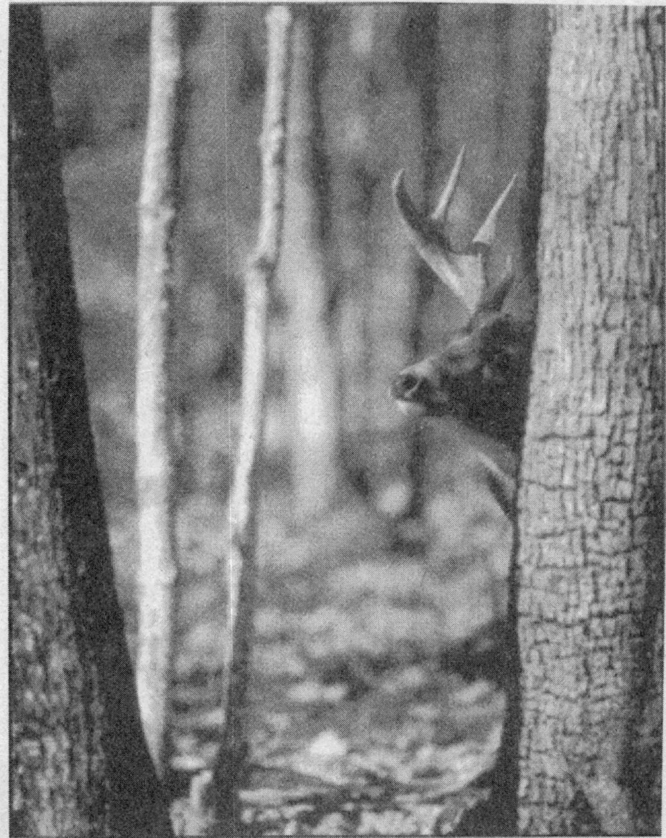

A buck behind every tree? Maybe . . . if the demand exceeds the supply.

The does trigger the rut, and the New Moon helps determine the timing.

depending on its timing m the fall. For example, a lunation with a New Moon arriving a week earlier than a traditional peak rut date balances off the minute traces of extra daylight. The net result is an early rut. For those interested in predicting future rut hunts, here's Scriver's formula. If a New Moon:

- Is "on time," coinciding with optimum daylight for estrous release: The rut will be electrifying for a short spell. The length of day is ideal for peak rutting, and so is the dark of the Moon. The frenzy will soon subside as does become bred and come out of estrus.
- Hits late: Most hunters will complain of a sub-par rut: however, chase activity will occur a week later, after a lot of hunters have given up prematurely. In states like Michigan, Minnesota and Wisconsin,

many bucks will be harvested during the firearms season, with not enough remaining to service late-estrous does. Fewer does bred in November leads to an accelerated rut in December.

- Arrives a week early: The rut should be "decent," according to Scriver, arriving earlier and maintaining a fairly even keel. But if it's two weeks early, like it was in 1994 (November 3), rutting activity hits a moderate level and spreads out, with not much intensity. "The days are shorter, but the nights are darker," Scriver says. "The net effect is no change translated through the pineal gland. By the traditional rut date of November 15, daylight will be short enough to trigger a trickling rut, which will be spread out."

Don't forget the weather, either. A prolonged spell of thunderstorms and dark, overcast skies during the fall suppresses general deer activity "I believe deer become depressed much like humans," Scriver says. "But a day or two after the clouds lift, the bucks often go bonkers; they've been cooped up at a time when they're free spirits, and if a few does come into a short period of heat, look out. This 'false heat' will quickly reverse itself, however, so you really have to stay on top of it."

Now that I've got your attention, here are a few New Moons to back-date:

| Year | October | November | December |
|---|---|---|---|
| 1993 | 10-15 | 1 1-13 | 12-13 |
| 1994 | 10-5 | 11-3 | 12-2 |
| 1995 | 10-24 | 11-22 | 12-22 |
| 1996 | 10-12 | 11-11 | 12-10 |
| 1997 | 10-31 | 11-30 | 12-29 |
| 1998 | 10-20 | 11-19 | 12-18 |
| 1999 | 10-9 | 11-8 | 12-7 |

## The Full Moon & The Rut

There are two kinds of rattlers in Texas—snakes and antler-bangers. If you don't want to be lopped into the former camp, better learn the real secret to rattling the most dominant breeding buck in an area. It boils down to waiting for a Full Moon to overlap the rut. Four factors give you the best odds of the year for bagging the buck of many lifetimes.

First off, the Moon is underfoot at midday, so does will be up and feeding, whether or not they're in estrus. Of course, bucks know this, and they'll be on the prowl.

Second, the bright intensity of the Full Moon guarantees increased midday activity. "From 20 years of studying deer at night during Full Moons," Bob Zaiglin says, "I've witnessed a repeating sequence: Deer bed and feed all night long. Up at midnight, down by 1 a.m. Back up again at 3 a.m., and so on . . . " Deer seem to be unusually uncomfortable, and I suspect it's because of their perceived vulnerability to predation in the extra-bright light of the Moon.

Third, a Full Moon overlapping the rutting cycle is double trouble for dominant breeding bucks. "During the rut, bucks push does out in pear flats [cactus), running them ragged," Zaiglin says. "By sunrise the does will be holed up, and around midday they want to get up and flex, go to feed. Meanwhile, bucks continue pestering them. The typical three-day period of an estrous doe is no time to slack off at midday. Over the years, I and many of my clients have taken some impressive trophies at this time."

Which leads to the most important reason trophy hunters concentrate on this lunar period: The demand for does far exceeds the supply. "This fall, go out on a Full Moon night, and count the bucks you see," Scriver says. "I bet there won't be many.

But if there was a hot doe out there, don't you think the bucks would be after her? Heck, they'll chase a doe in the middle of the day, if she's hot. But the fact remains, not many does will be in heat during the Full Moon. Two weeks later, you'll see some bucks chasing some does for sure."

No wonder rattling is a waste of time during the peak breeding season—when the supply of hot does is at its peak. A week or two later tells a different story. "The bucks are ornery because they can't find any action," Scriver says. "They've been running all night, and no doe will stand for them. They're on edge. A slight provocation could trigger them. Rattling when a Full Moon overlaps the rut can be deadly, if you happen to hit it just right."

## Rattle Their Cage

In sum, during the Full Moon only bucks at the top of the totem pole get to breed. If you bump into a hot doe at this time, you've got a serious chance at a Booner. There will only be a handful of does in heat—the majority cycled during the New Moon—so the nature of the game has changed. Before, the supply met the demand; now, the demand exceeds the supply. The average hunter should be successful the first time around; savvy hunters could score now when the big boys will have been primed for a week or two.

The tactic of rattling is neither a science, nor an art. It's strictly a matter of timing, as alluded to earlier. Ideally, you want to rattle in a buck when he's on his feet and not preoccupied with a steady date. Larry Weishuhn, a former Texas state biologist, wholeheartedly agrees. Though he has successfully spotted bedded bucks in the distance and gotten a response from a rattling sequence, he'd much rather hunt an animal that's on the move. "It seems that once a buck decides to hole up for the day, he gets into a twilight-zone-type of mentality. Doo-do-doo-do. He isn't going to get up unless something really sparks a fire under him. I'd much rather rattle a buck I know is actively seeking does. That's one reason why I've hunted by the Moon for so many years."

Rattling also works best with a balanced deer herd. The two extremes of Texas and Canada are ideal candidates. When does badly outnumber bucks, the competition is next to nil, and the bucks rarely square off.

When it comes to rattling m the big woods, you can dismiss the need for low-impact scouting. Quietly erect a portable treestand along a hot rub or scrape line, and wait for the Full Moon to peak underfoot (typically 1 to 3 p.m.). Then rattle a pair of antlers, fairly softly at first, gradually increasing in intensity. Bang them together for 15 to 45 seconds. If you don't strike a responsive chord, try again in about 15 minutes. Then relocate, if you haven't sighted a whitetail within an hour or so.

Two final thoughts. Technically speaking, bucks do not grunt when they fight (the tending grunt is associated with a buck courting a doe); however, an adjustable grunt call still does the job in spite of the apparent contradictory message. But keep it simple. I've heard some so-called deer callers hit more notes than Whitney Houston, and I wonder what the deer think.

Last, add a decoy to your rattling sequence. Delta markets a realistic portable buck decoy that can be packed down and easily transported. (Delta/B-K Industries, 117 E. Kenwood St., Reinbeck, IA 50699; 319-345-6476.)

## It's A Shoo-in

Now there's a right and wrong way to rattle a buck in the North Country. Like many hunters, I've learned all of the wrong ways. I'm starting to learn the fine line separating good, better and best techniques.

A good technique, for example, is doing my homework ahead of time to locate key traditional rutting territories. This should put me m an excellent position to trigger a buck before or after the rut peaks. A better technique is adding the Moon's influence to ensure that the buck is on his feet and most likely to investigate (compared to a buck bedded deep in the thick stuff). The best technique, however, is injecting efficiency. As noted bowhunter Dwight Schuh aptly points out, big-woods deer are neither as predictable, nor as plentiful as their open-country counterparts.

Dwight Schuh rattled in this nice tall-tined Montana buck from a treestand.

"I add a key wrinkle to the basic system," Schuh said. "I go to the bucks, instead of assuming they'll always come to me." The success of Schuh's strategy pivots around mobility. When I bowhunted with Schuh in Illinois recently, I watched him leave camp with his daily needs on his back. He didn't return until well after dark. With the help of his famous Dwight Schuh backpack, marketed by Fieldline, he could stuff needed accessories—from a survival kit to raingear—into a pair of removable Polar fleece-covered packs. Just as important, he strapped a super-lightweight portable treestand to his lightweight nylon composite frame.

"If a bowhunter rattles from the ground, even with the help of a buddy cleverly disguised off to the side, he might get a lot of sightings," Schuh explained. "But if he isn't elevated from the ground, he won't get many shots. I'd rather get one shot from, say, one or two encounters, than never draw my bow while sighting a dozen bucks that end up circling and blowing me off."

It's hard to argue with Schuh's success: This celebrated bowhunter rattled up a pair of handsome bucks last year without trying.

# The New Rut Rules

In the good old days, my Grandpa used to lick his chops when a chilly northwest wind signaled the first hint of fall. He knew, both intuitively and from experience, that the whitetail rut is best time of year to kill a hat-racked buck, as he used to call it. That's still true, but in spite of the Information Age we live in, many hunters head for the same woods with the same tactics on the same dates year after year. Talk about a rut!

It's high time for a change. I've learned a great deal since my theories on the rut were published back m 1995 in my book, MOONSTRUCK! In fact, I believe it's now possible to predict not only the rut, but each phase of the rut. This, in turn, tells us what to do as well as what not to do as deer undergo key physiological and behavioral changes in the fall.

Now it's time to take rut-hunting to its highest level. There are new rules to the game.

## Predicting the Rut

I admit to being possessed when it comes to figuring out how to time the rut. But I've got cold logic backing up my obsessive compulsive nature. If I really know when the breeding season kicks off, I will also know where to hunt and how aggressively I dare hunt. That, my friends, is the Whole Nine Yards. Ever wonder why it's possible to spook deer with rattling one day, yet rattle in the buck of a life a week later? You're about to get the straight scoop. The starting point is realizing that each rut phase presents both barriers and openings; discern the difference and you're razor-close to being at the right place with the right stuff.

Is the rut really that predictable? Two distinct factors say it is. The first is decreasing daylight, known as photoperiodism. Suffice to say, thanks to her pineal gland, a whitetail doe is capable of "monitoring" light intensity at remarkably low levels. When daylight reaches a prescribed minimum threshold, she prepares to enter estrus. Following the Fall Equinox in September, daylight contracts as darkness expands. This is why deer in North America always breed in the fall (and why deer in the Southern Hemisphere breed during our spring, which is their fall). But because daylight hours diminish more rapidly in northern latitudes, particularly above the 40th parallel, rutting activity is generally more concentrated the farther north one travels.

A graphic illustration of this principle is the sunrise/sunset tables for the cities of Minneapolis and Houston, located near the middle of the Central Time Zone. According to the U.S. Naval Observatory, during the week of October 24-30 for a typical year, sunrise times for Houston change from 7:29 a.m. to 7:33 a.m. whereas Minneapolis sunrises change from 7:40 a.m. to 7:48 a.m. The sunset times also change—five and nine minutes, respectively for the two cities. While the net difference over one week's time may seem insignificant—Houston loses about nine minutes of daylight, Minneapolis loses 17 minutes—the RATE of change for Minneapolis is nearly 100 percent greater.

Obviously hunters can do little about photoperiodism. But keeping tabs on changes m moonlight intensity can mean the difference between a buck on the ground and a grounded hunt. Deer are biologically equipped to respond to changing lunar periods. Consider that the illumination of a Full Moon is about the same as twilight. It can get complicated, but the latest research suggests that the first New Moon following the second Full Moon after the Fall Equinox typically overlaps peak breeding among white tails. As one researcher described the process, "the sun cocks the [rut's] trigger, the moon pulls it." What this means to hunters is that it's now possible to time rut-phase hunts years in advance, since these lunar periods are predictable. This forms the basis for the Deer Hunters' Red Hot Rut Guide, which predicts specific rut dates for the four hunting phases of the rut over a five-year period.

Radio telemetry work suggests that deer are cued to the position of the moon, but does the moon affect the timing of the rut? If so, how?

As I said, knowing "when" can also mean knowing where and knowing how. Such as timing the high tides of activity while avoiding the neap tides. Or matching hunting tactics more precisely to each and every phase of the rut. That includes getting a grip on the best time to make amends: successfully hunting the elusive "second rut" phase. Again, this is based on the fact that, during the rut, deer don't act like Dr. Jekyll one week and Mr. Hyde the next. Quite the contrary, deer behavior changes predictably throughout the fall, much like children entering various stages of development. But before we re-examine rut phase tactics, let's re-check our data.

## Researching The Rut

Any theory on the timing of the rut must be based on solid evidence. In recent times a few skeptics have suggested that the rut is not cyclical, as I maintain, but is constant (that is, occurs on the same dates each fall). Several variables—road kills, penned deer, conception dates—have been used to support this theory. Each is subject to misinterpretation, even by dedicated students of the whitetail. Consider the examination of fetuses removed from road kill does in hopes of back-dating conception dates. The basic technique of measuring the size of a fetus to determine its age—and therefore

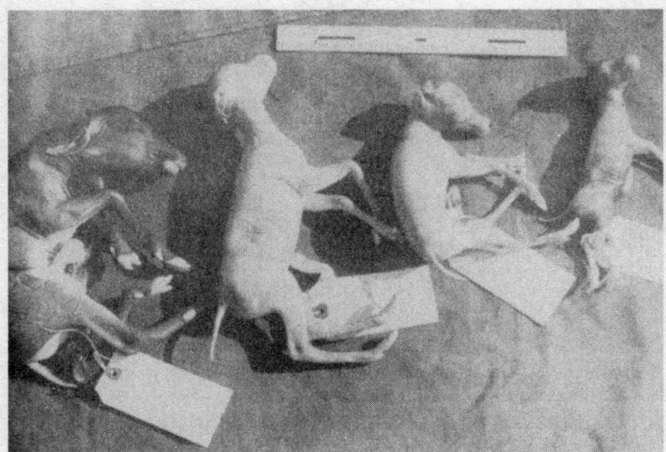

Researchers have examined fetuses, removed from road kill does, in hopes of back-dating conception dates. The basic technique is imprecise.

when it was conceived—is imprecise, at best. The main problem is erratic fetal growth, particularly toward the end of the cycle. This is common among warm-blooded organisms, including humans. I still remember the day I whisked my nine-month-pregnant wife to the maternity ward and blurted to the receptionist, "It's our due date." The tart response was predictable: "That date is only an educated guess," the nurse replied. "Come back when your wife is in labor." Of course Coric had been in labor for several hours and was miserable. I just used the wrong terminology to describe her plight.

And so it is with back-dating road kill fetuses to reach a so-called "conception date." Even with the latest formulas, this method is a plus or minus 10 days-to-two-weeks affair. Which just won't do because that's about how much the rut varies each year. What about observations of penned deer? I certainly make it a point to network annually with several "deer farmer" friends to keep tabs on how the rut is progressing with their herds. But I'm very careful when comparing notes from enclosure to enclosure, to make sure the "biostimulation effect" doesn't skew my data. Research seems to indicate that the more contact bucks have with does, the more biostimulation—the exchange of hormones and pheromones resulting in an involuntary response—occurs and the more does are likely to cycle in a concentrated manner. Of course the reverse is also true—less contact between the sexes means a more variable and "diluted" rut cycle. So unless studies involving captivity deer control this key variable—specifically how many bucks are grouped together with how many does, and in what proximity and for how long—the conclusions are likely to be off the mark

Academia notwithstanding, it's always helpful to know what's going on in the real world. After all, reality is reality. When I first considered how the moon's position might affect hunting tactics,

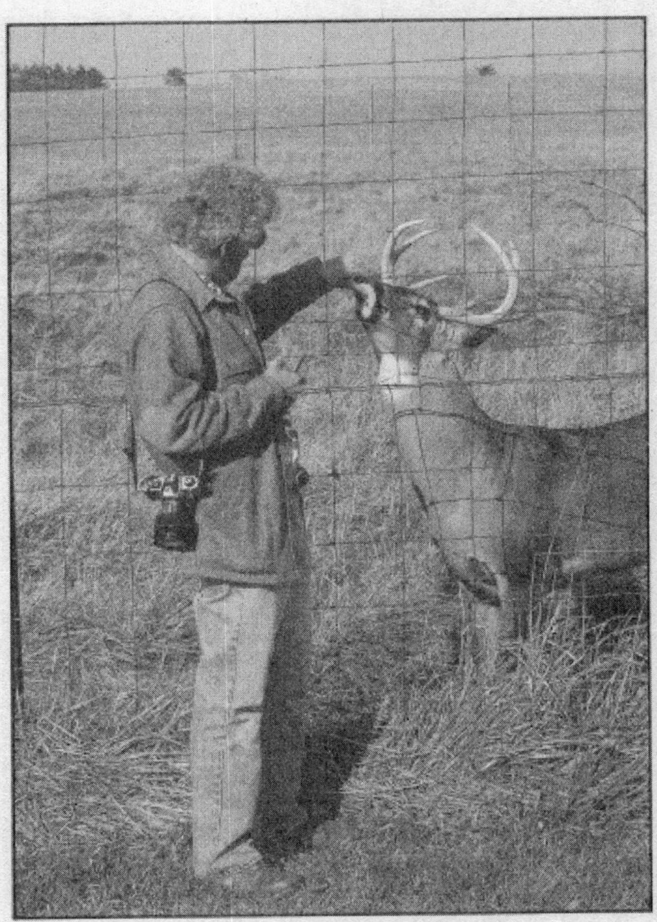

Data derived from captivity deer can be skewed if the "biostimulation effect" isn't considered.

I gathered harvest data from several states in the Midwest and South where deer kills are registered. I quickly discovered that success rates for the majority of days within any given lunar month were surprisingly low, and that most deer were harvested on a handful of "favorable" days. That's why the Moon Guide can be used like a report card for grading future dates—days that list Area A are better than those listing Area B which are rated higher than those listing Area C.

You can easily verify this locally. Go to any deer registration station and note how many deer are checked m during, say, a Full Moon period. Unless it's during the rut, you're going to encounter depressingly low numbers. But return a week or so later during a Quarter Moon phase, and the number of registered deer will increase appreciably. Almost always, almost everywhere. This hunter success-lunar calendar relationship isn't puzzling if you give the moon due credit. During Full Moon periods the moon is underfoot during midday and overhead around midnight, translating into more midday movement and less activity associated with dawn and dusk. Conversely, Quarter Moons are overhead and underfoot early and late in the day—when hunters are hunting hardest and when deer are most active. Makes sense to me.

I embarked on a similar path to verify the validity of my new rut theory. Besides charting rutting dates of deer raised in captivity, I compared the success rates of bowhunters and gun hunters in Illinois. Harvest data in the Hoosier State is particularly meaningful because its shotgun slug season falls in the third week of November. If my hypothesis proves correct, the deer harvest for Illinois' opening 3-day gun weekend should be higher in years with a late rut and lower when the rut falls early. In other words, hunter success rates should be proportional to the level of buck activity. If, on the other hand, there is no such correlation, there will be little fluctuations—and certainly no pattern—in the Illinois gun harvest; the naysayers would be correct in saying the rut falls on the same dates year after year.

Well, well. As I suspected, a consistent pattern emerged paralleling the predictions of the Deer Hunters' Red Hot Rut Guide debuting in 1996–97. The Rut Guide makes bold predictions for the four main hunting phases of the rut, providing specific dates as well as unique game plans tailored for each phase. Below is the Illinois harvest record compared to my predictions published in various magazine articles as well as within the Red Hot Rut Guide:

| **Year** | **IL Gun Harvest** | **Change** | **Prediction/Reason** |
|---|---|---|---|
| 1994 | 63,014 | –7% | Down; very early rut |
| 1995 | 71,986 | +2% | Up; late rut |
| 1996 | 59,412 | –9% | Down; early rut |
| 1997 | 61,937 | +4% | Up; late rut |
| 1998 | 70,015 | + 12% | Up; later rut |
| 1999 | 66,761 | –5% | Down; early rut |
| 2000 | 73,425 | +9% | Up; later rut |

These predictions were made public and are well-documented. For example, my rut forecast for the fall of 1997 in Buckmasters called for an increase in the Illinois gun harvest, "since rutting activity will coincide with that hunting season," I wrote. A closer look at 1998's New Moon falling on November 19 is especially revealing. It just so happens that breeding was winding down and bucks were running out of available does when the slug gun season hit. I believe the 12 percent increase is a reflection of accelerated buck activity more than variables such as favorable weather or high hunter turnouts. More important,

Remote photography (infrared sensors) at baited sights prove little: bait piles "noctumalize" deer.

this insight tells me we can take rut-hunting to a much higher level.

The real key to understanding the rut is the principle of "rut economics." Simply stated, when the demand for does exceeds the supply, hunting is best. This axiom holds water across the board, regardless of geography. Take the pre-rut, when daytime buck activity is nearing an annual peak; bucks are "primed" by alluring new odors in the woods but their makers are elusive. Only problem is, which bucks are most active, the monarchs we all dream about or adolescent bucks jockeying for position on the right-to-breed merry-go-round? The pre-rut can be good to hunters who wisely plan ahead ... but the next rut phase can be downright explosive! Too bad most hunters, never heard of it.

## Coming to Terms

While some writers use adjectives such as chasing and seeking to describe segments, or phases, of the rut, I feel these terms are misleading and may actually do more harm than good. Fact is. during any phase of the rut some bucks will appear to be "seeking" does and some will appear to be "chasing" them around. In fact, I've arrowed bucks that were literally on the tails of does in all four rut stages.

So terms are important, and the Trolling Phase is highest on my list. It's such a tremendous window of opportunity that every sane deer hunter should learn as much about it as possible. In short, if you study the rut with an open mind and have no ax to grind, you'll discover that, from a hunter's perspective, there are actually two peaks of activity, not one. I've never seen anyone report on this phenomenon, and it's high time the hunting community gets in on it. his twin-peak discovery has remained a mystery for so long largely because it's disguised. One reason is misinterpreting the Peak Breeding stage of the rut (when most eligible bachelors have hot dates, and hunting prospects dwindle as bucks pair off with receptive does). During this phase, the supply (estrous does) exceeds the demand (dominant breeding bucks). Unfortunately, it's toward the end of a typical rut cycle and most hunters mistakenly assume the rut's over. But be at the right place at the right time a week or so later (hunting seasons permitting)., and you'll see buck activity spring to life overnight. The Trolling Phase blossoms right after the does have been bred out, and it's a mad scramble for bucks to find another sex partner. So when you see a heavy-racked buck on a dog-trot in the distance, grab your binoculars and see if he's in the "troller trance." His glassy eyes, stiff gait, ruffled coat, and slobbering tongue says he's under the spell.

## Formula for the Rut: 3-Year Cycle

The lunar formula popularized by the Rut Guide offers the only reasonable explanation for annual fluctuations in rutting activity. We've long known that the New Moon was a special key to the rut. Back in 1932, for instance, the federal government commissioned a study on the reproductive habits of the Indian Buffalo; from 2,457 first-hand observations of mating buffaloes, peak breeding almost invariably overlapped the New Moon. This makes perfect biological sense, as it ensures the propagation of the whitetail species. For example, if whitetails breed on essentially the same dates year after year, weather could wreak havoc with localized populations. Indeed, herds could be extinguished in some regions of the country. Spring flooding, the hurricane season, and delayed green-up caused by late-arriving springs in the snow belt are just a few examples.

On the other hand, the Full Moon-to-New Moon "cycle" ensures the rut will fall early on the breeding calendar some years, the rut will fall late some years, and some years the rut will be "on time." Early, late, middle; early, late middle. This cycle all but guarantees that during the lifetime of a healthy adult doe, at least one year-class of fawns will survive to carry on this unique synchronized breeding characteristic. It also means this neat pattern can empower hunters to cope with ever- changing whitetail patterns. Since the advent of the Rut Guide, hunters all over the nation have reported exceptional results in matching specific tactics to specific rut phases.

But don't take my word for it. Hear what brothers Mark and Terry Drury, game call experts and popular video producers, have to say. Their livelihood depends on successfully videotaping hunting scenes in the wild, and their schedules revolve around whitetail deer nine months out of the year (their only respite is targeting spring gobblers). Mark Drury is gifted with a photographic-type memory, and when I first shared my lunar theories on the rut, he spit out specific details of deer kills like it was last week. It didn't take long for him to make the 'lunar connection."

Mark Drury's impressive Illinois buck, arrowed on film in October 1998, marked the beginning of his "moon-hunting" tactics.

Over the next several years the Drurys made it a point to hunt with, not regardless of, the moon. It's safe to say they're now hooked on Moon-Hunting. "We don't plan any hunts these days without first checking out [moon times]," says Terry. "[These times] are way too significant to ignore, and I think [leaving them out] is the downfall of many game plans. I've seen too many hunts, especially those revolving around food sources, turn out as predicted by the [Moon Guide]."

"Nothing always works, of course," adds brother Mark. "But the correlation between deer activity and peak lunar times and phases is becoming self-evident. I agree with Terry. I encourage hunters to consider both rut predictions and daily movement predictions m their trip planning." Riveting testimony to the potency of properly timed hunts can be seen in a new series of Drury Outdoors video productions. A good start is *Walk the Walk*.

Another key point is that rut phases are predictable to the week—and almost to the day—in the 39 whitetail states experiencing a November rut. This group includes the states of Kansas, Oklahoma and Montana which average

Terry Drury is a firm believer in hunting both favorable lunar feeding periods and favorable moon phases during the rut.

three to seven days later than predicted dates for the other November-rut states. Five others—Alabama, Florida, Mississippi Louisiana, Texas—are exceptions to this rule and must be handled on a case-by-case basis; some geographic regions experience a December rut and some a January rut. (Texas has an October, November and December rut, depending on the area!) But even states with later ruts can benefit from annual predictions: If the rut falls earlier than normal in the "November Belt." it will fall earlier than normal m December-rut and January-rut states. It isn't voodoo mathematics.

The ability to predict each rut phase is priceless. Now, for the first time, hunters can match game-specific strategies to unique windows of opportunity.

## The Prerut Phase

Technically, the whitetail rut begins with the hardening-off stage of bucks shedding velvet; bachelor groups break up as dominant breeders settle into discreet "territories." This is not the easiest time to pursue trophy whitetails. We want to put the microscope on the phases of the rut that unveil chinks in a buck's armor. The first—and most celebrated—phase is the Prerut. This period is characterized by an increase in nocturnal buck movement followed by a slight increase in daytime activity. A mid- to late-October Full Moon often stimulates after-dark buck activity; bucks respond to hormonal increases with increased rubbing and scraping. Daytime activity is spurred by the first olfactory clues released by does nearing estrus.

Now here's a little secret. If you know when bucks are most likely to be rubbing trees and tearing up scrape lines, you'll also know when and where to intercept bucks: near trees scarred from previous years. So-called "multiple-year rubs" are a surefire tip-off that bucks will continue to rut m the same general areas. Naturally, sheds provide additional incentives. So plan ahead. Set stands and prune lanes

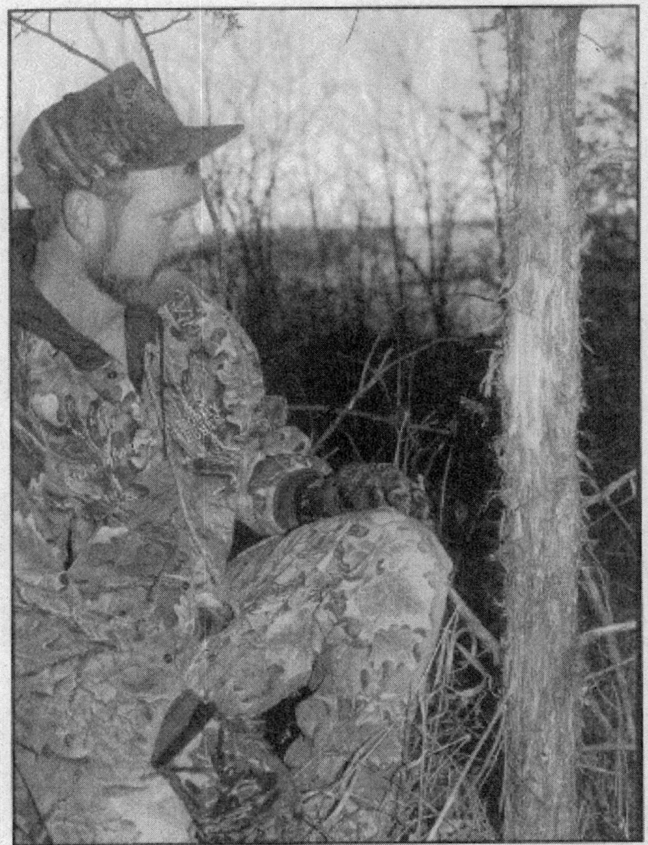

Steve Snoop, with J & S Trophy Hunts, admires a "multiple-year rub." This is where it's at for the prerut.

BEFORE the first sign-post markers appear. Plunk your fanny and wait for rubbers and scrapers, and you could score big early in the rut cycle. The rule of the prerut is: Hunt rubs and scrape lines as they emerge, not after they're obvious.

## The Peak Breeding Phase

When breeding peaks, bucks have little trouble locating receptive does. Bucks don't have to do much looking, let alone chasing, and hunter opportunities nose-dive. The problem is exacerbated in many parts of the South, where deer often exceed the carrying capacity of the land and does drastically outnumber bucks. Put another way, when bucks don't waste any energy to satisfy their mating urge, you won't see many during hunting hours. Needless to say, this renders aggressive rattling and calling tactics useless.

But during this fickle phase you must also alter your game plan when dealing with fairly balanced herds. For starters, the conventional wisdom of hunting high-traffic areas gets tossed out of the window Right now any buck worth his headgear isn't about to share his female companion, so he alters his daily routine to reduce contact with other deer. I know it's the peak of the breeding season when I see bucks quartering does into the darnedest places—from desolate drainage ditches in the middle of plowed fields to sloughs and swamps; from brushy rock piles and isolated fence rows to dried up potholes and ponds. These are the best places to hunt, not fresh scrapes or grooved trails.

When bucks are paired off with does, think "isolation."

Meanwhile, a possible alternative is intercepting a buck traveling between hot does. But, frankly, this is a good time to conserve energy, bide your time, and keep a sharp eye on the rut's progression. You really want to be primed and ready for the next phase. Hence, the rule for peak breeding: Think low traffic, interception & observation.

## Post-rut "Trolling" Phase

My all-time favorite time to be in the whitetail woods is, by far, the short but oh-so-sweet Trolling Phase. It's a rarefied period when bucks are so desperate to locate estrous does that even Boone and Crockett-class specimens risk exposure to danger. "The prerut is okay for lots of buck action, but the trollers are what I'm after," says Mike Weaver. "These bucks can't find any more willing does, yet they're used to breeding. This combination can be the downfall of a buck that probably won't make a single mistake the rest of the year. Even though [the troller] should lay low and recuperate when his nose tells him there are no more hot females around, he isn't quite ready to give up breeding. So he trolls from one doe family group to the next." No wonder so many monster bucks are killed by hunters that never knew of their existence! I'm convinced these rogues were merely caught out of position in unfamiliar territory during the Trolling Stage.

Now's THE time to turn up the heat. Start by picking the best venues to rattle. Remember, if the wind's right, you can rattle on a calm, clear morning and let the magic sound of clashing antlers do your walking—if it's the right time, bucks will travel considerable distances to investigate. By the way, my field notes reveal a statistical advantage for mornings over evenings (3:1); the period between 8 a.m. and 9 a.m. has also been more productive than the crack of dawn.

Let me repeat: Rattling can be so effective on trollers that your entire game plan should revolve around rattle-friendly spots. The combination of elevation and funnels—to increase carrying distance and intercept corner-cutters—is unbeatable. Trollers almost always follow the terrain, rather than wind direction, when covering ground at a rut-crazed clip.

A final caveat is how to spend time. I say spend it lavishly. Most hunters are programmed into hunting mornings and evenings and resting up midday. Don't do that now. Instead, hunt hard all day. You never know when a troller might show up. Don't chance missing out. Hit the woods during this phase rested up, bring plenty of refreshments, and commit to a predawn to post-dusk vigil. So the troika for trollers: Hunt funnels, rattle aggressively, hunt hard.

## Second Estrus

The so-called second rut is supposed to hit when a subsequent wave of does supposedly enter estrus for a second time in the fall. It's supposed to be an excellent time to see trophy whitetails on the prowl again. But if theory lined up with reality, we wouldn't need all the excuses: Too cold (or too warm); too wet (or too dry); deer patterns switched (or didn't switch enough); the farmer planted the wrong crops (or harvested them too early). And so it goes with the second rut.

It's hard enough predicting the primary rut, and here we are dissecting the elusive second rut. But after thoroughly researching this topic, I'm convinced the second rut is legitimate if you know when breeding peaked during the primary rut. In addition, some interesting correlations have emerged that tell us what to expect. For one, the intensity of a given year's second rut will generally be the opposite of its preceding primary rut. During a recent rut cycle, for instance, the main rut was hot for most hunters, whereas the second rut was hardly a whisper throughout much of the nation. But the following year the second rut was unusually intense—better, in fact, than the diluted primary rut. No one can say for sure why this happens, but it probably has to do with concentration levels of estrous does. Whenever a significant number of does are not successfully bred during the primary rut, more estrous does will be available the following month. This seems to stimulate aggression between bucks and may make the second rut as intense as the first in some years.

You can succeed during the Second Estrus if you know how to time it.

The intensity of any second rut is influenced by a trio of other factors. One is the fawn crop. In most states, fawns experience their first estrus about a month after mature does, typically mid-December throughout much of the whitetail range. A bumper crop of female fawns can stimulate sudden and unexpected buck aggression. When I see a lot of triplets, rather than twins or singles in the summer, I take note. Besides fawn-watching, observe nature: The year following a heavy mast crop usually improves fawn survival, as do years of abundant rainfall.

Second, we must factor in does failing to conceive after copulation during the primary rut. Ungulate research at major eastern university indicates that approximately 25 percent of female deer fail to become pregnant the first time they mate in a given fall. It's interesting to note that this percentage is higher during draught. Diet also has an impact on a doe's reproductive capacity—those animals feeding on an abundance of soft mast and other food sources high in nutrients are going to be more fertile, other factors being equal. Third, balanced deer herds will always provide more action the second time around than unbalanced herds. In years when rut intensity is lowest, I still get favorable reports from hunters who manage to hunt blue ribbon lands blessed with a lot of mature bucks. More adult bucks during the second rut means more competition for breeding rights, pure and simple.

In years in which the primary rut is slow, subsequent phases are usually fast-paced. When that happens, bucks like this will cut corners just as they did during Trolling Phase.

The main key to "second chance" rutting bucks is capitalizing on a peculiar bedding habit of theirs. During the primary rut, bucks typically relocate bedding areas: from security cover segregated from does to immediately down-wind of traditional doe bedding areas. Breeding bucks pull this stunt so they can keep tabs on estrous does and be the first on the scene when it's prime time. These "temporary bedrooms" are easy to spot, because they're punctuated with an abundance of rubs and scrapes.

Well, this predictable buck movement reoccurs during the second rut. You're on the right track if you can locate FRESH rutting sign: scraped trees with the sap still running; scrapes pungent with buck odor; and over-50-mch beds. If fresh rutting sign is hard to come by, there might be a shortage of second-estrus does. Switch to the waiting game: Set up shop near primary food sources richest in protein. Late-season does zero in on the best available food sources—winter wheat, rye and oats—and bucks won't be far behind. Meanwhile, tone down rattling sequences and rely more on tending grunts; the sound of a buck on the trail of a hot doe can be irresistible to a lusting buck ... if the demand for does exceeds the supply. So the rule for the second rut is Hunt fresh rut sign and key on nutritious food sources. Just don't over-hunt these hotspots, or you'll "nocturnalize" deer and shipwreck your game plans. The rut is a helter-skelter time of year when dedicated deer hunters are as wired as the deer. Put these rules for the rut to practice, however, and you shouldn't get short-circuited. In fact, with a little luck you just might make the connection of a lifetime.

**Mitigating Factors**

The moon is not exactly a panacea for the Rut Blues. Unfavorable weather can be a disease for which there is no cure. For example ocean patterns such as La Nina and El Nino can lead to balmy weather with above-normal temperatures and heavy doses of cloud cover. This throws each phase of the rut off, causing delays in projected rut dates. Moreover, the intensity of the rut slacks off measurably when the moon is clouded over and daytime temperatures make a buck feel a guy in wool longjohns during the month of August. Bottom line: Pray for clear skies and normal temperatures for November and December!

The best strategy for hunting the rut is keeping in touch with feeding does and knowing where bucks are during the breeding cycle. The Moon Guide and Rut Guide are invaluable planners.

# EXPERT TIPS
## What Animals See and How They See It

Judging the trophy status of bears can be notoriously difficult, even when the bear is close. When my guide on a British Columbia spot-and-stalk bear hunt whispered that the bear we had just glimpsed slipping through a stand of stunted pines 30 yards or so away was not quite the trophy black bear we were looking for, I relaxed. When the bear passed through an opening and paused momentarily to look our way, the guide got a better look at his big, square head and small, wide-set ears and changed his mind.

"Go! Go! Go!" he whispered frantically, pushing me forward. "That's a good bear! Get up there!" The bear turned and dropped into a small ravine, and I quickly nocked an arrow and began moving forward. Thinking the bear was probably running full speed in the opposite direction, but keenly aware it could also be moving in our direction, I brought my bow to full draw as I approached the lip of the ravine. I peeked over carefully and spotted the bear, hardly 10 yards away and broadside. It lunged forward a few steps toward a thicket, then, inexplicably, stopped and stared in my direction. I don't believe animals think, but if I were asked to caption a photo of that situation, the caption would be "Wait a minute. I'm a bear. I'm not the one who is supposed to run." In one motion I put the sight pin behind the bear's shoulder, touched the release, and watched the fletching disappear in the sweet spot.

That was the first day of a weeklong hunt, and I spent most of the rest of the week photographing bears. It was a remote wilderness area, early enough in the spring that the big boars were just coming out of hibernation, and they were hungry. On several occasions over the next few days, with the guide sitting beside me toting a .45 caliber carbine, I sat photographing bears from close range. In each case, the experience was similar. The bear would raise its head from time to time to look at me, then go back to eating. When it "huffed" at us, or got inside 25 yards or so, the guide would tap me on the shoulder and we would slowly back away.

Many hunters assume bears have poor vision, but recent studies suggest they see color, and many biologists are convinced their vision is at least as good as ours. Hunters observe that bears seem to glance at them and then look away, and assume the bears don't see them. My experience in British Columbia, and numerous similar experiences since then, convinced me that, in most such cases, the bears do see the hunter. In a remote wilderness area, though, bears seldom encounter humans, and are not likely to be threatened by anything but a bigger bear. I suspect they see hunters, but just aren't intimidated by them. Many animals, including canines, perceive staring as a threat and will turn their eyes from another animal if they don't want a confrontation. Hunters often think that because a bear looks at them and then looks away, it hasn't seen them. That may be, but it could also be the bear is simply avoiding the kind of long, intense stare that for many species is a prelude to a fight. In less remote areas, where bears come into more frequent contact with people, especially in areas of heavy hunting pressure, they do seem more likely to run without hesitating.

Regardless of how their vision compares to that of humans, the vision of most species rarely compares to their sense of smell. While defeating the olfactory abilities of most game animals is somewhere between difficult and impossible, defeating their eyes is usually less challenging—the obvious exceptions that come to mind being pronghorns and turkeys. (Fortunately for bowhunters, turkeys have virtually no sense of smell.) The vision of pronghorns is often compared to that of 8X binoculars and, like most animals, they are quick to spot motion. Moose and wild hogs are often cited as having poor vision, but even they are far from blind, and the hunter who underestimates their vision is going to be seen by them sooner or later. Every hunter has been spotted by a wary old buck or a smart doe as the hunter crossed a field or other opening, made their way down a logging road, or, for that matter, still hunted through a hardwood forest. The hunter whose tree stand has him silhouetted, or which simply leaves him exposed with inadequate cover, is likely to be spotted as well.

A number of strategies can help hunters evade the eyes of their quarry, but before we examine some of these, let's take a close look at exactly how animals see and what their optical capabilities are. Generally speaking, vision occurs when light enters the eye and is absorbed by various specialized cells at the back of the eye. These cells transmit signals to the brain, which interprets the signals as sight. Color is a function of the wavelength of light reflected from the objects we see. The entire spectrum of wavelengths includes ultraviolet at the short end and infrared at the long end. Humans and other primates are rare among mammals in that they have very sophisticated color vision, and can see the entire wavelength with the exception of the extremes at both ends. We cannot normally see either infrared light or ultraviolet light.

Structurally, most mammals' eyes differ from a human's in several important respects. At the back of the eyes of all mammals are two kinds of light-sensitive cells: rods and cones. Rods function in very low light and allow some degree of night vision. Cones operate in brighter light and allow daytime vision and the perception of color. Human eyes have three types of cones, which are sensitive to short wavelengths (blue), middle wavelengths (green), and long wavelengths (red). Most species of mammals have more rods than humans, but fewer cones. This suggests they have better night vision, but poorer daytime vision. The specific cones they lack are those that perceive the longer (red) wavelengths of light. Both physiology and behavioral studies suggest that most mammals can see shades of blue and green, but not red and, like some color-blind humans, they probably cannot distinguish between green and red. Large mammals have larger pupils than humans, to admit more light, further improving their vision in low light. In addition, they possess a reflective layer at the back of their eyes called a tapetum. (The tapetum is what shines so brightly in the headlights of a vehicle.) This reflective membrane further increases the light available to the eye, again improving night vision. We mentioned earlier that humans cannot see the ultraviolet end of the color spectrum. That is because we have a filter that blocks almost all ultraviolet light. One advantage of this is that it enables us to see fine detail better than most animals. Because most mammals lack that filter, they can probably see better in the UV spectrum than we can, but they do not perceive small details well.

What does all this mean, in general terms, for the hunter? To begin with, it means hunters needn't hesitate to wear blaze orange in most situations. Where legal, the blaze orange camo patterns are probably effective. The issue of UV vision has to do with the fact that most modern detergents have UV brighteners in them, to make clothes appear whiter and brighter. The concern is that hunting garments that have been washed in detergents with UV brighteners will be highly visible to game animals. An entire industry has sprung up to provide hunters with special, non-UV detergents and spray-on products developed to remove UV residues from clothing that has been exposed to it. While I'm not aware of any independent studies proving that deer readily distinguish garments washed in UV detergents, their ability to see that portion of the color spectrum suggests that, in low light, they probably can see such garments better. Using the products designed to eliminate it certainly can't hurt, and might very well make a difference.

All the data available about how animals see is useful, but like all scientific information, it leaves some questions unanswered and leads to even more questions. Here is one that I have long pondered: If game animals have superior low-light vision, why have I, on so many occasions, been able to approach very closely to grazing deer when heading to my stand or leaving it in low light? Apart from remaining downwind of them and pausing whenever they raised their heads, I took no particular efforts to conceal myself, and have often managed to walk to within 20 or 30 yards of deer, usually when they were feeding in groups. Even more mysteriously, this seems to happen not in the darkest situations, but on those occasions when I'm late getting to my stand—before sunrise but after first light—or when I've left a stand early in the evening, after sunset but well before hard dark. I've even had deer approach me in such low-light situations, seemingly out of curiosity. On one occasion I arrowed a big Kentucky doe that approached me in a meadow at dusk. She appeared to spot me from nearly 100 yards out. When I knelt and nocked an arrow, she sneaked in, stopping several times to bob her head and paw the ground, but eventually approached to within 40 yards and offered me the shot. Never have I walked up on feeding deer like this in broad daylight. I've discussed this phenomenon with many hunters including, most recently, well-known white-tailed deer hunting expert (and my publisher) Peter Fiduccia. Peter, along with many other experienced hunters, has made the same observation.

Despite this puzzling behavior, the tendency of many pressured species to become almost exclusively nocturnal, together with their ability to run full speed through thickets on the darkest night, indicates that, as the physiology of their eyes suggests, they see very well indeed in low light. How well do they see in the light of day? I suspect they see better than many hunters give them credit for. Turkey hunters like to say that a deer sees a man in the woods and thinks he's a stump, while a turkey sees a stump in the woods and thinks it's a man. There is some truth in that old saw, but I suspect it has more to do with the tendency of deer to rely more on their keen sense of smell than on any inability to see well. Most game animals that have not been heavily hunted, or that are simply not alert, will probably not see a motionless hunter standing against a tree or behind a sapling. Once alert, any animal, even bear and moose, is quick to detect the slightest movement and will probably spot the human silhouette, or the unconcealed face or hands of a hunter. And, as increasing numbers of hunters are learning, deer, bears, elk, and even moose will learn to look for hunters in tree stands.

Aside from the fact that most animals, once alerted, can use their eyes very effectively, experienced hunters have learned that one way to increase their success ratio is to avoid overhunting the same spot. Perhaps more to the point: Don't continue to hunt a spot from which you have you have been picked off. Any game animal that has been spooked in a given location will be extra wary for some time when approaching that location. They will learn to avoid certain spots. In the case of deer, there is some evidence that they communicate alarm with their interdigital glands, leaving scent on the ground that other deer immediately recognize as a danger signal, putting them on alert. Many hooved game animals have similar glands and engage in similar behaviors, and it is possible that most herd animals have similar means of alerting one another to danger.

One of the more efficient—and effective—game/hunting operations I've been fortunate to hunt with is at Enon Plantation, a wellknown bow-only deer hunting plantation in Alabama. The fact that it is bow-only is incidental; any hunting operation could benefit from similar practices. Hunters at Enon routinely see numerous deer on each morning and afternoon hunt. What's more, the deer tend to venture into food plots during daylight hours on a regular basis, and usually seem to be relaxed. At the opposite extreme, I've hunted at operations in which plenty of tracks and other sign indicated the presence of deer in good numbers, but they're rarely seen venturing into food plots during the day, and when they do, they are extremely wary. How does Enon do it? I observed two ways. First, there are numerous tree stands over a large area. No stand gets hunted frequently, and, because of the wide choice of stands available, there is never a temptation to hunt a stand for which the wind direction is not right.

Second, Enon controls how stands are hunted. Hunters are driven directly to their stands, which they can access by taking only a few steps. They are asked to remain in their stands until a vehicle returns to pick them up, and told that only then should they leave the stands. Because of this approach, any deer that are in or close to the food plot (and there are usually at least a few), run off at the approach of the truck. They never see the hunter enter or climb down from the stand. Even when a hunter sticks a deer, the folks at Enon suggest he remain in his stand, awaiting the arrival of the vehicle before taking up the trail. These precautions mean that not only are hunters rarely seen entering or leaving their stands, but also they don't contaminate the area with scent. If the guides at Enon suspect a stand has been compromised—if a hunter reports deer looking up and spotting him, for instance—they either relocate that stand or give it a long rest. The result is that deer at Enon travel more during daylight hours, and tend to be relaxed most of the time.

## Motion Detectors

We've seen that few animals have good color vision, and that their enhanced night vision tends to come at the expense of an ability to see details. On top of that, the placement of their eyes on either side of the head gives them a very wide field of view, but decreases their depth perception. They make up for these disadvantages by being motion detectors. As every bowhunter knows, one of the chief challenges of bowhunting is drawing the bow without being seen. Nearly every bowhunter has a story or two about a trophy that was in range but picked up the movement and bolted when the hunter started to draw his bow. Bowhunters learn to wait before drawing until their quarry's head is hidden behind a tree or brush, or at least until its attention is focused elsewhere. There are several ways hunters can minimize the problem of having their movements spotted. The obvious one is overlooked by more than a few hunters: Don't move. In a society that values productivity over just about everything else, standing still, sitting motionless, or even walking very slowly can be a near impossibility for many modern hunters. Hunting situations may at times require moving fast, but the hunter who cannot remain nearly motionless for long periods is at a real disadvantage, and probably spooks game he never knows is there.

There are two keys to remaining still. The first is comfort, and the second is relaxation. We'll look at these in another context later in the book; for now, suffice it to say that both are underrated. However, the hunter who is not comfortable will have to rely on a tremendous amount of discipline to remain motionless, and the hunter who cannot relax totally in the outdoors will be a less effective hunter.

## Camouflage

It's a rare hunter these days who ventures afield without camouflage clothing. Even our guns, bows, and gear are camouflaged. Now and then someone makes the observation that, as recently as a generation ago, hunters, including the most successful ones, ventured afield without camo clothing. That is only partly true. While they may not have worn the kinds of patterns that are popular with hunters today, they tended to avoid light-colored clothing, preferring darker colors, often green or brown. Red was a commonly seen color, too, often in plaid. The old-timers understood that game animals did not seem to distinguish red, and felt that plaid tended to break up a hunter's outline. I also recall, from my earliest childhood hunts with my father, being admonished to wear gloves and to keep the bill of my hat low over my brow to keep my white face shaded.

By the same token, our fathers' generation also didn't hunt from tree stands and rarely, if ever, used the kind of fully enclosed ground blinds available to hunters today. Few experienced modern hunters would deny that tree stands or ground blinds offer significant advantages in many hunting situations.

One well-known outdoor writer of my acquaintance, who also acts as a guide on frequent occasions, enjoys hunting without camo. He wears dark clothes and takes other measures to avoid being spotted by game. He gets an extra kick out of tagging animals and ribbing his hunting buddies who are dressed head-to-toe in the latest camo patterns.

The real question, though, is not whether it is possible to tag a trophy animal while not wearing camo. It most certainly is. The question is: Does wearing camo clothing and using camo gear give the hunter an advantage, if not in every situation, at least in some of them? While I would not hesitate to go hunting without camo if there was no camo available to me, I'm also inclined to seek every edge I can get, especially when bowhunting. It's just too darned hard to get within bow range of a trophy animal to do otherwise.

Breaking up a hunter's outline and wearing dark, nonshiny clothes are important, but if I could camouflage only one part of me, it would be my face. Second choice would be my hands.

On a hunt with my friend Vince in Tennessee several years ago, I paused before entering the woods to put some camo paint on my face and hands when I noticed Vince grinning at me. I had to laugh, because I knew exactly what he was grinning about.

"I guess you don't need any of this," I said.

"No, I don't think I do," he said.

Vince, if you haven't guessed, is black. Apparently he found it amusing to watch a hunter pull what looked like a makeup kit from his daypack, flip it open to the mirror in the lid, and start applying camo paint to his face.

The fact is, though, unless you have a very dark complexion, you need to cover your face and hands with camo paint or a head net of some sort. A hunter can be wearing camo head to toe, but if his skin is white and his face and hands are not camouflaged, they will shine through the woods like a full moon on a cloudless night.

Since there are no limits on how much camo I wear, I generally wear it head to toe. Does the pattern matter? In many situations, it probably doesn't. I will wear any pattern as opposed to none, but when I head out west to hunt sage country, I try to wear a pattern that blends better with the lighter colors of that area—if possible, one designed to imitate sage. If I know I'll be hunting primarily in spruce forests, I wear a pine pattern. The fact is, I do 80 percent of my hunting in mixed hardwood forests, and have found patterns, such as the popular Mossy Oak and Realtree, to be effective in environments ranging from southern swamps to northern forests to wide-open prairies. Still, more than once I've been caught in a camo pattern that seemed far too dark, too light, too green, or too brown for the area in which I was hunting. There are some excellent all-round camo patterns available, such as ASAT, which tend to reflect the colors around them and conceal hunters in every imaginable environment.

Camouflaging gear is probably less important than clothing, the exception being blinds or anything that shines or is highly reflective. Some blinds, though printed in camo patterns, are made from fabrics that will shine in the sun.

Remaining undetected by game animals is far more than a matter of wearing camo, climbing trees, or hunting from blinds. (Later we'll look more closely at hunting from tree stands as well as ground blinds.) Whether avoiding the eyes of the hunter's quarry is instinctive or learned behavior could be the subject of a good debate, but a surprising number of hunters take little care to remain unseen. A few years ago a book high on the bestseller list was, *Everything I Need to Know I Learned in Kindergarten*. I cannot quite say that I learned everything I need to know about hunting in kindergarten, but that is about the age at which my education as a hunter began. My father took me along with him hunting in the woods of southwestern Ohio and southeastern Indiana, and the basic lessons I learned on those outings are things every hunter should internalize. I can almost hear my father's voice when I think of them:

"When you come to a field or an open area in the woods, don't walk through the middle of it. Skirt around it. If you have to walk through it, don't waste time; get through it in a hurry."

"Walk in the shadows and out of the sunlight as much as you can. When you stop to look around or take a break, stay in the shade."

"Be careful about brushing against saplings and small trees when you walk, and don't hold on to them when you climb up a hill. An animal will hear and see that sapling shake for a long ways through the woods."

"Try not to walk down ridgelines or stand out on points, where you'll be exposed."

"Avoid walking down game trails and logging roads if you can. Animals use them, too, and will spot you. They'll also pick up your scent long after you've gone."

"You can usually get away with slow movements, but rarely with quick ones. When you look around, turn your head slowly. If you've got to scratch or get something out of your pocket, do it slowly."

"When you stop, stop behind cover that will hide you, but that is not too thick to prevent shooting."

"Use the terrain as much as possible—ravines, hills, creek bottoms, even large rocks or downed trees—to move without being seen."

"Keep in mind the time of day, the time of year, and the weather, to avoid spooking animals. Don't walk through a likely feeding area or bedding area at a time when you might expect game to be there."

"A man standing upright can be seen for a long ways. Stay low when approaching game—hunker down at a distance, drop to your knees as you get closer, and crawl if you need to get very close."

To the experienced hunter, these behaviors are automatic, and require no thinking. And yes, I can think of numerous hunting situations that represent exceptions—times when shaking a sapling, moving quickly, or walking down a logging road might be the right thing to do. They're good general rules, though, and most hunters would be better hunters for following them unless there is a good reason not to.

## Concealing Tree Stands

It's surprising how many hunters spend hours scouting and picking the perfect location for a tree stand, but give little consideration to keeping the stand hidden. Make no mistake: Game will spot hunters in tree stands. In fact, it happens all the time. Sometimes the easiest way to understand how to do a thing is to look first at how not to do it. Let's take a look at the worst-possible tree stand setup. We'll assume we're dealing with a deer-hunting scenario here, since the great majority of tree stands are used by deer hunters. The same reasoning could apply to other species that might be hunted from a tree stand.

Our hypothetical stand is ten feet high, on the side of a mediumsized tree with no limbs until about twenty-five feet up. It's on the side of a hill, facing uphill, with a well-used trail straight ahead, and a cluster of scrapes off to the right, which in this location is to the south.

Problem one with this stand is that it is not high enough. I say this as someone who is not all that comfortable with heights. Height matters. Sorry to all those who want to think that eight, ten, or twelve feet is high enough—it's not. Ask yourself this: If height does not matter, why are we climbing trees anyway? Actually there are several reasons, but the main one is to get above the normal line of vision of deer. Deer can and will learn to look up into trees, but it is not something they routinely do. By getting above their normal line of sight, we can more often remain unseen by deer. It's that simple. How high is high enough? Opinions vary, but my own experience tells me that at somewhere above 15 feet, a white-tailed deer becomes less likely to spot a hunter, and the likelihood decreases further at 20 feet or above. Experimenting with deer I did not intend to shoot, I have literally waved my arms and remained unseen by deer when I was hunting from 20 or more feet. And yes, I have also been spotted at that height and higher, and yes, I have taken deer from stands as low as eight feet. Over the years, though, I have been spotted far more often at heights below 15 feet.

Some hunters would argue that fifteen feet is an adequate height, and a few of the best deer hunters I know would suggest that the magic number is closer to 25 or even 30 feet. But I do believe this: the bowhunter at less than 15 feet is better off on the ground. On the ground, he can use terrain and cover to his advantage. Perching 10 or 12 feet up in a tree simply makes him more visible to his quarry, unless he is fully enclosed in a blind. (In which case, why bother climbing the tree?) Though our focus here is on visibility, many hunters also believe that when they are at greater heights, deer are less likely to catch their scent. The theory is that in some situations the hunter's scent will be carried over the head of deer approaching close to the stand.

A related problem with our hypothetical tree stand is its location on the side of a hill. In hill country it's not always possible to avoid such a location, but the hunter needs to keep in mind that, even if he is 20 feet up a tree, deer on the uphill side will, at some point, be at eye level. That may be unavoidable, but a hunter should at least see to it that a trail, logging road, scrape, or rub line is well below eye level, to decrease the likelihood of deer walking by the stand at that level. A stand facing east is not necessarily a problem, but the hunter should be aware that if he plans to hunt this stand in the morning he may, depending on the steepness of the hill, find himself looking directly into the sun. Morning stands facing the rising sun to the east, or evening stands facing the setting sun to the west, can leave the hunter nearly blinded for a good while on clear days, and can be downright uncomfortable.

Hunters are often advised to position stands in such a way that deer are more likely to be looking into the sun, but I have some doubts about the soundness of that advice. First, the primary consideration—far and away—is wind direction, and the likelihood seems low that the perfect setup with regard to wind, among other factors, will position hunters so that deer are likely to be looking into the sun to see the stand. What's more, if the sun is behind the hunter, he is likely to be casting a long shadow. If concealment behind the hunter has him completely shaded, this is not a problem. But if so much as the top of the head or one arm is at any time touched by sunlight, the hunter's slightest movement will be exaggerated by a giant shadow on the ground. It's far better if no portion of a hunter's shadow extends into the area where he expects to see deer. Finally, our hypothetical tree has no limbs until the twenty-five-foot mark. That is just the kind of tree many of us look for when using climbing stands, but it leaves us hanging out there in the great, wide open, where deer—especially mature deer—are almost sure to spot us. Drawing a bow without the movement being picked up can be all but impossible in a stand of this sort. In this kind of stand, even the absolutely motionless hunter can and probably will be seen by deer, unless he is at heights beyond the comfort and safety level for most of us.

There are fixes for that problem, including various camo skirts designed to conceal hunters in tree stands. Trimming limbs and properly positioning them around the stand with wire or nails can help address the problem, in areas where hunters have permission from landowners to do this. There are also artificial limbs on the market that can be used in these situations to help provide concealment. Also among products that can be useful here are umbrellas such as Eastman Outfitters' Sta-Dry Umbrella. From the perspective of a deer looking up, these provide a background to which hunters can blend in, and simply keeping hunters shaded makes them less visible. Decoys can be useful, too, by helping to keep the attention of an approaching deer on the decoys and away from the hunter, though decoys in themselves are no substitute for some degree of concealment.

Many hunters turn an otherwise excellent stand into something less than that by overpruning. Some judgment is called for here. It's an exercise in frustration to sit in a stand with inadequate shooting lanes that require an animal to stop and position itself in one of two or three spots for the hunter to have a good shooting opportunity. At the same time, overpruning can call attention to the hunter and leave him exposed. There is a happy medium between adequate concealment and adequate shooting lanes, and only good judgment and experience will tell the hunter when that point has been reached.

## Eye Contact

Is eye contact an issue in concealment? Though some hunters might scoff at the idea, most veteran hunters have reached the conclusion that many prey species understand that when eye contact is made, they have been spotted. More than a few hunters have stopped to scan a nearby deadfall or thicket, only to have an animal that was hidden there bolt the moment eye contact was made. Among many species of animals, staring is recognized as a threat, and animals, including most canine species, will show submissive behavior to a dominant member of their own species by turning their heads and looking away. More often than not among canines, two animals staring at one another is the first step toward more overtly aggressive behavior which usually leads to a fight. It doesn't seem at all out of the question that prey species should have evolved in such a way that they recognize—through eye contact—when they have been spotted.

Hunters have developed some interesting approaches to this problem. One, of course, is to avoid staring (at least when the quarry is close) by not looking directly at the animal, but looking to one side instead. Ultimately, it's difficult for a hunter to avoid looking at what is about to become a target. My friend Chip Hart, with whom I cohost The Big Outdoors radio program in Cincinnati, swears by glasses, developed specifically for the purpose, that allow hunters to see perfectly while completely hiding their eyes with a camo pattern. Many hunters—and I confess to doing this myself on occasion—try to squint in such a way that they can still see, but the whites of their eyes are mostly

A good ground blind might be the ultimate in concealment, hiding movement, and even reducing sound and scent.

hidden. It would be difficult to prove that these methods work, but it's hard to imagine they can hurt.

We've already mentioned that most animals are great motion detectors. The best concealment is unlikely to work if a hunter makes exaggerated movements. It's important that the stand be arranged in such a way that movement can be kept to a minimum. That limb partway around the tree trunk might be suitable for hanging a daypack on, but only if it can be accessed without requiring gymnastics. It could be that I fidget too much, but I frequently access my daypack for water, snacks, calls, or other items. Bows and rifles, too, should be in easy reach. Holders attached to stands work very well. My own preference when bowhunting is the EZ Hanger, but there are similar devices that can be affixed to the tree over the hunter's head, with the bow hanging immediately in front. With this arrangement, a hunter can get his bow in hand with only the slightest movement. Still other hangers and organizers are available for hanging calls and other accessories. There is nothing worse than frantically digging around in a daypack or a pocket for an item that has become suddenly very necessary.

One of the more interesting approaches to reducing the likelihood of being spotted in tree stands involves the use of dummies. I've seen this trick used most often in tripod stands where concealment options are limited, but it can be used in any tree stand. A simple, homemade dummy of some sort (usually consisting of an old jacked stuffed with pillows or straw, with an improvised head wearing a hat) is left in the stand when it is not occupied. The idea, of course, is that a deer spotting the stand will become accustomed to the general shape of a hunter in it, and will not react to the real thing. I can't speak to this from personal experience, never having tried it, but it seems like a good idea.

## Ground Blinds

The first hunter probably used ground blinds of some sort. Even four-footed predators will remain hidden behind deadfalls, thickets, or trees, waiting to pounce on any prey species that walks by. Humans simply improve on that tactic by, in effect, creating their own deadfalls, thickets, or trees. They can considerably improve on the "blinds" that occur naturally, and enjoy the huge advantage of being able to put them wherever they want them. (That is only an advantage if they know where to put them, but we'll get to that later.) The corollary to this is that prey species have learned that predators like to use cover for setting up ambushes, and many of them have learned to avoid danger areas, or to pass by them with extra caution. A young goose or turkey might wander close by a big tuft of grass or a row of standing corn, but older ones will usually give them a wide berth, preferring to remain out in the open where they can see all around.

Deer and some other game animals are a little different in that they often prefer thick cover for concealment, relying heavily on their keen sense of smell to avoid danger. Still, mature animals are wary enough to be cautious around anything new or unnatural in their environment. This suggests two keys to success in using a blind for hunting: (1) make sure it's not "new," (2) try to make it appear as natural as possible. Both things are very doable for the hunter willing to take a little time. Making it not "new" is as simple as setting it up in advance. Even a blind set up in the middle of a wide open meadow or pasture is something animals will become accustomed to if they see it repeatedly. How long that takes depends on how often the animals pass by it, and probably a little bit on the individual animal itself and how wary it is. Longer is better, but the hunters I know who are consistently successful from ground blinds prefer to have a blind in place at least several days before hunting from it. That is not always possible for any of several reasons, and in any case, that strategy tends to negate one of the chief advantages of using a ground blind, which is mobility. Many of today's newer blinds, which are designed to be set up and taken down very quickly, allow hunters to observe everchanging travel patterns and take advantage of their observations by setting up a blind for an ambush.

This leads us to the other key to success in using a ground blind—making it appear as "natural" as possible. I use the term "natural" here, because it is the kind of jargon with which hunters are familiar. On a farm in South-Central Ohio is an abandoned barn. It's surrounded by thick, second growth penetrated only by a network of well-used game trails. I have used that barn as a blind on several occasions. There is also a rusted-out, old pickup truck in the corner of a field close to where a logging road enters the field, and I have spent a few hours sitting in that truck, too. There is nothing natural about either of them, but deer accept them as part of the landscape because they have been there a very long time. Making a blind appear natural is mostly a matter of breaking up an unnatural silhouette. Cover behind the blind helps, but it can be important to have some cover in front of the blind, as well. In many spots it is possible to set the blind up in such a way that some natural cover is all around it, and that may be sufficient. In other cases, hunters will have to manipulate the habitat a little. A log or limb on the ground in front of the blind can help anchor it and keep it from flapping, as well as break up an unnatural straight line along the ground. Additional concealment can be had by leaning a few limbs, real or artificial, against the blind. Many blinds have ties at strategic locations to facilitate this process. By backing off and looking at the blind, it's not hard to tell when the silhouette is less discernible.

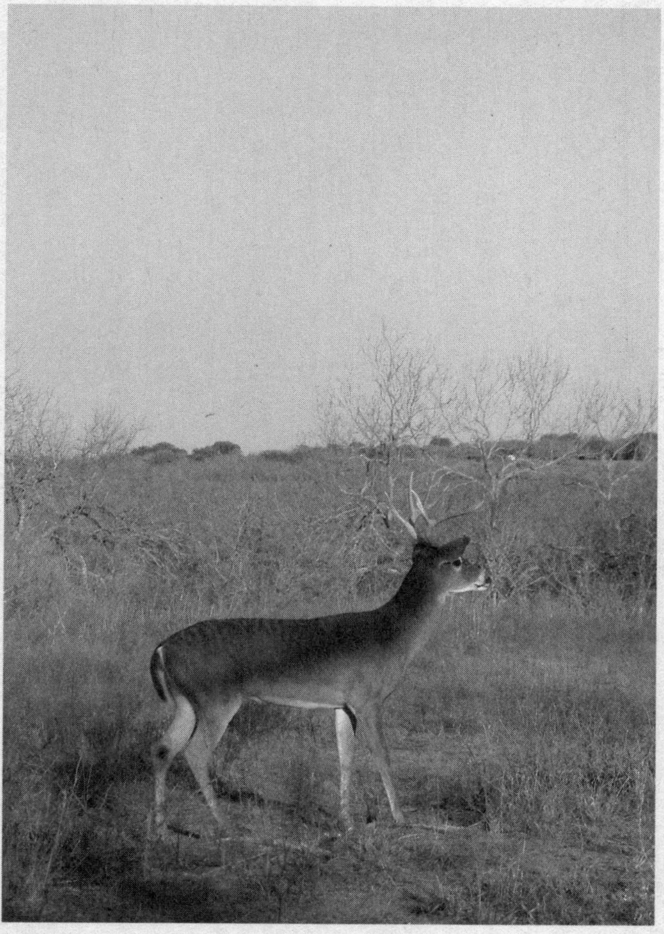
The ears and the body language of this buck suggest something is approaching from across the clearing. Is it another buck?

As with providing concealment for a tree stand, some judgment is in order. The idea is to provide concealment while insuring that adequate shooting lanes are available.

Keeping blinds shaded can be helpful here. Aside from the fact that blinds in direct sunlight can get uncomfortably warm in all but the coldest weather, sunlight will make any unnatural aspects of the blind more visible. Also, as we mentioned earlier, some fabrics reflect sunlight, creating a very unnatural shine. When a given environment or location requires setting up a blind in the open, it becomes increasingly important that it remain there for some time before being hunted. While a fully enclosed blind can go a long way toward concealing hunters, sharp-eyed game animals can still pick them off if they can see inside the blind. One way to avoid that is to keep the interior of the blind dark by putting it in the shade. Better still, many newer blinds have black interiors for this purpose. A hunter wearing camo or dark clothing, whose face and hands are covered, will be virtually invisible from outside the blind unless he gets very close to the opening. This is another advantage of comfortably large blinds. It can be impossible to stay back from the opening in a smaller blind, and a smaller blind may even require that the arrow be extended outside the window, which is a real disadvantage.

There is some concern that shooting windows can be problematic in blinds with black interiors. From outside the blind, these windows, when open, appear as large black spots, and there is reason to believe that many animals shy away from these—in fact, the folks who developed Double Bull blinds are convinced that this is the case. They recommend keeping the shoot-through camo mesh netting in place. Hunters inside the blind can see through the netting, but from the outside the netting blends in perfectly with the camo pattern of the blind. I've shot through them on numerous occasions and noticed no loss of accuracy. There is one important limitation, though. Not all mechanical heads will work with shoot-through netting, since the netting will open the heads prematurely. In general, L-shaped or wing-blade mechanicals won't work, while other designs such as the Rocket Steelheads will work. I would highly recommend trying any mechanical heads before shooting them through the netting in a hunting situation. String trackers will not work with the shootthrough netting.

Finally, there is the issue of scent and ground blinds. Some hunters have suggested that ground blinds tend naturally to reduce scent, since they block the wind and may tend to contain some scent inside the blind. A few of the newer blinds actually include the same carbon-impregnated fabrics as Scent-Lok suits. At least one blind I'm aware of—Scent-Tite—is sealed and actually vents the hunter's scent through a tube high into the air. I've never used a Scent-Tite blind, but have seen some impressive demonstrations in which deer, following a bait trail put down for demonstration purposes, walked completely around the blind, eating as they went, and showed no awareness of the people in the blind.

# Insider Tips to Patterning Bucks

Larry Kline first saw the buck that would take him on a three-year quest while shining deer, a legal activity in Wisconsin. Right then and there, he decided that he wanted that animal. Later, after a scouting camera captured an eerily foggy picture of the buck, he became known to Larry's family and friends as the Ghost Buck. The buck's ability to vanish for long periods of time made the name fit even better yet.

"My dad had been telling some of our friends that I was obsessed with taking this buck," Larry told me. "The truth is that I was. The Ghost Buck had become a part of my entire family's life, and I wanted him bad. I was obsessed, but I viewed it as a healthy obsession."

Patterning the Ghost Buck took Larry Kline on a three-year quest before it finally ended in success.

Because of the big-woods setting the Ghost Buck lived in, sightings for Larry were rare. Instead, he had to focus on determining food sources, reading sign and making educated guesses. In his three years of hunting this magnificent animal, he had passed up many Pope & Young-class bucks, and he'd yet to see the Ghost Buck a single time from stand!

Then Larry got the break he needed. Checking his scouting camera on a morning before the season opened, he saw that he'd captured the Ghost Buck's photo. He intently studied the Imageof his property, doing his best to correlate the location shown with an idea about how the buck was using the ground. The more he studied the photo, the more convinced Larry became that the big deer was using a strip of jack pine that separated two of his food plots.

It made sense that the buck was using the strip for cover as he traveled to his bedding site after a night of feeding. Larry hoped to encounter the magnificent animal using the stand at the narrow point of that strip.

Opening morning found him perched in that stand. As he peered through the jack pines, he caught the movement of a large-bodied deer approaching. When it raised its head, Larry almost couldn't believe his eyes. There, working its way toward him, was the Ghost Buck. Several minutes and many frazzled nerves latter, the hunter put a killing shot on the local legend.

If I had a nickel for how many times I've heard "experts" talk about patterning bucks, I'd be a rich man. Whether it's in print, on TV or in seminars, the term is knocked around more than a tennis ball at Wimbledon. Ironically, for all the talk, they rarely ever say anything.

When you think about it, it makes sense that most experts have little of value to contribute. Frankly, patterning bucks takes time and effort. When TV personalities are expected to produce piles of antlers each season, most simply can't afford to invest the resources it takes to pattern one or more bucks. To a certain extent, publication deadlines impose the same constraints on many writers. I'm not saying that some experts don't actually pattern bucks. But I have no doubt that far more of them toss the term around simply to make themselves appear to be better hunters.

Patterning bucks takes work, woodsmanship, dedication and time. Even then, you are bound to strike out on far more bucks than you'll smash homers on. Still, it can be done. Furthermore, it's made far more doable if you understand the tricks of the trade.

## OBSERVATIONS

The first step toward patterning a buck is identifying him. Certainly, large rubs, tracks and beds can all indicate that a mature animal is present, and there's absolutely nothing wrong with setting up on sign alone. However, if a hunter is going to dedicate the time and effort to a specific buck, he wants to see what he's after.

You might get the initial view of the buck in many different ways. Perhaps it is a distant sighting while you're hunting—a buck you kick up while walking to the stand—or a chance sighting while you're driving home from work. For those purposefully striving to find bucks to pattern, investing some morning and evening hours, slowly cruising back roads or past known food sources, is a common practice.

Another method is setting up to perform long-range observations of specific areas. For some reason, many seem to believe that such observations are exclusively for hunting food sources and farm country, and that there's no benefit for big-woods hunters. That's simply not true.

For one thing, observing some common big-woods food sources, such as overgrown meadows and clear-cuts, is not only possible, but also highly recommended. Additionally, once leaf-off occurs, one can often get up high and observe the woodlands below. Yes, that means sacrificing a hunting opportunity, but it can be well worth it.

When performing long-range observations, employing several tips can be very helpful. The

Treating long-range observations with the same respect you'd treat a hunt, such as paying attention to wind direcion, helps ensure that these activities go undetected by the bucks you're trying to pattern.

first group revolves around keeping deer ignorant of these activities. Before blundering out, analyze the area to be observed and carefully select a location that will lend itself to helping you remain undetected. That translates to keeping the deer upwind at all times and having enough cover to keep you hidden.

Personally, I find pop-up blinds very valuable for hiding me during observations. In less than a minute, a high-quality blind can be slapped up and ready to use. The cover and ability to move they provide are some of the little things that can make a difference.

Another factor in remaining undetected is getting in and out. When practical, select vantage points that you can reach by crossing as little deer habitat as possible. Not only does this limit the risk of bumping deer, but it also minimizes the odds of them picking up any scent that may have been left behind.

Take the same scent-reduction steps that you would before going hunting. Even when everything is set up perfectly, deer have a tendency to show up where they aren't supposed to, and wind directions change. Having observation efforts educate deer to being hunted is a deadly sin that can greatly reduce your odds of eventual salvation—harvesting the buck.

Selecting observation posts that offer a good field of view is also important. Good fields of view can mean either complete coverage of the area or zoning in on a specific spot. For example, if forced to choose between seeing 90 percent of a field or watching the 10 percent that's hidden in a corner, it's often better to watch the 10 percent.

Speaking of watching effectively, a good spotting scope is extremely helpful. Though binoculars can work, once light begins to fade, a spotting scope's extra magnification can make the difference between positively identifying a spectacular buck or discerning that it's only a large-bodied deer.

When used properly, scouting cameras can be excellent tools for revealing the bucks on a particular property and giving you insights into their patterns.

Finally, when a targeted buck is seen, note the trail he's using. This may sound basic, but it's easy to get so caught up in the animal that the details are lost. Once the animal is spotted, find a landmark that will allow you to pinpoint his location later. Employing these tips can make observations far less disruptive and far more beneficial.

## LOCATING MR. BIG WITH CAMERAS

As shown by Larry Kline's success, trail cameras can be powerful and beneficial tools. That is, assuming they are quality units and used properly.

I have no doubt that any deer has the potential to be trained to accept a flash and noisy camera as harmless. Some don't even seem to care the first time they experience an up-close photo session with these potentially harmful units. However, some mature bucks have no tolerance for anything out of the norm and won't stick around for the training session.

Though they most likely won't abandon the area, they are apt to avoid the location where the camera is set. I've seen this firsthand.

When choosing a scouting camera, I look for several features. First, above all else, it must be quiet. Camera noise is unacceptable. Next is reliability. If I'm going to base decisions on what a camera reports, it better not misfire or miss shots. That also encompasses the triggering time. A second may not seem to be much time, but if it takes that long to snap a photo, an amazingly high number of rear-end shots will be the result. Though one can easily argue both sides of whether a standard flash scares deer, I prefer an infrared flash. It has the ability to capture more readable night photos at a distance, and is undetectable to deer. Finally, I can't even imagine ever using a film-based scouting camera again.

Setting scouting cameras behind the scrape and shooting out over it captures both the bucks working the scrape and many of the deer investigating it from a distance.

Digital is simply so much easier, faster and cheaper than having to develop film.

My next great concerns involve the users. Though checking pictures is fun, every time we step into the woods, we are leaving sign of our activities. Repeatedly checking those cameras can be very harmful to our hunting efforts.

Cleaning the camera, taking odor-control steps, avoiding trails, and timing the trips during mid-day hours are steps in the right direction. Next, apply my three-strikes rule: After setup, I refuse to take more than two more trips to the camera location. Commonly, I'll return a week after setup and yank the unit then. After all, if Mr. Big hasn't passed within seven days, I probably don't want to hunt that location anyway. Occasionally, I'll either leave it one more week or I'll reset the camera there later to see if the buck's patterns now include that area. However, I'll never make more than three consecutive trips to the same location.

To break down placement techniques, let's look at three examples of sites to monitor: food and water sources, trails and scrapes.

A very quick and effective way to get an idea of the caliber of animals living in an area is to monitor prime food and water sources. Begin by placing a scouting camera at sites that show the heaviest signs of feeding or watering. If the area is too large for one setup to do it justice, either employ more than one or relocate the unit after a week or two. After covering one food or water source, move to the next. Even on relatively large properties, this rotation scheme provides very good coverage in just one or two months.

When food sources aren't a good option, scouting units can be set up on trails. In this case, setting the scouting camera about four or five yards off to the side, with its coverage area cutting across the trail, is far less intrusive than aiming it down the trail.

Finally, there's the scrape method. Because many scrapes are worked after dark, and a high percentage of them are used sporadically at best, scrape hunting can be a very frustrating experience. Trail monitors certainly can't guarantee success, but they can at least tell us that a mature buck is working the scrape and whether the activity ever occurs during shooting hours.

Setting the camera behind the scrape, so that it shoots out over the scrape and also covers deer passing by in front of it, is commonly the best placement. That way, you'll capture pictures of deer working and many just investigating the scrape.

When using all of these placement strategies, my primary goals are to find the buck I'm after, note the time he's there, and find his track. To help locate tracks on trails, I'll often rake a small portion clean of debris. It may surprise some to note that I rely far more heavily on scouting units to locate my buck and get his track than for patterning.

## TRACKING BUCKS

Tracks are what I rely on most for gathering details on a specific buck's pattern. Whether I saw him first during observations or in a photograph, one of my primary goals is to then scour the area and find his track.

When I locate a track, measuring the length and width of the hoof, along with a tip to dewclaw and stride measurement when possible, gives me the foundation of the buck's fingerprint. Taking it a step further by noting the shape of the tip, chips in the hoof and any other visible characteristics, I can now track that animal almost anywhere it goes. Of course, the four hooves are not identical, but their size and overall shape characteristics are usually close enough to generate a match.

The ability to track a buck is extremely beneficial. Let's say that in early September we document the track of an animal we spotted in an alfalfa field. Later we find a track leading from a bed and pull out the tape, along with our track notes. Just that quick, we can often identify the animal. In October, we find the same track in a line of scrapes along the edge of a swamp. November turns another up in the bean field a mile away.

The point is that when tracks are documented, they can fill in a lot of the missing puzzle pieces required for patterning that buck of a lifetime. Literally, anywhere that buck leaves a track, we can tell that he was there.

Many green fields and trails don't provide adequate surfaces for collecting tracks but, luckily, simply clearing the litter from a three-foot section of the trail will correct that. Now we no longer have to guess if that buck is using a specific trail. He will show us for certain. By scrubbing it clean periodically, we can even tell how regularly he travels it.

Most often kicking a patch clear with a rubber boot is enough. To do an even better job, a garden rake can be used. This not only clears the trail, but also breaks the soil to provide an even better medium for collecting tracks. When all else fails, dirt can be brought in to improve conditions that simply won't work otherwise.

"Track catchers" are so powerful that they are the reason I don't rely heavily on scouting cameras as patterning tools. Not only are track catchers free, but I can place as many as I need at any given time. That allows me to blanket an area one time, come back a week later and, in one shot, have all the answers I need.

It isn't unusual for a hunter to be able to pinpoint the trail a buck uses to enter a food source.

Unfortunately, it's also common for the trail, as it works back into the woods toward bedding areas, to split into several branches. That leaves the hunter guessing which bedding area the buck is using.

Armed with a rake, the hunter can create a track catcher on the main trail and just up from each split. Returning a week later, he can check the main trail for the buck's track. If it's there, he can check the track catchers on the splinter trails. Based on which one holds tracks, the hunter now knows one of the locations where Mr. Big is bedding.

Simply put, strategically positioned track catchers throughout a habitat are invaluable tools for monitoring the activity of a fingerprinted buck. Any time you question if the animal is using a trail, crossing, funnel or almost any confined area, track catchers can provide the answer.

As with the scouting cameras, care must be used to minimize disturbances. Using the three-strike rule, avoiding stepping on trails, cutting odors, and only going in at mid-day, when deer are most likely bedded, all are important steps. Following these guidelines, you will receive the full benefits from this patterning tactic.

## FOLLOWING IN HIS FOOTSTEPS

In areas that receive a blanket of snow, a buck's entire world becomes a giant track catcher. A day or two after a fresh snowfall, getting out and finding the targeted buck's track provides an incredible opportunity to nail down precisely what he has been doing. All one must do is follow his trail backwards.

Taking that direction ensures that the buck isn't reacting to your pressure and that he was indeed moving naturally. From this natural movement, you can easily identify his travel routes, food sources, bedding sites and anything he may have done.

Granted, even following the trail backwards is no guarantee that you won't bump into the monarch, which definitely makes this an aggressive and somewhat risky in-season tactic. However, when nothing else seems to be working, time is running out and you don't know where he is, it can lead to results.

Luckily, bumping him once typically won't kill your chances. Bucks seldom alter their long-term patterns based on one relatively harmless encounter with humans. On the plus side, bumping him in this way alerts you that his pattern is relatively stable

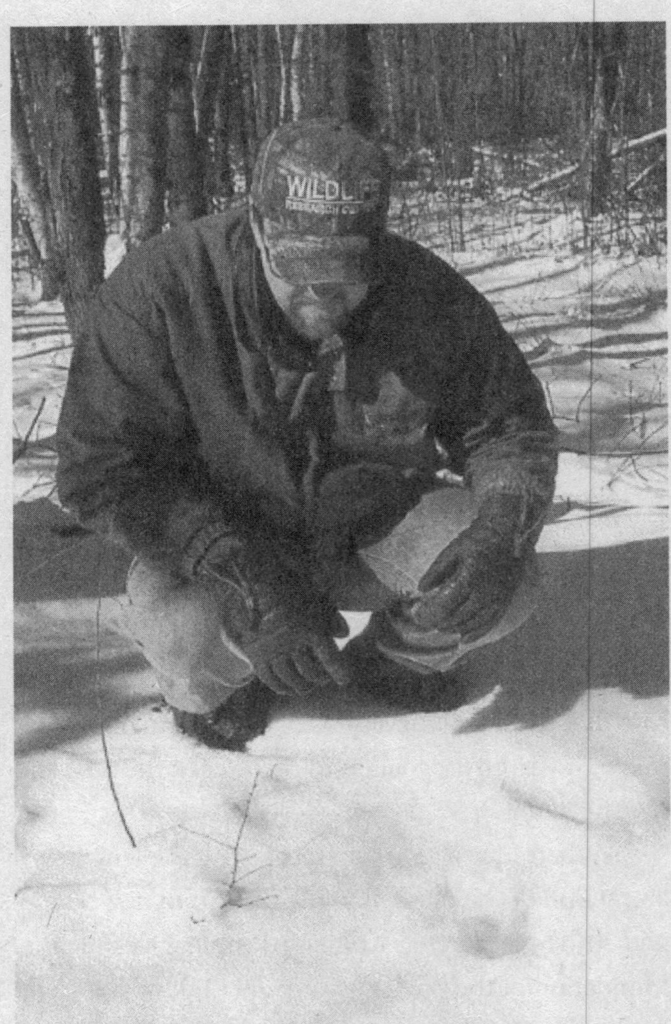

Backtracking a buck in the snow can reveal everything the buck did for as long as the track can be followed, and provide priceless insight into his life.

and that it's advisable to modify hunting strategies immediately to capitalize on your findings.

Backtracking in the first weeks after season ends eliminates any concern, but it does require a little more analysis. Assuming his survival, along with no major changes occurring to the habitat or with food sources, chances are very good that the buck will be following those patterns next late season. The real question becomes whether he does the same things during the earlier phases of season; that's where woodsmanship and common sense help to provide answers.

For example, if old rubs happen to be intermittently marking his travels, chances are good that he used that same route earlier in the year. Some food sources, such as soybeans, sorghum and corn, are used for much of season. However, if the area holds only alfalfa fields buried under the snow and he happens to be feeding on woody browse, chances are strong that he'll be feeding on alfalfa during much of next year's season. Also, relatively short-lived food sources, such as mast crops, must be figured into the equation. Still, even if all these findings only produce his patterns for next late season, they put the hunter much farther ahead of where he previously was.

## RECORD KEEPING

Another important and often-overlooked aspect of patterning bucks lies in record keeping. The logs I keep are grouped into two categories. One covers my overall hunting activities, including scouting notes, such as locations that show deer activities and places I want to check in further detail. In many ways, this is much like a journal, summarizing what I found and want to remember for the future.

I also log deer sightings and the details of each hunt. Regardless of whether it's an afternoon conducting long-range observations or a morning on the stand, the entry begins with a description of exactly where I was posted and how I got in and out. It then includes details on the conditions, including temperature, wind direction and speed, cloud cover, notes on any precipitation that may occur and the moon phase. As of late, I've even begun including barometric pressure, and whether it's rising, falling or constant.

Next comes the information on the stars of the show. I try to include a description of each deer I see, naming them if they have recognizable traits. I include what time period I observed them, where they were and what they were doing, all in specific detail.

For example, instead of merely noting that I saw a young buck feeding, I'd write that I saw a 2.5-year-old eight-point, scoring approximately 100 inches. He entered the field five minutes before sunset—specific references to sunset and sunrise provide a better timeline than citing the hour on the clock—from the trail in the northeast corner. He spent the first eight minutes eating acorns under the cluster of oaks before feeding his way steadily out to the middle of the alfalfa field.

I include the same sort of notes in my logs on specific bucks—logs dedicated exclusively to the activities of individual animals. Having one source of information on each buck is more effective than sifting through the general logs in an attempt to find information specific to him. Because these logs are kept on my laptop, I also copy them into my general logs. That makes it easy for me to maintain a master general hunting log file and then break that into logs for each property I hunt.

The final piece of the puzzle to truly patterning a mature buck comes from plotting his sign and sightings on a map. Granted, it may be impossible to pattern him during the rut, but with the aid of a map, we can come pretty darn close to nailing him down during the other phases of season.

For any phase of season, filling in every gap of a buck's life strictly from our findings is a tremendous challenge. However, when it is mapped out, along with plotting a property's thick protective cover and food and water sources, it's much easier to apply educated guesses and deductive reasoning to piece things together.

To make it better still, marking our findings on three clear overlays—one for early season, the lull and scraping phase; another for the chase and breeding phases; and the last for post rut and second rut—gives us the opportunity to see how his patterns change throughout the season. With that, we can compare and contrast each phase, gaining valuable insight into the best stand locations for each.

## DIVIDING YOUR EGGS INTO SEVERAL BASKETS

Even with all of this, finding more than one buck is extremely helpful. A lot can happen to mess up bucks that seem practically gift-wrapped. Locating more than one gives you a safety net in case things go haywire.

My own experience several seasons ago is a good example of that. In the days leading up to the opener, I'd located five good bucks, two of which were living on land open to public hunting. The other three were calling a parcel of heavily hunted private land home. Though the ground was restricted, as many as five hunters could be found sitting in various trees at one time.

With a pretty good handle on all the bucks' patterns, my stands were set and I was ready for the opening day. Knowing that the largest, a 10-point I'd estimated in the low 160s, routinely fed in a small grassy meadow, I began the season there.

Sitting in stand that first afternoon, I was more than a little disappointed to spot three other hunters. With a smidge more than an hour of shooting light left, they drove their ATVs into the meadow and started snooping around for places to hang their stands. Amazingly, though the meadow was just over an acre in size, they never saw me slip my stand out of the tree and make the long walk back to my truck. Before opening day was over, I knew the location would be trashed beyond repair. Such is life when competing with others on hunting grounds.

With four bucks still remaining on my list, the following afternoon found me targeting the one feeding on the oak ridge. Though also on public lands, I was confident that I'd have the ridge to myself. The acorn drop in the area was early and very light that year. Because the ridge was a pain to get to, as well as the rest of the oak woods being void of acorns, I didn't believe other hunters had put in the work to find this secluded patch. I was right.

It wasn't long before the ridge was covered in deer. With ample shooting light left, I spotted the large eight-point cresting the ridge. He was well out of range, but I watched him feed until dark. Since the area was covered in does and fawns, I didn't dare risk attempting to call him within range.

Over the next week, I hunted the stand three more times. With so many deer feeding on the limited acorns, I knew the location would be picked dry fast. That knowledge, as well as a low-impact route to and from my stand, convinced me to hunt the location hard. So long as I could keep the deer ignorant, I would continue to hunt the ridge until they exhausted the acorn supply. After one more close encounter with the eight, and just over a week into season, the acorns were gone. Not surprisingly, the large eight vanished with them.

During the period of time I was hunting the acorns, I was also alternating trips to the private land. I even passed on a shot opportunity at the smaller of the three bucks I'd targeted, because the other two more impressive bucks were flirting with the edge of my shooting range at the time.

Just under two weeks in, with the desire to fill my tag growing stronger, I shifted to hunting the 3.5-year-old nine-point—the same buck I'd passed the week before. As luck would have it, a well-placed stand delivered an easy shot opportunity. A short tracking job later and the buck was mine.

Finding and targeting more than one buck was key to that season's success. As of writing this, in three of the past four seasons I've been able to tag out early. During each of the three seasons I was successful, I'd located two or more mature bucks to hunt. Though few of us have enough access to private lands to do that, adding public lands to the equation makes it possible for nearly anyone.

## CONCLUSION

Truly patterning a buck takes work and scouting smart, but it can be accomplished. The tools described here can all be extremely helpful. However, I'd be lying to you if I claimed that I've ever used all of them together on a single deer. Personally, I rely on observations, sign, track catchers and my logs far more than scouting cameras and mapping sign. Still, all are great tools for hunters to have at their disposal, to be used as needed.

In fairness, I must also point out that one rarely knows every detail about any buck. The majority of the time, patterning involves discovering small pieces of a buck's life and using that info to generate educated guesses on how to most effectively hunt him.

Further complicating matters is that buck patterns rarely stay the same throughout the season. So when a kink in a buck's armor is found, hunt it smart and fast, before his patterns shift.

Follow that advice and use these tools, and you just may accomplish the ultimate in bowhunting deer. Effectively patterning and arrowing a specific buck takes your game to the next level—to the apex of the sport.

When used properly, scouting cameras can be excellent tools for revealing the bucks on a particular property and giving you insights into their patterns.

# Hunting the Wind: What Most "Experts" Won't Tell You

As we approached the downed 146 4/8-inch 10-point, I exchanged high fives with my good friend Tom Indrebo. At first glance, it was one of those rare bucks that had fallen in place almost effortlessly. I knew his bedding sites, food sources and routes connecting them. Based on the wind direction, I could even predict the route he'd take on a given day. I had the buck nailed.

When most hunters speak of hunting the wind, they are referring to keeping the deer upwind of their stands. That's understandable. Not allowing deer to enter their odor stream is a prerequisite to having a successful hunt. However, there are already ample teaching resources available to instruct hunters on how to safely hunt the wind. Heck, I covered it some myself in my first book.

For Tom Indrebo and me, determining how this buck was using the wind for protection was a key to harvesting him.

Furthermore, you already know that I don't worry about having bucks downwind, so I'm not going to cover all that here.

Instead, I'll invest this space in discussing how bucks use the wind and how we can use that to our advantage. For the life of me, I have no clue why this aspect of hunting the wind isn't covered in more detail. Bowhunting pioneers Gene and Barry Wensel are the only others I'm aware of who ever tackled the subject in any real depth.

I'm not pointing this out to say no one else has ever truly covered it. It is possible that they have and it slipped by me. My true purpose for bringing this up is to provide a belated yet very sincere thank-you to the Wensel brothers. I stumbled across their lessons on hunting the wind when I was still in my early stages of bowhunting. They helped me take my game to a new level.

Learning how bucks use the wind is one of those little details that truly can make that much of a difference. When reading the rest of this chapter, remember that deer rely much more heavily on their noses than humans ever could. In many ways, their sense of smell is every bit as important to them as our eyes and ears are to us. Sure, on a small level, deer communicate through grunts and bleats, and they relate to the world visually. However, they really talk to each other through odors. They may question their other senses. They rarely doubt what their noses tell them.

## USING THE WIND FOR SAFETY'S SAKE

To illustrate how bucks use the wind in their routine, everyday activities, let's look more closely at how the taking of the 10-point Tom and I were celebrating at the beginning of this chapter came together.

It really all began in early August, when Indrebo gave me a farm to rip apart for his clients and myself. It offered two major sources of cover. One was a strip of woods that followed a meandering creek slicing through a crop valley. The other was a large, steep-wooded ridge flanked on both sides by crop fields. Studying the topo maps, I found several likely locations for later in season. However, I knew the only way to pick early-season stands would be to observe the crop fields.

Because of the setting, observing with a spotting scope from the truck was the best approach. I could watch one valley until just about dark and then flip to the other side for a quick viewing. I saw the 10-point buck feeding in the north valley that first time in.

To be more specific, my logs show that the temps were in the high 60s, the skies were partly cloudy and the wind was out of the southeast. I spotted a total of three does, five fawns and three bucks feeding on the alfalfa in the north valley. Two bucks were yearlings and the other was the 10. The south valley held two does, three fawns and two yearling bucks.

Over the course of repeated observations, I saw two bucks that would score higher than the 10 and another that was slightly below. To be honest, the reason I targeted the 10 was because of his regular appearances.

Taking it a step further, my logs also showed that he used the wind direction to select which valley he visited for feeding. When winds came from northerly directions, he selected the north valley. Conversely, he fed in the south valley when winds had southern origins. Putting that together, I believed I had a good chance at arrowing him.

Mid-day, still a couple of weeks before season's opening, I set out to place stands to take him. I'd already noted the areas where he entered the field on both sides of the ridge. The problem was that, though they were relatively close, he didn't use the same trails each time. It was entirely possible that I could get the side right, but have the buck enter the field out of bow range.

Because of that, I decided to conduct one hard scouting and stand-hanging trip. With two stands strapped to my back, I began walking the edge of the woods along the south valley. Mid-ridge, a point dropped off the side to serve as a natural route between the food and the bedding on top. Based on his field-entry points, I believed it was a good bet that he was traveling that point. I was not disappointed. In fact, I traced the buck's old rub line all the way up the point to his bed. With large tracks indicating the line was still active, I knew I was onto something good.

Surveying the area, a large oak was positioned perfectly on the crest of the point, providing an easy shot to the rub line. With a low-impact route in and the tree being only 150 yards from his bed, I hung the first stand in the oak.

When further scouting revealed a second bedding site and rub line, suddenly it all made sense. The buck was bedding on knobs jutting from opposite sides of the ridge. With a wind from the south, he would bed on the north side. That enabled him to use his nose to detect danger approaching from on top of the ridge and use his eyes to scan for danger lurking on the ridge side below. Then, late afternoon, he could rise, crest the ridge and drop into the south valley. That way, as he approached the field, he could keep the wind in his face and scent the food source for danger. When the wind had a northern angle, he could bed on the south side and mirror this action in the other direction. In either case, he was using the wind to keep himself safe to the fullest extent.

On both sides, he followed his trail from his bed down most of the ridge side. As he neared the field, he'd break off to use one of several trails to enter the food source. I believe these various routes were selected to fully utilize his sense of smell. In other words, he'd finish his entry to the field by taking whichever splinter trail allowed him to scent-check the field best under the current wind direction.

After slapping up a stand on the opposite side, just before the trail broke, I was set. Returning to the farm early in the season, a quick check of the wind told me which stand to sit. To be safe, I climbed into the stand extra early. Even with the day producing high winds and the breeding phase still a long way off, I knew being so close to the bedding area could lead to early movement.

It all started coming together a full hour before dark. Catching movement out of the corner of my eye, I saw the mature 10-point trotting down his now freshened rub line.

Already positioned, I was ready when the buck stepped out from under the oak's branch. Settling the pin high behind the front shoulder, I sent the arrow driving into the buck's vitals. He crashed away, but I knew he wouldn't go far.

Of course, this situation was more cut-and-dried than most. In settings with limited food or cover, if bucks only fed when they could travel into the wind to get to food, they'd eventually die of starvation. Along those lines, there are other times when a buck simply wants to feed on acorns worse than he wants to eat browse in a clear-cut. If traveling from his bedding site to the acorns involves walking with the wind at his back, he'll do it more often than not.

However, knowing that they'd prefer to walk directly into or quartering into the wind is information that hunters can use to their advantage. All else being equal, keeping that in mind when selecting which stand to sit can up the odds of meeting Mr. Big on a given day.

On the flip side, bucks almost always use the wind when deciding how and where to bed. At the very least, they have the strong tendency to bed with the wind at their back and use their eyes to protect their front side. That makes sense from a survival standpoint.

This knowledge can be applied in broken or rolling land. When a buck is rotating between several bedding sites, the wind direction can dictate which he selects. The safety advantage of beds that simultaneously offer a good view of the front and wind coverage of the back is tremendous. Applying that knowledge makes it much easier to predict where a buck will bed and what stand sites are most likely to produce encounters with him during his travels to likely food sources.

In a nutshell, outside of during the chase and breeding phases of season, buck movement is mostly between bedding and food and water. When one doesn't have a good reason to select one stand site over another, analyze which covers the trail that provides a buck the ability to use the wind most to his advantage. Though that won't always lead to sitting on the right trail, it will far more often than strictly relying on random luck.

## LOVE IS IN THE AIR

As helpful as playing the wind during the non-rut related phases of season can be, it's even more so during the scraping, chase and breeding phases. That is when hunters can gain an incredible advantage.

Many of the best-producing scrapes are those located on the downwind side of bedding areas. With a single pass, a buck can check both his scrape and the bedding area for a doe entering estrus early. In that scenario, it isn't a coincidence that the hottest scrapes on a given day are often dictated by the wind direction.

To fine-tune stand placement for hunting these scrapes, I strive to set up 20 yards downwind of them. Any buck that wants to check the scrape must either come to it or pass downwind of it. It isn't uncommon for bucks to check these scrapes from 10–40 yards downwind. Such a stand placement allows me to catch all of that activity. More than once, this strategy has provided me with shot opportunities at bucks checking scrapes from a distance.

As helpful as the wind is for checking scrapes, it's even more advantageous for checking does. Though bucks may seem to be moving at random during the rut, there is often method to their madness. To maximize their breeding opportunities, bucks must effectively cruise as many doe concentrations as is practical in a swift and efficient manner. The wind is a tremendous aid in accomplishing that.

When determining how to set up on doe-bedding areas, start by selecting the downwind side.

For example, as opposed to running wildly around a field, sniffing doe after doe, one pass on the downwind side of the field lets the buck know if any are ready. While doing so, he can also scent-check the trails for any hot does that have recently entered or exited the field.

All of this makes the downwind side of prime food sources a good place to sit. To further stack the odds, stands placed 15–20 yards in, off the inside corners of these fields, can be great choices. The hunter can cover the bucks cruising the edge as deep as 40 yards inside the woods, intercept those walking the actual edge of the field as well as any bucks that may be following a doe on the worn trails entering the field that most inside corners possess.

Bucks often cut just inside those corners when getting from one side of the field to the other. Doing this provides the quickest route that offers the safety of cover. All of these things can be taken advantage of when hunting the downwind corners of fields that are being used as food sources.

Finally, as was the case while scraping, running the downwind edges of doe-bedding areas is the most effective means for a buck to scent-check the bedded does. Placing stands 20 yards off the edge, covering the best entrance/exit trail, positions the hunter to intercept most of this movement, as well as providing the chance that a hot doe will lead a buck past the stand.

The story of an Illinois buck I took is a good example of how this can pay off. During a spring scouting trip, I'd found an area where the mature woods had been selectively logged. One patch along a ridge finger had been logged harder than

By factoring in what wind directions would make the stand location the best, I was able to take this wide, high-beamed nine-point on the stand's first sit.

the rest. The combination of the thicker regrowth, extra downed tops and view of the more open creek bottom below all resulted in a prime family-group bedding area.

On the surface, it seemed like bucks could be working it from any side. However, further analysis revealed that the wind direction would be the key. When the wind blew down the point, it created one best route for roaming bucks. By skirting the lower edge, they could scent-check all the does, the bedding area, and use their eyes to scan the creek bottom below.

The first November morning providing this wind found me in that stand. My sit was short and sweet.

Around 8 a.m., the large-bodied, high-beamed nine-pointer appeared. As I had hoped, he was skirting the lower edge of the thicket. Coming in on a string, his head alternated between tilting up to check the wind and turning back to use his eyes to scan the creek bottom below.

At about 30 yards out, I drew and settled my knuckle behind my ear. Coming to a stop, he intently scanned the creek bottom for does. Turning just a bit as he did, I let the arrow fly. As the arrow sank in, the buck took flight for the creek bottom. Folding as he neared the bank, the wide, chocolate-racked buck was mine.

## USING SCENT WITH THE WIND TO SEAL THE DEAL

In some situations, bedding areas are too large or don't offer one obvious spot to set up. That's when one pulls out the scent to help focus deer activity around the stand. This is exactly what I did to create a focal point while hunting an otherwise non-focused bedding area in big timber.

Lying between a creek bottom and ridge top, right in the middle of a large stand of timber, was a large doe-bedding area. One problem with the setup was that the bedding area went on for nearly a half-mile and held numerous potentially good stand locations, but not one that would cover the majority of bucks cruising by. The other problem was that bucks were also running the valley on the opposite side of the ridge.

For the best odds, I needed to do something to concentrate the buck activity near my stand. On my way in for the first morning's sit, with the wind

Applying how bucks use the wind to your scent strategies makes scents far more effective. Scents can even be used to reel in bucks before they hit the hunter's odor stream.

blowing up and over the ridge from the bedding area, I paused on top of the ridge to place an estrous urine-soaked scent wick. Reaching to place the wick on a high branch, my hope was that the alluring odors would filter down the other side of the ridge. The goal was to draw bucks up from that valley, but not allow them to locate the source of the odor.

Drawing bucks to the top of the ridge was a good start. Still, because the ridge top was out of shooting range, I needed to lure them farther to get the shot. To do this, I placed two more wicks at 20 yards on both sides of the stand, forming a scent triangle.

Now I had a chance of drawing deer to my stand from the opposite side of the ridge. Upon reaching the top, with the two flanking wicks producing odors, chances were good that, if the buck traveled down the ridge in either direction, he would pick up one of their odor streams and be lured in for the shot. Furthermore, the wicks should draw in any bucks simply cruising the ridge. In either case, they would already be looking for hot does. The scent would simply sell a buck the lie that one was in the bedding area waiting for him to come get her.

Less than an hour after shooting light emerged, I spotted the 150-inch buck on the ridge top. Feverishly scent-checking the air, it was obvious that he was intent on locating the doe whose scent had drawn him up the ridge. With the odor now wafting above his nose, he eventually gave up and began walking the ridge top away from my stand.

His defeatist attitude changed quickly the moment he hit the odor stream of estrous scent from the wick flanking the left side of my stand. He was coming in on a rope; I prepared for the shot. Less than 10 minutes later, as I walked over to where I saw the buck crumble, I was thankful that I'd gone the extra mile in using scent to take advantage of how cruising bucks use the wind.

## RELYING SOLELY ON THE WIND

In fairness to those who are either unable or unwilling to take odor control to the extreme, I should point out ways they too can use these techniques.

Under most of these settings, stands can be placed to take advantage of the way bucks use winds, while still being positioned so that the wind blows from the stand at an angle, quartering toward, but not directly across the buck's most likely approach routes. Granted, because winds often shift and bucks don't always show up where they're supposed to, this is riskier than taking odor control to the extreme. Additionally, there will be many wind conditions that make this approach too risky for a stand site. However, multiple stands can be set to increase the likelihood of a huntable quartering wind occurring.

Another option, when hunting scrapes, feeding locations and doe-bedding areas, is placing stands downwind of where one believes the buck will pass. Unfortunately, because these cruises only occur frequently during the scrape, chase and breeding phases of season, well-established trails don't often exist. Instead, the hunter is hunting a more general area downwind of a point of interest. Because bucks are more randomly passing through the general area, relying on staying downwind of most bucks to remain undetected usually translates into a comparatively higher percentage passing through so far upwind that they're out of shooting range.

Still, this technique and placement strategy can work. For example, let's look at applying this to intercepting bucks scent-checking the downwind side of bedding areas. If the most likely path skirts 20 yards from the edge, placement 35 yards from the edge will work. Now you can safely cover the path, as well as have decent odds of the odors flowing over the heads of bucks that pass just downwind of the stand.

When hunting scrapes, placing the stand 40 yards downwind is often safe and will intercept many of the bucks checking from downwind. Though it doesn't provide a shot to the scrape, a grunt or two may lure those bucks into range.

Scent can also be used to our advantage. Placing scent out 20 yards from both sides of the stand can potentially reel bucks cruising downwind before they hit the hunter's odor stream. Of course, it's also always possible to coax those that are too far upwind closer for the shot with a grunt or doe call.

Hunting upwind of a buck's bedding site is the trickiest. Even using a quartering wind, chances are high that it will momentarily shift to the bedding site. That shift can be disastrous. The trick is setting up far enough away from the bedded buck to remain undetected through the wind shifts. The farther an odor travels, the less likely it becomes that the currents will deliver it to a buck's nostrils, and the more it dissipates before it arrives. Although bucks can smell objects from 500 yards away, odds are good that the distance will stop him from picking you up when a rogue shift in wind direction occurs.

Though taking odor control to the extreme makes these techniques easier and more successful, relying on the wind to keep you safe can be effective. The cost is placing a higher premium on choosing a stand location that's better for the hunter's wind than the buck's ability to use it.

## CONCLUSION

Learning to take advantage of how bucks use the wind may not receive much exposure, but it sure provides the savvy hunter with a tremendous advantage. As a matter of fact, that just may be why it's barely, if ever, covered in detail. Because of its effectiveness, perhaps the "experts" who have picked up on its power want to guard this secret for themselves. If you give it a try, you just may begin to understand why.

# Mastering Hunting from the Ground

I first saw the incredible main frame 10-point standing a mere 20 yards away, as if he materialized out of thin air. With our blind covered in snow and tucked in next to a round bale, the buck that would easily score somewhere above the mid 160s scanned the field, oblivious to our presence. Whispering to my cameraman not to move, I waited for the monster whitetail to spot the decoy placed 50 yards behind the blind. Hidden by the angle, the buck dropped his head and began pawing through the 18 inches of snow cover, exposing the alfalfa that was hidden below.

After he swung his body around to a broadside position and dropped his head to feed, I began to make my move. Already in position, I slowly raised my bow no more than three inches before the slammer's head snapped up and he began staring a hole through me. With just enough time to realize that I needed to be at full draw already to take this animal, two powerful bounds removed him from my life.

I chose to begin this chapter with the events of this painful bowhunt because it effectively illustrates the benefits what the better pop-up blinds on today's market can deliver. After all, I was stuck in a situation where hunting from a tree wasn't an option. The sign showed me the place I had to be and my pop-up blind allowed me to effectively set up there. For several minutes, a grizzled old buck lingered within 20 yards of my blind. Heck, he even stared right past it for nearly a minute, never having a clue that it was out of place. If that doesn't state how effectively blinds can open doors to otherwise nearly unhuntable locations, as well as their ability to help hunters go undetected, I don't know what would.

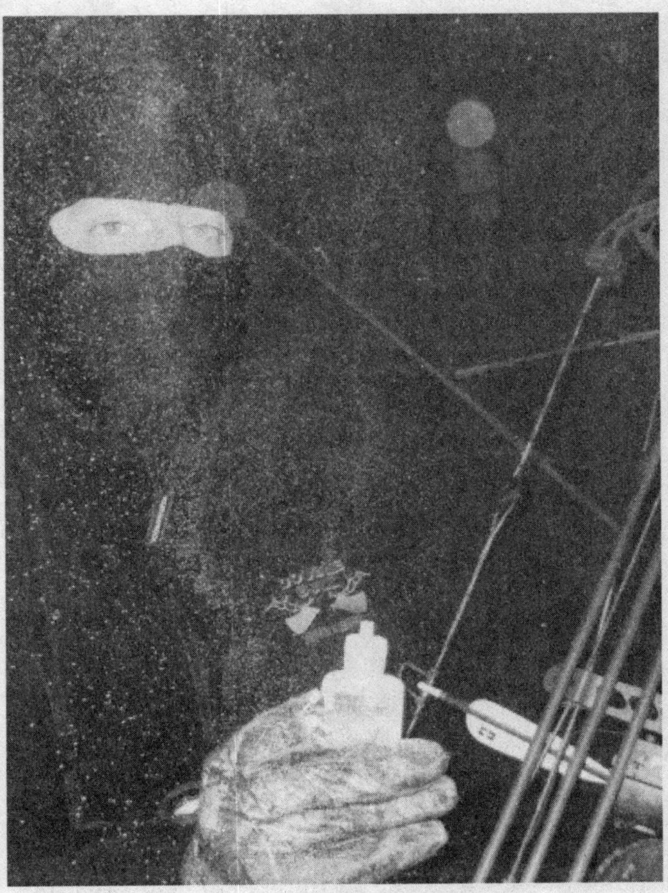

Because of the ability to seal the back side of the blind, air can be forced to flow around it, as opposed to through the blind. This provides scent advantages when deer are downwind.

That hunt also clearly points out the importance of following certain guidelines. The old buck didn't spook at the blind. He spooked at me. Worse yet, it was all my fault. He caught the movement of my uncovered hand. Apparently, he didn't believe that the color of pasty white skin should be floating around inside an otherwise black blind. Simply wearing dark gloves or covering the windows in shoot-through mesh would have allowed me to arrow that buck. Learning that painful lesson has enabled me to never repeat that mistake again, and to arrow several other great bucks I would never have had a chance at otherwise.

## BENEFITS OF POP-UP BLINDS

As already stated, one of the greatest benefits of pop-ups is their ability to be placed nearly anywhere. Many locations simply don't allow for standard treestand hunting methods. Luckily, since the advent of pop-ups, every location is safe to slip a stand into.

A reality of hunting is that many of the largest bucks live in areas not easily hunted. Often, they call the thickest, nastiest tangle their homes. Whether that's a tag-alder or cedar swamp, a young pine plantation, a clear-cut regrowth, a pocket of sage or the tangle of thorns that could slice you to shreds, such settings don't often provide suitable trees. The same lack of trees commonly occurs in the more open grasslands of the Western states, where deer can often see danger approaching from what seems like forever away. Pop-ups provide an effective hunting alternative in all of those cases.

They can even be used to help hunters who have issues with getting winded go undetected. Of course, it's always safer for hunters to be downwind of their prey. Still, the beneficial effects of closing windows on the upwind side and sealing the bottom of the blind with debris can reduce the airflow enough to allow them to go unnoticed. This is because sealing the upwind side of the blind causes the airflow to go around, rather than through it. In some situations, that's just the edge needed to tag a mature buck.

## SETUP CONSIDERATIONS

When selecting the best location for a blind, one must understand what causes deer to spook at such structures. Aside from not keeping them odor free, I believe the biggest culprit is the element of surprise. I don't believe that deer find blinds particularly threatening. Like a round bale in the middle of a field, it's simply another inanimate object in their world. If given the chance to study it from a distance, they'll often dismiss it as harmless. However, if a deer turns a corner in the woods and finds a new round bale 20 yards away, it's far more likely to turn inside out in an effort to vacate the area. The same is true of blinds.

Considering where deer are most wary helps remove the element of surprise. A prime example is when a deer is approaching an open food source. That same old doe that was calmly walking the trail 200 yards back in the woods is now taking a few steps, stopping and scanning every inch of the landscape before her. If anything is remotely out of place, after a series of stomps and head bobs, she will likely vacate in a hurry, alerting anyone who cares to listen with her barrage of snorts. This tendency makes hiding a blind along the edge openings a challenge.

Conversely, while traveling the transition zone between feeding and bedding, deer are far more relaxed. In such areas, hiding a blind is more easily accomplished. First, try to find some hanging branches that you can slip the blind under, located 15–20 yards on the downwind side of the

Trimming the lower branches and snugging a pop-up blind under limbs of evergreens is a great technique for breaking the roof outline.

travel zone. Being set off the deer's natural line of sight helps.

Just like with tree stands, being in the shadows also helps. However, keeping the sun out of the hunter's eyes is even more important. During both early morning and late afternoon, because of being on ground level, having the blind's openings oriented toward the sun commonly causes the hunter to look directly into it. Obviously, that can seriously impact the ability to shoot.

A further complication is that having the sun shining directly into the blind creates other serious problems. One of the advantages of quality blinds is that their dark interior helps to hide the hunter. If sun shines directly into the blind, the hunter becomes highlighted and items such as the bow, arrows, hunting heads and other objects are likely to produce reflections.

Keeping the blind in the shadows is one solution to hiding both it and the hunter inside. At the very least, the blind must be positioned so that the sun is off its back side during the hunt.

The next great culprit when it comes to revealing blinds is not brushing them in well enough. If it's in a relatively open location where deer can see it from a distance, doing nothing but popping it up and placing it next to any available cover will work. However, when blinds are placed in thicker cover and deer have a high probability of not seeing them until they are 50 yards or less away, they must be brushed in well to break up their outlines for best results.

Draping the top of the blind with a matt of overhanging branches goes a long way toward blurring the outline. If a suitable tree doesn't exist, snug it into the best available cover and either cut branches for the top or use a concealment product, such as the synthetic branches made by PMI. Breaking the roofline is critical for placing blinds in cover.

Along with using cut limbs or synthetic branches, a great way to break the roof outline is to remove enough of the lower branches from an evergreen to be able to slip the blind underneath (always check to see that it's legal to cut branches and/or get the landowner's permission before doing so). By snugging it under a natural mat of limbs and allowing them to hang over the side, the blind blends in very well. Placing a smattering of natural or synthetic limbs around the outside, paying particular attention to the corners, further aids the blending process.

Remove all the debris from the inside of the blind's floor and use it to seal the bottom around the outside. Doing so helps further blend it in, along with reducing airflow and allowing more silent movement inside. The combination of placing the blind out of the deer's line of sight, breaking the roof and effectively blending its sides dramatically reduces the element of surprise and promotes relaxed shooting opportunities,

Another method of removing surprise is placing the blind in relatively open areas. When deer can see the blind from 50 or more yards away, they have the opportunity to survey it for potential danger, As in the comparison made earlier, the first time they see a round bale in a field, they most often analyze it for a period of time and then dismiss it as harmless. Though a certain percentage of deer will spook from this placement method, I've personally used is successfully several times to fool mature bucks.

## HIDING THE HUNDER

The last steps involve hiding the hunter waiting inside the blind. Unlike being perched 25 feet in a tree, deer can spot unmasked ground-level movement much easier. Luckily, there are ways to counter this. For those shooting fixed-blade and certain expandable heads, using shoot-through mesh is a huge help. The mesh reflects light, which eliminates the unnatural dark holes in the blind and helps hide movement.

Additionally, the windows on the back of the blind must be closed. Doing this eliminates having the hunter's silhouette created by backlighting. Blinds that have viewing ports and silent, easy-opening windows have a tremendous advantage here. Unfortunately, deer don't always realize that they aren't supposed to approach from a certain direction. When they do, the viewing port allows the hunter to see them, whereas the ability to open the windows undetected provides the opportunity for the shot.

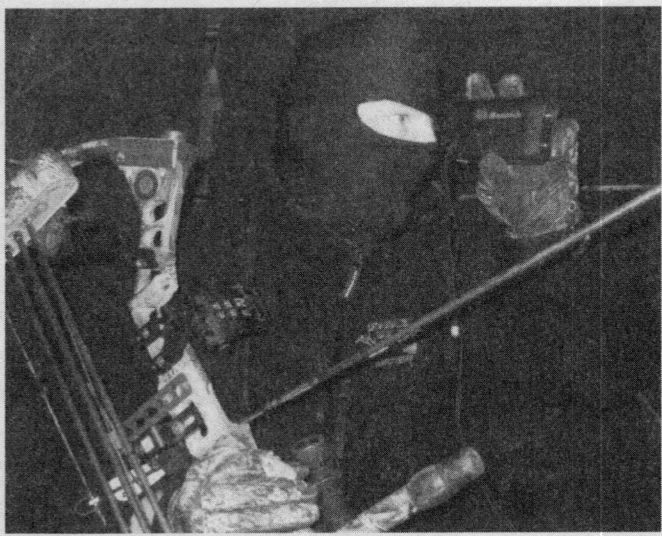

Wearing black when hunting from blinds helps the hunter stay swallowed up by the shadows.

The final component of undetected movement is wearing black. The only pop-ups I'd recommend hunting deer from all have interiors that are colored black. It makes staying hidden and moving so much easier to get away with. Wearing black allows the hunter to further blend into the dark interior. Because his face must be lined up with the opening to shoot and his hands are closest to the deer, wearing a black facemask and dark gloves is of particular importance.

The main drawback I've found to hunting from blinds is that it gets darker inside faster than when hunting from stands. Though the deer can still be seen easily, the pins on sights tend to disappear. Those planning to hunt from blinds much should strongly consider using sights with superior light-gathering abilities. Though I've never used them myself, I'd guess that lighted pins, where legal, would also be a good choice. Luckily, simply being aware of this issue and addressing it removes the potential for losing legal shot opportunities due to not being able to see the pins.

## THE IMPORTANCE OF PRACTICE

To get the most from the blind, it's a very good idea to practice shooting from it until you are comfortable shooting from a sitting position and slipping arrows through the blind's opening. Though clipping the bottom of the opening is one of the few blunders I've managed to avoid, my good friends, blind-hunting visionaries Keith Beam and Brooks

Johnson, have done it more than they'd care to admit during the first few years they hunted from blinds. Unless you practice shooting from them, it can be easy to forget that the arrow must clear the bottom of the blind's opening.

Also, if you're planning on using the shoot-through mesh, highly recommended when deer hunting, use it while practicing. Though I've never had it significantly affect arrow flight when shooting fixed-blade heads, I've found it's always best to test these things before it matters!

## SEALING THE DEAL WITH DECOYS

Just following what we've covered thus far will enable readers to use blinds effectively. To really push their effectiveness over the top, consider pairing the blind with a deer decoy.

Decoys are great complements to blind hunting because they draw the deer's attention away from the blind. Though concealing blinds along openings can be challenging, placing a buck decoy 40–50 yards out in front of the blind makes pulling that placement off much easier.

When hunting stands, I like to place a buck decoy facing the stand, approximately 20–25 yards out. That way, when the buck circles it to make eye contact, he typically provides a 10- to 15-yard shot opportunity. With doe decoys, a placement of 15 yards away, in a broadside position, fairly consistently produces 15-yard shots as the buck approaches from behind to mount her.

Though those placement strategies are pretty universally accepted for tree-stand hunting, I believe that they must be tweaked for hunting from ground blinds.

First, I use buck decoys almost exclusively when hunting from blinds. One of the reasons for this is that I want the decoy placed as far away from the blind as I can get it, while still having it produce buck encounters within shooting range.

If the blind is hidden along the edge of a field, I can get away with placing the decoy 40 yards out into the field. Along with putting it out farther than normal, I also alter its position so that it's quartering toward the blind, as opposed to facing it directly. That way, if any deer become curious about what the decoy is staring at, their attentions aren't drawn directly to the blind.

The first advantage to using the decoy as a buck is that, as stated earlier, the investigating buck will most often circle to face a buck decoy. Though the distance varies, this act most often brings the buck another 10 yards closer to the blind, resulting in a 30-yard shot opportunity. Since I'm comfortable with this distance, and I want to keep the buck as far out as practical, I find this placement to be the best balance between the two.

Because deer are already on the alert when approaching fields, they are snore likely to notice blinds located along the edges. Because of the high likelihood that they won't notice them until they're too close for comfort, the surprise factor leads to a dramatic increase in negative responses.

Because doe decoys aren't routinely circled, they tend not to draw bucks closer than their position.

When the blind is placed out in the open, such as next to a round bale or a clump of brush, it's often possible to cheat the decoy out another 10 yards farther. If the blind is placed between the woods and the decoy, the bucks will most likely angle past the blind, maintaining eye contact with the decoy the entire way. That placement also typically results in 30-yard and closer shot opportunities. If shots 20 yards and closer are the goal, moving the decoy 10 yards closer in on either of these setups will most often accomplish that.

Though I haven't come right out and said it yet, I'm guessing that most readers have already figured out why I want to keep the deer away from a field-edge blind setup. The closer they get, the more likely they are to notice the blind is out of place.

That's more or less the same reasoning behind exclusively using the decoy as a buck. Does tend to congregate around other does. When hunting from a blind, not only are you risking that the does will get nervous because the decoy isn't moving, but there's also the risk that they'll spot the blind. Since does don't investigate bucks very often, going the buck route minimizes the chances that the setup will be swarmed by troublesome does.

Speaking of the lack of movement making deer nervous, there are a few things you can do about that. One is to purchase a remote-controlled, robotic decoy. Legal in most states, it gives you the ability to control head and tail movement, making these decoys much more effective.

Another option, where legal, is to attach a moving tail to a stationary decoy. These are relatively inexpensive devices and, though they aren't as good as the robotic decoys, they do add a level of realism. The completely legal, virtually free option is to tack unscented tissue paper to the ears and tail area of the decoy. By doing that, the tissues flicker in the wind, simulating moving ears and a flickering tail. Any of these options are helpful and can provide wildly exciting blind-hunting moments.

## SLIPPING INTO COVER

Of course, though pop-up blinds offer great advantages, owning one isn't a prerequisite to hunting from the ground. For years before their acceptance, countless hunters successfully took deer from the ground without them. Heck, one of the first bucks I ever took with a bow came when I was hiding behind a deadfall.

When selecting a location to hide, use many of the same guidelines as you would for selecting a tree for a stand. You want to be 15–20 yards off the animal's line of sight and have a surplus of back cover. Backing into the top of a deadfall, a clump of brush or even using tall grass will work. However, for those concerned with the wind, it's even more critical that this ambush spot be downwind of the deer.

Though many hunters may cringe at the idea, sitting on the ground, using nothing but Mother Nature as concealment, can be an effective hunting tactic.

After that, the biggest tricks are to remain motionless and only draw when the buck's looking away. I'm not trying to pretend that hunters won't get busted, but they really can pull this off much easier than most believe. When all else fails, don't be afraid to try it. You just may be pleasantly surprised by the results.

## CONCLUSION

Following the guidelines in this chapter will allow readers to get the most from hunting on the ground. Take it from me, not only does adding this tactic greatly expand the number of locations one can effectively hunt, it's just plain a rush to be nose-to-nose with an unsuspecting buck! Try it and see for yourself how addicting that can get.

# Consistently Scoring on Public Land

When Wisconsin hunter Jeff Severson saw the buck approaching, he couldn't believe his eyes. There, sneaking through a creek bottom, was a buck that would gross score well over 220 inches! More amazingly still, a group of duck hunters was sitting on a pond, pounding away at the skies, merely 100 yards away.

Although he already had an impressive number of Pope & Young bucks to his credit, Jeff knew this one was in a class all its own. Even later, as he walked up to his downed trophy, Severson was amazed.

Certainly, the unbelievable rack was part of the amazement, but where the buck was calling home was every bit as mind-boggling. Despite gaining exclusive bowhunting access for himself and his small hunting party to thousands of acres of prime Kansas farms, he'd taken this buck from land open to public hunting. Even more amazing, the nearby pond and grass fields were hammered hard by hunters. Yet both the area's sign and reports from nearby farmers all confirmed that the monster buck had called this easily accessed swath of cover home.

As a matter of fact, the only reason Jeff was hunting the area that day was because the duck hunters told him about the deer they saw there. Even with all the sign in the area, Jeff was reluctant to hunt it. With the nearly constant blasts from the shotguns so close to the small patch of cover, he'd decided to give himself only until 8 a.m. before calling it quits.

Jeff Severson poses with the net 220-inch non-typical monster he took off public land.

Frankly, Severson didn't really buy that he was going to encounter a shooter buck there, and who would blame him? After all, what self-respecting mature buck, let alone a world-class monster, would call an easily accessed sliver of cover on public land overrun with duck and pheasant hunters home? Particularly when the buck had endless miles of seemingly better options to choose from. My answer to that is, a very smart buck!

Hunting lands open to public hunting is a vastly different animal than hunting tightly controlled private lands. Often, the same tactics TV and magazine experts preach as deadly are just that, when used on heavily hunted public lands; deadly to your chances of taking a good buck.

Though many hunters fall into the trap of believing that mature bucks don't exist on these public grounds, at least not on the ones they hunt, that belief is incorrect a high percentage of the time. Whitetails are extremely adaptable creatures. It's that very trait that leads many hunters to the incorrect conclusion that the big bucks have either all been killed or relocated off the public ground that they hunt.

The reality is that the bucks able to reach maturity have adapted to avoid hunting pressure, often making them all but invisible during season. Don't believe me? Consider this: In the last three years, I've written 14 stories profiling world-class bucks. When I say world-class, I mean bucks grossing over 190 inches as typicals and over 210 inches in the non-typical category. As I said, world-class bucks. Of the 14, four of them have come from lands open to public hunting. That's just over 28 percent!

Now, I'd be the first to admit that there are a lot more great trophy-hunting opportunities to be had on private lands than on public. Heck, I sincerely believe that it's easier to take a Pope & Young buck on many of these tightly managed pieces of private ground than it is to take a yearling buck on many pieces of public ground. However, as my non-scientific sampling and personal hunting experiences illustrate, mature bucks certainly do live to old age on pieces of public ground.

The first trick to taking these mature bucks involves forgetting most of the "cool" hunting tactics you read about and watch on TV. Most of the people teaching them either rely on outfitters to set them up on bucks or hunt such tightly managed ground that they have almost nothing in common with what the average hunter must do to take a good buck. Next, one must avoid hunting like everyone else.

The author was able to take this buck by targeting an easily accessed sliver of cover that all the other public-land hunters ignored.

## GOING WHERE "THEY" AREN'T

Let's begin this exploration of public-land hunting by addressing that last concern. It only stands to reason that, since a buck successfully eluded the hunting masses to reach maturity, the same tactics that the masses use aren't going to work well on him. Therefore, to be successful, one must break out of the norm.

Doing so begins with the critical first step of hunting where other deer hunters don't. When you pull up to a parking lot overflowing with the trucks of other hunters, it may be hard to believe that there is such a place, but most tracts of public land do have areas that deer hunters rarely step foot on. Finding those pockets is the key.

When scouting public land, the first thing I look for is not pockets of deer; it's the areas that other hunters won't be in. Having hunted public lands every year since I was 12, including tracts in a half-dozen different states and provinces, I've found that these pockets fall into a handful of different groupings.

When most hunters think of getting away from everyone, their minds drift to hiking miles back in to a deer stand. When the area is expansive enough, that certainly is one method. Truth be told, though, even getting one mile from the closest vehicle access point is almost always enough to have the woods to yourself. I have become convinced that hunters must suffer from a rare and highly contagious affliction that causes them to multiply the distance they walk to stands by the minimum of a factor of two. That would explain why so many sincerely believe that they're at least a mile back in, but almost none are over a half-mile from the road.

The next grouping of overlooked pockets runs off the same principle that causes remote areas to go unhunted—the areas that go untouched because they require more physical exertion than most hunters are willing to endure. Three settings that I've hunted immediately come to mind as fitting in this group.

The first was a nice piece of ground in the west-central portion of my home state of Wisconsin. The piece has everything going for it: sizable woods, agricultural land and high deer numbers. Because of that, it comes as no surprise that it's also heavily hunted.

Around a quarter-mile off the crop field, running the length of the property, is a deep gully. Trust me, it truly is a pain to cross, but the rewards were worth it. When I hunted that area, I passed hunters almost every time I was heading to my stands. Yet I never saw a single other hunter on the other side.

Not surprisingly, I did see four Pope & Young qualifying bucks the year I hunted back in there. Frankly, I would have taken pokes at three different bucks in the high 120s, if it hadn't been for the pain that getting them out would have been. Another reason I passed them was the 150-plus-inch 10-point that narrowly escaped me. Because he never had a clue I was there, I held out hope that I'd eventually take him. Though I saw him three separate times, two close calls and a distant sighting was all I have to show for it. Still, unless the hunters I spoke to on the field side of the ravine were keeping it a secret, not one of them ever saw any of those bucks there.

I had a very similar experience when hunting in Illinois. There, a square mile of timber was open to hunting. Because one had to sign in and out each day, I can tell you that the place was crawling

Being willing to cross water barriers can open the door to pockets of virtually unpressured public lands.

with other hunters. On the worst day I hunted it, I counted 32 other names. Still, I never saw a single hunter from my stand.

The reason was because three huge ridges ran north-south, paralleling each other. With the only access permitted to the land being from the east and west, despite being less than a half-mile walk in, I knew that I'd have the center ridge to myself. It took two gut-busting, lung-searing climbs to get there, but doing that also resulted in numerous encounters with bucks, including one that can thank an unseen branch for saving his life.

The third location involved a slashing of poplar regrowth, resulting from a quarter-mile-wide strip along the road being clear-cut seven years before I hunted it. Anyone who has ever walked a quarter-mile through a seven-year-old poplar slashing with a tree stand on his back understands that it truly is the definition of hell on earth.

However, the back-side edge, where the slashing met with mature woods, produced several excellent stand sites. For what it's worth, I can tell you that dragging the nearly 300-pound buck I shot from there back through the slashing was harder than walking in with a stand.

The point of these three examples is that most hunters aren't willing to cross major obstacles. Though I had to temporarily agree with their reasoning as I dragged the buck through the slashing, each time I look at him on my wall I remember the rewards of having those types of areas all to myself, despite the hordes of other hunters perched in the easier-accessed sections.

The next grouping of often-untouched pockets also includes an obstacle: water. For some reason, most hunters won't cross water that goes above their rubber boots. Simply slapping on a pair of hip boots or jumping in a canoe has opened the doors for me to many untouched pockets of land on the other side.

Lastly, there's the group that rarely requires extra work to get to—pockets that are often located near the easiest access there is, and are simply overlooked by other hunters. As was the case with Jeff Severson's magnificent buck, sometimes that is due to the established presence of humans. Whether it's because the pocket is close to a house, next to a highway or surrounded by pheasant and duck hunters, bucks learn fast which human activities are a threat and which aren't. Because these human activities drive other hunters away, they also often draw the big bucks in. Spending their daytime hours surrounded by humans in such places, they often live without experiencing a hint of deer-hunting pressure.

Another common type of overlooked area consists of small pockets of trees where there are abundant larger woodlots. That's the perfect description for the area I took another nice public-land buck from. The setting was a large chunk of public land in the central portion of Wisconsin. With big timber and swamps on both sides of the road, everyone ignored the 40-acre native-grass field. About halfway down it, right along the road, stood a small chunk of woods. Because it was impossible to get in and out without clearing any deer inside, it was left alone. However, a quick scout of the area revealed that most deer were bedding in the grass.

Right after climbing into the stand the first time, even before first light, the images streaking through the tall grass were unmistakable. With the deep, telltale grunts following shortly after, there was no denying that the buck dogging the doe was a good one. Over the painfully long 10 minutes it took for shooting light to arrive, they would flash through my field of view numerous times.

Finally, I could make out the buck. Seeing he was a good 10-point, I swiftly decided to take the first ethical shot opportunity he presented. I just

When on heavily hunted grounds, instead of keying on deer sign, focusing on avoiding other hunters will most often put you where the mature bucks live.

needed the doe to lead him back toward the half-acre square of woods my stand sat in.

Before long, she decided to cooperate. From well over 100 yards away, she put on a buttonhook maneuver and made a beeline to my stand. I came to full draw as she approached and I waited until the buck entered the 20-yard mark. With the doe to my left, I voiced a fawn distress call, believing my best chance of stopping the buck lay in stopping his prize.

Mirroring her every move, the buck froze behind her. All that was left was settling the pin behind his front shoulder and willing the arrow to fly true. A series of frantic bounds later, my buck crumpled on the other side of a dirt road. Once again, going where other hunters weren't enabled me to take a good buck out of heavily hunted public grounds.

## HUNT CLOSE TO THE BED

The next method of differentiating yourself from the others is, when the tract of land is heavily pressured, forget about hunting the food sources, forget about hunting the funnels, forget about hunting the impressive sign. Mature bucks conduct almost all of the activities those stands are set to take advantage of after dark.

Instead, find his bedding area and, just like during the lull phase, hunt as close as you can get without him knowing you're there. Remember, these bucks aren't like the ones you commonly read about or see on TV They survive heavy hunting pressure by not making themselves easy targets. Along with avoiding areas with deer hunters when possible, that also means they don't move much when deer hunters are in the woods.

I've recently been seeing a lot of press from an outdoor writer who sings the praises of hunting

Public lands can offer great hunting opportunities, assuming you don't hunt like everyone else.

public land during mid-day. He believes that bucks move then because other hunters aren't in the woods.

Though I do admire his hunting abilities and he honestly is one of only a handful of "experts" who hunt in a way I respect, I still must disagree with him. I do fully agree that hunting mid-day is productive on both lightly and heavily pressured public lands. However, on the heavily pressured lands, unless you are lucky enough to have a relatively large pocket to yourself, it has always been my experience that the mature bucks rarely venture far from their bedding areas at mid-day, morning or evening. During legal shooting light, they're close to their beds or they're already dead. So you must also be close to their beds to arrow them.

There are two notable exceptions to this that I've found. One is during bad weather. I believe that some of these bucks have been trained to realize that bad weather drives hunters from the woods. Because of this, they tend to move more freely during periods of heavy winds or rain. That makes those good conditions for hunters to be in the woods.

Don't get me wrong. I personally believe it is unethical to shoot a buck during heavy rains. I've had bucks run close to 200 yards on double-lung hits. During a heavy rain, even finding them would be difficult. If the shot is off at all, with all the blood washed away, it is like trying to find a needle in a haystack. However, the second the rain starts letting up, I want to already be in position!

The other exception is hunting doe-bedding areas during the rut. Even heavily hunted public-land bucks sometimes fall prey to having the desire to breed overpowering their better judgment. Not only will they abandon the safety of their bedding areas to stay with a hot doe, they'll also get up and follow her if she insists on moving. That makes setting up on her bedroom a good option.

When he absolutely, positively refuses to move during daylight, it's time to go in after him.

This strategy hinges on beating him into his bedding area. That may require being in stand as much as two or three hours before first light. Even if you beat him in, chances are high that it will still be dark when he returns to his bed. That means you'll now have to remain undetected until shooting light arrives. If he's bedded within shooting range and in the proper orientation, the shot can be taken then. If not, it demands waiting until he eventually stands to relieve himself. This is a demanding and risky tactic that should be saved as a last resort, but it can work when he is only willing to move after dark.

## DON'T DRAW ATTENTION

Keeping with the theme of hunting differently from others, heavily hunted land is not the place for calls, decoys or rattling. These bucks survive by avoiding anything out of the ordinary. Since this survivor has resisted coming to every other hunter's calling and rattling efforts, don't be arrogant enough to believe he won't be able to resist yours.

Along the lines of keeping a low profile, this is also not the place to trim large shooting lanes. Just because these warriors avoid hunters during the day doesn't mean they aren't being educated by them during the night. You can bet that he's investigated the disturbances created by freshly hung stands many times before. I can't tell you how many times I've tracked deer in the snow that purposefully make wide arcs around other hunter's stands. Believe me, they know what's up when the ground is suddenly littered with cut branches and a three-foot-wide lane magically appears.

As on more lightly hunted lands, I strive to do any significant clearing of lanes in the spring. Even then, I do far less pruning on heavily hunted public lands. Besides, it isn't legal to prune anything on many public lands. When placing stands during season, I never nip more than a branch or two, even when legal. When I'm forced to do that, I use a pruning tool to avoid leaving fresh sawdust behind, and I remove the branches from the area. The last thing I want is to raise a buck's curiosity and have him come in to investigate the area after dark.

Between following my odor-reduction techniques, limiting pruning to a minimum and not leaving curiosity-raising sawdust behind, I lower the odds of having to pass the sniff test.

## TOOLS OF THE TRADE

Several products and tools can make hunting public lands easier. The first are a mountain bike, bike light, rack and bike lock. With a rack on back to strap your bow to and a light to show the way, a mountain bike can let you get way back in much easier than walking on many of the larger tracts of public land.

However, when you're either hunting way back in or on the other side of difficult obstacles to cross, you must remember that, assuming you're-lucky enough to arrow Mr. Big, you also have to get him out. That's where a good deer cart can come in very handy. They may not work well in seven-year-old poplar slashings, but they can save many sore muscles in a lot of other settings. As a side note, when there's snow on the ground, the kid's long plastic snow sled works even better.

Lastly, though it should be a given that the hunter already has studied a topo map to help him find the unhunted pockets, he should also bring that map out hunting with him. Along with a flashlight and compass or GPS, topo maps are very helpful if you get turned around. For any of you who have tracked many deer after dark, you fully understand how easy that can be. The difference between doing so in farm country and on a large tract of public land is a slight inconvenience verses a long night in the woods.

## CONCLUSION

When you really think about it, there are two categories of mature bucks that most of us will encounter over our hunting lives. There are those that are exposed to heavy hunting pressure and those that endure moderate pressure. The tactics you read about in many articles and watch on a lot of TV shows will work, to various extents, on the properties experiencing moderate pressure, such as many family farms or your typical lease.

Truth be told, a lot of these hunting methods are ideally suited for hunting the third category of mature bucks: bucks that receive extremely light and tightly controlled hunting pressure. For the minority of hunters who are lucky enough to chase these bucks, almost everything they try is more effective. Unfortunately, most of us will never experience that kind of hunting.

When deciding on hunting strategies, the first step is determining which group the bucks you're hunting fall into. Then you can truly analyze which strategies make sense. Taking this critical step gives hunters a fighting chance on any piece of whitetail ground.

Luckily, despite what many hunters believe, mature bucks do exist on many tracts of public land. Just remember that they are true survivors and our hunting tactics must be tailored to that fact. Find the pockets where other hunters aren't; set up near the buck's or does' bedding areas, depending on the phase of season; take advantage of the times other hunters aren't in the woods; and, above all else, don't draw attention to yourself. Do those things and you just may be surprised at how many mature bucks your area's public lands hold.

Last, but certainly not least, don't forget your map and compass! If you spend much time in the big woods, you'll thank me for that piece of advice later.

Studying topo maps will help you find the pockets not touched by other hunters. Having a compass will help you get back out again!

# Wallhanger Whereabouts

So much for the when and how. *Where* are the whitetail knockouts? Two words: Near and far. Head north, head south, but don't forget the prairies. Although anybody can tag a nice deer just about anywhere these days, statistics don't lie. Here's the lowdown on where you want to plan your next vacation.

## Canadian Deer, Eh?

Soon I'll be compromising my standards as I cross the northern border to hunt whitetails. Yep, I'm heading for Canada, the land of the racked giants. What's wrong with that? After all, every well-heeled trophy seeker—from the Dick Idols and Gordon Whittingtons to the Charlie Alsheimers and David Morrises—make annual treks to the land of sky-blue waters to rattle up Boone and Crockett monsters. Well, for one thing it's a big-buck proposition, all right— costs typically run $2,000–$3,000 or more. Truthfully, I enjoy hunting public lands in the Midwest with friends and family just as much (I have done so successfully for nearly 30 years; all it costs me is the price of a license, food and transportation). Besides, my home in northern Minnesota is every bit as picturesque as Canada's forested provinces.

Moreover, one must hire the services of a guide or outfitter to hunt super-whitetails in Alberta, Manitoba or Saskatchewan. Though I'm going to enjoy a pair of hunts with some folks I can't wait to meet in the next couple of years, the stigma of a guide expecting favorable press—no matter what—is not always worth the hassle. And guides can mess up.

For example, one time I hunted my fanny off with a guide in South Dakota who simply had not done his homework. He failed to make proper connections with a particular landowner who inexplicably decided to let his cattle roam precisely the creek bottoms we had hoped to bowhunt. To make matters worse, those dang cattle followed us around like Mary s little lambs, spooking deer out of cover and into the prairie (where we couldn't get close).

Now, I like the guide and continue to recommend his services to my readers. But the episode raises a valid point: When you pay to hunt with someone, you better know what you're getting into. Don't leave anything to speculation. Find out ahead of time the basics—style of hunting, clothing needs and accessory requirements. More important, find out if the guide or outfitter is flexible. This alone could make or break your hunt. A case in point is a Canadian booking in which Myles Keller found himself hunting November hotspots in October. Myles didn't feel free to improvise, so he bit the broadhead. Frankly, Myles is not the kind of bowhunter who needs a chaperon. Just give the guy the lay of the land, and he'll finish the job. So because some provincial regulations require close supervision of non-residents at all times, I suggest you get a good handle on what you can and cannot do on your dream trip.

And what a dream trip it can be. Long before Milo Hanson's new No. 1 whitetail made Saskatchewan a household name, big-buck zealots sneaked discreetly over the border to harvest the spoils of North America's largest-bodied deer. Indeed, Bergmann's Rule decrees that the higher the latitude, the larger the homeotherm. Alaska moose are bigger than their Maine counterparts: Manitoba elk are bigger than their Colorado brethren; even Minnesota raccoons weigh substantially more than their Louisiana cousins.

These Northern giants are among the largest of 30 individually documented subspecies of white tails, and they stand head and shoulders above the rest in two respects. Their massive surface area maintains core body heat more efficiently in the frigid zone, and a larger body consistently grows larger antlers; evidence of the impressive *mass* of Canadian whitetail racks shows up in the record books every new scoring period.

But there's another reason you should take a Canadian trip in the near future: Thanks to unseasonably mild winters in recent years, the deer herd continues to expand in many regions. And, as any hunterbiologist can tell you, an expanding whitetail herd means disproportionately high numbers of record-book animals. This is why Illinois has been hot, why some river systems in Ohio continue to grow eye-popping racks, and why Kansas is hot today.

Want to score in Canada? The boreal forest "bush" is governed by a few key fundamentals. Heed their calling and dine on venison sausage (the big ol' buck's too tough to fry, anyway), or ignore them and sip on stone soup.

- Go prepared to hunt all day, no matter how cold the weather. Harvey McDonald, with Elusive Saskatchewan Whitetail Outfitters, states flatly that deer in his neck of the woods tend to be active during middle-of-the-day hours. He cited the psychological comfort of the timbered bush that makes deer feel safer than usual during daylight hours. Then there's the comfy afternoon temperatures that give deer an added incentive to feed before nightfall. A mid to late-afternoon Moon time in Saskatchewan, where baiting is currently legal, is almost cheating.
- Forgive the broken record, but let's not forget the Moon. Is it any wonder that the much-traveled David Morris, founder and publisher of *Game & Fish* Publications, meticulously schedules Canadian hunting trips around a Full Moon during the rut? It works: In mid-November 1994, he rattled to gun a dandy Boone & Crockett buck at lunchtime. Not coincidentally, on the very next day hundreds of miles away, nationally respected whitetail photographer Charlie Alsheimer rattled up a 170-class Booner, again at midday.
- Relatively few deer in wall-to-wall cover doesn't sound like very good odds. Fortunately hunting rut sign works because of the even buck-to-doe ratio. Hang a portable along a fresh rub or scrape line, especially one situated along funnels and in strip cover. And don't forget the grunt tube.
- Discriminating bowhunters should hunt agricultural areas early—starting in late-August. (Remember Don McGarvey's Alberta monster arrowed in September.)
- Rattles rub 'em the right way. It's no secret that in some camps, such as Classic Outfitters in Alberta, rattling accounts for 50 percent of bucks sighted. Find last year's rutting corridor with this year's rubs, and you might call in the buck of 10 lifetimes. Again, deer in forested regions with

Check out these massive Manitoba sheds, eh.

balanced buck-to-doe populations rely more on signpost and auditory communication than deer in agricultural lands where the herd is typically top-heavy with female deer; a surplus of does reduces competition among bucks, so what's to fight over? Conversely, does are spread pretty thin up North, and the guy walking silently carrying big rattle-bangers is playing the odds.

Put it together—good midday movement, the most comfortable time of day, the call of the mating season, the pull of the Moon—and it's airtight! Remove the Moon from the equation, however, and you'll be scratching and clawing to redeem your hunt.

So what else is new, eh?

## Texas: Similar But Different

The deer population in Texas—nearing 4 million—exceeds all other states, and hunting is a $1.5 billion industry—an impressive figure compared to the $289 million hunters spend in my home state of Minnesota. Although only 80,000 archery licenses are sold annually in the Lone Star State, bowhunting is spreading rapidly Because the state is only 2 percent public lands, most hunters belong to clubs that lease hunting rights on private ranches. Many of these lands are intensively managed for deer. You may not get what you pay for, if you don't take advantage of the Texas scene.

Larry Weishuhn needs no introduction to Texas hunters. As a former state biologist, consultant to several ranches and a frequent contributor to popular literature such as *Texas Trophy Hunters*, Larry knows "deer hunting biology" as well as anyone. When I asked him how he hunts Texas by the Moon, he didn't skip a beat.

"In many respects Texas deer are similar to [those in] other areas," he began. "Even though we don't have the lakes and streams and prolific acorn-bearing oaks that hunters typically associate with whitetail strategies, we hunt bottlenecks and funnels just like everybody else. But the ones I rely on are a little different: a unique patchwork of low-growing bushes and tall brush. It's hard to put into words, but once you get a feel for it, you'll know what I'm talking about.

"Feeding areas are a bit different, too. Almost anything that's green is considered food to deer. And while some ranchers put out bait, most of it's available 24 hours a day. So it's a lot like acorns on the ground in a big white-oak stand. In north-Texas, Spanish acorns are important, and in the brush country down South, everything is browse, browse, browse.

"My hunting strategy is fairly simple, actually. I like to hunt hard all day, even though I know that peak deer activity periods coincide with Moon position. I routinely head out before dark, and usually won't show up till after sunset unless I've got my buck.

"Down here, food sources are very important to a hunter. For instance, bucks tend to eat a lot of prickly pear [cactus] during December in one of my favorite areas. I think it's because [the cactus] is fairly palatable, high in vitamin A and carbohydrates. And it's pretty succulent, providing much-needed moisture. In some areas bucks—not all of them, but certain individuals—will continue to return to the same clump of prickly pear to feed just about every time they pass through the area. They do this year after year. Find one of these clumps that's been eaten down and you can set up a tripod [treestand] and wait them out or rattle, it the timing is right.

"As I said, I find that my most productive rattling occurs when the Moon's up. I've called in way more bucks at this time; when the Moon pulls [on a buck's] instincts to fill his rumen, he'll be up and moving and more inclined to investigate the sound of antlers. So I'm definitely mindful of those peak times and I always try to be in key areas when they occur.

Larry Weishuhn, one of the country's original Moon hunters, with one of eight bucks he killed in 1994 (next time you see Weishuhn, ask if he's had a "falling out" with Robert Goulet).

"Stillhunting areas I know hold bucks, based on the frequency and size of rubs and scrapes, is a good way to work myself into position, especially if the peak feeding times are, say, midday or early afternoon. If there's something out there deer really like to eat, so much the better. And, by the way, water can be critical in Texas, too. We're blessed—or cursed, depending on your point of view—with highly fluctuating water levels. This turns some stock dams and ponds into a food plot of sorts—when water levels recede, the perimeter sprouts with tender forbs. If the Moon's right and surrounding coveris adequate, big bucks are apt to water and feed right on schedule [with the Moon].

"Stillhunting, glassing and sitting periodically all work in conjunction with predictable habits of Texas whitetails. Another thing: Hunting out of a vehicle is legal in Texas. I'm not talking about 'road hunting' here, but extensive use of a 4 × 4 to quickly eliminate unproductive areas."

"What throws many non-resident hunters off," said Bob Zaiglin, "is the diverse habitat of Texas. Eastern Texas is quite similar to the Southeastern United States—some hardwoods, some pine stands. The [central] Hill Country is a smattering of dense thickets—scrub oak, juniper, dense shrubbery—in a rolling, broken 1andscape. Farther north, it's basically grown up antelope country: mesquite, scattered hardwoods and brushy draws. Here, forbs are especially important.

"South Texas' famous brush country doesn't have the forbs, but with all the nutritious browse, the deer don't need it. Finally, the southeast coastal region, the King Ranch area, is mostly sandy-loam soils where deer subsist more on forbs and less on browse species. So it's a very dynamic, changing

Jerry Johnston, publisher of *Texas Trophy Hunters*, thinks that the "lunar effect" is the hottest topic in the whitetail world since rattling.

environment you must become familiar with to hunt properly."

What food sources do bucks seem to prefer? According to Zaiglin, the number-one choice of the brush country's successional stage growth is Granjeno, which is 21 percent crude protein. Also: lime prickly ash (an aromatic, thorny bush), LaComa and acacias legumes (nitrogen-fixing plants high m crude protein).

"Bucks can bed and feed in the same area because of all the cover," Zaiglin said. "However, shade m the semi-arid region is critical, and persimmon and taller-growing plants are important for preventing long-distance movements during heat-of-the-day periods."

OK, besides feeding and bedding areas, what about transitional habitat? "Bucks bed up in the thickest country we have for protection from coyotes," Zaiglin said. "When deer move, they feed along the way, so their 'transition zone' is also a feeding zone. They have an inner bedding area and an extended transitional feeding zone, because the brush country's forage species are so abundant and varied that they enhance [the deer's] nutritional opportunities. These bucks are not dependent on hardwoods or grainfields with all of the nutrient-rich browse."

A final key to Texas is fresh rain following a drought. Natural regenerated forage—brand new terminal shoots—are preferred by deer over anything, including corn, Zaiglm says.

## A Prayer For The Prairies

A recurring nightmare has plagued me for about 25 years. My wife thinks it's hilarious, but the dream is so real I often wake up in a cold sweat. Ooh, I'm shivering at the mere thought of it, as I recall the details:

I'm before a judge, having been cited for some sort of game violation. (One time it was having too many arrows in my quiver; another time I was charged with hunting too many states in the fall; still another time I was hauled before the court when a virused computer declared my license number null and void. The details change, but the theme remains constant: constant haranguing by the law.)

"Well?" asks the judge, leaning over a shiny oak bench. "Well, what?" I ask.

"I'll have you in contempt of court, if you smart off one more time like that," he snaps. "Well… how do you plead?"

The words roll off my tongue without me having any control over them. "No contest, your honor. I'm not guilty. I mean, this law isn't.

"You can't plead no contest ***and*** not guilty," the judge interrupts. "Make up your mind."

Fumbling for politically correct words for this most delicate of moments, I respond," What I mean is, your excellency . . . "

"Guilty!" the judge declares, slamming a gavel in my camouflaged face. "I'll teach you to flatter me. Excellency huh? I sentence you to . . . "

At this, a hush falls before the court. Babies stop crying, toddlers quit fidgeting, the bailiff no longer jingles keys in his pocket, even the court reporter stops reporting.

"I sentence you to one," the judge continues, pausing for effect, "and only one habitat to hunt deer for the rest of your life. Well, Mr. Murray? Speak up now. Which shall it be?"

One habitat? Gee. Does he mean what I think he means?

Fingers tap loudly on oak veneer, first the pinkie, last the forefinger. "Well?"

"That's easy. Omnipotent One," I say. "I'll take the prairies. You know— Kansas, southern Minnesota, Nebraska, the Dakotas, Texas, Colorado, Manitoba, Saskatchewan, Alberta . . . "

As absurd as this sounds, I got off easy. Whitetails are fun to hunt anywhere— from the deep woods of Maine or Minnesota to a Georgia beanfield or a Kansas wheatfield—and the prairies top my list. Three reasons:

First, prairie deer are large-bodied animals compared to other subspecies of whitetail deer, and therefore grow impressive racks. The ***dakotensis*** and t***exanus*** subspecies account for a disproportionate percentage of record-book racks (the ***borealis*** subspecies is close behind).

Second, whitetails often reach full maturity in open, largely uninhabited spaces of the prairies, and this, along with genetics and nutrition, is a prerequisite for growing impressive headgear. (Speaking of nutrition, the nutrient-rich soils of the prairie make it the breadbasket of the world.)

And third, hunting the prairie environment is never dull. You get to see lots of deer. Prairie deer occupy a unique niche in the whitetail world, one that presents uncommon opportunities and obstacles. Joe Admire, a soft-spoken outdoorsman from Tulsa, Oklahoma, has studied these deer for 30 years. Here are some "admirable" tips:

- Get the jump by scouting in late summer when deer are bunched up and feeding contentedly in the open. The mature, dominant bucks break timber and feed in fields. Alfalfa is their top food choice, and you'll see a lot of big bucks because they typically bed in draws several miles away to distance themselves from roaming cattle and ranching operations.
- Open the season between feeding and bedding areas (during a favorable Moon). This is how I arrowed that Nebraska eight-pointer I mentioned earlier. "Take a stand on the edge of the cover so you can see which trails the bucks are using and which ones the does are sticking with," Admire says. "Then you can glass and hunt at the same time."

One important footnote: Some prairie seasons don't open until October. Roll with the punches. "One September morning I saw 13 Pope and Young bucks in a particular coulee," Admire says. "But by the time the season opened, they'd vanished. When October rolls around and acorns begin to fall, the deer completely change their patterns. They file into the draws and coulees that are closest to oak stands.

Hunt the prairie like Oklahoman Joe Admire, and you might nail a buck like this one that netted 166 2/8.

And bucks become nearly nocturnal at this time. You probably won't see a single book buck until the first does go into heat." (Incidentally, a typical prairie diet preference goes like this: alfalfa, beans, sunflowers, milo, corn and winter wheat.)

**Bucks In Your Pocket**

Jim Hill has a few good bucks to his credit, thanks to the praine country of southern Minnesota and the eastern Dakotas. Here are a few pocket pointers:

- Come prepared to "scramble around like a coyote," as mentioned earlier. Hill thinks most bowhunters blow it on prairie deer by not maintaining a super-low profile. Sew knee pads on your trousers. Get used to looking for sand burrs and other prickly plants (to know the sting of pain is to Deify crawl over a toy cactus.)
- To avoid being made out by sharp-eyed prairie deer, take *a* hard, close look at your outer garments. Hill agrees with Myles Keller that most camouflage patterns are too dark; they show up as a distinct "human blob" on the landscape. Patterns that work well for conventional treestand hunting usually won't do out on the flats. Backland (All Terrain) is surprisingly effective as is Realtree All-Purpose Grey.
- Develop a glass eye. Hill, like Myles, typically spends days on end just watching for deer to take the same route a couple of days in a row. "Once you bump deer in the sparse cover of the Dakotas and southern Canadian provinces, the bucks will exchange brushy bottoms for open hills," Hill says. "They'll bed where they can wind you from behind yet spot you a mile away. You're cooked."
- Look for patterns Involving potential ambush points. For example, prairie white-tails tend to follow "structure" from point A to point B-a dimple in the landscape, a fenceline or a tree or two. When a buck passes near a certain geographic landform more than once. Hill says, you better take note.

Especially keep the element of surprise on your side when hunting out-of-the-way pockets, Hill says: "Most of these deer have never seen a human in this stuff, and that's why they hole up out here. If you're sneaky, you can score."

Noted last words from a notoriously sneaky guy.

- Now, forget about bucks and key on does. "What does do in October is pretty much what they'll be doing during the rut," Admire says. "The bucks are into the same basic routine, often bedding in close proximity to one another, but again, you just won't see them. They're beginning to set up rub and scrape lines near the concentration of does." For the first time, bucks become territorial; so if you monitor individual doe groups, you can keep in touch with the bucks.

- By the end of October (sometimes the first week of November), buck groups totally break up. You'll see individual animals in the search mode, and if you've done your homework as explained, you could be in for a treat. This is the time period that Admire and his son, Joe Jr., recently arrowed three Pope and Young bucks within a week. "It's as good as it gets," the studious bowhunter maintains.
- During the rutting peak, hunting can be decent, but luck can work against you. For example, Admire believes that when a mature doe goes into heat, a dominant breeding buck has "first rights" in the pecking order. Because does bed predictably in low pockets at night where air currents settle—providing the safest zone for deer—a buck has little trouble locating her. He'll lead her away from the rest of the herd to avoid competition from rival bucks. This occurs mainly at night for about seven or eight days in a row; the buck will probably breed four or five does during that time.

This goes on largely unnoticed, and it often "takes place out in the prairie, away from the cover" you're hunting, Admire says. While the rut "can move deer into your lap, it has a way of working against you."

How true. While hunting with Bird-n-Buck Outfitters during the 1993 rut, I found myself in the same stand Joe Jr. had taken his pair of Pope and Young bucks 10 days earlier. Though I had three nice bucks within bow range in three days of hunting—and I saw another half-dozen in the distance chasing does—the deck seemed stacked against me. Every buck zoomed through my area in pursuit of a hot doe. Close but no Havana. So:

- If you don't score on a big buck in early November, your best bet during the rut is simply waiting it out. "Don't do anything foolish such as wandering off for greener grass. Or hopscotching from stand to stand," Admire says. "You'll only end up telegraphing your presence. Be patient." Hunt hospital clean, and play the wind by setting up several stands to cover a hot area like the back end of a stock dam—a classic Oklahoma funnel (ditto for an elbow or bend at the base of a steep wall).
- Hunt hard from Thanksgiving to Christmas. The key is making two factors work together—a shortage of breedable does and predictable feeding patterns. The first period occurs immediately following the peak of the rut. Bucks take chances when searching for late-estrous does; for a week, maybe 10 days, big bucks have had their way, but not now. So they go looking instead of waiting. Be smart and set up where bucks can look for does most efficiently.

"Late-estrous does like to bed m thickets near the rims and edges of coulees, not down in the timber," Admire says. "I've watched bucks work these thickets just like bird dogs, sniffing out patch after patch. When they find a receptive doe, the two pair off and disappear."

In some years, you won't see many big bucks in this search mode, but in other years they seem to be fairly common. Environmental factors such as drought and storms may be chief influences on how "spread out" the breeding season becomes. So is the timing of the New Moon.

# Recovering Wounded Deer

One of the most important elements to becoming a good tracker of wounded deer is to become intimately familiar with a deer's anatomy. This includes knowing everything you can about its internal organs and its skeletal, muscular, arterial, and cardiovascular systems. It is also crucial to learn all you can about the deer's hide. Understanding where certain hair has come from on the animal will help you identify or ID the part of the body you hit. Knowing deer hair ID will help you make an educated guess at the hit sight and as to what the deer will do, where it might go and how long it might take for the deer to bed down or expire.

Understanding the skeletal structure of a whitetail is probably one of the most crucial elements to eliminating the possibility of wounding

Understanding how to track a blood trail effectively will end in a recovered animal. Also learning to interpret all the other clues left by a wounded buck is equally as important to a successful recovery.

a deer to begin with. This is especially true for the bow hunter, who might put a broadhead through bone. There are times when a broadhead or a projectile does not penetrate the body cavity and the wound ends up being superficial. A good wounded-deer tracker has a chance of recovering the deer with a skeletal or muscular wound if the proper tracking techniques are employed from the onset. For instance, if you identify that the buck you shot has a superficial wound, your first obligation is to follow the deer to the best of your ability in order to recover it. Stay on the blood trail until it absolutely evaporates and all other sign is hopeless to find.

Remember that recovering a deer that has been hit in a non-vital area requires persistence and patience. Equally important, it requires an in-depth understanding of the wound itself. Wounds from different parts of a deer's body often leave different types of blood sign. The color of the blood can range from very dark—almost black—to light pink. Each of the different colors provides a clue as to where the deer was hit. Understanding the colors will help you quickly determine how to track the buck you are after.

This buck's tracks indicate he was walking slowly without concern for his back trail. I was able to keep a slow pace and concentrate on scanning the woods ahead of me carefully.

For instance, bright, red, crimson-colored blood calls for immediate tracking. While pinkish-colored blood, especially with tiny bubbles in it, indicates that the deer was hit in the lungs and should be allowed to rest before pursuit.

## Know Your Deer Hair

The same holds true when identifying deer hair and determining from which part of the body it came. Once a deer is hit, a good tracker marks the exact spot (or as close to the exact spot as possible) the deer was hit and immediately seeks to locate the hair that has fallen from the impact of the broadhead or bullet. Here is where a lot of novice blood-trail trackers make their first mistake. They often look for blood before looking for hair. A good tracker always looks for hair first.

I can recall wounding a deer high in its back. I knew this was where I had hit the deer because of two clues I picked up when I approached the location where I shot the deer. First, there was an absence of blood and there was a lot of hair on the ground. Looking closely at the hair, I noticed it was very coarse, hollow, long and was dark-gray with black tips. I suspected it was hair from the top of the deer's back. To make sure, I checked my pocket-sized deer hair ID chart. This is a wallet-sized portfolio with deer hair laminated on white, business-size cards with descriptions of each type of hair and from which part of the body it came.

I confirmed that this was hair from the top of the deer's back. This also explained why there was no blood at the site of impact.

Often, deer that are hit high in the back won't begin to bleed until they run 25 to 50 yards. Knowing this, I began to slowly and carefully search for more sign as I picked up the track of the running deer on hard ground. It was easy to see the direction the deer took from the scattered leaves and kicked-up dirt left behind. Within 100 yards, I found blood and was able to follow it until I found the wounded buck in a bed. I shot him as he stood up.

Upon closer examination, I found I hit him above the spine and while the wound was enough to slow him down, it wasn't a killing shot. The buck would have eventually recovered. By being able to identify the hair and knowing that the blood trail was not far ahead of me, I was able to get a second chance at this buck.

## Go Slow –Be Vigilant

When following a wounded deer, I can absolutely guarantee that all good things come to those trackers who are extremely patient and even more diligent. Following the trail of a wounded deer requires a hunter to move slowly and observe all sign when moving forward. This includes not allowing too many of your hunting buddies to join in tracking the animal before you have established some crucial evidence: where the buck was hit (by locating the hair), the color of the blood and the direction in which the deer moved off (whether in snow or on bare ground). By letting others help you, no matter how good their intentions, crucial sign will be unintentionally disturbed or eliminated when too many hunters join the search too early.

Some of the best advice I can give is to simply focus on the job at hand. Stop. Take a deep breath. Begin at the precise location where the deer was shot—this bears repeating. Once you've located hair and blood, it's important to remember to keep looking for blood in places other than on the ground. Look for sign on branches, brush, and hanging vegetation. Your next task will be to determine whether the track you're following is from a walking or a running deer. Never assume anything about the wounded animal you are following.

## Lots of Blood Doesn't Mean Dead

One of the biggest misnomers and errors when following a blood trail, is thinking the heavier the blood trail, the greater the possibility the deer was

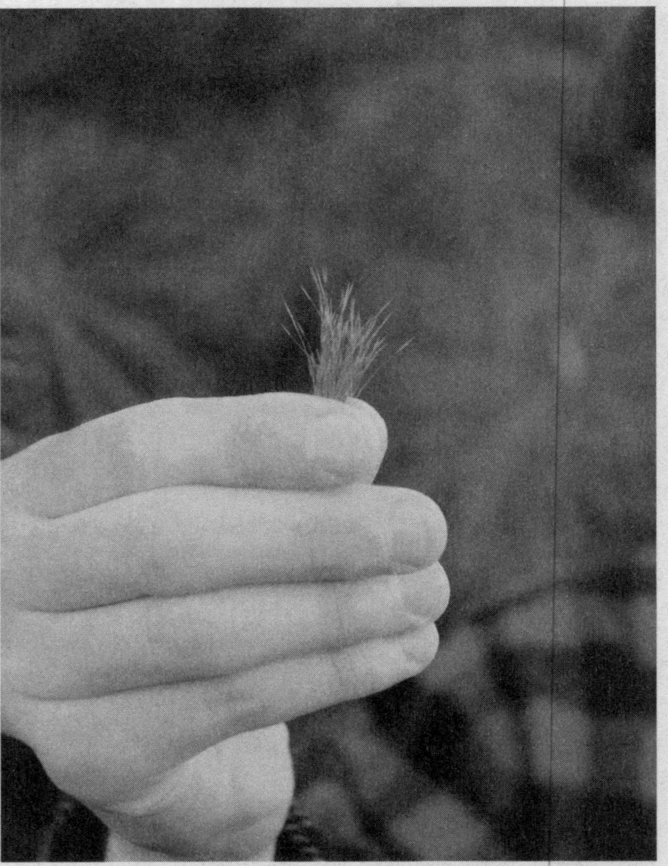

This hair indicated that the buck was shot high in the back. Being able to identify what part of the body the hair you find at a hit site is from, will help you know where the buck was hit, which will help you decide on how to track it.

fatally hit. Through experience, many of us learn this is not always the case. Many times a deer leaves a lot of blood sign, especially when the wound is superficial, but isn't fatal.

Years ago, I shot a buck from a difficult angle from a tree stand. My bullet hit the buck and I saw the buck go down. I watched it for several minutes as it laid motionless and thought it was mortally wounded. As soon as I lowered my rifle, the buck jumped to its feet and ran off. Upon approaching the site of the hit, I took my time to look for hair and blood. I find plenty of hair and an immediate blood trail. The deer hair was stiff, very coarse, dark-gray with dark tips, and was about 2½ inches long. It indicated the buck had been shot in the brisket. I knew then and there that I would have a long tracking job and would have to pay strict attention to the trail ahead if I was to get a second shot at this buck.

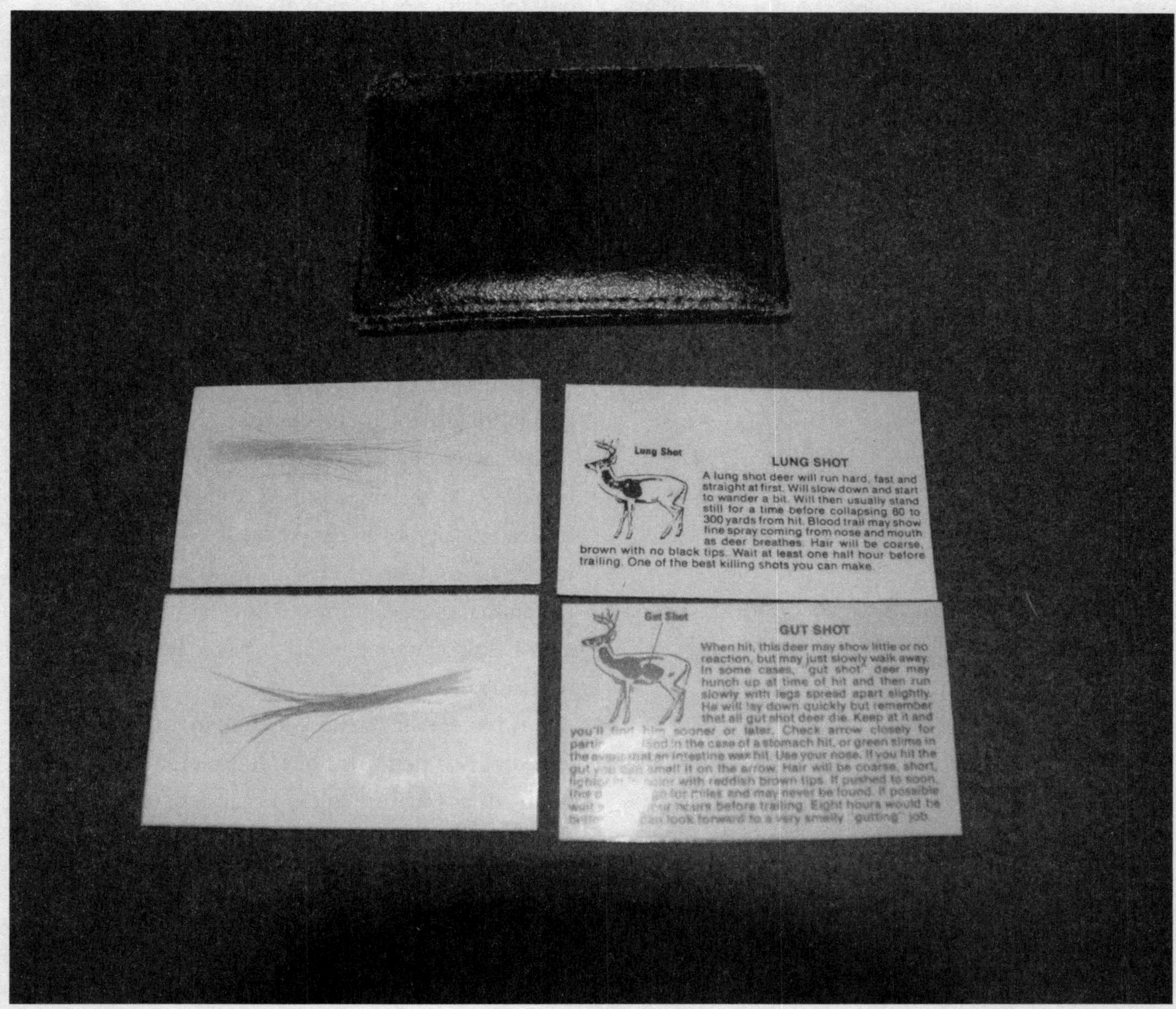


This deer hair chart has over a dozen hair samples identifying where on the deer's body they come from and suggestions on how to track the deer according to where on the body the deer was hit.

My cousin, Ralph, joined me on the trail and we tracked the buck for several hundred yards. After we had been on the trail for a long time, the buck's wound appeared to have stopped bleeding. This left us with following only his tracks on the bare ground and through a few patches of snow that were left here and there. Occasionally, we found a droplet or two of blood in areas where he stood still to watch his back trail. The buck actually passed within 20 yards of 14 of our tree stands along his escape route! Take a moment to think about that. I am not exaggerating when I tell you that this buck passed 14 of our tree stands. This is a classic example of Murphy's Law when it comes to following a wounded buck. Somehow, they instinctively know where to go and where not to go in their attempt to escape.

Get to know the neighbors surrounding your hunting land. Offer to help post their property. If they won't let you hunt, at least they may let you track a wounded deer on it.

The only stand he did not go by, of course, was the stand my wife Kate was sitting in. Eventually, the buck's trail took him on to private land. Unfortunately, we did not have permission to hunt this property. As we stood there discussing who would go back to ask for permission from the landowner, we heard a single shot ring out from the woods less than 100 yards ahead of us. As it turned out, the owner of the neighboring property shot the buck.

Understanding the blood, hair, and track sign that we were looking at enabled us to pursue the buck for a few hours. If he didn't go on to private property, we would have eventually gotten a second opportunity to finish him off.

Some of the most frequently asked questions about trailing deer are about when and where a deer will bed down, do they circle, do they travel up hill or down hill and do they go to water? It is important to note that there are no absolutes when it comes to the behavior of a wounded deer, especially a mature buck. As any seasoned hunter knows, big bucks have a tenacity for life and because of this, they tend to "die hard." I have found that the body weight of the animal often determines how far it will move after being wounded before it has to bed down or succumbs to its wound.

I remember shooting a buck in my hometown in a spot I named The Bowl. It is a unique area that often attracts mature bucks because of its extreme cover. One time, a buck about 50 yards from me was walking slowly across the Bowl. I stopped the buck with a blat call and I took my shot. I could clearly see that I hit the buck in the boiler room and was absolutely sure I would recover him within a short distance from where I hit him. When I checked the location of impact, I found blood and hair that supported the fact that I had made an excellent shot. Again, I was confident I would find the buck only a short distance away. But I did not.

I followed a heavy blood trail until the end of the day when it got too dark to trail him any further. I did everything right. I gave the buck enough time to bed down. I stayed on the track and moved slowly and methodically, keeping my eyes out in front of me. But each time I got close to the buck, I either saw or heard him slip away. I decided to let the buck bed down overnight. I was quite sure I would find him the next morning.

I picked up his blood trail at first light the next morning. To my utter amazement, I found the buck bedded, but still alive. He strained to get up. But he was, for all intents and purposes, dead on his feet. One final shot put the buck down in his tracks.

After I field dressed the buck, I was amazed to see that I hit the buck squarely in the boiler room. The bullet entered through the rib cage, took out a lung and ricocheted into the liver. How the buck survived for the length of time it did, still amazes me today.

I have experienced similar situations like this with mature bucks over the years. The old adage, "Big bucks die hard," should be remembered by anyone trailing a mature wounded whitetail buck. Whether it is hit with a broadhead or a bullet, a big deer's tenacity for life enables it to perform feats that younger deer simply can not. The point to remember here is that you should never become disillusioned when you hit a big buck well, only to find a long and arduous tracking job ahead. The fact is big deer have more stamina than their smaller brethren and use the energy in amazing ways.

Despite being double lung shot this buck managed to travel several hundred yards to where I found him dead. Knowing to track him slowly from the sign he left paid off in big dividends.

## Bedding Down

Deer that are severely hit try to bed down in thick cover as soon as they can. Even when shot in open hardwoods, a deer often moves to the security of a dense area before it beds down. This behavior some-times changes if a deer detects that a tracker is following it. Through my years of tracking wounded bucks, I have found they even seek out certain types of dense cover. My long-time hunting companions, Ralph and Leo Somma, have substantiated this. Both of these hunters have tracked their fair share of wounded deer. Ralph lives and hunts in an area in New Jersey loaded with horse and agricultural farms surrounded by dense cover. Leo, on the other hand, lives and hunts on the eastern part of Long Island. The area he hunts is also filled with dense cover. We also have a wide variety of terrain on our farms in upstate New York. Leo's farm has a lot of dense cover on it. They both told me that bucks they tracked, whether they were in New Jersey, Long Island, southern New York state or even central New York state, headed to thick cover soon after being hit. Believe it or not, dense cover includes standing fields of corn. We have all found that a wounded deer will head to standing corn. Standing corn, to a wary old buck, represents security. He instinctively knows that he can hide there safely. Be cautious when tracking a wounded deer into standing corn. It's hard to locate blood in a cornfield when the ground is bare. Be observant as you enter the corn and look for blood smeared on the stalks and leaves of the plant.

Other times, wounded deer will head to the thickest cover around. The pursuers will either pass him up or find it hard to penetrate the cover to disturb him. I have often seen bucks use this type of cover to bed in when they know they are being pursued after being hit. As soon as they enter cover like this, they will bed down. Whenever you find a bed with blood in it, be vigilant. I always recommend standing in the spot and slowly eyeballing the area carefully before picking up the trail again. Oftentimes, bucks will rise from a bed, go 30 yards, and because of the wound, bed down again. Paying attention to this detail can often put a wounded buck in your sights.

## Up- and Downhill

There seems to be a never-ending controversy about whether or not deer travel up- or downhill after being wounded. It is similar to the argument about whether or not all wounded deer immediately head for water. I can only relate what I have witnessed with the deer I have tracked.

I have trailed many wounded bucks up the side of a mountain, despite the fact that most experts will tell you that a wounded deer rarely, if ever, heads uphill. I discovered that deer that head uphill after being wounded leave a blood trail as they climb that is less than the blood trail found on level or declining ground. Why? I don't know. But it is a fact.

My wife, Kate, shot a buck at the base of a mountain behind our old house on opening morning. She called on the radio to let me know that the buck ran off into the pines. She was going to wait 15 minutes and then pick up the blood trail. About a half hour later, she called me back to let me know she was about 200 yards into the blood trail and it was heading half way up the side of the ridge. Kate mentioned that she was worried that the buck was not mortally hit because the blood sign was dwindling. Knowing that even a heavy blood trail lessens as a buck goes uphill, I asked her to stop and wait.

We picked up the blood trail and we followed it another 200 yards up the ridge to the first plateau. I asked Kate to stay behind while I slowly and methodically poked my head over the top to look around the plateau for more blood sign. Following the trail, I picked up a lot of blood within 75 yards. Kate re-joined me and again we took up the trail. The blood remained significant for another 100 or so yards until the buck once again started up again towards the next plateau.

As we reached the second table, the buck must have been running out of gas, as he was only bedded 30 yards from where he walked onto the plateau and was laying with his head flat on the ground.

Kate never even had to take a finishing shot. The buck expired in his bed, within minutes thereafter. Upon field dressing him, we found that Kate's shot was indeed a fatal wound and should have left a significant amount of blood throughout the entire trail. The fact is that it left an easy-to-follow blood trail only on flat ground.

Although it is crucial to have snow to track a buck effectively in many parts of the country, in places where soft, dry soil exists like in Texas, deserts and beaches, and in the red clay of the south, a deer print is also easy to follow. I tracked this Wyoming buck for two hours over dry loose soil before I found him bedded down in a patch of scrub oak.

Another interesting fact about blood trails of wounded deer going up- or downhill is that for some oddball reason, deer do not seem to bleed any less when going downhill. The blood trail always seems to be as significant as it is on flat terrain. I have never been able to put my finger on exactly why this is, or why a deer bleeds less going uphill.

You would think the mere fact that the deer is exerting itself walking uphill would make its heart race more and thereby pump out more blood. But that's just not the case.

A different case was documented on a TV show I produced in Canada in 1988. Viewers saw a large-bodied, 140–155 class buck break the rules about traveling uphill after being shot. I shot the buck in the chest and he immediately took off in high gear through the woodlot. The camera followed the action as the buck ran through the woods for about 100 yards, down an embankment, through a small stream, and then up a very steep embankment on the other side, heading toward an open field.

As the buck started up the steep hill, it was noticeable that his back legs were giving way. Yet, he continued his ascent with a mindset that seemed irreversible. Just shy of the top of the hill, about 50 yards above the stream, the buck's life force began to ebb. He collapsed. To our surprise, he then staggered to his feet and turned to look down toward the stream. At that point, I thought he was going to head downhill to the water. Instead, he tried to climb the last several yards uphill. Within a dozen yards, the buck's back legs slowly gave out and he slid all the way back down the hill and into the stream.

I believe he died on his feet as he tried to climb the last few yards to the steep embankment. Why the buck chose to run up this steep hill rather than stay on level ground or run along the stream is beyond me. But, what it did prove is that, once again, every deer's reaction to being wounded is unique. Hunters must keep this in mind when trailing a wounded animal. Nothing about wounded game is written in stone.

## Seeking Water

What I found out about wounded deer heading for water is like the rest of the adages about wounded deer: nothing is ever written in stone. Most fatally hit deer do not immediately head toward water. They are simply not thinking about liquid at this point. Instead, they are preoccupied with escape and survival. It isn't until a deer begins to become feverish that it will actually seek water. Most of the time, this occurs when a deer has either a fatal wounded that may not result in death right away or has just a minor wound. In either case, the wound is severe enough to raise the temperature of the deer. This is the only lesson I have learned about wounded deer and water.

# TROPHY STORIES
# Don Baldwin [Michigan]

***198 2/8 Net P&Y Michigan Non-Typical 23-Point Whitetail***

Don Baldwin, a Michigan whitetail archer, feels mixed emotions when he looks out his kitchen window and gazes upon the new subdivision being built behind his house, in a field where once he spent every free hour scouting or bowhunting deer.

On the one hand, that field was where he had bagged his best buck to date: a huge non-typical 23-pointer with an uncannily symmetrical rack that netted a P&Y score of 198 2/8. Baldwin's main-frame 12 point is something of an anomaly; almost each of its non-typical, scoreable points has a match on the opposite antler.

On the other hand, Baldwin knows that the land would have been developed someday, despite his own wishes to the contrary. Seeing the earth finally penetrated and the building begin to take shape motivated him to search for his own hunting property.

The man soon found the acreage of his dreams, a nice chunk of land that encompassed several hundred yards of shoreline on the bay that gives his home part of Michigan—Bay County—its name. He just purchased the property and has already taken a couple of good bucks, and he has high hopes of bagging other big whitetails there during future seasons.

When the backyard field was still Baldwin's favorite hunting spot, he relied on his wife, Kristy, to keep him apprised of the deer she spotted while he was at work. Kristy Baldwin, although not a hunter, had an eye for the big bucks that sometimes showed up in the field and, occasionally, even in their yard.

"You won't believe the buck I saw in our driveway today," Baldwin remembers her once saying. "He looked like an elk!"

"The next time we saw that buck was November 4, 2001," Baldwin said. "Earlier that morning I'd seen some smaller bucks in the field, so I planned to hunt there that afternoon.

"I went out that evening with a plan to rattle in one of the bucks I'd spotted earlier in the day . . . set up at about 4:30 p.m., which didn't leave me much time for bowhunting, since it gets dark fairly early at that time of the year."

Baldwin had set up on the ground and positioned himself behind a hedgerow, but toward one end of the cover, where the brush had grown up into an almost impenetrable thicket. "As I completed my first rattling sequence, I noticed a huge deer standing in the field about 100 yards distant," he said. "I couldn't make out antlers, but I watched the deer until he suddenly turned and ran back into the woods."

Using his natural voice, Baldwin immediately snort-wheezed, and the deer raced back out of the woods. "I could hear him grunting and I could see how his neck hair was bristling," the bowhunter recalled. "He raced around the end of the hedgerow and halted 15 yards from me.

"I thought I was having a heart attack, I got so excited," Baldwin said. "I had trouble drawing my bow, and when I finally did, the buck ran off about 20 yards and stood there, stamping his hoof. I continued to grunt, snort-wheeze and slam the rattling horns on the ground.

"The buck really got hacked off. He raced along the fencerow—downwind of where I was standing–jumped the fence and stood there, but wouldn't come closer than 55 or 60 yards. I don't think he smelled me—I was wearing Scent-Lok, plus I'd sprayed down with Wildlife Research's Scent-Killer—but he suddenly lost interest and left."

The rubber-kneed archer had been crouching within spitting distance of the buck for 15 minutes. "I had plenty of time to look him over," Baldwin said. "I know his antlers were much larger then than during the following season in 2002. Each tine was at least six inches longer, plus I believe the rack then sported at least 50 additional inches." If that estimate is correct, the buck's 2001 rack would have grossed 260 points.

Although he wondered what had happened to the big non-typical during the remainder of the season, Baldwin never saw the buck again that year. He spotted several other nice bucks, but nothing close to the whopper that inhabited his big-buck dreams.

It wasn't until September 30, 2002 that Baldwin spotted the big whitetail again, in the same place where they'd had their earlier confrontation.

Baldwin, in the meantime, had amended his bowhunting plans and decided to hunt from a tree stand rather than from on the ground. "I placed the stand where I thought I'd have a chance to intercept bucks crossing the field," he explained. He was determined to hunt each day of the season, if that's what it took to bag the buck. Beginning October 1, he was in his tree stand by 4 p.m. each workday, and remained there until dark.

"I was in my stand on the evening of October 7 when a nice big 10-point buck ran past and into the woods," Baldwin said. "That buck would have scored about 150 Pope & Young points.

"My theory is simple: When you see a big buck, you must do everything in your power, short of spooking him, to get the buck," Baldwin continued. "I climbed down out of the stand, crawled across field, and then did some soft rattling and buck-grunting.

"I didn't realize it at the time, but the huge non-typical was running with that 10-pointer. As I was rattling and calling, the larger buck slipped up behind me, winded me and raced off in the opposite direction."

Five days later, Baldwin encountered the big buck again. "On two separate occasions, as I climbed down from my stand at dark, I failed to see the big buck running toward me," he said.

Don Baldwin grew up deer-hunting teeth in Michigan, where baiting deer remains a legal method of hunting. "I didn't know any better," he said. "I'd kill deer, but never the size of buck I'd hoped for. Only after I learned how to match your tactics to whitetail habits and behaviors did I understand that bait makes big bucks suspicious, and that rarely will they [respond to] bait during daylight hours."

The big non-typical was proving to be a tough nut to crack. "I'd decided to make the area near my stand more attractive by scattering some corn about," Baldwin explained. "I thought if the buck did come past the stand he might be distracted enough by a handful or two of corn that he'd give me a good shot."

Baldwin didn't realize that the buck had discovered the corn several evenings before. "Only after I'd bumped him a few times and then looked back, after I'd left the field, did I notice him feeding on the corn," he said.

"It all made sense at that time. The buck was patterning me! I think he was bedding on the field edge and waiting until he saw me climb out of my stand. When I did so, the buck would get up and make a beeline for the corn."

Once Baldwin understood what the buck was doing, he was able to make a plan of his own. "The next evening I climbed out of the stand 30 minutes before dark," he said. "I made a lot of noise, too, then I climbed back up and climbed down again just for good measure. The second time I reached the ground, the rattling horns were still dangling around my neck and my bow was still clipped to its haul-rope. I looked up and saw the buck coming!

Don Baldwin's heavy-horned whitetail buck nets a remarkable 198 2/8 Pope & Young points.

"Have you ever tried to shoot a bow with rattling horns slung around your neck?" Baldwin asked. "Believe me, it's almost impossible to do so."

The archer was standing at the base of a willow tree, about 6 feet in diameter, around the base of which he'd wisely cleared the earth of brush and fallen leaves.

"I'm standing near the tree like a statue with the buck feeding on the corn just seven yards distant," Baldwin said. "I was behind the hedgerow, so the deer was oblivious to my presence. I also picked out an opening that I could shoot through, if the chance arose. 'How am I going to pull this off,' I wondered."

Don Baldwin did what any bowhunter worth his whitetail salt would do–he improvised.

"Each time the buck lowered his head to feed, I'd slowly move the rattling horns until they finally were laying upon the ground. I did the same with the bow until I'd unclipped it from the rope and an arrow was nocked on the bow-string.

"The buck looked up. Maybe he heard me nock the arrow; I'm not sure. I just stood there, until the moment was right. The buck was still standing seven yards distant, but quartering toward me. My shot would have to be perfect."

Baldwin then aimed through the hole he'd found in the hedgerow, zeroing in on the tiny "gateway to the heart" between the buck's brisket and front leg. The arrow hit precisely where he'd been aiming.

The archer had the presence of mind to run out of the hedgerow so he could follow the course taken by the mortally wounded animal until it entered the nearby woods.

"I asked Bud Lesor, my neighbor, to help track it," Baldwin said. "By this time it had started to sleet and rain."

The two men picked up a blood trail where the buck had entered the woods. The deer expired after traveling just 100 yards from the hedgerow where Baldwin shot him.

Bud Lesor reached the deer first. He grabbed hold of its antlers and said, "Oh, my God, this buck is huge!"

Baldwin, by then, was running on pure adrenaline. "I yanked that buck up into my truck by myself," he said. "It weighed 207 pounds field-dressed, but felt light as a feather."

The next hour passed dream-like. One vehicle followed Baldwin's pickup truck until it stopped just so its occupants could get a better look at the mature seven-and-one-half-year-old buck with the mighty rack sticking above the truck's bed. As news of Baldwin's bowhunting feat spread, the madness escalated. Soon, more than 50 friends, relatives and neighbors were milling about on the family's driveway and admiring the fallen monarch of Bay County.

Michigan's Don Baldwin outwitted this big 23-point non-typical when Baldwin started his evening hunt in a tree stand, but climbed down and shot the buck from the ground.

Don Baldwin believes the real secret to his eventual success might have been the big old doe whose home range encompassed the archer's hunting area.

"Each fall one big doe would always have with her two buck fawns," Baldwin commented. "The fawns had small nubbin-type antlers, but their bases were huge—two or two-and-one-half-inches in diameter—as though someday they would become really big antlers.

"I've heard that certain bucks remember a particular doe and return to breed her each year, and that's what I think happened in this case. The big non-typical remembered the old doe and would move into the area each fall during her estrus cycle."

The year after Baldwin shot his big buck, a neighbor mentioned that he'd seen a vehicle collide with a big doe. "I worried that it might be that big doe, and it was," Baldwin said. "When I next saw her, most of her hindquarters had been stripped of hide. She died soon afterward."

Don Baldwin started bowhunting when he was 12 years old; 22 years later, he scored on the big non-typical buck. During the interim, he'd used his bow to bag five other bucks, although none would have scored much higher than 100 P&Y points.

Taking his record-book whitetail has motivated Baldwin to raise his sights. "Most guys I know are happy to take one-and-one-half-year-old bucks," he said. "Bucks older than a year-and-a-half become nocturnal, especially once firearms season begins. That's why the best chance an archer has of bagging a big buck is before the gun season.

"I've had quite a bit of success by going out to hunt later in the afternoon and then rattling, calling and snort-wheezing bucks off of their beds," Baldwin continued. "The tactic is especially effective during the last few days of October and the first few days of November."

In 2003, Baldwin's success continued when he shot a 12-point, 130-class P&Y buck. In 2004, the archer briefly switched to a different broadhead, only to watch it glance off the shoulder of a big 14-pointer that subsequently escaped.

"That buck had split brow tines, a 23-inch inside spread, and would have grossed about 170 P&Y points," Baldwin recalled. "I've since gone back to my NAP Spitfire. I've never lost a deer that I'd hit with that head."

Baldwin went on to bag a heavy-racked eight-pointer at 4 p.m. on November 4, 2004. "I rattled and snort-wheezed the buck out of his bedding spot in some cattails growing on the shoreline of my new hunting property," he explained. The buck scored 128 P&Y points, and dressed out at 230 pounds.

Like most of his bowhunting brethren, or at least those who still operate from a realistic perspective, Don Baldwin simply loves to hunt whitetails.

"I still get excited, whether a buck will score 125 or 150," he said. "That's not what's most important. Being out there and wondering what you'll see next is what makes bowhunting so great."

And keeps Don Baldwin—and others like him—coming back for more, season after season after season.

## BOWHUNTING STATS

### HUNT PARTICULARS

**Superbuck:** 198 2/8 Net P&Y Michigan Non-Typical 23-Point Whitetail
**Hunt location:** Bay County, Michigan
**Date:** Oct. 17, 2002
**Time:** 6:45 p.m.
**Habitat type:** fallow field and hedgerow
**Weather:** Overcast, front moving in, began to sleet; 45 degrees earlier, but 32 when I shot.
**Ambient temperature:** 32 degrees
**Wind direction:** Southerly
**Wind speed:** 5 m.p.h.
**Sunrise:** 7:52 a.m.
**Sunset:** 6:49 p.m.
**Moon phase:** Waxing gibbous, with 88% of the moon's visible disk illuminated. Full moon would take place on Oct. 21, 2002.
**Moonrise:** 5:28 p.m., on Oct. 16, the preceding day; 5:50 p.m., on Oct. 17. (The moon had been up for 55 minutes when Baldwin shot his buck.)
**Moonset:** 4 a.m.
**Duration of moonlight:** 10 hours, 32 min. from moonrise to moonset. Actual nighttime illumination 9 hours, 11 min.
**Tree stand:** No; on ground
**Tactics used:** Rattling, calling
**Scent-Lok?** Yes, "plus I'd sprayed down with Wildlife Research's Scent-Killer."
**Had you seen that buck before?** Yes
**Private ground or public?** Private
**Yours or someone else's?** Someone else's
**Outfitted or permission and self-guided?** Self-guide

### EQUIPMENT

**Bow:** PSE Firestorm; 70#, 65 percent let-off; 29-inch draw length
**Sight:** Trophy Ridge Flat-liner with peep
**Rest:** Tiger Tuff two-prong
**Release:** Cobra caliper with custom handle (due to carpal-tunnel problem)
**Arrow:** Gold Tip 3555
**Feathers or vanes:** Vanes
**Broadhead:** NAP Spitfire three-blade expandable
**Optics used:** None

### BOWHUNTER'S Q&A

**Occupation?** Owner of an auto mechanic shop
**Years hunting?** 22

**Years bowhunting?** 22
**Competition shooter?** League shooter; Saginaw Valley Archers Association
**3-D Shooter?** Yes
**Number of days spent scouting yearly?** 30
**Number of days spent bowhunting yearly?** Every evening that I can, which means most evenings by 4:30 p.m.
**Number of states, provinces, countries bowhunted in an average year:** One
**Most likely to bowhunt in:** Michigan
**Other than whitetails, I've bowhunted for:** Turkeys
**Estimated number of bow-killed whitetails to date:** 12
**Largest-racked whitetails:** 205 6/8-gross non-typical, 132-gross 11-point, 128-gross eight-point
**Tactics used:** Tree stand hunting, stalking, still-hunting, ground blind
**Favorite tactic:** Tree stand
**If you could hunt only one time of day . . . ?** Evenings. I also think the midday hunt, from 10 a.m. to 2 p.m., is good.
**Why?** I really haven't had much luck during the morning hunt. It probably depends on where you're hunting, but if you're hunting near a food source, which most people do, deer gravitate toward those areas in the evenings. I try to avoid bedding areas because you never know when deer will be traveling through them. My ideal stand site will be located somewhere between a current food source and a bedding area.
**Tree stand particulars:** I enjoy hunting on the ground, but when I use a commercial stand I prefer hang-ons. It takes too much labor to use a climbing stand, plus you have to cut off all the cover [branches] so you can climb up. I like to be at least 20 feet high in a tree, and sometimes as much as 30 feet. If I can position my stand that high, I find that deer never spot or wind me. My favorite stand is in a willow tree with multiple big branches growing off the main trunk. Once I'm in position on one of those large branches, I look like just another limb.
**How do you blend in?** I'll always place my stand so that I blend into the background, which is usually comprised of other trees. I leave in place most of the branches that are growing beneath my stand. When I position a stand like this, I'm never silhouetted.
**Rattle?** My successful rattling comes later in October and early November. Earlier in the season I may tickle the antlers together to make light sparring sounds, but I rarely have much luck during the pre-rut period.
**Real antlers or synthetics?** Real. My current set is an eight-point rack that would score about 140 P&Y. I've cut off the brow tines, then put rubber around the antler bases. I wrap the rubber with camouflage tape and then, early in the season, paint the wrappings with primer, painting well before archery season begins so that the smell dissipates. I use a good-sized rack for rattling, since it seems like the size of your antlers almost predicts the size of buck you'll rattle in. Last season I used 130-class antlers for rattling, and that's the size of buck I seemed to rattle in.
**Calls?** Late October and early November is the best time to use a snort-wheeze call. If you're hunting in an area occupied by at least one mature buck, I guarantee you that if you use the snort-wheeze, he will respond. I snort-wheeze every time I rattle. If I reach my stand at 2 p.m., I'll rattle and snort-wheeze in at least three or four different sessions of about five minutes each. I start each session with a couple of grunts, wait a few seconds, snort-wheeze, make another, responsive grunt [as though two bucks are behaving antagonistically or aggressively toward one another], tickle the rattling antlers lightly, then slam the antlers together. I'm always trying to make my rattling and calling sound as realistic as possible. If

I'm on the ground, I'll stomp my feet and bash the rattling horns in the bushes and against tree trunks.
**Mock scrapes?** I've never had much luck with them.
**Mock rubs?** No
**Commercial or homemade scents?** I believe estrus-doe urine scent wafers work very well. I used them once and hadn't been set up for five minutes when a buck I'd been patterning came running out to investigate the scent. Know your area, and then place them so that their scent blows into cover where bucks may be bedded, feeding or traveling.
**Scent-Lok:** Yes
**Trail cameras?** I've used lessexpensive, film trail cameras but haven't had much luck with them. I don't plan to buy an expensive model because I worry that it might be stolen. I've lost tree stands to kids who obtain their own gear by finding it in the woods.
**Recent equipment upgrades:** Mathews Switchback
**Braggin' rights:**

- I enjoy hunting with my Dad, Don, whenever our schedules permit it.
- My son Nathan will be 12 this year, and so I'm really looking forward to hunting with him. Nathan shoots in archery leagues and does very well. He's also eager to hang deer on the wall like his dad does. He'll be a far better hunter than me because I'm planning to teach him everything I know about whitetails and their habits. I hope Nathan will be able to benefit from what it's taken me so long to learn on my own.
- My daughter Madison, eight, is very dainty but I'm already teaching her about archery and how to shoot a bow. She likes to do things with her dad, so I think she'll become a hunter, too. That will be great if she does.
- My wife, Kristy, is very understanding once deer season rolls around. She knows deer hunting is what I love most, so if she sees any big deer she will always let me know where and when she saw it. I don't give her any grief about her bingo playing, and so she tolerates my deer hunting.

**TOP BOWHUNTING TIPS**

- I set up my stands depending upon where I find old sign from preceding seasons. Bucks tend to use various terrain features as they travel through the woods. As they travel, especially during the rut, they'll leave sign in the form of old scrapes, scrape lines and rub lines.
- I never scout during the rut or at any time during the season. When archery season begins, my stands are already set up and everything is ready for me. I might have to fine-tune a stand by moving it 15 yards or so, perhaps to position it closer to a trail that they've started using, but other than that I try to create no other disturbance.
- If you see a buck during the rut, do everything in your power to get him, even if it means coming down out of your stand to do so. The chances that he'll come back again or that you'll see him again are practically nil.
- The best time to call or rattle, in my opinion, is during the evening hunt. Bucks at that time are rested up and ready to go, and so more susceptible to being called or rattled in.
- Use some kind of yardage marker at every stand. Fumbling with a laser rangefinder while a deer is right in front of you is never a good idea. Once I started using yardage markers, I started killing deer.

# Mick Hellickson [Texas]

***182 6/8 Gross P&Y Texas Typical 14-Point Whitetail***

Mick Hellickson landed his dream job when he was hired to be the chief wildlife biologist for the fabled King Ranch of Texas. Hellickson, an Iowa native who as a youngster was first turned on to hunting by his next door neighbor, started out hunting pheasants, moved on to shotgun hunting for whitetails, and then drifted into whitetail bowhunting. Bowhunting for whitetails soon became his passion. He especially enjoys spot-and-stalk bowhunting on areas available to him as a member of the King Ranch Employee Hunting Club.

Before readers' imaginations start running amok with possibilities, Hellickson, like all full-time employees, must pay dues to belong to the club. Members also are limited to hunting in certain pastures only, and those pastures must be reserved ahead of time. What's more, employees are allotted just five days of deer hunting each year.

Regardless, King Ranch deer hunting is fantastic, whether the hunt is for one, five or 20 days, and Hellickson realizes it. His interest in hunting there may be greater than that of other employees, since he manages the ranch's quality deer program.

Hellickson first attracted the notice of the Texas deer community after he co-authored, together with Drs. Larry Marchinton and Charles DeYoung, a landmark study that focused on whitetail buck breeding behaviors. The intensive three-year telemetry study analyzed movement patterns and behaviors of 130 radio-collared bucks of all ages.

Rattling was especially important to the study's authors. "Any buck that responded to rattling would be offering its own unique perspective to its breeding behavior," Hellickson said. "If more than one buck responded, we hoped to determine each buck's relative dominance within the local hierarchy."

Hellickson hoped that by altering the variables, both volume and the amount of time spent rattling, he would be able to determine which type of rattling sequence would attract the greatest number of bucks.

The study not only served as the preliminary research for the doctorate in wildlife biology that Hellickson eventually earned, but also made him something of a rising star in whitetail circles. That was especially true in Texas, where rattling is king of the whitetail-hunting techniques.

Rattling works well in Texas because buck-to-doe ratios are managed carefully to produce a perfect biological climate for them to work in. A buck for every doe–or nearly so–keeps rutting bucks in good physical condition, since one dominant animal isn't worn out from breeding 10, 20, or more does in a single season. A buck for every doe means a buck must actively seek out any doe in or about to enter estrus or else risk not breeding at all. Rattling simulates the noise created when two whitetail

Seems like they grow everything bigger in Texas, as archer Mick Hellickson displays his 182 6/8 gross Pope & Young typical 14-point buck.

bucks battle it out; rattling during the rut raises buck curiosity levels because the possibility exists that the "battle" is being waged for an estrus doe.

No wonder that Hellickson enjoys rattling even now, years after the study's completion. But he doesn't limit his bowhunting to that which is accompanied by rattling. He's more eclectic in his whitetail-bowhunting techniques and actually prefers spot-and-stalk hunting over any other tactic.

Spot-and-stalk came to the rescue on November 14, 2004, the day that Hellickson used his Martin Firecat compound to bag his largest whitetail to date, a 14-point buck that gross-scored 182 2/8 P&Y points as a typical.

Each summer, Hellickson conducts a spotlight deer survey to determine which pastures–blocks of hunting land–are holding the best bucks. Last August, he videotaped four or five superbucks, any one of which he gladly would have arrowed if given the chance.

"King Ranch employees are allowed to reserve two pastures at a time, each of them for a single day of hunting," Hellickson explained. "I knew which two pastures I'd spotted the largest bucks in, so I reserved one pasture for each of two consecutive days. I'd teamed up with another employee and he reserved the second pasture, again for each of two consecutive days."

Hellickson and his friend would be able to hunt Pasture 1 on Days 1 and 2 of their hunt, then move to Pasture 2, which had been reserved by Hellickson's friend, on Days 3 and 4. A third friend also joined the two men for their hunt.

Hellickson put the moves on Buck #1, but missed him. He then started to stalk Buck #2, but ran out of daylight.

"In Texas, we hunt safari-style out of the same vehicle," Hellickson said. He explained that ranch hunting etiquette provides the hunter who reserved the pasture being hunted with the right of first refusal: If a big buck is spotted, then the person who reserved the pasture has the option of going after it or not.

That day the three of us walked into a rather large live oak motte, and then went our separate ways," Hellickson said. "We each slipped through the motte for about three-fourths of its length before meeting again. The third member of our party then told us that he'd spotted one of the big bucks I'd videotaped in August, together with two smaller bucks. The smaller bucks prevented this guy from shooting at the big buck.

"That's when the other guy, the hunter who had reserved the pasture, said that he wanted to try for the big buck. Which was his right, of course.

"I warned him, 'The big buck is running with another buck, one with a large-framed rack but fewer points,'" Hellickson said. "'Don't shoot the wrong buck by mistake.'"

The second man slipped back into the motte and began to stalk the bucks. "He shot the wrong buck," Hellickson said. "While he and the third guy field-dressed that buck, I went after the big buck, the one he had been after when he made his mistake."

Hellickson moved slowly into the motte. He knew that the big buck probably would be with a smaller buck, since three animals had been banded up together and the other archer had killed one of the three. He continued to stalk through the trees, remaining alert to any movement that could tip him off to the bucks' presence.

"When I finally spotted the bucks, they were browsing on oak stems, tips and leaves," Hellickson said. "It had rained hard the night before. I could move ahead without making a sound because everything was damp.

"The wind was in my face, so that was also a point in my favor. I'd move forward only when the buck's head was down and he was feeding. The smaller buck generally stayed between me and the larger deer, and that also worked in my favor. Little by little, I closed the distance."

Hellickson stayed close to the bucks and at last the larger buck decided to bed down. "Soon afterward the smaller buck bedded between the larger buck and me. I waited for about 10 minutes, and then the smaller buck got up and again began to feed. As that buck moved away I slipped in as close as I dared to the big buck."

An oak motte is a magical place made up of many tiny-leafed trees with twisted trunks and high, over-arching boughs. Live oaks hold their leaves even in winter, and the net effect of walking within a motte is almost an otherworldly experience.

When the archer had closed the distance to a mere 20 yards, he realized that the opportunity before him was as good as it was liable to get. The big buck remained bedded and facing away from him. The man slowly raised his bow, aimed and triggered his release. Hellickson's 100-grain Thunderhead pierced the animal behind its right shoulder, slammed into the ground and then exited the buck's left shoulder. The buck leaped to his feet, ran 30 yards, began to totter and fell to the earth, dead.

The entire stalk, from start to finish, had taken one hour.

Hellickson borrowed a phrase from George Carlin, and used it to express his feelings about this, his most memorable bowhunting experience. "'Life is not measured by the number of breaths we take, but the number of moments that take our breath away,'" he said. "This was one of those moments."

## BOWHUNTING STATS

### HUNT PARTICULARS

**Superbuck:** 182 6/8 Gross P&Y Texas Typical 14-Point Whitetail
**Hunt location:** Kenedy County, Texas
**Date:** Nov. 14, 2004
**Time:** 12:30 p.m.
**Habitat type:** Live oak motte
**Weather:** Overcast and warm
**Ambient temperature:** 60s
**Wind direction:** Southeasterly
**Wind speed:** 5 to 10 m.p.h.
**Sunrise:** 6:50 a.m.
**Sunset:** 5:41 p.m.
**Moon phase:** Waxing crescent, with 7 percent of the moon's visible disk illuminated. New moon had occurred on Nov. 12, 2004.
**Duration of moonlight:** On Nov. 14, moon was up and visible for 10 hours, 26 minutes. Moon was up when I shot the buck. Nighttime illumination for Nov. 13, from sunset at 5:42 p.m. until moonset at 6:39 p.m.: 57 minutes.
**Moonrise:** 9:12 a.m. on Nov. 14. 8:01 a.m. on Nov. 13

**Moonset:** 7:38 p.m. on Nov. 14. 6:39 p.m. on Nov. 13
**Tactics used:** Spot and stalk
**Commercial or homemade scent?** No
**Scent-Lok?** No; was downwind
**Had you seen that buck before?** Yes; I'd seen him once before in August 2004.
**Private ground or public?** Private
**Yours or someone else's?** King Ranch ground
**Outfitted or permission and self-guided?** Self-guided

EQUIPMENT

**Bow:** Martin Firecat; 72#; usually 70 to 75#; 65 percent let-off; 31 1/2-inch draw length
**Sight:** Three fiber-optic pins, with peep
**Rest:** Two-prong rest
**Release:** Scott Gator-Jaw
**Arrow:** Easton Aluminum XX75
**Feathers or vanes:** Vanes, with uni-nock
**Broadhead:** NAP 125-Thunderhead chisel-point with bleeder blades
**Optics used?** Bushnell Laser-rangefinder

BOWHUNTER'S Q&A

**Occupation?** Chief Wildlife Biologist for the King Ranch in Texas
**Years hunting?** 33
**Years bowhunting?** 22
**Competition shooter?** None recently
**3-D Shooter?** No
**Number of days spent scouting yearly:** I'm in the field about half of every year.
**Number of days spent bowhunting yearly:** 15
**Number of states, provinces, countries bow hunted in an average year:** One
**I've bowhunted in:** Texas, Iowa, Ontario, South Africa, Georgia
**Other than whitetails, I've bowhunted for:** black bear, turkeys, greater kudu, blesbok, gemsbok, zebra, nyala
**I've hunted whitetails in:** Texas, Iowa, Georgia
**Estimated number of bow-killed whitetails to date:** Between 40 and 50
**Largest-racked whitetails:** Hellickson has other archery superbucks to his credit as well, including those with gross scores of 165 4/8, 161 2/8, 159 6/8, 154 4/8 and numerous others that gross between 131 1/8 and 150 5/8, most taken in Texas.
**Tactics used:** Tree stand, stalking, still-hunting, ground blinds
**Favorite tactic:** Spot-and-stalk; it's the most challenging, too.
**If you could hunt only one time of day . . . ?** Mornings, especially the first hour of daylight.
**Why?** Activity is high at that time, and if things don't work out you have the rest of the day.
**Tree stand particulars:** Tripod stand; also fixed position.
**How do you blend in?** I try to place my stand in a tall mesquite tree so that I'm in the branches, where I blend in. I have a short, 10-foot-tall tripod.
**Rattle?** Anytime during the peak of the rut is a good time to rattle a lot. Before the rut and after the rut, it depends on the situation. If we know a particular buck is in the neighborhood, we may try rattling to see if we can bring him in.
**Real antlers or synthetics?** Real; 150-class sheds. You get more volume out of real antlers.
**Commercial or homemade scents?** No
**Scent-Lok?** No
**Mock scrapes?** No
**Mock rubs?** No, although I make the sound of a buck making a rub sometimes while I'm rattling by rubbing an antler against the base of a tree.
**Trail cameras?** Yes. I've used a lot: StealthCam, DeerCam, Leaf River, Deer Tracker, and I think I like Non-Typical's DeerCam film camera the best. It's the easiest to use and the quality of the camera in the unit is the best. Leaf River digitals are also very good.

**Recent equipment upgrades:** No; in fact, my new equipment failed and I had to go back and get my old bow to shoot that buck.

**Braggin' rights:**

- My Dad, Willis Hellickson, and a neighborhood friend got me interested in hunting. I started out hunting pheasants and it just grew from there. I return home to Iowa to shotgun hunt whitetails and pheasant each fall. Then, when I draw a turkey tag, I return in the spring to hunt turkeys.

**TOP BOWHUNTING TIPS**

- There's no silver bullet or magic bullet; it's basically time spent in the field. The best hunters are those who spend the most time in the field.

# Carl Osterlund [New Jersey]

***179 5/8 Gross P&Y Non-Typical 17-Point New Jersey Whitetail***

Carl Osterlund, a New Jersey taxidermist and big-buck bowhunter, is well aware of the corollary of Murphy's infamous Law that states, "Stuff happens." If Osterlund had not been acquainted with that adage before New Jersey's 2002–2003 archery deer season, afterward he most certainly would have been familiar with it.

Osterlund began hunting with his father, Carl Sr., also known as "Bob," when the youngster was about 12 years old.

"Wild quail and pheasant were plentiful back then," Osterlund recalled. "Dad and I had bird dogs, and we enjoyed hunting birds with our dogs. The other boys I knew played sports, while I'd go to south Jersey with my father and we'd hunt quail with my uncles."

At the age of 17, Osterlund's life changed dramatically. "I met some boys who were interested in bowhunting, and they got me interested, too," he explained. "I shot my first archery deer, a doe, that year. Ten days later, I bagged a button buck. That was it for me. I knew I'd be a whitetail bowhunter for the rest of my life."

Whitetails so intrigued Osterlund that as a teenager he'd spend countless hours watching the animals interact while they fed or mingled on local golf courses. He discovered the advantages of off-season scouting, and successes soon began piling up, one after the other. By 1990, he no longer gun hunted at all. He's taken 168 archery whitetail bucks to date, and there's no indication that he plans to slow down. A record like his would be quite a feat anywhere, but it's downright spectacular for an archer from an Eastern Seaboard state."

After I became a bowhunter, I could no longer keep my mind on quail, even when I was out hunting them," Osterlund said. "I'd get sidetracked by a scrape, rub or other sign, and by the time I finished examining it, my Dad and uncles would be a half-mile away."Whitetail deer continue to enthrall Osterlund even today. He once rescued a one-and-one-half-day-old buck fawn whose mother had been killed by a car and raised it as a pet. He soon grew attached to the fawn, and the fawn returned his affection.

"He was so tame as a baby that he'd walk into the house and through my taxidermy shop," Osterlund said. He was my buddy."

He built a pen in his backyard where the buck fawn eventually became a beautiful 160-class non-typical buck. "When the buck's horns were hard, I wouldn't enter his pen unless I had a stick for protection," Osterlund said. "But once his antlers had dropped, he'd go back to being my buddy. He'd lay his head in my lap so I could scratch his ears while I sat on the ground in his pen and ate my lunch."

The buck was six-and-one-half years of age when he died of a bacterial infection of the rumen, although Osterlund had spared no expense trying to save him. The veterinarian did everything he could think of, but in the end, it simply was time to say good-bye.

Osterlund, who works at a newspaper in addition to doing taxidermy work, knows whitetails. He hunts them, studies them, has raised them and even loved one special buck. You might say his life revolves around these fascinating animals. (His wife, Gail, is also fascinated by animals, but in her case they're the horses she rides, trains and sells.)

The Osterlunds own a nice piece of property, but Carl, ever diligent, obtains hunting permission from other landowners, too. In 2001, he spotted a great non-typical buck on land owned by someone else. The archer scouted the buck; he never got a shot, but the man knew the buck often used this one particular piece of ground on which he had permission to hunt. Then the land was sold to people who did not allow hunting.

In early 2002, the land again changed hands, and Osterlund was gratified when the land's new owners not only gave him written permission, they had the permission slip laminated for him.

Osterlund now concentrated on taking the big non-typical buck, a deer that previously had been videotaped by one of his friends. Working two jobs makes it difficult to bowhunt on a daily basis. But Osterlund knew that if hoped to take this buck, he had to set aside time in which he would focus on nothing else. From November 2002 onward, he spent every Saturday in his tree stand, from sunup to sundown.

Saturday, January 3, dawned cold, damp and foggy, with temperature hovering in the low 30s. "The ground and leaves were soaked, which meant I was able to get into my stand without alerting every animal in the woods," Osterlund said.

The sky was still dark when he reached his stand. He kicked back fallen leaves to reveal the bare earth in a spot about eight yards downwind of the stand, then sprayed Wildlife Research's Dominant Buck and Golden Estrus Urine on the barren ground.

"When the wind is blowing from north to south, my strategy calls for applying both scents somewhere to the west of where I'll be waiting," Osterlund explained. "That way, if a buck responds to my calls and circles downwind to scent check the area, he'll encounter the smell of the buck and doe urines before he reaches any human scent that may be drifting about. A buck will often hesitate when he scents the urine, and that hesitation can buy an archer some time."

The morning had started on a high note: Osterlund had briefly spotted two white deer rumps that quickly vanished into the undergrowth. The next five hours passed slowly, and the bowhunter had just started eating his lunch when he heard a sudden snapping sound beneath his stand, as though something was standing or walking on a branch or twig.

Osterlund's latest Ohio bow kill is a dandy that grosses 151 4/8 Pope & Young points.

"I turned and saw two deer," Osterlund said. "One was a doe. The other was the big non-typical buck. The doe walked almost directly under my stand, but the buck bedded in heavy brush about 22 or 25 yards in front of me."

Since the buck had bedded down facing the archer, there was no good shot to be made. Osterlund's only viable alternative was to continue waiting and hope a better shot would develop.

The doe hung around for a while, and then wandered off and into some nearby cattails. When the buck noticed that he'd been abandoned by his lady love, he rose from his bed and started following the doe."

The buck circled downwind, but hit the scent of the doe and buck urines I'd sprayed on the ground. He started sniffing around, and then he must have smelled urine on my boots, because he followed my trail to the tree.

"The buck now was almost too close," Osterlund said. "If I tried to shoot straight down, my movements or noise might spook the buck, and that concerned me."

Osterlund started to draw, but was unable to shoot. The buck, meanwhile, remained directly beneath his stand.

"So many things could go wrong," the man said. "The arrow might slip off the rest, or hit the bow, almost anything could happen and often did."

The buck continued to snuffle about beneath Osterlund's stand, so the archer finally decided to shoot and let the chips—or buck—fall where it may.

"When I drew, the bow's lower limb hit the stand's seat cushion, so I was unable to come to full draw," Osterlund said.

He slowly released the tension on the bow, then re-nocked an arrow, balanced on one foot, and with the knee of his other leg, he slowly lifted the stand's seat upward until it had folded back upon itself and was out of the way. With the seat folded back, Osterlund placed the proper pin on the buck's boiler room, fired his release and saw the arrow penetrate the buck's body behind the shoulder blades.

"The buck jumped slightly, made three bounds and stood there," Osterlund said. "I saw the blood running out of the exit wound, so I knew I'd hit him. The buck began walking down the main run to where the doe had crossed. He waited there, for about a minute, then he turned and went into the cattails where I'd last seen the doe. When I saw the buck stumble on the other side of the cattails I thought was finished. But he regained his composure and then disappeared into the brush."

Osterlund remained in the stand, worried that any noise made while climbing down might further spook the wounded whitetail.

"I finally decided to go home," he said. "I didn't want to push the buck, so I called a friend, Rich Novotny, and asked if he could help me search for the animal."

By the time the two reached the spot where Osterlund had shot at the buck, it was completely dark. Despite the darkness, the pair found a good blood trail, but it gradually petered out. The men got down on their hands and knees, gripping their flashlights in their mouths, searching for the miniscule blood specks that revealed the path traveled by the wounded buck.

"I would have been really depressed if I hadn't gone through this same thing on other occasions," Osterlund admitted. "I knew that occasionally a bit of tissue will break loose inside the body cavity and clog the exit wound to prevent the free flow of blood. That's what I was thinking when I heard Rich say, 'Here he is.'"

Osterlund at first was unable to make out either the buck's outline or antlers, because they blended so well with the darkened terrain and flashlightlit brush and saplings.

"When I finally got close to the buck, I stared at the rack in a state of awe," Osterlund said. "I couldn't believe how big he was."

After field-dressing the buck, and noting how Osterlund's arrow had sliced through liver and lungs before exiting the animal's chest, the two men each grabbed onto an antler for the long drag home.

"We were dragging the buck along the ground when, suddenly, the left antler, the one I was holding, simply came off of the buck's head," Osterlund remarked, still sounding somewhat astonished by this application of Murphy's Law within his own bowhunting life. "If it can happen, it will" isn't something one generally associates with trophy buck antlers, especially a buck that would have ranked as the number-three all-time New Jersey archery buck. And yet it happened, as Carl Osterlund can sadly attest.

The moment the buck's antler slipped off its pedicle, the rack ceased to be a potential record and became just another single-antlered buck. A buck that has cast one antler is not eligible for the record books.

Rising levels of testosterone in a buck's blood signal the antlers to grow and then harden. Hardened antlers mean that the buck is ready, willing and able to breed. Blood testosterone remains at a level sufficient to support hardened antlers until no more does are in or entering estrus. At that point, blood testosterone drops precipitously, and soon the antlers fall off.

Osterlund's big whitetail was tending a doe minutes before it was shot. It's hard to believe that the buck didn't have enough testosterone circulating in its blood to retain its hardened antlers, at least until the doe had been bred.

As Osterlund began to cape out the buck, he noticed a large fighting scar gouged deeply between the antler bases. "The wound was badly infected, particularly toward the left pedicle," Osterlund said. "I think that's why the antler dropped off."

Had he and Novotny not dragged the buck by its antlers, the rack might have remained intact. The reality, however, is that there is no way of knowing whether or not it would have stayed that way. The antler still might have fallen off while the animal was skinned, butchered or caped. It might even have separated from the pedicel while being scored. No one knows what might have been, only what is.

Osterlund's trophy whitetail was aged at about six-and-one-half years of age, and dressed out at 158 pounds. The rack's inside spread was 15 6/8 inches. The largest basal circumference of each main beam was six and twoeighths inches, and the rack had 17 points that would have been scoreable under other, happier circumstances. As it was, the rack was scored anyway, and its gross P&Y score of 179 6/8 made Carl Osterlund one very happy archer, regardless of the circumstances surrounding New Jersey's hard-luck buck.

## BOWHUNTING STATS

### HUNT PARTICULARS

**Superbuck:** 179 5/8 Gross P&Y Non-Typical 17-Point New Jersey Whitetail; 170 2/8 Net P&Y typical (see color insert)
**Hunt location:** Monmouth County, New Jersey
**Date:** Jan. 3, 2003. (This was the only buck I've ever killed during the January bow season.)
**Time:** 12:00 p.m.
**Habitat type:** Woods and pastureland in the suburbs.
**Weather:** Foggy, damp; it had been misting lightly, but a warm front would move through shortly.

**Ambient temperature:** Low 30s Wind direction: Southwesterly
**Wind speed:** 1 to 2 m.p.h.
**Sunrise:** 7:19 a.m.
**Sunset:** 4:42 p.m.
**Moon phase:** Waxing crescent, with 1 percent of the moon's visible disk illuminated
**Moonrise:** 8:16 a.m.
**Moonset:** 5:30 p.m.
**Duration of moonlight:** The New Moon had occurred on the previous day, Jan. 2; there was no moonlight to speak of.
**Tactics used:** No mock scrape per se, although I'd roughed up the leaves somewhat and sprayed Wildlife Research's Dominant Buck urine on them. I'd also sprayed the company's Golden Estrus doe urine on the ground.
**Tree stand:** Set at 18 feet. Commercial or homemade scent? Wildlife Research Golden Estrus
**Scent-Lok?** Yes
**Had you seen that buck before?** Yes, twice before. My friend Brian Perry captured the buck on video during the summer. By using a gradual process of elimination, I was finally able to locate him again while the archery season was still in progress.
**Private ground or public?** Private
**Yours or someone else's?** Someone else's.
**Outfitted or permission and self-guided?** Self-guided

## EQUIPMENT

**Bow:** Mathews Q-2; 72#, 70 percent let-off; 27 1/2-inch draw length.
**Sight:** Tru-Glo three-pin fiber-optic sight, with peep
**Rest:** Trophy Taker's Shakey Hunter Drop-away
**Release:** Scott caliper (hand-held)
**Arrow:** ICS Carbon 340
**Feathers or vanes:** Quick Spin Vanes
**Broadhead:** 100-grain Rocky Mountain Premier expandable broadheads
**Tree stand:** Fixed-position Baby Gorilla
**Optics used?** None

## BOWHUNTER'S Q&A

**Occupation?** I work in the transportation department at a newspaper; I also own a taxidermist shop called All Game Taxidermy.
**Years hunting?** 32
**Years bowhunting?** 29
**Competition shooter?** Yes, years ago.
**3-D Shooter?** Only for fun on a course I've put in on my farm.Number of days spent scouting yearly: It's difficult to say. I'll go out a couple of days each week during the weeks leading up to bow season. I'll spend even more time scouting or looking for sign during the post-season.
**Number of days spent bowhunting yearly:** Every day during archery season
**Number of states, provinces, countries bowhunted in an average year:** Two or three
**I've bowhunted in:** New Jersey, New York, Maine, New Hampshire, Vermont, Pennsylvania, Ohio, Illinois, Wyoming, Colorado, Utah, Kentucky, South Carolina, Quebec, Manitoba, Saskatchewan
**Most likely to bowhunt in:** New Jersey, Ohio, Colorado
**Other than whitetails, I've bowhunted for:** Pronghorn antelope (SCI 85 1/8, 74 2/8), mule deer, elk (two P&Y-class bulls)
**I've hunted whitetails in:** New Jersey, Pennsylvania, South Carolina, Illinois, Ohio
**Estimated number of bow-killed whitetails to date:** 168
**Largest-racked whitetails:** 179 5/8 gross P&Y non-typical 17-point (New Jersey); a 168 P&Y Maine buck; 151 1/2 Ohio eight-point (2004), plus 10 other P&Y whitetails.
**Tactics used:** Tree stand, still-hunting, stalking, ground blinds

**Favorite tactic:** Tree stand

**If you could hunt only one time of day . . . ?** I enjoy hunting evenings when I'm hunting elsewhere, but when I'm hunting in New Jersey, mornings seem to be best, possibly because it's such a heavily pressured area.

**Why?** In New Jersey, a lot of other archers will sleep in rather than get out into their stands before first light.

**Tree stand particulars:** My favorite is the Baby Gorilla fixed-position stand. Fixed positions are safer than climbers and easier to camouflage.

**How do you blend in?** I'll position my stand within branches that can be used for cover, plus I'll also cut branches, if I need to, and hang them from the stand's carrying straps or wherever else they will do some good.

**Rattle?** I don't rattle when hunting.

**Real antlers or synthetics?** N/A

**Commercial or homemade scents?** Wildlife Research Dominant Buck and Golden Estrus Urine. I've put the buck urine on one pad on my foot and the estrus urine on the other to simulate a buck following a hot doe's track. One buck raced across my scent trail, locked up and slid for about four feet, sniffed my trail and then walked directly to my tree.

**Scent-Lok:** Yes

**Mock scrapes?** Yes. I'll make them so that if the deer approach from the north, for instance, with a westerly wind that might prompt them to try to circle my stand to the south, the deer would pick up the scent of the mock scrape before they would get downwind of my position. Doing this can buy you time.

**Mock rubs?** No

**Trail cameras?** I have them but don't use them. My buddy Rich Novotny uses mine and his and sets them up for both of us.

**Recent equipment upgrades:** I added a shooting loop.

**Braggin' rights:**

- I bought my wife, Gail, a bow and during her first year of shooting, she did so well that a team comprised of she and I and a friend competed in an indoor 3-D target league. We finished in third place. Gail possesses great natural ability, plus she's an extremely fast learner. My wife totally supports my bowhunting. When I get a deer, she's the first person I'll call. I'll then call my father.
- I'm something of a bowhunting loner, but when I go bowhunting out of state, I'll often travel with my buddies, Tom Santomauro or Chris Erickson.
- My father still enjoys rabbit hunting with the beagles that he and two of his friends own. They have a lot of fun doing that. Dad doesn't bowhunt, but he'll visit during the firearms deer season. He'll hunt with a gun and I'll use my bow in the woods near my home. I always look forward to our time together.

**TOP BOWHUNTING TIPS**

- I shoot my bow every single day of the year, and use the best form possible as I do so. Doing this makes perfect archery form become a part of your subconscious.
- I'm a big proponent of scent control; it's crucial if you want to be a successful trophy whitetail hunter.
- When you can hunt every day, I don't believe the moon is much of a factor. I've taken good deer when the moon phase was at its absolute worst.

# Dan Perez [Illinois]

***174 5/8 B&C Net Typical Illinois 10-Point Whitetail***

Go ahead; talk with Dan Perez, if you must, but limit your conversation time to a few minutes at most, or risk your *own* bowhunting sanity. That's because this Illinois archer is *consumed*by the topic of giant whitetails. To say Perez breathes, thinks and dreams whitetail deer would be an understatement. The man's essence, his very being, is predicated upon the parallel existence, in his universe, of whitetail bucks sporting mind-boggling headgear.

As driven as he is in everything he does, Perez attends to his daily deer-hunting duties with single-minded intensity. Every facet of every day finds the man focused on the buck or bucks that soon will be added, should all proceed as planned, to his impressive collection of trophy-class whitetails.

Let's begin with a discussion of scouting. When asked how many days each year he spends scouting, Perez replied, "At least 300 days each year."

He attempts to explain away his bowhunting fanaticism, but how do you explain an obsession? Especially one at which you excel?

Obsessed Perez is, with over 250 bow-killed whitetails to his credit to date, 25 of which have sported racks that garnered scores higher than the minimum needed to qualify for P&Y. His largest bow kill is a big typical 10-point that scored an enviable 174 5/8 net P&Y points.

Perez once hunted in a tree stand that he'd hung 45 feet high. "I had to hang it that high," he explained. "The tree was leaning, so to allow me to stand up straight I had to go higher."

This bowhunter not only scouts in some way, shape, or form 300 days each year, he names each of his stands and maintains a log with data that helps him decide which stand to hunt each day based upon wind direction, past deer sightings and other factors.

He also hangs many stands, mainly because he believes that using a particular stand less will increase the odds of a trophy buck either using or remaining in that stand's general area.

"After I've hunted a stand, I'll usually let it rest before I return to it," he said. "The key is to keep each stand site as fresh as possible." Perez readily admits that some circumstances could cause him to abandon this reasoning and head back to a stand sooner than he ordinarily would.

Dan Perez has given plenty of thought to the topic of taking trophy whitetails. "Most hunters make the same mistakes over and over," he said. In his estimation, some of the most egregious errors include:

- Not hunting an area where big bucks live
- Hunting a stand when the wind is wrong
- Failing to control human odor
- Being too noisy while approaching a stand
- Approaching a stand when the wind direction is unfavorable

- Over-hunting or under-hunting a stand ("I'll never hunt the same stand two days in a row. Conversely, some archers often slip into their stands, wait an hour or two and then leave. They'll rarely be there when the buck finally shows up.")
- Lack of mental toughness ("Too many bowhunters fall apart when a shot finally presents itself. Bowhunting requires mental toughness. Concentrate. Take time to plan your shot.")
- Rattling too much ("If I sit in a tree stand for four or five hours, I might rattle two times that entire time unless I can see the buck.")

Perez's first encounter with his biggest buck was memorable, mainly because he went home empty-handed.

The weather that day was blustery and cold. A stiff northwesterly wind had been blowing so persistently that Perez turned his back to it. As he waited there, facing the trunk of the giant white oak in which he'd placed his stand, he noticed a big 10-pointer enter a soybean field about 100 yards distant. "That buck was something of a local legend," Perez said. "Other bowhunters had nicknamed him 'Tall Tines.'"

Perez watched as the deer fed for a short time out in the beans, then moved on into the timber on his side of the field. When the big deer disappeared from sight, the archer grunted four times in an attempt to locate it again.

"No sooner had I finished with the last grunt than I spotted the buck again. Tall Tines was now approaching me from behind my stand, which was also the downwind side."

This was not good, Perez knew. "My heart was pounding and my mind racing," he recalled. "Tall Tines, meanwhile, had closed the distance between us to a mere 12 yards." Unfortunately, the buck then stopped. He stood there, standing stock-still, directly behind the huge oak tree while he focused his attention on the scene in front of his position.

"There was no way to reach around the tree with my bow and release an arrow with any accuracy," Perez said. "I was in no position to move even a muscle."

He remained totally motionless, but the jig was up. After what seemed like an eternity to the man, the big buck sensed that something was wrong. With no further ado, the animal simply turned and fled back in the direction from which he'd come.

That scenario haunted Perez during the entire off-season, filling his thoughts with the various "wouldas, couldas, shouldas" that might have applied to the situation.

When the following season got under way, he was waiting in the same stand while again mulling over the circumstances of that previous occasion together with what might have been done differently.

Dan Perez displays the tremendous 174 5/8 Illinois rack from his largest bow-killed typical whitetail.

"I suddenly glimpsed movement in that same bean field," Perez said. "When I turned my head to get a better look, I saw a big-bodied buck, its head close to the ground, trailing behind a couple of yearling does. When I looked through my binoculars, I couldn't believe my eyes. It was Tall Tines!"

Perez was well aware that the pre-season had not progressed to the point where the two young does would be interested in any advances the big buck might make. Knowing that boredom would soon set in and cause the buck to leave, Perez slammed together his set of rattling antlers and then ground them into each other furiously.

"The buck stopped what he'd been doing immediately, and stared back in my direction," he said. "I stopped rattling and put the antlers away."

Tall Tines wasn't ready to abandon the does for another 30 nervewracking minutes. "Only then did he finally travel right down the tree line and directly for my stand," Perez said.

The big buck covered about 80 yards and then dropped down into a hollow where the archer lost sight of him. Moments later, Tall Tines reappeared on a ridge slightly opposite from where he'd been.

"I knew the buck was going to circle downwind," Perez said. "To keep my excitement under control, I kept repeating to myself, 'He's going to wind me, he's going to wind me.' I had to, just maintain my composure."

As the big deer continued its downwind circle, the bowhunter's anxiety attained critical mass. "The buck was just 10 feet from being directly downwind of me when he altered direction and headed straight toward me," he said.

Against all odds, the big buck had avoided walking into vagrant aircurrents that likely carried at least some of the archer's telltale human scent. Against all odds, Tall Tines was now proceeding, at a rapid walk, through tangled thicket of vines and brush.

Perez calculated the course the big buck was traveling and chose an opening to shoot through that the buck seemed fated to enter.

"I was at full draw before the buck ever reached it," he said. "When he'd moved about a quarter of the way through it, I grunted with my natural voice. The buck stopped; it looked in my direction. I steadied my 30-yard pin right behind his right shoulder and released the arrow."

The broadhead hit home, and almost instantaneously the buck reacted. It tossed its hindquarters high above its head, swapped ends and then slammed into a tree. Tall Tines crashed into the ground, clambered back to his feet and smashed through the brushy tangle of vines until Perez could no longer see him.

"I waited there, following his progress by listening to the snapping of branches and the popping of limbs," he recalled. "Then all was silent."

He knew Tall Tines was down, but he continued to wait quietly for about 15 minutes before he climbed down from his tree.

"I hit the ground and didn't even worry about searching for a blood trail," Perez said. "With the excitement that so often accompanies anticipation, I stalked onward to where I'd heard the buck's last loud crash. Forty yards into that maze of vines and brush, my best buck ever was lying sprawled out in a shallow swale."

Perez's pursuit of this outstanding Illinois whitetail had concluded on the highest possible note. As the comprehension of what had just transpired flooded through his consciousness, the grateful archer sat down on a nearby log where he relived the entire episode in his mind. "I waited there with the old buck for more than an hour before I even considered moving him," he said.

Such are the ways of those who revere large bucks, both whitetail and mule deer, above all else but God, country, family and friends. These bucks assume a place of tremendous importance in their lives, providing a focus and meaning that often defines them for the rest of their days. Like the advertisement says, for such people, an experience like Perez's truly was "priceless." Even now, each time Perez passes the mount of that massive, heavy-horned buck, he never fails to think of the very first time he saw him.

"He was standing in that bean field, with the sun's golden evening light glistening off those huge antlers," Perez said. "It was so cold, the steam of his breath before him blurred a portion of his face. And yet I'll never forget that moment, and the way he looked."

In this way, Dan Perez, and bowhunters like him, revere the animals they take, and bestow upon them their own measure of immortality.

## BOWHUNTING STATS

### HUNT PARTICULARS

**Superbuck:** Illinois 174 5/8 B&C Net Typical 10-Point
**Hunt location:** Illinois
**Date:** Nov. 2, 1977
**Time:** 5 p.m.
**Habitat type:** Timber/crop field (Note: Timber areas were extremely rugged)
**Weather:** Cool and overcast
**Ambient temperature:** 55 degrees
**Wind direction:** Northwesterly
**Sunrise:** 6:33 a.m.
**Sunset:** 5 p.m.
**Moon phase:** Waning gibbous; 64 percent of the moon's visible disc illuminated; moon was not up when I shot this buck.
**Moonrise:** 9:31 p.m. (Nov. 1); 10:25 p.m. (Nov. 2)
**Moonset:** 11:52 a.m. (Nov. 2)
**Duration of moonlight:** 9 hrs. 2 min. between the night of Nov. 1 and early morning Nov. 2
**Tree stand:** Set at 18 feet
**Tactics used:** When I saw the buck dogging some does at a distance from my stand, I rattled loudly.
**Had you seen that buck before?** Yes; we'd had a three-year relationship during which I'd spotted him, but only one other real encounter.
**Private ground or public?** Private
**Yours or someone else's?** Someone else's
**Outfitted or permission and self-guided?** Permission and self-guided

### EQUIPMENT

**Bow:** PSE Mach 8
**Sight:** PSE pin sights
**Rest:** TM Hunter
**Release:** Scott caliper
**Arrow:** 420-gram carbon shaft, 28-inches long
**Vanes or feathers:** 3.20 pro-fletch vanes
**Broadhead:** PSE Brute 125, which had four fixed blades

### BOWHUNTER'S Q&A

**Years hunting?** 40
**Years bowhunting?** 40
**Competition shooter?** At one time, yes
**3-D Shooter?** At one time, yes
**Number of days spent scouting yearly:** 300; I think, plan, plant food plots, breathe and sleep trophy whitetails.
**Number of days spent bowhunting yearly:** 70
**Number of states, provinces, countries bowhunted in an average year:** Two or three
**Other than whitetails, I've bowhunted for:** Black bear, mule deer, elk

**I've bowhunted whitetails in:** Illinois, Missouri, Iowa, North Dakota, Montana, Georgia, Nebraska, Texas, Florida, Kentucky
**Most likely to bowhunt in:** Missouri, Iowa, North Dakota
**Trophy-class whitetails taken to date:** 25 that exceed a P&Y gross score of 125 points; of that number, including my 174 5/8, another that grosses 171 2/8, one that grosses 170, two in the high 160s and four in the high 150s, plus a passel of 140-plus bucks.
**Tactics used:** Tree stand, stalking, still-hunting, ground blind
**Favorite tactic:** Tree stand hunting
**If you could hunt only one time of day . . . ?** I've been equally successful during mornings and evenings
**Tree stand particulars:** My favorite brand is Loggy Bayou because they're lightweight, quiet, solid, safe, and easily hung. I never used wooden stands because I believe they're too dangerous, and I never hunt in a tree without a stand.
**How do you blend in?** I'm very conscious of being skylined, so I prefer hanging my stands in trees with a wooded background as well as lower cover that will help disguise my presence.
**Rattle?** Depends on the circumstances
**Real antlers or synthetics?** Real; shed antlers
**Commercial or homemade scent?** No
**Scent-Lok:** Robinson Outdoors' Scent-Blocker
**Mock scrapes?** No
**Mock rubs?** No
**Trail cameras?** No; I enjoy fooling with them, but would never set one up where it might alert deer to my presence, especially if I'm trying to harvest a big buck in the area. They're great if you're able to slip in to replace film or chip without leaving human scent behind. Field or food plot edges would be good spots to set up trail cameras.
**Recent equipment upgrades:** PSE Primos Bow, 29-inch draw length; 80 percent let-off; 280 fps IBO; Carbon Force arrows; Tallon-100 broadhead; Scott Little Goose release aid; Vibra-check stabilizer.
**Braggin' rights:**

- My best bowhunting buddy is my son, Danny Perez.
- Anyone who'd like to learn more about my bowhunting style and big-buck tips should either read my book or attend one of my "Mossy Horn Seminars," which I put on in various locations around the country. Interested parties are welcome to email me at Dperez@pse-archery.com.

Ilinois archer Dan Perez hunts out whitetails where they live and then sets up nearby.

**TOP BOWHUNTING TIPS**

- Never examine a scrape by walking up to it. Use binoculars from a distance to check scrape activity. Harvesting a mossy-horned survivor means first respecting his scrapes.
- When this season closes, start next season's scouting. When woods and brush are naked of cover, the lay of the land is exposed. Every deer trail, bedding area, travel corridor and possible funnel situation can be easily identified.
- Study aerial maps before you enter new hunting areas. Zero in on crop fields located well away from roads, and identify unpromising areas.
- Study deer sign to locate whitetail high-traffic areas. Zero in on secluded crop fields, funnels, pinches (tighter funnel situations) and saddles.
- Hang stands based on the three "Ws," when, where and wind: When do deer use the area, where do they approach from or go, and how does the wind factor into the equation?
- Save your best stands-such as those positioned along a funnel that connects bedding areas-for bowhunting closer to the rut's peak period, and then hunt them sparingly.
- "Staging areas," places where mature bucks linger until dark in cover before heading out to feed, are great places to hang tree stands, especially if a trophy buck appears only after it's too dark to shoot.
- When watering holes freeze over, create your own. Carry a sledgehammer in your vehicle for breaking ice, avoid hunting nearby for the next 12 to 18 hours, and then make your move.
- During the rut and pre-rut periods, the best big-buck bait is does. Concentrate your efforts wherever you find the most does.
- During both the early and late seasons, my favorite low-impact scouting strategy is glassing favored feeding areas from a distance.
- Hunt ridgetops on windy days. Hunting hollows or canyons will plague you with swirling, unpredictable wind currents. The best tree for your stand is the one that will offer you the greatest number of possible shots while providing the least chance of being spotted or scented by your quarry.

# Russell Thornberry [Alabama]

***148 4/8 BTR Semi-Irregular Montana 12-Point Whitetail, Compound Bow Category; P&Y Gross Score: 166 1/8***

Who hasn't waited for the chance to draw back on a true trophy whitetail? Let's say an 11-point behemoth, with double drop tines, no less, wandered in front of your stand, like one did for Russell Thornberry on an early October day back in 1996.

"I closed the jaws of my release around my bowstring," he recalled. "As the buck walked past me and angled away, I started to raise my bow for the shot." But then a seemingly disembodied voice–an unwelcome reminder of Thornberry's reality at that time—whispered, "Don't shoot!"

At first, with a cockeyed optimist's irrational glee, the bowhunter took the whispered warning to mean that the cameraman in a nearby tree stand had spotted an even bigger buck for him to shoot. No such luck. The cameraman had halted him, in the midst of what would have been a perfect shot, Thornberry believes, to let him know there wasn't enough light to film the scene.

"There was the best buck I'd ever been in bow range of, and to be instructed not to shoot because of camera and lighting constraints was almost too much to comprehend," Thornberry said, still indignant almost a decade later.

"Welcome to the wonderful world of Deer TV," he said later, sarcastically expressing his warring

This 321-pound British Columbia buck is the largest bodied whitetail Russell Thornberry has ever arrowed. The huge body size dwarfs the 150-inch plus rack.

emotions that day. The seesaw battle raged between Russell Thornberry, avid whitetail archer who escaped to the woods to rejuvenate his spirit and recharge his batteries, and Russell Thornberry media celebrity, whose professional life was dedicated to helping to instill an awe and love of nature in others.

Thornberry has what most whitetail-hunting fanatics would consider a "dream job" as the editor-in-chief of three popular hunting magazines, *Buckmasters Whitetail Magazine*, *Rack*, and *Gun-Hunter*—all part of the Buckmasters media empire. Yet the man has never lost sight of what makes hunting and bowhunting most meaningful to him.

"At this stage of my life, hunting is more about *how* I do it than *if* I do it," Thornberry said. "I compare it to my fishing. I might be able to use a spinning rod to fill the boat up with fish, but catching fish isn't the point. If I couldn't use my fly rod, I simply wouldn't go. Some people don't care how they do something as long as they're doing it. For me, *how* I do it makes all the difference."

The anglers among us know that fly-fishers are a different breed; they care more about substance than result. A dedicated fly angler wants to catch fish, yet is usually unwilling to compromise on the means used to accomplish that end.

So it is with Russell Thornberry, the bowhunter. "My finest hunting memories are based upon the amount of drama and intensity involved in when an animal was taken," he said. "It's not merely a question of how big the buck was, but how hard or how long I had to hunt for him."

Discovering that he prefers using a bow when hunting whitetail deer comes as no big surprise. "Bowhunting for whitetails is special to me," he said. "An archer must deal both with the limitations of the equipment and the drama that unfolds as the deer approaches to where you might get a shot. I plan to be bowhunting until I'm too weak or decrepit to pull back the string. Bowhunting is a part of me."

This native Texan was stirred early on by an atavistic urge to hunt with a bow. He was still a tyke when he cut down a limb in his grandmother's backyard, fitted it with a string and began loosing stick arrows at anything unlucky enough to cross his path. "Between that homemade bow and my many slingshots, I became a pretty deadly shot on rabbits," he said.

The more scientific aspects of the sport, such as how to increase arrow speeds and the use of higher-tech materials, failed to interest Thornberry until he was about 13. "I got my first solid-handled fiberglass bow," he recalled, "and I promptly used it to shoot out a window.

"The greatest shot I ever made, one that remains so today, took place during those early days," Thornberry said. "I'd spotted a jackrabbit hunkered down in the brush about 70 or 80 yards away. I reckoned the trajectory, aimed up at the sky and let 'er rip. I was totally surprised when the arrow came down and hit that rabbit right between its shoulder blades."

However sporting that long-distance shot might have been, and despite the fact that male bunnies and deer are both properly termed "bucks," a rabbit hardly qualifies as a superbuck. So although Thornberry grew up in big-whitetail country, the path he followed to his current home in Alabama, and his leadership role with Buckmasters, which is located there, was rather circuitous.

"I began thinking during my junior high school years about what I wanted to do," he said. "I loved to hunt and fish, so I tried to figure out some way to work them into my career. I thought about becoming a game warden, but decided that wasn't for me. I was a big kid and a fairly good football player, and in Texas, that [combination] rules. I decided to see how far playing football might take me."

Thornberry excelled at the sport until his sophomore year in college. "I was out hunting with a friend when he handed me his .22 rifle," he said. "As he did so, he kept his finger on the trigger . . . somehow fired the rifle and shot me in my foot. That accident extinguished my dreams of someday playing pro football.

"I wandered about rather aimlessly for a while, but eventually I found myself back on track, thinking about hunting and fishing. I drifted into big-game outfitting in Alberta, Canada, and I soon began writing articles about my experiences. I was in the right place at the right time, at the start of the Canadian whitetail-hunting boom. As a Canadian outfitter, I was able to call attention to some of the best whitetail hunting for some of the largest-racked and bodied bucks on the continent. I truly believed that the Canadian whitetail-hunting experience was something special, and it was later proved true. That love of what I was doing, and why, came across in my writing. Without making any particular plans to do so, I'd gradually become one of the most qualified big-buck hunting writers in western Canada."

Thornberry's unique perspective on the topic soon had magazine editors and book publishers clamoring for his submissions. He began toying with the idea of devising a new scoring system for deer antlers—one that would be more fair or even-handed than those already in existence. The scoring systems established and used by B&C and P&Y rely a great deal on a rack's side-to-side symmetry when calculating net score: Does one side match the other, tine for tine, circumference for circumference? If not, deductions are taken, whether the rack is typical or non-typical—something Thornberry found frustrating. An inordinate emphasis on symmetry, he once commented, "penalizes many animals for growing antlers the way the good Lord intended them to grow."

After much thought, he arrived at a radically different antler-scoring method. Originally called The Alberta Trophy Deer Record System, this method did not penalize for lack of symmetry. Instead, scoring was based upon mass, or the total inches of antler upon a buck's head at the time the animal was taken or its rack picked up. Thornberry's method would eventually become the framework for Buckmasters' Trophy Record System, a method that has become increasingly popular among those who take huge bucks, whether they qualify for other records books or fall short due to another system's rigid demand for symmetry.

When Buckmasters' founder and CEO, Jackie Bushman, began casting about for a respected, high-profile individual to take the helm of a new deer-hunting magazine he envisioned, Thornberry was already well known in whitetail-hunting and publishing circles. The fact that he was Bushman's first choice was no surprise, and it has proved an inspired decision.

Today, Thornberry's name is synonymous with a high degree of hunting ethics, and an outdoor philosophy that are consistent with the way he lives his personal life, and which shine through in the pages of the publications he controls.

At a time when high-fenced big-game shooting operations seem to be gaining in popularity, Thornberry and Buckmasters have taken a stance that aggravates some folks on both sides of the issue.

"I'm not mad at fences," he said. "I'm mad at any kind of hunting that makes it impossible to be fair to the animal. There are many kinds of hunting in the world conducted inside fences. Some of it is actually more difficult because of the fence, while others are shams.

"With more high-fenced hunting opportunities being provided each year, we felt it was Buckmasters' duty as a company to define 'fair' as it related to a high-fenced situation. We're so committed to our definition that an operation that wants to advertise with Buckmasters first must prove that it meets our criteria.

"People all over the world have erected fences in an attempt to control hunting and the taking of quality game animals; America is no different. It's just been some time coming. I don't think we can stop it, although people are going to try."

Thornberry hopes that defining reasonable high-fence parameters and not being totally inflexible about them will help convince others that just killing an animal means nothing; circumstances of fair chase, whether within a high fence or outside of one, is what makes hunting a worthwhile endeavor.

This spirit of pragmatism puts Buckmasters and Thornberry at odds with B&C and P&Y in principle. Neither club allows an animal taken within the confines of a game-proof or high-fenced enclosure to be entered in their respective record books, no matter how large.

Thornberry, however, used the Kenedy Ranch, a Texas operation consisting of than 460,000 high-fenced acres, as a hypothetical example of the dilemma confronting record-books keepers as they attempt to determine which hunts are fair chase and which are not. Having hunted on Kenedy property, he said, "I believe a hunt there to be fair chase in every sense of the words. Why should those animals be ineligible for record-book listing?" But he knows there is no easy solution to this problem, and it will continue to plague ethical hunters and affect the non-hunting public's perception of hunters into the foreseeable future.

The same careful thought that he's given to fair chase and high fences was put to equally good use years ago, when he established the personal moral and ethical codes that define his hunting and bowhunting life. Those precepts came in handy once the corporate push to make him an on-camera hunting celebrity began.

"I cannot reconcile myself to being *required* to shoot something," he said. "And I refuse to make a business out of my personal hunting. Shooting something simply so that an animal will die for the camera filming it just isn't for me.

"I get around that by never planning a two- or three-day hunt," he said. "I make certain that if I'm going to be filmed, I'll have enough time to succeed on my own terms. That means a minimum of 10 days for any bowhunt. In 10 days, I feel I'll have a good chance of finding a deer that's big or unique enough that I'm excited by it. I refuse to shoot any animal because someone else wants me to; I'll only shoot it if I *want* to shoot it."

Yet compounding Thornberry's ethical dilemma is the fact that he's often hunting private land or with an outfitter by invitation. "I also feel compelled to shoot the best animal possible to attract people to that outfitter or guide's service. That's an added pressure," he said.

An archer bound by such constraints, even of his own making, can easily spend a minimum of 90 days bowhunting each year. Ninety days is a lot of time, and Thornberry has taken a lot of deer. Yet the fact that he's taken just 16 record-book whitetails that he considered worthy to be listed as his own true "trophies" illustrates the difficulties involved, even for an archer of his caliber, to connect on a trophy whitetail. Sixteen bow-killed trophy whitetails during a career that, to date, has spanned 52 years speaks volumes, especially when you factor in the difficulty of archery hunting with a cameraman in tow, like the one who put the kibosh on that shot at the double drop-tine 11-pointer, discussed at the beginning of this chapter.

Amazingly, Thornberry is reluctant to play that card. "A cameraman may have been a disadvantage early on," he said. "Analog film had its draw-backs; namely, the best 20 minutes for hunting, both early and late, didn't provide light good enough for filming. That was totally frustrating. Opportunities arose that I couldn't take. But things eventually changed for the better."

With the advent of digital cameras, the lighting problem was resolved. "The capabilities of cameramen also improved to the point where I no longer mind being filmed, at least not while hunting from a tree stand," Thornberry said.

He plans about a half-dozen trips each year with the intention of using acceptable archery footage in upcoming shows. The remainder of his bowhunting time is personal, when he doesn't have to concern himself with the camera, weather, or even if deer are moving.

That's a far cry from his week in Montana in 1996, when, with a sickening feeling, he watched the buck of his lifetime stroll calmly past his stand and couldn't do a thing about it. Thornberry had been so disgusted, he couldn't help wondering, "What am I doing here?"

The next morning, Jackie Bushman, who'd accompanied him to Montana, had a similar chance at a big 10-point that paused broadside 10 yards in front of him, and again the dreaded "Don't shoot" was heard, putting the brakes on any potential shot.

Later, Thornberry and Bushman talked about whether letting good bucks walk was wise, from either an entertainment or educational perspective.

"Viewers want to see the real thing," Bushman argued. "Not something staged to replicate circumstances."

"I'd never considered my personal hunting time as entertainment for a viewing audience," Thornberry said. "Hunting has always been a private, solitary endeavor; an encounter between me and the deer. With a cameraman and a potential viewing audience, I now realized it would never be the same. It would no longer be hunting for hunting's sake; it was hunting for the sake of others."

Thornberry had reported his triumphs and detailed his failures in hundreds of articles, but always after the fact. "My readers never interrupted me or made my hunt more difficult," he said. "Hunting on my own, with no distractions, was suddenly a luxury."

Filming caused other problems, particularly during Deer TV's early years. "If light wasn't good enough to film various set-up scenes, or if tracking occurred when the camera was unable to 'see' anything, viewers complained that shots look 'staged,' and with good reason," Thornberry said. "Some scenes would have to be re-shot on another day, sometimes when the light or weather were totally different."

To feed *Buckmasters' Television* needs each year means serving up 26 deer-hunting shows in a fairly brief period of time–filming that must be completed when whitetail hunting is legal in North America. "That's pressure," Thornberry stated. "People may think it's all fun, but believe me, it's not."

After letting the 11-point walk, Thornberry's big-buck luck seemed to desert him. He spotted several small bucks that he decided not to take, and then a respectable eight-pointer walked by in easy range. The light was good, and after plenty of soul-searching and rationalization, Thornberry decided to "go for it."

His shot appeared to be perfect. The buck leaped forward into some thick brush, where it disappeared. "I waited for a crash, but never heard one," the bowhunter said. A minute later, Thornberry saw the eight-pointer walking calmly down a trail to his left, browsing along the way. He consoled himself by thinking he might still get a chance at the double drop-tine buck.

Meanwhile, Bushman had arrowed a beautiful 10-pointer, his best bowbuck ever–good enough for the record book–and flew home the next morning. Thornberry stayed behind with the camera crew for one last try at one of the bruiser bucks that remained healthy and relatively undisturbed.

"My cameraman and I decided to head back to where Jackie had been hunting," Thornberry said. "A number of good bucks had been feeding nearby before he bagged the 10-point. Sure enough, a little past daylight, the same buck group returned to feed in the same place."

The archer spotted several excellent eight-pointers, two good 10-pointers, and a heavy-beamed

12-pointer, which gained two of those points courtesy of the rack's long, split brow tines, one on each side.

"That 12-pointer was to die for," Thornberry said. The bucks fed nearby for about 15 minutes, crossed a dry wash, and disappeared into the nearby brush. Once the deer had been gone for a reasonable length of time, Thornberry and the cameraman walked over to where the animals had been feeding.

A huge cottonwood tree with a twisted trunk leaned rather precariously about 30 yards from the spot. "It was leaning so badly that setting up one tree stand in it wouldn't work, and two would definitely be out," Thornberry recalled. The archer viscerally understood, however, that this tree presented him with his best, perhaps only, hope of taking the 12-point. "I envisioned myself standing in the tree's highest fork, safety straps around each trunk section, waiting like in a crow's nest on a sailing ship."

The following morning, Thornberry borrowed the rancher's extension ladder, positioned it against the tree's trunk, and left the area. The next morning found the archer climbing silently into the fork and securing his safety belts. The cameraman carried the ladder away; the plan was for him to wearing head-phones and manning a position about 100 yards distant, from which he'd try to film the action. Communication between archer and technician would be via a remote microphone attached to Thornberry's camouflage clothing.

The archer was settled into the fork of the big cottonwood well before first light and had drifted into daydreams when he heard the crunch of leaves below his stand. Two does and the big 12-pointer were walking directly below him.

Thornberry grabbed his bow, slid his hand in its sling, released his homemade rubber-band arrow holder, and clipped his release on the string. During this time, the buck had covered 30 yards. Thornberry positioned the pendulum sight's top pin behind the deer's right shoulder and squeezed his release's trigger.

"The arrow connected and the buck bolted into the nearby willows. He came out to my left, his head held low, and I knew he was hit hard. Not wanting to take any chances, I shot again, this time getting both lungs. The buck jumped back into the willows and vanished from my sight."

Only after the drama died down did Thornberry realize that he'd never activated his remote microphone. He had done the unforgivable–shot a big buck off camera. When he tried to turn on the mic, though, the red light was gleaming, which was even worse in Thornberry's mind. It had been on all the time, and he had failed to warn his cameraman that the deer was nearby and he was going to shoot.

Luckily, the cameraman had seen the buck just before Thornberry did. He got the camera turned on in time and filmed the whole event.

They found the buck lying not far from the willow patch. The cameraman, who had filmed Bushman a few days earlier, recognized the deer as the same one that he'd warned Bushman not to shoot in poor light. In other words, thanks to Deer TV—or perhaps in *spite* of it—RussellThornberry took his best bow buck ever: a typical 10-point, with high, heavy tines and "trash" enough, in the form of matching double brow tines, to make any discriminating whitetail archer happy.

The big buck scored 148 1/8 using the BTR system, and grossed 166 1/8 when scored using the P&Y method. Any way you score it, it's one for the books.

"I don't own hunting land," Thornberry reflected. "One of my life's greatest joys is to go somewhere new to hunt and figure out, in a set amount of time, what deer are doing to an extent that I'm able to take a good buck. I don't have all hunting season to learn a buck's pattern. I have 10 days after I've been dropped into his world. That's what I've been doing my entire life, and it's a huge challenge for any bowhunter, no matter how skilled he or she may be."

## BOWHUNTING STATS

### HUNT PARTICULARS

**Superbuck:** 148 4/8 BTR Montana Whitetail; 166 1/8 gross P&Y typical
**Hunt location:** Richland County, Montana
**Date:** Oct. 12, 1996
**Time:** Daybreak
**Habitat type:** Timber, near crop field (sugar beets)
**Weather:** Clear
**Wind direction:** Westerly
**Sunrise:** 7:12 a.m.
**Sunset:** 6:13 p.m.
**Moon phase:** New moon
**Duration of moonlight:** There was negligible illumination; moonrise and sunrise occurred at the same time—7:12 a.m.—on the morning I shot this buck.
**Tactics used:** No trees suitable for a stand, so I waited in the crotch of a cottonwood tree, 33 feet off the ground
**Had you seen that buck before?** Yes; at the beginning of that hunt
**Private ground or public?** Private
**Yours or someone else's?** Someone else's
**Outfitted or permission and self-guided?** We were hunting with permission on Montana landowner tags. We found bucks by ourselves.

### EQUIPMENT

**Bow:** Jennings Buckmaster
**Sight:** Pendulum
**Rest:** New Archery Products flipper rest
**Release:** Scott
**Arrow:** Easton 2317 aluminum shaft, 660 grains, 31 inches
**Feathers or vanes?** Vanes
**Broadhead:** Patriot two-blade, fixed, cut-on-contact

### BOWHUNTER'S Q&A

**Years hunting?** 52
**Years bowhunting?** 52
**Competition shooter?** No
**3-D Shooter?** No
**Number of days spent scouting yearly:** 30
**Number of days spent bowhunting yearly:** 90
**Number of states, provinces, countries bowhunted in an average year:** About eight
**I've bowhunted in:** British Columbia, Alberta, Saskatchewan, Quebec, Old Mexico, Alaska, Yukon, the Northwest Territories, Florida, South Carolina, Alabama, Texas, Mississippi, Louisiana, Ohio, Kansas, Iowa, Illinois, Montana, Pennsylvania, Wyoming, Idaho.
**Most likely to bowhunt in:** Kansas, Illinois, Iowa, Texas, Saskatchewan, British Columbia
**I've hunted whitetails in:** British Columbia, Alberta, Saskatchewan, Texas, Kansas, Iowa, Illinois, Mississippi, Louisiana, Alabama, Montana, Pennsylvania, South Carolina, Ohio, Wyoming, Idaho
**Other than whitetails, I've bowhunted for:** Canada moose, Alaska Yukon moose, grizzly bear, black bear, Rocky Mountain elk, red stag, mule deer, black-tailed deer, alligator, bison, caribou
**Estimated number of bow-killed whitetails to date:** About 200
**Largest-racked whitetails:** 131 1/8 P&Y; plus the following with BTR scores, which do not include the inside spread credit: 128 5/8, 109 6/8, 108 2/8, 131 6/8, 122, 117, 116 7/8, 113 2/8, 148 1/8, 147 3/8, 116 4/8, 121, 119, 138 3/8

**Tactics used:** I've about done everything.
**Favorite tactic:** Tree stand and ground blinds
**If you could hunt only one time of day . . . ?** It depends upon the moon phase and its impact on deer movements
**Why?** Feeding patterns shift depending upon moonrise, moonset, and phase
**Tree stand particulars:** I like a climber's versatility for ambushing bucks where they haven't been hunted. If I know I'm going to be spending long days on stand, then I prefer a spacious fixed-position stand for both comfort and staying power.
**Rattle?** I rattle from pre-rut through post-rut
**Real antlers or synthetics:** Real
**Commercial or homemade scent:** Commercial; doe-in-heat lure
**Scent-Lok:** Yes
**Mock scrapes?** Yes
**Mock rubs?** No
**Trail cameras?** No
**Recent equipment upgrades:** My affiliation with Buckmasters means I have many bows. I'll generally update my equipment annually with a new Jennings (our sponsor) bow.
**Braggin' rights:**

- My son Darren and my son-inlaw Barry are both hunters. My best bowhunting buddy is my lifetime hunting and fishing friend, Gary Sitton.

# Mike Weinerth [New York]

***182 3/8 Gross P&Y Typical 11-Point New York Whitetail***

When New York State's Mike Weinerth starts a discussion about bowhunting, the first thing he says is, "My best hunting stories are of fumbles and misses."

It turns out that Weinerth's not kidding, although he could have qualified his statement by amending it to "Some of my best hunting stories are of fumbles and misses." Because when he had to make his shot count, that's what he did, at least on his second try.

Mike Weinerth is one happy fellow. After talking to him for a while, you're happy, too. He bubbles over with joy as he describes how his parents, Tom and Linda Weinerth, raised him and his sister to appreciate everything about the outdoor life.

"If I were to describe how I came to know what I know about hunting and bowhunting, I can only say that I'm just a little chum fish feeding off scraps dropped by a shark," he said. "I'm the little chum and my father, Tom, is the shark, the ultimate predator. I can't begin to describe all the big bucks that he's tagged during the years, and he took them back when hunting was far tougher than it is now."

Still, it's Mike Weinerth who bagged one of the largest bow-killed bucks ever taken in New York State. And while the tale is one that could easily have been imagined by the Farrelly Brothers or the scriptwriters of Saturday Night Live, it's all Weinerth, all the way. Had someone videotaped his escapade, it might have won top prize on America's Funniest Home Videos, and yet the bottom line is this: His strategy worked. No matter how many obstacles appeared, Mike Weinerth surmounted each in its turn.

Weinerth's tale begins at about 10 a.m. on October 23, 2002. The weather had soured badly and the skies finally opened up in an absolute downpour. The drenched archer finally admitted to himself that he'd had about all the fun he could stand for one day, and climbed out of the tree stand he'd placed on private land in central New York. Once he reached the ground, he started trudging back to where he'd parked his truck.

"As I walked through this field of stubble, I noticed a huge buck about 250 yards away," Weinerth recalled. "The buck was busily feeding on the other side of an island thicket in the middle of the stubble field, and so he didn't spot me."

Weinerth said that the "island" was perhaps 30 yards wide and 70 yards long. It hadn't been cultivated because it was full of huge boulders, grown trees, shrubs and brush. Much of the vegetation was festooned with vines.

Using the island as cover, the bowhunter hurried across the field toward the feeding buck. "The rain was falling so fast and furiously, I didn't have to worry about [the buck] scenting or hearing me as I approached," he said.

While scurrying toward the buck, he stayed alert for some type of clearing in the thicket through which he might be able to shoot. He found one such opening; the big buck was standing, just 30 yards away, on its other side. Weinerth drew back his bow, aimed, and shot.

"The arrow went 'thwack," he said. "I saw the buck jump and then slowly walk away." Weinerth remained where he was until he saw the buck enter a thicket and disappear into the brush.

"I found my arrow immediately," he said. "It was sticking in a tree near the other side of the island, right in line with where the buck had been feeding. The shot probably would have been good had the tip of the expandable point not latched onto a small, dangling grapevine along the way. The grapevine slightly deflected the arrow from its course."

When Weinerth told his tale of bowhunting woe to his buddies, they didn't believe him. "I told them I'd just had a shot at a giant buck and they laughed and said, 'Sure, you did!'"

Trophy-whitetail bowhunters rarely give New York, New Jersey, New Hampshire or Pennsylvania a second thought when they're planning hunting trips. And yet the northeast has a long and storied history when it comes to hunting whitetail deer. Many hunters believe that the big-buck hunting in this area will continue to improve, since more and larger New England bucks have been reported recently than at any time in history. The region also is rife with hunting clubs and rod-and-gun clubs, and the social aspects of these organizations are a focus for many hunters and bowhunters—like the Weinerths—whose lives revolve around hunting and the outdoors.

Mike Weinerth, in fact, mentioned his clubs well before the discussion turned to the man's giant whitetail. "That's a big part of hunting in this part of the country," he said, referring to his affiliations.

He is the founder and president of New York's Mahogany Ridge Hunting Club. "We've got 100 members who hunt in the southern tier of New York State," he said. "Our members have sponsors, we make our own club videos and, thanks to one of our members who owns his own state-of-the-art video studio, we last year put out our first public video. The club is mainly social in nature, and we get together for wild-game dinners, compete in a turkey-hunting contest and big-buck competition, and generally just have fun together."

Weinerth also belongs to Weedsport Rod and Gun Club. "It's phenomenal," he said. "We've got 400 members, archery ranges, trap-shooting facilities, rifle ranges and other places were we shoot and fish."

Members of Mahogany Ridge and Weedsport had plenty to talk about in the days that followed Weinerth's remarkable bowhunting accomplishment. The story of how the archer bagged his buck traveled like wildfire, since so many of his bowhunting buddies had been integral to the plot.

"I hadn't forgotten the big buck I shot at the year before," Weinerth said. "When the 2003 season got under way, I was hoping to see that deer again. On the morning of October 28, 2003, I was bowhunting in a bottleneck of timber," he said. "After I finished the morning hunt, I decided to leave my climbing stand in position so I could return that afternoon.

"I walked out to where I'd parked my old '86 hunting truck, got inside, started the engine and began driving slowly. I could hear the muffler fall off, but it didn't fall all the way off.

"I turned toward town, and while I'm driving down the road, the muffler is dragging along beneath the truck. Sparks are flying and I can hear a terrible

Mike Weinerth's New York superbuck totaled 182 3/8 gross Pope & Young typical points as an 11-pointer.

clattering noise. As I'm driving, I spotted Trent Sears, one of my hunting buddies, and the two of us pulled our vehicles off the road so we could talk. I asked if he would cut off the muffler, but he didn't have any tools. We then drove to Elbridge, where a couple of other buddies, Donny Schoff and Lance Godfrey, were working on a house.

"Donny and Lance cut off the muffler, and after we'd talked for a while, I got into my truck and prepared to drive away, but the engine died. I tried but was unable to get it started. I'd been planning to drive over to my friend Alan Slater's house, but without a truck, I wouldn't be going anywhere. I then phoned Annette Young, my girlfriend, and waited until she was able to drive over to pick me up. I left all my hunting stuff in the old truck, got into Annette's Blazer, and we drove off."

Weinerth dropped off Annette at her house. He planned to return to his own house, on the far side of the bowhunting spot where he'd left his climbing stand that morning.

"I was driving down a main road, but I'm always searching for deer or deer sign as I'm doing so," Weinerth explained. "I looked into this one field and noticed a deer's body, with a huge set of antlers, lying in a gully about 80 yards away. Was the buck dead? Was it wounded? Or, was it simply bedded down? I didn't know.

"I turned the Blazer around and approached from the opposite direction. When I drove past the second time, I looked again and saw those huge antlers swing around to the side like a rocking chair. The buck was alive!

"I had no equipment, nothing. I turned the Blazer around again and drove it as fast as I dared back to where I'd left my dead truck, bow, Scent-Lok, and almost everything else. I had to pass a New York State Trooper barracks, and I'll bet the Blazer was doing 90 or 100 m.p.h. I didn't care; I just wanted to get my stuff and get back before the buck decided to get up and move.

"I reached town and discovered that the road had been blocked," Weinerth continued. "Just my luck that they'd chosen that moment to pull giant tankers out of a gas station. I had to wait; my truck and gear were on the other side of the roadblock."

Weinerth reached his truck after what seemed, in his words, like "an eternity." "I put on my gear, grabbed my bow and then raced the Blazer past the Troopers' barracks in the opposite direction. I was nearing the field and the gully when a combine pulled out in front of my vehicle.

"'Can't anything go right?' I wondered, as the combine chugged slowly down the road and then turned onto a side road," Weinerth said. "At that point I was totally hacked off. I sped about 100 yards further, pulled the Blazer off of the side of the road and parked.

"I couldn't see the buck from where I'd parked, and I wasn't even sure the animal was still there. A south wind added to my problems, since it was blowing past me and to the gully where I hoped the deer was bedded."

Weinerth would have to move diagonally across the field in his approach to the gully. He'd be traveling blind, since he had no way of knowing whether or not the buck was still there. His only option was to proceed as though it was, and hope that the puzzle pieces would eventually come together in satisfactory manner. Little did he know that salvation would come in the form of a previous frustration—the combine.

"I was wearing my Scent-Lok and yet I was worried as I started across the field," Weinerth said. "Big old bucks won't tolerate any unexplained human scent, and I knew it.

"That's when I suddenly realized how the combine might help me out. Its driver was traveling so slowly that the fumes and noise of the machine would help mask my scent and the sounds of my approach as I neared the gully. The smelly smoke that the combine was spewing out, together with the terrible racket it made, had to be distracting for the buck, if he was still bedded in the gully. When I got to within ten yards of the gully, I came to full draw, and then stood up so that I could peek up ahead. The buck was lying 30 yards ahead of me in the gully, staring back at the combine.

"I shot immediately," Weinerth said. "At the same instant, the buck shifted its body so that shot hit further to the rear than where I'd been aiming. As the buck jumped to his feet, I noticed a bloody area toward its rear end. In that spot was my arrow. The buck then ran around a knoll at the end of the gully and, when it did, I couldn't see where it went or what it was doing.

"I sprinted about 500 yards to a nearby swamp, where I believed I had a chance to cut off the buck if it had managed to escape. I waited, but no buck ever came past me. After 10 or 15 minutes, I walked back to the gully to search for blood or another sign of a hit. I spotted the buck just 20 yards from where he'd been when I'd shot him.

"I think I went crazy for the next several minutes," Weinerth said. "I hadn't yet started to field-dress the buck, but I tried to drag it around, for no reason whatsoever except that it seemed like the thing to do. I could barely budge the buck; its live weight was estimated to be 270 pounds. Even after it had been field-dressed, it weighed 215 pounds.

"I wanted to field-dress the buck, but I didn't have my knife. I got my cell phone and called both Alan Slater and Trent Sears to ask if they'd come over and help me. When they arrived, they each told me, 'Man, that's a record book buck.'

"Believe me, that deer saw more counties and bars dead than it ever did while alive."

Unbeknownst to the archer, the shot he'd made at the huge 182 3/8 gross P&Y buck was the last shot anyone would take with the bow he'd been using. In other words, it was a good thing he didn't need to take a second shot, because his bow's cable was so badly frayed that it nearly separated."The bow was no longer made, so I was unable to replace the cable," Weinerth explained. "I'm just fortunate that the cable lasted as long as it did."

He makes no apologies for his zany whitetail bowhunt, "I think craziness actually helps when you're trying to bag a big buck up in this country."

Crazy hunt or not, Weinerth remained on top of the world about his big buck nearly two seasons later, despite feeling that the wrong archer, perhaps, bagged the trophy buck."I know it sounds funny, but I wish my Dad had harvested this buck," he said. "What a fitting way to top off [his] lifetime of hunting. My Dad deserves a buck like mine more than anyone else in the world."

Weinerth hesitated, and then added, "But I'll take it."

He is grateful to both his parents for raising him to love the outdoors and hunting. "On the day that I was born, my Dad killed a nice buck," he said. "Back when I was just a little kid, my Dad would come back to the house and ask me to help drag his buck out of the woods. I'd ask, 'How big is it, Dad?' and he'd say, 'Just a spike.' But when we'd reach the buck, it would always be a nice eight- or ten-pointer."

Tom Weinerth, Mike's father, is of the old school of hunting and bowhunting. "He won't use Scent-Lok," his son explained. "He works the wind, period.

"My father taught me how important wind direction is when you're hunting whitetails. That's especially true in the areas where we hunt in New York, because heavily pressured deer are extremely sensitive to human scent.

Weinerth's mother, Linda, has taken plenty of whitetail bucks herself. In addition, she's the state's top-ranked female trap shooter.

As the twig is bent, so does the tree incline. Perhaps that's why Weinerth is such a "bare-bones" archer—one who has rigged his bow to be so rugged that it can be dropped or abused and still shoot accurately, every time.

After enduring a serious blood infection that prevented him from hunting the entire 2004 season, Mike Weinerth realized that there was no time like the present for him and his Dad to expand their whitetail-hunting horizons.

"We'll be traveling to Indiana and Illinois this fall," he said. "As of now we can harvest three bucks apiece: archery tags for both states and a shotgun tag for Indiana. If we draw shotgun Illinois tags, we'll be allowed to take four whitetails out of state, as well as two New York bucks, one with a gun and one with a bow."

Life is good, if you're Mike Weinerth. He loves his job at Meyers RV Superstore where the management allows his to structure his schedule so that he can hunt the entire New York bow and gun seasons. He's surrounded by family and friends who, like Weinerth, love hunting and the outdoors as much as the air that they breathe.

His giant New York whitetail may have been his life's high point to date, but Weinerth doesn't intend to rest on his laurels. He's got a great role model who's been leading the way and showing his son how it's done for as long as the younger Weinerth can remember.

If all goes well, perhaps Mike Weinerth will be there when his role model, his father Tom, bags a whitetail trophy as big or bigger than the one Mike bagged on that wacky autumn day in 2003.

## BOWHUNTING STATS

### HUNT PARTICULARS

**Superbuck:** 182 3/8 Gross P&Y New York Typical 11-Point Whitetail
**Hunt location:** Onondaga County, New York (near the Finger Lakes)
**Date:** Oct. 28, 2003
**Time:** 9:30 a.m.
**Habitat type:** Cornfields, beanfields, swamps and hardwood thickets
**Weather:** Clear and warm; blue skies.
**Ambient temperature:** 50 degrees
**Wind direction:** Southerly
**Wind speed:** 5 to 10 m.p.h.
**Sunrise:** 6:35 a.m.
**Sunset:** 5:04 p.m.
**Moon phase:** Waxing crescent; 14 percent of the moon's visible disk illuminated
**Moonrise:** 10:35 a.m.
**Moonset:** 7:20 p.m.
**Duration of moonlight:** Moon set at 6:32 p.m. on the preceding day, so there was no visible moonlight

that night. Moon rose on the morning I killed this buck, approximately one hour after it was shot.
**Commercial or homemade scent?** None when I took my biggest buck.
**Scent-Lok?** Yes; Scent-Lok is an absolute necessity.
**Had you seen that buck before?** Yes; I missed him the previous year.
**Private ground or public?** Private
**Yours or someone else's?** Someone else's
**Outfitted or permission and self-guided?** Self-guided

EQUIPMENT

**Bow:** Golden Eagle Carbon Hawk; 75 lbs. 65 percent let-off; 28-inch draw length
**Sight:** One homemade fiber-optic pin
**Rest:** Carolina Archery's Whisker Biscuit. This is the best investment an avid bowhunter can make. I can hang almost upside-down from my stand and still be able to shoot without fear of having my arrow fall off the rest.
**Release:** Yes; an old release, and I forgot its name.
**Arrow:** Easton Carbon Epic 340
**Feathers or vanes:** Vanes
**Broadhead:** 85-grain expandable; not sure which one, but think it was a Jackhammer
**Optics used?** Simmons monocular

BOWHUNTER'S Q&A

**Occupation?** RV salesman at Meyers RV Superstore
**Years hunting?** 23
**Years bow hunting?** 23
**Competition shooter?** No
**3-D Shooter?** No
**Number of days spent scouting yearly:** Every chance I get all year long. I begin the day after the season ends, and don't stop until the day the next season begins.
**Number of days spent bowhunting yearly:** 40 to 45
**Number of states, provinces, countries bow hunted in an average year:** One
**I've bowhunted in:** New York, Pennsylvania; I'm also bowhunting in Indiana and Illinois.
**Most likely to bowhunt in:** New York
**Estimated number of bow-killed whitetails to date:** 20
**Largest-racked whitetails:** 182 3/8
**Tactics used:** Tree stand, stalking, ground blind, still-hunting
**Favorite tactic:** Tree stand
**If you could hunt only one time of day . . .?** Morning (But I enjoy bowhunting any time.)
**Why?** If you hit one, you don't have to worry about following it up. Plus, deer are still on their way back from bedding areas, and if you plan properly, you should be able to sneak into your stand without them knowing you're there.
**Tree-stand particulars:** I prefer using a Lone Wolf climbing stand. It's lightweight, easy to pack and easy to climb with.
**How do you blend in?** I use surrounding branches, weeds and brush; basically, I'll use anything I can that won't hinder drawing the bow or my shot.
**Rattle?** Rarely
**Real antlers or synthetics:** NA
**Commercial or homemade scents?** Local homemade doe or buck urine
**Scent-Lok:** Yes; I wouldn't be without it.
**Mock scrapes?** Yes. I even have a deer foot I'll use to make mock scrapes, but only what I call "scrub" bucks have ever come in to my mock scrapes.
**Mock rubs?** No
**Trail cameras?** Yes, film. I use it for scouting, but I think I'm going to upgrade because I'm not happy with the results so far.
**Recent equipment upgrades:** I now shoot a High Country bow.

**Braggin' rights:**

- Having a family that supports me in my hunting, bowhunting and fishing is one of the most important things in the world to me. My mother, father, sister Tammy and her husband, Kevin Simmons, all hunt, and we enjoy sharing hunting stories.
- I have so many great bowhunting buddies, including my father, that it would be impossible to list them all. I'm so fortunate that I have them and we share common bonds that keep us close and, I hope, always will.
- And my girlfriend, Annette, well, I just love her a lot.

**TOP BOWHUNTING TIPS**

- Hunting wind direction is very important.
- K.I.S.S.—Keep It Simple, Stupid—that's what I try to do. The easier the hunt, the happier I am.
- If they're pressured, then the bucks may move and I'll go with them.
- Make sure your equipment is tough enough to stand up to hard use; that's important in case a shot materializes after you've inadvertently dropped your bow.

# BONUS TIPS
## 43 Tips for Bowhunters

*Taking a deer with a compound or recurve bow is, to many, the ultimate accomplishment in hunting. These tips can help you do it.*

1. Because arrows outfitted with hunting broadheads often fly differently from arrows outfitted with field or target tips, it pays to practice with the same broadheads you'll be hunting with. You'll occasionally have to replace the razor-blade inserts when they become too dull for hunting use, and you may have to replace the whole broadhead if it doesn't have inserts. If economy is important, practice with field tips during summer, then switch to broadhead practice as the season gets closer.
2. When you buy a new bow, fine-tune it by shooting through a large sheet of white paper tacked to a square wooden frame (place straw bales behind the wooden frame to stop the arrows). When you examine the tear holes, you can determine if your arrows are fishtailing or porpoising in flight. Ideally, you want to see a round shaft hole surrounded by perfect fletching cuts. If you're getting tail-high cuts, tail-left cuts, and so on, the remedy is to either slightly move the plunger button in or out, or adjust the arrow rest. Because every bow and each brand of arrow rest is different, consult the owner's guide for exact fine-tuning techniques.

To take bucks like this, you must spend a good deal of time prior to the season fine-tuning your equipment.

3. Strive for the most realistic shooting practice. Shoot arrows at life-sized 3-D foam deer targets, not at straw bales with bull's-eyes. And don't simply place the deer targets out in the open. Position them in shrubbery, under low-hanging tree branches, and in close proximity to other cover, to simulate actual shooting conditions.

4. The most common causes of an arrow wobbling in flight are an untuned broadhead, an untuned nock, or a bent arrow shaft. Use an inexpensive tabletop device called an Arro-Check to fix the problem. Lay the arrow on top of the device's opposing bearings, and spin it rapidly. If the tip of the broadhead scribes a wide circle, replace it with a new one. Now check the nock the same way, and replace it if necessary. If the arrow still wobbles in flight, the shaft has a minor bend that the naked eye cannot see. Either take the shaft to your pro shop, to have it straightened out or remove the broadhead and discard the defective shaft.
5. When a deer jumps the string, it instantaneously crouches to load its leg muscles with springed tension in preparation for flight. When it does this, the arrow frequently flies over its back. It never actually sees the arrow and attempts to duck it, however. Instead, it's reacting to the sound of the bowstring being released. Even though an arrow from a compound bow travels at an average of only 250 feet per second, sound travels at 1,088 feet per second, so the noise of your bowstring reaches the deer five times faster than the arrow itself. Dampen your bow noise with string silencers, but also remember to aim slightly lower. To achieve the recommended lung shot, for example, the aiming point should be the heart.

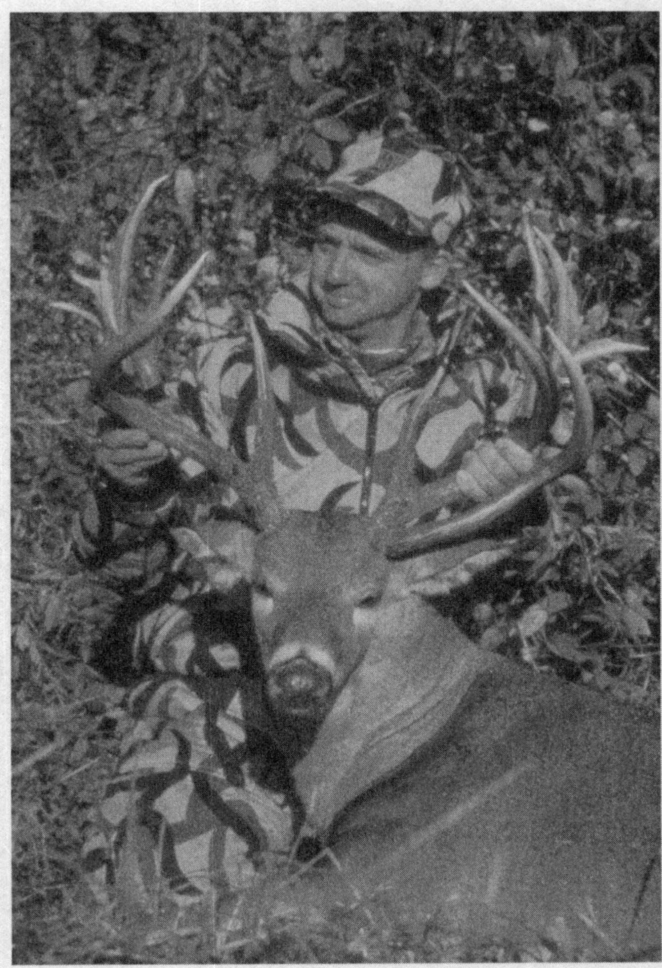

As a general rule, bowhunters take bigger bucks than those who use firearms, but not necessarily because they're better hunters. It's because most states' firearms seasons don't open until after the mating period when bucks are most vulnerable.

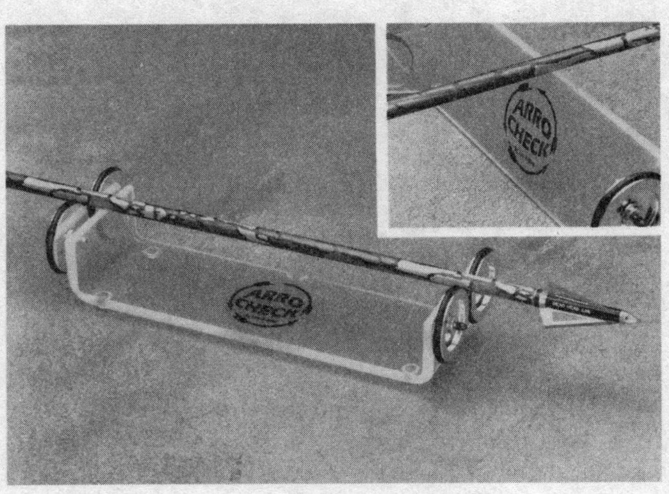


It's easy to diagnose arrow problems with an arrow spinner made for the purpose.

6. When you engage in shooting practice, wear the same clothing you'll be wearing while actually hunting, not casual clothes. The hunting clothes will undoubtedly be heavier and bulkier, and this will slightly change the way you hold and draw your bow.

7. The cams and wheels of compound bows have an annoying habit of squeaking at precisely the wrong moment. Some hunters lubricate them with silicone spray, but this attracts dust and grit. It's better to use a small pinch of graphite powder. The cable guard may also squeak upon occasion, but due to the wear of the cables on the guard, graphite powder will quickly wear off. Keep a pencil stub in your pocket, and frequently blacken that part of the cable guard contacted by the cables.
8. How high should a bowhunting stand be? Let the shape of your chosen tree answer that question. If the tree looks like a straight, naked utility pole, a stand height of twenty-five feet or more may be in order. But if the tree has a multiple-forked trunk and many gnarled branches at a lower height—both of which will adequately break up your body outline—then hanging your stand at only eight or ten feet may be sufficient.
9. A bowhunter's ideal shot at a deer comes when the animal is standing broadside or quartering slightly away, which exposes the largest organ, the lungs. Don't settle for less or be too impulsive to shoot; deer tend to dawdle around, and in many cases they'll eventually offer the shot you want.
10. Even with a finely tuned bow, broadheads that have replaceable razor-blade inserts with cutout vents tend to fly more accurately than broadheads with solid-surface blades. The latter often plane a bit, especially in brisk breezes, causing the hunter to miss his point of aim.
11. If you know your shot at a deer was not as accurate as you would have liked, how long

This is your shot!

Turkey feathers are more forgiving— but plastic fletching is better in inclement weather.

should you wait before following the blood trail? The rule of thumb is half an hour if the shot was in the front half of the animal, and three hours or more if the shot was toward the rear. An exception to this rule occurs during inclement weather. Then, you must take up the trail immediately, or rain or snow will quickly obliterate it and eliminate any chance for recovering the animal.

12. What's the best type of arrow fletching, turkey feathers or plastic vanes? Both have benefits and shortcomings. Turkey fletching is more forgiving when you make mistakes such as not smoothly releasing the bowstring, but in inclement weather feathers tend to become matted. Plastic vanes won't correct even a slight bit of arrow wobble, but they're immune to moisture. Just bump the arrow shaft with your finger, and water droplets will fall away.
13. Many bowhunters hang a grunt tube and binoculars around their necks, but these can cause problems when you're attempting to draw. It makes more sense to stow these items in large cargo pockets, so that they don't get in the way.
14. A peep sight on your string can shift after numerous shots if it's not permanently secured in place, and this will, of course, destroy accuracy. Many veteran bowhunters like to tightly wrap dental floss on the string immediately above and below the sight and then liberally paint the floss winding with clear nail polish or superglue to make it durable and prevent it from unraveling.
15. Buying a hunting bow from a department store or through a catalog is beneficial only from the standpoint of getting a good price. You need more than that, and it's rare to get a bow custom-fitted to your needs through such retail outlets. That's why many serious hunters prefer to deal with a local pro shop. You may pay a bit more, but the draw weight of the bow will be adjusted exactly as you want, arrows can be custom-cut in accordance with your measured draw length, a bow sight or custom arrow rest can be installed, and future tune-ups or repairs by a factory-authorized dealer are a breeze.

Work on your angles by shooting from an elevated vantage point such as your garage or house roof.

16. When you're shopping for a new bow at a custom archery shop, shoot several models and brands on their indoor target range (another

Put a dab of fluorescent paint on your sight pins to see them better in low light.

service not offered by department stores and catalogs). High-tech compound bows are fitted with a wide variety of wheels and cams come in too many designs to mention here. As a result, one bow model may draw easily and be perfect for target archery but be far too noisy and therefore unsuitable for deer hunting. Another bow's wheels may be dead quiet on the draw, but its breakover point—the point at which the draw weight suddenly lessens—may be unacceptable for your hunting purposes. You have to decide on these and other factors to satisfy your personal hunting needs, and the only way you can do this is by actually shooting and comparing numerous bows.

17. If you'll be bowhunting from a high tree stand, don't practice across level ground. Shoot from a stand hung in a tree in your backyard, from the roof of your garage, or from some other elevated vantage to master the acute downward shooting angles. Likewise, if you'll be hunting from a ground blind, practice while kneeling or sitting on a stool.
18. If you're commonly on stand at the crack of dawn or at dusk, and you have difficulty seeing your metal sight pins in the low light, switch to plastic glow pins. Or dab a bit of fluorescent paint onto each metal pin. If you use lighted sight pins, be sure to change the battery at the beginning of each season and keep a spare in your fanny pack.
19. Which is better, a cutting-tip broadhead that you must sharpen, or a chisel-point broadhead with replaceable razor blades? Cutting-tip heads penetrate more easily because they begin severing hair and hide the instant the broadhead makes contact with the animal. Chisel-point broadheads, on the other hand, must push through the hair and hide before the razor blades can do their cutting work. Balance this against the fact that sharpening cutting-tip broadheads takes a good deal of time. Plus, they must be sharpened often because repeatedly pulling them out of a quiver and shooting them at targets quickly dulls them. Chisel-point broadheads need no time-consuming sharpening, though—just slip new ones in place.
20. Should your broadheads be turned in their arrow-shaft sockets until the blades are perfectly in line with the fletching? Engineers for broadhead companies say no. If, by coincidence, the blades end up perfectly aligned with the fletching, fine. But a less-than-perfect alignment is also fine; any effect upon arrow trajectory or flight will be so minimal that you'll never notice it.
21. Unless you practice throughout the year, it's wise to release the draw weight of your compound bow before putting it into off-season storage. Do this by making four to six turns of the limb bolts to lessen the stress on the limbs and

reduce stretching of the string. Simply unstring a recurve or long bow after each day's hunt or practice session.

22. The risers and handles of compound bows are made of lightweight metal composite materials. If they come into contact with an aluminum or carbon arrow, a metallic clinking sound is created that will put nearby deer on full alert. Pad your arrow shelf, sight window, and handle with moleskin or felt that has a self-adhesive backing. The material also makes the handle warmer to hold in chilly weather.
23. Bow-tuning problems associated with erratic arrow flight can often be traced to a cheap arrow rest. It's false economy to spend $350 on a new bow and then slap on a $2 arrow rest. Check the catalog of the company that made your bow, and you'll undoubtedly find a wide array of arrow-rest options. The higher-quality rest you select, the better accuracy you can expect.
24. In hot weather, never leave a long or recurve bow in an enclosed vehicle for long periods of time. These bows commonly have wood and/or fiberglass laminations, and excessive heat may cause the glue between the component layers to melt, ruining the bow. Some compound bows with solid-metal limbs and risers may also warp just enough to destroy accuracy.

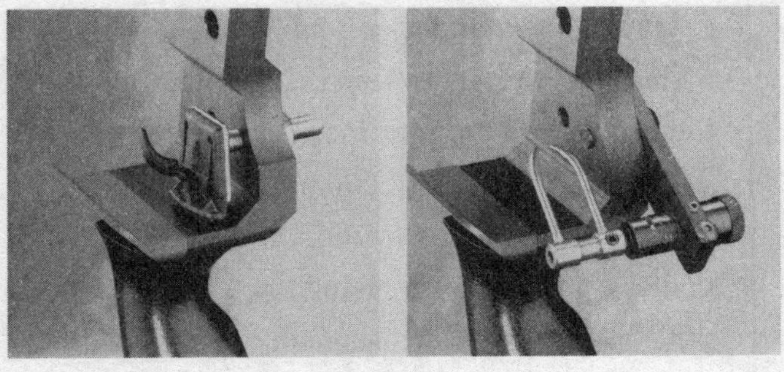

Buy a quality arrow rest. Two common styles are shown.

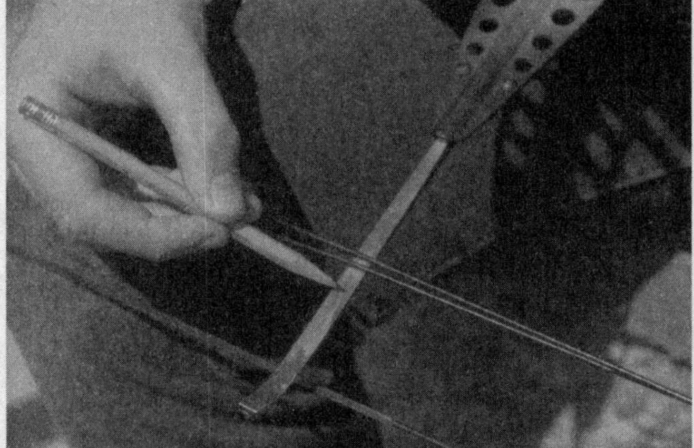

Graphite on cable and string guards prolongs their lives and eliminates squeaks.

25. The key to shooting accuracy is acquiring an intimate familiarity with your equipment, and this means regular practice throughout the year. Practice your shooting in small, untiring doses. It's far more beneficial to practice for twenty minutes every day of the week than to engage in a single four-hour marathon session on a Saturday morning.
26. How many pins do you need on your bow sight? Some hunters have only one, set at twenty yards. They then restrict themselves to shots of no more than thirty yards, which makes the slight aiming adjustment easy. Other hunters use four pins set at ten-yard intervals. It's a matter of individual preference.
27. Compound-bow hunters often own two identical bows, one of which is kept in camp as a backup. The reason is that it's very difficult to replace a compound bow's broken cable or string in the field; most such bows must be repaired at an archery shop with a bow press. Meanwhile, a backup bow set up exactly the same way as the damaged bow can save an otherwise ended hunt.
28. Wear an arm guard in cold weather when you're bulked up with heavier clothing. Otherwise, a

released bowstring may slap against the sleeve of your bow arm and send the arrow flying wildly away.

29. A belt pouch can be used to support the lower limb and wheel assembly of your compound bow. When you're standing, you won't have to constantly strain your muscles by trying to hold your bow vertically, ready to draw and shoot. Moreover, when the moment of truth arrives, and a deer is within shooting range, the only movement necessary is raising the bow a few inches to clear the pouch. Such minimal movement will reduce the chances of alerting the deer to your presence.
30. Broadheads weighing 100 to 135 grains are recommended for most whitetail deer hunting situations.
31. As a rule, the best fletching twist for right-handed bowhunters is right helical; for left-handed bowhunters, it's left helical. In either case, a four-inch-long fletching is recommended for stabilizing a carbon arrow with a broadhead; five-inch fletching works best for aluminum arrows fitted with broadheads. Far less satisfactory results come from using straight fletching or fletching of less than four inches long and intended solely for competitive shooting with target points.
32. If your turkey-feather fletching becomes matted or bent due to exposure to moisture, allow it to dry thoroughly. Next, hold it briefly over the steam coming from a teakettle spout, which will allow the feather fronds to spring back to their original shape.
33. Many bowhunters think they can gain greater arrow speed—and thus a flatter arrow trajectory in flight—by increasing a bow's draw weight. This is true, but all bows have an upper draw-weight limit, and in all cases, the higher the limit selected, the more difficult the string is to draw and hold. One solution is to use an overdraw, a shelf that extends back from the bow handle. This shelf allows you to use arrows that are shorter and therefore lighter in weight, increasing your arrows' speed and flattening their trajectory without increasing draw weight.
34. When you're using a recurve or long bow, deaden the twanging sound your bowstring makes upon release by tying two acrylic yarn puffs or rubber cat whiskers onto your string, one of them ten inches from the top limb and

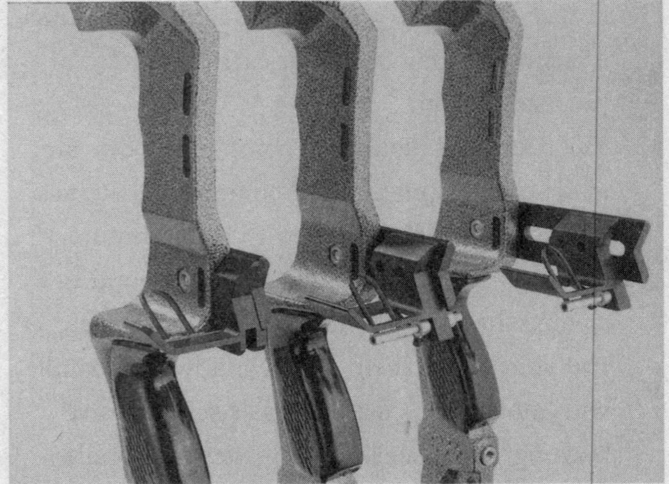

Overdraw shelves come in a variety of sizes.

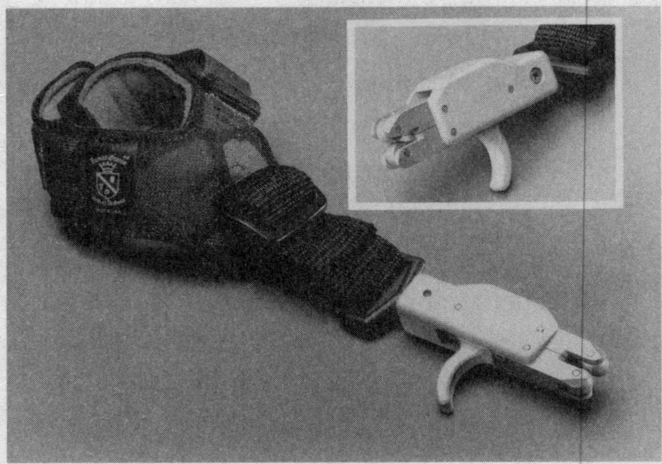

A mechanical bowstring release is generally smoother than shooting with a glove or tab, and it yields greater accuracy. But you must occasionally maintain it by removing grit and grime from the moving parts.

the other ten inches from the bottom. With an overly noisy compound bow, you may have to use four silencers: two on the string and two on the cable.

35. If you use a shooting tab or a three-fingered glove, small traces of perspiration and grime will eventually roughen the leather's surface, and this will begin to cause a stuttered string release that impairs accuracy. To cure this, place a teaspoon of unscented talcum powder in your hunting jacket pocket, and occasionally place your shooting hand in your pocket. A tab or glove with a fine coating of powder will give you the silkiest shooting release imaginable.
36. If you shoot with a mechanical shooting release, use a can of compressed air to blow out dust, pocket lint, and other debris that's sure to have accumulated in the trigger mechanism. Then, add one drop of unscented oil to the inner moving parts.
37. The weakest part of any bow is its string, because of minor but continual fraying. To prolong the string's life, rub it with beeswax several times each season. Put some on your fingertips, and then vigorously rub the string between them until you can feel heat being generated, which means the wax is softening and penetrating the strands. Whenever you have any doubt about the string's integrity, immediately replace it. You *do* have a spare on hand, don't you?
38. One advantage that carbon arrows have over aluminum shafts is that they cannot be inadvertently bent; either they remain perfectly straight, or they break. Aluminum shafts become bent from shooting, penetrating a deer, or hitting the ground when a shot is missed. You should either discard damaged arrows or have your local archery shop put the shafts on an aluminum-arrow straightener.
39. If you plan to build one or more ground blinds, buy a roll of lightweight camouflage cloth. Inexpensive and available in all the popular patterns and colors, the cloth can be cut to length and thumbtacked between two trees. A few strategically placed branches help break up the blind's rectangular shape; all you have to add is a stool to sit on.
40. What's the longest shooting distance a bowhunter should attempt? Only the distance that he has regularly practiced and at which he is confident he can execute the shot with accuracy.
41. Be aware of an important mechanical glitch that arises when shooting with sight pins—you have to hold your bow nearly vertical. If you

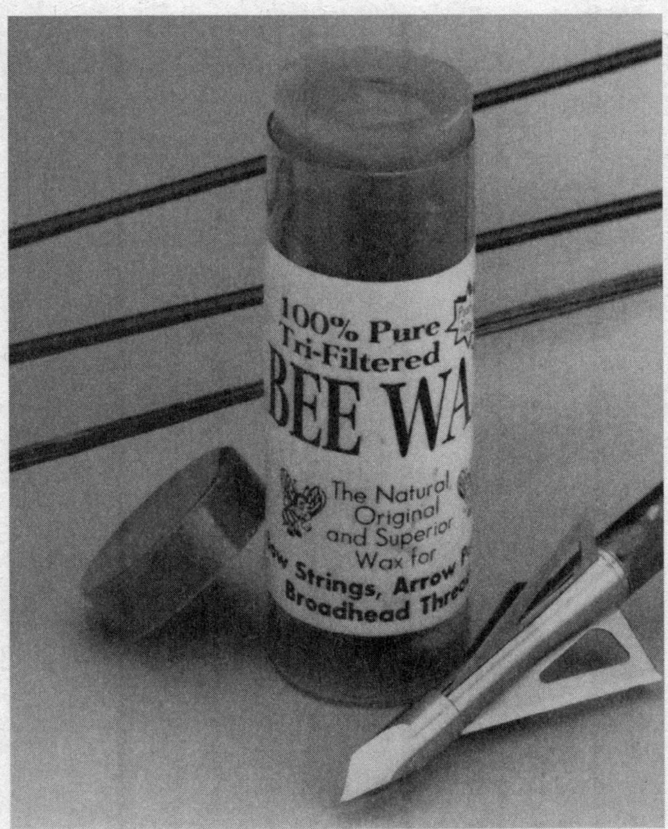

Get into the habit of applying beeswax to your bowstring several times a year.

Carbon arrows won't bend; they're either straight, or they break.

Roving is an excellent way to fine-tune your shooting ability away from the target range.

try to cant your bow slightly to the right, you will shoot considerably low and to the right. And depending on whether you're a right- or left-hand shooter, you'll probably hit the animal too far forward or too far to the rear. That's why there is an increasing trend among bowhunters to no longer rely on sight pins, but to learn to trust instinctive shooting.

42. When using either a compound bow, recurve, or long bow, the bow arm should never drop the moment you release the arrow because this will cause the arrow to fly low to either the right or left, depending on whether you are right- or left-handed. This is called plucking, and it's detrimental to accuracy.
43. Once you become adept on the shooting range, continue your practice afield. The value of roving, as it is known, is learning to estimate distances. Using a judo head instead of a broadhead or field point, shoot at leaves, tiny patches of moss, or pinecones on the ground. It is equally important to shoot uphill, downhill, across ravines, through holes in cover, in brightly illuminated places, and in shadows.

# Part 4

# *Big Game, Small Game*

# Introduction

While deer, and especially whitetails, are the quarry of choice for the majority of bowhunters, there is that special cadre that casts its eye at other quarry, big and small, dangerous and not. In this section, you'll get all the information you need to know on stalking black bears (or hunting them with hounds), calling moose into bow range, hunting turkeys in the spring, going after small game such as rabbits, bowhunting for bugling elk in the high country, sneaking up on bedded mule deer in rimrock country, plus setting up for a shot at a trophy antelope buck on the plains. Whitetails may be the ultimate quarry to most of us, but you haven't lived until you've called an enraged bull elk into bow range. Steam spewing from his nostrils as he lets loose yet another bugle, so close that it makes your ear ring; then you wait until he passes behind a tree, giving you a chance to draw. Then, you make the shot. You want an adrenaline rush? Look no further!

—Jay Cassell

# Bears

Bear bowhunting seldom lacks in challenge or excitement, whether you're following a pack of trained bear hounds, spotting and stalking a bruin across a salt grass flat in Alaska, stand-hunting over a bait in Saskatchewan, or calling a ravenous bear with a predator call in Arizona.

Bears are unique animals that have many habits and characteristics totally different from other big game. They are the only species of big game that spends the cold winter months in hibernation. They are soft-footed, silent, solitary animals that prefer the most rugged terrain and inhospitable, impenetrable jungles of brush and vegetation, negotiating and surviving in this habitat with ease.

Black bears come in many different color phases, ranging from light blonde to reddish or cinnamon, chocolate brown, and coal black. Black bears on Kermode Island, off the coast of British Columbia, have evolved into a predominantly creamy white color, and the rare "glacier" or "blue bear" phase near Yakutat, Alaska, is a beautiful and unusual bluish-gray color.

There are areas of Canada, Alaska, and the eastern United States where the bears are predominantly black, and getting a color-phase bear is a rarity, while in central and western Canada and the western United States, color-phase bears make up about 40 percent of the population. One spring I had a sow bear bring three beautiful blonde-colored yearlings into a bait site with her when she appeared in the early spring. She abandoned the cubs in mid-June, when she was ready for breeding, and by September, two of the cubs had shed their blonde fur and were dark brown, while the third remained a light-blonde color with dark lower legs, a phenomenon I had never witnessed before.

Grizzlies and brown bears (actually the same species) vary in color as much as black bears but display the grizzled or variegated-colored hair that gives them their name. I've observed black bears that had a grizzled-color appearance and grizzlies that were solid brown or black, so color is not a reliable species identifier.

The most dependable identification characteristics are the roman nose of a black bear, compared to the dished-in face on the grizzly, and the rounded shoulders of the black bear as opposed

Like a lot of other big game, black bears prefer southern exposures for feeding grounds when they first leave their dens.

to the grizzly's predominate hump. A black bear's claws are short, and if they show at all in the tracks they will be very close to the toe pads, while a grizzly's claws are long and usually leave a mark at least an inch or more in front of the toe pad.

When a bear first rouses from its long winter's nap, it's pretty lethargic. Its feet are very tender (I've heard that bears completely shed their footpads during hibernation but haven't observed this personally), and their digestive system needs reconditioning. For the first few days, they stay close to the den, resting and nibbling. As time progresses, they venture farther and spend more time satiating their growing appetite. A spring bear may spend four hours a day roaming and feeding, while a fall bear preparing for hibernation will spend four hours a day resting or sleeping and 20 hours voraciously feeding on anything that doesn't bite it first.

Bears are completely omnivorous and have an amazingly varied diet, from bugs to berries and grass to the grossest carrion around. They are also very efficient predators and are very capable of killing other big-game critters. There are several studies that show black bear predation on elk calves to have a major impact on elk populations in areas of the west.

One spring, I had a bowhunting client who almost called me a liar when I told him that black bears were very capable game killers and especially effective on elk calves. As we were approaching a bear bait for his late afternoon hunt, I spotted a pile of fresh bear sign in the trail, and right on top of the pile was the small, undigested hoof of a calf elk. The proof is in the poop, you might say.

The black bear's secretive, reclusive nature and preference for impenetrable habitat would make it an exceptionally difficult adversary for a bowhunter, if it weren't for the bear's escalating appetite after it comes out of hibernation in the spring. Spring has long been a favorite time of year for hunting bear. It's generally the only hunting season available at this time of year, and the bear's pelt is thick and glossy after being protected from the elements and light during the winter's hibernation.

## BEAR BAITING 101

According to the last Pope and Young biennial records, over 60 percent of the bow-killed black bear are taken with the use of bait. Baiting spring bears is not rocket science and it's a technique that can be mastered by most bowhunters. There is, however, a tad of injustice to such mastery.

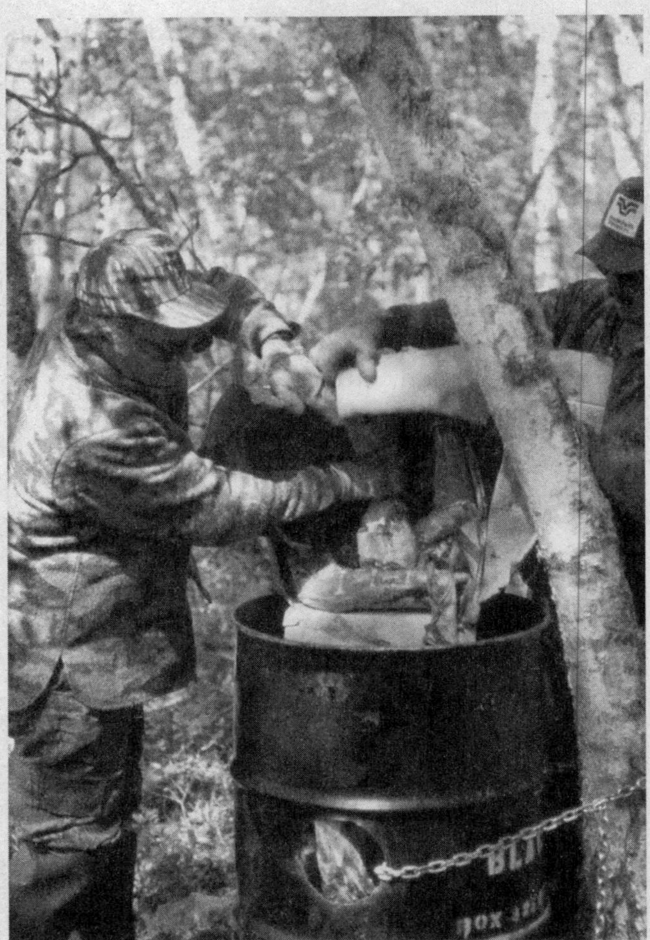

Baiting for black bears still requires a bowhunter to be very careful with movement. Even though a bear is coming in for the food, he is very wary and will spook easily.

An accomplished golfer, tennis player, or even fisherman is often referred to as a master of his sport. Just think how you'd be referred to as an accomplished baiter.

I never claimed to be a good bear outfitter or guide, but I was a good garbage hauler and scrounger, and that equated to success when it came to killing bears consistently for clients and myself. I've often heard comments that bears like nothing better than a maggoty, rotten carcass to feed on, and I can guarantee you that nothing is further from the truth. Bears are very persnickety eaters when they have a choice.

One spring I worked as a conservation officer for the Colorado Division of Wildlife and was inquisitive about every aspect of bear behavior. I placed the fresh carcasses of road-killed mule deer and elk alongside those of a horse, steer, and sheep at one of my well-used bait sites, where there were several bears actively feeding. The bears completely ate the deer and elk carcasses before touching the horse. I replaced the remaining steer and sheep carcasses with more recently deceased ones, and even with the fresher carcasses, the bears completely cleaned up the rapidly ripening horse before starting on the steer.

They completely cleaned up the bones and bits of meat from the other carcasses before touching the sheep (which shows good taste on their part, as I feel the same way about mutton). I've also watched bears pick through a large box of edible scraps from a café, much as you and I would pick out our favorites on a buffet line. They scrounged out the chicken and meat scraps first and then moved to the fish, fruit, eggs, toast, rolls, pie, cake, etc. Potatoes were generally the last edibles munched.

In my experience with over 30 years of baiting, citrus fruits and lettuce are a total bust for bears. Fish is another item that some swear by, and I suppose if you have an inexhaustible supply it will do the job, but I've found that fish rots quickly and gets ruined in short order by flies and maggots. It's just not worth the effort.

I used to haul several trailer loads of killer ponies from Texas each spring to use as bear bait (probably a felony in this day and age) because I always wanted fresh meat or bait on the site when a client was hunting. A bear that leaves a bait still hungry, with the bait completely gone, is a lot less likely to return regularly, and I wanted them to know there was always something to eat when they came back . . . regardless of the time of day.

My favorite bear baits were edible scraps from the local cafés. I would pay the kitchen help a couple of bucks per five-gallon pail and then freeze the scraps for later use. Bears would walk right past a fresh horse or colt carcass to get to the edible scraps; they were easy to haul and use and didn't rot down or attract flies too badly.

For several years, I got loads of "end-of-run" candy from a company and was afraid I might be creating a population of diabetic bears. One of the best baits I ever used were 50-pound blocks of hard candy from the Jolly Rancher company in Denver. At the end of a production run, they would empty the machines into a plastic bag inside a box, creating a solid block of candy.

I put these sweet chunks in the bottom of the barrel, where a bear could scrape off a smidgen of the candy—just enough to pique his taste buds and keep him working the bait, even when all the other goodies were gone. The bears couldn't get the solid blocks through the holes in the barrel, and a block of candy would last all season, making sure there was always a bit of delectable and appealing bait left in the barrel. Unfortunately after a couple years, the company went to computerized candy making and did away with this long-lasting, fly-free, easily handled, un-spoilable, indestructible, and irresistible form of bear bait.

For a number of years, in addition to edible garbage, I hauled pickup loads of outdated pastries and bread for bear bait. To add to the drawing power of these delicacies, I poured old honey, diluted 50 percent with water, over the whole mix. Honey is a great additive to all types of bear bait, and a good supply can be obtained from any beekeeper at a reasonable cost. The old honey keeps well, and if it turns sugary or solid, just adding hot water will make it pourable again.

I have burned honey on many a bear bait and had bears walk right up to the dense black cloud of cloyingly sweet smoke and actually burn their noses on the hot honey can. The past few years, I've added smoking scent sticks to my bear-baiting set-ups, as the dense, sweet, berry-flavored or anise-flavored smoke carries for considerable distances downwind.

The pungent smoking scent sticks can also be placed on both sides of the tree stand to help mask your scent or confuse the bear's sensitive olfactory organs at close range.

Grease is another additive that can enhance your bear bait. I've poured used grill and cooking grease from cafes and barbeque restaurants very effectively to enhance bread products for bear baiting. Grease garbage and bread products are great for advertising your bear baits far and wide. A bear stirring around a greasy bait site gets his paws and leg hair coated with the odiferous, oily stuff. When the satiated bruin saunters around his domain he leaves a strong, moisture-resistant scent trail clinging to everything it brushes up against. Any bear crossing or passing downwind of this trail has little trouble backtracking it right to the source—your bait site.

I know of several bear hunters and outfitters that simply dump grease on rotten logs or pour it on the ground and consider this a bear bait. Sure, bear will hit the grease site and dig around, licking up bits of greasy dirt and vegetation, but they aren't going to hit such a site regularly enough for my money, or that of my clients.

When I first started bear baiting, I simply dumped or placed my bait on the ground and then built a V-shaped corral of logs behind the bait to force the bear into position. If I was using a carcass of some kind, I wired or chained it to a tree to keep the bear from dragging it off. Birds and other critters devastated my baits, so I eventually switched to 55-gallon barrels with 7-inch diameter holes cut in both sides and a chain run through the holes and around a tree in a way as to keep the barrel locked in the upright position. The snap rim lids made filling these barrels a piece of cake and yet kept the bears out. During our first year of bear baiting in Saskatchewan, we figured we lost 70 percent of the fresh meat scraps on some of our baits to the hordes of rapacious ravens and crows. It didn't take long to switch to bird proof barrels for all of our baits.

The bear could easily dig and pull small quantities of bait through the holes but the ravens, crows and magpies were limited to scraps left on the ground. Barrels also made for a cleaner bait site and were a good gauge of a bear's size and trophy potential, as will be discussed later in the chapter. It didn't take the province of Saskatchewan long to realize the benefit of bait barrels and they are now required for baiting bears in the province.

Also, bear-bait placement is critical to the success of your venture. You can put the best bait in the world where a bear doesn't travel or is unlikely to locate the bait and your chance of success will be between zero and none.

Because bears prefer heavy cover, that's where your bait should be. However, there are several other factors that can increase your chances of success in placing a bear bait. Bears, like other big game species, require food, water, and protective habitat, so confine your baiting to areas near the other two essentials.

Bears, like other big-game species, require food, water, and protective habitat, so confine your baiting (food) to areas near the other two essentials.

I like to have a bait at the edge of, or near, a small clearing or opening for one simple reason. The ravens, crows, and magpies that can raise havoc with loose bait can also be your best advertising agents. When I first start bait, I place loose scraps where the birds can see it from the air. Their raucous racket will often attract bears that cannot see or smell your bait.

I don't want my bait site in the open or where a bear has to cross large open areas to get to it. A bait in such a location might get hit, but only late at night when the bear feels protected by the cover of darkness. Keep your baits close to escape cover and near a source of water, where the prevailing wind can carry the scent into the cover and the birds can advertise the bait's presence to every bear within hearing, and you'll earn your master's badge in baiting in short order.

Stand placement over bait is also critical to the success of a bear bowhunt. Remember, a bear has a very discerning nose and hearing as keen as any big-game animal. Many people would have you believe a bear has poor eyesight, but I don't subscribe to that theory at all. I have had bears pick up my camouflaged form at several hundred yards on numerous occasions. I think their vision is much better than they are given credit for, and I will continue to operate under that assumption until I can be convinced otherwise. I feel that a very high percentage of the bears taken over bait are fully aware of the hunter in the stand, but simply don't give a darn, as long as the hunter doesn't make any quick, noisy, threatening movements.

Wind is without a doubt the most critical factor in placing a bowhunting stand. The distance from hunter to bear is generally 20 yards or less, and a slight whiff of pungent human scent at that distance can put even a dominant old boar on red alert. I generally put my bear tree stands 16 feet above the ground and in a position where the least likely avenue of approach is behind the stand. In Saskatchewan, we were hunting along the lakeshore, so it was easy to place stands where we had both the prevailing breeze and the open shoreline working for us.

If you have to make a choice, choose the stand location with the wind in your favor at the time you will be bowhunting from the stand. Quite often, the prevailing breeze is from one direction during the day, and then it will switch directions toward evening. Make use of this anomaly to get your stand where the wind works for you. You can use scent blocker or eliminator and wear the best scent-suppressing clothing—all this helps—but the real key to success is hunting with the breeze in your face.

I constantly make use of a small, plastic squeeze bottle filled with scented talcum powder to check the wind currents and breezes from the stand location at a time of day when I will be hunting from the stand. A very simple procedure, but an extremely important one that can make the difference between a huge bear rug on the den wall or a blow-up photo of your mother-in-law.

Another crucial factor in choosing a bear stand location is the light direction. The best time to bowhunt bears over bait is in the late afternoon, so place your stand where it's fully shaded during the prime time. You certainly don't want to be lit up like a store window mannequin in the late afternoon light, where your slightest movement will be illuminated and intensified.

Once your stand is in position, inspect it thoroughly for the slightest squeak or scrape and get your bow and gear hangers situated where you can place and retrieve your equipment with a minimum of movement. The less disturbance you make when getting in and out of the stand, the better your chances of success.

'Course, there are exceptions to every rule. As a bear hunting guide and outfitter, I'm able to spend much more time working the baits on a regular basis than an individual hunter. Sometimes this can be used to a client's advantage.

In Colorado and Canada alike, both my guides and myself make little attempt to approach a bait site quietly and often drive a truck, boat, or four-wheeler as close to the bait as possible. We rattle the bait cans and barrels noisily while baiting and leave as much scent around as possible before leaving with a maximum of racket. This habituates the feeding bears to both noise and human scent around the bait. It also tunes them into the fact that when they hear the noise, they'll find fresh food at the bait. I make it a point to *never* go to the bait without leaving fresh enticement.

Sometimes bears can get a little too keyed to your arrival and departure, and numerous times in Canada when we were hunting wilderness areas where bears had little if any human contact, we'd pull up to the bait in a boat or on a four-wheeler and literally have to chase the bears while we were baiting the bait. Several years ago, Larry, one of our guides, got chased back to the boat by a big boar that met him at the bait. That evening, Larry accompanied a hunter back to the bait armed with a shotgun and pepper spray, and the client killed the 19-foot bear half an hour after Larry dropped him off.

When we take a client to the bait by boat or four-wheeler, we drive as close to the stand as possible and leave the engine running while we bang and clatter around, adding a bit of fresh bait to the can while the bowhunting client slips into the stand. When he is situated, we leave the site, making no effort to be quiet. Numerous times, before our truck or boat is out of sight, a hungry bear will be approaching the bait. Proper advertising pays off.

Anti-hunters have been quick to jump on bear baiting, hound hunting, and spring bear hunting in general as unethical, unsporting, and detrimental to the burgeoning bear populations. Which is total hogwash. Unfortunately, they were able to get this issue on ballots in several western states and convince the uneducated and unwashed masses, through lies and misinformation, that bear numbers were declining and spring hunting killed an abnormally high number of females with cubs. Consequently, spring bear hunting of any kind has been eliminated in many of the prime bear-producing states of the western United States, such as Colorado, Utah, and New Mexico.

## FALL BEAR BOWHUNTING

The fall of the spring season has meant a spring in the fall season, with more bears roaming the western states than ever before. Bowhunting fall bears is a totally different proposition from hunting spring bears.

When a bear comes out of hibernation, it will spend four hours feeding and moving and up to 20 hours sleeping or resting. In the fall, the process is reversed, with the bear active and feeding up to 20 hours a day, taking minimal down time for rest or sleep. This gives a bowhunter who is willing to put in the time and effort ample opportunity to take a prime fall bear.

Food is the chief motivator for fall bears, so the obvious tactic is to bow-hunt near food sources such as berry or acorn patches and grain fields. Water is also a critical element in many areas during the fall season, and man-made tanks, springs, and seeps are also superb places to ambush a thirsty fall bruin. When you can locate a water source adjacent to a food source, your chances of finding and arrowing a fall bear increase dramatically.

The best time to ambush a fall bear in a feeding area or waterhole is during the late afternoon. Even though bears actively feed most of the day and are out and about at daylight, the mature bears likely will confine their feeding and movement to heavy cover during the daylight hours.

The warmer the weather, the less likely a fall bear will be found in the open during the day. The morning dew and dampness of the vegetation will generally fulfill a bear's water needs until later, after his siesta. In hot, dry weather, a bear may slip into a waterhole to slake his thirst mid-day, but the behavior is unpredictable, which makes waiting for one an iffy proposition at best.

The erratic, swirling mid-day thermals are another reason to stay away from a honey hole until the odds are loaded in your favor. When you find a prime fall bear ambush location, be patient and hunt it only when the conditions are the best possible. A woods-wise trophy bear can be as leery and spooky as a whitetail buck. Let him know you're in the area hunting him and lurking around his favorite feeding or watering spot, and he'll pull stakes and vacate the area in short order.

Shot placement is critical on a bear, as it has a thick layer of fat and a long coat of hair.

## CALLING BEARS

Calling bears with a predator call is a way of hedging your bets during the autumn season and adding a whole new challenging dimension to your fall bear bowhunting. I carry several predator calls with me at all times during the fall and have called in a number of bears for clients and myself.

Fall bears are dominated by their appetite, and the alluring sounds of an animal in dire trouble might just bring them within bow range. For fall bear calling I prefer a call with a deep, raspy tone that imitates a deer fawn, calf elk, or big-game animal in distress. My favorite bear calls are the Circe/Lohman triple voice call, the Burnham Brothers Black Magic, and the Critt'r Call magnum.

Bears may respond to calling on the dead run or saunter in to the call with aggravating slowness. Bear calling takes a lot more effort than other types of game calling, as the best results come from almost continuous calling. Bears have a short attention span, and when the calls sound stops for extended periods of time, they lose interest and stop coming. When I set up to call bears, I stay for an hour to give a distant bear time to get within sight. Once a bear is spotted responding to the calling, I adapt it to his actions. When he stops or slows down, I call louder and more frantically. As long as he's headed my way, I make my calls just loud enough for him to hear, which keeps his attention focused.

Bear calling can keep the hackles on the back of your neck standing straight up, especially when an approaching bear suddenly disappears in the brush and you know he's close, but can't see him.

My first bear-calling adventure was the most potentially dangerous situation, with a darn good lesson. I was working on Afognak Island, Alaska, as a stream guard for the Alaska Department of Fish and Game at the time. I'd seen lots of cross and silver fox on the beaches and along the streams scrounging and decided to call some in for movies.

I picked a bright sunny morning, and as soon as it was light enough for filming, about 4:00 a.m. there, I eased my skiff into a small inlet and hiked a couple hundred yards to the edge of a clearing that was several hundred yards long and about one-hundred yards wide. I scrunched back under a spruce, got my camera ready for action, and ruined the peace and quiet of the morning with an agonizing series of distressed rabbit squealing and squalling calls.

The ear-ringing sounds had barely been absorbed by the impenetrable underbrush and moss-laden trees of the forest when a huge brown bear bounded out of the trees across the clearing from me and stood with his head swinging back and forth, trying to locate the source of the enticing sounds. One look at the size of that huge, hungry predator was all it took for the ignoramus source of those sounds to slither soundlessly and speedily away from the clearing, my tongue stuck to the roof of my mouth, and the predator call buried deep in a jacket pocket. As soon as I got a short distance from the meadow, I ran like heck to my boat, expecting at any minute to be overrun by the 700-pound fox I'd called up. If that bear had come in behind me while I was calling, there's a good chance I wouldn't be writing this book.

Any bear attracted to a predator call, expecting to find something warm, fuzzy, and edible to munch, has to be treated as a potentially dangerous adversary, whether it's a black bear or grizzly. Prudent precautions should be taken to make sure you end up the victor and not the victim. In northern Saskatchewan where I operated a black bear hunting camp, the backcountry bears rarely encountered humans and were "king of the bush," with little innate fear of man or beast. We had a number of close encounters and our clients either carried magnum canisters of potent pepper spray or a 12-gauge stoked with 3-inch magnum No. 4 copper-plated buckshot loads as back up. The same advice would be well taken when you're setting up to call bears with a predator call.

Calling with a partner is an excellent method of fall bear hunting and two sets of eyes are always better than one for spotting an incoming bruin. Several years ago, I had a bear-crazy client and his wife bowhunting elk with me in southwestern Colorado. When one of my guides stated he'd seen several different bears along a road while bringing his elk hunters in for a midday break and breakfast, I decided we'd better take a look. I figured there must be a steer carcass or a patch of ripe service berries near where the bears were spotted. It was noon when we got to the area and a gorgeous brown phase bear ran across the road in front of my truck to vanish into the dense oak-brush above the road. The sight of the bear had my client couple hot-wired to the limit, and as I drove another half mile down the road, they were jabbering non-stop about trying for the bear that evening. "Got a better idea," I stated as a pulled into the shade of a ponderosa along the road. "We'll sneak back and set up, and I'll call the bear in for Jerry to shoot." I quipped confidently.

Half an hour later, we'd eased to within 200 yards of where the bear had crossed and set up on an oakbrush-covered bench. I put the client 20 yards in front of me and had his nervous wife sitting by my side in the shade at the base of a huge ponderosa pine. I'd advised Jerry that if the bear came on the run, I'd stop calling when the bruin was in position for a shot, which should stop the bear. My plan worked almost too well. The first series of agonized squalls brought the bear into an opening 100 yards away, and when I cut loose again he came bolting right at Sharon, the hunter's wife, and me on the dead run. When he was 30 yards out, I cut back on the volume and intensity of my calling, which slowed him to a fast trot. When the bear hit the 15-yard mark, I stopped calling, and by the time the bear stopped, he was facing a very nervous Sharon and me at 10 yards. He was also broadside to Jerry at 10 yards. The instant he came to a full stop Jerry's arrow zipped through him non-stop and successfully ended the confrontation—much to his wife's relief.

Hunting bears with hounds is an exciting adventure and requires a hunter to be in top physical condition. Also, remember to practice shooting that will simulate shooting a treed bear.

## BEAR HUNTING WITH HOUNDS

Not many bowhunters are in position or have the time to raise and train a pack of bear dogs. Consequently, they miss out on the challenge, frustrations, camaraderie, and rewards in seeing such endeavors come together in forming an efficient bear-hunting team.

Clients hiring an outfitter that hunts with hounds also do not get to see the hunts average out the way the dog man does. I've had clients whose hunt was over the first morning after an easy, quick chase and cooperative bear. Several of these unenlightened bowhunters complained they would never hunt with hounds again because the bear didn't have a chance against the well-trained dogs. Little do they know.

The next hunter may spend five days of trudging over mountains and through canyons listening to the distant dogs trailing a hound-wise bear on hot, dry hillsides without ever seeing a hair of the bear. Some of these clients have left camp with their tail between their legs vowing never again to try and hunt the abominable, "un-bayable" black bear unless it's from a tree stand over a bait.

Only the outfitter in any hunting situation gets to see enough action and different situations to have any comprehension of what the "average" hunt is like.

The best advice I can give on preparing for a bear hunt with hounds is to get yourself in good physical condition, because the longer you can last on the hunt, the better your chances of bringing home a trophy bear.

Feet are the first to go on a bear chase. Most bowhunters have probably spent the winter months in front of the TV without tromping around much, keeping their legs and feet in condition. Spend some time climbing the bleachers at the football stadium or up and down the gravel piles at a local gravel pit with a hefty pack on your back. A little conditioning at home will make a big difference when it comes to negotiating rough country on a bear chase. Don't plan on breaking in a new pair of lug-soled boots (a prerequisite on a hound bear hunt) on your hound bear hunt; do it at home where the consequences won't be as disastrous.

I've had pro football players and marathon runners who thought they were going to die on a bear chase because their legs, feet, and muscles weren't conditioned to climbing over logs and rocks while hiking up and down the mountainous terrain that a black bear calls home.

A black bear can outrun a horse on flat ground and has the stamina to stay ahead of a pack of bawling bear dogs all day long, especially if he's survived previous hound hunter encounters. When a mature bruin is being pursued by a pack of hounds, he'll head for the most inhospitable habitat he can find and negotiate the rugged terrain with ease. Most bear chases are determined by Murphy's Law, so you can bet the better shape you're in, the closer to the truck the bear will tree. If you're looking for a tough, day-after-day, ass-dragging bear hunt with hounds, just show up for the hunt out of shape and hoping for a quick, easy time of it.

Practice your shooting on the ground, but also do some shooting that will simulate shooting a treed bear. I've had good bowshots shoot up all their arrows at treed bears without drawing blood because of the excitement, bear fever, and the impossible angles involved.

When you go on a bear chase, take a *full* quiver of arrows, and if you've got any apprehensions, have your outfitter or guide carry an extra handful. My guides and I have walked many miles retrieving extra arrows from the truck or camp because a shook-up bowhunter couldn't seem to get an arrow and a bayed bear in the same place at the same time.

When still-hunting black bear in the fall, their color variations blend in well with the tans and browns of fall vegetation. Unlike when you are hunting a deer, you won't see the white flicker of a tail or a white rump patch that gives a deer away.

## SPOT-AND-STALK BEAR HUNTING

Spot-and-stalk is the ultimate challenge in bowhunting any species. When you're dealing with hairy critters that have the equipment, ability, and often the temperament to do serious damage to your tender young body, spot-and-stalk hunting for bears takes on a whole new dimension. It is the leading method for taking grizzly, brown, and polar bears and is equally effective on these species in spring and fall alike.

The first prerequisite for successful spot-and-stalk bear hunting is to see your adversary *before* it sees you. Bears may not have the best eyesight in the realm of big-game animals, but I've seen them pick out a camouflaged hunter at 100 yards and disappear in a heartbeat on more than one occasion.

I've had several grizzly licenses in Alaska when bowhunting other species and blown several stalks on them. The times I've been in a situation to arrow one of these tremendous trophy animals, they had me pinpointed. Shooting a black bear at point-blank range when he knows you're there may not be real smart, but doing the same with a grizzly or brown bear is more like suicide.

Good binoculars and a spotting scope are essential to spot-and-stalk bear hunting and the propensity for letting your eyes do the walking until you spot a stalkable bear. Once you spot a shootable bear, be patient, take your time to watch his movements and plan your stalk to the last detail. Keep the wind and sun direction in mind and use your spotting scope to study terrain features you can use to get within bow range of your quarry. I would venture that over 90 percent of the blown stalks on big-game animals are due to impatience and "pushing the envelope" to get the shot. Patience is next to godliness when it comes to spot-and-stalk hunting, especially when your adversary is armed with formidable teeth, claws, and attitude.

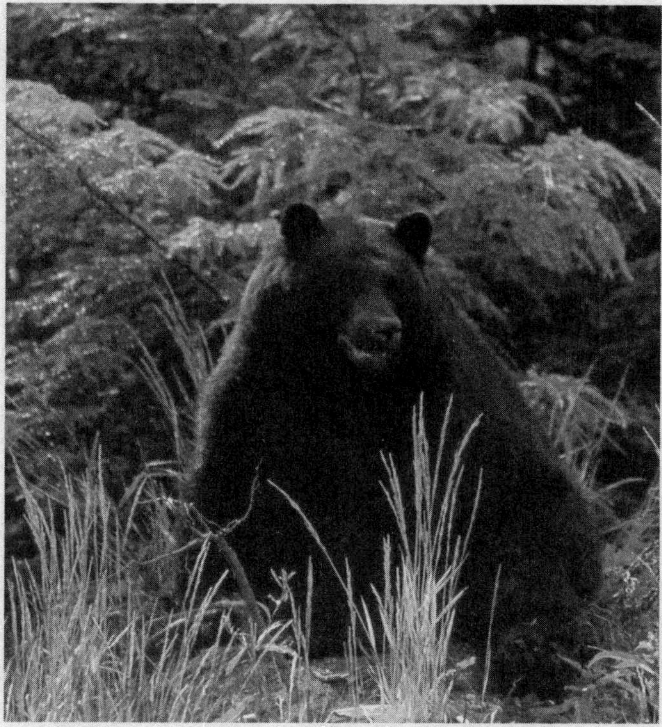

When bears first emerge in the spring, they are intent on eating and will be in places where spring growth is abundant, along stream banks, ponds, lakes, and swampy areas.

## JUDGING TROPHY BEARS

Bears are without doubt the toughest big-game animals to judge for the record book. It's extremely hard to accurately determine the size of a bear's skull under a thick covering of hide and long hair, especially if you haven't encountered many bears in the wild under hunting conditions. When I first started guiding and outfitting for bear hunters, I bought a spring scale to get an accurate weight of all the bears killed. I got rid of the scale after the first season because all the bears weighed less than half what the hunter estimated, and I figured it was better for business if they claimed to have killed a 400-pound behemoth bear rather than one that actually weighed 160 pounds on the scale.

"Ground shrinkage" is probably more acute with bear hunters than any other type of big-game hunting. We used 55-gallon drums for bear-bait containers and advised our hunters that, if the top of a standing bear's back reached the second ring on the barrel, it was an average-sized bear. If the top of its back was between the second ring and the top of the barrel, it would be close to record-book class. And if the top of its back was *above* the barrel top . . . shoot quickly.

A large boar bear is easy to judge because of its massive bulk, low-slung build, and broad, heavy head. A lean, gangly, leggy young bear is equally easy to judge. It's the large, bulky females with their hefty build and smaller skulls, and the equally bulky mid-sized males with skulls that might just make the record book, that are the stinkers to judge down to the last inch.

To add to the confusion, there are long, lean, lanky bears that aren't very impressive looking, with long skulls that will measure better than they appear, and then there are short, stocky bears that look

Bears spend time looking for insects in downed trees and under rocks. Still-hunting with the wind in your face in potential feeding areas will get you a bow shot like this.

massive, with short, wide skulls that measure less than appearances indicate.

There isn't any magic formula for accurately judging the difference between a bear with a skull measuring 17 3/4 inches and one with a skull measuring 18 1/4 inches that qualifies for the Pope and Young record book.

Any bear, regardless of skull measurement, is a trophy. The condition and color of the pelt may be more of a determining trophy factor than skull size to many bowhunters, myself included. I've often had clients take a smaller bear with a prime, unblemished pelt or different color phase over a larger animal with a scruffy, badly rubbed hide. Beauty is definitely in the eye of the beholder when it comes to bear pelts. The only person you have to please on your bear hunt is *you.*

Bears are tough critters with tremendous vitality and endurance. Couple these factors with the sometimes impenetrable habitat in which they thrive, and it's not hard to see that a bad hit or inferior equipment is going to lead to a less-than-desirable experience and a lost animal.

I've had bowhunters take bears with longbows, recurves, crossbows, and compounds, so any bow you can shoot well will do the job on a black bear when a good broadhead is properly placed. Several of my lady clients have made clean kills on large bears with 42-pound bows, shooting two-bladed, razor-sharp, cut-on-contact broadheads.

Bows and arrow shaft type are not critical as long as you can put the arrow where you want it. But broadheads are extremely critical, and so am I. I prefer a cutting type broadhead to penetrate a bear's thick fur, heavy muscle, and fat layers, and my clients and I have made many clean kills with these heads. I do not like mechanical broadheads for anything other than turkeys and did not allow them in my bear-hunting camp, nor do I allow them in my whitetail camp in Iowa. There are simply too many things that can go wrong for me or one of my clients to take a chance on wounding and losing a bear because a mechanical broadhead malfunctioned.

Almost all the wounded and lost bears I have encountered over the past 40 years of bear hunting and guiding have been hit too far forward. I admonish my clients constantly to keep away from the massively muscled and heavy-boned front shoulders. The likelihood of recovering a bear hit too far back is much greater than a front-end hit bruin. Bears are built similarly to humans, and their lungs extend much further back than most hunters think.

Proper shot placement and a razor-sharp broadhead are critical to penetrating a bear's thick layer of fat and into its vitals for a clean kill shot.

A sharp forward-angle shot behind the shoulder can be deflected by the outside of the rib cage, or can slice along it, exiting the front of the chest. Unless the shooter is lucky enough to cut open the brachial artery down the inside of the front leg, the bear is going to get away.

Several years ago, I had a client make just such a shot on a gorgeous blonde-colored bear while bowhunting with us in Canada. He had a video camera mounted in the tree behind him and got a perfect shot of the hit and the bear running off. After watching the video numerous times and seeing the arrow strike in a seemingly perfect hit behind the shoulder, the hunter was convinced we would find his bear. I wasn't. I'd trailed the bear for a quarter mile, then lost the blood trail entirely and figured the hit was non-fatal. However, I don't give up on a wounded animal easily, and the following morning, six of us did a grid search for four hours where I'd lost the blood trail. I became even more convinced that, despite what it looked like on video, the hit did little damage to the bear.

Late that afternoon, the bowhunter killed the very same bear on the same bait. The previous hit had gone in behind the front shoulder, grazed off the ribs and exited through the front of the chest . . . just what the blood trail indicated. Both entrance and exit holes were sealed over and were starting to heal. If we hadn't seen the bear on video and identified it by its unique markings and color, we might have missed the 24-hour-old wounds entirely. Bears are unique and tough animals. Treat them with the respect they deserve and you'll never have an unsuccessful bear bowhunt.

# Moose

Moose are the largest member of the deer family and sport the largest antlers of any animal in the world. Not only is bowhunting moose an exciting challenge, but the meat is superb and those antlers make an awesome trophy.

There are four subspecies of moose recognized in North America. The largest is the Alaskan-Yukon moose. An adult bull carrying antlers in the fall, just before rut, can be eight feet tall at the top of the shoulder and 11 feet from nose to tail, with a hefty weight of 1500 pounds. As the name implies, this gigantic deer is found throughout Alaska and the Yukon Territory.

The second-largest subspecies is the Canada moose, a term applied to both the western and eastern animals. The western Canada moose ranges from Ontario to British Columbia, while the eastern Canada moose ranges from Ontario to Newfoundland and down into Maine. These two subspecies overlap in northwestern Ontario, a prime area for moose hunting. An adult Canada bull moose carrying antlers in the fall, prior to the rut, can be seven feet at the shoulder and 10 feet nose to tail and weigh in at 1250 pounds, very much in the heavyweight class.

The fourth subspecies, the Shiras or Wyoming moose, found from Colorado and Utah northward through Wyoming and Montana, is the pigmy of the group, but still big! An adult Shiras bull sporting antlers during the fall can stand six feet at the shoulders, be nine feet in length, and tip the scales at 1000 pounds. All moose are BIG!

Moose have considerable attributes that make them a tough adversary to bowhunt under any conditions. Their long-legged, ungainly appearance, with a huge shnozz, dangling fuzzy bell, and humongous rack, may foster the impression of a dull-witted and lethargic critter. Not so. Moose may not exhibit the sneakily alert look of a whitetail buck or the majestic demeanor of a bull elk, but the moose's survival equipment will rival those of any biggame animal.

A moose's first lines of defense are its extraordinary sense of smell and hearing. That stupendous shnozzola can discern the slightest tinge of human scent in the air at phenomenal distances and smell edible greenery under several feet of water.

A bull's hearing is keen enough to pick up the soft, low frequency moans of a cow a mile or more away and the soft snap of a twig at 100 yards. This I know from personal experience. A moose's ears work independently of each other, so it can be checking both the front and back door at the same time. When moose tune in on a sound they want to investigate, they zero both ears and can pinpoint the slightest sound with uncanny accuracy.

Experienced moose bowhunters can also vouch for the acuity of the moose's eyesight. Their daytime vision is equivalent to a human's, but in the dim, early morning, late afternoon, or dark timber light, their vision is far superior to a human's. Their eyesight is highly tuned to picking up the slightest movement, and like their ears, the eyes work independently of each other. A moose's height gives him an elevated perspective that is often underestimated by bowhunters.

On my first Alaska moose bowhunt, I got within 70 yards of a huge bull that was feeding in alders and willows and quickly realized that, from his lofty viewpoint, he'd be able to see down into the dense cover and probably spot my movements. The only thing I could do was trail along behind him and wait for the right opportunity to close within bow range. It never happened.

Even though the monstrous bull was casually munching his way through the dense creek bottom willow and alder thickets, his long-legged strides atop dinner plate-sized splayed hooves allowed him to move faster than I could unobtrusively follow through the thick, noisy brush and spongy, boot-sucking tundra. The last sight I had of the bull was as he strode purposefully across the tundra a quarter mile ahead, headed for another creek in the next drainage, completely unaware of my pursuit.

According to the Pope and Young record book, calling is the most successful method of getting within bow range of a bull moose, and decoying (where possible) can make calling even more effective. To effectively call and decoy moose, one needs to be aware of the major difference in rutting tendencies between the Alaska-Yukon moose and their Canadian and US cousins.

Because of the vast expanses of tundra and more open alder- and willow-covered country, the Alaskan moose is not nearly as vocal as the Canada moose. Biologists tell us that this may account for the larger antler growth of the Alaska-Yukon moose. Moose living on the tundra make more use of their antlers in communication than do woodland moose.

The Alaska-Yukon bulls stake out the mating areas, tend to be more territorial in defending these areas, and gather harems of cows through calling, perfuming themselves regularly in rut pits and wallows, and making showy antler displays. The bulls hold their cows in brushy creek bottoms, along lakeshores or timbered ridges and side hills, where they can keep an eye on them and run off any interloper bulls that try to horn in on the action. Alaskan-Yukon bulls don't spend as much time or energy roaming their territory looking for cows as do the Canada bulls. They spend their time keeping the competition at bay, their harems intact, and their girls well serviced.

A caller trying to lure an Alaskan bull into bow range should use aggressive tactics and bull sounds to incite a jealous bull. Several Alaskan moose guides I know mix a few cow calls with their bull grunts in hopes of stoking a rutting bull into enough of a jealous rage to leave his harem and come looking for a fight.

One Alaskan outfitter uses a small set of lightweight, fake moose antlers to decoy harem bulls to him by flashing and rattling the antlers in the brush to imitate another bull in the herd bull's territory. According to him, when this method works, the action is fast and furious and certainly not for the faint hearted.

An Alaska bull's huge antlers play an important part in letting other bulls know they are in the country and just how big they are. I've glassed several bulls at a distance challenging each other by simply swaying their heads back and forth to show their opponent the size and width of their antlers. Quite often, this antler display is enough to determine the outcome of the confrontation without any physical contact. In the low Alaskan and Yukon vegetation, a large bull's antlers flashing in the sun can be seen for several miles by both hunters and

Carry a small squeeze bottle filled with talcum powder when spotting and stalking moose. Their very sensitive nose will pick up your scent in an instant, so keeping yourself downwind of your quarry is of utmost importance.

other moose. This visual signaling alone probably plays a greater role in attracting both bulls and cows than hunters realize.

Several studies have been conducted that strongly indicated decoying with a large set of fake antlers worked with bulls that carried equally large or larger antlers, but would spook bulls with smaller antlers. I would love to bowhunt Alaskan bulls with a lightweight, pop-up cow decoy of some form and a small pair of antlers. There's no doubt such a combination could put a trophy bull right in the hunter's lap.

## CANADA AND SHIRAS RUT

The Canada and Shiras moose rut is very different from the Alaskan-Yukon moose rut. The main rut usually starts sometime near mid-September, give or take a week depending on the location. It is the cow that controls when mating will take place. Just before coming into estrus, solitary cows stake out breeding areas approximately one-and-a-half to two square miles, and start to advertise their presence by calling for bulls and frequently urinating to leave their scent for the roaming bulls to find. Cows will defend these areas against other cows and try to drive off any cows encroaching on their mating areas. Cows generally prefer territory around ponds, beaver dams, lakeshores, meadows, or logged areas during the breeding season. Naturally, these are prime locations to set up for calling bulls.

The Canada and Shiras bulls, on the other hand, have home ranges that may cover as much as 16 to 18 square miles, with the ranges of various bulls broadly overlapping each other. During the rut, they travel these ranges in search of cows to breed. Rutting bulls are not constant travelers, they often stop in a particular area for long periods of time listening for cows that might be calling. Once the bull hones in on a vocal cow, they travel together until she comes into estrus. When the cow allows copulation to take place, they may breed several times during a 24- to 48-hour period, then the bull leaves to find a new cow. Cow moose that do not get bred in this main rut period will come into estrus again 25–28 days later and start calling and trying to attract a bull all over again. Some Canada and Shiras cows have been known to breed as late as November.

## CALLING AND DECOYING CANADA MOOSE

Alex Gouthro is a Canadian moose outfitter and guide, with 30 years of experience guiding hunters and bowhunting moose himself, and he is probably one of Canada's most knowledgeable and proficient moose callers. Alex believes the use of a moose decoy, combined with good calling, is the deadliest combination possible for a bowhunter.

Pulling a Canada bull within 70 yards by calling is okay for a rifle hunter, but it doesn't cut it for a bowhunter. After several years of trial and error, Alex finally got a decoy designed that works well for his type of calling and hunting. Alex's silhouette cow moose decoy is life-size, cut from four-inch thick Styrofoam, and divided into three parts for portability. The realistic body, long-nosed head, and prominent ears present a profile that looks like a cow moose from a distance, particularly during the early morning and late afternoon hours.

As with any decoy, Alex believes that movement is the key to effectiveness. To accomplish this, his moose decoy mounts on a lightweight pipe stake through the center, with 30-yard pull cords attached to the head and tail of the decoy. Pulling on the cords swings the decoy back and forth on the pivot stake and allows Alex to fully control the position of the decoy from his calling location. He can swing the decoy to keep it broadside and more visible to an incoming moose or simply move it back and forth to give the impression of life-like action.

Another Canadian moose guide uses a painted foam taxidermy head form of a cow moose. He carries the moose head strapped to his chest with a shoulder harness. This decoy is equally effective when properly used, and has produced many close encounters for the outfitter and his clients. Several have put the outfitter into hasty retreat mode with an overly amorous Canada bull.

## MOOSE CALLING

In addition to the decoy, moose calling tools consist of a birch bark calling horn and a dried scapula or shoulder blade bone. Moose megaphones can be the traditional birch bark, plastic, fiberglass, or rolled linoleum. They should be 14 to 16 inches long, with a mouthpiece one and a half inches in diameter, and the bell end five to six inches in diameter. The moose horn simply amplifies the caller's voice and imparts a moosey timbre to the noise. There are also several excellent commercial moose calls on the market that use a reed or diaphragm to produce cow and bull sounds rather than the human voice. The horn can even be used to simulate a cow moose urinating by pouring water from it onto the ground or into a lake, stream, or pond.

A moose or domestic cow scapula is used to imitate the sound of a bull raking his antlers in the brush or knocking against a tree. A scapula isn't as traditional as a set of real moose antlers, but it's a heck of a lot lighter, less cumbersome, and still has a "ring of bone" sound, almost as good as the real thing. In lieu of a scapula, a canoe paddle also works well for imitating the antler action of a rutting bull, and some may find it even easier to use.

Moose calling falls into two categories: passive and aggressive. Passive calling consists of making cow calls to let the bull know there's a cow in the area. Wary, older, trophy-size bulls often approach the caller cautiously and generally downwind to let their nose verify the presence of the cow or danger. Bulls may respond from a distance by grunting an answer and continue grunting as they approach the caller's location. These are the easy ones. More cautious, mature bulls are liable to come in as silently as a morning fog and suddenly appear right in the caller's lap. Amazing how such a huge animal, with such an awesome set of headgear, can move like smoke through the dense timber and brush, but bull moose seem to manage it with ease.

A responding bull may announce his presence by smacking his antlers with single knocks against a tree or by loudly thrashing them in the brush. The single knocks generally indicate a cautious bull that wants the cow to come to him. Use passive calling tactics with this bull.

The bull thrashing trees and brush with his antlers is aggressive and claiming the cow's territory for himself. If passive tactics don't work, use the scapula, pretending to be a small bull raking his antlers in the brush or limbs. I've also had several bulls come to my calling, grunting every step of the way, leaving little doubt as to their whereabouts.

The sheer size and intimidating nature of a rutting bull moose can often turn an avid hunter into a gibbering wreck and leave a guide wondering if he shouldn't take up guiding bird watchers.

Several years ago, Alex called up a nice, 50-inch bull that came in for one of his clients. The bull was creating a major ruckus, raking bushes and trees and grunting loudly. He was deadly serious about intimidating any other bulls in the area.

Alex hand signaled his client to move closer to him and coaxed him into squatting behind a clump of three-foot-high bushes. Alex then proceeded to call the bull past the shooter, broadside at 16 to 18 yards. *Five times!* The bull would stalk up to the decoy, stop, and eye the fickle female, waiting for her to make some move. Alex was so close, he didn't dare twitch the control cords. Getting no response, the bull would move off until Alex cow called and moved the decoy to entice it back.

As the bull stalked past, the petrified shooter would peek over the bushes and then hunker back down. The bull eventually got tired of going in circles with no visible encouragement from the cow, and wandered off to look for a more cooperative date. When a very exasperated outfitter inquired as to why the hunter hadn't taken a shot, the flustered client blurted, "The bushes were in the way."

Alex pointed out that the bushes were not all that tall and it would have been easy to shoot over them. "Well you didn't tell me that," the thoroughly distraught, badly whupped bowhunter retorted.

As with other big game, the call of a cow in heat will quickly bring in a love-sick bull moose. One of the oldest and most reliable calls is a birch bark megaphone.

When a reluctant bull hangs up back in the woods or approaches following a cow, switch to more aggressive calling tactics. Use soft bull grunts and the scapula to imitate another amorous bull competing for the favors of the cow. These tactics simulate a smaller, younger bull that won't intimidate the target bull and are especially effective later in the season, after most of the cows have been bred and the bulls are hunting hard for the next encounter. Patience and perseverance are probably more important in moose calling and decoying than any other type of hunting.

## THE PERFECT MOOSE-CALLING SEQUENCE

Move quietly into position on a good crossing, travel-way, or along a lakeshore at least an hour before legal shooting time. Carefully set up your decoy, if you are using one, set out scented rags or canisters or light up your smoke scent sticks, and place them downwind of your blind or tree stand.

After everything is set, walk slowly and noisily around in the brush, slightly downwind of your stand, and splash loudly in any nearby water to simulate the sounds of a feeding or active cow, just in case there is a bull within hearing. After the racket making, get into your blind or tree stand and wait for things to settle down, listening for any bull sounds.

If nothing develops after 15 minutes or so, make a couple of soft communication grunts, using your cupped hands rather than the megaphone. Continue the cow-in-heat calls every 20 minutes, gradually increasing the length and volume of your calling for one or two hours. If there's no action and you're set up near water, quietly leave your ambush, fill your calling horn with water, and loudly pour several containers full into the water, to simulate a cow urinating. The urination procedure can be repeated every hour or so. If nothing develops by mid-morning and you feel the need for a break, move quietly out of the area, leaving your scent equipment in place. If using a decoy, lay it on the ground and cover with brush.

Float hunting waterways for moose is an enjoyable hunting strategy that will also allow you to take in some stunning scenery. Just make sure the bull is not in the middle of a bog or stream when you release your arrow.

When you return for the afternoon bowhunt, do so with caution, as occasionally a bull will move into the area during the mid-day lull, looking for the source of earlier moose sounds, and he may still be there. The late afternoon session is much the same as the morning hunt, and if you don't do any good, don't get discouraged. Whether you plan on bowhunting the location again or not, vacate the area as quietly and unobtrusively as possible. Even a bull moose spooked by accident may become more difficult to hunt because of it.

A bull moose, for all his size and bulk, can move almost soundlessly through the thickest timber and brush. Add the disturbance of even a slight breeze, and a distant grunt or antler cracking against the brush or a tree may be muted or obliterated by rustling vegetation. I try to cut down on the chances of an unheard encounter by using a pair of Walker's game ears to amplify the sounds around me. The ability to hear the slightest out-of-place, stealthy step or subtle antler scrape may make the difference between success and being snookered.

Partner calling, where the second hunter does the bull imitating while the first does the cow calling, can add even more realism to the ambush, because the simulated cow and bull sounds are coming from two different places. This double teaming will often coax even the wariest of bulls to sidle in close enough for one or the other to get a good bow shot.

Bulls accompanied by a cow can present a whole new challenge to calling moose. If a bull is following a cow, chances are good she has *not* been bred, and aggressive calling may get the bull riled up enough to come relatively close for a shot. If the cow *has* been bred, the bull will be in front of her leading the way and ready to find another receptive cow. In this situation, passive calling with seductive cow-in-heat groans, and even the calls of an agitated cow begging for attention, may pull the bull into shooting position.

As with elk calling, when a responding bull is arrowed and starts to leave, a flurry of excited hyper-cow calling may stop the bull and hold him in the area until he drops.

Most of the same tactics used for calling and decoying Canada moose are equally effective for the Shiras moose in the lower 48. The Shiras subspecies cows also establish their own territories and the bulls cover a lot of ground in their quest to locate a breedable cow. Pre-season scouting to locate the cows' home ranges or core areas and travel ways, or corridors within their area, can provide ideal locations for calling during the season. Unfortunately, no manufacturer makes a moose decoy that is realistic looking and easily transported in the mountainous terrain the Shiras moose roam, so decoying these moose is generally not a viable option.

## SPOT-AND-STALK MOOSE HUNTING

Spot-and-stalk bowhunting is almost on par with calling for producing record-book moose for bow-and-arrow toting hunters.

Spotting moose is a heck of a lot easier than stalking moose. I've flown over thousands of square miles of prime moose habitat in Alaska and Canada and seen hundreds of humongous trophy bulls from the air. Unfortunately, you couldn't get to a high percentage of them from anywhere, and most of them will live and die without ever having encountered a single hunter.

The first axiom for a successful spot-and-stalk bowhunt, as mentioned before, is to locate your antlered adversary *before* it becomes aware of you. An animal the size of a moose, with its massive headgear, is often easy to spot from a distance in the swamps, tundra, timber, or brush country it calls home. Finding the same critter when you're engulfed in the same impenetrable tangle of moose habitat, at the same level, is a whole different ball game.

Good binoculars are essential for locating moose at a distance and a spotting scope can be invaluable for long-range trophy judging and finite route planning of your stalk. Once a shootable moose is located, don't let the excitement and anticipation override your patience and planning. It's easy to do and disastrous to success. Generally, you'll be hunting with a guide or partner on a moose hunt. Take the time to work out a system, whereby one stays put in a well-marked, visible location, while the other stalks the moose. Work out a fully understood set of signals, so the stalker will be able to ascertain the bull's position relative to his own, its activity . . . bedded, feeding, moving, etc., and the unexpected appearance of other moose (bulls or cows).

Impatience blows a major portion of the stalks on big game, so take your time and do it right. If the wind changes direction, the moose relocates, or anything unforeseen happens, don't hesitate to back off, reconnoiter the situation, and start over . . . even if you have to wait another day.

Since visibility is often very limited when stalking moose in heavy cover, wind becomes

Spotting moose is hard work. The country moose live in is huge, but they move through rough, log-strewn bogs and sloughs with amazing speed and ease.

even more important, and I make constant use of my powder bottle to keep the slightest trickle of breeze working for me. A string or feather on your bow won't register slight updrafts or downdrafts, and these are often erratic enough to carry your scent the wrong direction. Use your powder bottle.

## MOOSE BOWHUNTING GEAR

Moose are my kind of target . . . *big!* A bull moose is not exceptionally hard to kill with a well-placed, razor-sharp broadhead. However, as big as they are, it just takes them a bit longer than smaller big game to realize they are dead and supposed to fall over. Any type of bow, 50 pound and above, shooting cut-on-contact, razor-sharp broadheads, will make clean kills on the largest moose when the arrow is put into the huge heart-lung zone of a moose.

The large size of the kill zone on a bull moose (30 inches by 30 inches) gives a bowhunter a bit more leeway on range and a 50- to 60-yard shot on a moose equates to a 20-yard shot on a whitetail buck . . . *if* you conscientiously practice and become proficient at these longer distances.

The moose's enlarged dimensions and overall size make range determination a critical factor in moose hunting, and the best tool to take the guesswork and chance out of this important aspect is an accurate rangefinder. Never leave home without it!

Clothing can go a long way toward making or breaking a moose bowhunt, as the weather where these beasties live during the fall can range from miserably hot to miserably cold and wet. The hot weather can be combated by stripping down to the essentials, but for the wet and cold weather, you'd better have effective rain gear and warm, dry, layered undergarments.

All outer garments should be in a camouflage pattern and color that blends with the background, including gloves and facemask or camo paint. Moose country generally isn't plagued with cockleburs, burdock, and some of the more clingy, poky weeds of whitetail country, so my choice is wool outerwear, with thick or thin (depending on temperature) wicking-type underwear. (I hate wool against my tender skin.) Whatever clothing you choose should be soft and quiet as well as warm and water resistant. Scent Lok has come out with items of clothing that are ideal for moose hunting under a variety of conditions, and they help cut down on the amount of human stinkum floating around the moose habitat.

Moose are water creatures, which means your footgear should be waterproof, insulated, and of sufficient height to keep your feet warm and dry. Unless, of course, you have to cross a lake to get to your moose; then a boat would be nice.

When you walk up to a dead bull moose, your first thoughts are going to be, "What have I done and how far is camp and transportation?" You can have all your portable, packable, and foldable meat saws for smaller critters. I want a razor-sharp, full-sized, steel-handled axe at hand for quartering a moose.

Taking a trophy bull moose with a bow and arrow is an awesome accomplishment, and one that every bowhunter should experience. Sinking your teeth into a sizzling, sputtering, fat-dripping, succulent, two-foot-long, campfire-broiled moose rib ain't a bad experience either.

# Turkey

Thank God turkeys can't smell (I thought to myself) as the cantankerous gobbler "spit and drummed" to his heart's content a few yards from where I knelt comfortably, arrow strung and ready for a shot, and my aggravation grew. Half an hour later, I was still kneeling, but not nearly as comfortably nor as ready for a shot. I realized I'd been had by the longbeard, and there wasn't a thing I could do about it. The bird was so close, I didn't dare blink, and there wasn't room in the tight little blind to even think about turning around for a shot. That was the first time I had a gobbler near enough I could actually hear it breathing.

Two afternoons previous, I roosted the bird on the Ponderosa-studded slope. I'd found the ideal place for a set-up under a drooping spruce tree, just above an irrigation ditch where the gobbler scuffed the dry dirt to powder with his strutting and wing dragging. When I found the strutting ground, and even before I'd decided to ambush a turkey from under the adjacent spruce, I had already smoothed out the drag marks and tracks in the dirt so the area wouldn't show any fresh use. Old habits die hard.

The following morning, I was hidden in a cavernous pocket under the evergreen, 15 yards from the strutting ground, in perfect shooting position. As I listened to the vocal tom fill the valley below with his deep-throated gobbling, I just knew I was going to arrow that longbeard. Wrong! I'd tree-called softly in the paling gray of pre-dawn and gave a couple of quiet clucks just before fly-down time and was answered immediately by the "hot-wired" gobbler. I heard him fly down, hit the ground 200 yards up the hill, and the gobble a quarter of a mile in the opposite direction.

I made the beginner's mistake of chasing that ridge-running tom, and several other gobblers in the area, around the mountainside until late morning, without getting close enough for a shot. To add insult to injury, when I got back to the blind to pick up a call I'd inadvertently left, there were fresh strut marks all over the knoll in front of my blind. Thirty yards farther down the ditch, I found an even more heavily used strutting area covered with fresh tracks, feathers, and droppings. I figured I had him

Movement is a turkey hunter's biggest concern. A camo blind is an ideal tool to help conceal movement from keen-eyed turkeys.

cold now and proceeded to build a tight little blind in the oak brush, where I had a 10-yard shot to the strutting ground. I filled in the backside of the blind with thick oak and spruce branches, and even roofed it over so I would be kneeling in the blind's darkness, invisible to the sharp-eyed gobbler.

The second morning's scenario was much the same as the previous day, only I called a lot more aggressively, hoping to pull the tom away from his hens to the strutting area and make my bowhunt short and sweet. No such luck. This time, when the irascible gobbler strayed off with his harem, I stayed put, bound and determined to wait for him, or another one of the gobblers I could hear in the distance, to come investigate my calling.

I yelped excitedly on my box call every 20 minutes for the next three hours and got an occasional distant gobble to answer. My butt was numb and my patience had about petered out when my seductive yelping got a response from the ridge behind me. Within a few minutes, the sneaky tom was strutting, not on the strutting ground where he was supposed to, but right in back of my blind. That blooming bird kept me locked up and motionless while he strutted back and forth in the grass and weeds a few yards from the rear of the blind. His "spittin' and drummin'" and raucous gobbling in my ear aggravated me for over an hour as he moved back and forth and around the side of my blind, but never ventured out in front where he was supposed to go. Then he silently vacated the premises.

Not one to give up without a fight, I returned late that afternoon and set up in the shadowy confines of my first blind. On my second series of yelps, a gobbler answered from the hillside above and sounded off every minute . . . until he strutted onto the top of an irrigation dike at 10 yards and got skewered by a Thunderhead tipped xx75. I love it when a plan finally comes together in spite of the turkey's unpredictability and contrariness.

## WILD TURKEYS IN THE UNITED STATES

Wild turkeys can now be found from the tip of Florida to the woods of Maine, from the rainforests of Washington to the brush country of south Texas, and the populations are thriving and spreading with each season.

There are four species of wild turkey found in the United States. The eastern turkey, as the name suggests, is predominately found east of the Missouri river. With the preponderance of cereal grains, mainly corn and beans, found in many of the Midwestern states, these turkey populations are increasing tremendously and, if anything, the overwhelming number of birds make them tougher to hunt than those in states where the population densities are much lower.

The Osceola subspecies is found only in Florida and is a similar-colored, smaller version of the eastern bird that has adapted to the swamps and sloughs of the Sunshine State.

Merriam's turkeys are the Western subspecies, found from the Dakotas west to California, Nevada, and New Mexico. Evidence discovered in the early Native Americans' southwest cliff dwellings (dating back several thousand years) shows that not only were Merriam's hunted by these early bowhunters, but the turkeys were also raised in captivity. The Merriam's turkey, with its contrasting white-tipped tail and body feathers, is without a doubt the most striking of the turkey species.

Rio Grande turkeys are mainly found in Texas, but have been transplanted (or transplanted themselves) to the surrounding states of Oklahoma, Colorado, New Mexico, and southern Arizona.

In addition to these four subspecies, Mexico boasts a couple more (if you are thinking of getting the world slam of turkeys with your bow and arrow). The Gould's, colored much like the Merriam's and probably pretty close relatives, live on the rugged slopes and timbered areas of Mexico. The Ocellated turkey is found farther to the south, in jungle-covered areas of the Yucatan, and has much different habits from the rest of the turkey clan, as well as brilliant, iridescent, greenish plumage with bright blue spots, similar to that of a peacock.

In order for us as hunters to rationalize getting skunked on our bowhunting ventures, we often anthropomorphize our adversary as being super intelligent and educated to the point of being unkillable, when in reality, most of their escapes are just plain luck or habit.

Several years ago, Bill Winke and I were hunting turkeys on a private ranch in Texas when we thought we'd run into a cagey, crafty, hunter-wise old tom. We gotten the gobbler going shortly after sun-up and he'd sounded off at every call we threw at him, obviously interested and coming to investigate. When the gobbler got 200 yards out in the dense brush he stopped coming but kept on gobbling with enthusiasm at our combined calling efforts. This went on for over an hour while Bill and I discussed his reticence to come the rest of the way in to our best calling efforts. We figured he might be henned up or maybe was just call shy. Either way, it was obvious he wasn't going to come to us so we might as well try going to him. He was making enough racket, so it was easy to keep him located as we circled out through the brush to approach him from another angle. When we got to the edge of the brush within 100 yards of the still gobbling gobbler and spotted him, we both broke out laughing. Our super cautious, henned up, hunter-wise adversary had run into a three-foot-high woven wire fence and was pacing back and forth along a 50-yard stretch completely baffled as to how to cross it. So much for turkey smarts. We quickly set up on the same side of the fence the bird was on. The first series of calls brought the gobbler running our way so fast that Bill almost missed him at 15 yards.

The main thing that separates the killability of the different turkey subspecies is simply hunter pressure. Generally, eastern turkeys are hunted much more than the other birds, but put a lot of pressure on a Rio Grande gobbler or Merriam's, and you will have a turkey that is equally difficult to call in and kill.

Almost all the turkey species follow the same year-round lifestyle pattern. In the winter, the mature gobblers are generally found in bachelor groups from two to 30 or more birds, while the hens and young of the year, along with the jakes, feed, loaf, and roost in much larger groups.

As the weather warms, the gobblers start separating and attaching themselves to groups of hens or roaming around looking for unattached hens. As the breeding season gets into full swing, the gobbler hierarchy will have been established and a group of hens will usually be accompanied by a dominant breeding gobbler and one or more subdominant birds. During the early part of the spring breeding season, the hens and gobblers will roost together and spend the early morning hours together, at which time breeding occurs. This is usually the most difficult time to call in a mature longbeard, as they are all pretty well "henned up."

Prior to the onset of actual breeding, the hens will have located a well-hidden nest site. When they get into breeding mode, the hens stay around the gobblers in the morning until they are bred, then sneak off to lay an egg. They will lay one egg a day while still roosting with other hens in proximity to the gobblers. When there are several eggs in the nest, the hen will start spending most of the day on or around the nest and sit on the eggs at night. During the morning, they will move to the gobbler to breed and then go back to their nest and eggs.

Gobblers are the most vocal and responsive late in the season, when almost all the hens are on the nest and only spend a short time each morning with the toms. During this phase of the spring season, the "hot-wired" toms gobble more on the roost in the morning to let the nearby hens know where they are, and then, after flydown time, they vocally advertise their whereabouts so the hens can find them.

When the hens abandon the toms and head for their nests by mid-morning, the toms really get vocal and respond readily to late-morning calling. During the late afternoon they gobble going to the roost and really fill the woods with their loud advertising once they are safe in their trees for the late afternoon. This should be the very best time for a bowhunter to seduce a gobbler into bow range. However, if I have learned one thing in my bow-hunting and outdoor career, it's Mother Nature's propensity for throwing a monkey wrench into sure things.

In Iowa and Nebraska, where I guide spring turkey hunters, the burgeoning turkey population, with lots of gobblers and even more hens, coupled with an equally elevated populace of turkey nest-destroying predators, has created a frustrating late-season problem. Over 50 percent of the turkey nests we find in the spring get hammered by varmints, such as coons, possums, fox, or coyotes. This puts the hens back to square one, starting the process all over again, which means that many late-season re-nesting hens are back roosting with gobblers and spending time with them until they get enough eggs laid to start full-time nesting. It puts a whole new spin on late-season hunting and can make the gullible gobblers of the normal late season as "henned up" as early-season birds.

Fortunately for bowhunters, turkey hunting has undergone some major changes that make it a whole new ball game now compared to 10, 20, or 30 years ago.

The turkeys are still the same sneaky, unpredictable, wary, contrary critters they've always been, but the expanding and booming turkey populations, superb equipment, and unlimited turkey-hunting information available have brought about a new level of turkey bowhunting and greatly increased a bowhunter's chances of taking a hefty gobbler with a stick and string.

While there have been some major changes in turkey bowhunting techniques and equipment to help a modern day bowhunter be successful, the basics of turkey hunting are still pretty much the same as they were when the American Indians tangled with them. A turkey bowhunter has to know the rudiments of turkey habits, idiosyncrasies, scouting, calling, and hunting techniques, before venturing into the woods after one of the toughest and most challenging trophies a bowhunter can pursue. Hunting turkeys with a shotgun is tough enough, but when you decide to take on these feathered phenomena with your bow and arrow set, you've bit off a real mouthful. The turkey's eyesight and hearing are exceptional. Considering the fact that turkeys are right at the top of the menu on every predator's list, from great horned owl to bobcats, it's little wonder all turkeys are constantly on the alert, convinced that every unusual movement or shape in the woods is potential danger. Consequently, turkeys (especially gobblers) harbor little curiosity about unknown objects they can't readily identify as harmless parts of their environment.

Fortunately for all of us, a turkey's sense of smell is almost non-existent. If turkeys could smell, there certainly would be a whole lot fewer of them on dining-room tables at the end of the spring season, and bowhunting them would be a real exercise in futility.

## CAMOUFLAGE

Good camouflage and its proper usage are more important to a turkey hunter than with any other type of bowhunting. You're going to have to blend perfectly with your surroundings or a gobbler will spot your outline in a heartbeat and be long gone by the time you get your bow drawn. It's never been easier to find a camouflage pattern to match the background cover you'll be bowhunting, from the palmetto swamps of Florida and rock canyons of Wyoming, to the rain forests of the northwest. Background is the most important aspect of your cover, and a full head net, or face paint and gloves, are mandatory for bowhunting turkeys without a blind. I make use of several different camouflage patterns during the course of a season, as the background color and vegetation changes in the locations where I'm guiding and hunting.

Movement is the turkey bowhunter's real nemesis. Imitating a lovesick hen with seductive calling pinpoints your location precisely for a sharp-eyed gobbler with the homing instincts of a laser guided missile. The slightest movement, drawing and releasing, while a gobbler is looking your way is an invitation to disaster and a running shot at a rapidly departing gobbler.

## TURKEY CALLING TACTICS

Calling turkeys is not as tough as many turkey hunters would have you believe. Many books, videos, and articles deal with the specifics of how, when, and where to call spring gobblers. Take the time to study the available information and supplement what you learn with plenty of practice before the season; it'll go a long way toward the success or failure of your spring gobbler hunt. Don't get caught up in all the hype and wonder of turkey calling. Keep your patience lengthy and your calling brief, rather than vice-versa, and you'll be much more successful.

Learning to yelp and cluck on a box call, or a simple-to-use, push-pull type box call, is all that's needed to put you in the ball game bowhunting turkeys. Mastering a diaphragm call is a tougher proposition, but something that will make calling turkeys, especially for bowhunting, a bit more effective. With a diaphragm mouth call, you can make turkey sounds while you are in the process of

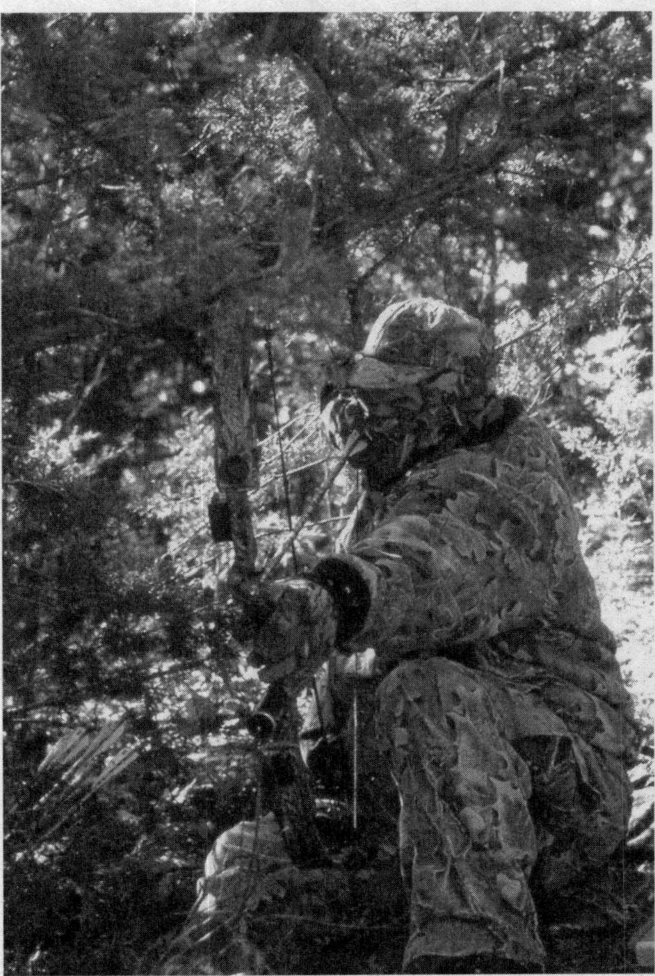

A turkey's eyesight is sharp, so dressing in full camouflage from head to toe is essential to success.

drawing and holding on an incoming bird, without undue movement. On several occasions, I've been clucking and purring softly and had a gobbler walk within a few yards before I took the shot.

When I set up to call, I use a combination of three calls. During the initial calling phase, I use a box call. The box call is almost foolproof and can produce loud, distance-covering sounds or quiet purrs and clucks for close-up use. A box call can make almost all the turkey sounds, such as yelps, clucks, purrs, cuts and even gobbles. My two favorite box calls are a Heartbreaker made by Will Primos and a handsome and realistic-sounding custom box made by Albert Paul of Greenville, Mississippi.

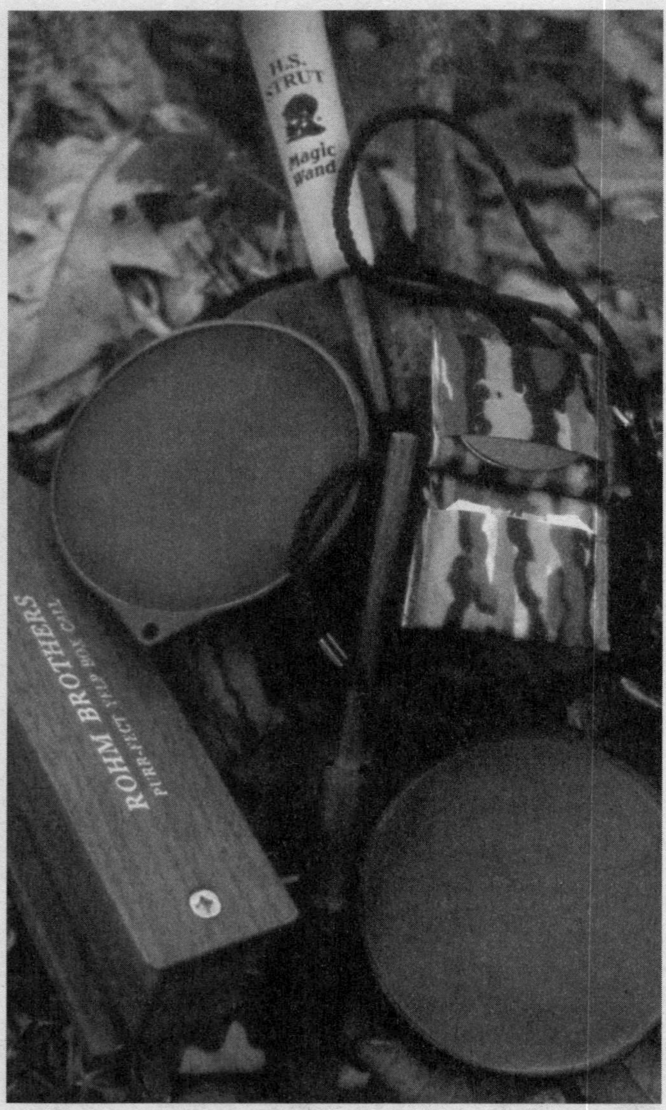

An experienced turkey hunter knows it's a good idea to carry a few turkey calls when afield. Some days the turkeys will respond more readily to one call versus another.

I also use several scratch-type slate calls made by Quaker Boy and Knight and Hale for soft purrs and clucks when a gobbler is getting close. I've pretty much settled on one diaphragm call the last couple of years: The Quaker Boy jagged-edge diaphragm's raspy sounds seem to get results better than any other diaphragm I've used, and I'm not one to change a winner. The diaphragm mouth call is a bowhunter's best friend, as you can keep calling with both hands free for drawing and shooting.

When I sneak in and set up to call a gobbling tom off the roost, I usually call very softly and let the gobbler carry the conversation. If he is with hens and the hens start sounding off, then I try to match the hens' calling, sound for sound, because if I don't get them curious or mad enough to come, the gobbler isn't going to come either. Let the gobbler's reactions or actions dictate your calling tempo and volume. Loud, forceful calling scares or turns off a lot more turkeys than soft, seductive calling combined with infinite patience. If you err, do so on the side of moderation rather than overzealousness.

One of the most successful methods of bowhunting spring turkeys is pairing up with a partner. One hunter does the calling while the second tries to ambush the turkey when its attention is on the caller. The key to making this plan work consistently is picking your calling location with turkey habits and preferences in mind.

Turkeys will generally follow the path of least resistance in responding to a call or traveling from location to location. This characteristic makes easy travel routes, such as old logging roads, four-wheeler paths, cattle and game trails, narrow corridors in

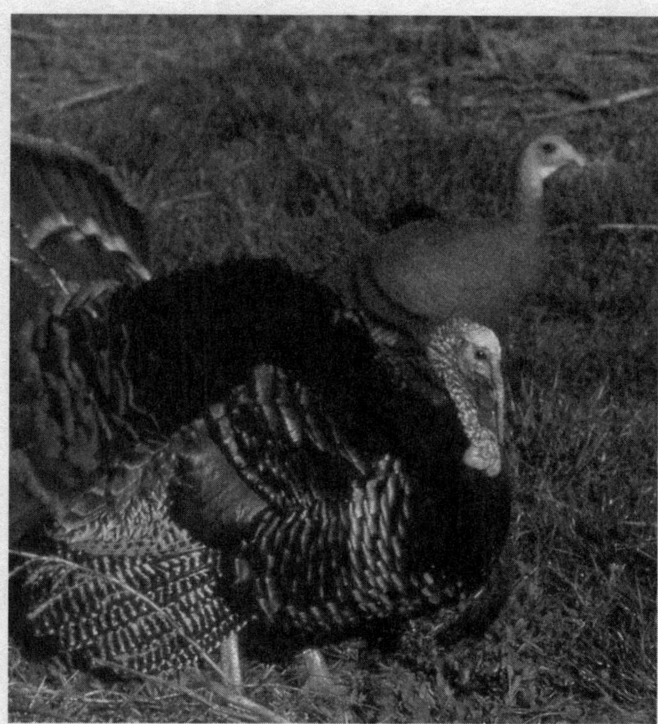

A hen decoy will help add to the illusion when you are making seductive hen calls to bring in that boss gobbler.

meadows, and open ridge tops, ideal places to try to draw a gobbler past a waiting bowhunter. When you set up to call a springtime tom, take your time and remember three of the most important aspects of ambushing a turkey: *location, location, and location.*

Set up where the advantages are yours and plan your ambush with care and thought before you ever make the first call. Turkeys have very little, if any, curiosity, and once they sense the slightest possibility of danger, they're history. You can swing a turkey off his chosen path of travel or direction, but it's darn difficult to get one to backtrack, so take the time to make it easy for a gobbler or his harem to come to your calling set up. Let patience work for you and against your feathered adversary.

## DECOYS AND DECOYING

Some 30 years ago, I discovered the value of a turkey decoy for getting a gobbler's full attention and bringing him "up close and personal," at full strut, so I could photograph him. At that time there wasn't a turkey decoy on the market, and my pride and joy was a full-bodied mounted hen turkey, christened Henrietta. I wore the feathers off several skins carting this decoy over the mountainous terrain of Colorado and through the brush country of Texas on my quest for the ultimate turkey photo and to help fill my tags.

No longer do turkey hunters have to cart around a solid, bulky, full-bodied decoy that is forever snagging on brush and making more noise than hail on a tin roof. With today's lightweight, collapsible, realistic foam decoys or a photo-realistic, fold-up decoy, there is no reason a turkey bowhunter should take to the woods without several stuffed into his turkey vest or daypack, unless you're hunting a state where they're illegal, like Alabama.

My turkey vest contains Feather Flex's love triangle of two jakes and a hen, plus a Higdon Motion-Hen decoy with a flexible head and neck that can be manipulated with a pull string from 30 yards away. I also carry several photo-realistic Montana pop-up strutting gobbler decoys.

## DECOY MOVEMENT

The lightweight Feather-Flex decoys swing seductively on their pointed anchor stakes in the slightest breeze, giving them life-like action to catch the eye of a distant gobbler. However, a stiff breeze can cause these ultra-light decoys to spin erratically and even blow off the stakes. Either of these occurrences will put an approaching gobbler into instant escape-and-evasion mode! To keep this from happening, simply screw a small wire connector nut down on the point of the stake, protruding through the decoy's back. This lets the decoy move seductively but holds it securely on the stake in the stiffest wind.

Just as movement can be a great attractant for a decoy set-up, too much of a good thing will spook the gobbler in a heartbeat. To prevent decoys from spinning or swinging back and forth too erratically, I *always* place two sticks or stiff weeds six to eight inches apart on either side of the tail. The stakes allow the decoy to swing back and forth enticingly, but eliminate a full spin or excessive movement. If there's no wind to provide movement, the Higdon hen decoy will provide enough action and realism to your decoy set to convince that reluctant tom to slip into bow range.

A motion decoy of some ilk will often con a gobbler away from hens or convince a reluctant tom to come that last few yards for a close look. Quite often the movement of the hen decoy will lure the gobbler's curious harem to your set-up, with the gobbler tagging along. A multiple-decoy set-up, with swinging or moveable decoys, is equally deadly when used on a travel-way between a roosting area and feeding area, or when set up right in the bird's loafing area. When located where there is long-distance visibility, I've pulled birds for half a mile without making a sound on my calls.

There are a number of motion-producing devices on the market, some practical enough and some questionable. Several of the small battery-operated units are very effective when used with lightweight foam or plastic decoys, and add just enough movement to calm a spooky tom's nerves and bring him to you. In a number of states, the use of any electronic devices for calling or attracting turkeys is illegal, so check your state laws before using such a device.

## TURKEY DECOYING TACTICS

The best set-up I've used for consistently pulling in a lone, dominant gobbler, or both the dominant and sub-dominant birds, is setting out two jake decoys and a hen. The aggressive jake has a bright-red head, while the passive jake's head is muted gray. I try to position the aggressive jake decoy so it's between the hen and the approaching gobbler and 10 to15 yards slightly to the left of my shooting position (it's just the opposite for a left-hand shooter). This combination makes it seem like the aggressive jake is challenging the incoming gobbler by keeping between him and the hen, just inviting a confrontation.

I put the passive jake decoy off to the side, away from my position, to coerce the challenging tom closer to me and away from the second jake: the path of least resistance. The challenging gobbler will generally circle the hen and approach the jake from the front, presenting an ideal side or rear-end shot. Patience is tough at this point, but waiting for just the right moment is essential to making a killing shot. Make sure your decoy set-up is on level ground so, when the challenging and usually strutting tom turns tail end to you, he can't see over his fanned tail and catch the movement of your draw.

If I'm bowhunting a gobbler in an area where there has been little hunting pressure, I'll often use a single hen placed in an open area with maximum visibility from the most likely direction of the gobbler's approach. Good visibility is a vital part of successful decoying, so choose your decoy locations for maximum exposure. I try to set the decoy or decoys so the tom will pass my shooting position on his way to the decoys. With his attention on the decoys, he is less likely to pick up my camouflaged form or any slight movement I might make in getting into final shooting position.

When the dominant gobblers are "henned up," and later in the season when hunting pressure has educated many of the gobblers roaming my hunting area, I may add a couple more hens to my decoy set-ups. If I'm sure a gobbler is with hens, I'll often use

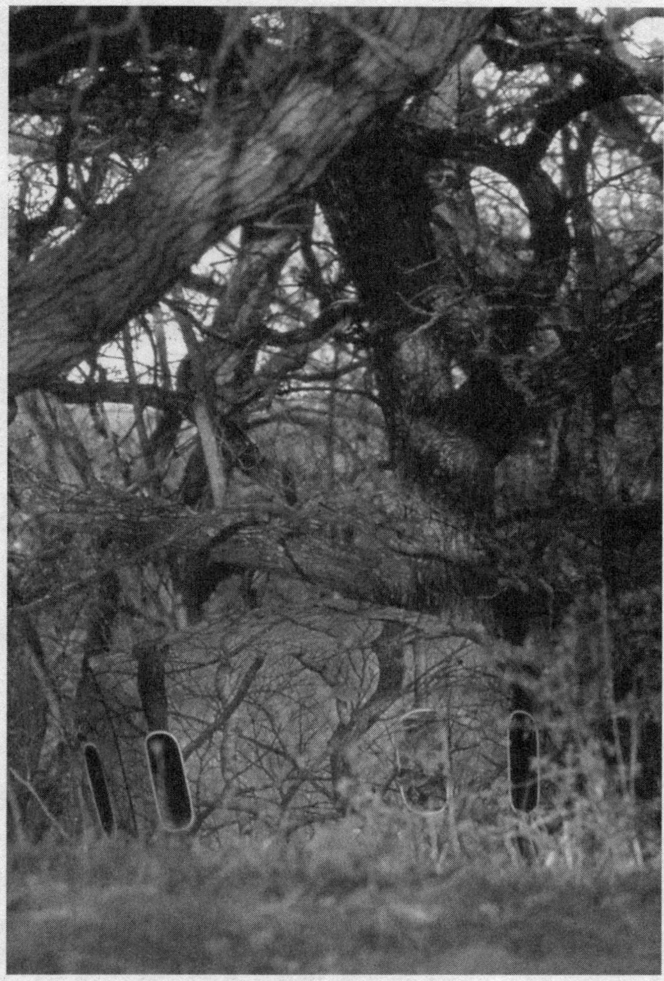

Some gobblers come in to your calls making all sorts of noise and sounds. Others come in on the sneak and don't make a sound at all. Blinds will help conceal a hunter's movement when a turkey surprises you and you have to get into shooting position.

a decoy set-up with three hen decoys and the two jakes, and use several different calls to convince the tom these hens are hot to trot and waiting for him to come and take care of their needs.

The double-jake-and-hen decoy combination is extremely deadly in the late season, when the hens are nesting and the gobblers are roaming in late morning, mid-day, and late afternoon, looking for available hens. Even a wise old Alpha gobbler spotting this set-up will often throw caution to the wind and stomp in to kick butt and take hens!

## TURKEY BLINDS

Today there are numerous superb, lightweight, portable pop-up blinds on the market for the turkey-hunting enthusiast to choose from. In the past, I've used the Double Bull, Invisiblind, Hide-Out, and Seneco blinds for turkey bowhunting and photography and had excellent results with all of them. Each of these blinds is sturdy, portable, lightweight, and quick to set up under hunting conditions.

Unlike deer and other big game, turkeys tend to accept a newly placed blind as part of the environment immediately. This means you can cart a pop-up blind along and set it up wherever and whenever needed to provide instant movement-hiding cover. Each spring on our Iowa turkey hunting leases, I set up a half-dozen blinds along the edges of food plots, watering areas, strutting grounds, and travel routes, for use by bowhunters and gun hunters alike. All it takes is a couple of decoys, some adequate calling, and lots of *patience* for these blinds to prove effective.

Blinds are effective for getting youngsters and beginners involved in bowhunting turkeys. They provide these inexperienced hunters with an almost foolproof hide, where they can get away with movement that would decimate their chances of getting a close-in shot at a turkey without them.

Utilizing a blind for bowhunting turkeys has taken many of the rocket-science aspects out of the equation. When modern-day pop-up blinds are combined with calling and decoy set-ups, the only variable left is the bowhunter's shooting ability and resistance to "turkey fever."

## FALL TURKEY BOWHUNTING

Spring isn't the only time of year turkeys can be bowhunted, and I've taken a number of gobblers during the fall season in conjunction with deer and elk bowhunting, as well as specifically bowhunting turkeys.

Fall turkey bowhunting is a different proposition from spring hunting, as the birds (especially gobblers) are far less vocal than in the spring. This means you're going to be more dependent on your knowledge of turkey habits, daily movements, and habitat features: where they can be ambushed while traveling, feeding, or watering.

My favorite fall turkey-hunting method is to set up on a waterhole or food plot and ambush them as they come to feed or water. This type of bowhunting is ideal for making use of a blind. Turkeys have very set time-frames when it comes to feeding and watering, and a few days' scouting and glassing likely areas should allow you to pattern the birds well enough to choose a good site for your blind. Set the blind where there is little chance of being skylighted or outlined by the early-morning or late afternoon sun. Ambushing fall turkeys is a waiting game, and I've found the best way to make time pass is to read a book while you're waiting for turkeys to come.

Turkeys can be called in the fall, but the technique is quite different from springtime turkey calling. Generally, fall birds are in family groups of hens and poults, and bachelor groups of gobblers. The trick is to break up these groups by chasing after them, sicking your dog on them, or trying any other tactic that will spook the birds into flying in every direction.

Once the birds are scattered, set up near the point of dispersion and be patient. I generally sit quietly and wait at least an hour before starting to call. Call with a short series of plaintive yelps interspersed with the "kee kee run" call of a lost young bird. These calls will attract hens, poults, and gobblers alike. Be patient; it may take another hour before you pick up the movement of birds sneaking silently back to join the vocal birds. A couple of hen decoys in this situation will help draw the cautious birds into bow range. The returning birds are going to be spooky and looking for the slightest movement, and a blind will help greatly in keeping them from spotting your ambush.

An even more effective method of scattering fall turkeys is to locate the roost area of a group or two of turkeys. Just at dark sneak into the roost and scare the heck out of the birds, scattering them in every direction. The following morning, sneak into the area and set up. Start calling as soon as the woods come alive and call every 20 minutes for at least a couple hours. Stay alert, because incoming birds probably won't make a sound approaching your location.

I have, on occasion, had an old hen fill the woods with her coarse yelps in answer to my lost-turkey calls, as she tried to call me to her rather than come to me. Gobblers will occasionally pull this same stunt, but if you keep up your lost calls, they will eventually work their way to you. Fall turkey bowhunting isn't all that popular, and I can assure you that competition will not be a problem. The challenges and experiences are just as exciting as spring hunting, and fall turkey bowhunting adds another dimension to your fall deer and elk bowhunting.

## KILL SHOTS

A turkey gobbler is certainly not in the same category as a bull elk for toughness, but they are *tough*. Nothing works better for bowhunting turkeys than a razor-sharp broadhead, properly placed. This is where a mechanical broadhead is advantageous. Several of my clients and I have used the Spitfire 100 Gobbler Getter, manufactured by New Archery Products, with good results from a 65-pound bow.

I've had several turkey-hunting acquaintances swear by head-shooting turkeys with blunts, and I have little doubt that a turkey shot this way is going to stay down for the count every time. However, I have trouble hitting bull elk at times and have missed the whole blooming turkey more than I like to admit, so hitting a turkey's weaving, bobbing head is totally out of my league. I try to put my arrow high in the center of the body mass, where it will get into the backbone, rib cage, and base of the wings to break bones and anchor the bird on the spot. A turkey shot through the breast will run or fly off, and it's tough to blood trail a flying turkey.

The only shot to take on a strutting turkey is to wait until it turns away, then use the base of the tail as an aiming point and try to put your arrow just above the white bull's-eye. I don't recommend a broadside shot at a strutting gobbler. Wait until he comes un-puffed and then drive your arrow slightly to the rear of the wing base to anchor them. Turkeys are tough. Take your time and make your shot count, because you aren't likely to get a second chance. A heavy-bearded, long-spurred trophy gobbler is a gorgeous addition to any trophy room and one a bowhunter can be proud of.

# Small Game and Non-Game

It was everywhere, just as the lady in the village had told us, as Chuck and I slipped slowly through the undergrowth, trying to avoid the stickey bushes and impaling cactus. There were fresh tracks and trails in the sand and trails leading to the obvious den holes at the base of huge trees scattered through the dense jungle. An hour of sneaking quietly through the jungle-like forest hadn't netted us a single sighting of our elusive quarry.

We finally edged out onto a well-traveled trail between the little village and the nearby river, where we plunked down on a rock to contemplate our next move. A few minutes later, a leathery-skinned, old timer came down the trail with a water-filled olla precariously balanced on his shoulder, eyeing my bow and arrows with more than a bit of suspicious curiosity.

Fortunately, Chuck Cadieux, my partner in this questionable endeavor, spoke passable Spanish, and after a couple of minutes of listening to Chuck haltingly explain our unsuccessful bowhunting endeavors, the old man broke out in a toothless grin, set down the water jar, and motioned us to follow him.

Our chuckling guide led us back the way we'd come, to several large trees with gaping holes in their roots, worn smooth by four-legged critter traffic. Our guide started circling the trees bent almost backwards as he scanned the treetops.

"Alla alla," chortled the oldster, pointing upward. Sure enough, spread out on a limb, soaking up the hot sunshine, was our bowhunting quest: a huge, three-foot-long Iguana. Well . . . no wonder we couldn't find them. Nobody told us they spend most of their time living in the trees.

I'm not sure if one would classify Iguana lizards as small game, but a fresh lime-marinated and broiled lizard, dolloped with homemade salsa and washed down with an ice-cold brew, rivaled the best cottontail or squirrel I'd ever eaten.

Bowhunting small game can provide bowhunters with plenty of action, unbeatable shooting practice, and some delectable table fare. I've often wished that cottontail rabbits weighed 100 pounds or so or that deer tasted like cottontail.

I got a good start bowhunting bunnies in my hometown of Luverne, Minnesota, when I was nine years old. I had a small bow and a bunch of arrows made from dowel rods and tipped with homemade steel broadheads. I'd chased rabbits all over the neighborhood for several years before I finally hit my bunny "bonanza," a couple of blocks off Main Street.

The railroad ran through town, and there was a grain elevator alongside the tracks. There was always an abundance of spilled grain that attracted lots of pigeons (also fair targets) and cottontail rabbits from the nearby woods and old buildings. There were several piles of 20-foot by six-inch pipes laying alongside the tracks, providing an ideal hidey hole for the cottontails.

It didn't take me long to realize I could sneak up to a pipe and carefully check to see if it harbored a rabbit. If it did, I'd block the ends with rocks hauled up for just that purpose. Then I'd slip around and shoot into the open pipes until the rabbit expired . . . kind of like shooting fish in a barrel. As I proudly toted bow-killed trophies up the main drag, I got lots of comments on my prowess with a bow at nine years old, and the end result was a lot more important than the method. Don't think my folks ever did figure out how I provided so many bunnies for the table with my bow and arrow set.

Small game and non-game can provide beginning youngsters with bowhunting challenges commensurate with their size and abilities. When my son Blain was three, I got him a stout Bear Cub bow and made him some arrows. We lived on a ranch with several hundred acres of sage brush-dotted pastureland that was alive with Richardson's ground squirrels, or "picket pins" as they were more commonly known.

Bowhunting small game is perfect for youngsters as it sharpens their shooting skills with plenty of action.

Blain would spend hours every day in the pasture around the house, stalking and shooting at the brazen little gophers. Most days he had to be seriously threatened to get him in the house for meals. It didn't take him long to mutilate and destroy his small supply of wooden arrows, so I took time one late afternoon to make him up a dozen classy little arrows, with full cresting and fluorescent orange fletching . . . figuring they'd be easy to find.

By noon the following day, he'd lost all but one arrow. With a seemingly endless supply of arrows in the little quiver, the tyke would shoot one arrow one way, another in a different direction, etc. Due to the bright colors, it only took the rest of the family three hours to gather all his arrows. From that point on, I gave him one arrow to hunt with. That way, he'd have to keep track of it every shot, and not let the overwhelming population of gophers exhaust his supply.

I never will forget the day he came running to the house with his first "big-game kill." I'd originally tipped his tiny arrows with cut-off 25-20 brass that made very effective and indestructible blunts. He swore he'd hit several gophers without killing them and wanted broadheads like his dad's arrows. I took several bent Bear Razorheads, ground them down to fit his arrows and put a razor-sharp edge on each.

We already had several safety discussions, and he was only allowed to take one arrow hunting. The second day, he came thundering up on the back porch holding his first gopher. Seems he'd missed a dozen or so and figured he had to get close, so he nestled into a thick clump of sage a few feet from a picketpin mound and waited. When the curious and probably overconfident gopher poked his head up, Blain slowly drew and put his arrow through the gullible gopher at less than *five feet* That kind of patience and perseverance makes good bowhunters.

There is nothing that will make a better shot out of a bowhunter than lots of shooting under hunting conditions, something that most bowhunters don't get. They practice and practice at paper targets or on a field range, shooting at full-bodied targets. There is no such thing as bad practice, but shooting at living targets, under actual hunting conditions, just can't be beat.

When I first started bowhunting in northern Colorado, I was lucky to live in an area that had a thriving population of cottontail rabbits, jackrabbits, picketpins, and prairie dogs. It was easy to grab my bow, a quiver of arrows, and head out in the pasture or drive a short distance to the nearest dog town. No limit, no season. At that time, rangefinders were a thing of the future, so the shooting was superb practice for judging range as well as learning what your bow and arrow were capable of at varying distances. It was this small-game and non-game bowhunting and shooting that made me a life-long instinctive shooter. The unlimited experience taught me the rudiments of range judgment and the effectiveness of long-range shooting.

Over the years, there have been a number of occasions when my big-game bowhunting suddenly took a back seat to small-game hunting with bow and arrow.

## COTTONTAIL RABBITS

Cottontails are, without a doubt, the most popular small-game animal for gun and bowhunters, and at one time provided more meat volume for the hunter's table than whitetail deer. With the increase in whitetail numbers and the decrease in small-game hunting pressure, I doubt if that is still true, but cottontails are still number one on the small-game hit list.

There are numerous subspecies of cottontail rabbits, ranging from the largest swamp cottontail, weighing up to six pounds, to the pigmy cottontail, weighing a pound or less. Cottontails thrive from the east coast to the west, Mexico to Canada.

Snowshoe hares are cousins of the cottontails, but their propensity for changing from the dull brownish-gray summer pelage to white in winter puts them in the hare family rather than the rabbit clan.

I've bowhunted snowshoes in conjunction with bowhunting elk in the mountains of Colorado and whitetails in the birch, aspen, willow, and alder thickets of Alberta, Canada. One fall, I bowhunted whitetails in east-central Alberta during a full moon and unseasonable warm weather, which limited deer movement to the very early morning hours and late afternoon. The dense birch and alder thickets around camp were alive with snowshoe hares, providing

Before heading out on your next deer hunt, bring along extra arrows because bowhunting cottontails is a fun activity during your mid-day break.

hours of challenging and rewarding bowhunting during the long mid-day lulls.

Bowhunting bunnies and snowshoes is a great way to spend a sunny winter afternoon and a true test of your stalking and shooting skills, especially if you're bowhunting snow country. A missed shot at a rabbit or hare on snow-covered ground usually means down time searching for your arrow, or a lost arrow. So not only do you have to stalk carefully within bow range, you have to choose an angle that will give you the best chance of recovering your arrow should you miss. Of course, nobody plans on missing.

Cottontails and snowshoes are easily anchored with rubber bludgeon blunts, steel blunts, judos, or broadheads. Judos work the best in brushy country and are also very worthwhile when hunting in snow. When I'm bowhunting big game in good cottontail or snowshoe habitat, I generally carry two of my hunting arrows tipped with judos or rubber blunts for any unexpected encounter with these furry delicacies. To make sure I don't grab a blunt by mistake in the heat of action and try to kill a bull elk or buck with it, I carry the blunts with the feathers down and tips up where I can see them.

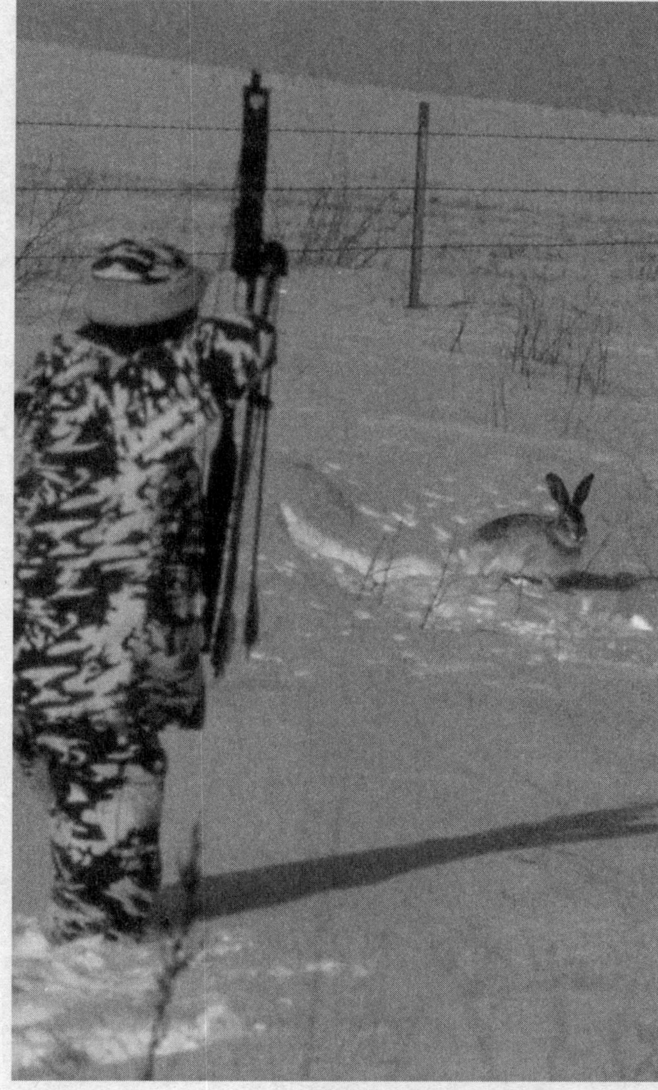

Jackrabbits are tough critters. I prefer hunting them with razor-sharp broadheads or judo points.

## JACKRABBITS

If I had to choose my favorite small-game or non-game bowhunting target, it would be the jackrabbit. I've bowhunted jackrabbits from Mexico to Canada, and they never fail to give me all the bowhunting challenge a person could ask for. In addition to an exciting, action-packed bowhunt-ing challenge, jackrabbits can also provide some of the best hunting and shooting practice possible to hone your spotting, stalking, shooting, and ranging skills under actual hunting conditions.

There are four subspecies of jackrabbits in the United States. The common black-tailed jackrabbits found in the semi-arid west and southwestern United States stay the same dull-brown and white color year round, blending perfectly with the desert and brush country background they call home.

The white-tailed jackrabbit's range is farther north, from northern California eastward to Iowa, Kansas, and Minnesota. The white-tailed jackrabbit is actually a varying hare rather than a rabbit. It's lighter in color than its southern cousin and turns almost pure white in the winter, to blend it into the snowy background.

One of the most action-packed methods of hunting white-tailed jackrabbits in winter, when they are herded up in prairie shelterbelts or sagebrush and greasewood creek bottoms, is by pushing or driving. A couple of bowhunters sneak into the downwind end of the cover, and one or two more move through the patch, trying to stalk close enough for some shooting of their own. In the process, the drivers will move the jackrabbits to the standers, for plenty of fast action shooting. During the peak of jackrabbit populations in the Dakotas, I've seen several *hundred* jackrabbits come pouring out of a half-mile-long shelterbelt.

The antelope jackrabbit is found only in the desert regions of southwestern New Mexico and south-central Arizona. And the fourth subspecies, the white-sided jackrabbit, is limited to part of one county in New Mexico.

Jackrabbit populations are generally cyclic, with years of abundance when there seems to be a jack under every bush, and lean years, when finding a jackrabbit is as tough as locating a Pope and Young muley.

Jackrabbits are tough critters, and you don't need to feel over-bowed using your regular big-game bowhunting gear for them. In fact, bowhunting jackrabbits in conjunction with Texas whitetail, Wyoming antelope, Colorado mule deer, or even Arizona elk is an excellent way to fine-tune your shooting during the hunt.

I prefer either broadheads or judo points for jackrabbits. Black-tailed jackrabbits, with their thinner southern hides and fur, are easier to kill with blunts or judos. But the northern whitetails, that are bigger and heavier with dense winter fur, call for razor-sharp broadheads for consistent clean kills.

## SQUIRRELS

Next to cottontail rabbits, squirrels are probably the most sought-after small-game critters with bow and gun. Find good whitetail country and you'll find good squirrel hunting. It is fast becoming a lost art, and seeing a squirrel hunter in the woods is getting to be a rare occurrence, except in the south and southeast, where gun hunting for squirrels is still a popular pastime.

The fox and gray squirrels are found from a bit west of the Missouri River to the east coast, with a wide variety of color phases occurring in each species, from pure white albinos to a coal-black melanistic phase. Alabama has the most unique color-phase fox squirrels, with black and white faces, tails, and legs and every combination thereof. I got more engrossed bow-hunting these gorgeous squirrels one fall than I did on my deer hunt. Never did get one of the critters for my den.

Patience is the key to getting one of these skittish, jumpy tree climbers into bow range. bowhunting squirrels from your deer tree stand is about as good as it gets. You can shoot at a

When you're up in a deer stand, be sure to have a few arrows tipped with rubber blunts. They're ideal for some quiet squirrel hunting and you won't be leaving any arrows stuck high in surrounding trees.

dozen squirrels over the course of a morning or late afternoon bowhunt without spooking a single deer. You can make use of your regular big-game bowhunting equipment to fine-tune your tree stand drawing. A close miss on the squirrel-sized target should mean a good hit on a deer-sized target, if you pick the same-sized spot. If you're careful about your squirrel shooting, there's little chance of announcing your presence to deer in the area. Just be sure to carry enough ammunition in your quiver.

If you're specifically bowhunting squirrels, the best bet is locating a prime food source, such as a cornfield or oak tree the squirrels are hammering. Squirrels don't like to venture too far into the open. Find a corner or cul-de-sac where the squirrels can feed close to cover. Building a ground blind a couple days prior to bowhunting, or better yet, utilizing a pop-up ground blind for concealment, is ideal. These little fuzztails have super vision and will pick up the slightest, quick movement; they'll run first and look later.

If it's legal to use a feeder in your hunting area, you've got it made. Set up your blind 10 to 15 yards on the downwind side of the feeder, take lots of arrows, a fold-up chair, and a good book and enjoy a day of great squirrel hunting.

Stalking squirrels and picking them out of the trees with your bow and arrow is about as challenging as small-game bowhunting gets. This type of squirrel hunting is a great way to gain knowledge of your bowhunting area, improve your still-hunting and stalking skills, and keep your arrow supplier happy. It's also a great way to bowhunt with a partner. Use binoculars to spot feeding or moving squirrels. When a squirrel is located, one bowhunter tries to stalk close for a shot while the other keeps the squirrel in sight. If the squirrel spooks, the stalking bowhunter keeps the squirrel treed until the partner arrives.

Rock chucks and other small non-game critters can provide a full day of quick shooting and fun.

The best way to get a shot at a treed squirrel is for one bowhunter to stand quietly on one side of the tree while the other circles out from the tree. The squirrel will usually try to stay on the backside of the tree, and when it moves around to stay out of sight of the moving bowhunter, the standing bowhunter should have a shot. Good camouflage is essential for spot-and-stalk squirrel bowhunting.

For this type of squirrel hunting, I prefer a rubber blunt and try to take shots where there's a tree trunk or limb behind the squirrel, in case I miss (which is generally the case). A broadhead or judo will stick in the tree, and you can kiss another arrow goodbye. Unfortunately, I don't always follow my own advice and have arrows sticking in trees in just about every prime whitetail and squirrel-hunting state in the country.

There are rock chucks, prairie dogs, groundhogs, gophers, and a host of other small non-game critters running around the country, just waiting to test your bowhunting mettle and provide you with all sorts of opportunity to sharpen your bowhunting techniques and skills. Don't leave home without extra arrows.

# Elk

Bowhunting elk can be the ultimate adrenaline rush. They are big, majestic, loud animals that can have massive antlers. The elk is arguably the perfect species for bowhunters who want an action-packed adventure. On the flip side, returning home year after year without fresh elk meat or even a close call can be bitterly disappointing.

As an avid elk hunter who has guided more than a hundred clients on hunts for these awesome animals, I have learned that successfully bowhunting elk requires three main things:

1. Getting in range
2. Drawing undetected
3. Proper shot placement

It sounds so easy, just three little things. However, each one has prerequisites. Before breaking down these three main requirements, let's look at some average success rates.

Anybody can bowhunt elk. Go buy a tag, grab your bow, and head out. Obviously, this is as much effort as thousands of bowhunters put into their hunts, since the average archery success rate—including both bulls and cows—in most Western states hovers around 14 percent for both guided and nonguided hunts. Based on these numbers, your average hunter has only a slim chance of ever harvesting an elk.

I point this out because I feel that most people have the misconception that bowhunting elk out West is pretty easy. Heck, just flip on your TV and watch one of the elk shows, and you can see guys calling in and shooting tremendous elk. Some popular DVDs on the market also show one monster bull after another being called into big, open meadows and harvested. Realistically, unless your pocketbook is extremely deep or you have drawn a limited-tag area, your hunt will not be so easy. Statistics from a three-year period show archery success rates for Colorado, Wyoming, Oregon, Washington, Idaho, Montana, and Utah averaging about 12–15 percent. These numbers include bulls and cows and both guided and nonguided hunts on both public and private land. In states such as Nevada, New Mexico, and Arizona, these numbers are slightly higher due to the limited number of tags available.

What statistics don't show are the opportunities lost—for example, close calls, missed shots, and hunters winded, spotted, or busted while drawing their bows. If lost opportunities were included in the statistics, those success rates would be a lot higher.

So what makes the difference between routinely harvesting an elk and falling into the majority of elk hunters who go home empty-handed every year? There are a lot of factors that come into play, some major and some minute, but they all fall under the three main requirements listed above. My goal in this chapter is to help you improve your odds on your next elk hunt.

## GETTING IN RANGE

Getting in range sounds pretty obvious. To be able to shoot an elk you must first get in range. Now let's look at how to get that elk within bow range and how not to screw up once he is there. Let's call bow range from point-blank breathing in your face out to 30 yards. This is the critical distance where everything usually pans out or not.

To get within bow range of elk, the most effective and common methods include:

1. Calling: Emulating the sounds of a calf, cow, or bull to lure an elk into range.
2. Still-hunting: Slipping quietly through the woods, hoping to either sneak into range undetected or spot an elk moving toward you and wait or position your- self for a shot.
3. Stand hunting: Waiting in one location for an elk to come into bow range.

## CALLING

Let's start with calling. In my opinion, this is the most overrated way to lure an elk into bow range. Any elk that is coming in to a call is ultra-alert. It is looking for another elk, so the odds of getting busted are increased exponentially. Also, since elk use their sense of smell to follow and locate each other, they usually circle downwind of the calls. That said, on those occasions when it does work, when a bull or a cow reacts to your calling and runs into bow range, it is an exciting experience that you will never forget.

Before sharing my suggestions on calling elk, I want to share a story of an elk hunt in Colorado that we captured on video. I was with two friends, and just minutes before we had watched two raghorn bulls sparring in a small clearing about 300 yards away. Now the three of us slipped through the aspens looking for a good spot to set up. I checked the wind, and then moved into an area where I had enough room to shoot. I slowly knelt down by a small aspen tree and started breaking finger-sized branches off a fallen limb. I cow-called softly while my friend Scott cow-called from his position 20 yards behind me.

We had cut the distance in half and quickly set up in a small stand of aspens. We knew the bulls were alone and were counting on them wanting to join up with a few lonely and vocal cows. It wasn't going to be easy—Scott was carrying a video camera and my friend Brian was also with us. Brian was set up to my right and Scott was between and behind us, where he could tape the action if the bulls came in. Scott cow-called again and I broke a few more small branches. We were doing our best to sound like a small group of cows grazing through the aspens, softly calling to one another.

Suddenly, through the trees I spotted the top of a rack as one of the bulls made his way toward us

One of my guides, Luke Robb, called this bull in for client Daryl Mull.

through the white-trunked aspens. He was followed closely by the other bull, which stopped to rake an aspen limb with his antlers. The wind was still in our favor, and the two bulls continued toward us, confident they were about to meet up with some cows, not two bowhunters and a cameraman. As the lead bull closed to within about 30 yards, he stopped and looked around. I was sure one of us would be spotted any second. I tried to make myself small as I hid behind my bow and the small aspen tree. Although I couldn't see them, I was sure Brian and Scott were also trying to stay calm and blend into the brush.

The young bull continued slowly forward, heading directly toward me. If he continued on his current path, he was bound to spot one of us at any moment. I slowly started to draw my recurve. The bull was now only about 20 yards away and instantly spotted the slight movement. He jumped and took a few steps to my left, which turned him broadside to me. Luckily the young bull hesitated while I finished my draw and released. The arrow struck the bull just above the heart, and he ran only 40 yards before he stopped and collapsed in front of us. Our setup had worked perfectly, and Scott captured all the action on video.

Although on tape this whole sequence took less than four minutes, it had taken years of botched setups and hundreds of hours afield to help tip the scales in our favor. What follows is a list of tips and tactics I have used to call in elk while hunting and guiding. Just remember that calling does not work all the time. Wind is by far your toughest obstacle, because most elk will attempt to circle or come in downwind.

## NOISE

It's a fact; elk make noise when they walk through the woods. Don't misunderstand me: they can move quietly when they want to, and I've watched bulls that thundered into a setup sneak away without making a sound. But generally, when elk are comfortable, they make a lot of noise: branches snapping, antlers scraping brush and trees, legs and hooves breaking branches or hitting logs and rocks as they walk along. Sometimes they really make a racket. Use that knowledge when you are calling. Noise adds realism. It's tough to get used to because generally when bowhunting silence is your main concern. However, if you are trying to convince a bull or cow to come join you and the only noise is your calling, oftentimes they will hold up out of range. So next time you try calling, add a little noise to your routine. Try breaking a few small twigs or raking a tree with a branch. It may just be enough to cause that elk to rush right in.

## STOP CALLING SO MUCH

Overcalling is a common mistake. It's hard not to scream on that bugle tube again or to send a few more cow calls down into the draw. I've learned the hard way that less is best.

Elk have great hearing, and both their calls and yours travel a long way. If an elk is going to come in or respond, usually just a few cow calls (a few being three or four) or a single bugle is all it takes. This can be especially true on public land, where most elk have already heard the latest in new elk calls long before you ever put on your pack.

I once watched a friend of mine on public land spook a bull into the next county by overcalling. From my vantage point above him, I watched as the whole show played out. A bull was heading up over a ridge, and I was trapped on the opposite ridge so I couldn't move without being spotted. The bull was alone and heading into the timber when we both heard my friend's two cow calls float up from

This bull was busy raking a tree when I slipped up to 19 yards and saved the tree's life.

the draw between us. I watched as the bull turned completely around and started heading rapidly down the ridge toward my buddy. He couldn't see the bull from his location and cow-called again three more times. The bull continued heading toward him but slowed down noticeably. The third time he called, the bull bolted back up the slope and into the timber. He had obviously heard too much. I truly believe that had he stopped after the first two calls, the bull would have trotted right down into range. As it was, overcalling blew that elk out of there, and my buddy never even knew the bull was around. I think this scenario happens more than we realize.

The lesson here is to give elk time to respond to your calls. They may be coming in silently from a few hundred yards away, so make sure you give them enough time. I have often been surprised by elk that came in to my calls as much as an hour after I had let out a few pleading cow calls. I try to wait at least 30 to 45 minutes before moving or calling again from the same area. I prefer using a cow call over a bugle and usually use only three to four cow calls at a time.

Diane Kinney is an avid bowhunter who hunts with a recurve. Her story proves how effective calling can be in the right situation.

"It was down to the last hour of the last day of my elk hunt, when two bulls stepped out into the meadow across the valley from where we were. I could tell they were bulls, but not how big. I cow-called to get the attention of my guide, Dick Louden. From where he was he couldn't see them. He understood immediately and started calling; the bulls started our way across the meadow into the valley below us and then they disappeared from view into an arroyo. Not knowing where they would come out, I was standing with an arrow nocked, using a pine tree that made the perfect cover for my 'ground blind.' The sound of rolling rocks in the arroyo was the first thing to give away their position. Suddenly there was an elk rack coming up and out of the arroyo, but I realized it was not a legal bull as he passed. I didn't have time to be disappointed when the second set of antlers came into view. This bull was legal and trotting past me at 11 yards. As the realization that the bull was legal flew through my mind, as if on its own, my recurve came up, the string came back, and the arrow was in the air. I heard a CAWACK as the arrow hit hard. The bull's gait changed, he slowed, went about 100 yards, and went down. He never got back up. It was by far the most exciting

Diane Kinney from Pennsylvania and her bull that guide Dick Louden called in.

fifteen minutes of my life and an experience I will never forget."

## BUGLING

In my opinion, bugling is probably the most overused calling technique. I bugle only sparingly unless the bulls are really cranked up. More often than not I've seen bulls gather up their cows and run when challenged by another bull. If the bull doesn't run and responds, I try to wait for him to bugle again before calling so I can gauge how worked up he is and mimic everything he does. Occasionally a bull will come screaming in no matter what you do or how often you do it, but generally I try to err on the quiet side. If he wants to fight, don't worry, he will find you.

If you find yourself trying to work one of those stubborn herd bulls that won't come in, try this radical technique. Sneak in as close as you can without spooking the bull or his cows. Then let out your best bugle. If the bull herds up his cows and takes off, you follow. Run up as close as possible without being spotted (terrain obviously plays a role in this method) and then try cow-calling three or four times. Not just a short mew. Stretch it out a bit like a pleading, whining cow. Meeeeeewww. If all goes as planned, the bull will spin around and drop back to pick you up, thinking that he has inadvertently lost one of his cows. In the right situation, this can be a great way to lure in an old bull that usually wouldn't come in to your calls.

Don't forget that most elk coming in to a call will try to circle downwind. So if you're calling by yourself, try to use the terrain to your advantage. Try to force the elk to come in upwind of you, or set up anticipating them to circle downwind. If you practice your calling and hunt during the "prime time" for your location, you may have the most exciting close-range encounter imaginable. When calling, I've had the best luck with two people, one caller and one hunter. I like using two different cow calls to try to simulate more than one elk.

## SETTING UP

How you set up when calling will often mean the difference between success and failure. One common mistake is not being set up at all. I have (on more than one occasion) been embarrassed in front of a client when I have gotten busted by a bull charging into range after I had let out just a few calls, hoping to locate a bull. What I have learned is to always be ready and never to call without first being in position to shoot, just in case a bull or cow you don't even know is there charges in. When pair hunting, I like to have the hunter 20 to 60 yards upwind in front of the caller. Exact positioning varies and depends on the elk's position, obstacles, and terrain. In general, if I know the elk's exact position, I like to place the shooter a little farther out between the bull and the caller. If I am calling blind or have no idea if there is an elk within earshot or where it may be located, I prefer to have the shooter within 20 yards upwind of the caller. In certain situations or on heavily pressured bulls, having the shooter downwind of the caller can work great as the bull circles to confirm it's an elk he is hearing.

Since most calling for elk is done from the ground, you must use the terrain to your advantage. Most eastern whitetail hunters are used to hunting from tree stands. It is a whole different ballgame when you're on the ground trying to get drawn on an animal that is wired and looking for any movement. My friend and fellow guide Jake Kraus once had one of our clients set up on a bull that was coming in. He told the hunter to kneel by a tree and wait to see if something responded to his calls. Due to cover, Jake was only a few feet away from our client. A bull responded and started coming in. Jake whispered, "Get ready," and to his shock the client stood up! The bull instantly spotted the movement and bolted down the ridge. When Jake asked why the hunter stood up, the reply was, "I always stand up in my tree stand to shoot. I've never shot kneeling down."

Using cow elk decoys is a great way to lure in bulls to bow range.

If you're going elk hunting, you had best practice shooting your bow leaning, kneeling, sitting on your butt, and standing on one foot. Okay, the last one is an exaggeration, but not by much. Also practice shooting at steep up and down angles. When you do set up to call and stand, kneel, or sit waiting for an elk to come in to your calls, pay attention to your surroundings. I have often kicked myself for setting up in a position that prevented me from shooting when an elk did come in. You want to be concealed, but not so much so that you restrict your ability to turn, draw, and shoot if the shot presents itself. Pay attention to the position of the sun and always set up in the shade or shadows when possible. Whenever possible, I like to set up with my back to a large tree and with a few other large trees directly in front of or off to both sides of me. They can be great vision blockers and can give you the chance to draw quickly without being detected when the bull's eyes are obstructed by them.

Another thing to try to avoid is calling from too open an area. Elk realize something is up real quick when they hear calls and can't see an elk when they know they should. If you must call from an open area with little cover, try using a decoy. Even some

My 14-year-old son Seth and his cow elk taken at a waterhole.

of the partial decoys that show just an elk rump or head work great.

Another trick for luring in stubborn elk on pressured land is rattling. I like to use a set of 5 x 5 sheds in areas where I don't have to pack them in too far. Since hunters rarely rattle for elk, it can sometimes fool a bull into range. If you must call from an open area with little cover, try using a decoy.

Rob Evans of Wisconsin with his water hole bull and guides Jake Kraus and Cam Keeler.

## DECOYING ELK

Elk decoys can be a real asset when you're bowhunting. I like the Montana Decoys and usually use the full silhouette with the head up in the alert position. I have also had luck with their partial silhouette decoys that show a hard angling feeding cow or the one that just has an elk rump silhouette.

Decoying can work any time of the season. I have had luck early in the season when it is pre-rut and have lured both cows and bulls into range. Early in the season, late August to about September 10th, elk usually come in slow and usually circle downwind as they approach.

I have also had success using decoys as confidence builders if elk were hanging up in the trees before coming out in a meadow. One or two decoys set up in a mountain meadow or in an agriculture field can build confidence and signal that all is clear.

The peak of the rut is when I use a decoy the most. It seems a rutted-up bull just can't stand seeing a lone cow out there; they just have to come over to check her out. I have even used it to "run and bow." What I mean by that is if I have a bull moving his cows away from me either because he is slightly spooked or I bugled and he is just trying to avoid a fight, I will often go as quickly as I can toward him without spooking him. When I am as close as I can get I will set up the decoy and cow call. A bull will often spot the decoy and think one of his cows is missing and swing close to run her back into the herd. Get ready, the action can be fast and up close when using a decoy in this manner.

Decoys can really help dupe a bull into coming in close. In fact this past year, Luke Robb, one of my guides at Fulldraw Outfitters, called in a bull that actually came up and pushed the Montana Decoy

This big bull has been doing some serious fighting. He is just dropping his head to get a drink. Now, if he would just turn broadside . . .

with its nose. I can't say I have had them touch a decoy but I have had them within ten yards of it.

Late in the season, when elk are more cautious especially in hard hunted areas of public land, I tend to use the decoy to convince elk everything is just fine. I like to cow call softly but usually not until the elk have seen my decoy.

For me a decoy is something I always have with me, and the past few years I would say I use it fifty percent of the time. They don't always work but they do enough that I always have one with me, and sometimes it makes the difference between getting a shot or not.

## RATTLING

Another trick I have used for luring in stubborn elk on pressured land is rattling. Just like rattling for whitetails, rattling for elk can bring a bull running in. When rattling for elk, get aggressive. If you have ever seen two bulls fight or even two young bulls sparring, then you know they make a lot of noise. I try and emulate that. I like to use a 5 x 5 set of sheds. The disadvantage to rattling elk is that the sheds are more difficult to carry and I usually only use this method if I am hunting within a mile of my truck. When rattling I slam the sheds together as loud as possible. I also hit brush and trees, and stomp my boots. This method works best if you have two people and one keeps up the rattling while the other stands ready with the bow. After a good loud two to three minute rattling sequence, I like to wait five minutes and try again. If nothing comes in after three rattling sequences, I wait quietly for another ten minutes before moving. Although most elk will come in quickly, I have had them sneak in quietly as well. Most circle toward the downwind side, so set up for the shooter to watch that direction. I also like to have the shooter set up a little closer to me when rattling—usually only ten to fifteen yards away. By keeping the shooter close if a bull just runs straight in to the rattling without circling, he is still in range. Since most elk hunters rarely rattle for elk, you can have success with the method even in hard hunted areas. Just be careful: If another hunter is close by, he may come running in too. Some orange, even when bowhunting, can help avoid a dangerous situation.

## HUNTING WATER

Another method that can be used with great results is hunting water holes. Find water holes the elk are frequenting by looking for well-used trails with fresh tracks leading into the water. Elk will usually head to water first thing in the evening after being bedded up all day. If the weather is warm, I will sit all day over water. Often, you can catch elk slipping in early in the morning or during the heat of the day for a drink and to cool off. If your area doesn't have water holes or small ponds, you can often find certain spots on creeks or rivers that are favored watering areas.

We often set clients up on water holes in warm weather with great success. A few years ago, I was guiding a fellow from New York named Tommy Bender. Tommy is one of those guys who can tell jokes all day long and never repeat one. I wouldn't describe him as a super-patient guy, but he wanted an elk with his bow in a bad way. Problem was that the hunting was slow and the bulls weren't talking much. Since the weather was warm, I suggested he sit at a small water hole I knew about. I could tell the idea of sitting 12 hours didn't really appeal to him, but he said he would give it a try. When I walked in to pick him up that evening, a huge grin met my flashlight beam. He was fired up and talking fast. He explained that a group of elk came in to the small pond just as the sun was setting. He made a perfect shot on the bull and was as proud as he could be with his first archery bull.

Another client, Rob Evans, who is an outdoor writer and avid bowhunter, joined us for an elk hunt. Once again, the conditions were warm and his guide, Cam Keeler, set Rob up in a blind by another water hole.

Rob said: "After just an hour of sitting, I got so warm I stripped down to my skivvies. The heat had me nodding off, but I was jogged into consciousness by the sound of thundering hooves. I dove for my bow and came to full draw as the first cow jumped into the water. Nine more followed, but I didn't see a bull. Then I heard the sound of running hooves again, and a bull ran to the edge of the water shaking his rack. The shot was thirty-four yards, and my arrow blew through the bull's lungs. My first elk made a small circle and crashed dead into the water."

These are two perfect examples of what can happen if you find an active water hole and wait patiently. I am convinced that waterhole hunting is a great way to harvest an elk, especially in the arid western states. Our two oldest teenage boys have both taken elk over waterholes at under fifteen yards.

I spotted this bull in his bed. After an almost two-hour stalk, I was able to put an arrow into his chest.

## WALLOWS

When scouting or hunting, always look for wallows. They are usually found in swampy areas or sometimes in or near creeks or drainages. Rutting bulls will roll around in these wet depressions and cover themselves in mud and urine. This strong smell helps attract cows and warns other bulls of their presence. Some wallows are used only once, while others are commonly visited and used by more than just one bull.

Wallows are generally easy to spot. The ground and grass around them are usually gouged by the hooves and antlers of rut-crazed bulls. If you don't spot one of these small muddy depressions, you can often follow your nose to them. One of my favorite wallow stories happened while guiding Brian Brochu from New Hampshire. Brian owns an archery shop and is an experienced bowhunter. I had found an active wallow while guiding a client earlier in the season and suggested Brian give it shot. We tried calling a bull in early that morning with no success. So around 10:30 in the morning, we quietly sneaked into the wallow. Brian set up on the ground, and 30 minutes after I left, a beautiful 7 x 7 bull walked in to roll in his wallow. Brian drew back and made a textbook shot on his very first elk hunt.

When you find an active wallow, don't pass on the opportunity to hunt it.

## SETTING UP ON WALLOWS

Carefully choose the best location to conceal yourself. Take into consideration where you think the elk are coming from and wind direction. Tree stands, ground blinds, and pop-up blinds are all good choices to use for your ambush.

My favorite setup is the Double Bull pop-up blind because it's tough and can be set up quickly. Blinds are also a plus because they help contain your scent.

A bull will come—it's just a matter of time. Although some people like to call from a stand near water or a wallow, I prefer to remain silent. It is easy to spook a bull that is coming in silently when you rip off a few poorly timed calls.

I don't believe you can ever eliminate human scent, but you can try to reduce and mask it. Clean clothes, rubber boots, and a clean body will help even more. Remember that concealment and scent elimination are the keys when hunting water or wallows because the animals will be close, and more often than not there will be more than one set of eyes and many noses to deal with.

Client Bob Wood took this bull from a treestand over a waterhole.

## TREESTANDS

I think a lot of Eastern hunters who come out West for an elk hunt would have more success if they stuck with what they know. Almost every bowhunter I know cut his teeth hunting whitetails from a treestand.

The reason so many hunters take to the trees for whitetails is because it works! It also works great on elk. For hunters who aren't used to hunting from the ground, I think sticking to a hunting method they know would increase their odds. Some of the best elk our clients and my own family have taken have been from treestands. The odds of getting busted are greatly diminished and it also helps get your scent off the ground with a little help from good air currents. An interesting elk statistic is that at my outfitting business, for every ten elk we call into bow range for a client bowhunting the ground, with a guide calling, we harvest one. An even more interesting stat is that for every ten elk that walk by in range of a treestand, we kill seven. That is a big difference in success rates and that is exactly why I am a big fan of treestand hunting for elk. The kill rate being one out of ten on calling is because it is so easy to get busted on the ground. Most of my clients get nailed trying to draw their bows. Others get spotted just standing there and others get winded or heard. Oftentimes it is a combination of reasons. I feel the difference is that when you call elk, it is looking, listening and smelling for another elk that is supposed to be there. They are on high alert and every sense is alert. When walking by a treestand the elk are relatively relaxed and it is much easier to draw and shoot undetected. If your stand is placed well you also usually have a good broadside shot. When calling, shots are usually rushed and they are rarely perfect broadside shots. I am still a fan of calling, but I think your odds of

My client Wright Harrell shot this 316 bull from a tree stand. He was set up between the bull's feeding and bedding area.

success are increased in a tree, especially if you are not accustomed to elk hunting or hunting from the ground.

## OTHER SETUPS FOR ELK

For other great stand locations, try trails between feeding and bedding areas. Elk, like whitetails, have favorite bedding areas. They also take advantage of agricultural plantings such as clover or alfalfa, where available. Although hunting from the ground near these trails works well, a tree stand gives you a huge advantage with elk. Unlike whitetails, which have learned that danger often lurks in trees, elk are still tree stand illiterate. I usually try to set two stands for different wind directions on one trail. Bear in mind that wind direction in the mountains is tricky business. One general rule of thumb is that wind currents are usually going downhill early in the morning, then switching to blowing uphill by mid- to late morning.

When hunting active trails from tree stands, don't be disappointed if you don't see anything for a day or two at a time. Elk rotate and often use different trails to get to and from their feeding and bedding areas. Usually they will have multiple main routes they frequently use. Be patient. If you're on a well-used trail, the odds are you will get your opportunity. I also try to place my tree stands on the fringes of bedding and feeding areas. Too much scent at either one can ruin your hunt. Elk don't take much pressure before moving to a new area. Stand-hunting near one of these areas is often the most effective way for a bowhunter to harvest an elk. Unlike a calling situation, the elk aren't as wired, straining to spot any movement or hear a noise. A bowhunter can usually take his or her time and shoot at a relaxed elk as it passes by feeding, on a trail, or coming into or leaving its bedding area. It might lack a little of the excitement of calling in an animal, but it is a great way to put a backstrap on your plate.

## ESCAPE ROUTES

This method usually works best on public or private land where there is other hunting pressure. Like most animals, elk have areas they repeatedly use to escape hunting pressure. Finding these areas is sometimes as simple as looking at a topo map of your area and determining where you would go to leave all the people behind. Sometimes it's a matter of trial and error and hunting the same place over and over and noting the differences between where you see elk on opening day and where you find them five days later. Usually these are two totally different locations.

My friend Blye Chadwick and I once lucked into a great escape route on public land when a rifle hunter friend of Blye's told him where the elk usually go to elude pressure from hunters. We decided to try the area on opening day of bow season and watched as at least 60 elk, a few of which were great bulls, all went down the same steep trail heading to another, more remote area. I managed to take a cow out of the group at 5 yards, but more important, I learned an efficient method of setting up and letting the elk come to me. I've had luck hunting escape routes only during the first few days of the season. After that, most of the elk have already moved to their new areas.

When hunting a good escape route, I try to stay on stand all day. Usually these trails lead to more remote areas or areas where the thickest cover or timber can be found.

It's not the size of the elk, it's the size of the experience that matters. Here is my wife Michele with her bull that guide Jake Kraus called in to 10 yards. She used a 48-pound bow, and the bull dropped in sight 70 yards away.

## STILL-HUNTING

Still-hunting can be an extremely effective way to slip undetected into bow range of an elk. Fortunately for the still-hunter, elk are big animals and therefore usually make noise when going through the woods. Most elk guides I know prefer to stillhunt elk if they are with a client who is in reasonable shape who can move slowly and quietly through the woods or run if need be.

Oftentimes elk may be vocal, which makes them easy to locate, but they won't respond to calls. This happens a lot on heavily pressured private or public land. Being mobile often allows you an opportunity to slip up quietly on vocal feeding elk. I have also run into range of elk that hesitated before running, thinking I was another elk approaching. I would only try the run technique on elk that are moving away from you that you can't cut off or catch up to quietly.

Still-hunting requires patience. When I am still-hunting, it usually takes me approximately ten minutes to go 50 yards. That's about one minute for every 6 steps. Slow and steady with no sudden movements is the key. I also stop every few yards to slowly scan the area with my eyes for any movement. I have used this method to harvest both bulls and cows for myself and have also used this method with clients to slip into bow range.

Oftentimes, you will spot elk feeding or walking and can wait for them to come to you or move slowly to cut them off. Full camouflage is the key to utilizing this method effectively. That includes a head net or face paint on your head and hands as well.

One of my favorite times to use this method is when it is raining, snowing, or windy. It really tips the odds in your favor. The key is how slow you can go. I have found that I have never spooked an elk by going too slowly, but I have sent a few hauling by getting impatient and going too fast.

I have successfully still-hunted clients into range of a lot of elk. Unfortunately, since I am usually guiding during elk season, I don't have much time to hunt elk for myself. When I do have a little time, I like to still-hunt if the conditions are right. Since I also love elk meat, I am not picky and usually shoot the first elk I slip into range of. My friends have accused me of having a lucky horseshoe . . . I

Guide Jake Kraus and Steve Memmott from Hoyt with the bull Jake called in for him.

These two bulls are probably 30 years old.

will spare you the graphic details on where they think it's hidden! I just sometimes seem to be in the right spot at the right time.

My largest bull to date was shot while still-hunting. I was being followed by a cameraman because we were trying to capture an elk hunt on video for Easton Bowhunting on The Outdoor Channel. As luck would have it, we slipped up on three bulls feeding in a secluded meadow. It was early in the season, and the bulls were still hanging out together. There was a small, barely legal 4 x 4 and two 6 x 6 bulls in the meadow. The 4 x 4 was closest and I told the cameraman I would happily shoot him if I could crawl into range. While I was crawling closer, one of the bigger bulls swapped places with the little guy and I had no choice but to harvest the big bull. I am convinced that had I not been wearing a head net and crawling slowly, that bull would have lived another day. Remember that when still-hunting, the slower you go, the better off you are.

Another plus to still-hunting is that you can cover more country. I have often found great stand locations while slipping quietly through elk country. As the old adage goes: "There is more than one way to skin a cat." There are also lots of different theories and methods on how to hunt elk. The ones I have outlined here have all worked for me. However, as all elk hunters know, no method is foolproof when it comes to bowhunting elk.

## DRAWING UNDETECTED

Okay, you've done it. Your heart's pounding and you're not sure why, but you're also holding your breath. An elk is within bow range—one of the biggest and most impressive game animals in North America. You can already taste those 2-inch-thick steaks. Geez, wait till your buddies see this elk! All you have to do is draw your bow. The shot is a piece of cake. Wait, oh no, what happened? He's gone!

It's happened to me, and as an elk guide I have watched it happen to a lot of clients: getting busted trying to draw.

In my experience, this happens more often than not when you're on the ground in a calling situation. For example, the bull or cow is coming in with every sense alerted. It's straining its highly tuned ears for any sound. Its huge eyes are searching for any movement. As soon as you try to move or draw, wham, you're busted. It's the exception when you get to draw and shoot undetected.

A beautiful 7 x 7 bull my oldest son Jeb—seventeen years old—harvested at a waterhole.

In talking with other experienced elk guides, I have found that they all share similar experiences. I asked longtime friend and elk guide Jake Kraus about his strategy and success rate on calling. He likes to call elk from the first day of the season to the last. He is the best caller I have ever heard and prefers calling to other methods of hunting elk. Here is what Jake had to say:

"When a bull screams within earshot, it makes the hair on the back of your neck stand up! The ability to interact with a wild animal such as an elk is a blast. Not every animal will come flying in on a string. Calling elk is a sport that requires finesse and strategy. It is all about when to call, when to keep quiet, which call to use, and when to use it. If you do it right, you're on your way to a close encounter. Make a mistake and you won't see a thing.

"As with most big game species, female vocalizations are really what the male is listening for during the rut. My twelve years of guiding experience has taught me to use my bugle tube sparingly. I tend to use bugling most frequently as a locator call, and that's it. Using a cow call is by far my favorite and most successful tactic for rutting and nonrutting elk. I'll often emit soft calls every minute or so as I sneak through the woods with a client, probing new areas or experimenting in spots that I know hold elk. A cow call is the best call to use, particularly if you know the herd is sensitive to calling pressure. Once a bull is located, cow calls can either be used to coax the bull to your position or to instill confidence as you move in on him.

"This may sound easy on paper, but remember you are dealing with a wild animal whose senses are put to the test every day. Getting elk to respond to your calls is fairly easy. Getting them in bow range, standing still with a clear shooting lane, and getting a shot without being seen can be very difficult. To further complicate things, by calling you have told the elk that there is something out there. Now the animal is coming in looking for the source of the call. Simply put, the odds are not in your favor. Each year I personally guide anywhere from ten to fifteen archery elk hunters and spend every day of the archery season in the woods. In my experience, I would say that only one of every ten encounters ends with success. It's inevitable that you are going to get 'busted,' but if you keep putting yourself in those close encounters, it is going to happen eventually."

When Steve Memmott, the manufacturing manager for Hoyt bows, came out on an elk hunt with us, I sent him with guide Jake Kraus. He loves to call elk, and I knew Steve would be in good hands. The first morning of his hunt, Jake got a bull screaming with his seductive cow calls. The bull was so worked up he jumped two fences to get to them. The bull got nervous when he didn't see his hairy beauty as he closed within range, so he started to turn to leave. Jake turned him broadside with another cow call, and Steve smoked the bull at a little over 30 yards. His first guided elk hunt only lasted about fifteen minutes, but they were all action-filled.

So what can you do to get drawn undetected? Start with camouflage. It doesn't matter if you're on the ground calling, still-hunting, or in a tree stand. This is one of the most important things you can do to help your odds. It's simple. Put on a head net and gloves or face paint on your head and hands, and also wear a good, broken-up camouflage pattern. Don't wear anything noisy. Cotton, fleece, and wool are tough to beat for stealthy materials. I have watched helplessly as elk have bolted from clients when their noisy clothing gave them up.

Quiet down your bow. I once had a client draw his bow as a bull came walking past him heading toward me. I had just bugled again, and the bull was coming in pissed. My client did everything perfectly. He waited until the bull's head was behind a tree and drew. I was about 20 yards away from him on that cold quiet morning and I heard his aluminum arrow screech across his rest. The bull didn't hesitate. He dropped and whirled out of there without ever presenting a shot.

Use moleskin on rests and risers to quiet contact between arrow and rest and to avoid an accidental "clank" on the side of a wooden or metal bow riser. Also, practice quietly removing an arrow from your quiver. These are small things that can save a hunt from being unsuccessful.

Another common mistake is drawing while the elk is not yet at a good shot angle. When possible, wait to draw until the elk is in a position to shoot. I have sat and watched with sympathy as clients who drew too soon had to finally let the bow down, their arms shaking with fatigue when a bull or cow hesitated before coming close enough or stopped when they caught a glimpse of movement. It happens every year, usually more than once. Waiting to draw until the animal is at a good shot angle increases your odds of getting a shot if the animal locks up for some reason. Whenever possible, it is best to wait to draw until the elk's eyes are completely or at least partially obstructed by trees or brush.

The draw itself should be smooth and controlled. If you can't draw your bow slowly straight back to full draw, you need a lighter bow. Every year I see hunters who have to put their bow arm up in the air like they are going to shoot at a star. Then they yank the bow down while jerking back the string. I would rather see hunters shoot a 45-pound bow that they can draw smoothly rather than struggle with a 60-pound bow that is too heavy.

The final key to getting drawn undetected is controlling your nerves. It's easy to come unglued around elk. I have had clients do some crazy things when elk walk into bow range. It doesn't seem to matter if they saunter into a water hole or stroll past on a trail. There is just something about elk that can cause even an experienced hunter to come unstuck. Sometimes it's a situation where a big bull is bugling in your face and ripping up trees . . . well, if that doesn't rattle you then you probably need to quit hunting!

My favorite experience where a hunter "lost it" was in southern Colorado. I was guiding a client on a private ranch and we had a bull pretty worked up, but he wouldn't come down to us. So we slipped up the mountain into some aspens. I set the hunter up in front of me and I let off a bugle. I was just putting the tube down when we could hear this bull come running down the mountain bugling and hitting every tree he could on the way down to us. My client got up and started back down the mountain in a hurry. I jumped up from behind a tree as he came past me and said, "What are you doing? He's coming in." He said, "I know," and kept going. As far as I know, he hasn't been out West elk hunting since. Although this was an extreme example, nerves can cause you to freeze up, or act irrationally.

The best realistic practice I have seen is one of the "interactive" target systems. They can be found at some archery and/or gun retail shops. Watch elk shows on TV or rent elk DVDs. They will help you get used to how elk move and react. Shooting 3-D competitions, or just shooting with people watching you, will also help you shoot under pressure. One coach I knew who trained some Olympic shooters would throw firecrackers around to help his students practice under pressure. That may be a little extreme, but you get the idea. Improving your shooting will also increase your odds of bringing home some elk meat.

## FIELD-JUDGING ELK

Field-judging a typical rack is much easier than field-judging a nontypical rack. Since the large majority of trophies have typical racks, I have included tips and score sheets for scoring typical animals only. These should be used as a rough guide only. The best way for you to improve your own judging skills is to guess the score on friends' mounts, or anywhere you can observe different mounts, and see how close you are.

Any elk with a bow is a trophy, but for those looking for a record-book bull, here are some tips on what to look for. To make the Pope & Young record book, an American elk must score a minimum of 260 inches after deductions (see scoring sheet). Although there are many measurements that apply to the total score, field judging must usually be done in a few seconds. For a quick snapshot of whether a bull will make the book or not there are a few references that will help.

First check to see if the bull has six points on each side. The majority of bulls that make the record book minimums have six relatively symmetrical points on each side. Next look at the length of the main beam. Tine length can add a lot of score in a hurry, so look for a bull with good tine length. The third and fourth points are usually the longest so a quick check of these is a good indicator. If you can roughly total 55 inches by adding all the tines on one side you probably have a bull that will make the minimum if his main beams aren't real skinny. You are looking for a main beam that is 40 inches or more. Also look at width or inside spread between the main beams at the widest point. If it looks to be 30 inches or wider you probably have a contender.

I spoke to my good friend Lee Kline about rough judging in the field. Lee has been an Official Pope & Young scorer for over 35 years. Lee said the best way is to count the number of seconds between your breaths after you see the bull. If it is less than one second or you stop breathing completely . . . Shoot . . . it's a good one!

## FACTS ABOUT ELK (*Cervus canadensis*)

Elk are often referred to as wapiti, which comes from an Indian word meaning "white rump." Mature cows average 500 pounds, while bulls average 700. Elk calves are spotted at birth and gradually lose their spots after one to three months. Only the males have antlers, which they shed each year near the end of winter. New antlers are grown every year and can grow at a rate of an inch a day. The rut (breeding season) takes place from mid-September to mid-October. Their average lifespan is 15 years.

## EQUIPMENT SUGGESTIONS

Elk are large, big-boned, tough animals. I advise a minimum of 45 pounds bow weight with a minimum arrow weight of 450 grains. Razor-sharp broadheads are always a must. I also suggest staying away from flimsy, thin-bladed broadheads with less than a one-inch cutting diameter.

Elk meat is also hard to beat on the dinner table. I enjoy elk a lot of different ways, but here's one of my favorite recipes, which is great if you're having some friends over for dinner.

## ELK ROAST STUFFED WITH GARLIC AND PARSLEY

Serves 6-8

This recipe works best with a boned piece of elk rump.

4- to 5-pound elk rump roast
4 cloves of fresh garlic, chopped
2/3 cup chopped fresh Italian parsley
½ teaspoon salt
½ teaspoon pepper
½ cup olive oil
1 cup red cooking wine
2 cups beef stock
4 to 6 potatoes, peeled and quartered
3 to 4 peeled carrots, cut into 2-inch chunks
2 medium onions, quartered

In a bowl, combine the garlic, parsley, salt, and pepper. With a sharp, thin (½-inch) boning knife, make two or three knife-size holes the length of the roast. Push the parsley mixture into the holes the length of the roast, reserving one tablespoon of mixture. Place the roast in a roasting pan, and rub olive oil and leftover garlic and parsley mixture all over the roast. Let sit overnight in the refrigerator.

Preheat the oven to 375 degrees. Place the carrots, potatoes, and onions around the roast and coat with some of the garlic, parsley, salt, pepper, and olive oil. Add red wine and 1 cup of beef stock. Cover and roast using a meat thermometer to the desired doneness. I suggest medium rare (which is usually about 125 degrees F). Remove the roast and let sit for 30 minutes before carving. Remove the drippings and vegetables and process in a food processor. Add leftover beef stock until it is the proper thickness for gravy. Slice thin and serve.

# Mule Deer

Of the five huntable species of deer in North America, mule deer, in my opinion, are the most impressive. Besides tipping the scales as one of our largest deer, their antlers can be huge. When you combine these incredible physical characteristics with their keen sense of smell, incredible eyesight, super hearing, and an uncanny ability to avoid humans, it is no wonder that many bowhunters consider a mature mule deer buck to be one of the most difficult species to harvest with a bow.

Before skipping this mule deer chapter in search of easier prey, read on for tips on how to bring home the bacon and an impressive rack from one of these Western giants.

There are many reasons why a trophy mule deer is a difficult animal to hunt with a bow. One is that mule deer are found in huntable numbers in only 16 states. That is a far cry from the 43 states that have seasons for white-tailed deer.

I harvested this trophy buck using the spot-and-stalk method, and captured the hunt on video.

The upside is that—thanks to stricter management in several Western states—the opportunity for a bowhunter to harvest a mature mule deer is as good as ever. Especially for the bowhunter that is willing to go the extra mile . . . literally.

## SPOT-AND-STALK

In my opinion, the spot-and-stalk technique is one of the most efficient ways for a patient, slow-moving bowhunter to harvest a mule deer. This method is most successful when the stalk is made on a single animal that is bedded down. In my experience, the two best times of year to stalk bedded mule deer are early in the fall and during the rut. The advantage to early fall is that the heat during the day causes the deer to bed down early and get up late. When the weather is hot (70-plus degrees during the day) deer usually stay in their beds most of the day, getting up only occasionally to reposition, urinate, defecate, or drink.

The rut is another great time to catch a buck bedded. Oftentimes during the rut, an exhausted buck will bed down during the day for a few hours of badly needed R and R. In most Western states, the mule deer rut falls later than the whitetail rut. In southeastern Colorado, for example, the peak of

Guide Jake Kraus, Dwight Schuh and me with Dwight's trophy buck taken on a spot-and-stalk hunt.

I took this mule deer over a waterhole in New Mexico.

the rut falls in early December. In any case, a buck that is bedded for a long duration, whether due to heat or exhaustion, offers a great opportunity for a bowhunter. Before stalking, you must first spot the animal you're after. The two ways to find a bedded muley are to watch a deer bed down, or to spot a deer that is already bedded. When glassing for mulies in early fall, I rarely see a "mule deer" as such. It is usually a branch that doesn't look right, the flick of an ear, the twitch of a tail, a horizontal line that isn't a fallen tree, or a black spot that turns out to be a nose.

Using a spotting scope or binocular efficiently takes practice. Most guides I know, myself included, have a particular technique we prefer. We use a systematic grid to cover an area efficiently. Some prefer scanning an area from side to side or from top to bottom. I usually do a quick scan, first glassing anything that looks suspicious. Then I start to comb the area from side to side, bush by bush, tree by tree, and rock by rock. It takes patience and good optics, but once you master the art of glassing effectively you will feel naked without a good pair of binoculars and a spotting scope.

Although I have taken bucks and also guided bowhunters to bucks that I spotted once they were already in their beds, whenever possible I like to watch deer come into their beds in the morning. One reason is that it is easier to spot a deer that is moving. The other is that watching mulies approach their beds gives you a lot of additional information you can use to your advantage. For example, you get to see where the deer came from. Odds are it will be heading back to that area when it gets up in the evening. Another huge bonus is that you can see if the deer you're after is alone or if there are others that are bedding down in close proximity.

In early fall, bucks will oftentimes hang in small bachelor groups. Spotting two to seven bucks together is not uncommon. Unseen deer are one of the top reasons stalks don't pan out. I have closed to within bow range of several bucks that never knew danger was close by until one of their unseen travel partners blew the whole gig. The key to a stalk working out is to know what you're up against. Multiple animals increase the difficulty level exponentially. Oftentimes, due to wind direction, your target, other animals' locations, or the time of day it is best to pass on a stalk instead of blowing the deer out of the area or alerting them to your presence.

It is usually better to wait until things are right and make one good stalk than to try to force things to happen. Wind is always a huge factor in making a successful stalk. Wind currents can be tricky, especially in the mountains or rough country. A very general rule of thumb is that wind currents usually travel downhill in the morning and start turning and moving uphill as the temperature rises about mid-morning. In the afternoon they usually switch and start going downhill again.

Before stalking in on a bedded mule deer, study the terrain and choose the best path that will keep you hidden. Also try to choose a landmark near where your target is located. Once you move, everything looks different. I once made what should have been a perfect stalk on a bedded buck, but somewhere along my route I unfortunately mixed up the rock that the buck was bedded by. When I crept up in range of the wrong rock and the buck wasn't there, I assumed I had been spotted. I quietly headed back across the canyon to my pack and spotting scope and was upset to find that the buck was still bedded in the same spot. I had sneaked up to within approximately 40 yards of the buck while stalking up on the wrong location. I wish I could tell you that this has only happened to me once! A hunting companion can be extremely helpful in situations like this. By working out a series of hand signals, a hunter can often be signaled into range.

Another tip that helps when stalking any bedded animal is to use a rangefinder. I will use a rangefinder to measure the distance between the animal I am stalking and an obvious landmark in front of or behind the animal, depending on my planned direction of approach. The taller the object, the better you will be able to see it. Then, as you are stalking, you can keep track of how far you are from your intended target by checking the range to your landmark.

When stalking, quiet clothing and equipment are a must. Patience is also a good attribute to have. I have watched many bucks slip away unscathed when hunters tried to rush in too quickly.

A few years ago, my guides were impressed when Dwight Schuh (longtime editor of *Bowhunter* magazine) and his hunting buddy Larry Jones pulled off a textbook stalk at our camp. They were taping a mule deer show for *Bowhunter Magazine TV,* and Larry was acting as cameraman. On their third day of hunting, the wind really kicked up. They had seen some great bucks from our tree stand but couldn't close the deal. A few days prior, my guide Jake Kraus had glassed several different rut-weary bucks bedding down in a steep draw. The draw was thick with overgrown brush, making it a perfect bedding area. Jake went and grabbed Dwight and Larry from their tree stands and pointed the draw out to them and suggested they try sneaking down along the edge of the draw with hopes of catching a buck in his bed. After a few hours of slipping along and glassing for bucks, Dwight spotted what he thought might be an antler tine in the thick brush. Dwight and Larry took off their shoes and made a great barefoot stalk. On video, Dwight shot what ended up being a record-class buck at 15 yards in his bed.

Six things worked out to make that stalk successful: they had a bedded buck spotted; it was the middle of the day, so the buck was probably going to be down for a while; they had a constant wind in their favor; they took their time; they moved quietly; and Dwight made a great shot. If you're willing to work for it and adapt to the situation, the spot-and-stalk method can help you fill your next mule deer tag.

## HUNTING WATER

Oftentimes out West, the biggest mule deer bucks are found in the high desert badlands. Sometimes these areas look more like antelope country than prime mule deer habitat. There is a line in a song I think of when I am hunting or guiding in the high desert plains: "Where the deer and the antelope play." Rest assured that they were not singing about whitetails in that song. Water can be the key to having a successful mule deer hunt. Even if there is a lot of it, all animals have their favorite places to drink. Mule deer are no exception.

I have spent days trying to find out where mule deer I have seen are drinking. Sometimes it is an obvious location, such as an irrigation canal, creek, river, or pond. But sometimes it is like a treasure hunt trying to find the small seep in the rocks or the last puddle in the bottom of a dried-up old river or creekbed. Some of the biggest bucks I have ever seen were drinking out of windmill-driven, metal cattle tanks that are out on the plains, 30 miles from the nearest tree. I have also watched bucks come into alpine lakes 2,000 feet above timberline. The one constant is that all mule deer have to drink.

They also all have favorite places they return to repeatedly. I prefer to scout these areas from a distance whenever possible. A spotting scope is invaluable when glassing water holes from a distance. Although I prefer to hunt over water in hot weather, I have had luck hunting mule deer over water in single-digit weather as well. I have video taped and photographed mule deer breaking ice with their front hooves in favorite areas on ponds and rivers. The point I am making is that by glassing and scouting for fresh sign and tracks, you can open up more options in your mule deer playbook. River crossings are another water option. By walking rivers or creek edges, you can often find frequently used areas. Usually these are places where the water is shallow or crossing is easy.

If the weather is hot, after finding a frequently used watering location, I like to set up for an all-

Hunting over water can be a productive way to harvest your deer. Above, a group of does drink in early September and, below, a young buck breaks the ice to get a drink during a frozen December.

A blind setup near water or an active trail is another great mule deer tactic.

day sit. Wind direction, concealment, and being comfortable are my biggest concerns. In open country, just getting into position without blowing the deer out of the country can often be tricky. In these situations, I prefer to set up and leave in the dark. When possible, I take advantage of one of the quick pop-up blinds on the market, such as the Double Bull blind. They help contain scent and make it more comfortable to sit all day. Other times, I will try to take advantage of any natural cover, or build a small, low-profile brush blind. When possible, I also like to have multiple setups for different wind directions. A comfortable chair with a back is also helpful when you are going to be sitting all day. Mule deer drink at all times of the day, especially when the weather is hot.

Sometimes when hunting water, you just have to improvise. Last year, while hunting for mule deer in another location with cameraman Michael Leonard, I spotted a nice buck up and moving in the hot midafternoon sun. I guessed he was heading down toward some water and green grass that were located at the bottom of the ridge he was on. I quickly changed the game plan. I wanted to try to get in range of this buck. It was early in the year and there hadn't been a freeze yet, so all the leaves were still on the willows and other trees by the water. We used the thick cover to sneak around and get between the buck and the water. There was a good trail coming down the mountain, and I felt confident the buck would use it. I set up only about 20 yards from the trail, and Mike set up behind me with the camera. I figured the buck would be on us any minute, so we stayed frozen and quiet in our spots just off the trail.

Time dragged on as the mosquitoes busied themselves making us miserable. In my haste, I had left behind my pack with the repellent in it. When you're dumb you gotta be tough, so we both suffered in silence waiting for the buck to show up. After almost two hours, I figured that the buck had either seen us or winded us. I whispered to Mike that we might as well pack it in. As I stood up to leave, I spotted the buck. He had taken another route and was below us by the water. How long he had been there is hard to say. I drew back and shot quickly. I was rewarded with a resounding thump and a beautiful mule deer whose antlers were still wrapped in velvet.

If you're hunting out West and the weather is hot, consider sitting by a water hole all day. If the weather is mild or cold, try to hunt water in the mornings or evenings. It may help you fill your tag on your next bowhunt.

## GO HIGH FOR SUCCESS

Although not the most commonly used method for hunting mule deer, tree stands can be highly effective in certain situations. I often use them during the rut on the eastern plains, where mule deer like to funnel through the few strips of trees found along most waterways. I also like to use tree stands when I am hunting near agricultural plantings. Mule deer, like elk, will often travel long distances to feed on alfalfa, clover, wheat, and other crops.

Visibility is one big advantage to being in a tree stand. Plus, if the deer doesn't walk by within range, you can sometimes slip down when conditions are right and make a stalk. Unlike whitetails, which are becoming educated to tree stands, mule deer are still very susceptible to a well-placed stand. The two downsides to tree-stand hunting for mule deer is that mulies are more nomadic than most white-tails. This makes stand placement difficult, and that's why I use them only in certain situations. The other downside is that, out West, it can be a long walk from the truck to where you are hunting.

As I mentioned, we often use tree stands during the mule deer rut when guiding clients for trophy bucks. When guiding Lon Lauber a few years ago, the day before his hunt started, I showed him a tree stand I wanted him to hunt. Lon is an experienced bowhunter and a highly accomplished outdoor writer and photographer. When Lon saw the tree stand I had set up low in a cottonwood tree, he flat-out told me he didn't want to hunt there. It just didn't look good to him. I encouraged him to try it for one full day, and if he didn't like it, I would move him to another stand or we could try stalking a buck. Lon grudgingly agreed to try my spot out for one day. At about noon on the first day, Lon called me to come get him and the largest mule deer buck he had ever taken. Lon explained that it had been slow all morning when he spotted two bucks chasing a doe. The doe led them right by his stand, and Lon nailed a trophy mule deer. Two days later, I put another client, Tom Rothrock from Indiana, in the same stand. Tom also shot a big Pope & Young mule deer.

Before the week was over, three of my four clients harvested Pope & Young bucks, all out of tree stands. The largest that week was a 181-inch monster taken by Todd Wickens, also of Indiana. Todd had seen a few bucks hanging around near some thickets while chasing does, so we set up another stand. Todd's stand was only about 6 feet up, and he nailed the monster buck with a great shot at only 12 yards. The moral to these stories is that while they're not that popular, tree stands can be highly effective for your mule deer hunt if the situation looks right.

## SIT FOR A SHOT

Sitting and waiting can be a highly effective way for bowhunters to get into range. One of my largest mule deer with a bow was taken from the base of a cottonwood tree where I had been sitting patiently waiting for hours. I had seen the big buck on multiple occasions and knew he was a true giant. It was a mid-December morning during the peak of the rut when I spotted him following a doe into a dense weed patch. There was some alfalfa planted close by, and I hoped that the doe would lead him into the field that evening. I slipped into the field's edge and set up with cameraman Chris Butt to try to wait the deer out. The wind was in our favor, and all we could do was hope my guess would pan out.

Before the sun had even hit the horizon, the doe stood up and started leading the giant buck in my direction. The buck hesitated to rake over a small sapling. While he raked the tree, I could see that

this was truly a monster deer. When the buck finished, they slowly made their way toward the field's edge where we were crouched. I tried to maintain my composure as they walked into range.

Lon Lauber harvested this trophy buck with me from a tree stand set up in a large cottonwood tree.

Tom Rothrock of Indiana harvested this trophy mule deer with me from a tree stand. When it was only eight yards away, Tom dropped the string on this Pope & young buck.

I slowly drew my bow and shot. The arrow passed through the buck's lungs in the blink of an eye. I truly think he didn't have any idea what happened. He took a few staggering steps toward the doe and collapsed. The buck grossed just over 191 inches and netted 186 2/8 inches. This buck, and others I have guided clients on, proves that sitting on the ground, on a log, or on a small stool in high-traffic areas can really pay off, especially in open country where cover for stalking or trees large enough for a tree stand are slim to none.

Todd Wickens of Indiana harvested this huge buck with me. He grossed 181 and netted 175 5/8 inches. He was taken from a tree stand at 12 yards.

## RATTLING AND CALLING

Mule deer bucks, in my opinion, are not nearly as aggressive as whitetails. So some tactics that work great for whitetails do not get the same response from a mule deer. But that doesn't mean that they don't work at all.

I have guided clients who have successfully rattled up trophy mule deer. I have also had some success rattling in bucks myself. From what I have experienced, mule deer come in much more slowly than whitetails and often need a lot of coaxing. The bucks I have rattled in usually had to hear multiple rattling sequences before they would come to investigate. I have had a few young bucks run in, but the old guys seem to really take their time. I have had the best results when trying to call in an animal I have already spotted. The advantage to working an animal you can see is that you can gauge the buck's reaction. If he ignores you, keep making a ruckus.

Once a mule deer buck starts coming in, I stop rattling. I only start up again when the buck stops for longer than 30 seconds or changes direction. In the open country where mule deer are generally found, I really work the antlers hard, frequently crashing the antlers loudly together. This helps the sound carry farther. So always remember to include

My largest mule deer with a bow. He was taken using the sit-and-wait method. For the curious, this monster's gross score was 191, net 186 2/8.

a pair of rattling antlers in your bag of goodies, but be prepared to rattle more than you ever would for a whitetail.

It is also advantageous to try bleating or using a decoy where practical. Whether I am rattling or not, I always include a doe bleat in my pack. You don't need a special mule deer call. Just take along your whitetail doe bleat tube or one of the tip-over can bleats. I have caused rutting bucks to veer over to investigate when they think a hot doe may be just around the next tree or clump of sagebrush. Mule deer bucks do grunt very similarly to whitetails, and I have heard one snort and wheeze just like a whitetail as well. Although I have tried grunting, I have always had the best luck with a doe bleat or rattling antlers.

## DECOYING

Just as with decoying any other animal, I have had mixed results trying to decoy mule deer. The deer may react positively to the decoy and come in to investigate, they may totally ignore it, or they may run out of sight. In states where it is legal, I get a lot more reaction with a 3-D target covered with a tanned mule deer hide than any other type of decoy. No matter what type of decoy you use, it is always best to try it on overcast days. Bright sunny days make almost all decoys shine and look unnatural. I like to use a decoy during the pre-rut or rut. I also prefer using a doe over a buck decoy. I feel that more bucks will come in to a situation where they are looking for love rather than a fight.

The biggest drawback in decoying mule deer is the open country they live in. Setting one up without being spotted is the first obstacle. The second is that if mule deer have a long time to look at a motionless decoy, it seems to unnerve them. It is just not natural. For best results, try setting up where the buck won't see the decoy until it is already within 50 to 100 yards. Also, using a doe bleat in conjunction with a decoy will help improve your odds of luring a buck in.

Guide Cam Keeler sews a green mule deer hide over a 3-D target to make a realistic-looking decoy.

## SETTING UP ON A RUB LINE

Mule deer bucks don't make scrapes like whitetails. The biggest scent posts they make are their rubs. You can use this to your advantage if you find the right rub.

Trappers know that if there is only one small bush or tree in a field, every male coyote that passes by will go out of his way to pee on it. Mule deer bucks seem to have the same mentality when it comes to certain rub trees. I call some "one-time" trees, those that have been used only once when a buck was walking by, or it was made early in the season when a buck was working off his velvet. Other rub trees seem to be used as major scent posts, where passing bucks commonly stop to joust and, more important, to leave their scent. I have video taped and watched as multiple trophy bucks have come in over the course of a day to leave their scent on the same rub tree. This is even more applicable in open areas, where there are only so many small trees or bushes for them to leave their marks on. These scent post rubs are usually easy to identify because they get visited frequently, and so the tree or bush gets more ragged-looking every day. These are great spots to hunt, when you can find them. I usually try to set up downwind as far away as I am comfortable shooting, since a lot of bucks will circle or approach these trees from the downwind side.

An exhausted buck takes a break during the peak of the rut. Notice his swollen neck.

## FIELD-JUDGING MULE DEER

For a typical mule deer to make the Pope & Young minimum, it must score 145 inches after deductions (see score sheet in Appendix A). For rough judging, I look for a typical 4 x 4 or larger, not counting brow tines, since these are usually small if the rack has them at all. Next I look at width. An average mule deer has a 21- or 22-inch gap between ear tips if they were laid out horizontally.

If the buck's inside diameter is as wide as his ears, that's a good start—keep measuring. If I can make 30 inches out of the buck's G-2, G-3, and G-4, it is a good one that should make the minimum. Remember that deep, tall forks add score quickly onto a mule deer rack. This is a quick method I use to figure out if a buck is going to make the minimum score. But there are exceptions, and if the buck's main beam or circumference measurements are weak, he won't make it. If he is symmetrical, he should make it just fine. I look at brow tines as bonus inches that, if present, will just add to the score. The main thing to remember is that if you harvest any mule deer—buck or doe—with a bow, you already have a trophy. A big rack is just icing on the cake.

## FACTS ABOUT MULE DEER (*Odocoileus hemonius*)

Larger than whitetails, blacktails, or Coues deer, mule deer get their name from their large, mule-sized ears. Mature does average 100 to 200 pounds, while mature bucks average 200 to 300 pounds. Their average lifespan in the wild is 9 to 12 years. Only the bucks have antlers, which they shed every year near the end of the winter. Mule deer antlers usually branch to form two forks. Fawns are spotted at birth and lose their spots after one to three months. The rut falls in late November to early December. Mule deer are often noted for their peculiar, high-jumping gait: all four hooves leave and hit the ground at the same time.

## EQUIPMENT SUGGESTIONS

Mule deer are large, and shots are sometimes in the open. A flat-shooting, fast bow is advantageous. Because of their size, I suggest a minimum bow weight of 45 pounds, with an arrow weight of no less than 400 grains. As always, razor-sharp, sturdy broadheads are a must.

Mule deer meat is excellent. There are a lot of great ways to prepare it, including jerky, roasts, steaks, and stews. The recipe I have included below is just one of many great ways to enjoy your mule deer meat.

## PEPPER STEAK MULE DEER STIR FRY

Serves 6-8

You can use any piece of your mule deer for this recipe.

2½ pounds of mule deer meat, sliced across the grain into thin, 2-inch-long strips

6 small cloves of garlic, chopped

½ cup olive oil

2 green bell peppers, cut into strips

1 red bell pepper, cut into strips

8 green onion stalks, sliced into diagonal strips (use the entire onion, even the white and green leafy parts)

8 ounces sliced mushrooms

1 cup sherry

2 cups beef broth

½ cup soy sauce

3 tablespoons cornstarch

In a wok or large fry pan, heat half the olive oil on high heat and sauté half the chopped garlic for half a minute, then add the meat in batches and sauté quickly until medium rare (do not overcook). Remove from pan. Add the rest of the oil, and sauté the rest of the garlic for half a minute, then add the green and red pepper strips, sliced green onion, and sliced mushrooms. Cook for approximately two minutes on high heat. Add sherry and beef broth, and cook for two more minutes on high heat to bring to a boil. In a small bowl, combine soy sauce and cornstarch and stir until fully mixed. Add to boiling vegetable mixture, stirring constantly as it thickens. Add back the cooked meat, stir to cover with mixture and remove from heat. Serve with rice.

# Antelope

Imagine sitting in a small blind in the desert, drops of sweat beading on your forehead and the thick, sweet smell of sage hanging in the air. An isolated water hole lies 20 yards out in front of you, its precious contents steadily evaporating in the heat. Tracks made by delicate hooves pockmark the dirt around the water, and you know it is just a matter of time.

If you have never experienced the thrill of bowhunting for antelope or can't wait to go again, read on for tips on how to plan your archery antelope hunt.

Antelope are truly a Western success story. Hunted almost to extinction in the old days of market hunting, pronghorn antelope are now thriving thanks to progressive game management programs.

The great news for bowhunters is that they are now found in huntable numbers in 16 states. Of these, the four that generally stand out with the highest population numbers are Wyoming, Montana, Colorado, and South Dakota.

After deciding which state you want to hunt, call the game commission and ask for one of the state biologists or a game warden who works in the plains area. Both can be excellent sources of information and will often give you the locations of the best public land to hunt. I have found that game wardens will often give out the names of farmers and ranchers in their area who allow hunting on their property. Once you choose an area to hunt, get a detailed topo map of the region and mark all the natural or manmade water holes. Again, biologists, local wardens, and landowners can be very helpful with this step and save you the extra legwork.

A lone pronghorn buck silhouetted against a Western sky.

## WATER HOLE HUNTING

When choosing a location to set up a blind, my guides and I check all the water holes for fresh tracks and numbers of fresh tracks. Then we rank the different locations on a map according to our findings. We pay special attention to small water holes that are far from any other water sources. These remote places, when found, can be extremely productive. Ranking fresh tracks and numbers of tracks will help you discover which water holes the antelope prefer. Usually it will be where they can check for danger at a distance before coming in to drink.

Also pay attention to where around the water holes the majority of the tracks are. I have found that most water holes, whether they are manmade (dugout ponds or metal cattle tanks) or natural water sources such as creeks, rivers, or springs, have specific areas where the antelope prefer to drink. Sometimes the reason one area is favored is easy to identify, for example, the terrain or easy access to the water. At other times, it is subtler, for example, firmer ground or better visibility from the antelope's eye level. Whatever the reason, it is always advantageous to learn exactly where on the water source the majority of the antelope drink.

Whenever possible, I prefer to hunt areas with very limited options for water. I also prefer to hunt small dirt tanks or manmade cattle tanks. Smaller water sources are easier to hunt, and blind placement is not so critical. On the flip side, I have hunted large lakes, ponds, and canals where blind placement and scouting the well-used areas is absolutely critical. Make a mistake in these locations, and the closest look you get of an antelope may be through your binoculars.

Pronghorn hunting over water is a game of patience. Big bucks are just as likely to drink at noon as they are at dawn. So arrive early and be prepared to stay until sunset if you are up to the challenge of a day in the desert heat in hopes of arrowing a big buck coming in for a drink. Weather plays a huge role in whether your hunt over water will be successful or not.

If the weather is hot and dry, antelope hunting at a popular water hole is the way to go.

I harvested this antelope when he came to drink at the metal stock tank in the background.

My own patience and determination were put to the test a few years ago while hunting antelope over water. My cameraman, Mike Leonard, was sharing a blind with me. We were attempting to tape an antelope hunt over a water hole for an episode of Easton Bowhunting. I explained to Mike that during a normal dry year, odds were high that we would harvest a buck in a short period of time. Sitting in a small, hot space for almost 15 hours a day is not for the faint of heart. It can take a toll on the most determined hunter. Since I assumed the weather would remain hot and dry, I passed up a few pronghorn bucks during the first few days of the hunt.

A few rain showers made things a lot rougher than I had counted on. After nine straight 15-hour days without another opportunity, Mike and I were starting to show signs of the fatigue and mental torture that only an antelope blind can dish out. Whether it was the heat, dehydration, cramping back muscles, or lack of sleep, it mattered little. We were close to giving up. What started out as a trophy buck hunt quickly turned to a "whatever is legal and comes into range" hunt.

Nine days turned into fifteen, and the fifteenth day of our hunt started out as so many others had. We could see quite a few antelope around us in the distance, but nothing was coming in to drink at our small water hole. It seemed that the many small depressions and gullies in the area were still holding water. The day was slowly dragging on when we heard the sound of running hooves. I grabbed my recurve bow while Mike went for his camera. In an instant, our lonely water hole was teeming with antelope. I was starting to draw my bow on a big doe only about 10 yards away when a large buck walked into my shooting hole. He was about 20 yards away and broadside. My recurve bow jumped in my hand, and my carbon arrow flew right through the buck's chest. The buck bolted from the edge of the pond, dying less than 50 yards from the water's edge. We had spent 15 days—approximately 220 hours—trying to harvest an antelope. I don't advise that type of marathon, but you can bet I was proud of that buck. I'd hunted as hard for him as I had any animal I have ever taken.

Wet weather can shut down water hole hunting in a hurry. If bad weather rolls in, I usually just wait until it dries up before going back out. This is easy for me, since some of my best antelope spots are only a 30-minute drive from my house. For many hunters, however, waiting until it dries out is not an option. In those situations, we either try other strategies detailed later in this chapter, or wait at the water holes anyway, hoping that some antelope will still come in out of habit. I have learned that some antelope get used to drinking at certain locations and will sometimes revisit them even when other water is readily available.

Sometimes pronghorns visit these water holes because the best grass can often be found near areas that have water, even during the driest years. At other times, it seems they come in just out of habit.

In 2006, my wife Michele had been busy during the first few weeks of antelope season. She

I harvested this 77-inch Pope & young antelope after waiting 15 full days at a blind near a water hole.

Me and my wife Michele with her first Pope & young antelope, taken with her recurve bow. The trophy buck was shot when he came in to a cattle tank.

was helping our cook feed clients and was also busy helping the guides get hunters out to their blinds. When she finally had a few days to hunt herself, the weather was not cooperating. Another big rain left puddles all over the prairie. Every small depression and road ditch had water in it. I suggested she wait until things dried out, but she had only a few days free and decided to try it. On the fifth day, a large buck literally walked around other water holes to drink at the tank where she was hidden. At 18 yards, she harvested her first Pope & Young buck with a recurve.

Some hunts just seem to be easy and quick. Others can be very difficult and long. A few years ago, I was excited to have Michael Waddell from Realtree Road Trips join us for an archery antelope hunt. Michael had never harvested an antelope with a bow, and he was excited to try hunting them. The evening he arrived, I took Michael and his cameraman out to try a spot-and-stalk hunt. I found a large buck bedded in some tall sage, and Michael and his cameraman made a great stalk on him. They closed to about 70 yards before the buck spotted them and fled the scene.

Michael Waddell and his beautiful Pope & young buck, which he took while hunting with me in southeastern Colorado.

The weather was hot, so we advised Michael that we thought their best bet would be to wait it out at a water hole. On the evening of the third day, a nice buck meandered slowly toward the water hole where they were hidden. Michael said he was as excited as he has ever been with any animal. The buck came in to drink, and Michael made a textbook shot, dropping the animal within sight of the camera. That night he told me that sitting in that blind for 15 hours a day was one of the toughest hunts he had ever experienced. When it comes to sitting over water, it is usually the patient hunter who scores.

## TREESTAND

YES. It has been used, can be used, and I have done it. Although it is rare in the wide open country antelope generally inhabit, getting above an antelope in a treestand or a windmill is a deadly effective way to shoot them. The first antelope buck I ever harvested was taken from a platform I had in a windmill. Platform may be a bit of a stretch. What

Keep an eye out for snakes and scorpions when antelope hunting.

it really consisted of was two 2 x 10 boards cut to fit between the support struts of a windmill. Although I was only about ten feet off the ground, the buck never looked up when he came in to the water tank. The reason is that antelope just aren't used to danger from above. Besides the odd golden eagle now and then, antelope have always had to watch for danger from ground level. Because of this they are highly susceptible to bowhunters that get above them.

The past two years I have harvested my archery antelope from a cottonwood tree I built a small "platform" in. This one counts as a platform because I actually used a piece of half inch plywood in the tree. The tree is only twenty yards from a cattle tank and my seven-year old son and a cameraman were in the tree with me when I shot the last one. The disadvantage to a windmill stand or in rare cases a treestand for antelope is the sun beating down on you can get rough. I suggest a sombrero or an umbrella! If you have a prime water location with a windmill or a tree by it, try climbing up to fool these sharp-eyed prairie goats. It works.

A treestand I built over a waterhole to hunt antelope out of.

## HOT WEATHER GEAR

Since pronghorns are usually hunted in temperatures that can exceed 90 degrees, take lots of fluids with you. A small cooler filled with frozen water bottles will help quench your thirst and keep you hydrated as the day heats up. Stick with loose, comfortable, and quiet clothing. You want to blend in with the black background of the blind, so wear black or camouflaged shirts. Camouflage is also important on any body parts that may be close to the opening of the blind, such as your hands or your face. Keep in mind that dangers may include snakes and scorpions, although dehydration and lightning strikes usually pose the biggest risks you will encounter.

## SETTING UP ON WATER

Ask permission before building a blind on private land, and check hunting regulations before erecting a blind on public land. Most ranchers and farmers won't mind you setting up blinds, as long as you don't build a permanent structure. The three most common blinds used for pronghorn hunting are partial pit, self-constructed above-ground, and manufactured pop-up blinds. Don't worry if your blind seems to stick out like a sore thumb. Pronghorns adapt quickly and will often ignore obvious objects by water holes, provided they aren't overhunted.

My favorite is the Double Bull pop-up blind. It is lightweight and can be set up in minutes. This is an obvious advantage if you decide to move or set up multiple blinds quickly. Make sure that your blind is as dark as possible inside—any penetrating light makes you easy to spot. After your blind is completed, you should cattle-proof it. Often, where you find pronghorns you will also find livestock that utilize the water holes. A simple and effective way to protect your blind is to drive four T-posts into the ground off the corners of your blind and wrap two strands of barbed wire around them.

## SPOT-AND-STALK OR DECOYING

Although bowhunters take more antelope over water than by any other means, torrential rain can ruin such a hunt in a hurry. Fortunately, there are other options. The spot-and-stalk method is tough, since the open prairie that antelope generally inhabit usually offers little cover. This makes it difficult for any predator to sneak up on this sharp-eyed animal. Therefore, full camouflage is a must for trying a stalk. I also advise wearing knee and elbow pads for protection from hot, sun-baked ground and cactus. Broken terrain or pockets of tall sagebrush can be used to your advantage. I have managed to get within range of a few bucks by using deep draws or dry creek beds to slip up undetected.

But getting in range is only half the battle. Drawing your bow undetected is usually one of the most difficult things to do. Practice drawing horizontally and raising your bow slowly. You may have to drop some bow poundage, but it could make all the difference.

Torrential rains flooded the plains, leaving one of my antelope blinds under five feet of water. In rainy weather, try another tactic besides water hole hunting.

For hunters wanting to try another method, there is always decoying. It has been my experience that this is a win-or-lose proposition, with losing being the more common result. Don't misunderstand me: antelope can be and are decoyed in, and it is a rush when one comes charging at you attempting to run off the artificial intruder, often from as far as half a mile away. It is just that the window of opportunity for this method to work is small, and the best results are obtained at the peak of the rut in areas with a high buck-to-doe ratio. So include a decoy in your gear, but be prepared to leave it at camp if your timing is off. Another decoy that can work is an artificial cow or horse. I have had mixed results with these "confidence" decoys, but if you're looking for a project give it a shot.

## HUNTING OVER SCRAPES

Another option for speed goats (a common nickname for antelope) is hunting them over scrapes. As the rut approaches, antelope bucks make a series of scrapes. They also become territorial and constantly patrol their areas to keep out intruders. These scrapes can be seen dotting the prairie and are commonly found in dirt roads or dirt openings out on the prairie. They are similar in size to whitetail scrapes, and prong-horn bucks usually urinate and defecate in them. We have successfully guided clients by placing blinds within bow range of antelope scrapes. So if the sky opens up and your blind gets flooded, try setting up on an antelope scrape. It may save the day.

Here is a story written by one of our clients, Daryl Quidort, about his scrape hunt:

In the predawn darkness, the pickup lurched and bumped through yet another huge puddle, which was flooding the two-track. It had been raining steadily for days. In fact, this part of Colorado had received more than its average annual rainfall in just the past three weeks! There was standing water everywhere. One rancher told us there were full stock tanks on his land that hadn't held water in 20 years.

"And this is the year I picked to come hunt thirsty antelope at water holes," I thought glumly as we followed the muddy wheel ruts in the truck's dim headlights.

Antelope hunting at water holes is normally a hot, dry ordeal. Spending 14 or 15 hours a day, from daylight to dark, in a blind situated near a desert water hole takes fortitude and dedication.

Daryl Quidort and his Pope & young buck taken by waiting at an antelope scrape.

"It's like being in solitary confinement!" one hunter exclaimed. "You can't leave the blind in this open country without spooking all the game within miles. You just have to stay in there and tough it out." Of course, when antelope are coming to the water and the hunter is having action, the day doesn't seem so long.

Sunrise was a bright pink promise on the horizon as we pulled up to the water hole where I planned to spend the day hunting antelope. The headlights revealed the portable blind sitting in 6 inches of water.

"Look at that," Fred's guide muttered in his slow, Western drawl. "All this rain raised the pond." After a short discussion, we decided I should try another spot near some scrapes.

With my binoculars, I studied the scrapes about 25 yards out in front of my blind. I had seen antelope scrapes several times in the past, but never understood them or considered hunting them. Usually found out on open, treeless areas, they look and smell quite a bit like whitetail deer scrapes. I was sure they played an important part in the antelope rut, but I didn't know how. Hopefully an antelope buck would give me a demonstration before the day was over.

About 1:00 p.m., I saw two white specks appear out on the plains. By 1:10 p.m., two antelope bucks were standing 100 yards away, nervously looking my way. They were small bucks, their horns barely as long as their 6-inch ears. After trotting back and forth a couple of times, they both raced away at high speed. I wondered if they were afraid of the blind or afraid a larger buck might catch them near the scrapes.

A few hours later, I looked up from my magazine to see a nice antelope buck heading my way. I quickly grabbed my bow and quietly moved the stool out of the way. On my knees, with an arrow nocked and my recurve in ready position, I froze as the buck smoothly picked up speed. He was running right at me. Then, swerving gracefully to his right, the antelope sped past the blind and out of my sight. Without moving a muscle, I waited patiently for him to return—but he didn't. "That's it?" I wondered.

After a time, I slowly opened a small peek hole on a side window. The buck was standing about 60 yards away, shaking his ears and kicking a hind foot under his belly, trying to rid himself of the mosquitoes. Suddenly, he ran toward the scrapes again. This time he sped right past the blind, only about 20 yards away, but going at full speed. Fifty yards out, he stopped, whirled around, and came back. Trotting up to the scrapes, he stopped and sniffed the ground. Then he started pawing the earth with a forefoot.

It would have been interesting just to watch him, to see what his scraping ritual consisted of . . . but I came here to hunt antelope. I shot. The buck's reflexes were to drop and spin away at the sound of the shot. But my arrow got there first.

I know I was fortunate (darn lucky, according to my friends) to get a nice Pope & Young antelope during a rainy-season water hole hunt. Hopefully, if I make this type of bowhunt again, I won't run into such wet circumstances. But if I do, at least now I know what to do when it rains. I'll hunt antelope scrapes.

## FENCE CROSSINGS

Fence crossings are the last little gem in my antelope hunting repertoire. These crossings have also saved a few foul-weather hunts for me. In most Western states, antelope will go under a fence—as opposed to over it—90 percent of the time, even when being pursued by predators. This has always seemed odd to me, since antelope are excellent jumpers and can clear a fence easily. I have heard it theorized that this is because fences in the West are a relatively new addition to the landscape and are still few and far between in many states. Most antelope may simply have not adapted to jumping over any obstacles they may encounter. Sadly enough, in the future, as fences become more frequently encountered obstacles, antelope will probably become accustomed to jumping over them.

Since they prefer going under rather than over fences, there are always certain places along fence lines where you will find well-worn trails. Antelope often walk quite a ways to use these favored crossing spots where, due to the terrain or a broken strand in the fence, it is easier to go under. If you find a good one, don't pass up an opportunity to harvest

A trophy antelope gives me the stare-down.

your buck there. If the farmer or rancher doesn't mind, you can make your own fence crossing. Just use a few twists of bailing wire or twine to raise the bottom wire by tying it to the one above it. It may not be good to hunt until the following year, but you can bet that the antelope will find and use it.

When approaching a fence crossing, antelope usually stop for a few seconds before going under. That is a perfect opportunity for a bowhunter to take a standing broadside shot. Blinds should be set up near the fence, as far away as you can comfortably shoot. For example, if you're comfortable shooting out to 25 yards, set up the blind 25 yards from the crossing.

Years ago, I shot a beautiful young buck at a fence crossing. I found an active fence crossing and set up a blind about 20 yards from the trail. The weather had been pretty bad, so the water hole hunting was slow. I climbed into the blind early the next morning. After only a couple of hours, a group of young bucks came walking across the pasture heading toward my ambush point. When the lead buck reached the fence, he stopped to look things over. My arrow passed through his chest, and a short sprint later he fell within sight of my blind.

My largest antelope, harvested in Colorado, netted an impressive 79 inches.

I feel that fence crossings are not nearly as productive as water holes in hot, dry weather, but they do provide another enjoyable way to hunt the prairie speedsters.

When hunting antelope, remember that they have incredible eyesight that they rely on to a fault. Although they have great hearing and olfactory senses, in most cases they just don't seem to believe that danger is there unless they can see it. Their eyes are their main means of defense. If you can fool their eyes, you are on your way to harvesting what is, in my opinion, the most desirable Western big game animal.

## FIELD-JUDGING ANTELOPE

For bowhunters interested in trophy antelope, it is important to be able to accurately field-judge a buck. To make the Pope & Young record book, antelope must have a minimum score of 67 inches. Antelope can be difficult to judge, because they have few measurements and no width measurement. This means the few measurements that they do get have a large bearing on your final score. Instead of trying to break down the intricacies of measuring, I will detail how to quickly judge whether you are looking at a trophy animal.

On average, an antelope's ear is 6 inches from tip to base. If the antelope has horns that are 13 inches or longer, you may have a contender. So the first thing I do is quickly look to see if the antelope's horn is a little longer than twice the length of his ears. Don't forget that an antelope's main horn is often curved at the tip, so this will add to the length. I have seen some with 4 inches of curl-over, so keep that in mind.

Next, look at the prong, or cutter, as it is often called. Again, use the ear for a reference. If there is more than half an ear showing, or 3 inches, keep

These three antelope does are enjoying a drink during the heat of the day.

looking. Circumference is the next thing to look at. Antelope horns are oblong rather than round, making them wide at the sides and thin in the front and back, so to rough-judge mass you want to try to get a side view if possible. Instead of looking at and trying to guess all four circumference measurements, I look at the widest or thickest part of the horn, which is between the base and the prong. If it looks like it is 2 1/2 inches wide, it probably has close to a 6- to 7-inch base. Unless it gets really skinny really quickly at the top, it should make the minimum.

Other things I look for are prongs that start above the ears, or really heavy mass that carries the length of the horn. Of course this is a quick, rough way to estimate if what you're looking at will make the record book. I think if you shoot any antelope with a bow, you already have a trophy. Large horns are just icing on the cake.

## FACTS ABOUT ANTELOPE (*Antilocapra americana*)

Antelope, or pronghorns as they are commonly called due to their two-pronged horns, are as unique as the open prairies they call home. Evolution helped these animals adapt to the prairies they live in by developing many different distinguishing characteristics. One of the most notable is their headgear, which they shed every year in November or December. Although called a horn, it really isn't a true horn, since true horns—like those of bighorn sheep or Rocky Mountain goats—grow continually throughout the animal's lifetime. Antelope bucks have a bone core that is covered by a black outer sheath made of keratin. Keratin is a tough, insoluble protein substance that is the chief constituent of hair, nails, horns, and hooves. Oddly enough, about 40 percent of mature doe antelope also grow horns, but unlike the buck horns, which average 13 to 15 inches in height, does' horns rarely grow more than 4 inches long. When antelope shed their horns in November or December, a new sheath, wrapped in hair, is already beginning to grow. Unlike antlers, which grow from the base, antelope horns grow their sheaths both up and down, starting from the tip of the core.

Although they appear huge on the open prairies they inhabit, antelope bucks average only 120 pounds, while the smaller does average 105 pounds. They are equipped with lightning speed, which helps them outdistance their predators, since hiding in the open isn't really an option. The fastest land animals in North America, antelope can achieve speeds of up to 60 miles per hour for short bursts, and they can maintain speeds of 30 to 40 miles per hour for long distances over uneven terrain.

Pronghorns also come equipped with spongy, hollow hair that provides layering warmth in the subzero temperatures and blistering winds they face in the winter. In the summertime, temperatures on the Western plains and deserts often exceed 100 degrees. When the weather turns warm, antelope shed their spongy coats, which helps to cool them down. Additionally, they can cause their remaining hairs to stand upright, which helps air circulate close to the skin, keeping them from overheating.

Their protruding, side-mounted eyes allow them close to a 270-degree field of view, which makes slipping up on one undetected very, very difficult.

Antelope fawns are born with muted brown and white coats that become more pronounced and obvious as they mature.

As you can see, antelope are uniquely suited for only one type of habitat. If we ever lose the large tracts of open prairies and grasslands, I fear we will lose or endanger one of the most impressive animals that shares the West with us.

Even if you never plan to bowhunt for antelope, next time you're out West, take a drive out to see one. A large herd running in unison across a seemingly endless prairie is truly a sight to behold.

## EQUIPMENT SUGGESTIONS

Antelope are small animals, so arrow penetration is rarely an issue. I advise a minimum of 40 pounds of bow weight, with 9 grains of arrow weight per pound of your bow. For example, a 40-pound bow would require a 360-grain arrow. And as always, a razor-sharp broadhead is a must. Choose a quiet bow that is as short as possible, whether you are shooting a traditional bow or a compound. Shorter bows are easier to maneuver inside a blind.

## GRILLED ANTELOPE BACKSTRAP

Allow 6–8 ounces per serving. This marinade works great with elk and deer also.

1 cup soy sauce

½ cup olive oil

½ cup A1 Steak Sauce

4 large cloves of garlic, chopped

½ cup chopped onion

1 tablespoon Jane's Krazy Mixed-up Salt or similar seasoned salt with garlic

2 tablespoons Grill Mates Montreal Steak Seasoning

In a non-metallic container, combine all the ingredients. Add whole antelope backstraps. Make sure the marinade covers the meat. Marinate backstraps overnight. Discard leftover marinade.

Grill to desired doneness. Slice across the grain into ½-inch-thick slices. Game should never be overcooked, as it has less fat than beef. Medium rare to medium is our preference.

# Part 5

# *Regional*

# Introduction

The whitetail deer inhabits every state in the U.S. except Alaska and Hawaii. Its range also extends well into Canada, and south into Mexico and beyond. Its ability to thrive in areas as extreme as the arctic cold conditions of northern Saskatchewan to the Florida Keys and Mexico attests to its adaptability.

Most whitetail hunters understandably hunt in their home state. Maybe they belong to a hunting club, or own property that they hunt, or perhaps they have been given permission to hunt private lands. Time constraints, work schedules and family obligations also factor in to how far we may stray from home to hunt.

In the East, hunters encounter a variety of terrain, from the snow belt to the farm belt to mountains to mixed hardwoods and print forests. In the more open West, whitetail hunters not only encounter mountainous terrain, but also wide open spaces, prairies, and vast agricultural areas.

Simply, the whitetail is capable of living almost anywhere, and as a hunter, you owe it to yourself to try different areas, difference terrains, different states and provinces. When you do, you'll realize that some of the tactics you used back home aren't worth much in this new spot; but some are because, no matter where it lives, a whitetail is a whitetail.

In this section, authors J. Wayne Fears and Larry Weishuhn talk about the value of scouting East and West. We also included a chapter by Peter J. Fiduccia on mast and browse, and that can apply to whitetail anywhere.

—Jay Cassell

# East

I remember as a teenager following an old master deer hunter around hoping to pick up his deer hunting tricks. As we would walk across the hills, he would read deer signs like a scholar reads a book. Every track, trail, rub, and dropping gave him a hint as to how to properly plan his hunt. After several of these scouting trips the old hunter would get a twinkle in his eye and tell me that he knew where he was going to kill his buck. Sure enough, each year he scored and usually in the area we scouted.

## PRESEASON SCOUTING

Scouting a month or more before deer season opens is good for learning the terrain; however, your more serious scouting should take place as near the season as possible. Eastern deer habits have a way of changing just as hunting season opens. They begin switching from late summer foods to fall foods. Colder days mean that bedding areas will change. The rut is coming on and the bucks are becoming restless. The later you scout, the more accurate and up-to-date your finds will be and you stand better odds of being at the right place at the right time on opening morning.

As you scout your deer hunting area looking for signs, it is advisable to carry a U.S.G.S. topo map or aerial photo with you. Using a topo map or aerial photo to record your findings on gives you an excellent "memory bank" to use for planning hunts. By marking trails, bedding areas, feeding areas, and scrapes on the map you will see a system appear before your eyes. This map will tell you where to locate your stand, or where best to stalk. Topo maps and aerial photos can be downloaded by going to website: www. terraserver. microsoft.com.

There have been many magazine articles and books written on what to look for when scouting so we won't go into the details of basic signs in this book. However, we will give you some pointers so the signs will not mislead you.

***Deer Droppings:*** One of the signs that mislead many beginning hunters are deer droppings. To the novice, deer droppings mean "deer are here!" This may or may not be true. Let's look at a few facts. Deer droppings come in two basic shapes—round and oblong. At first glance they look like rabbit droppings; however, rabbit droppings are smaller and are much more fibrous than those of the deer. Fresh deer droppings are shiny black and are moist for the first day. Older droppings have a dry and dull appearance. Fresh deer droppings are a sign that deer are using the area. However, don't get excited and think that when you find several piles of deer droppings that the area contains a lot of deer. Wildlife researchers have found that a deer may deposit droppings up to 12 times a day.

***Deer Tracks:*** The deer sign that has more myth associated with it than any other of the signs is the track. Many hunters think that all tracks are fresh; others think that deer tracks always lead to a deer; while others claim to distinguish a buck track from a doe track. In many cases, none of these are true. Deer tracks generally tell you one thing—deer have been there. Do not be misled by numbers of tracks as one deer can make a lot of tracks. Do not waste your time trying to distinguish buck tracks from doe tracks. Contrary to the opinion of many hunters, there is usually little difference. In the far north, some hunters can distinguish a buck track in the snow after studying the trail for a distance, but this is the exception. Large tracks, or tracks showing the dew claws, may be made just as much by a running doe or a heavy doe as by a buck. While tracks are an important sign, they are limited as to what they tell you.

***Feeding Areas:*** Deer food in the East may not be considered a deer sign by many hunters; however, I think it should be treated as a sign when scouting. When scouting for deer signs watch for preferred deer food such as white oak acorns, Japanese honeysuckle, greenbrier (smilax), or a field of soybeans, wheat, or oats. These foods attract deer. When you find a deer food area look for fresh tracks and fresh droppings. If you find these signs together, you may have found a place for a stand. Mark the food area on your topo map for future reference. Also, look for deer trails leading into the food area and mark these trails on your map. These trails make good stand sites.

***Bedding Areas:*** Deer beds are a difficult sign to find and to read when found. Wildlife researchers have found that bed locations vary considerably with individual deer and are distributed widely throughout the home range of the individual deer. In addition, bedding sites vary by habitat differences. On a cold, sunny day deer like to bed down in the warm sun in a dry place such as in a broom sedge field. During periods of bad weather, such as cold, rainy, windy days, they like to bed in dense evergreens, protected from the elements. Once hunting pressure is on, you will find beds in the edge of thick brush where the deer can see danger coming. One jump will usually assure them a safe exit. Preferred bedding sites can vary widely from deer found in Michigan cedar swamps to deer found in Virginia mountains to deer found in flat southern pine forest. The one thing that is common with all sites is that bucks like the thickest sites they can find.

***Deer Trails:*** A sight that excites most deer hunters is a well-worn trail or runway, as some hunters prefer to call them. Eastern deer trails are best described as paths of least resistance followed by deer, bucks going around obstructions and, if possible, does going under them whenever encountered. Some are as long as a mile; others are as short as a few yards across a stream or saddle between two hills. Some are used for only a month or so and others are known to exist for years. Generally speaking, the most common deer trail found is one that begins as several faint trails, leading from bedding areas, which come together to form a more prominent trail that leads to a favored feeding area. As long as the food in the feeding area is available, the trail will be active. When the food supply is exhausted, the trail may be abandoned.

There are many animals that make trails, so the deer hunter will do well to scout a newfound trail for fresh deer droppings and deer tracks. One fall, I was hunting with a youngster in West Virginia on his first deer hunt. The second morning, he came rushing into camp exclaiming that he had found a heavily used deer trail leading from a wooded ridge down to a small lake. I got my bow and followed him back to the trail. Indeed, it was being used, but not by deer. My young friend had found a trail made by beavers dragging saplings and small logs into the lake. Confirm your trail. Make sure that you are spending your days watching deer trails and not beaver, cow, or fox trails.

The hunter who finds a good deer trail should mark the trail on his topo map. More than likely it will join up a bedding area or feeding area you have already marked. If not, it may lead to such areas.

***Rubs and Scrapes:*** Perhaps the best signs to the buck hunter are fresh rubs and scrapes. One buck may make many rubs. I like to find rubs when scouting because it means I am in a buck's territory. I especially like to find large trees, eight inches or larger in diameter, rubbed as this is usually done by larger bucks.

Scrapes are a better sign to find as bucks often return to scrapes to freshen up the scent he has left there as a part of the mating cycle. Active scrapes can be a good place to take a stand.

Through preseason scouting can be some of the most valuable time you can spend in preparation for the hunt. Learning to read signs and keeping a detail record of your findings will generally spell the difference between success and failure during the coming deer season.

As I learned from the old hunter, preseason scouting is not a deep, dark secret. It is simply knowing what to look for and the ability to put the signs together to plan a successful hunt. By using a topo map as an aid, you too can put the clues together to solve the mystery of where old mossy horns can be found.

## ARMCHAIR SCOUTING

This was the worst whitetail hunt I had been on in a long time. A friend had given me permission to hunt his 1200-acre farm that was located in the southern part of Mississippi. Because I had been on a number of back-to-back hunts, I did not have the opportunity to drive down to the farm and scout the property.

On the opening morning of deer season, I had driven three hours to be on the farm at daybreak. I easily found the front gate of the farm. As dawn was breaking in the east, I left my truck and started walking toward the north. The landowner had told me there was a creek up that way with a lot of

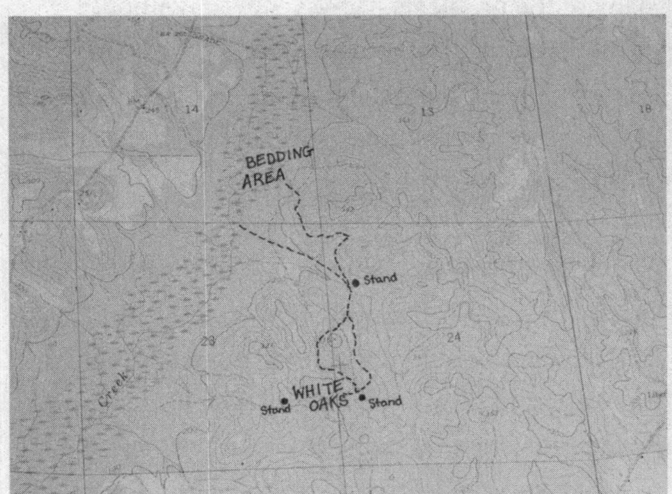


By carefully plotting out scouting clues on a good topographical map, a hunter can find the pattern that helps tag that elusive trophy buck. To obtain a detailed U.S.G.S. topographical map of your hunhting area, access: http://stoegerbooks.mapcard.com

acorn-bearing oaks growing along the bank where the deer fed every morning.

In the dim light, I made my way north. As I walked, the vegetation became thicker, and soon I was barely able to move through the thick tangle of cane and greenbrier. It was obvious I was in a thick creek bottom swamp without an oak in sight.

It was long after sunup when I reached the creek, which more properly should have been called a river. My clothing was torn from the walk through the briers, and I was soaked with perspiration. I found a few small oaks but no acorn-bearing trees. To make matters worse, the swamp was so thick I could not see 20 yards in any direction. I decided to sit down and catch my breath before walking back through the jungle.

As I sat cursing my bad luck, I heard barking dogs running in my direction. Soon the swamp was filled with the howling of a large number of hounds. Obviously, someone was conducting a deer drive nearby. My so-called stalk hunt was ruined.

What went wrong with this hunt? If I had had time to scout the property, I could have avoided many of the problems. However, even without on-site scouting, my situation could have been improved had I taken the time to exercise a strategy for learning new land that many experienced hunters call "armchair scouting."

Even if you scout out a tract of land in person, you would be wise to talk to those who visit or travel near the property regularly. In the East the deer population density is greater than in the West, and deer territories are much smaller. By interviewing those who live or travel near the property you can learn much about the patterns of the deer.

If, in today's fast-paced world, hunters learn of new hunting grounds but do not have the time for preseason scouting, they can put armchair scouting to work. It can be a fun-filled adventure in itself, like solving a mystery. Here is how to go about it.

Obtain a U.S. Geological Survey topographical map or aerial photo of the area. Once you have a topo map and/or an aerial photo of your hunting property, you are ready to get more current information. You can do this by telephone.

Begin by calling the landowner or his agent, such as a farm manager, managing forester, or land manager. Since this person is on the land regularly, he can possess a wealth of information about the property. Ask questions such as: Are the boundary lines marked? You do not want to get onto another

No matter if you're a bowhunter or rifle hunter, droppings, combined with other sign, can provide some idea as to what the deer are doing.

person's property. Does anyone else have hunting rights on the property? It could be that you are sharing the area with many more hunters. How do the deer hunters in the area hunt? Remember the experience I had with the deer-hunting dogs. What land management practices are planned for the next few months? You do not want to plan a hunt along a ridge that is going to be clear-cut the week before the season opens. It would, however, be great to learn that a field is planted in alfalfa that should be about four inches high on opening weekend. Where has the owner/ manager been seeing most the bucks? I leaned the locations of some of the best bucks I have taken simply by asking someone who worked on the property.

Be sure to have your topo map and/or aerial photograph in front of you as you interview this person. It will make understanding his directions much easier. If he talks about a deer trail leading from his apple orchard across a creek and onto a ridge running parallel to the railroad, you can see it all in front of you and even mark it for future reference.

Next, call the county Agricultural Extension Service agent in the county where the property is located. He is familiar with the entire county and can give you valuable information on the local deer population, what crops the deer are feeding on, hunting techniques used by hunters in the area, local butcher and freezer information, and often current deer information on the property itself. Once a county agent saved me a lot of time by telling me there was a new landfill adjacent to the property where I planned to hunt, and the landfill had attracted a large number of feral dogs that had chased the deer off the property.

One of the most valuable calls you can make is to the state Department of Natural Resources wildlife biologist who works in the area. He can give you approximate rutting dates, deer population estimates, foods the deer favor, local problems you might encounter such as heavy poaching, problems with conflicting hunting interests, land management problems such as a recent clear-cut, late fall prescribed forest burning, etc. Many times the biologist can suggest hunting techniques and strategies that are unique to that area. The same thing is true if you place a call to the local conservation officer. He knows the local area well and is up-to-date on the deer situation in your area of interest.

One word of caution: These people are busy and cannot sit around listening to all your deer hunting stories. When you call any of these officials, be well organized and have your questions written down. Be courteous, and do not waste his time. I have usually found these people willing to share helpful information with the caller who is well organized and gets to the points quickly.

Be creative in your research. One year when I was in college and did not have the time or financial resources to physically scout a small farm, I tried to call the landowner and officials listed above. Due to meetings, sick leave, etc., I could not find anyone to talk with. Out of desperation, I called the rural mail carrier who drove daily on roads that passed on two sides of the farm. It turned out he was a hunter who told me about a nine-pointer he saw on a regular basis. As he described the area over the phone, I marked the road crossing on my topo map. That Thanksgiving I found the trails the buck used at the road crossing just as the mail carrier described, and I took the buck the second morning.

This is not in any way to imply you should not spend time on a new hunting property scouting for sign and getting to know the lay of the land. However,

Ben Lee (left), Wayne Fears (center), and Fred Bear (right) examine a rub during the early part of the bow season.

in those cases where an actual visit to the property is impossible, do not give up scouting. Simply purchase a topo map and aerial photo, study them, and put in some time on the phone putting the clues together that will solve the mystery of where you can find a buck. More often than not, the information you compile will put you on the property knowing it almost as well as if you scouted it in person.

## POSTSEASON SCOUTING CAN BE VERY REVEALING

Many years ago when I first started guiding hunters on spring gobbler hunts, I made it a point to start my scouting as soon as the deer season was over. The month of February and the first half of March found me in the woods looking for turkey sign and watching turkeys. The very first year I started this early intensive turkey-scouting program, I noticed something that caught me by surprise. While looking for turkey sign, I was finding an enormous amount of fresh deer sign. I was finding the hidden areas where big bucks spend the winter after the pressure of hunting season had pushed them into deep hiding.

I found 2-month-old rubs and scrapes in areas that had been totally overlooked by hunters. In March, I found shed antlers and saw signs of heavy feeding on smilax and honeysuckle. Early that spring I jumped bucks that still had their racks, in areas so difficult to get to that I hadn't bothered to hunt there that fall.

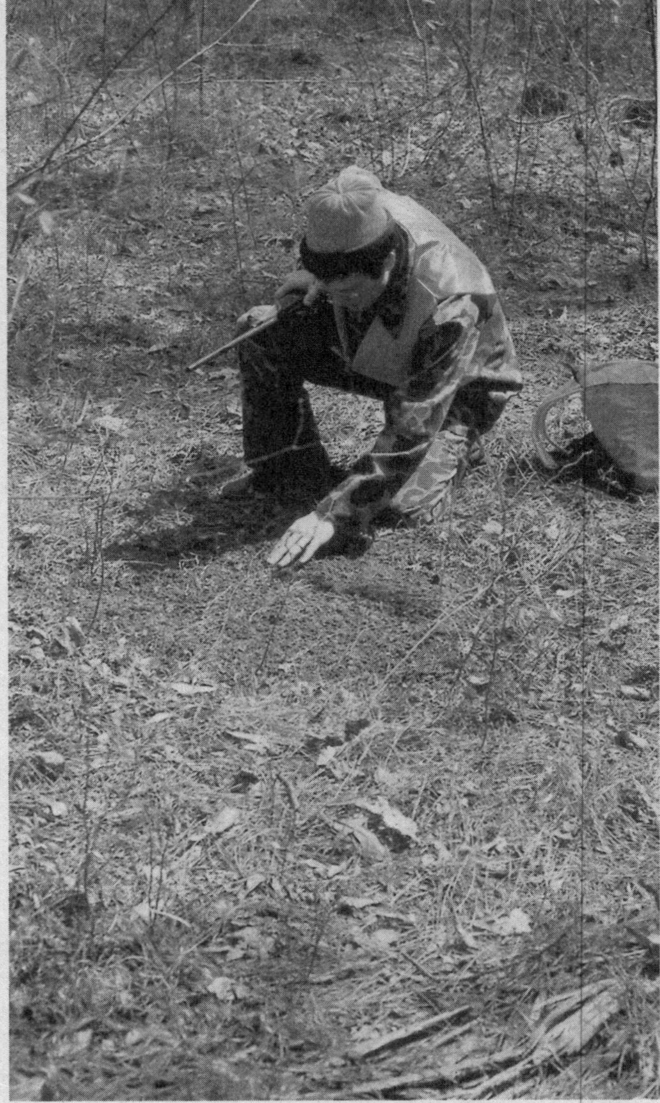

A rifle hunter examines an active scrape. This can be a good place to look for a stand location.

This discovery of buck wintering grounds sparked an idea that was to be a great hunting aid the next season. Throughout the entire turkey-scouting period and turkey season, I kept a set of notes on my findings and sightings. By April, I had located several pockets of land that obviously had been retreats where bucks spent the winter. It was my plan to go into these areas late in the next deer season and do some intensive hunting.

The next fall I waited until midway through the deer season and started hunting my newfound areas. The results were three nice bucks. When I was asked by my friends how I had found these deer, my answer was "postseason scouting." You can bet I got some strange looks.

In order to understand why postseason scouting is valuable, one must first understand what is happening. In many states, such as Alabama and South Carolina, the deer seasons are long, and even in states or areas where the deer season is shorter, a lot of hunting pressure is brought to bear on the bucks. Big bucks react to this pressure by reducing their daylight activity until most become nocturnal. As the pressure continues and these night-traveling bucks are jumped from their hiding areas by roaming hunters, they begin to seek areas where human pressure is less.

At the same time that hunting pressure is causing mature bucks to move to new locations within their territory, a natural occurrence is adding pressure. Late in the year, the fall food crop gets scarcer, especially during years of poor mast production. The fall crop of acorns and other nuts, soft mast, corn, soybeans, and a lot of the green browse play out late in the deer season. The green understory vegetation which has provided a lot of cover is disappearing.

These two factors combined cause the bucks to change their diets and to seek more cover. This usually means a move to areas that are thick and contain food such as smilax, honeysuckle, mushrooms, and low-growing twigs. In many cases, this is a move into moist, low areas with rich soil, such as beaver swamps, creek bottoms, and along rivers. In some cases, this can be a move to thick

People who frequent your hunting territory, such as rural mail carriers, can give you important information about buck movements and location.

fencerows or wood lots adjacent to fields planted in winter pasture crops such as wheat, oats, or rye. The bucks lay up in the thick areas during the day and feed in the adjacent fields at night.

I have seen bucks move into an area of young, thickly planted pines during this period. They move out of the pines at night but hold up tight in them during the day. In addition, I have seen them move into a thick pocket of vegetation in the middle of a clear-cut.

I do not want to sound like bucks in the East go great distances to seek new hideouts during the winter, for this is not necessarily so. They simply seek out the overlooked corners and pockets of habitat that is in or near their territory where cover is abundant and food is nearby. They stay in these wintering areas until the hunting pressure is gone and spring brings out an abundance of food throughout their territory. Then they move out to roam their home range.

Postseason scouting should begin as soon as the deer season ends. The first step is to try to find the overlooked habitat that the big bucks may have retreated to. More often than not, it will be an area that is extremely thick with understory vegetation. This may be a creek bottom that is thick with cane, vines, etc. It could be an area in an old stand of planted pines where the blackberry vines are so thick that it has kept hunters out. An island thick with cover in a river or swamp can often hold a buck or two.

In many situations, the cover doesn't have to be so thick. More open woods near buildings or in areas that are not hunted can be good wintering grounds. Many years ago when I worked on the Swannoochee Wildlife Management Area in south Georgia one of the largest bucks on the area spent the hunting season around the check station where there was no hunting. When I owned Stagshead Hunting Lodge in Alabama, we had a huge buck that spent the hunting season around the shooting range. There was a lot of shooting but no hunting pressure.

At another hunting lodge I once owned, a road makes a loop around several thousand acres of wet flatwoods. It is a mile from one side of the loop to the other. One year while postseason scouting, I found a pocket of relatively open woods in the center, which was the winter home for these big bucks. Hunters, during deer season, had only hunted the first one-quarter mile of woods off the loop road. The center of the loop was wet and muddy. No one bothered to go into the center. Since there was plenty of browse in that area, the bucks were living "the good life" without being bothered by man.

To find areas such as this, try to put yourself in the place of the bucks. Where would you go to be safe and yet be close to food? Answer that question and do your postseason scouting there.

Signs to look for during this period are similar to signs you would look for during a preseason scouting trip with an exception or two. Since the bucks—and often retreating does as well—are confined to a smaller area with thick vegetation, they will create more visible trails than they normally would. Often by following these trails, I have found the main wintering ground. While in most cases the rut will be over, be observant for rubs and scrapes.

One sign I look hard for in the spring are dropped antlers. It is a sure sign that you are in a buck's home. I mark it on a topo map for future reference. Usually I find only one antler since the buck rarely sheds both at the same time or in the same place.

If you hunt several areas, you would be wise to mark the postseason sign you find on a topo map. After several seasons of scouting, these records will become valuable when you are planning a mid- to late season hunt.

Once you have found a lot of postseason sign and may have possibly seen bucks during your scouting trips, your work is complete until the next deer season. When the season opens you can hunt the areas you regularly hunt. Save the wintering grounds for the last part of the season when the hunting pressure in on. The hunter who knows where the big bucks spend the winter knows the best places to hunt during the latter part of the next season.

# West

If you had seen my two daughters and me running through the woods, converging toward a spot on the ground some 30 yards away, you might have thought we had just spotted a five-dollar gold piece and were running to be the first to claim it. Theresa, my older daughter, was in the lead for a short while. I was gaining and just when victory was in sight, Beth, the younger daughter, ran between us and claimed the prize.

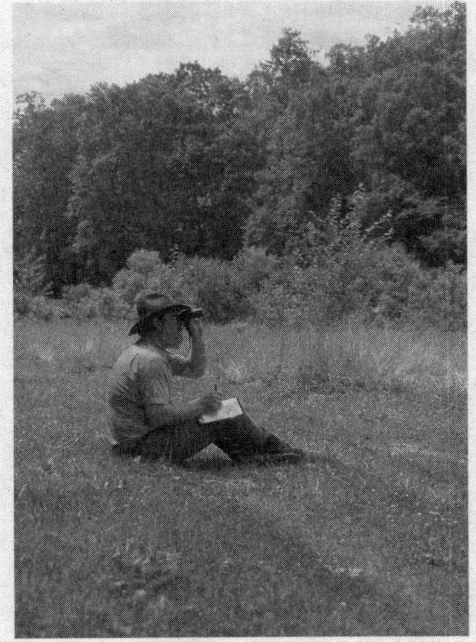

What was it? Why a matched set of shed antlers from a four-year-old typical twelve-pointer that we had seen a few times before deer season had opened three months earlier. That had been the last time he had been seen. Throughout the six-week-long Texas whitetail season neither we, nor any of the other hunters on the property, had seen that buck. I had been concerned that he might have died, but here was proof that he had indeed survived the season. Chances appeared excellent he would produce even bigger antlers the coming fall. Before the afternoon's shed hunt was over we had collected no less than 20 recently cast antlers which provided considerable information about the sizes, ages, and whereabouts of particular bucks.

The early spring Saturday afternoon antler hunt had become a weekend ritual. Both daughters, then ages 12 and 10, loved spending time on the ranches I managed, and thoroughly enjoyed shed hunting. It was sort of like searching for Easter eggs, only more exciting. To them and me it was great fun spending time together engaged in friendly competition to see which of us could find more cast antlers, while gathering considerable data about the local deer herd and particular bucks.

## SCOUTING DATA

Quite a few years ago I started recording information about the different ranches I managed and hunted in spiral and loose-leaf notebooks. Generally, my first step was to procure a map of the property, either a topographical map from the U.S. Geological Survey, or an aerial photo from the Soil Conservation Service—now called the U.S. Natural Resource Conservation Service. If a no quality map was available I hand-drew a map of the property with all the pertinent landmarks. Occasionally, even if there was an aerial map, I still hand-drew an enlarged section of certain parts of the property.

On the map I recorded as much deer sign information as possible, with special notes within the body of the notebook about what was seen, what was found, where and when.

Information that was marked on the map included concentrations of particular types of vegetation, water sources, trails, location of shed antlers, rubs, scrapes, unused deer stands, suspected bedding areas, current feeding areas, and deer sightings.

Not only did the notebooks and maps serve as storage for scouting reports, they also recorded patterns to help in interpreting the information collected.

## WHEN TO SCOUT

I do most of my on-site scouting in western deer habitat beginning a couple of weeks after the season closes. By then the deer have started to settle down and have returned to their natural patterns.

During the late winter, if there is not a tremendous amount of snow on the ground, you can still see where bucks had established scrapes. Even with snow on the ground you can still determine where scrapes were by looking for overhanging branches that were "nuzzled" by bucks. Rubs are visible at this time and show recent use. Trails are obvious, and there is a good chance you might catch glimpses of bucks. Depending upon where you scout, you might also start finding some cast antlers.

Postseason scouting gives you a pretty good idea of what is left after the season closes, does not overly upset the deer, and will give you a pretty good idea where to start hunting when next fall's season rolls around.

A detailed topographical map is a valuable tool in planning your hunt.

With mature bucks, if you put too much pressure on them, especially right before the season opens you can cause them to completely change their normal habits, including going totally nocturnal. That is why I try to do much of my scouting postseason. During late summer and early fall most of my scouting is done from "afar" with binoculars, or simply spot-checking to be certain food sources haven't changed, water holes haven't dried up and there haven't been any other major changes to the habitat that would cause deer to change their fall habits.

Whitetails throughout most of the West are not migratory, like they can be in the northern portions of the East such as in northern Michigan and possibly elsewhere.

## SHED ANTLERS

Throughout the western whitetail deer range, much can be learned from the cast or shed antlers. A lot of critters, such as rats, mice, squirrels, and rabbits chew on cast deer antlers. The sign of their chewing can be seen on the antlers and can be distinguished from other animals chewing on them, by looking at the rather small and chisel-like teeth marks. However, if you find fairly recently cast antlers and they show considerable sign of having been chewed on by a larger animal, such as a cow or a deer, it tells you the area you are in is probably deficient in such minerals as calcium, phosphorous, or trace minerals. If you find such chewed upon sheds, and it is legal to do so in that area, consider setting up some mineral licks. Will they do great wonders for the deer herd and antlers? Simply let me say, it certainly won't hurt!

Finding freshly cast antlers tells you the deer that dropped them made it through the hunting season. It also tells you where that deer was at a certain period of time. Mark where you find sheds on your map.

Interestingly in Mexico, South Texas, eastern Colorado, and Wyoming, as well as in Alberta we have often found sheds and the following season killed the deer which dropped them within less than a quarter of a mile of where the sheds were found.

In southern Texas I have on several occasions found sheds and then the following fall killed the buck that cast them within less than 100 yards of where they were found. No, those deer weren't behind high fences!

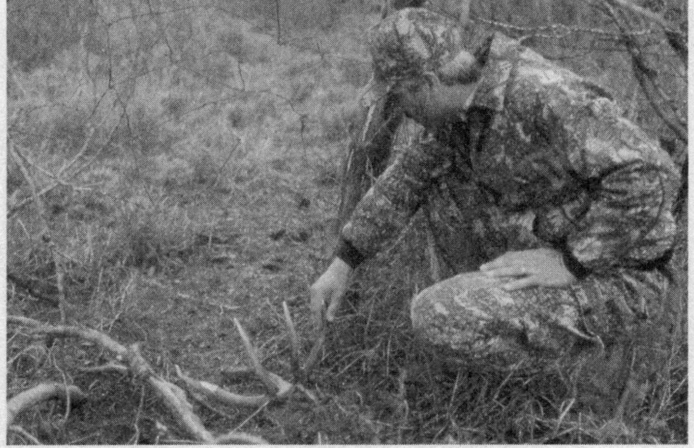

Finding freshly cast antlers tells you that the buck that dropped them made it through the hunting season.

The size of the antler will give you a pretty good clue as to how big and how old the buck that dropped them is. Small antlers generally come from young deer, bigger antlers from "coming" bucks, and big antlers from mature deer. However, you can also be a bit more specific as to the age class of the buck that dropped them.

Yearling deer generally produce no more than little 4 by 4 racks, most are smaller. Thus they are easy to determine. Two- and three-year-olds and most four-year-olds produce bigger racks and may have several points per side, decent main beam lengths, good mass and tine length. To confirm such antlers were cast by that age class of bucks, grasp the antler and turn it upside down, so that you are looking at where the antler was attached to the skull. Compare the rough pedicel attachment area below the burr to the diameter and circumference of the main beam just above the burr. In most two- and three-year-olds and some four-year-olds the pedicel attachment area and the diameter and circumference of the main beam are nearly the same size.

If the antler is big, again turn it upside down and compare the size of the attachment area to the beam just above the burr. If the buck is in his prime, say from four to seven years of age his shed antler will have a sizable pedicel attachment area and the diameter and circumference of the beam just above the burr will be even bigger.

When the buck starts going downhill because of age (and some bucks as long as they continue on good, daily nutrition may continue producing big antlers until they are 10 or 12 years old or older) he will have a large pedicel attachment area, but the beam just above the burr will not be as large.

What's interesting especially where bucks have a tendency to live to maturity and beyond is to find sheds from the same buck in serial years. Then you can really notice the above and also see how he progresses from year to year. Shed hunting can be great fun and highly rewarding!

## TRACKS

During a seminar an attendee asked me if there was a sure way to determine the difference between a buck track and that of a big-footed doe. My reply? "There certainly is! You can always tell if they are still standing in those tracks!" For a second that brought numerous puzzled looks. I then continued that in my opinion sometimes you might be able to tell the difference due to size, bucks being larger, but after years of following around big-footed deer I have yet to determine a sure way by simply looking at tracks. Chances are if you spot a track and there is a smaller track following or walking off to the side, it's a doe.

While rifle hunting, Larry Weishuhn examines deer tracks along a trail that leads to an active feeding area.

Several of the biggest bucks I've taken from northern Canada to below the Rio Grande had relatively small feet, especially when compared to some of the tracks I watched does leave.

A single deer can make a huge number of tracks and three can make it look like 30 have been in the area. What I try to determine from looking at tracks is where did they come from and where are they going and if it's worthwhile for me to try to set up an ambush spot near a trail.

Where I do pay particular attention to tracks is when I find a trail where deer have been entering a food plot or feeding area. Once I find such a trail I back-track the trail to try to find where two or more trails converge. That's where I'll look for tracks that look like they were made by a deer that stood around and waited for other deer to come by on their way to the food source. Find such a set of tracks and it's a pretty good bet it was made by a mature buck. Rather than expose himself to danger in the open field, he'll hang back where the trails come together to check every doe that comes past. He may also feed in the food plot, but chances are he'll do it only after dark.

Near where I find such tracks as mentioned is where I'll set up an ambush point, perhaps a tree stand or quite possibly simply sit in a tree where I can see the area. Tracks as a whole indicate the presence of deer, especially if they appear relatively fresh.

## DROPPINGS

Several years ago I was involved in a research project that tried to determine the relative worth of pellet count deer surveys, a system that was once used to get a handle on the local deer population where other census methods were useless. Back then biologists determined the average whitetail dropped 12 pellet groups per day. Thus by counting the number of pellet groups within a given area and dividing by 12 they hoped to determine the local deer density.

My part of the program was to determine the validity of this assumption and also determine where deer generally defecated relative to bedding and feeding areas. The trend among the deer we watched, which were in about a 10-acre enclosure, tended to drop pellets most often shortly after they left their bedding areas. They would stand up after having been bedded for a while, stretch and then drop a pellet group. What this told me was that if one found numerous pellet groups, both fresh and old, in an area, it was likely close to the deer's bedding area. Finding such pellet groupings has often helped me establish where deer bed, if indeed bedding and feeding areas are specially separated.

Rubs on larger trees can be an indication of big bucks. Larger bucks tend to prefer bigger trees.

Interestingly in a fair bit of western deer range, bedding areas and feeding areas can be one and the same, rather than the distinctive separation of the two found in eastern habitats. Quite frankly I do not pay much attention to deer droppings when scouting, other than trying to determine the location of bedding areas.

## FEEDING AREAS

Deer foods and feeding areas vary greatly between western whitetail habitats. In the Southwest, most of the low-growing brush and the weeds or forbs that grow between them are at worst at least decent deer foods. A bit farther north and west things really don't change all that much other than these areas may have various varieties of oaks which produce acorns. A bit even farther north and west forbs, some woody browse, limited mast producing trees, and agricultural crops provide the primary food source. That situation extends well into Canada. In the extreme northwestern whitetail range, within the Provincial Forest of Canada limited mast producing trees and woody browses and vines as well as spring and summer forbs provide food for white-tails.

The common food sources that run throughout most of the western whitetail's habitat are agricultural crops such as corn, milo, soybeans, wheat, barley, alfalfa, and other similar row and hay crops. These food sources are often bordered by creek bottoms and drainages, CRP grasslands, plum thickets, cattle pastures, or thickets of various sorts.

If you want to learn some of the primary food sources of deer in the area you hunt, contact your state's local wildlife biologist or game warden. He can generally give you a good idea as to what deer eat and when.

During the hunting season when someone kills a deer, I will often ask to be the one to gut it. There is method in my madness. I always try to evaluate shot placement and terminal bullet performance, for one thing. But the other thing I do is once the rumen has been removed, wearing rubber gloves as one should when gutting deer, I'll make a slit in the rumen to see what the deer has been eating. Usually there are bits and pieces of vegetation large enough to determine what they have been eating. And while I may not be able to identify the plant by name, I can get a pretty good idea of what the deer just ate. It may be from something I've seen while hunting. If the rumen contains an abundance of a particular plant, I'll know that I want to hunt in the area where such plants are in abundance. Scouting never ends!

## SCRAPES

Have you ever watched a buck make or refresh a scrape? It is most interesting the ritual a buck goes through. Generally he approaches it from downwind, where he can scent if another buck has been there. Quite often bucks do to scrapes what male pet dogs do to car tires and corners of their territory. They stake claim to it, but then every other male dog that comes by will attempt to "X-out" the previous "visitor." By approaching downwind the buck can smell if the scrape has been visited by another deer since he was last there.

If indeed it has been visited by another buck, or he feels the urge to refresh the scrape, he approaches the pawed-out area under an overhanging branch and generally "nuzzles" or chews a bit on the overhanging limbs, possibly rubs his forehead on the overhanging branch or carefully tries to rub the area right in front of his eye on the branch. He may also "horn" the overhanging branch a bit. Then standing in the pawed-out area below the branch he will generally paw the ground three to five times with each the left and right foot, seldom more and seldom less. The ground freshly pawed, he will step forward, draw his two hind legs kind of under him and then urinate on his legs so the urine trickles down his legs, over his hocks and tarsal glands. He may also while the urine is trickling down, rub his hocks together. When finished the buck walks away. Sometimes I have also seen bucks defecate in the scrape.

The purpose of the scrape may be in part to mark territory, although whitetails as a group are in the truest meaning of the word not territorial. One or many bucks may use the same scrape.

Scrapes generally are most actively maintained during the tail end of the pre-rut, just before the peak of the breeding season.

Some bucks return many times to the same scrape and others may only visit a particular scrape only one time. Incidentally it's been my experience that whenever you start seeing active scrapes from that point on bucks start responding to rattling horns.

Certain scrapes tend to be actively used only a short period of time while others are actively used fall after fall. The longest I have personally seen a scrape be used year after year is 15 years and counting. Every year I have had access to the property the scrape has been actively used.

In scouting these are the type of scrapes I look for and pay particular attention to. Usually very active scrapes are obvious even during the late winter when I do most of my personal scouting.

Research tells us that most of the scraping activity is done by bucks after dark, as high as 75 percent of all scraping activity takes place under the cover of darkness.

## RUBS

Rubs are the surest sign of bucks in an area, outside of finding shed antlers and actually sighting bucks.

I personally look for big rubs when scouting because big bucks tend (although not always) to make big rubs. I also look for rubs on trees which show signs of having been rubbed in the past. It's been my experience that some bucks frequently return to rub on the same trees year after year. Finding a good, recent rub which has been previously rubbed in years past catches my interest, especially if it is on a sizable tree and is made a bit higher from the ground than most.

Rubs, as scrapes, are generally made along travel routes. Thus pay attention to which side of the tree they were made. Then start looking for more rubs on that same side of the tree beyond where you found the first one. These "rub lines" will clue you as to the travel route the buck takes and also the direction he usually travels. Research tells us that many whitetail bucks tend to travel in somewhat of an egg-shaped pattern. Mark the rubs you find on your map of the property to try to determine travel routes of bucks.

By looking at the surface of the rub you can get a pretty good idea about the kind of antler the buck that made it has. If the rub's surface is relatively smooth, chances are good the surface of the buck's antlers, especially close to the base and around the brow tines, is also very smooth. If the surface of the rub exhibits deep gouges, chances are pretty good the buck that made it has antlers that have "kicker" points near the base and around the brow tines.

People who work in a hunting area, such as this cowboy, can give valuable information about a buck's location.

If there is underbrush on either side of the tree beyond where the rub is being made, look for scarring on the limbs and branches. Finding where antler tine tips scarred them may give you a clue as to how long the buck's tines are and the width of his spread.

When scouting pay attention to rubs, whether you are scouting postseason or making a quick reconnoiter through your hunting area in the fall just to be sure things have not changed.

## DISTANT SCOUTING

Not all of us are so fortunate that we live close to where we hunt. This is especially true if we are considering going on an out-of-state whitetail hunt. If you can't spend some time in the area there are ways to scout it just the same, but by long distance.

If possible when hunting a new or distant area I try to procure a topographical map of the area. Then once I get such a map I start calling people in the area, perhaps rural mail carriers or school bus drivers who frequently drive through the reasonably immediate area I hope to hunt. I'll do my best to learn about the terrain to determine if indeed it is as I have pictured it in my mind based on the topo maps. If possible also contact someone who has previously hunted in the area, but don't always put too much faith in what you hear from fellow hunters. If you called me and asked about a particularly favorite hunting area, I'm probably not going to tell you everything I know.

If you're going to hunt in relatively open country, look for drainages on your map and low saddles on ridges that provide access from one creek bottom to another. Remember also that the biggest bucks in otherwise open prairie country are often found in small coulees and rills quite some distance from denser creek bottom country.

Try as best as you can to learn about the lay of the land and where bucks have been sighted in the past. Ranch hands and those who tend western crops are good sources if you can find them.

Quite often a western whitetail hunt may be a guided or outfitted hunt. If you have done your homework and have selected a good outfitter or guide, listen to him concerning how he suggests that you hunt.

If you have enough faith in him to pay him good money in order to hunt with him on his property, have enough faith in him or her to hunt and do as they suggest. It's their home turf and if they are "worth their salt" and have your trust in booking with them, do as they suggest and in most every instance you're going to have a successful hunt.

# Mast and Browse Plants

## Some Common Mast And Browse Plants Preferred By White-Tailed Deer

**Definitions: Mast**

Fruits or nuts used as a food by wildlife. Hard mast includes acorns, beechnuts, pecans and hickory nuts. Soft mast includes fruits such as apples, blueberries, raspberries and persimmons.

**Browse**

The current annual growth of vegetation consumed by deer. This includes the stems, buds and leaves of woody plants and all plant material from forbs or herbaceous growth. Most woody browse consumption occurs during fall and winter.

**SPRING**

- American beautyberry
- Blackberry
- Blueberry
- Common persimmon
- Crab apple
- Flowering dogwood
- Greenbrier
- Hawthorn
- Japanese honeysuckle
- Oak
- Plum
- Poison ivy and poison oak
- Pokeweed
- Red maple
- Red mulberry
- Sassafras
- Virginia creeper
- Wild cherry
- Wild grape
- Willow
- Yellow poplar

**SUMMER**

- American beautyberry
- Apple
- Aspen
- Blackberry
- Blueberry
- Elderberry
- Flowering dogwood
- Fringetree or Old Man's Beard
- Greenbrier
- Japanese honeysuckle
- Jewelweed
- Pear
- Plum
- Poison ivy and poison oak
- Pokeweed
- Red mulberry
- Sassafras
- Strawberry bush
- Striped maple
- Sumac

- Virginia creeper
- Wild cherry
- Wild grape
- Wild rose
- Yellow poplar

**FALL**

- American beautyberry
- American beech nuts
- Blueberry
- Common persimmon
- Flowering dogwood
- Greenbrier
- Honey locust
- Japanese honeysuckle
- Oak
- Pecan
- Plum
- Red raspberry
- Sassafras
- Strawberry bush
- Sugar maple
- Sumac

**WINTER**

- Aspen
- Blueberry
- Greenbrier
- Japanese honeysuckle
- Mushrooms
- Northern white cedar
- Oak
- Red maple
- Striped maple
- Sumac
- Yellow poplar

Note: It's important to note that scientific evidence has recorded the consumption of well over 700 species of plants nationwide by white-tailed deer, and the above short lists only represent some of the preferred species; consumption of each item varies with soil type, timber stand condition, and land use, and may only comprise a small portion of any individual deer's diet. The amount of plant utilization depends on its regional availability, the preference of the deer in that particular area, and the types and availability of other foods.

## How to Fertilize Mast-Producing Trees

**Method No. 1 - Granular Fertilizer**

- Fertilizing a selected mast-producing tree is more than a matter of scattering a handful of fertilizer at its base. There are two methods of fertilizing your selected trees. The first is the use of 13-13-13 granular fertilizer.
- This should be applied in early spring. Apply it at a rate of 2 pounds per 1,000 square feet of crown. A mature white oak with a crown measuring 80 by 80 feet, or 6,400 square feet, would require about 13 pounds of fertilizer.
- You want to apply the fertilizer from the edge of the drip line, that is, the outer edge of the farthest tips of branches from the tree trunk, to within 3 feet of the trunk of the tree.
- If there are a lot of leaves and limbs on the ground in the fertilized area, you will want to take a rake with you to rake them away so that the fertilizer will come in contact with the soil quickly.

**Method No. 2 - Fertilizer Sticks**

- A second method is to purchase a box of fruit- or shade-tree fertilizer spikes at a nursery or garden supply store and follow the instructions on the box. They are more expensive than granular fertilizer but are easy to carry into the woods for use.

Results take time.

While this is a good way to increase the mast production of a selected tree, do not expect to see bushels of fruit appear on the tree the next fall. It is usually the third year with all other things going right, such as no late-spring frost, that you can see a significant increase in the fruit crop. Like most habitat management, it takes time. This, of course, is a long-term project that requires fertilization every year.

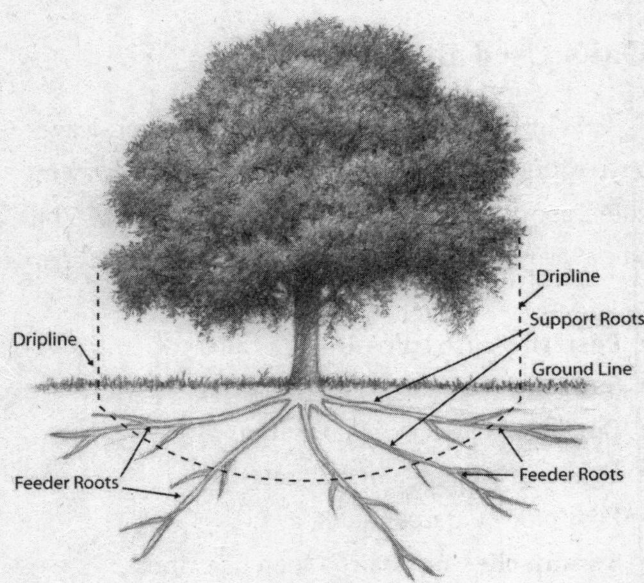


Drip Line

## Planting Bareroot Seedlings

Most state forestry agencies offer both pine-and hardwood-tree as well as shrub bareroot seedlings at reasonable prices. The seedlings are grown in a nursery bed until they are ready to be transplanted, and then they are lifted out without any soil around the roots and shipped to the landowner. They are usually shipped with moss or gel around the roots to keep them moist. Bareroot seedlings are less expensive than balled plants and much faster and easier to plant. When planted correctly, they can help improve the deer habitat on a property. Here is how to plant bareroot seedlings:

### SPACING FOR PINES

For pine, a 6-foot by 7-foot spacing is generally recommended and requires 1,000 seedlings per acre. For creating a bedding area, a spacing of 5 feet by 5 feet (1,700 seedlings per acre) is good.

For creating a corridor for deer, a spacing of 6 feet by 8 feet (900 seedlings per acre) is ideal.

### SPACING FOR HARDWOODS

For hardwood trees such as oaks, plant 40 feet by 40 feet to allow for large crowns when the trees mature.

### SPACING FOR SHRUBS

Follow instructions given by your state forester.

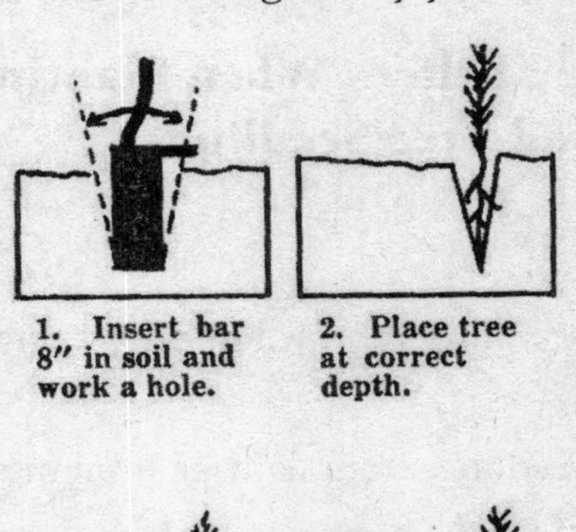

1. Insert bar 8″ in soil and work a hole.
2. Place tree at correct depth.


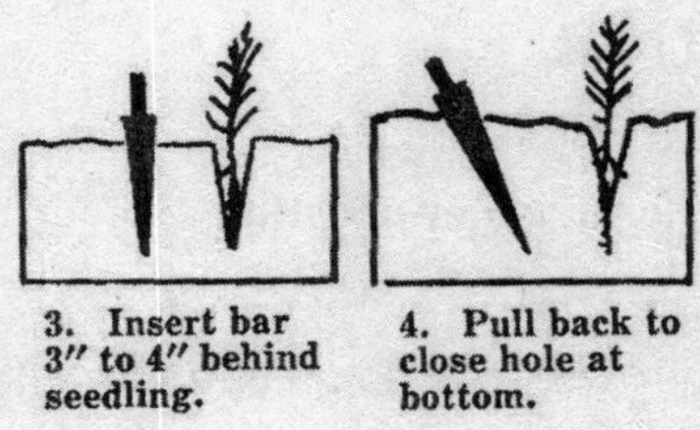

3. Insert bar 3″ to 4″ behind seedling.
4. Pull back to close hole at bottom.


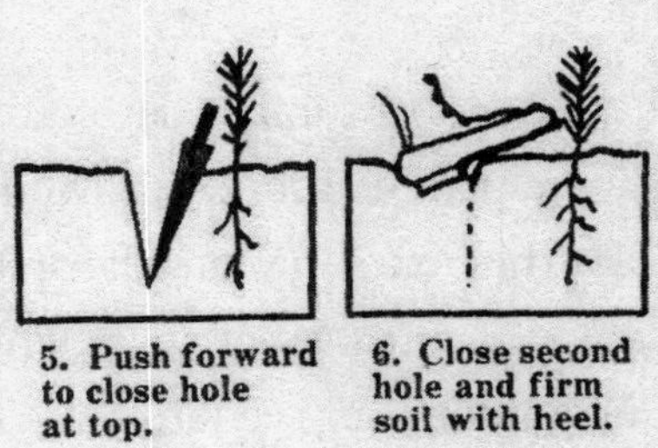

5. Push forward to close hole at top.
6. Close second hole and firm soil with heel.


Planting

- Use a dibble to loosen the soil to a depth of a few inches deeper than the length of the roots.
- Plant seedlings to the same depth they were planted in the nursery. There will be a color change on the stem of the seedling at this point.
- Be sure the roots are pointing straight down and not bent into a "J" shape.
- Insert the dibble about into the soil again 4 inches behind the seedling and pull back to close the first hole. Push forward to close the hole on top.
- Close the second hole and firm the soil with your heel.
- Keep weed competition controlled the first 2 to 3 years.
- Use a tree shelter on hardwoods.
- Fertilizer will help bareroot hardwood or shrub seedlings become established.

## Use Tree Shelters When Planting Hardwood-Tree Seedlings

### ADVANTAGES

- Protect seedlings from wildlife browsing and girdling.
- Protect seedlings from damage from mowers and weed trimmers.
- Help locate seedlings.
- Simplify herbicide applications.
- Improve survival.
- Improve growth, due to greenhouse effect.

### APPLICATION

- Tree shelters are long, tubular devices made of plastic that are placed around hardwood tree seedlings for the first 3–5 years after planting.
- Tree shelters come in a variety of heights. Select the right height for your seedlings.
- Hardwood seedlings usually require a 48-inch tree shelter due to rapid growth.
- In areas where deer browsing is a problem, the 72-inch shelter is better.
- Shorter tree shelters are available for protection from rabbits and small animals.
- Keep the tree shelter around the seedling until it has grown well out the top, usually 3–5 years.
- Tree shelters are available from many garden stores, forestry supply stores or www.plantra.com or www.nwtf.com.

## Oaks Used By Deer

**White oaks** - Acorns mature in 1 year; leaves have rounded tips on most species; bark is gray in color; acorn meat is white and usually sweet. White oak acorns are preferred by deer over red oak acorns.

- **Eastern white oak** - Quercus alba
- **Sawtooth oak** - Quercus acutissma
- **Bur oak** - Quercus macrocarpa
- **Overcup oak** - Quercus lyrata
- **Post oak** - Quercus stellata
- **Swamp chestnut oak** - Quercus prinus
- **Chestnut oak** - Quercus montana
- **Swamp white oak** - Quercus bicolor
- **Chinkapin oak** - Quercus muehlenbergi
- **Oregon white oak** - Quercus garryana
- **California white oak** - Quercus lobata
- **English oak** - Quercus robur
- **Durand oak** - Quercus sinuata
- **Bluff oak** - Quercus austrina
- **Chapman oak** - Quercus chapmanii
- **Basket oak** - Quercus michauxii
- **Virginia live oak** - Quercus virginiana
- **Oglethorpe oak** - Quercus oglethropensis

**Red (black) oaks** - Acorns require 2 years to mature; leaves usually have pointed tips; bark is dark; acorn meat is usually yellow and bitter, however they have higher fat content than white oak varieties.

- **Northern red oak** - Quercus rubra
- **Black oak** - Quercus velutina
- **Shumard oak** - Quercus shumardii
- **Southern red oak** - Quercus falcata
- **Swamp red oak, cherrybark oak** - Quercus falcata var.
- **Scarlet oak** - Quercus coccinea
- **Pin oak** - Quercus palustris
- **Northern pin oak, Jack oak** - Quercus ellipsoidalis
- **Nuttall oak** - Quercus texana
- **Blackjack oak** - Quercus marilandica
- **Turkey oak** - Quercus laevis
- **Buckley oak** - Quercus buckleyi
- **Bear oak** - Quercus ilicifolia
- **Georgia oak** - Quercus georgiana
- **Arkansas oak** - Quercus arkansana
- **Water oak** - Quercus nigra
- **Shingle oak** - Quercus imbricaria
- **Willow oak** - Quercus phellos
- **Bluejack oak, sand oak** - Quercus incana
- **Myrtle oak** - Quercus myrtifolia
- **Sand live oak** - Quercus geminata
- **Laurel oak** - Quercus laurifolia

The Quality Deer Management Association recommends, as with many things, managing for diversity of oak species. Because white oak varieties are highly preferred, but red oak varieties are more common on the landscape and provide deer and turkey with more carbohydrates prior to harsh winters, leaving about a 3:1 ratio of red to white oak varieties on your property.

## Prescribed Burn Plan

One of the best deer habitat improvement tools in a southern pine forest is the use of a controlled fire, called a prescribed burn. This intentional use of fire, usually in the late winter or early spring, does several positive things:

- It burns natural litter from the forest floor, allowing sunlight to hit the mineral soil.
- It scarifies seeds so they can sprout.
- It releases nutrients that can offer a quick production of grasses, legumes, forbs and other plant materials that deer favor.

A prescribed burn for wildlife management requires knowledge, skill and planning. Most of all, it requires experience. It is best to get your local state forestry department involved and/or a consulting certified prescribed burn manager if you think a burn is what your hunting property needs.

Assuming your pine trees are old enough to withstand a prescribed burn and the land can be burned in several small units, here is an example from Alabama of some of the things you will be required to put into your burn plan before you can request a burn permit. Since each state has different rules and regulations for a prescribed burn, you will want to check with your local forester for your state's plan requirements.

**Minimum Standards for Prescribed Burn Plan**

As required under the Alabama Prescribed Burn Act

1. **Personal information to include:**
   a. Name of property owner
   b. Owner's mailing address
   c. Owner's phone number

   d. Same information on individual preparing the plan and/or executing the burn
   e. Prescribed burn manager certification number
2. **Description of area to be burned:**
   a. County
   b. Section, township, range
   c. Acres to be burned
   d. Type and size of overstory
   e. Type and size of understory
   f. Fuel type and amount
   g. Topography
3. **Purpose of burn**
4. **Pre-burn information to include:**
   a. Needed manpower and equipment
   b. Firing techniques to be used
   c. List of areas around site that could be adversely impacted by smoke from burn
   d. Special precautions taken
5. **Range of desired weather information to include:**
   a. Surface wind speed and direction
   b. Minimum and maximum relative humidity
   c. Maximum temperature
   d. Transport wind speed and direction
   e. Minimum mixing height
   f. Dispersion index
6. **Starting time and completion of ignition**
7. **Sketch of area to be burned**
8. **Signature of burn manager, dated and notarized or witnessed**
9. **Burn permit number**

## Make a Deer Corridor

Deer corridors, by my definition, are strips of heavy cover that connect deer bedding areas to deer feeding areas. They are natural funnels for deer due to the fact that they offer safe cover when traveling during daylight hours. One example of a naturally occurring corridor may include a wide, thickly vegetated fencerow running between a plantation of young planted pines and a soybean field. Another possible example could be a streamside management zone, which is a wooded strip purposefully left after a timber harvest that runs along a stream and connects tracts of woodlands. Finally, a brushy ditch bank that runs between agricultural fields could be an excellent deer corridor.

Any strip of high-growing, thick cover that gives a buck a sense of security when it is traveling during daylight hours can become a corridor; thus, property with lots of corridors may potentially have more daytime buck movement due to the fact that bucks are more likely to feel safe to move about in these areas.

If your property lacks corridors, you can create a system of corridors within a few years. Each corridor can become a great place to hunt.

- Start by planning your future corridor system. Take a topographical map or aerial photo of your property and mark all known or suspected deer bedding areas. For mature bucks, these are usually the thickest areas with lots of ground cover. Swamps, wetlands, young planted pines and thick brushy areas are often choice bedding areas. Any thick area seldom hunted may be a potential bedding area.
- Next, mark deer feeding areas such as food plots, agricultural crops that offer highly desired food, patches of natural forage such as Japanese honeysuckle and Smilax, or groves of mast-producing trees. Connect the bedding areas to the food sources by following creeks, ditches, fencerows or any natural depression running between the two. These will be your potential corridor sites.

- With the corridor sites identified, the next step is to do whatever it takes to get the area to become grown up with thick trees, brush and high grass. Give the bucks a strip, at least 10 yards wide and head high, of vegetated cover to travel in and feel safe. A small creek bank, in many areas, will become thick quickly with alder, sweet gum trees, high grass and vines if it is not mowed or sprayed with herbicide. If you decide to do some cutting in these areas to advance vegetative growth, make sure you know what your states basal area laws are near streams or bodies of water, An unmowed strip on either side of a ditch, gulley or fencerow can also provide the same desired habitat.
- An annual application of 13-13-13 fertilizer at the rate of 300 pounds per acre broadcast throughout the corridor will help speed up the growth process.
- If you want to plant your selected strip in fast-growing cover crops, consult your county agricultural agent to ascertain what works best in your area. Consider planted strips in dogwoods, blackberry, switch grass and pine along fencerows and ditches to create a corridor. Every now and then, plant female persimmon, plum and crab apple to offer some soft mast in the corridor.
- If your property is open and flat, not having a depression connecting bedding areas to food sources, you can plant a 10-yard-wide strip of pines or cedars connecting the two areas. Within about 3 years you will have a good wildlife corridor, and it will get better each year.

Hunting corridors can be most productive for mature bucks, but a word of caution is advised. Since most corridors are narrow, too much hunting pressure will cause the bucks to quit using the corridor during daylight hours. Develop as many corridors as you can on a tract of land, and after hunting a day or two in one corridor, change to another corridor, giving each a break of five or six days before hunting it again.

## Restore Old Apple Trees

Many old farms and abandoned properties have overgrown orchards that at one time contained apple trees grown for consumption or sale. Often these old apple trees are still alive today and may be bearing a little fruit each year. If so, they can be improved to produce more fruit, and if they are not bearing fruit, with a little work they can be brought into production. Follow these steps and you will have a great food source for deer to use on your hunting land.

Here is a three-step method you can use to manage abandoned apple, pear or crabapple trees to bring them back into production for deer food.

**Step 1 - Tree selection**

If one exists, look for apple or fruit trees around the old farmstead on your property. You may also find apple trees in other parts of the old yard, as they were often grown in several areas. Finally, sometimes entire orchards have been overtopped by mature timber, so if you find a lone apple tree in the woods, take the time to look for others nearby. Once you have identified your fruit trees, select and mark with surveyor's tape the healthiest individuals. Remember, apples require cross-pollination to bear fruit, so there must be an apple tree of another variety nearby. They will cross-pollinate with crab apple trees, so leave as many apple trees as you can for this reason.

Apple trees require lots of direct sunlight to produce fruit, and they don't do well when there is a lot of competition from shrubs and trees growing under and near the tree. Remove all shrubs and

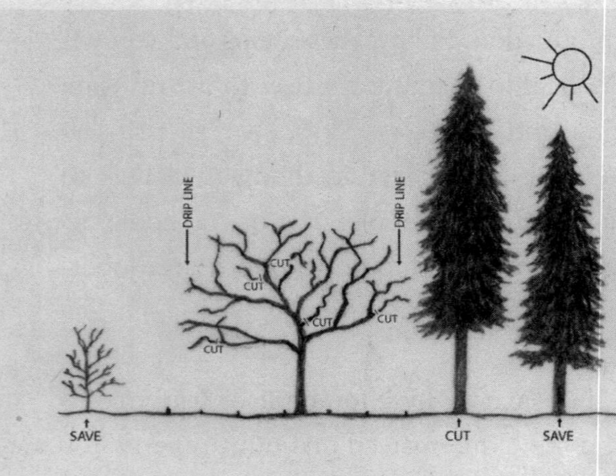


trees that are growing next to, growing under or overshadowing the apple trees.

**Step 2 - Pruning, year one**

Apples are typically produced on the youngest growth of apple trees, and old unmanaged apple trees have lots of limbs and branches that are not fruit producers. Pruning will be necessary to reduce the amount of old wood, encourage the growth of new wood and get sunlight into the tree. It is well worth the effort to prune your apple trees, as those that have been managed for 4 or 5 years will produce three to four times the fruit of an unmanaged tree.

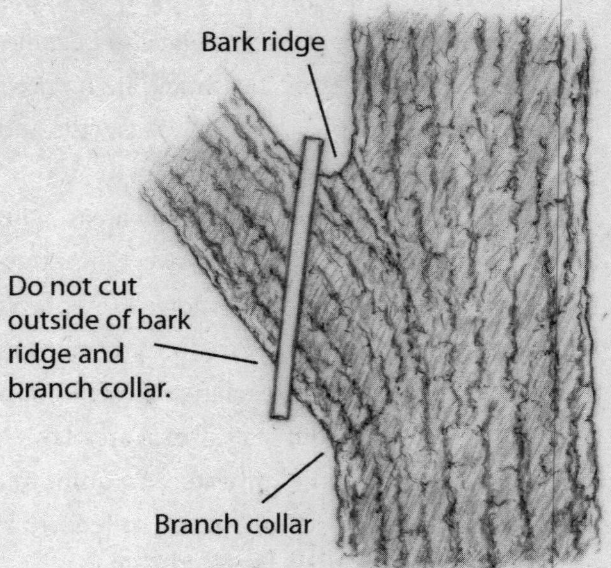


Always plan on doing your annual pruning in the early spring, after the last frost but before the tree blooms. For first time pruning on old trees, do about half of the necessary pruning the first year and the rest in the second year to reduce both disease transmission (fewer wounds) and any shock the tree may experience from the change in environment.

Start your pruning by removing all the dead branches and limbs from the tree. Using a pruning saw or pruning shears, cut the dead limbs as close to the living tissue as possible.

Next, in the tree's canopy remove no more than one-third of the limbs to reduce the tree's height and to let more sunlight into the tree.

Fertilize the tree with 3 pounds of 6-24-24 fertilizer in a band spread around the drip line. Do this each year.

**Step 3 - Annual pruning**

Open up thick clusters of small branches by pruning out those that are rubbing against one another, growing into one another or have died. Never remove more than one-third of the live growth of the tree.

# Part 6

# *From Field to Table*

# Introduction

While we all enjoy bowhunting for whitetail deer, other big-game animals, small game, and turkeys, it's safe to say we all equally enjoy the products of our labor—namely roasts, chops, steaks, burgers, and stew meat from a deer or elk, the tasty breast meat of a wild turkey, or the tender meat of a rabbit or squirrel. In this section, we have covered everything you need to know to put some great meals on the table—from field dressing, skinning, and quartering deer, to smoking wild game, to making jerky, and finally to making mouth-watering main courses. Enjoy!

—Jay Cassell

# Venison and Other Wild Game

Many hunters do not raise or butcher domestic animals, but instead hunt venison and other big game, and by necessity butcher and field dress the animal. I often wonder about hunters who don't do the complete process. Butchering a deer is a relatively easy process, and with my complete boning method, requires little in the way of tools or skill.

The main advantage of doing it yourself, however, is meat quality. When you take your deer to a slaughter plant you may or may not get back ground meat from only your deer. Some plants cut up carcasses and then grind meat in large lots instead of grinding the individual carcasses separately. Even if you've been extremely careful not to contaminate your meat while field dressing, perhaps another hunter wasn't as careful.

Small game and wild fowl are also pursued by many hunters. Squirrels, rabbits, upland game such as doves, quail and pheasant, as well as wild turkeys, ducks, and geese all provide excellent table fare. Unlike their domestic cousins, small game and birds are more lean, yet high in protein. Dressing small game and birds properly is extremely easy and they should be done as quickly as possible, especially in hot weather to prevent spoilage.

Wild game meat offers some health advantages. Following is a chart showing the benefits.

**THE SKINNY ON GAME MEAT**

| Type of Meat | Fat | Saturated Fat | Calories | Protein |
|---|---|---|---|---|
| Deer | 3.2g | 1.2g | 158 | 30.2g |
| Elk | 1.9g | 0.7g | 146 | 30.2g |
| Antelope | 2.7g | 1.0g | 150 | 29.4g |
| Lean Roast Beef | 14.3g | 5.7g | 249 | 27.0g |
| Lean Ham | 5.8g | 1.9g | 153 | 24.8g |
| Salmon | 5.8g | 1.4g | 163 | 24.5g |
| Chicken Breast* | 3.5g | 1.1g | 163 | 31.5g |

**SOURCE:** U.S. Department of Agriculture (for 3.5-ounce portions) *roasted, no skin

## Venison

### Choosing

Wild game meat, such as deer, elk, or moose, is some of the best red meat you can eat. First, it's leaner; actually it's a natural "grass-fed" meat, although deer tend to eat more of a variety of plants than just grass. Venison has about 2 percent fat, compared to beef with 30 percent fat. Just like with home-grown meat, selecting a wild game animal for food is also important.

Wild game, especially venison, is one of the healthiest meats. It's lean, with about 2 percent fat, compared to beef with 30 percent fat.

Younger animals are naturally tender, and females are usually less tough and have less gamey flavor than male animals. An old trophy buck, during the height of the rut, can be both tough and gamey. Old bulls are usually ground up into hamburger and old bucks should be as well. If you're trophy hunting, you'll be stuck with an older, tougher animal.

Just as with butchering domestic livestock, stressed animals produce lower-quality meat. A deer or other wild game that is hit poorly and runs a distance also has the chance of "fiery meat" due to the release of the same adrenaline and lactic acid as in domestic animals. Regardless of gun or bow, it's important to strike the vitals for a clean, quick kill. This is not always possible, but it's important to practice with your gun or bow and be proficient.

As with domestic livestock, younger animals are the best choice for tenderness and have a less "gamey flavor."

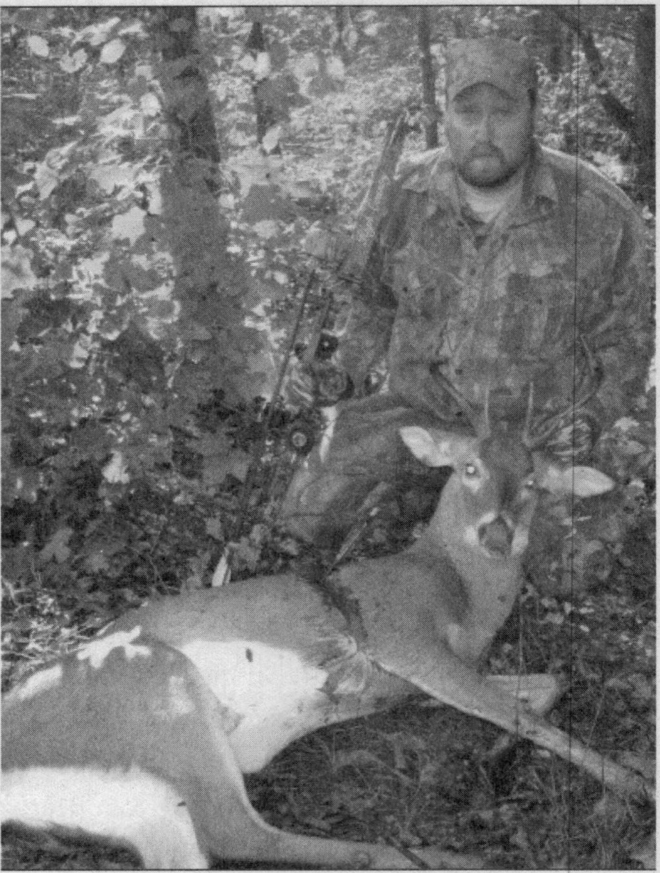

It's important to make a good killing shot, with a quick death for quality meat.

Then take only shots that will ensure a good kill. I don't take running shots because running deer are usually scared or running for a reason. Even if you do make a clean kill, which is rare, the meat may have an off taste.

Several years ago a friend and I were quail hunting on my property when my bird dog jumped a buck from a brush pile fairly near a major highway. The buck jumped out, lunged forward onto his front legs, which were both broken, tried to lunge again, falling over. My setter grabbed him by the tail and the battle began. I finally killed the buck with a knife, cutting his throat. Apparently the buck had been hit by an automobile on the highway alongside my property and had hidden in the brush pile for days. I called the Conservation Agent and explained the situation. "Go ahead and dress him and keep him," he replied. I did, but the meat wasn't fit to eat, almost powder dry and very strong tasting.

Many people find venison too gamey for their taste. Killed, field dressed, and processed wrong, venison can indeed be strong flavored. Venison has been a major meat source in our household for decades. We've learned to cook it in many different ways. Our guests often don't know they're eating venison as they comment on the great-tasting food. Venison, like beef, benefits from aging.

Aging creates more tenderness, but also requires consistently cool temperatures (staying below 40°F) for the length of the aging time. The carcass must also be quickly chilled down to 40°F before the aging period. The carcass is typically aged by hanging in a cool area with plenty of circulation and safe from pests such as cats, dogs, even coyotes. The carcass can be hung skinned or unskinned. Skinned carcasses will cool quicker. The carcass will form a hard, dry "skin" on the outside or "fell," the membrane covering the meat and keeping the meat moist. You can also cover the carcass with a cheesecloth game bag to provide some protection. Make sure the animal is properly field dressed and washed, and the body cavity propped open to get good air circulation. We typically hang deer for seven to ten days, but it depends mostly on the temperature at the time. If you don't have consistently cold weather, or the weather alternates between freezing and too warm, add the freezing time to the aging time. In hot climates hanging to age is not an option. The carcass can be quartered and placed in an old refrigerator to age. As there is no air circulation, you'll need to move the pieces around frequently to prevent blood pooling in one area. If possible, stand the pieces on end so they will drain properly.

**Field Dressing**

Proper field dressing is a major step in safe, quality venison. It's extremely important to field dress as quickly as possible after the animal has been killed to allow body heat to dissipate rapidly. Venison can also be heavily contaminated with fecal bacteria—the degree varying with the hunter's skill, location of the wound, and other factors. Take all necessary steps to avoid puncturing the digestive tract, a very common problem.

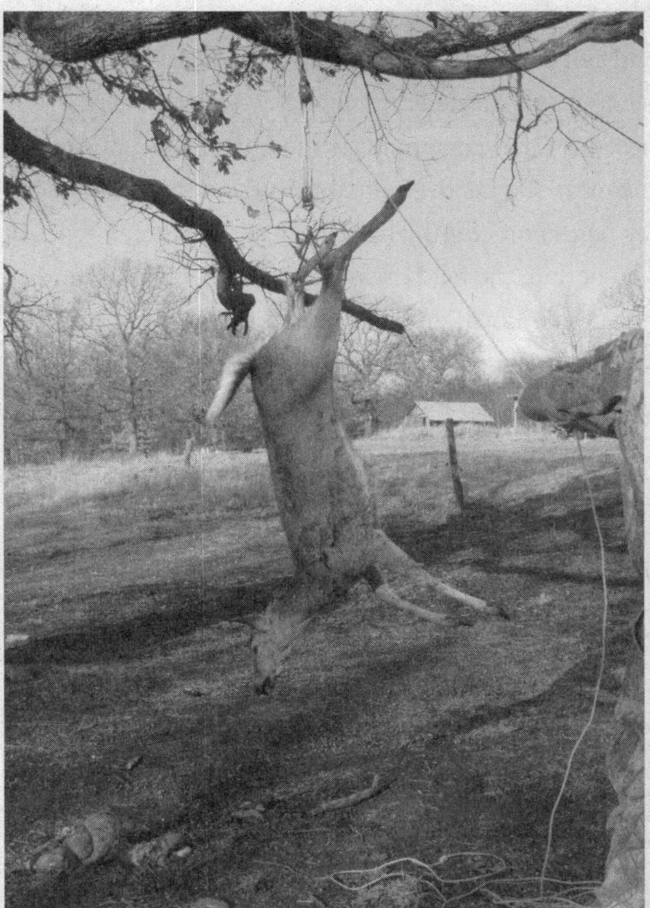

Venison is often hung to age, depending on the weather and ambient temperature, and then cut up.

Always have the necessary tools for field dressing readily available. In addition to a good skinning knife, you'll need a twelve-inch piece of sturdy string, a plastic bag for holding the liver and heart, and rubber or plastic gloves. Although the standard food-safe rubber gloves can be used, a better choice is "vet" gloves found at farm supply stores. These long plastic gloves come up to your elbows. This prevents getting blood and other matter on your hunting clothes, a common problem when you're reaching into a bloody carcass. These gloves can be carried in a plastic food bag in a pocket or in your hunting pack. My nephew Morgan also carries a small container of wet-wipes in his hunting pack. A drag harness or section of sturdy rope that can be fashioned into a drag is also handy.

Sticking or cutting the throat is not necessary and can contaminate the meat. Do not cut off the scent glands located on the hocks. This also isn't necessary and contaminates the knife blade and then the meat. Do tag the animal with the necessary game tag before proceeding to field dress. As with all types of butchering, the field dressing can be done in a number of ways. Following is the method I've used successfully for many years. Under the right circumstances I can field dress a deer in about three minutes.

Proper field dressing is the first key in safe and quality game meat. Do so as soon as possible after the kill.

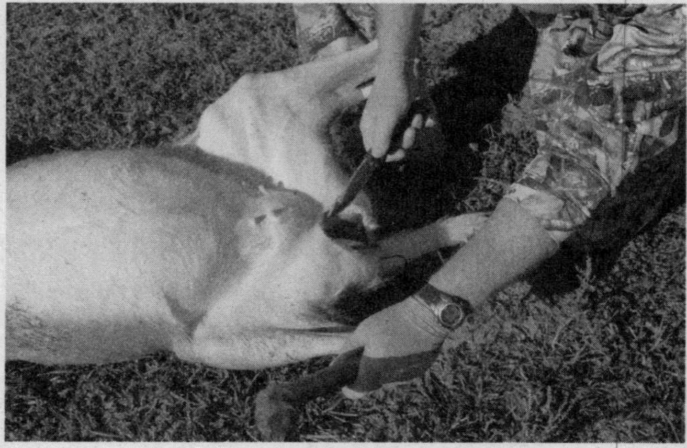

Roll the animal onto its back and prop in place or hold with your legs. Make a cut between the legs and down to the pelvic arch bone. Then continue the cut through the pelvic arch, being careful not to cut into the paunch or bladder.

The first step is to roll the animal onto its back on a flat spot. Sometimes that takes a bit of dragging here in the Ozarks where I live. You may even have to prop up the body with sticks or stones. Prop the head just a bit higher than the rest of the body. Straddle the animal facing toward the head. On small deer I place my legs inside their back legs to force the legs outwards and help hold the body in position. On bigger animals, I use one of my legs to force one of their back legs into an upright position. A buddy can be a great help in field dressing, especially by holding the animal in place. Check your local laws regarding leaving the genitals on the carcass. Some states require the genitals to remain on the field-dressed deer until the deer has been through a check station. Many states, these days, however, use electronic checking and this is not necessary. If a buck, and allowed by law, cut away the penis and scrotum, slicing to one side just through the skin, then peeling out and slicing the opposite side. Do not remove, but allow them to hang back over the anus. If a doe is still lactating and the udder is full, cut away and remove the udder, but do not cut into it. If the milk from the udder contacts the meat, it can create a strong taste. Make

Cut around the bung, or anus, from the rear of the animal. Pull out the bung and tie it off with a string.

The Hunter's Specialties Butt Out makes this chore quick and easy. Insert the Butt Out, then pull out the bung and tie it off.

a cut with the knife held fairly flat through the skin and muscle between the legs and down to the pelvic arch. Be careful not to cut into the paunch at the beginning of the cut. Locate the white line in the center of the pelvic arch and cut on it through the pelvic bone. On smaller deer you can do this with a sturdy skinning knife; on larger animals a game saw or hatchet is necessary. Push down on the inside of the haunches to further spread the pelvic bone apart.

From the rear of the animal, cut around the bung on the sides and back. Pull the bung out and tie it off with a string. This prevents getting fecal matter on the carcass through the remainder of the process. Or, you may prefer to cut around the bung and pull it out first before splitting the pelvic bone. Hunter's Specialties makes a great tool for this chore, the Butt Out. In this case the bung is pulled out as the first step.

Simply insert the Butt Out into the anal canal, making sure the handle is flush against the canal. Twist the handle until you feel the tool grab the membrane and then twist one half turn more. Steadily pull the Butt Out from the anal canal. This will pull out the canal membrane. Extract about ten to twelve inches of the membrane, and tie it off.

The next step is opening the paunch and can be the hardest part. However, if you have a skinning knife with a gut hook, this step is actually very easy. Starting at the point of the breastbone, make a small incision just through the skin and muscle, but not into the intestines.

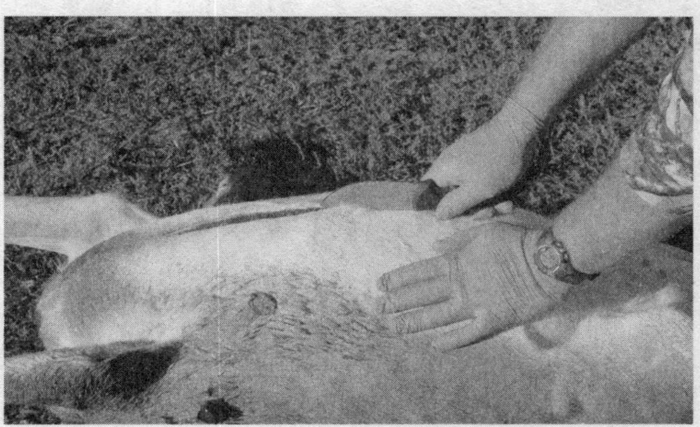

Using a knife with a gut hook, start an incision through the skin and muscles at the point of the breastbone and cut down to the pelvic cut.

Insert the gut hook in the cut and pull down, slicing through the skin and muscle. The gut hook prevents cutting into the paunch.

The paunch will steadily rise up and out of the animal as you make the cut. Continue the cut to join with the cut through the pelvic arch. There will be a fairly heavy muscle just ahead of the pelvic arch. Cut through this with the knife blade, again being careful not to cut into the intestines or the bladder, which lies just below the arch.

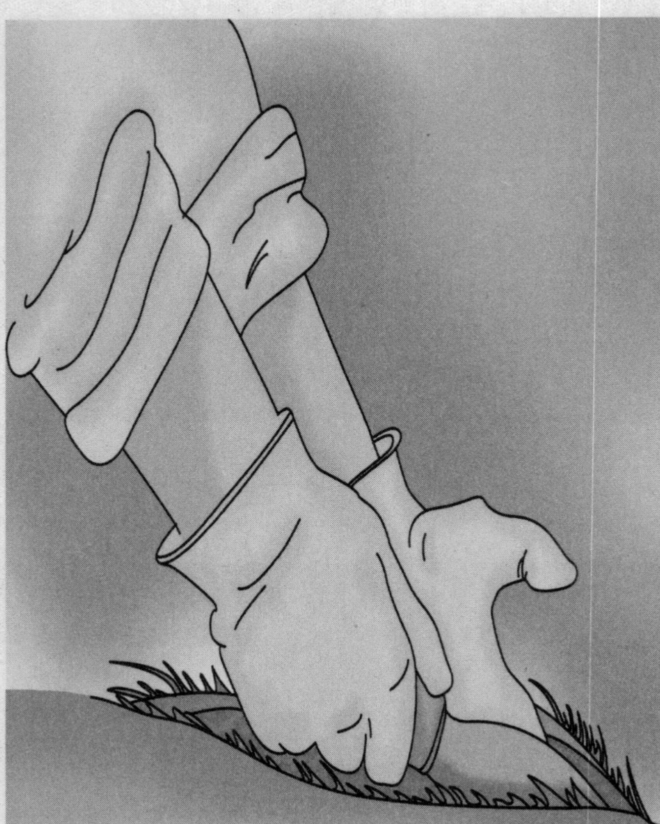

Or make the cut with a knife blade, pointing outward and up, using your fingers to push the paunch and intestines down and away from the cut. Be careful not to cut into the paunch.

Turn the knife around and make a cut from the tip of the breastbone through the center of the ribs up to the throat. This can be done fairly easily on a small animal. On larger animals you may need to cut through the skin with a knife, and then complete the cut with a meat saw. If you're dressing a trophy buck, do not cut high on the throat: just to the front point of the chest, in order to save the cape.

Reach up into the chest cavity and cut the gullet attachments. Pull the heart, liver, and other intestines from the cavity, cutting the skirt or diaphragm membrane as necessary. Be extremely careful not to cut into the tenderloins located just inside the backbone.

Roll the carcass over on its side and the entire intestines will fall out. Pull the penis and bung back through the pelvic opening and pull the intestines away from the carcass, cutting away interior attachments as necessary.

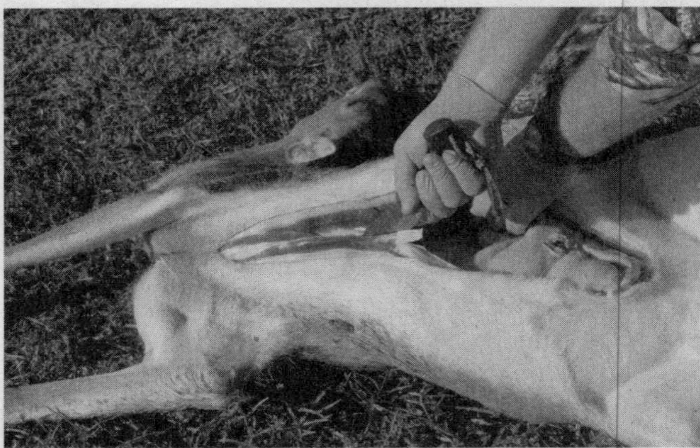

Turn the knife around and cut through the breastbone toward the throat. On larger animals you may need a saw or hand hatchet to cut the bone.

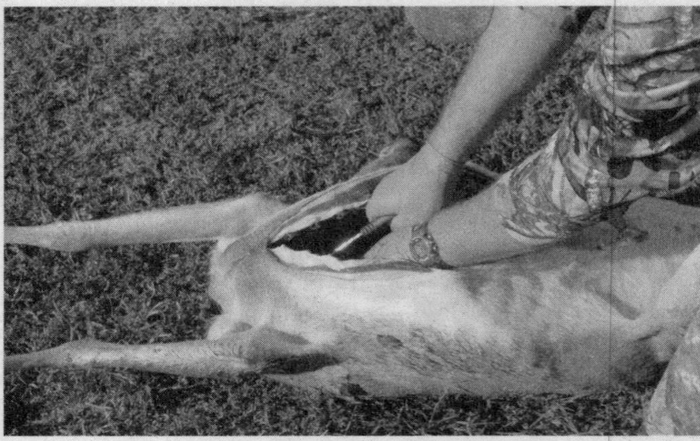

Reach into the chest cavity and cut the gullet and windpipe.

Pull the intestines, heart, and liver through the openings, cutting the skirt or diaphragm to release the heart and lungs.

Lift up on the head of the animal to allow blood that has collected in the cavity to drain out. If fresh, clean water is available, thoroughly wash the inside of the carcass.

Cut the liver away from the intestines, and cut away the gallbladder, cutting off a bit of liver with the gallbladder attached. Remove the heart. Place the liver and heart in a plastic bag. You're now ready to transport the animal. Keep the opening of the body cavity clean during transport.

### Processing

Deer, as well as elk and moose, can be processed in any number of ways. Moose and elk are normally processed in much the same manner as a beef. Deer are often processed in a variety of ways. Deer can be skinned, then cut up in the same basic method as for other domestic livestock, following the same basic cuts. Or, deer can be partially processed in that manner and other portions boned out. Or you can bone out the entire carcass, my favorite method. I'll describe the latter two and you can make your own choices.

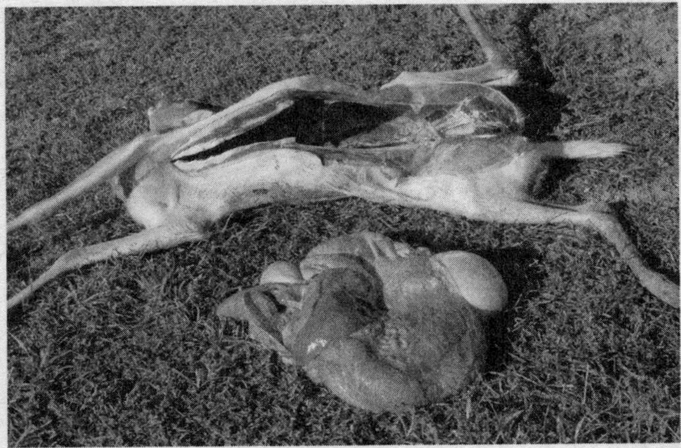

Roll the carcass over on its side and the intestines will fall out. Turn the carcass over on its belly to allow blood to drain out. If possible wash the interior with fresh, cold water.

### Skinning

If you're processing in the traditional manner, the first step is skinning out the carcass. Depending on the weather and the time I have available during hunting season (sometimes I have a half dozen or more deer to do), I'll skin before hanging and aging, or after. If the weather is ideal, I prefer to skin before hanging and aging and as soon as possible after the animal has been killed. The skin comes off easier while still fresh. If I'm skinning in the traditional manner, the first step is to saw off the rear legs below the hocks and the front legs in front of the knees. There is almost no meat on the legs of a deer. The main problem with skinning a deer is the brittle hair, which comes out easily and also cuts and breaks easily, with the result being hair on the meat. The method described results in the least amount of hair on the meat, although you'll always have some. Make all cuts from the underside of the skin and outward to avoid cutting hair as much as possible.

A cut is made in each hind leg between the hock and main tendon to insert a gambrel. The deer is then hoisted, head down, and high enough that I can easily reach the chest and front legs. Slide a skinning knife under the skin on the inside of a

Field deer are often field dressed and quartered at the same time in the field, for easier transporting.

front leg and make a cut on the inside of the leg, continuing to the field-dressing cut on the throat. Then skin out the front leg around to the shoulder. Repeat this for the opposite leg. Many people start at the rear and skin downward, but the hide falls down over the shoulder and front legs, making it harder to skin them. Once both front legs and shoulders have been skinned out, lower the carcass until you can easily reach the hind legs, but do not let the front of the carcass touch the ground. Slide the skinning knife blade in under the skin on the inside of the hams, from the initial field-dressing cut. Turn the

To skin in the traditional manner saw off the feet, make a cut behind the rear-left tendons and insert a gambrel.

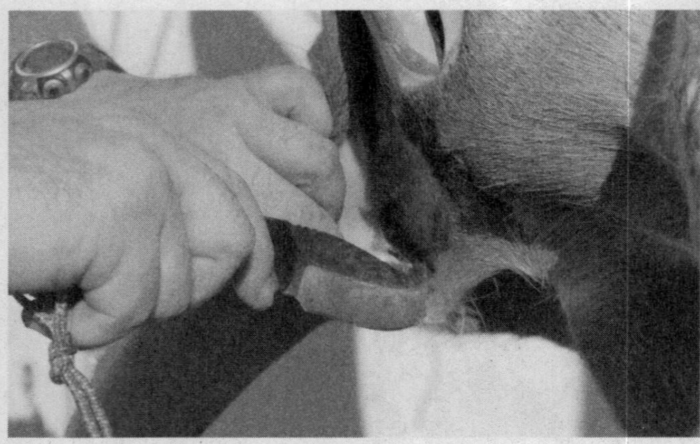

Hoist the carcass head down and make an incision in the inner skin of the front legs to the neck. Always cut from the underside of the skin to avoid getting hairs on the meat.

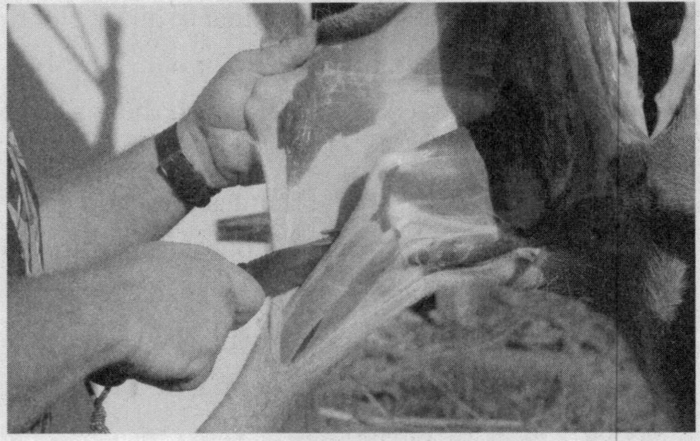

Skin out the front legs.

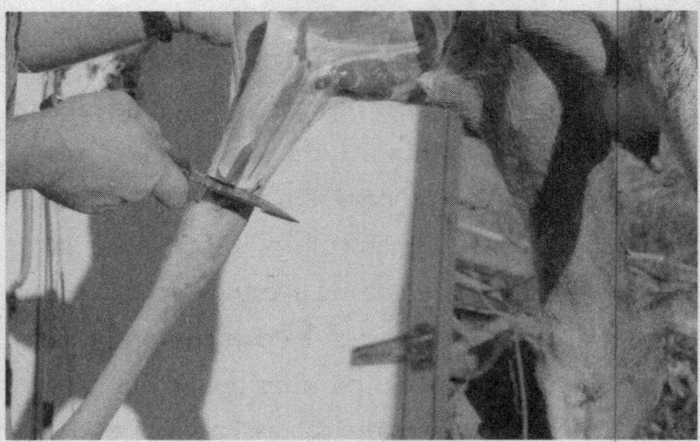

Make a cut encircling the skin of the front legs.

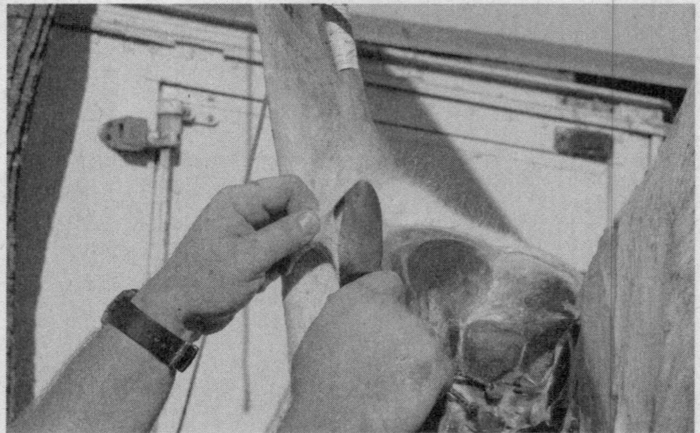

Skin out the hind legs, starting with a cut made from the inside of the skin on the inside of the hams.

blade sharp edge out and slice through the skin up to the cut made to remove the hind legs. Grasp the flap of skin on the inside, next to the pelvic arch, and peel it up over and toward the ham, using the edge of the skinning knife to help release the skin

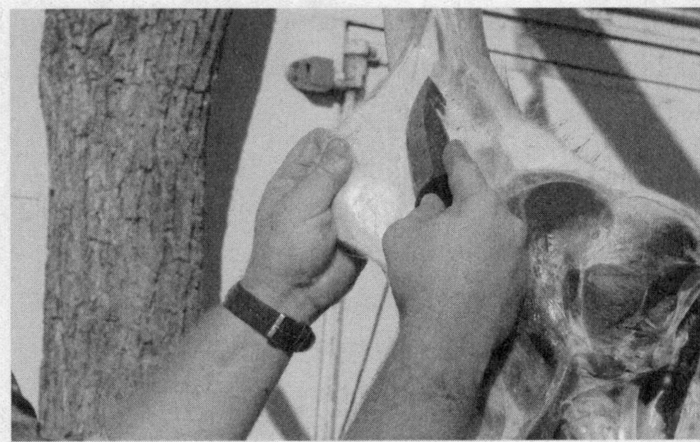

Grasp the flap of skin and pull back over the hams, using a knife to help cut away from the fell, or membrane, covering the muscles.

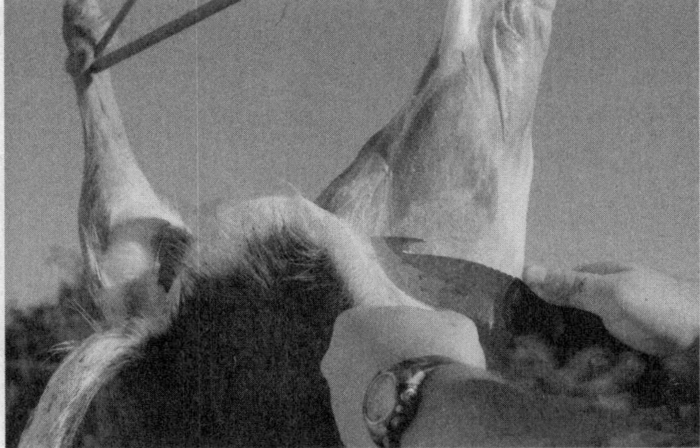

Skin over the back of the hams and cut off the tail.

from the membrane covering the muscle. Continue this process until you reach the back of the ham.

This is actually the hardest part of the skinning process as the skin sticks to the meat on the top of the ham. Grasp the skin on the outside edge of the ham and peel and slice it off until you reach the carcass side. Finish skinning out the back leg and repeat for the opposite leg. When you reach the tail, cut it off. With the tail free, as well as the skin from each leg, you can often peel the majority of the skin free. Grasp the hanging skin or tail and pull down. If the carcass is still fresh, the skin will often simply pull down almost to the shoulders. The skin will still stick in some places, mostly on the flanks and brisket. Use the knife with a sweeping, slicing motion to cut the skin away as needed. Be careful not to cut into the skin from the underside as you again risk getting hair on the meat. Be extra careful if you're saving the hide or the animal is a trophy buck.

Encircle the skin of the back legs.

You can usually peel the skin off the back and sides, using a knife only when necessary to help loosen the skin.

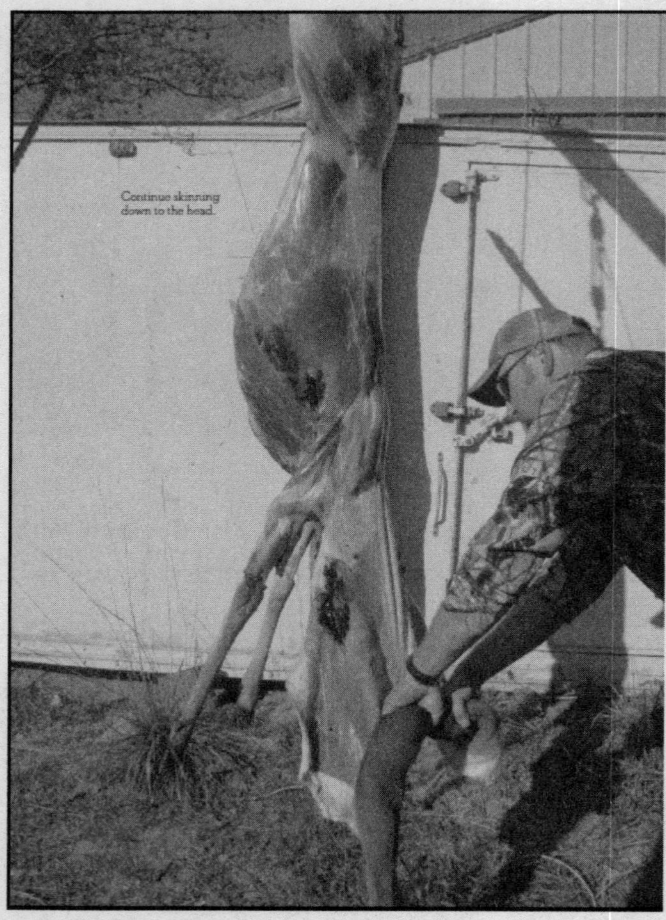


Continue skinning down around the shoulders and the neck until you reach the head. Remove the head at the atlas joint by cutting through the meat with a knife, then twisting off the head. If you have meat that has been possibly contaminated by fecal matter or shot area, cut it off, then wash the knife with disinfectant.

Remove the head at the atlas joint, twisting as needed and cutting through the tendons with a knife.

**Cutting Up**

Before you begin cutting up the carcass, have everything you need on hand. This includes a clean work surface, pans for ground-meat pieces, and a pail or other container to contain the discarded pieces, and paper towels to wipe your knife blade of hair.

You can divide the carcass into quarters in much the same manner as a beef or pork, producing two halves with two forequarters and two hindquarters. This results in loin chops, steaks, and ribs. A more traditional venison division is often used.

Begin the processing with the carcass still hanging by its hind legs, but do not split the carcass. The first step is to remove the front shoulders. The front shoulders come off easily. Grasping a front leg, pull the shoulder out and away from the rib cage. You'll see a division between the two. Using a long, boning-style butcher knife, slice between the two. Pull the shoulder upward as you slice and you'll see the cartilage move on the top of the shoulder. Continue cutting between the shoulder and rib

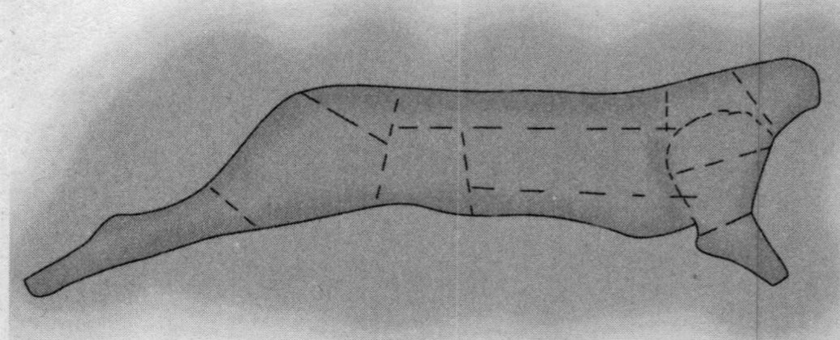

The carcass can be cut up in the same manner as beef but is traditionally cut into somewhat different cuts.

With the carcass hanging head down, grasp a front leg and pull it out and away from the body. Then, using a long boning knife, cut between the leg and body to remove the front shoulder. Lay aside and repeat with the opposite shoulder.

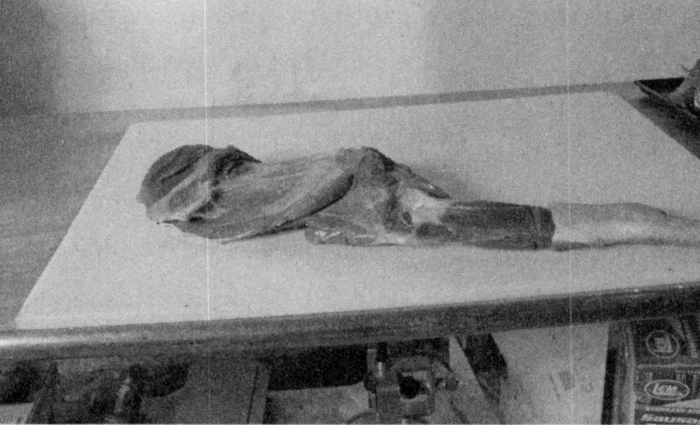

The shoulders can be cut into roasts or ground meat. The shanks can be used for ground meat or stew meat.

cage around the shoulder cartilage and it will come free easily.

Make sure the shoulder you're holding is secure when it comes free. The shoulder produces the traditional roasts and ground meat, while the shank portion produces meat for stews, soups, and ground meat.

The second step is to remove the loins from the backbone. Again a boning-style knife is the best choice. Make a cut down each side of the backbone as close to the backbone and as deep as possible.

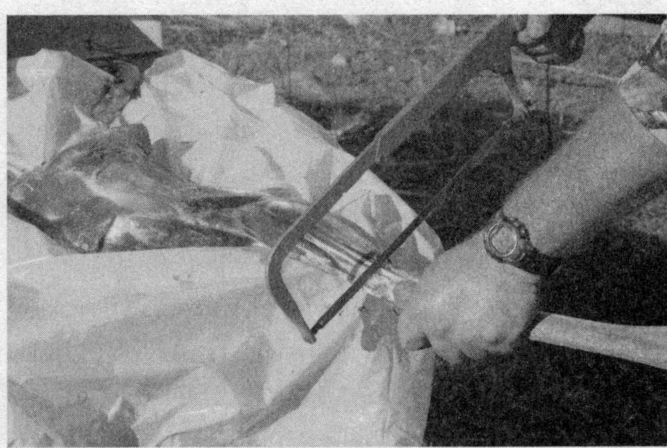

Saw off the front legs.

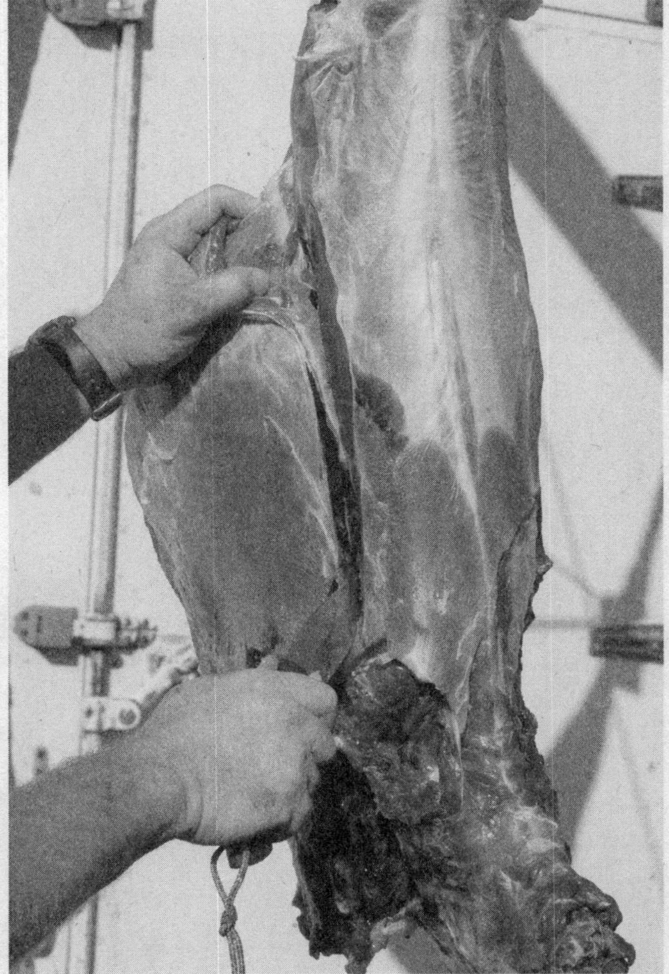

Quite often the loins are boned out. Make a cut following the rib cage.

Then insert the knife against the ribs and, starting at the top of the loin, slice along the outside of the ribs and to the backbone, meeting the first cut. Cut down to the end of the hanging front quarter. This produces a deer loin about eighteen to twenty-four inches long and two inches thick. Hold the meat strip with one hand as you cut it free with the opposite. This tender portion of the deer makes great steaks and roasts and is fantastic smoked. Repeat these steps for the opposite loin. Inside the carcass on either side of the backbone are the two tenderloins. Using a boning knife, peel them out. These are the most tender portions of the deer carcass. They make great "steak" hors d'oeuvres for the grill.

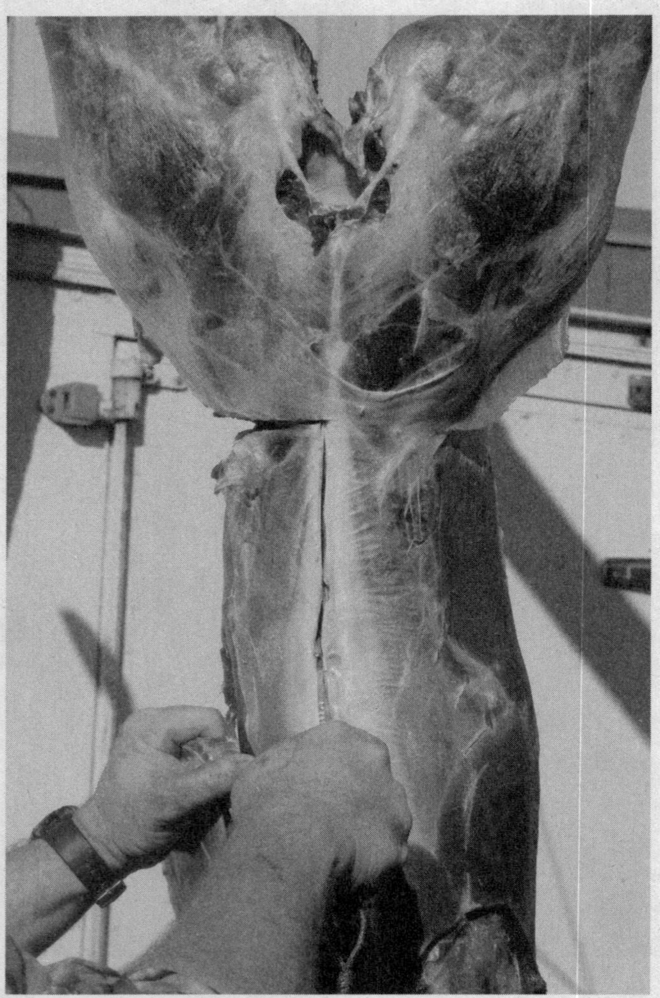

Then make a cut along the side of the backbone.

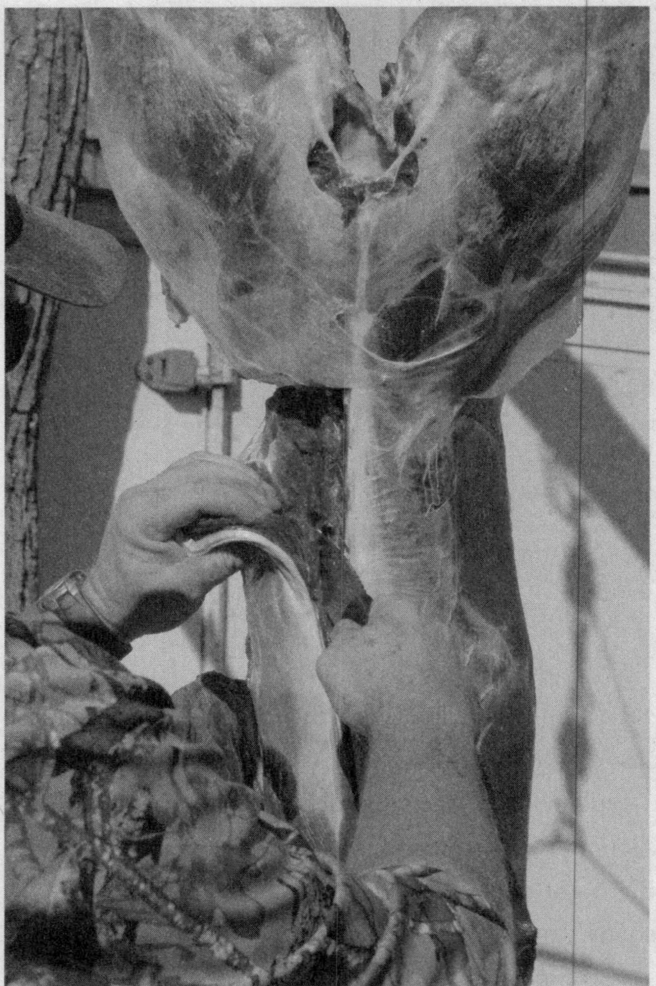

Peel out the loin.

The third step is to remove the hindquarters from the front quarter or rib cage. Cut the hindquarter off at the joint, starting the cut through the flank, making the cut on both sides to the backbone.

Cut through the backbone with a meat saw. Again be careful to not drop the front rib sections.

On a large deer you may want help in holding the front sections while making the cut, or slide a table or other support under the carcass. The hindquarters produce rump roasts, roasts, or round steaks. The shank produces soup bones, stew, and ground meat. Remove the hindquarters from the gambrel and place on a sturdy worktable. Saw

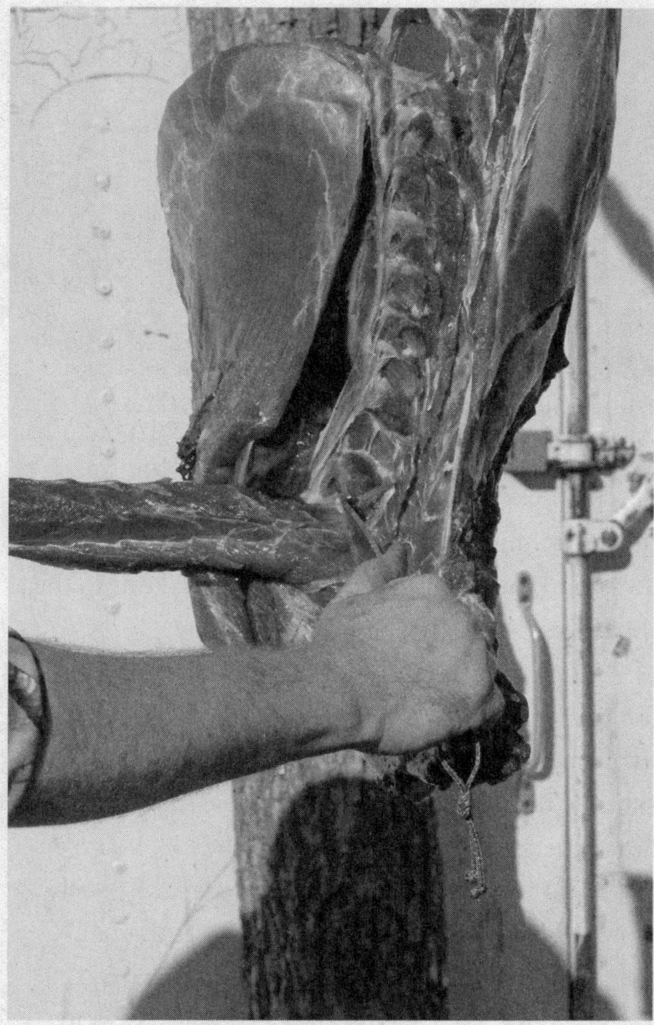

Finish cutting off the loin and then repeat for the opposite side.

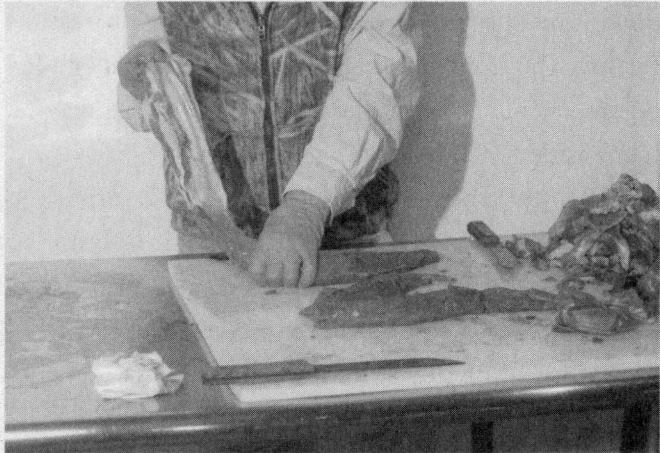

Peel the back fat away from the loin, using a boning knife to start the cut, then pull away with your hands. The loins can be left whole for smoking or cut into steaks for grilling.

Saw the backbone and rib cage away from the hindquarters.

down the center of the backbone to produce two hindquarters. Then bone out the meat, using a sharp boning-style knife. Simply cut around the bones to remove them, following the natural division lines of the muscles. Then cut into steaks or roasts as desired. The steaks will be round steaks as they are cut from the "round" of the hindquarter. You can also use a meat saw to saw the hindquarters into more traditional steaks.

The remaining carcass contains the ribs and neck. Lay the carcass on a table and saw off the front shoulder portion still left on the carcass. This can be made into a shoulder roast or used as ground meat. The neck is cut off and the meat used for stews, soup, or ground meat. Saw the ribs from the backbone, and then saw into three- to four-inch-wide strips.

**Complete Boning Out**

The third method is completely boning out the carcass. This is definitely our favorite venison dressing method. No bones are cut through. Not only do you avoid any possible health problems with CWD, but you end up with no bones to take up space in your freezer, and you don't even need a meat saw. You'll end up with lots of boneless loin, steaks, roasts, and ground meat. In this method the

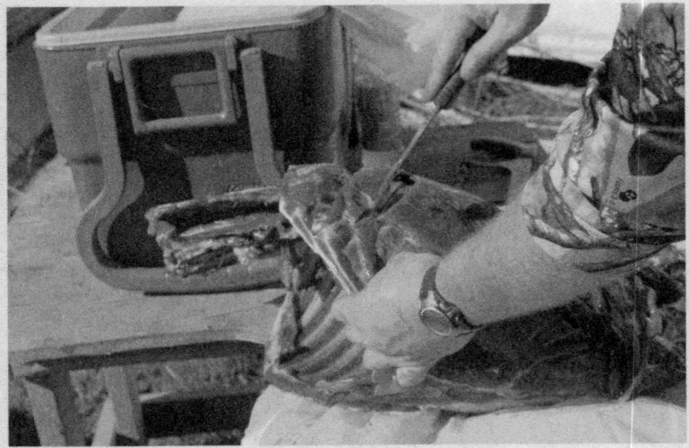
Remove the backbone from the rib cage and saw the rib cage into rib pieces. Or bone out the entire rib cage.

Take down the hindquarters and lay on a sturdy table. Cut into the traditional steaks and roasts or bone out the meat.

deer is normally skinned and boned at the same time, so the skin is left on during the aging process until you're ready to cut up the carcass.

If using this method with a young deer or antlerless deer, the head is even left on the boned-out carcass. Or, you can skin the animal in the normal manner, remove the head if a trophy buck, allow the carcass to age the desired amount of time, and then bone it out. I call this method one-step deer processing.

When using one-step deer processing, the legs are not sawed off before skinning. The deer is hoisted so you can easily reach the front legs and the legs are encircled with a cut just behind the knees, then a cut made on the inside of each front leg from

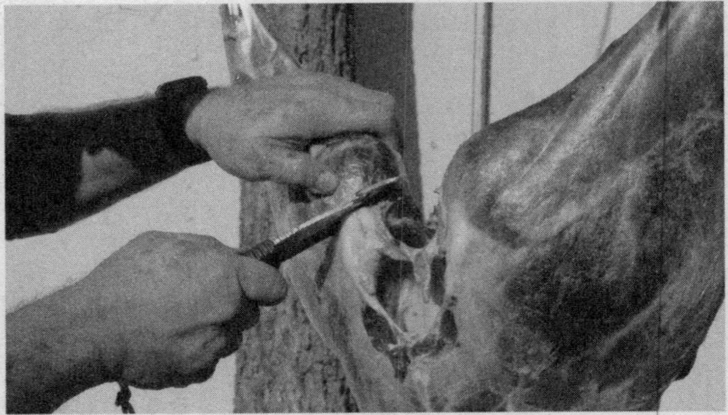
You can also completely bone out the carcass, leaving the skin and head attached for disposal and with no bones to fill your freezer.

the encircling cut to the throat cut made during field dressing. The front legs are then skinned out to the shoulders.

The carcass is lowered so you can easily reach the rear legs. Encircle the rear legs, make a cut from the ham field-dressing cut to the encircling cut and skin the hind legs down to the hams, then skin down the hams. When you reach the tail, you can either cut it off or skin it out. Either is fairly easily done. If you're saving the skin, peel out the tail.

Continue peeling and skinning down to the head. You can remove the head with the skin attached and leave the carcass to age, or continue the process. If the latter, merely allow the skin to hang down over the head and begin the boning process. Remove the front shoulders in the same manner as before, slicing between them and the rib cage. Lay them aside to be deboned later.

Remove the flanks. These have little meat, and are often bloody from the killing shot, but some meat can usually be salvaged. Cut away any bloody meat. The flank pieces are often used in ground meat or stews. Remove the loins by cutting between the backbone and ribs on the sides, beginning at the juncture or where the hindquarter ends at the backbone. Cut down toward the neck until you can peel out the loin pieces. Remove the tenderloins inside the carcass and against the backbone.

While the carcass is still hanging, lower it so you can reach the hindquarters easily and debone the meat from the hindquarters. This is fairly easy to do, if you follow the muscle joints, cutting around the bones with a boning knife as necessary.

Debone the neck. My nephew, Morgan, even likes to get the meat between each rib for his ground jerky. The final step is to debone the front shoulders. All that's left is the deboned carcass and skin.

Clean all pieces of meat to remove any hair. Cut away any bloody or excessively fatty areas, or those with gristle or excess sinew. The latter is a common problem with venison and other wild game.

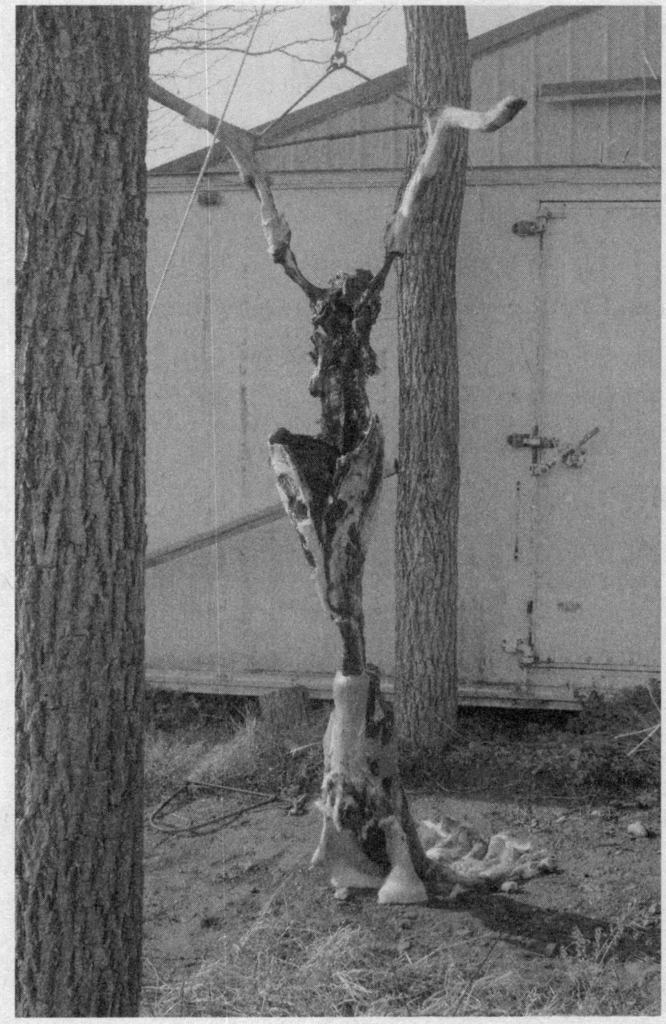
The resulting boned-out carcass with skin ready for disposal.

**Ground Meat**

We usually put all the boned meat into the ground-meat pot, except for the loins and tenderloins. These are saved for the grill or smoker. We also usually save one hindquarter to cut into round steaks for baked steak, Swiss steak, and stroganoff.

We eat a lot of ground venison in chili, tacos, taco salads, and summer sausage. For more on making your own summer sausage, see another one of our books, *The Complete Guide to Sausage Making.* We also make a lot of deer jerky from the ground meat. For more on making your own deer jerky see my book, *The Complete Jerky Book.*

Deer meat fat quickly becomes rancid, so cut all possible fat, sinew, and gristle from the meat to be ground. Then cut the meat into chunks or strips that will go through your meat grinder. Wear food-safe gloves at all times while working up and grinding deer meat.

Venison makes great ground meat for chili, tacos, and summer sausage. Make sure you trim off all fat and sinew.

**Getting Rid of Gamey Flavors**

Some people don't like the taste of venison, and indeed some venison meat can be quite strong. An overnight marinade can be used to help cut some of the gamey flavor. Some like to marinade roasts and steaks in milk. One simple marinade is soy sauce and lemon pepper. Or you can use commercial marinades. We like teriyaki marinade on our grilled loin steaks.

## Big Game

In addition to whitetail deer, other North American big game includes mule deer, antelope, the various bighorn sheep, mountain goats, bear, buffalo, elk, moose, caribou, javelina, and wild hog. The method of field dressing and butchering depends on the game species, the size of the game, and the location where killed. Regardless, the animal must be field dressed as quickly as possible. Smaller animals, such as antelope and small mule deer, can be field dressed in much the same manner as for whitetails. If antelope hunting in hot weather, quickly skin, gut, and quarter the carcass; then place the quarters in a cooler. If this is not possible, hang in the shade and cover with a cheesecloth game bag.

Bigger game, including elk, moose, buffalo, sheep, and goats, require a somewhat different approach due to their size and/or location of the kill. Again, the first step is to immediately field dress. A couple of sections of rope and a come-along can be used to help hold the legs up and apart for this step. You'll also need a sturdy knife and a packable game saw.

You can skin and then quarter the animal, or usually in the case of backpacking and horsepacking, leave the skin on until you get to camp, where the sections can then be skinned and placed in cheesecloth bags, and then into packbags for packing out. If you prefer to skin out the carcass and a handy and sturdy tree limb is available, you can partially hoist the carcass for skinning. Or leave the carcass on the ground—skin one side, roll the carcass over, and skin the opposite.

The carcass is then cut into quarters for easier transporting—whether on your back, horseback, by boat, plane, or other means. With this method you can reduce an elk to more manageable pieces between 65 and 130 pounds each. You can even cut larger animals into six or seven sections. If allowed, boning out the meat can reduce the weight even more. Make sure you understand the game laws in the state the animal is taken, regarding transportation of game meat.

There are several different methods of quartering. The first is to simply cut into four quarters. Bend a front leg and cut through the skin at the joint. Use a knife and saw to remove the lower leg. Repeat for the opposite front leg. Some like to remove the lower portion of the back legs as well, especially if backpacking. Some feel, however, that leaving them in place makes it easier to secure the back legs to a pack or pack frame, but they do tend to catch on tree limbs and brush.

Skin the neck and saw off the head. If the animal is a trophy, after field dressing skin out the cape, taking care to leave plenty of skin in place. If not a trophy, it's still best to skin out the neck area. Cut off the head with the cape attached.

Spread the carcass as much as possible and cutting from the inside to help prevent getting hair on the meat, make a cut between the third and fourth ribs on each side to the backbone. Using a saw cut through the backbone and complete the cut through the skin.

Make a cut through the skin, down the center of the backbone on the front half and peel the skin

Big game, especially the larger species often require a somewhat different approach to field dressing, especially those taken in the mountains and back country.

away on either side of the cut. Prop the half in place and saw through the backbone. Repeat for the rear half and you have four quarters ready to transport.

If you need smaller sections, say of a moose, it can be cut into six sections. After removing the head and lower legs, saw down the middle of the backbone to create two halves. Then cut just behind the front leg and just in front of the rear leg on each side. You can also cut off the neck creating seven pieces.

Several years ago a horse-packing guide showed me an alternative method of packing out elk quarters. It's quick and easy and doesn't require a packsaddle. Quarter in the same manner as before, but do not cut through the skin on the spine, leaving the quarters attached at the spine by the skin. The

Quite often you'll have to pack the carcass out on your back or by horse.

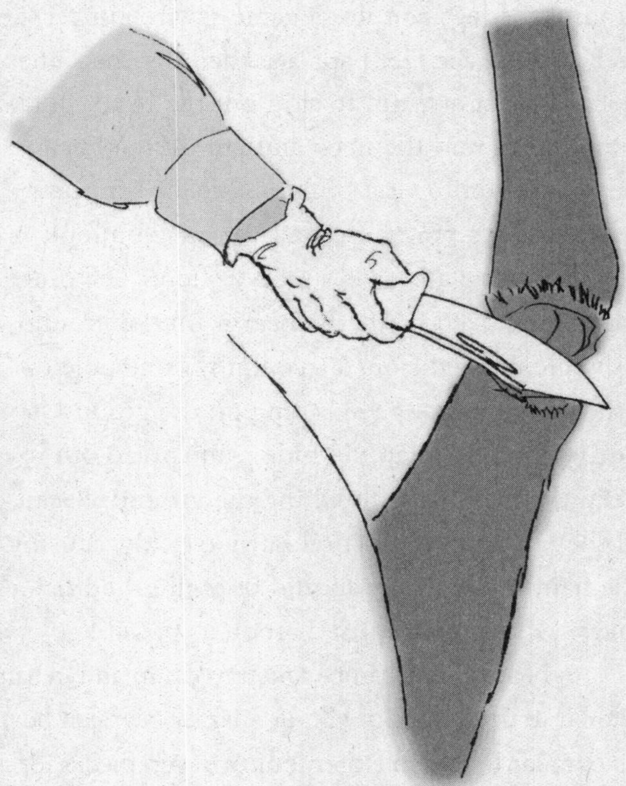

After field dressing, first step is to remove the lower legs. Use a sharp knife or a meat saw to cut through tendons.

entire half can be placed on a horse, skin side down and the legs of the carcass tied with a strap running under the horse's belly.

Wild hogs and javelinas are usually field dressed and skinned in the same manner that pork is. Wild hogs can carry diseases; make sure you wear protective gloves while field dressing, skinning, and quartering. Buffalo is done up in the same manner as for beef.

Some states require a bear be taken to a check station whole, or after field dressing. In either case, field dress in the usual manner. In many instances the bear skin, as well as the unskinned head is saved to be taken to the taxidermist. Continue the field dressing by cutting to the base of the chin and then make a cut in the hide from each paw to the centerline cut. Do not skin out the feet pads. Instead skin around the legs and use a game saw to cut off the feet, leaving the feet pads attached. By the same token do not attempt to skin out the head, but skin out around the neck and cut off the head. Bears have quite a bit of fat, especially on their backs and it's pretty greasy. Any way you look at it, skinning a bear is a messy chore. The hide can be removed while the bear is on the ground, or while hoisted from a tree limb, game pole or other item, although skinning on the ground is fairly easy, just keep the hide well spread out to keep the meat from touching the ground. Because of the fat, bear hides spoil fairly quickly, causing the hair to slip. They should be well salted or taken to the taxidermist as soon as possible.

A bear carcass can be taken to camp and cut up similar to deer, hogs or elk, or a larger bear can be cut similar to elk, in either four or seven pieces for transporting. In this case, first cut off the neck, then saw down the spine, finally cutting the two halves into thirds.

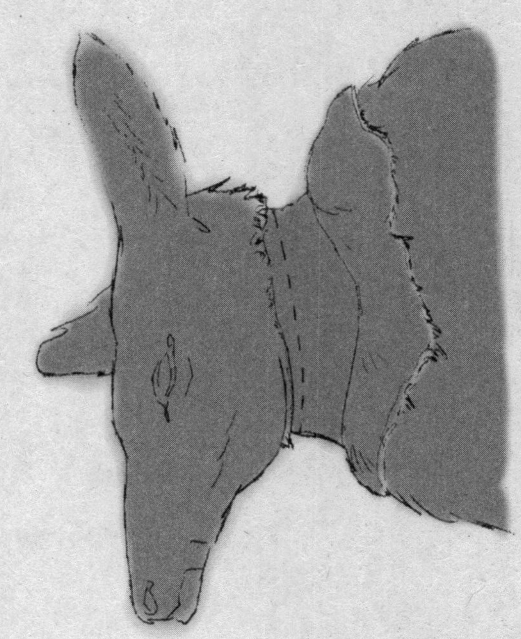

Cape the animal for a mount, or cut around the skin where the neck joins the head and cut off the head.

Spread the carcass and working from the inside, cut between the third and fourth ribs on both sides, cut through the skin as well. Then saw through the ribs and cut through the skin.

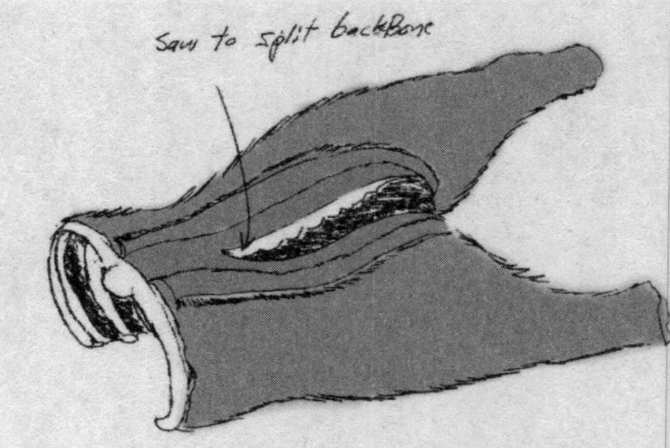


Turn the front and rear halves over and cut through the skin down the back bone. Peel back the skin on either side of the cut and use the meat saw to saw each half into quarters.

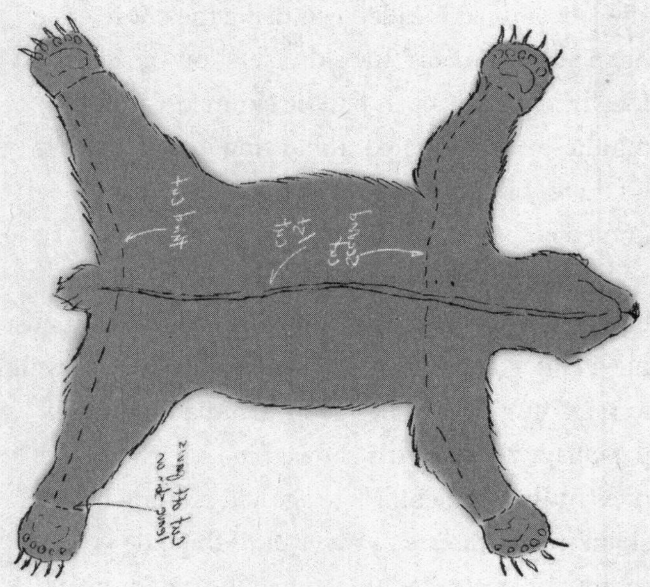

A bear is usually case skinned, leaving the head and feet attached to the pelt for the taxidermist. The carcass is then cut up similar to most other big game.

### Rendering Fat

The old timers often rendered the fat from game animals and used it for cooking. The taste will vary greatly, depending on the species and even the individual animal. To render, cut the fat into small, one-half inch chunks and slowly cook in a large skillet, pouring off the fat as it is rendered. Pour into sterilized fruit jars and keep refrigerated or frozen.

## Small Game

Many hunters grew up hunting small game such as rabbits and squirrels. Today small game hunting is still mighty popular. Both rabbits and squirrels make delicious eating.

Wild cottontails, hares, and even jackrabbits can be field dressed in the same manner as tame rabbits. Skinning in the case manner will result in a rabbit skin that can be tanned, and they do make great glove liners. Wild rabbits were common table fare on our Missouri farm in the '50s and I was taught a much simpler and quicker method of dressing them. It takes only seconds, and is a snap—pun intended. Make a cut just through the skin on the back of the rabbit. Grasp the skin on either side of the cut with your hands and simply peel both front and back off, leaving the skin on the head. Cut off the feet, tail and head. Make a cut from the anus and through the rib cage, severing the intestines at the throat. Give the carcass a swing and snap and the intestines will pop right out. Cut the intestines off at the anus and wash the cavity clean.

Caution: Rabbits can become infected with Tularemia, often called rabbit fever, tick fever, deer fly fever, or Pahvant Valley Plague. Caused by a bacterium, the disease can be transferred to humans by handling infected rabbits, or inhaling the bacteria on the fur, as well as eating the improperly cooked meat of infected rabbits. Although Tularemia is fairly rare in the United States, be wary of rabbits that appear sick, do not try to run away, or act strangely. The liver of an infected rabbit will have many tiny white spots, and it may also be swollen. The old-timers I grew up with wouldn't hunt rabbits until sometime after a hard freeze, feeling this killed the ticks as well as any sick rabbits. I don't, however, know of any scientific fact proving this. Regardless, to be safe, wear protective rubber or disposable plastic gloves while dressing rabbits.

Squirrels are an extremely popular southern table fare, but how they're prepared depends on the age. Young squirrels can be pan fried much like chicken and are tender and delicious. Older squirrels often take longer cooking to make them less tough and more palatable, and are more commonly used in stews and other means of slow cooking. Before you start dressing or skinning the critters, first determine whether they're young or old-timers. This can be done to some degree by

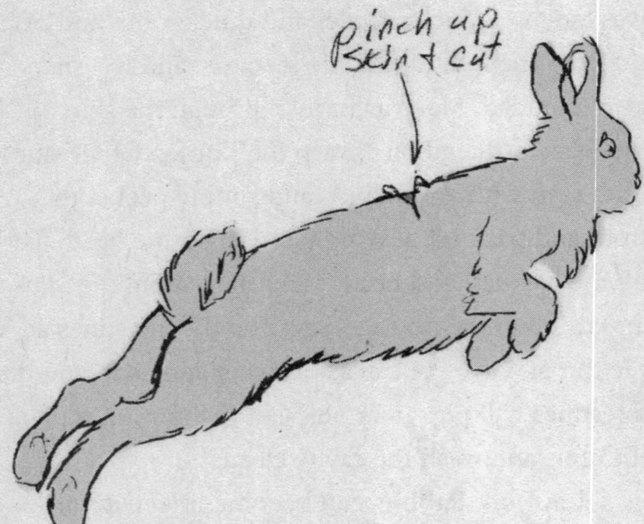


The simplest method of skinning a rabbit is to make a cut through the skin across the middle of the back. Next grasp the cut hide with both hands and peel the two skin sections off. Eviscerate, cut off head, tail and feet and you're done.

their size, but not necessarily, and grey squirrels will usually be smaller than fox squirrels. The testicles on older males will be fairly large. Young males will have less developed testicles. Older females will have darkened teats, with the hair worn off around them, evidence of nursing.

Of all the wild game, squirrels are some of the toughest to skin. Skinning as soon as you can after the animal is killed can make the chore easier. As the carcass cools, the skin "sets" on the animal. Ideally, the squirrel should be skinned within 30 minutes of being killed. If hunting in hot weather it's doubly important to skin and field dress immediately.

Squirrels also present another problem. The hair easily comes off and adheres to the flesh, almost like being glued in place. It can be a real mess trying to pick off the hairs. My good friend and hunting personality Brad Harris showed me a trick to help prevent the problem. He suggested soaking before skinning the carcass in water until the hide is thoroughly wet, Brad this to me illustrated on one hunt by dipping the animal in a creek. A bucket of water will also do. Regardless, make sure the hair and skin are soaking wet.

A squirrel can be case skinned, hanging from a tree limb or other item with a string tied around the back ankles. There is, however, an easier way I learned from my granddad many years ago. Sometimes called the Sioux Indian method, it's quick and easy once you get the hang of it. You'll need a good sharp knife.

Place the squirrel on its belly and bend the tail back. Cut from the underside of the tail and next to the anus, completely through the tail bone. Be careful not to cut through the skin on the top of the tail. Make two angled cuts away from the tail on the flanks, leaving a V-shaped section of skin attached to the tail.

Place the squirrel on its back and place your foot on the tail and as close to the body as possible. Grasp a hind leg in each hand and slowly pull the carcass up. This will take a bit of effort until the skin begins to pull off. As you pull, the skin will tear apart at the center of the belly. It will peel off the front legs and up to the head. You will have to work you finger under the skin around the legs and

Young squirrels can be tender, old squirrels tough. It's important to determine the approximate age. The teats on females will be blackened and the hair worn off. Older males have larger testicles.

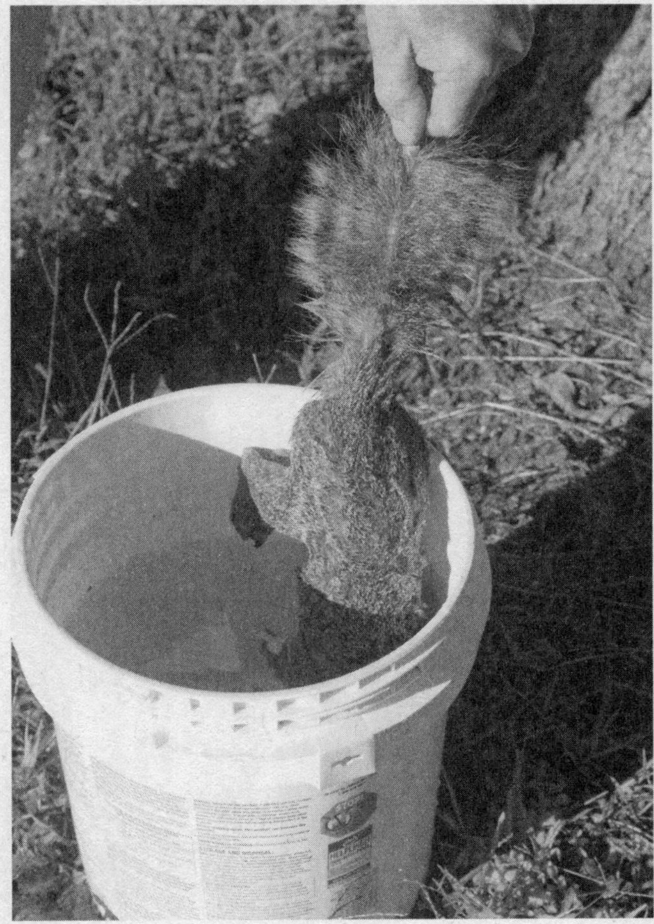

To keep hair off the carcass first dip and soak thoroughly in water.

Make additional cuts on the flank to leave the tail and a flap of skin.

With the squirrel on its back, stand on the tail, grasp a hind leg in each hand, and pull up to peel off the front half of the skin.

Place squirrel on its back and cut through the bone of the tail from the underside, but not through the skin on top of the tail.

Use your fingers to work the hide off around the legs and neck area.

between the legs and neck to completely pull the skin off to the front feet.

Stand on the tail and grasp the point of skin on the belly and peel it up. It may take both hands to peel the skin up and over both hind legs to the back feet. You should end up with the skin completely off the body, but attached to the feet and head. Cut off the feet, head and tail.

Make a cut through the pelvic bone and up to and through the rib-cage to the neck area, being careful not to cut into the internal organs. Pull out the internal organs and wash carcass thoroughly.

# Smoking Wild Game

## BIG GAME

Much of the game meat that reaches your table will probably be from large animals, and most of it from deer. The venison of the ubiquitous whitetail and the western mule deer counts among the most popular and flavorful of big-game meat. Smoking will allow you to enhance and vary the flavor of good venison and make older, tougher meat more fit for the table.

Curing and marinating offer countless new ways for you to enjoy your game. The extent to which you cure and marinate will depend upon personal taste and can only be determined by experiment.

**Curing and marinating**

You may already be using a cure on your game without even realizing it, for many hunters, when faced with the strong odors of some game meat, soak their catch overnight in salt water. Removing gamy odors and tastes is only one reason for using cures and marinades. A second reason is to flavor, and a third—and sometimes the most important—is to tenderize. It's not hard to see how these two preparations can be used effectively on almost any game animal you bring home.

Curing is a good way to deal with the meat of older animals. After all, you can't put the whole thing into stew. The action of the cure will break down the tough fiber of the meat and make it more palatable.

Just as with butcher meats, there are many different ways to use cures on game, not all of which are, in the strictest sense, curing. Simply rubbing the meat with dry-cure mix or seasoned salt before smoking, for instance, is often all that is needed to give a subtle flavoring to good meat.

Since game meats will vary greatly in the amount of tenderizing, flavoring, and deodorizing they need, curing time will have to be tailored to the meat. A few experiments on small pieces should let you know what cures work best.

Here are some general guidelines that you should follow in the curing of big game.

| CUT | CURING TIME | |
|---|---|---|
| | *Regular Cure* | *Hard Cure* |
| Chops and cuts less than 1 inch | 6 to 10 hours | 4 days |
| Steaks, 1 to 2 inches | 12 to 24 hours | 4 to 8 days |
| Roasts | 1 to 3 days | 8 to 12 days |

Use the same time for either brine or dry cures, overhaul several times during curing, and remove all salt from the surface of the meat following curing. If rinsing in water is not enough, soak meat ten to fifteen minutes, then scrub with a stiff brush. Allow plenty of time to dry.

Use marinades to take the place of cures. They will remove odors, tenderize meat, and add the flavoring of whatever seasonings you put in them. Most game meat will require basting and a marinade can also work well in this capacity. After picking up meat juices in basting, the same liquid will nicely flavor gravies or stews. If you are unsure of how marinade will taste with a particular game meat, experiment. You'll often be pleasantly surprised.

Smaller cuts of meat are usually marinated six to ten hours; roasts take about twenty-four hours. It is not necessary to cover the meat completely with solution. To ensure overall absorption, turn the meat several times. After marinating, allow one to two hours for the liquid to drain from the meat before smoking.

Most persons find the fat of big game has too strong a flavor. Body fat is also the source of much of the unpleasant smell associated with some meat. If allowed to remain on the flesh, the fat will impart this strong flavor as it melts during smoking. For this reason, it is best to cut away as much of the fat as you possibly can.

One possible exception to this is a very young bear. The fat of a young bear is not as strong as that of other large game. It may be left on the meat without appreciably altering the taste.

Because all this built-in basting material is cut away, and because few wild animals have much fat throughout their meat anyway, basting is usually necessary. Butter, margarine, or cooking oil serve well. Bacon or salted fat pork may also be used, draped over the meat to provide continuous basting. The area covered with bacon is not as readily exposed to smoke. To compensate, remove bacon during the last hour or two of smoking.

**Quick and Easy**

Cold smoking for flavor is the fastest way to enjoy smoked game meat. This can be done with or without a cure.

The cold smoking times given below are for a range of flavoring that will suit the average palate.

**Cold Smoking Big Game (Under 120°F.)**

| *Cut* | *Smoking Time* |
|---|---|
| Chops and cuts less than 1 inch | ½ to 1 ½ hours |
| Steaks, 1 to 2 inches | ¾ to 2 hours |
| Roasts | ½ to ¾ hour for each inch of thickness |

Meat smoked in this way must still be cooked before eating. Take it directly from the smoker and add to your favorite recipe.

**Hot Smoking**

Smoke cooking big game is easy using temperatures of 200° to 225°F. If your smoker can't reach this heat, lower temperatures are acceptable, but it will take longer to fully cook your meat. When possible, use a meat thermometer to determine when your meat is cooked to your satisfaction. That's the most reliable way of accounting for a smoker's variability of temperature.

As a general rule, your game will be fully cooked when internal temperature in the thickest part of the meat reaches 160°F. Gauge when smaller cuts are done by examining them. If you want a stronger smoke flavor, begin with a brief period of cold smoking.

**Heart, Liver, Tongue**

In some instances, these parts may well be the choicest meat you get off your game, and a good smoking will bring out the delicious best in them.

Prepare them as you would the same part from a domestic animal. The hearts of wild game are generally bigger than those of domestic animals, so slightly increased curing and smoking times may be in order. Tongue, especially, should be given a thorough curing and smoking.

**Jerky**

Any lean game meat can be made into jerky. Even lower-grade cuts will work well. If the meat is unusually tough, try slicing the jerky strips across the grain of the meat, as opposed to the regular, with-the-grain cut.

**Storage**

Big-game meat may be frozen at 0°F. or less with little loss of flavor. The larger the piece of meat, the longer it will last without deterioration. Be sure to seal each piece securely in good freezer wrap. Improper wrapping will cause freezer burn and drying out of the meat.

Here are some approximate time limits for the frozen storage of smoked game meat.

| | |
|---|---|
| Ground meat | 3 months |
| Chops and thin steaks | 5 months |
| Heart, liver, and tongue | 5 months |
| Cubes and stew meat | 7 months |
| Steaks | 9 months |
| Roasts | 12 months |

**Big-Game Characteristics**

Curing and smoking times for all animals can be judged primarily by the size of the cut of meat you're using. Individual animals, however, have characteristics that may influence how you prepare them. Below is a list of the most commonly bagged big game, giving tips about handling their meat.

**Antelope and Sheep.** The pronghorn antelope and the bighorn and Dall sheep can be classed together for the excellence of their meat, and no one could fault you if you were hesitant about tampering with their flavor. For a subtle taste difference that you're sure to appreciate, however, try a brief smoking of half to one and a half hours, after cooking. Mild cures also offer a good flavor variation.

**Bear.** The dark, coarse meat of this animal is fatty and subject to the trichinae parasite, just as is pork. Always fully cook or freeze under conditions that will make meat safe. The loin is usually the choicest cut. Roast the meat of younger animals. Braising or stewing is the best way to handle older animals that have developed tough meat.

All bear meat can benefit from a cure. Marinades are also good. Cold smoke roasts after cooking.

**Deer.** This most popular big-game animal provides one of the best smoked meats. Venison is excellent when simply smoked after cooking. Curing and marinating can also be used effectively to emphasize and vary flavor. Lengthy cures take too much moisture from the meat, so, unless you're preserving it, stick with flavoring cures or marinades.

The rump, shoulder, breast, or neck are good when braised; other cuts make good roasts. The liver and heart are very good eating. Cold-smoke or smoke after cooking. Smaller pieces may be hot smoked.

**Elk and Moose.** Although similar to beef in taste, the meat of these animals is darker and drier. Baste frequently or use bacon. Handle as you would venison.

Bear

## SMALL GAME

There seem to be two distinct categories of small game: (1) Those animals that nearly everyone considers edible; and (2) Those that most hunters would eat only on a bet

Most everyone would put rabbit and squirrel into the first category, but the acceptance of other small game as table fare fluctuates widely between geographic regions and between individuals.

Nothing short of a gourmet chef will do more for your small game than smoking. Combined with curing and marinating, smoking will tenderize, remove unsavory tastes and odors, add flavor, and retain moisture. With the help of your smoker, you may just find that all small game belong in that first category.

### Curing and Marinating

Animals living in the ground often acquire a musty, gamy odor that causes people to turn up their nose at the thought of eating them. Soaking in brine is an effective way of combating such unpleasant smells as well as helping the meat in various other ways.

Almost any small game will taste better if cured in brine. Six to ten hours is all that is required to cure parts; small whole animals—such as squirrel—need twenty-four to thirty-six hours. Larger whole animals—such as rabbit or woodchuck—should cure twenty-four to forty-eight hours.

Savory marinades can also be used. Wine, which is a central ingredient in many marinades, offers an excellent complement to the taste of small game. When game soaks in a marinade of wine and seasoning, the subtle flavor of the marinade is absorbed into the meat. All alcohol evaporates during the smoking or cooking process, but the flavor that remains is delicious, especially with rabbit, squirrel, or opossum.

Marinate parts about six to ten hours. Whole animals will have to soak eighteen to twenty-four hours. As with anything you're trying for the first time, it's best to make your first experiments on a few parts, rather than on a whole animal.

### Basting

Rabbit and squirrel, the small game that will most often find their way to your table, are both very lean and will need basting. Butter or cooking oil will work, but, for an extra special touch, use a marinade containing dry red wine. Place a small pan beneath the smoking meat to catch the marinade runoff and use this liquid later as a flavoring in stew or gravy.

Bacon is also a good basting material for small game when simply draped over a whole animal during smoking. Wrap with strips of bacon and fasten with a toothpick.

### Cook, then Smoke

A brief period of cold smoking after cooking is a reliable method of flavoring game. Smoking times of a half to two hours are usually enough for flavoring. Larger, whole animals will take up to four hours.

This fast method is also a good way of testing smoke flavor in meat. Say that you're looking for a way to spruce up the taste of woodchuck and have decided to try smoking. Cook the animal first with your favorite recipe, then take off some of the meat and smoke it at 100° to 120°F. just long enough to add a mild flavor. Compare the two.

### Cold Smoking and Hot Smoking

Only you will be able to determine what degree of smoke flavor suits you best with each type of game meat. That will involve trial and error. The cold-smoking times provided below are based on the amount of smoke necessary to achieve a range of flavors for a particular size of meat. With small game, there are really only two broad sizes of meat to work with—the whole animal, or parts of the whole animal. In neither instance is meat very thick. For most palates, a half to two hours will offer a sufficient range of flavor with parts. One to four hours, depending on size, will flavor whole animals.

Use temperatures of 100° to 120°F. Meat must still be cooked before eating.

Because meat is never too heavy on small game, it can usually be smoke-cooked in a minimum of time. Temperatures above 200°F. are best, but lower temperatures will do the job in a longer time. It is difficult to use a meat thermometer on small game, so inspection of the meat is the only way to tell when it is cooked. Meat will turn brown on the outside and lose its raw appearance on the interior. It will also become firm and will be somewhat loose around the joints.

## WILD BIRDS

Many hunters have had bad experiences with cooking game birds and consequently relegate them to stews or some other method of vigorous cooking that successfully masks their flavor.

There are cooking problems inherent in wildfowl to be sure. Taste-influencing factors, such as the bird's diet and its age, have left their mark before you even bring it home. Quick and proper field dressing is also important. But regardless of these influences, all game birds are good fare for your smoker. Their naturally lean, dry meat lends itself to preserving or cooking at low temperatures.

If you consider that your bird can be smoked after cooking, or the raw bird can be cold-smoked or smoke-cooked, add to this the variety of flavor combinations possible with curing and marinating and it's easy to see how your smoker opens up countless new ways to appreciate wildfowl.

### Curing and marinating

Both of these preparations are useful for flavoring, but more important with some birds is how they can be tenderized and how unpleasant tastes and odors can be removed. Either curing or marinating will go a long way toward making birds of questionable quality more palatable. Old birds can be tenderized appreciably in this way. Of course, even tender young birds can benefit from these effects.

Cure game birds as you would domestic fowl. Brining is best. Simply place bird—or parts—in a crock, cover with brine, and weigh it down to keep the meat submerged. Cure small birds overnight, or six to ten hours. Medium-size birds should cure one to two days, and larger birds—such as turkey, duck, or geese—one to three days. Overhaul several times during the cure.

The size of the piece in question will also have some bearing on the length of the cure. Frequently, game birds are cut into parts—breasts, backs, drumsticks, thighs—or simply halved or quartered. Unless unusually large, parts can be cured in six to ten hours. Halves may take up to twenty-four hours.

Marinades can take the place of cures for those who don't want a salt taste. They don't have all the preservative powers of a cure, nor do they tenderize to the same degree, but they work wonders at seasoning your meat.

Whole birds are difficult to marinate, so it's best to work with parts. To determine how marinades can affect the taste of wild fowl, and whether or not they suit you, experiment with several parts of your next bird. Using one of the marinades or your own concoction, soak them for varying lengths of time and use different marinades, then smoke-cook them all for the same amount of time and put them to the taste test.

### Basting

No matter how you smoke a game bird, it will require basting. Unlike their domestic counterparts, wild birds don't have layers of fat throughout their flesh to keep them moist during cooking. Consequently, you have to take greater care to keep the meat from drying out. For meat that will only spend a brief time in the smoker, basting with butter, margarine, or cooking oil will do the job. Birds that need special attention can be covered with bacon. Old birds will certainly need special attention, also birds that are especially lean, parts from which the skin has been removed, and almost any whole bird that will be in the smoker for an extended period of time.

To use bacon, drape the strips over the entire bird, just over the breast, or tuck them between thighs and breast. For birds suspended in the smoker, secure the bacon with toothpicks. Remove the bacon toward the end of the smoking period to allow skin to color.

**Giblets**

When dressing your bird, be sure to save the heart, gizzard, and liver. These tasty morsels should be simmered until done and then smoked. Simmering wild-bird giblets not only prepares them for smoking, but produces a savory stock that will come in handy in whatever recipe you use to cook your bird. Wings, necks, and even tough thighs can be simmered along with the giblets to produce this broth. The reason this liquid is so important with wildfowl is that the birds give up so little fat while cooking. The stock derived from the giblets is a natural for gravies, stuffing, or any necessary flavoring chore.

Smoke giblets at 100° to 120°F. for one to two hours. Dice the finished product for gravy or stuffing, make livers into pate, or create exotic hors d'oeuvres.

**Cook, then Smoke**

Many cookbooks call for wildfowl to be roasted, broiled, or braised. Birds prepared in any of these ways may then be cold-smoked at 70° to 90°F. for one to four hours. This time range provides a mild to strong flavoring.

**Cold Smoking and Hot Smoking**

If you have not cured your meat, rub it with seasoned salt before smoking. Spread parts, flattened small birds, or intact whole birds out on the oiled smoking racks. Smoke at 70° to 90°F. for one to four hours. The skin will turn a light brown. Remove and cook or finish cooking with a hot smoke.

Raise smoker temperature to 200° to 225°F. to smoke-cook. A meat thermometer should be used in whole birds to determine when they are done. Pieces, however, will have to be inspected. Incidentally, the tendons of a wild bird are stronger than those of a domestic bird. Twisting the leg to see if the joint comes apart is not a valid way of testing if a wild bird is cooked. Instead, press the meat to see if it is firm; also inspect the interior.

If you start your bird at a high smoker temperature, it may be cooked before it has had enough smoke. A preliminary cold smoking will strengthen the flavor.

Inspect meat periodically to check for drying. Baste several times before smoking. Lay bacon over whole birds or especially lean pieces. There will be little or no drippings from your bird, but a shallow drip pan is still a good precaution, if only to catch the basting runoff. Marinades are excellent to use for basting.

**Storage**

Usually the problem with game birds is that they do not contain enough meat. If you should be so fortunate as to have a surplus, it may be frozen without loss of flavor. Because there is so little salted fat to become rancid, cured wild birds hold up better under freezing than do cured domestic birds.

# Old-Time Jerky Making

No matter what the main ingredient was or is—mastodon, elk, deer, African or Australian game, beef, fish, you name it—the old-fashioned method of making jerky has been around for a long time. Old-time jerky is still easy to make and still provides a great food source. In the old days, jerky making was very simple. The Native Americans simply cut thin strips of meat from game they had killed, then hung the strips over racks made of thin branches. In the dry Southwest and the Plains, meat dried quickly and easily with the use of this method. In the North, a small, smoky fire was often used to speed the drying process. Not only did this help the drying process, but it also kept away the blowflies. In the Northwest, smoke houses were constructed to protect the meat and aid in the drying process. If the Native Americans had access to salt, it was applied as well. The Native Americans also dried salmon, placing them on long racks as they removed fish from the fish wheels in the rivers.

One of my favorite outdoor writers from earlier days was Colonel Townsend Whelen. This is his description of jerky making:

Jerky is lean meat cut in strips and dried over a fire or in the sun. Cut the lean, fresh red meat in long, wide strips about half an inch thick. Hang these on a framework about 4 to 6 feet off the ground. Under the rack, build a small, slow, smoky fire of any non-resinous wood. Let the meat dry in

The old-time method of jerky making using only the sun has been a tradition in many cultures, including those of the American West.

the sun and wind. Cover it at night or in rain. It should dry in several days.

The fire should not be hot enough to cook the meat since its chief use is to keep flies away. When jerked, the meat will be hard, more or less black outside, and will keep almost indefinitely away from damp and flies.

It is best eaten just as it is; just bite off a chunk and chew. Eaten thus, it is quite tasty. It may also be cooked in stews and is very concentrated and nourishing. A little goes a long way as an emergency ration, but alone it is not good food for long, continued consumption, as it lacks the necessary fat.

Following is a campsite jerky technique I learned from an old-time Wyoming big-game guide.

The traditional Native American method of drying meat for jerky consisted of hanging meat strips over racks made of thin branches. A small, smoky fire under the meat not only kept away insects but also added flavor and aided in the drying process.

One old-time method of preheating jerky strips was to place loops of string through holes cut in the ends of the strips. These were threaded onto a stick and dipped in a pot of boiling water.

A bag or "tent" of cheesecloth was often used to help keep off insects while the jerky dried.

He described his method of making jerky to me as we chewed on some while glassing for elk:

Cut the meat into strips, lay on a flat surface, and sprinkle both sides with black pepper. Lightly sprinkle with salt. Rub the salt and pepper well into all sides of the strips. Cut holes in the ends of the strips and thread white cotton or butchers cord through each hole, tying off into loops. Bring a pot of water to boil and immerse the strips into the boiling water for 15 to 20 seconds, remove, then re-dip.

Hang the strips to dry. If the strips are hung outside in the sunshine, cover them with a cheesecloth tent to keep off insects and make sure they're high enough so dogs and other critters can't get to them. The strips can also be hung on clothesline in a cold, dry room. The strips should be dry in 4 to 5 days.

Another traditional method involves the use of curing salt, an old-time product. It's easy to make your own curing salt. Take 1 pound of canning salt, 6 ounces of Prague powder, 3 ounces of sugar, and 2 ounces of white pepper. You can substitute brown sugar and black pepper. If you like hot jerky, add ground red pepper or cayenne pepper to suit. Mix all together and rub the mix over all the meat slices. Leave in a cool place overnight, then dry. In damp weather, the slices can be dried in an oven or meat smoker.

An old-time oven method is to lay strips in a glass dish, place a drop of Liquid Smoke over each strip, and use a pastry brush to evenly coat each strip. Sprinkle seasoning salt and seasoned pepper over the layer. Add a light sprinkling of sugar and garlic powder if you like garlic. Add another layer of strips, brush with Liquid Smoke, sprinkle with salt and pepper, then add another layer of strips. Continue adding and seasoning until the dish is full or you run out of strips. Cover the dish and set in a refrigerator or cool area (below 40°F) overnight. Dry in an oven set to 200°F or in a dehydrator.

## pemmican

Made from jerky, pemmican was also a staple food of the Native Americans. Another of my favorite old-time writers, George Leonard Herter, in his *Professional Guides' Manual,* published in 1966, stated, "Pemmican properly made is one of the finest foods that you can take into the wilderness or for a survival food in case of atomic bombing. Pemmican keeps indefinitely. Today, in our wonderful atomic age, pemmican is part of the survival ration of the newest United States Air Corps jet bombers."

According to Col. Townsend Whelen, "To make pemmican you start with jerky and shred it by pounding. Then, take a lot of raw animal fat, cut it into small pieces about the size of walnuts, and fry these out in a pan over a slow fire, not letting the grease boil up. When the grease is all out of the lumps, discard these and pour the hot fat over the shredded jerky, mixing the two together until you have about the consistency of ordinary sausage. Then, pack the pemmican in waterproof bags. The Indians used skin bags."

The proportions should be about half lean meat and half rendered fat. The Native Americans also added fruits such as wild grapes, dried berries and beans, corn, herbs, and other items. These added vitamin C, which prevents scurvy as well as other nutrients and gave the pemmican different tastes. To use, place the dried block of pemmican in water and bring to a boil. Herter suggests dropping in some chili powder, soaking some beans overnight, adding them, and then "You will have an excellent chili con carne."

If you want to try making pemmican, the following is a recipe to make approximately 10 pounds.

5 lb. jerky
½ lb. brown sugar
¾ lb. raisins or dried currents
4 lb. melted fat

Pound the jerky until it crumbles, and mix all ingredients together.

If you want to make a more modern version, first run the jerky through a food processor. Then, add ½ cup of raisins, ½ cup of salted peanuts, and ½ cup brown sugar for each pound of jerky. Other dried fruits such as cranberries can also be used. Sugar is optional, a matter of taste. The sugar can

Jerky was often made into pemmican by the Native Americans, utilizing suet cooked to render off the fat, then adding the fat, as well as fruits, herbs, and other ingredients to jerky that had been pulverized. Today you can use a food processor to quickly pulverize the jerky.

Add raisins or other dried fruits and nuts to the pulverized jerky, then stir in the warm, melted fat, adding only enough fat to hold the mixture together. A butter-flavored shortening is a good alternative to bacon grease or rendered suet.

also be replaced with chocolate or any other flavor of chips (butterscotch, semi-sweet, milk chocolate, and so on). Press the mixture into a pan, packing tightly. Pour melted suet or other fat over the mixture, using only enough fat to hold the ingredients together. It's easy to get too much fat. A modern alternative to melted suet or bacon grease is a butter-flavored shortening. Allow the mixture to cool and then cut into squares for storage and use.

To make a chili version, leave out the sugar and dried fruit and stir in chili seasoning with the ground jerky and fat. To use, add a chunk of the chili-flavored pemmican to a pot of cooking beans. This makes a very hardy camp meal.

For long-term storage, it's best to keep your jerky supply in the freezer and make pemmican just before consuming. Except for short periods of time, keep pemmican in the refrigerator, especially in warm weather.

It's possible to make jerky and pemmican using these age-old traditional methods, even in a remote camp, but always follow the safe food processing methods.

# Sliced Muscle-Meat Jerky

The simplest, traditional, method of producing jerky is to use sliced muscle meat. Almost any type of big-game meat can be sliced into jerky, including wild game such as deer, elk, moose, sheep, and antelope. Other meats, such as wild turkey breast, can also be made into jerky slices. Beef is a traditional sliced-jerky meat in many parts of the world, and buffalo was a favorite of early settlers and Native Americans.

In the 1970s I was a young freelance writer and book author with a family to feed. Since we lived on a farm in the Ozarks, venison was a regular food staple. I started making jerky in the old-fashioned, sliced muscle-meat method back then and have been doing so ever since. With several deer usually taken each season, most of one deer would end up being turned into jerky.

Traditional jerky was, and still is, made by cutting muscle meat into slices. Wild game such as deer and elk were and are popular meat choices. Beef is a traditional meat, while the Native Americans utilized buffalo.

## trimming and slicing

Traditionally I've used the hams or rear quarters of venison for old-fashioned, sliced jerky. The hams do provide good meat cuts for other uses, including roasts and hamburgers, but they also slice extremely well for jerky. Then, I use the butcher trimmings, left from cutting the sliced jerky, for ground meat, both for jerky and to cook in chili, tacos, meatloaf, and so forth. Once the rear quarters have been deboned from the carcass, cut the meat into long chunks by simply following the muscles where they are separated by sinew. Cut away any fat, as fat not only doesn't dry properly, but it adds a gamey flavor to the meat. Also cut away as much sinew as possible. Next, using a sharp butcher knife, slice the meat into thin strips, following the grain, not across it.

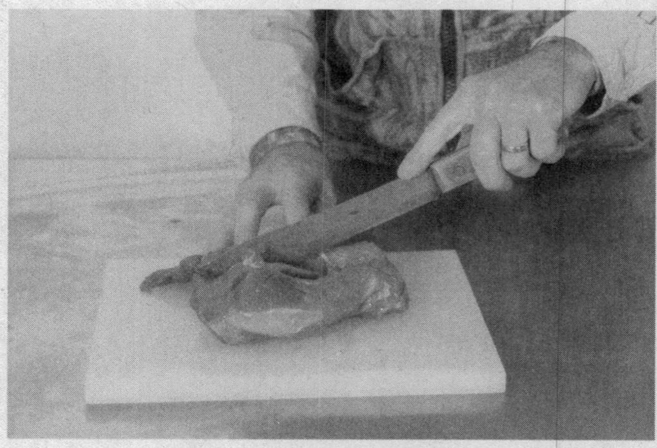

Once the meat has been deboned from the carcass, cut it into long chunks, following the sinew or natural muscle divisions.

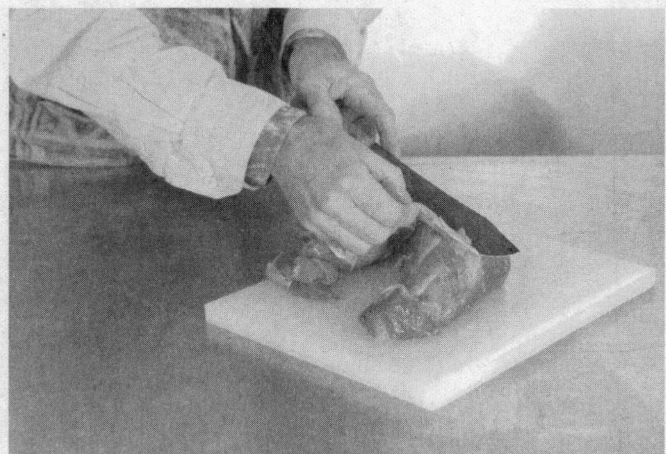

Cut away all fat and sinew.

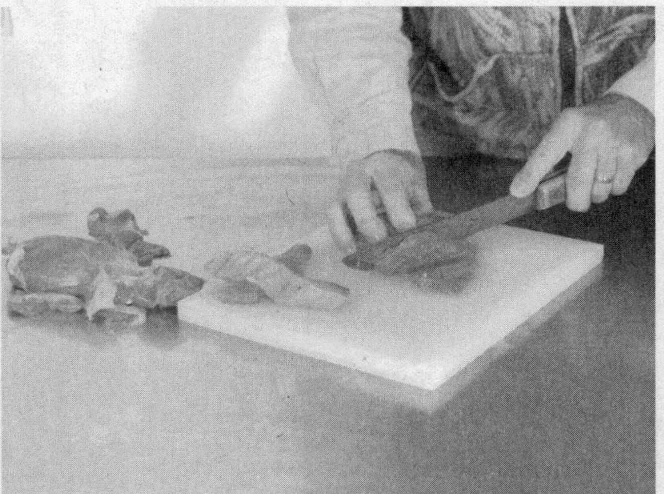

Then, slice into strips of the desired thickness.

Slice into strips either 1/8- or ¼-inch thick. Strips can actually be cut as thick as 3/8 inch, but any thicker and they become extremely hard to dry. The thickness is actually only a matter of taste. It takes longer to dry and cure the thicker strips, but they also tend to turn out less brittle when dried.

The Hi Mountain Jerky Board and stainless steel knife makes it easier to more consistently slice meat to the correct thickness and therefore results in a more consistent drying of the jerky. If a strip of meat is 1/8 inch at one end and 3/8 inch at the opposite end, for instance, it will be difficult for it to dry evenly. The board comes with a lip around the edge that allows you to slice 1/8- or ¼-inch thicknesses. Place the meat on the board and slice holding the knife with the flat side of the blade down on the edge lips.

The simplest and most consistent method of slicing meat is with an electric slicer. Regardless of the method used, for easier slicing, lay the trimmed meat pieces on a cookie sheet or other flat surface, place in the freezer until the meat is partially frozen, (usually about an hour to hour and a half) and then slice.

The Hi Mountain slicing kit includes a wooden board with raised edges to help guide the stainless steel knife (included) for precise 1/8- or ¼-inch slices.

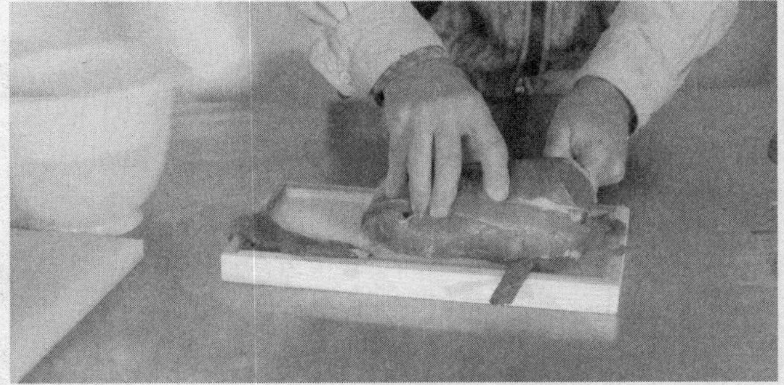

Place the meat to be sliced in the board, and slide the knife (flat side down) along the raised edges.

Frequently dipping the knife blade in cold water assists in slicing.

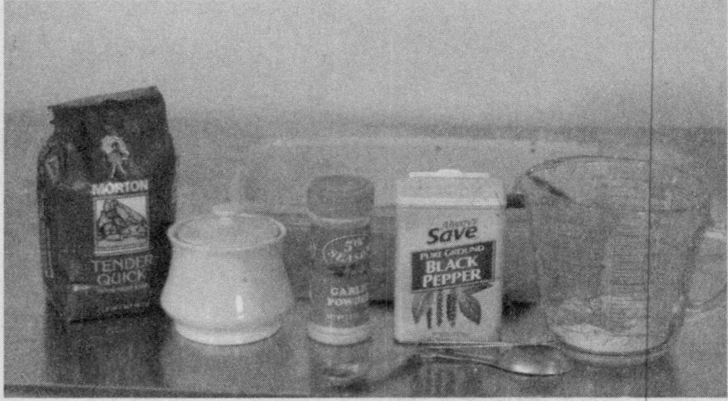

The meat can simply be dried, but in most instances, a cure or seasoning is added for flavor and can also be used to help cure the meat. You can make your own cure and seasonings by using a variety of curing agents and spices.

An electric slicer can be used to cut precise thickness slices fast.

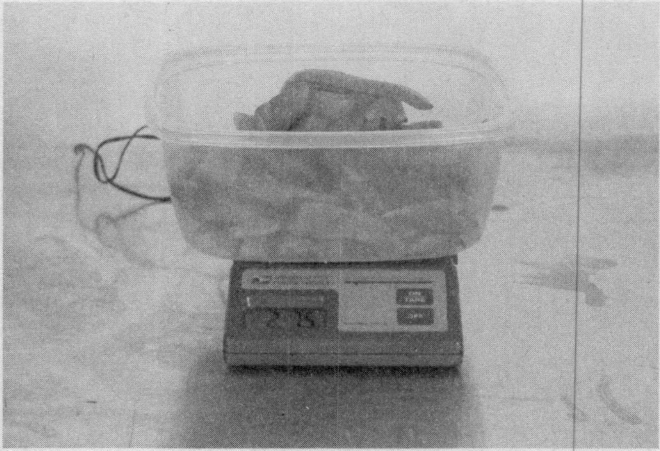
For most cure and seasoning mixes, you must know the exact amount of meat you're dealing with. We use our postal scale to weigh up to 10 pounds of meat.

## curing

Jerky can be nothing more than dried meat using a variety of heat and drying sources. Curing the jerky meat, however, not only adds to the preservation but improves the flavor. Jerky can also be made with a wide range of flavorings, depending on the seasonings and spices used. You can make up your own curing recipes, or use some of the wide range of cures and seasoning mixes available commercially. The latter often contain nitrites to aid in curing. Make sure you follow the recipe and use the proper amount of cure so you don't have too little or too much nitrite. In order to use any recipe, homemade or commercial, you need to know the exact weight of the sliced meat. Regardless, the commercially prepared cures and mixes allow you to make your own jerky with proven taste results. On the other hand, experimenting with homemade recipes is half the fun of making jerky.

Curing can be accomplished by using one of two methods: marinating the meat in a liquid marinade or using a dry rub to coat the meat. In most instances, the meat must sit a length of time before drying in order for the cure to work through. I've used both methods with good results.

The following recipes are primarily for venison, but elk, moose, antelope, or beef could be substituted.

## marinades

### Lawry Marinade

2 lb. meat, thinly sliced
2/3 cup Lawry's Seasoned Marinade or Mesquite Marinade

This is one of the simplest recipes I've used. Place 2/3 cup of Lawry's Seasoned Marinade or Mesquite Marinade and 2 lb. of meat strips in a resealable plastic bag or sealable plastic container. Mix until all meat strips are evenly coated. Place in the refrigerator for 2 to 4 hours. Remove, allow the meat strips to drain on paper towels, and then pat the surface dry with more paper towels. Sprinkle on Lawry's Seasoned Pepper or Garlic Pepper.

To dry, turn on an oven to 200°F, prop the door open an inch or so, and dry the meat. Drying can take anywhere from 2 to 6 hours. Check often for doneness. Jerky strips should feel like leather and bend but not break. The meat should be dried but not cooked. Store in an airtight container and keep in a cool, dry place.

### Burch Marinade No. 1

2 lb. meat, thinly sliced
1 cup of soy sauce
1 tablespoon garlic powder
1 tablespoon onion powder
Water to cover

I've used this simple marinade for almost 40 years. Many recipes contain salt as a curing agent, but other ingredients can be used to replace the salt. Soy sauce is substituted for the salt in this recipe.

The meat can be cured in one of two methods. Using a liquid marinade is very common.

The dry cure and spices are mixed with enough water or liquid to cover the meat.

Allow the meat to soak in the liquid in a non-metallic container, usually overnight.

Mix the ingredients; place them with the meat in a glass bowl, plastic container, or resealable plastic bag; and refrigerate for 12 hours or overnight. Remove, drain, and pat dry. Dry in the oven or a dehydrator. If you desire a spicier taste, add Tabasco Sauce.

**Burch Marinade No. 2**

2 lb. meat, thinly sliced Water to cover
1 tablespoon Worcestershire sauce
1 tablespoon salt
½ cup brown sugar
½ teaspoon black pepper
2 tablespoons onion powder or one large, fresh onion, finely diced
1 teaspoon garlic powder
Tabasco sauce to taste

Jerky is marinated to provide the taste and can be made as spicy or as mild as you prefer. Above is a very mild recipe we've used for years. Once the meat is sliced and all fat removed, place it in freezer bags, freeze for 60 days at 0°F to 5°F, and then cure and dry in an oven or dehydrator.

Place the thinly sliced meat in a bowl, cover with the marinade, and refrigerate for at least 24 hours. Stir occasionally. You can make the marinade spicier by adding soy sauce or teriyaki sauce and hotter by adding ground red pepper. Some folks like to add more sugar. You can also simply sprinkle additional spices onto the meat before drying, if you want even more flavor.

## dry rub cures

Dry rub cures normally consist of the dry ingredients sprinkled over and rubbed into the meat. The rub ingredients are then allowed time to work into the meat before drying.

**Easy-Does-It Oven Jerky**

**Meat, thinly sliced**
**Liquid Smoke**
**Seasoned salt**

This is a great recipe if you just want to try your hand at making jerky without a lot of hassle and ingredients. It's quick, easy, and tasty. All you'll need is meat, Liquid Smoke, and seasoned salt. Slice the meat into 1/8-inch-thick pieces. Brush a bit of Liquid Smoke on both sides of each piece and then dust each piece with seasoned salt. Place the coated meat strips in a covered container or seal-able plastic bag and store in a refrigerator. Allow the strips to marinate overnight. Remove and pat dry with paper towels to get rid of any excess moisture. Place cookie sheets or aluminum foil on the bottom of the oven to catch any dripping. Spray the oven racks with cooking oil and then hang the meat slices over the racks. Set the oven to 200°F and roast the meat until liquid begins to drip. Reduce the heat to 140°F, and dry the meat with the oven door slightly open. The jerky should be ready in 4 to 6 hours, but test frequently.

**Morton salt Jerky**

2 lb. lean beef or game, sliced
2 tablespoons Morton Tender Quick mix or Morton Sugar Cure mix in plain
2 teaspoons sugar
1 teaspoon ground black pepper
1 teaspoon garlic powder

One simple and easy dry-rub cure recipe I've used with extremely good results is the Morton salt jerky recipe. It is extremely mild yet long lasting.

In a small bowl, stir together the Morton Tender Quick mix or Morton Sugar Cure mix and the remaining ingredients. Place the meat on a clean surface or on a large flat pan, and rub all surfaces with the cure mixture. You can also put the ingredients in a bowl, and then rub the cure into each slice of meat. Place the rubbed strips in a plastic food storage bag, and seal shut. Allow to cure in the refrigerator for at least 1 hour. After curing, rinse strips under cold running water and pat dry with paper towels. Arrange meat strips on a single layer on greased racks in a shallow baking pan. Meat edges should not overlap. Place in a 325°F oven, and cook meat to an internal temperature of 160°F. Dry meat in a home dehydrator following the manufacturer's instructions.

A dry-rub technique can also be used. Mix the ingredients thoroughly.

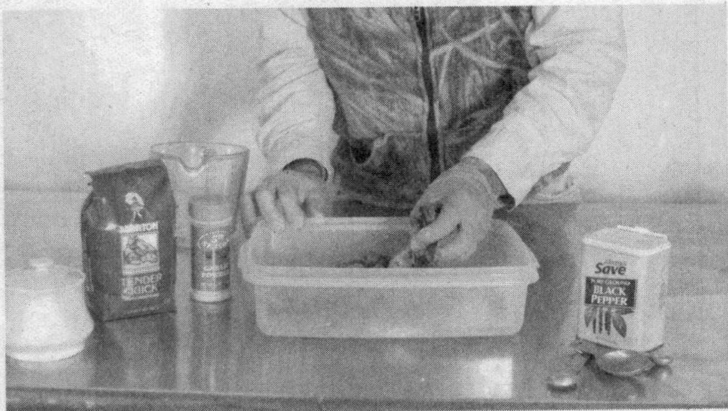


Sprinkle the ingredients over the meat strips and toss to coat well, or rub the mix into the meat surfaces.

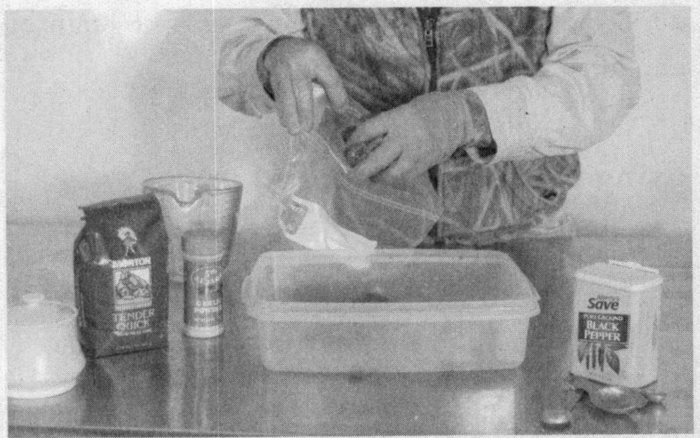


Place the rubbed strips in a glass or plastic container or zippered plastic bag to cure.

**Venison Jerky—Chef William's Style**

2 lb. venison roast
Cajun Injector Wild Game Marinade: Cane Syrup Recipe
Vegetable oil
Cajun Injector Cajun Shake

One of the most unusual jerky recipes is a combination of marinade and dry rub. This recipe is from Chef Williams, the founder of Cajun Injector Marinades. We found the recipe in an old pamphlet from Cajun Injector and have used it for years. The company doesn't make the Cane Syrup Recipe Marinade anymore, but their other marinades, such as Teriyaki and Honey, also work well with this recipe.

Inject the roast using 2 ounces of Cajun Injector Wild Game Marinade per pound of meat. Slice the roast into 1/8- to ¼-inch slices, slicing with the grain. Sprinkle with Cajun Shake. Brown the venison strips in hot oil in a large skillet, turning as the strips brown. Place in a dish and cover the strips with 8 ounces of Cajun Injector Wild Game Marinade and sprinkle with the Cajun Shake. Let the strips sit overnight in a refrigerator. Drain off the marinade and pat dry. Dry in a dehydrator or bake in a 150°F oven with door partially open for 8 hours or until the meat is dry.

## using prepared cures and mixes

I've experimented with a number of prepared cures and mixes and found them easy and fun to use. In all cases, the product comes in two packages: a cure and a seasoning. It's extremely important to follow the mixture amounts suggested by the manufacturer for the specific poundage of meat. It's also a good idea to make up small batches of jerky to test for taste. The following are jerky-making suggestions and methods from the products I've tested.

**Uncle Buck's Jerky Regular Seasoning and Cure**

Up to 10 lb. meat
2 cups water for every 2 lb. meat
8 teaspoons seasoning for every 2 lb. meat
½ teaspoon cure for every 2 lb. meat

Cut the meat strips 1/8-inch-thick and 8 inches long. To cure up to 10 pounds of meat, mix the cure packet and seasoning with 5 cups of water. For smaller batches, mix 8 teaspoons seasoning, ½ teaspoon of cure, 2 cups of water, and 2 pounds of meat strips. Mix well and marinate strips in solution

Uncle Buck's Jerky Seasoning and Cure provides a great way of making jerky with a sure-fire recipe.

Place the cure mix in water.

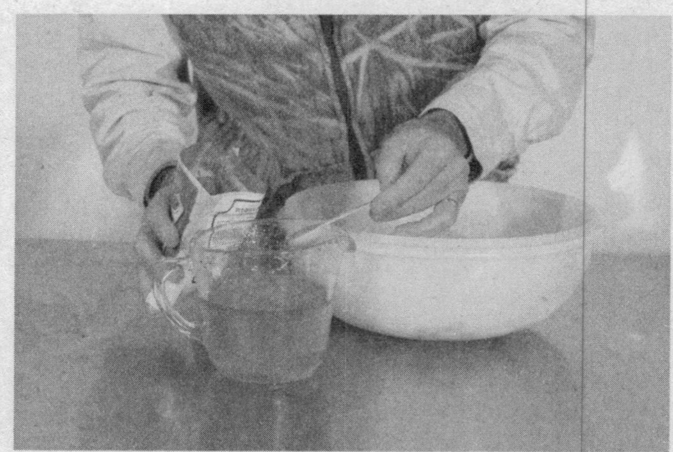
Add the seasoning mix and stir well.

Add the strips.

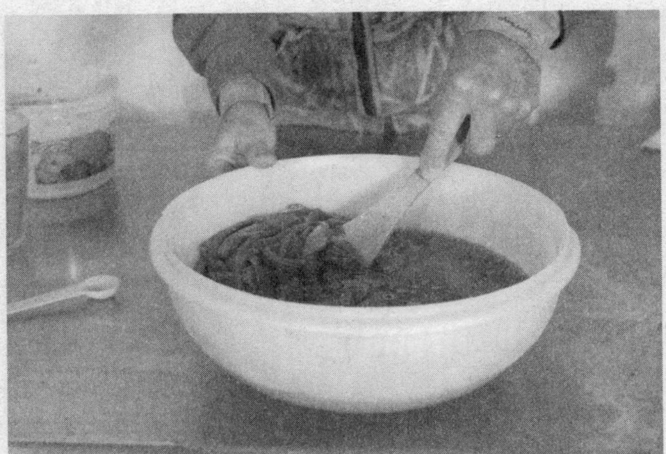

Stir well and refrigerate for 8 hours.

for 8 hours under refrigeration. Hang strips in oven at lowest setting with door open to the first stop until jerky reaches desired dryness. A dehydrator may also be used. This product is also available in hickory and mesquite flavors.

**Eastman Outdoors Jerky Cure and Seasoning**

Lean meat
3 teaspoons seasoning for every 1 lb. of meat
1 teaspoon for every 1 lb. of meat
Cure

Start with the leanest meat possible. Trim excess fat and partially freeze the meat for easier slicing. Cut along the grain into strips no more than 3/8-inch thick. Weigh the strips to determine how much seasoning and cure to use. Then follow the mixing chart using standard measuring spoons and a non-metallic bowl, mixing 3 teaspoons of seasoning and 1 level teaspoon of cure for each pound of meat. Gently toss the strips with the mixture. For best results, use the Eastman Outdoors Reveo to infuse maximum flavor into the meat. Cover the bowl, or place strips in a sealable plastic bag, and refrigerate for at least 24 hours. Use an oven, smoker, or dehydrator to dry. The Eastman Outdoors products are available in original, hickory, teriyaki, mesquite, and whiskey pepper.

**Hi Mountain Jerky Cure and Seasonings**

Hi Mountain Jerky Cure and Seasonings are old recipes, made without preservatives, and the dried jerky must be kept frozen or refrigerated. The company suggests you have fun with jerky. If you have meat that has been in the freezer for a while, for example, don't waste it: make it into jerky instead. Or, if you have a roast, try cutting it into 1-inch squares, and make jerky nuggets. Hi Mountain products are available in ten authentic Western recipes: original blend, pepper, mesquite, hickory, mandarin teriyaki, bourbon BBQ, cajun, cracked pepper and garlic, inferno, and pepperoni.

Cut the meat into strips of desired lengths and widths, allowing for shrinkage. Weigh the meat after cutting into strips and trimming. Now you know the exact amount of mix to use. Mix the spices, and cure according to the spice and cure mixing chart. Mix only the amount you need. Be sure to store the

Hi Mountain provides a wide variety of flavors in their line of cure and seasoning mixes that can be used with sliced jerky.

The cure and seasoning spices must be mixed together precisely according to the amount of meat being treated.

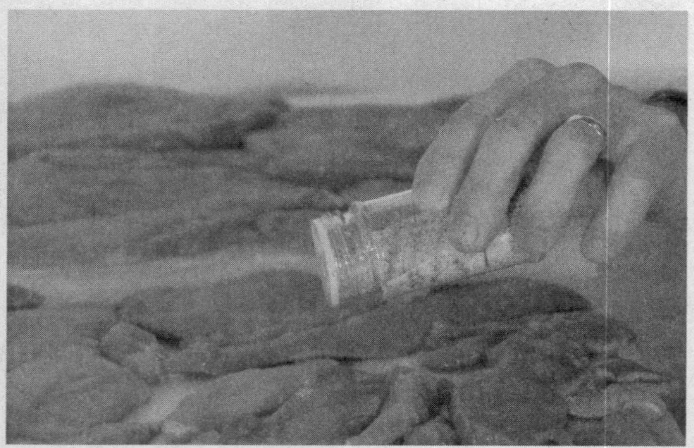

Hi Mountain provides a shaker bottle to apply their mixes. Apply to one side of the meat, turn, and apply to the opposite.

Thoroughly mix the meat and spices in a non-metallic bowl.

Place the slices in a non-metallic container or zippered plastic bag and refrigerate for the time specified by the recipe.

remaining unmixed spices and cure in an airtight container until needed. Hi Mountain recommends that you always make sure you mix the cure and seasonings exactly and correctly. Fluff the cure and seasoning before measuring. Always use standard measuring spoons, level full. Scrape off excess cure or seasoning with a table knife, leaving the measuring spoon level. Do not compact.

Lay the strips flat on an even surface. (If you have just washed the game meat, be sure to pat it dry before applying the cure and seasoning.) Using the blended spices and cure, apply to the prepared meat using the shaker bottle enclosed with the mixes. Sprinkle the first side of the meat strips with approximately half of the measured mix. Turn the meat strips over and sprinkle the remaining mix on the meat strips. If you can't get an even distribution on the meat, especially on the ends and edges, put all the seasoned strips in a large mixing bowl and tumble by hand until the cure and seasoning have been spread evenly over the entire batch.

Stack the strips, pressed together tightly, in a non-metallic container or a resealable plastic bag and refrigerate for at least 24 hours. Hi Mountain Jerky Cure and Seasoning is specially formulated to penetrate meat at the rate of ¼ inch per 24 hours. If thicker pieces of meat are used, increase curing time accordingly; for instance, cure 3/8-inch-thick strips for approximately 28 hours. Do not cure any meat less than 24 hours.

## drying

The following instruction for cooking or smoking jerky is from Hi Mountain: "Place foil or pan on bottom of oven to catch drippings. Lay the strips on the oven racks, making sure there is air between each piece (our Jerky Screens are perfect here). Place in the oven for 1 to 1¼ hours at 200°F with the oven door open just a crack. Taste the jerky frequently. When the jerky is cooked to your liking, stop cooking. The jerky is made with cure and seasonings, it does not have to be dry to the point where you can't chew it like store bought jerky. Remember, taste often while cooking or smoking."

Our oven door won't stay open just a crack, so I keep the door open with a wooden clothespin. A wooden stick of the desired thickness would also work. Another easy oven-dry technique is to insert toothpicks in the ends of the meat strips and hang the strips from the oven racks. This works, but they also fall easily, especially when you're trying to move the racks in and out of the oven.

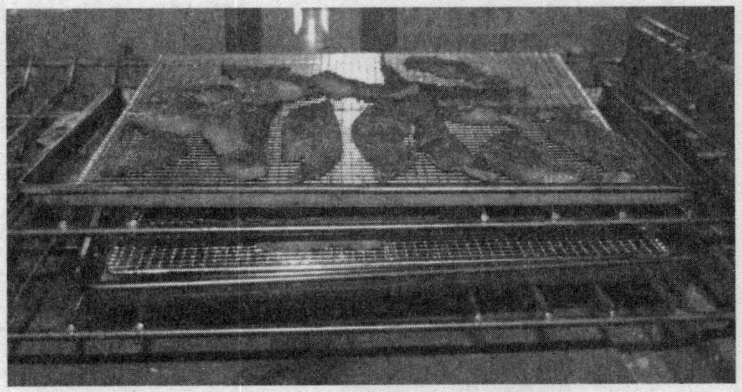

One of the simplest drying methods for the home jerky maker to use is drying in a kitchen oven with the door propped open slightly. Shown here are jerky strips on Hi Mountain jerky racks.

If using a smokehouse or smoker, Hi Mountain recommends experimenting. All home smokers are different in size, wall thickness, location (inside or

The jerky strips can be dried in several ways. The first step, however, is to place the marinated or dry-rub strips on paper toweling and pat dry.

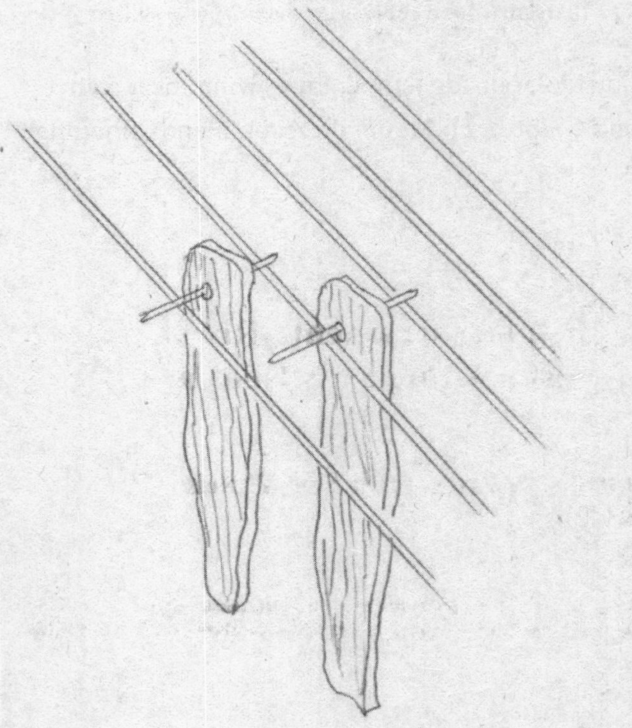

Jerky strips can also be suspended on ordinary oven racks using toothpicks threaded through holes in the ends of the strips.

Electric smokers that will reach temperatures of at least 140°F are also good choices for drying jerky strips.

A food dehydrator that will reach a temperature of 140°F is an excellent tool for dehydrating and drying jerky.

outside), outside temperature, wind, heat source, and so forth. Hi Mountain recommends smoking the jerky at 200°F for 1½ to 2 hours with smoke on; however, if your smoker will not reach 200°F, leave the meat in longer. Do not smoke for more than 3 hours until you have tasted the first batch. Do not overcook, and do not oversmoke. Too much smoke can produce a bitter flavor.

If using a dehydrator, Hi Mountain recommends that you follow your dehydrator instructions. Again, jerky does not have to be cooked so hard that you can't chew it. Test it frequently.

# Modern Ground Jerky

Although sliced jerky is the easiest to make, ground-meat jerky has become increasingly popular, not only with commercial jerky makers but with home jerky makers as well. Ground-meat jerky has several advantages. It's less chewy, and it can be made from lesser cuts of meat, as well as the small pieces of meat trimmings from butchering. To use all your butchered meat effectively, you might like to make both sliced and ground-meat jerky. Ground-meat jerky does require a bit more effort, and you'll need a means of grinding and extruding or shaping the ground meat.

Make sure you follow safe meat-processing procedures with ground meat because it's more easily contaminated. Cut away all fat and sinew.

Ground-meat jerky has become extremely popular. It's easy to do if you have a grinder, and it utilizes the less-choice cuts of meat.

## the meat

As with any jerky making, it's important to carefully follow safe meat processing methods, even more so with ground meat, as pathogens can be spread throughout ground meat. Also, as with all types of jerky making, it's important to cut away all fat and as much sinew as possible, especially with venison. Venison fat turns rancid, and sinew makes even ground jerky tougher to chew. Because the meat used is often butcher trimmings from carving out other choice cuts, including meat from the legs with lots of sinew and flank steak from the ribs with quite a bit of fat, it does take a bit more time and effort to ensure a good, lean meat for the jerky.

## grinding

Regardless of whether you use a hand or powered grinder, the meat should be cut up into chunks or strips that will fit readily into the grinder opening or throat. For hand grinders, the smaller

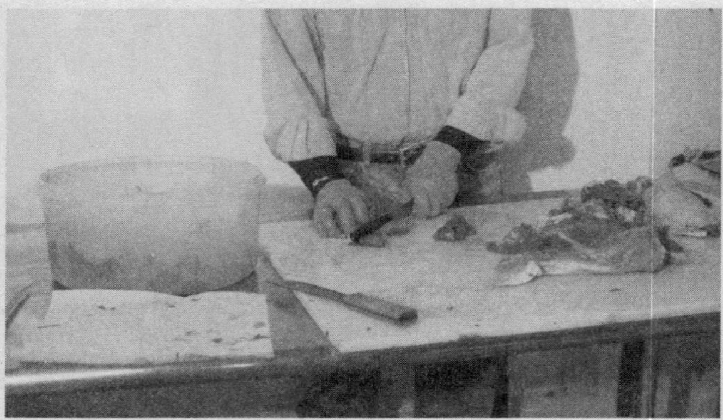

Before the meat can be ground, it should be cut into long strips or chunks that will fit down your grinder throat.

Grind the meat using a hand or powered grinder. The LEM meat grinder makes short work of the chore.

you cut the chunks or strips, the easier it is to grind. Make sure there are no bones in the meat to stop an electric grinder or damage the worm gear and grinding plate and blade. A bone will definitely stop a hand grinder, but it is less likely to cause damage. The meat should be 40°F or colder and free of gristle and sinew. Using the meat stomper, slowly feed the meat into the throat of the grinder head. Do not force the meat, and never use your fingers to push the meat into the head. Used properly, today's grinders are very safe, especially when compared to older versions like my granddad's big grinder with a big, wide, open throat. The family joke, "Don't get your tie in there," was really a reminder to all users to be extremely careful.

Grind the meat through the coarse plate first. We prefer our jerky made from coarse ground. If you want a finer grind, turn off the motor, and unplug the grinder. Next, remove the coarse plate, and clean the head of any sinew, fat, and gristle that has accumulated during the first grind. Reassemble the unit with the fine plate, plug the grinder in, and regrind the meat. If the meat mashes instead of coming through the plate in strings, unplug the grinder, remove all the meat from the grinder and plate, reassemble and tighten the grinder ring, making sure it's tighter than it was before, and begin to grind the meat again. When you're through grinding, run some saltine crackers through the grinder to help clean it out, then unplug the grinder, and disassemble the head. Wash all parts in hot, soapy water, and thoroughly rinse in hot water. Allow parts to dry completely. Spray parts with food-grade silicone to prevent rust and keep your grinder in like-new condition while stored.

## the cure

Although you can simply dry the meat, adding cure and seasonings not only provides a better

Regardless of whether you're using a homemade or commercial recipe, make sure you weigh the ground meat and use the correct amount of cure and seasonings.

means of preservation, but it adds taste as well. As with sliced-muscle meat, you can make up your own recipes or use any number of commercially prepared mixes. Many of the recipes in the muscle-meat chapter can also be used for ground-meat jerky. The following are a couple of homemade ground-meat recipes that we enjoy. As with muscle-meat jerky, ground meat must also be weighed for proper curing.

**Burch Ground Meat Jerky**

2 lb. ground venison
2 teaspoons Morton Tender Quick
1 teaspoon each garlic powder and onion powder
½ teaspoon each dried red pepper and ground black pepper, or to suit
¼ cup brown sugar

Mix all the cure and spices together. Place the meat in a glass or plastic container. Sprinkle a little of the spice over the meat, and mix well with your hands. Then, add more spice, and mix until you have all the meat well coated with the cure mix. An alternative method is to dissolve the cure and spices in ½ cup of cold water. Pour this over the meat and mix thoroughly. Place a cover over the dish or pan, and refrigerate overnight to allow the cure and seasonings to work into the meat. Extrude or roll the meat out onto the waxed side of freezer paper, a jerky rack, or dehydrator tray.

Curing and seasoning adds to the flavor and preservation. First mix the spices and curing agents together.

Next, spread the mixed cure and seasoning over the meat.

Thoroughly mix the meat and cure/seasonings together.

**Burch Ground Meat Jerky 2**

2 lb. ground venison
2 teaspoons Morton Sugar Cure (Plain)
1 tablespoon Worcestershire sauce
¼ teaspoon each black pepper, garlic powder, onion powder, Liquid Smoke

Another, less spicy ground meat jerky recipe is also a favorite. Again, mix the spices with a little water and then thoroughly incorporate into the meat using your hands. Extrude and dry as mentioned.

## commercial mixes

A number of commercial cure and seasoning mixes are also available. The following are some of the mixes I've tested and liked.

**Uncle Buck's Regular Jerky Seasoning and Cure**

Up to 10 lb. meat
4 teaspoons seasoning per 1 1b. of meat
¼ teaspoon cure per 1 1b. of meat
1 oz. water per 1 1b. of meat

The package will do 10 pounds of meat. Mix 4 teaspoons of seasoning, ¼ teaspoon of cure, and 1 ounce of water for each pound of ground meat used. Mix thoroughly until the mixture becomes tacky. Using a Jerky Cannon, squeeze strips on to a jerky rack. Place jerky rack on a cookie sheet, and dry strips in an oven at 200°F for 75 minutes on each side. Or, squeeze strips onto the racks of a dehydrator and dry, following dehydrator directions. The finished product must be refrigerated.

Purchased cures and mixes, such as the Uncle Buck's Snack Stick mix, are also available for making ground-meat jerky.

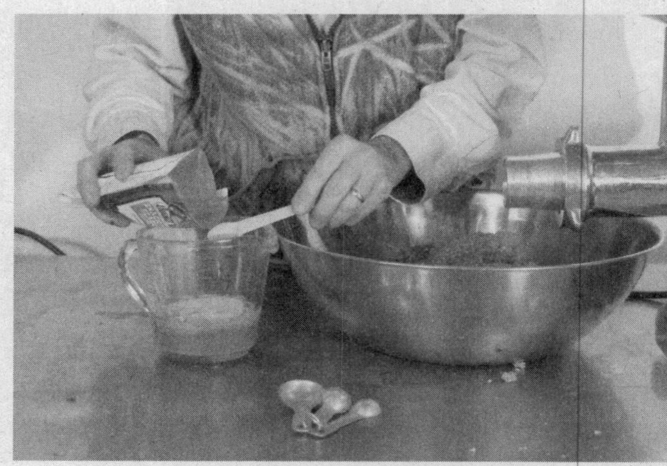

The cure and seasonings are added to cold water.

**Uncle Buck's Snack Sticks**

Up to 5 lb. meat
4 teaspoons seasoning per 1 1b. of meat
¼ teaspoon cure per 1 1b. of meat
1 oz. water per 1 1b. of meat

Another great tasting jerky is made with the Uncle Buck's Snack Sticks Seasoning. Extruded out into round sticks, this is a great homemade Slim Jim. The packet will treat 5 pounds of meat. According to the instructions; "Dissolve 4 teaspoons of seasoning, ¼ teaspoon of cure, and 1 ounce of water to mix with each pound of meat. Mix thoroughly until the mixture becomes tacky. Process using one of the following methods: Stuff into natural or collagen casings and smoke in smoker until internal temperature of meat reaches 165°F. Or make Slim Jims with a Jerky Cannon and shoot them onto a cookie sheet. Dry in an oven at 200°F for 75 minutes per side or until internal temperature of meat reaches 165°F. Finished product must be refrigerated."

The ingredients are mixed well, and then the cure and seasoning mix is poured over the ground meat and thoroughly mixed.

**Eastman Outdoors Jerky Cure and Seasoning**

5 lb. lean meat
1 oz. seasoning
1 oz. cure
1 cup cold water

Use the leanest meat possible. To each 5 pounds, add 1 ounce seasoning, 1 ounce cure, and 1 cup of ice-cold water. Mix in a non-metallic bowl for 5 minutes or until sticky. Cover the bowl, and refrigerate for at least 4 hours. Use the Eastman Outdoors Jerky Gun to extrude the meat into perfect strips or sticks. Package will do 5 pounds of ground meat.

**Hi Mountain Jerky Cure and Seasoning**

1 to 3 lb. meat
½ cup water per pound of meat
Cure and seasoning according to weight

Make 1 to 3 pounds at a time. Hi Mountain suggests you start with a small batch at first. Mix

Hi Mountain has a wide line of cures and seasonings.

Mix the cure and seasonings together and pour the mixture over the meat.

Mix well, and allow to cure overnight in a non-metallic container in the refrigerator.

cure and seasoning according to weight chart. Add 1 cup ice water per pound of meat. Mix meat, water, and seasoning thoroughly for approximately 5 minutes or until sticky.

## shaping the ground meat

Ground-meat jerky is commonly formed into thin strips or round sticks. You can shape the meat into a jerky product in a number of ways. One of the simplest methods is to place a ball of meat on a piece of waxed paper or the waxed side of a piece of freezer paper. Place another piece of waxed paper over the meat ball, and use a rolling pin or straight-sided drinking glass to roll the meat patty out to a uniform thickness of about 1/8 to 3/16 inch. Peel back the top paper, and use a kitchen knife to slice the rolled-out patty into strips about 1 inch wide. Take care not to slice through the bottom piece of waxed paper. Line a jerky rack or cookie cooling rack with freezer paper with the waxed side up. Transfer the strips to the jerky rack by flipping the waxed paper over onto the freezer paper and peeling the waxed paper from the back side. If using the freezer paper, dry the strips until the surface is sealed, flip this over onto a drying rack, and peel off the freezer paper. This gives the ground meat strips a little stability for each of the handling steps. When completely dry, tear or break apart the strips on the cut lines. The strips can also be flipped onto a dehydrator rack for drying.

Ground-meat jerky can be shaped into strips or sticks. Shown here are Slim Jim-style sticks.

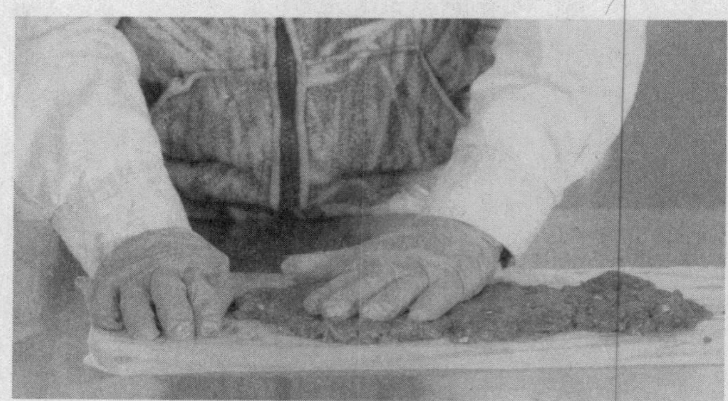

Ground-meat jerky can be shaped into thin jerky-style strips quite easily with waxed paper or the waxed side of freezer paper. Flatten a ball of cured and seasoned meat onto a piece of waxed paper.

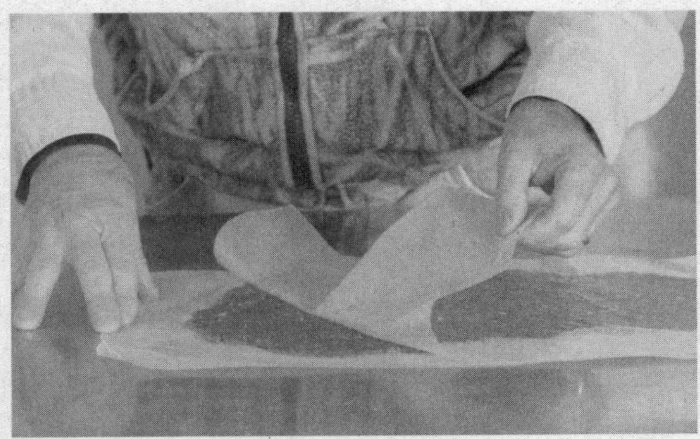

Place another piece of waxed paper over the meat, and use a rolling pin to roll the meat out flat to about a 1/8-inch thickness. Remove the top waxed paper piece.

Another method of creating the strips from ground meat is to line a sheet-cake or other baking pan with plastic wrap. Press the ground meat into the pan to a suitable thickness. Partially freeze the pan, remove meat from the pan, peel off the plastic wrap, and slice into strips. The partially frozen meat is much easier to work with and slice.

Extruding ground meat through a hand-held, ground-jerky-meat extruder is a very common and popular method. These tools resemble caulking guns, and most come with interchangeable tips—both a flat tip for jerky strips and a round tip for stick jerky.

With the meat ground and cured, wet your clean hands in cold water, then take about a cup of the ground meat and roll it between your hands to form into a roll small enough to slide down into the barrel of the jerky gun. Make sure the roll is wet enough to easily slide down into the barrel. Add more rolls until the barrel is full. Gently push the plunger down into the barrel, making sure to properly align the plastic plunger tip with the barrel so you don't damage the tip. Spray a jerky screen, such as the one from Hi Mountain, with a light coating of cooking oil. Pull the trigger gently to squeeze the strips or sticks onto the Jerky Screen, or extrude the sticks or strips out onto jerky racks lined

Use a kitchen knife—not a sharp knife—to separate the meat into thin strips. The meat strips can be flipped over onto a dehydrator tray for drying.

A jerky extruder, such as the Hi Mountain Jerky Gun, can also be used to shape the meat. These normally come with two tips: one for strips and one for sticks.

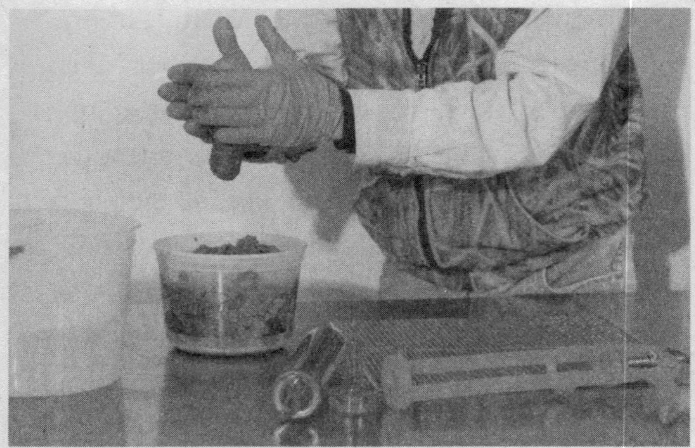

With wet hands, roll the cured and seasoned ground meat into thin rolls that will slide easily down into the jerky extruder.

Continue filling the tube.

Gently squeeze the handle to extrude the ground meat onto a jerky screen, such as that from Hi-Mountain.

The resulting extruded ground-meat jerky ready to dry.

with freezer paper following the directions above. Now you're ready to dry the jerky.

The ultimate extruder is the LEM Patty and Jerky Machine, an accessory that fits onto the LEM Grinder. The unit allows you to grind and then extrude large quantities of ground patties or jerky in either strips or sticks, depending on the plate chosen. The accessory extrudes four sticks or strips at a time. The Jerky Machine comes with a special extruding plate; a holder for a roll of waxed butcher paper; one roll of waxed butcher paper; and a pair of stainless-steel scissors. If you grind meat only one time, assemble the jerky machine head, and attach it to the grinder before you start grinding. If you grind twice, attach the machine head before the second

The LEM Patty and Jerky Machine is an attachment that fastens to the LEM grinder and extrudes sticks or strips of ground-meat jerky. You can grind and extrude at the same time or grind, mix, and extrude.

grind and use the extruding plate. The first step is to select the appropriate extruding plate, either the patty, jerky strip, or snack stick plate. Fasten to the front of the unit with the stainless steel screws.

Remove the retaining ring from the grinder. Attach the grinder adapter to the grinder using the retaining ring, as you would a stuffing tube. Mount the jerky machine head to the adapter and secure it with the winged bolts. Place the meat chute in position, and secure it with the winged bolts. Attach the waxed paper roll to the jerky machine head using the paper rod and winged nuts. Thread the paper between the jerky machine head and the meat chute. Make sure the paper unrolls counter-clockwise from the back of the roll to place the waxed side up onto the chute. Pull the paper down the meat chute about 3 inches. Start grinding or extruding. The extruded material will push the paper down the meat chute. When the meat reaches the end of the chute, stop the grinder. Use the stainless steel scissors to cut the strips and waxed paper to the desired length and slide them off onto cookie sheets.

The resulting jerky snack sticks on waxed paper and in pans, ready to dry.

We found it better to grind, then extrude. As you grind, the meat is forced out onto waxed paper.

When the sticks are the length needed, cut the paper and sticks with the stainless-steel scissors.

## drying

Ground-meat jerky can be dried using an oven, dehydrator, or smoker capable of reaching at least 200°F. Disease-causing microorganisms are more difficult to eliminate in ground meat than whole meat strips. Be sure to follow the dehydrator manufacturer's directions when heating the product at the end of the drying time. An internal temperature of 160°F is necessary to eliminate disease-causing bacteria such as E. coli 0157:H7, if present.

If drying in an oven, place the strips or sticks on jerky racks, positioned over cookie sheets to catch drips. We have also used cookie cooling racks as jerky racks. Preheat oven to 200°F and, with the oven door slightly open, heat for 1 to 2 hours or

Ground-meat jerky can be dried in an oven set at 200°F. Make sure the meat attains an internal temperature of 160°F

If using a dehydrator to dry the meat, follow the manufacturer's instructions. Shown here is a section of waxed-paper-shaped ground-meat jerky, ready for the dehydrator

until the strips crack but do not break when bent. Increase heat to 275°F until internal temperature reaches 160°F. Ground-meat jerky strips tend to stick a bit more than muscle-meat strips. It's a good idea to turn the strips over to ensure even cooking and to prevent sticking. If using a dehydrator, make sure you follow the manufacturer's directions on drying jerky.

# Main Meals

*Its an ill cook that cannot lick his own fingers*

William Shakespeare, Romeo & Juliet (1597)

Fall is the time of year when hunters are itching to be out of the office and in the woods. For us, the fall is our spring, our renewal. The woods come alive with vivid yellows, reds and oranges, and we savor the crisp, cool morning air as we inhale the unmistakable aroma of the woods that is never more pungent or exceptional than at this time of year.

How many times have you become enveloped by these moments and thought of the frontiersman or pioneer and what he must've felt and sensed during this time of year? Was he daydreaming of which route he'd take to his stand, what technique he would use to either rattle or call in a deer, or what game he might see on an upcoming elk or bison hunt? If you think about it, hunting's natural progression and our thoughts about the pursuit of game haven't changed much. After all, hunting season brings us in tune with Mother Nature as we strain to become one with the woods, fields and earth around us.

In the end, the heart of hunting revolves around its finale: the consumption of the game we take. For thousands of years, venison has served as a main meal for families across the globe. Venison satisfies our yearning for self-sufficiency by allowing us to take pride in our ability to hunt, clean, care for. preserve and cook our own food. It ignites the flames of tradition. Venison is a versatile meat that can be featured in elaborate gatherings, traditional holiday meals or quick dinners for the family. It also adapts well to international cuisines. The recipes that follow offer you a range of these choices, from simple to fancy, using ingredients you'll find right in your kitchen. The recipes are organized by the cuts of meat, starting with roasts, steaks and chops, and ending with ground venison and sausage.

## Roast Mustard Loin of Venison

*Serves: 8 to 12 * Prep Time: 10 minutes * Marinating Time: 1 to 2 hours * Cooking Time: 30 minutes*

- 4- to 5-lb. venison loin, well trimmed (you may also use 2 smaller portions)
- 2 to 3 cups Simple Marinade*
- ¼ cup plus 1 tablespoon olive oil, divided
- 1 cup Dijon mustard
- ⅓ cup chopped scallions
- ⅓ cup dry white wine
- ¼ cup bread crumbs
- 4 large cloves garlic, minced
- 1 teaspoon sea salt
- ½ teaspoon crumbled dried sage
- ½ teaspoon crumbled dried thyme
- ¼ teaspoon pepper

Measure venison loin against a large skillet, and cut into halves if necessary to fit skillet. Place venison in nonaluminum pan or bowl; pour marinade over and turn to coat. Cover and refrigerate for 1 to 2 hours, turning occasionally. Remove venison from marinade and pat dry; discard marinade.

Heat oven to 375°F. In large skillet, heat 1 tablespoon of the oil over high heat until it is hot but not smoking. Add venison and quickly sear on all sides. Transfer venison to roasting pan; set aside.

In blender or food processor, combine remaining ¼ cup oil with the mustard, scallions, wine, bread crumbs, garlic, salt, sage, thyme and pepper. Process until smooth; the coating should be thick. Spread coating evenly over venison. Roast to desired doneness, 15 to 17 minutes for medium-rare. Remove venison from oven when internal temperature is 5° less than desired. Tent meat with foil and let rest for 10 to 15 minutes before slicing.

**I sometimes like to use Myron's 20-Gauge Venison Marinade instead of the Simple Marinade. It is a very versatile, all-natural cooking sauce whose ingredients include soy sauce, garlic, red wine, rice wine vinegar, olive oil and spices. It has a rich, slightly malty flavor base, a pungent and peppery bite and subtle juniper flavor points, and works well for a variety of game and fish.*

## Spit-Roasted Leg of Venison

*Serves: 25 to 30 * Prep Time: 10 minutes * Marinating Time: 24 hours * Cooking Time: 2 to 3 hours*

*Here's a recipe for a deer camp full of hungry hunters. We enjoyed this at the Turtle Greek Camp in the Adirondack Mountains many years ago. While it was cooking , the aroma permeated the woods outside the lodge, where the younger hunters were prompted by the cook to maintain a vegilant watch over that fire!*

**Marinade:**

- 4 to 5 gallons white wine (enough to cover the venison)
- 4 carrots, sliced
- 3 onions, sliced
- 2 heads of garlic, peeled and sliced
- 1 tablespoon dried juniper berries
- 1 tablespoon whole black peppercorns
- 1 whole leg of venison (18 to 20 lbs.), trimmed of as much fat as possible
- Salt and pepper
- 1 lb. butter, melted
- Hunter s Sauce for serving, optional

In a nonaluminum container large enough to hold the venison leg, combine 4 gallons of the wine with remaining marinade ingredients. Add leg of venison, and pour in additional wine as needed to cover leg. Refrigerate for 24 hours, turning several times.

When you're ready to cook, prepare a hot wood fire. Remove leg from marinade and pat dry. Secure leg to a spit and season generously with salt and pepper. Strain marinade into large saucepan and heat to boiling; keep warm during cooking to prevent bacterial growth. Place spit over fire and cook for 2 to 3 hours, or until desired doneness, basting often with the melted butter and reserved marinade. The venison should remain slightly rare. Serve with Hunter's Sauce.

## Christmas Venison Roast with Baby Mushrooms

*Serves: 8 to 10 * Prep Time: 40 minutes * Cooking Time: 1 ¼ to 1 ½ hours*

- ¾ cup unsalted butter (1½ sticks), divided
- ½ cup minced shallots, divided
- ¾ lb. fresh spinach leaves
- ¼ lb. fresh baby portobello mushrooms, washed
- ½ lb. grated Swiss cheese
- 5 slices bacon, cooked and crumbled
- Salt and pepper
- 4-lb. boneless venison roast*
- 1 lemon
- 4 cups brown sauce
- 1½ cups red wine

First, prepare the stuffing. In large saucepan, melt 6 tablespoons of the butter over medium heat. Add ¼ cup of the shallots. Saute until translucent. Add spinach and mushrooms; cook about 3 minutes longer. Mix in grated cheese and crumbled bacon. Cook, stirring constantly, until cheese melts and mixture is well blended. Season to taste with salt and pepper. Transfer to medium bowl and place in refrigerator to cool.

Heat oven to 350°F. Butterfly roast, trying to achieve uniform thickness throughout. Season with salt and pepper; squeeze lemon juice liberally over inside of roast, picking off any lemon pips. Spread cooled stuffing evenly over roast. Roll up roast jelly-roll style, rolling with the grain of the meat. Tie roast at 1-inch intervals, using kitchen string.

Melt 4 tablespoons of the remaining butter in large stockpot over medium-high heat. (While a large skillet will also work, the sides of this larger pot will prevent grease from splattering on your stovetop.) Add roast and sear on all sides. Transfer to roasting pan. Roast to desired doneness, 15 to 20 minutes per pound. Remove roast from oven when internal temperature is 5°F less than desired; I prefer rare, so I remove it when the temperature is 125°F. Transfer roast to serving dish and tent loosely with aluminum foil; let rest while you prepare sauce.

In medium saucepan over medium heat, melt remaining 2 tablespoons of butter. Add remaining ¼ cup shallots and saute for about 2 minutes. Blend in brown sauce and red wine. Reduce heat and simmer, stirring frequently, for about 15 minutes. Check seasoning and adjust as necessary. Pass through fine strainer (or china cap) and serve with roast.

**Since you will be butterflying the roast, you need to start with a boneless roast that is in one piece (not a tied-together roast). Rump or round roasts work well in this recipe.*

## Adirondack Spinach Venison Roast

*Serves: 8 to 10 * Prep Time: 25 minutes * Cooking Time: 1 ¼ to 1 ½ hours*

- ½ cup unsalted butter (1 stick), room temperature, divided
- 4 cloves garlic, minced, divided
- 10 oz. fresh spinach leaves
- ½ lb. shredded Gruyere cheese
- Salt and pepper
- 4-lb. boneless venison roast*
- 2 tablespoons lemon juice
- 3 slices dry white bread, torn into small pieces
- 2 bay leaves, crumbled
- 1 teaspoon ground sage
- 2 slices uncooked bacon, chopped
- Half of a medium onion, chopped

In large skillet, melt 2 tablespoons of the butter over medium heat. Add half of the minced garlic and saute until golden. Add spinach and saute until wilted. Add cheese, and salt and pepper to taste. Cook for about 2 minutes longer, stirring constantly. Remove from heat and let cool to room temperature.

Heat oven to 350°F. While the spinach mixture is cooling, butterfly the roast, trying to achieve uniform thickness throughout. Season with salt, pepper and lemon juice. Spread cooled stuffing evenly over meat, keeping an inch away from edges. Roll up roast jelly-roll style, rolling with the grain of the meat. Tie roast at 1-inch intervals, using kitchen string. Place roast on rack in roasting pan. Sprinkle with salt and pepper, and rub remaining 6 tablespoons butter over entire roast.

In food processor or blender, combine bread, bay leaves, sage, bacon, onion and remaining garlic. Pulse on and off, or blend at medium speed, until all ingredients are mixed thoroughly, 30 to 60 seconds. Pat bread-crumb mixture firmly over top and sides of roast.

Roast to desired doneness, 15 to 20 minutes per pound. Remove roast from oven when internal temperature is 5°F less than desired; I prefer rare, so I remove it when the temperature is 125°F. Let roast rest for 10 to 15 minutes before slicing.

**Since you will be butterflying the roast, you need to start with a boneless roast that is in one piece (not a tied-together roast). Rump or round roasts work well in this recipe.*

## Venison Filet Wellington

*Serves: 5 to 8 * Prep Time: 45 minutes * Cooking Time: 10 to 15 minutes*

*Here's an elegant dish that will knock the socks off your deer-camp buddies. It may look complex, but it really is quite simple. From start to finish, Venison Filet Wellington will take about an hour. Read the direction at least once before preparing this dish, and you will see how quickly it comes together. Have all your ingredients ready, to make the assembly smooth and quick. Don't miss trying this recipe; it is well worth the effort.*

- 2-to 3-lb. venison loin, well trimmed
- 2 tablespoons clarified butter, room temperature
- 2 to 4 slices bacon
- 2 tablespoons butter
- 3 tablespoons olive oil
- 2 tablespoons chopped shallots
- ½ lb. fresh white or straw mushrooms, finely chopped
- 1 egg, separated
- 2 tablespoons cold water
- 1 sheet (half of a 17¼-oz. pkg.) frozen puff pastry, thawed per package directions
- Flour for rolling out pastry
- 1 cup shredded fresh spinach leaves
- ½ cup shredded Swiss cheese
- Hunter's Sauce

Heat oven to 325°F. Heat a large, heavy-bottomed skillet over medium-high heat. While skillet is heating, rub venison with clarified butter. Add loin to hot skillet and sear to a deep brown color on all sides. Transfer loin to dish and set aside to cool to room temperature. Meanwhile, add bacon to same skillet and fry until cooked but not crisp. Set aside on paper towel-lined plate.

While the loin is cooling, prepare the filling. In medium skillet, melt the 2 tablespoons butter in the oil over medium heat. Add shallots and saute until golden, stirring constantly; don't let the shallots brown or they will become bitter. Add mushrooms and saute until most of the liquid evaporates. Set mushroom mixture aside to cool.

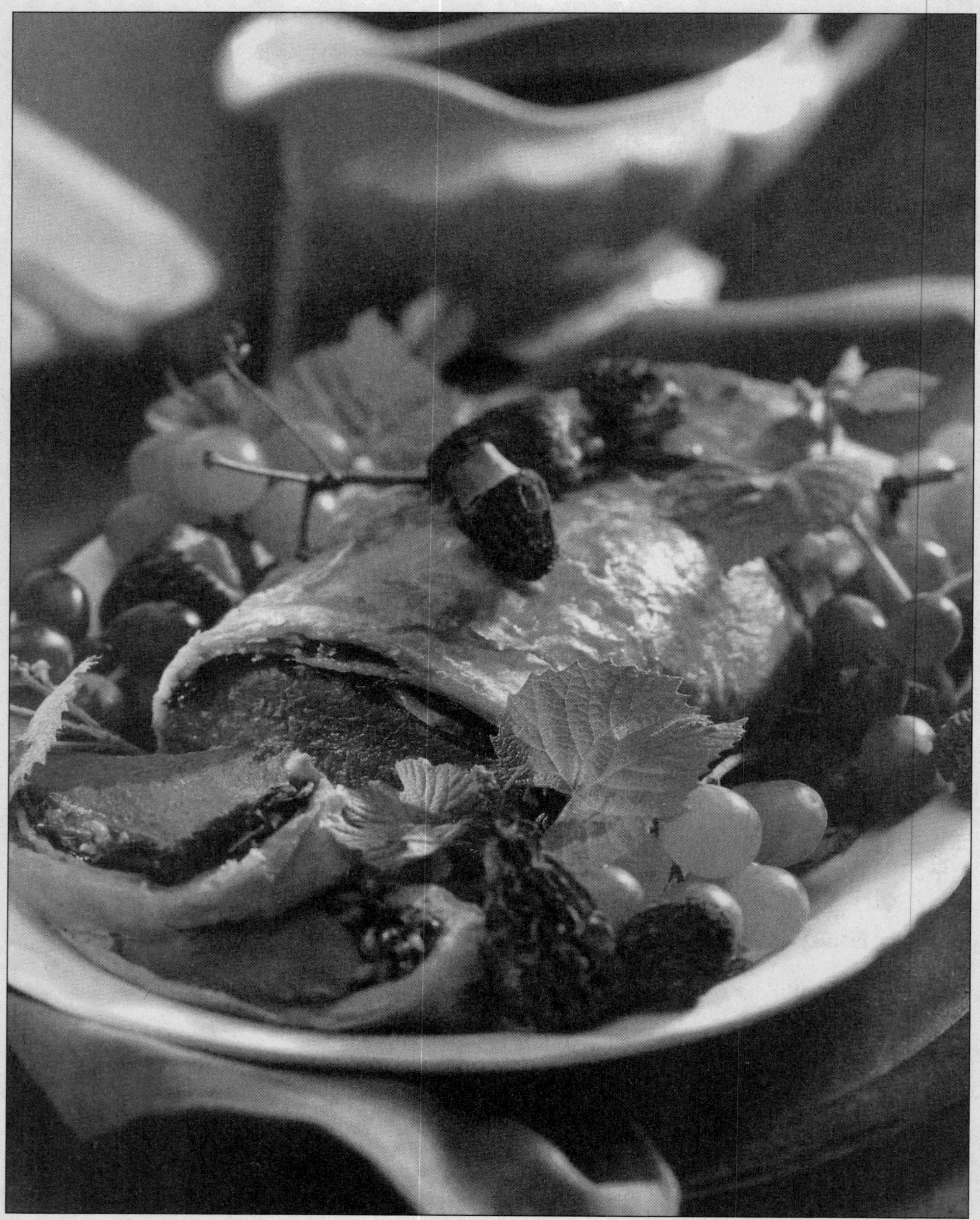

Beat egg white lightly in small bowl. In another small bowl, lightly beat egg yolk and water. Set both bowls aside.

To prepare the shell, roll out pastry on lightly floured surface to a rectangle 1 to 2 inches larger on all sides than the loin. Spread cooled mushroom mixture over the pastry, leaving 1 inch clear around the edges. Layer the spinach, cheese and bacon in a thin strip over the center; the strip should be about as wide as the loin. Place loin on top of bacon. Brush edges of pastry with egg white; this will help hold the pastry shell together while it is baking. Wrap pastry around loin and crimp edges very well to seal. Turn pastry-wrapped loin over so the seam side is down. Place onto baking sheet. Brush pastry with egg yolk mixture; this will provide a beautiful glaze to the Wellington.

Bake for 10 to 15 minutes, or until pastry is golden brown. The loin should have reached an internal temperature of 130°F. Remove from oven. Slice into individual portions and serve immediately with Hunter's Sauce.

**Kate's Cooking Tips**

*Clarified butter is regular butter from which the milk solids have been removed. Unlike regular butter, it won't burn even at high temperatures, so it is ideal for searing the venison in this recipe. To make clarified butter, melt a stick (or more) in the microwave, or in a small saucepan over low heat. Skim off and discard any foam from the top. Pour the clear yellow liquid into a bowl, leaving the milky residue behind. Cool to room temperature, then chill until hard. If there is any trace of milky residue in the chilled butter, re-melt and pour the clear yellow liquid through cheesecloth.*

*Here's a handy chart for internal temperatures of meat at various stages of doneness:*

| Amount of Internal | Doneness Temperature |
|---|---|
| RARE | 130° to 135° |
| MEDIUM-RARE | 135° to 140° |
| MEDIUM | 140° TO 145° |
| MEDIUM-WELL | 145° TO 155° |
| WELL DONE | 155° TO 160° |

## Venison Tenderloin Siciliano

*Serves: 4 * Prep Time: 10 minutes * Cooking Time: 10 minutes or less*

*Peter and I were hunting Rocky Mountain elk in northern New Mexico and stopped one evening in the beautiful town of taos for dinner. We dired on a version of this dish, and were fortunate enough to have the chef share the recipe with us. Although I have altered it over the years, this recipe is simple yet offers a deliciously rich flavor. Marsala, a sweet, fortified wine from sicily, can be found in your local liqour store.*

- 1 cup flour
- Salt and pepper
- 1 lb. venison tenderloin, cut into ½-inch-thick medallions
- 2 tablespoons butter
- 2 tablespoons canola oil
- 1½ cups mushrooms, sliced
- 3 tablespoons minced shallots
- ½ cup Marsala wine
- 1½ cups brown sauce or beef gravy
- 1 tablespoon chopped fresh parsley

Place flour in large plastic food-storage bag; add salt and pepper to taste and shake well to mix. Add medallions, 2 at a time, and shake to coat. Transfer medallions to a plate as they are coated.

In large skillet, melt butter in oil over medium-high heat. Add medallions and cook until browned on first side. Turn medallions; add mushrooms and shallots. Cook for about 2 minutes longer. Add Marsala and heat to simmering. Add brown sauce and parsley and heat to simmering again. Simmer for 2 minutes longer. Serve immediately.

## Chicken-Fried Venison

*Serves: 6 * Prep Time: 10 minutes **
*Marinating Time: 2 hours * Cooking Time: 15 minutes*

*Serve this classic southern - style dish with a brown sauce and garlic mashed potatoes.*

- 2 lbs. venison loin, cut into ½-inch-thick medallions
- 2 cups milk
- 4 cloves garlic, minced
- 1 tablespoon cayenne pepper, divided
- 1½ teaspoons black pepper
- ½ teaspoon onion salt legg
- ¼ teaspoon salt
- 1 cup all-purpose flour
- ¼ cup canola oil (approx.), divided

With flat side of a meat mallet or the bottom of a saucepan, pound medallions to flatten slightly. In bowl, combine milk, garlic, 1½ teaspoons of the cayenne, the black pepper and onion salt. Add medallions; cover and refrigerate for 2 hours.

When ready to cook, transfer medallions to a plate and set aside. Add egg to milk mixture and beat together. Return medallions to milk mixture. In large bowl, mix remaining 1½ teaspoons cayenne and the salt with the flour. Dredge medallions in flour.

In cast-iron skillet, heat 1 tablespoon of the canola oil over medium-high heat until hot but not smoking. Place 1 or 2 medallions at a time into skillet and cook for 2 to 3 minutes per side, until golden brown. Transfer to heated platter and repeat with remaining medallions, adding additional oil as necessary.

**Kate's Cooking Tips**

*When roasting venison, make sure that the roasting pan is slightly larger than the roast, but not too much larger. If the pan is too large, the drippings will spread out and burn.*

*Make sure that large cuts of venison are at room temperature before cooking. This way they will cook more uniformly.*

*When time allows, after cutlets are breaded, place them in the refrigerator for 2 to 3 minutes. I like to do this to "set" the breading before frying.*

## Blackened Cajun Medallions of Venison

*Serves: 4 * Prep Time: 10 minutes **
*Cooking Time: 10 minutes or less*

*Open the windows or turn on a powerful vent fan when you're cooking this, as it will produce a lot of smoke! This dish is excellent served with the Wild Rice Casserole.*

**Blackened Seasoning Mix**

- 2 teaspoons paprika
- 2 teaspoons crumbled dried thyme
- 1 teaspoon black pepper
- 1 teaspoon garlic powder
- 1 teaspoon cumin
- 1 teaspoon crumbled dried oregano
- 1 teaspoon sugar
- ½ teaspoon cayenne pepper
- ½ teaspoon salt
- 4 venison loin medallions (4 to 6 oz. each), ¾ to 1 inch thick

- 2 tablespoons unsalted butter, melted
- 1 tablespoon butter

In small bowl, stir together all seasoningmix ingredients. Pat medallions dry. Brush each side with melted butter. Sprinkle generously on both sides with seasoning mix, and pat to help seasonings adhere.

Heat large cast-iron skillet over high heat. When hot, add the tablespoon of butter. When butter just stops foaming, add medallions and cook for 2 to 3 minutes on each side, depending upon the thickness of the steaks. Serve immediately.

## Applejack Venison Medallions

*Serves: 6 * Prep Time: 10 minutes * Cooking Time: 20 minutes*

*I like to serve this with an gratin potatoes, and a dish of green peas garnished with pearl onions.*

- 6 venison loin medallions (4 oz. each), ¾ inch thick
- Salt
- ½ cup clarified butter, divided
- 3 tablespoons applejack brandy, preferably Calvados
- 1 large shallot, minced
- 1 teaspoon crushed black and red peppercorn blend
- ½ teaspoon cornstarch
- 2 cups beef broth (prepared from beef bouillon granules)
- 1 cup heavy cream, room temperature

Pat medallions dry and sprinkle both sides with salt to taste. In large skillet, melt ¼ cup of the clarified butter over medium-high heat. Add medallions in a single layer and sear on both sides. Transfer medallions to a plate; pour excess butter from the skillet and lower heat to medium. Return medallions to skillet and add brandy. Cook until brandy is warm. Remove skillet from heat and carefully ignite brandy with long-handled match. When flames die out, transfer medallions to plate; set aside and keep warm.

Melt remaining ¼ cup butter in same skillet over medium heat. Add shallot and peppercorns, and saute until shallot is translucent. Meanwhile, blend cornstarch and broth in measuring cup or small bowl. When shallot is translucent, pour broth mixture into skillet, stirring constantly. Cook until broth is reduced to about half, stirring frequently. Add 2 tablespoons of the reduced sauce to the cream and mix well (leave the cream in its measuring cup, or place in a small bowl); this raises the temperature of the cream to prevent curdling when cream is added to the sauce. Reduce heat under skillet to low and add cream mixture. Simmer until the mixture is reduced to saucelike consistency, stirring frequently. Return medallions to skillet and re-warm them briefly before serving.

## Venison Medallions with Herbed Cheese Sauce

*Serves: 2 * Prep Time: 5 minutes * Cooking Time: 15 minutes*

*Serve these tasty medallions with twice - baked potatoes and steamed broccoli.*

- 1½ cups all-purpose flour
- Salt and black pepper
- ½ cup Boursin herb cheese, or any soft herbed cheese
- ¾ cup heavy cream
- 2 tablespoons olive oil
- 6 venison loin medallions (3 oz. each), ½ inch thick
- ½ cup white wine
- Cayenne pepper

Place flour in large plastic food-storage bag; add salt and black pepper to taste and shake well to mix. Set aside. In small bowl, blend herbed cheese and heavy cream with whisk or slotted spoon; set aside.

Heat oil in heavy-bottom skillet over medium-high heat. Dredge medallions in seasoned flour. Add to skillet and sear well on both sides. Transfer medallions to warm plate; set aside and keep warm. Add wine to skillet and cook for about a minute, stirring to loosen any browned bits. Add cream mixture. Stir well to blend, and season with salt, pepper and cayenne to taste. Cook over medium heat, stirring frequently, until sauce thickens slightly; do not boil. Pour sauce over medallions and serve.

## Canadian Barren-Ground Caribou Tenderloin

*Serves: 2 * Prep Time: 10 minutes * Cooking Time: 10 to 15 minutes*

- 3 tablespoons canola oil, divided
- 3 medium yellow onions, thinly sliced
- 4 caribou or venison tenderloins (3 oz. each), well trimmed
- 3 tablespoons minced shallots
- ½ cup thickly sliced fresh mushrooms
- 1 cup heavy cream, room temperature
- ½ cup Madeira wine
- ¼ cup unsalted butter
- Salt and white pepper

In medium skillet, heat 1 tablespoon of the oil over medium-high heat until it is hot but not smoking. Add onions and saute until browned. Remove from heat; set aside and keep warm.

While onions are cooking, pound each of the tenderloin pieces with flat side of meat mallet until very thin. In large skillet, heat the remaining 2 tablespoons oil over high heat until it is hot but not smoking. Saute flattened tenderloins for about 1 minute on each side. Transfer to a warmed platter; set aside and keep warm.

Add shallots to same skillet and cook over medium-high heat, stirring constantly, for about 1 minute. Add mushrooms and saute until tender. Add cream, wine and butter. Cook until slightly thickened, stirring constantly. Add salt and pepper to taste.

To serve, divide onions between 2 dinner plates. Top each with 2 cutlets. Pour mushroom sauce over the top.

## Sweet Moose Loin Roast

*Serves: 12 to 14 * Prep Time: 15 minutes * Cooking Time: 1 to 1 ½ hours*

- ½ cup light molasses
- 1 tablespoon dark brown sugar
- 1 tablespoon sesame oil
- 4 cloves garlic, minced
- 3 tablespoons canola oil
- 4-lb. moose loin portion, well trimmed
- 1 teaspoon sea salt
- 1 teaspoon freshly ground pepper
- Horseradish Cream Sauce

Heat oven to 425°F. In small bowl, combine molasses, brown sugar, sesame oil and garlic. Mix well and set aside.

In large skillet, heat canola oil over high heat until it is hot but not smoking. Add moose loin and quickly sear on all sides; if the loin is too large for the skillet, cut it into halves and sear in 2 batches.

Place seared loin on rack in large roasting pan. Season with salt and pepper on all sides. Spread molasses mixture all over loin. Place in oven and reduce temperature to 350°F. Roast to desired doneness, 13 to 18 minutes per pound. Remove roast from oven when internal temperature is 5° less than desired; I prefer rare, so I remove it when the temperature is 125°F. Let meat rest for 10 to 15 minutes before slicing. Serve with Horseradish Cream Sauce.

## Roast Venison with Green Peppercorn Sauce

*Serves: 6 to 8 * Prep Time: 5 minutes * Cooking Time: 1 ¼ to 1 ½ hours*

- ¼ teaspoon salt
- ⅛ teaspoon pepper
- ⅛ teaspoon garlic powder
- 3-lb. venison roast, preferably boneless
- 2 tablespoons butter
- 2 tablespoons olive oil
- ⅓ cup canned or bottled green peppercorns, drained
- 2 cups light cream
- 1 cup beef bouillon

Heat oven to 325°F. Mix the salt, pepper and garlic powder, then rub over entire roast. In Dutch oven, melt butter in oil over medium-high heat. Add roast and brown on all sides. Place in oven and roast, uncovered, to desired doneness, 15 to 20 minutes per pound. Remove roast from oven when internal temperature is 5° less than desired; I prefer rare, so I remove it when the temperature is 125°F. Transfer roast to serving dish and tent loosely with aluminum foil; let rest while you prepare sauce.

Remove excess fat from Dutch oven. Place pan over medium heat on stovetop. Add green peppercorns, slightly crushing some of the grains. Add cream and bouillon. Heat to boiling, then cook until liquid is thickened and smooth. Season to taste with salt and pepper. Slice roast and serve with green peppercorn sauce.

## Venison Cutlet Delight

*Serves: 4 to 6 * Prep Time: 20 minutes * Cooking Time: 15 minutes*

- 1 cup all-purpose flour
- Salt and pepper
- 2 eggs
- ½ cups milk
- 1 cup Italian-seasoned bread crumbs
- ¼ cup grated Parmesan cheese
- 1 teaspoon garlic powder
- 8 venison cutlets (about 4 oz. each),
- pounded to ¼-inch thickness
- ½ cup canola oil (approx.)
- 1 can (10 oz.) whole asparagus, drained
- ½ lb. bacon, cooked and crumbled
- ½ lb. Swiss cheese, sliced

Heat oven to 400°F. Place flour in large plastic food-storage bag; add salt and pepper to taste and shake well to mix. In medium bowl, beat together eggs and milk. In large bowl, mix together bread crumbs, Parmesan cheese and garlic powder.

Pat cutlets dry. Flour each cutlet, dip into egg mixture, then coat with bread crumb mixture; transfer to plate in a single layer as each is coated.

In large skillet, heat about ¼ inch of the oil over medium heat until hot but not smoking. Fry cutlets in small batches until just browned on both sides, adding additional oil as necessary. Transfer browned cutlets to paper towel-lined plate.

When all cutlets have been browned, arrange in single layer on large baking sheet. Place 2 asparagus spears on each cutlet. Top each with a little crumbled bacon, then place a slice of Swiss cheese over each. Place in oven just until cheese melts, 1 to 2 minutes. Serve immediately.

## Steak with Caper-Mustard Sauge

*Serves: 4 * Prep Time: 10 minutes * Cooking Time: 20 minutes*

- 1 cup all-purpose flour
- ½ teaspoon salt
- ½ teaspoon pepper
- 4 boneless venison steaks (about 6 oz.
- each), well trimmed
- 2 tablespoons canola oil
- 1 medium onion, finely chopped
- 1 shallot, minced
- 2 tablespoons red wine vinegar
- ¼ cup beef broth (prepared from beef bouillon granules)
- ¼ cup nonfat plain yogurt
- 2 tablespoons drained and rinsed capers
- 1 tablespoon Dijon mustard
- 2 tablespoons chopped fresh parsley

Place flour in large plastic food-storage bag; add salt and pepper and shake well to mix. Pat steaks dry, and dredge steaks in seasoned flour.

In heavy-bottomed skillet, heat oil over medium-high heat until hot but not smoking. Add steaks and cook for about 2 minutes on each side for medium-rare, or as desired. Transfer steaks to platter; set aside and keep warm.

Add onion, shallot and vinegar to same skillet. Saute until vinegar has cooked away. Lower heat to medium and add broth, then yogurt. Simmer until mixture is reduced by half; do not allow mixture to boil.

Remove skillet from heat. Stir in capers and mustard. Blend together thoroughly, then pour over steaks. Sprinkle with parsley and serve.

## Curry Grilled Venison Steaks

*Serves: 4 * Prep Time: 5 minutes * Cooking Time: 10 minutes or less*

- 2 teaspoons salt
- 1 teaspoon coarsely ground pepper
- 1 teaspoon curry powder
- ½ teaspoon garlic powder
- 2 tablespoons red wine vinegar
- 4 boneless venison steaks (about 6 oz. each), ¾ inch thick, well trimmed

Heat broiler, or prepare grill for high heat by lighting coals or preheating gas grill. In small bowl, mix together salt, pepper, curry powder and garlic powder. Add vinegar to glass baking dish. Add steaks, turning to coat both sides. Sprinkle steaks with half of the curry mixture; turn and sprinkle with remaining curry mixture.

If broiling indoors, place steaks on lightly greased rack in broiling pan. With oven rack at closest position to heat, broil steaks for 2 minutes. Turn steaks and continue broiling for 2 or 3 minutes for medium-rare, or until desired doneness.

If grilling outdoors, grill for 2 to 3 minutes on each side for mediumrare, or until desired doneness.

## Venison Steak with Red Currants

*Serves: 4 * Prep Time: 30 minutes * Cooking Time: 10 minutes or less*

*While hunting red stag at a 5,000-acre ranch owned by the German baron Josef von Kerckerinck, I learned about the European fondness for pairing fruit with wild game—something I'd not encountered very frequently here in the States. Since then, I've created many delicious variations on this theme. If you're fond of such a flavor combination, I'm sure you'll enjoy this recipe as much as I do. If this pairing is new for you, give it a try; it will give your game a delicious new taste. As it turned out, I took a 16-point stag on that hunt; the meat was delicious with this recipe.*

- 2 cups red wine
- ½ cup sugar
- 2 pears, peeled, halved and cored
- 4 venison steaks (8 oz. each), well trimmed
- Salt and pepper
- 2 tablespoons butter
- 2 tablespoons canola or corn oil
- 2 shallots, chopped
- ¼ cup red wine vinegar
- 1 cup beef broth
- ¼ cup heavy cream
- ⅓ cup red currants*

In medium saucepan, combine wine and sugar and cook over medium heat, stirring constantly, until sugar dissolves. Increase heat slightly and cook until mixture is steaming but not bubbling. Add pears and cook for about 3 minutes. Remove pan from heat; set aside and keep warm.

Pat steaks with paper towel; season to taste with salt and pepper. In medium skillet, melt butter in oil over medium-high heat. Add steaks and sear on both sides. Cook until medium-rare, about 2 minutes per side. Transfer to dish; set aside and keep warm.

Add shallots to same skillet and saute over medium-high heat until fragrant; do not burn. Add vinegar, stirring to loosen browned bits, and continue cooking until liquid has cooked almost completely away. Add broth and boil until reduced by about half. Reduce heat to medium, stir in cream and simmer until reduced to saucelike consistency; stir frequently and remove skillet from heat temporarily if sauce begins to boil over. Add salt and pepper to taste. Add red currants to sauce and cook, stirring gently, until heated through. Serve steak with red currant sauce, garnishing each with poached pear half.

**Available in most gourmet markets and specialty food stores. Black currants, not as prominent in the food markets, also work well here. Just increase the amount to ½ cup.*

## Steak Au Poivre

*Serves: 4 * Prep Time: 10 minutes * Marinating Time: 2 to 6 hours * Cooking Time: 15 minutes*

*This dish is a favourite of mine; I serve it frequently when we have dinner guests.*

- 2 tablespoons coarsely crushed black peppercorns
- 2 tablespoons coarsely crushed white peppercorns
- ⅛ teaspoon hot red pepper flakes
- 8 venison loin medallions (3 oz. each), ½ inch thick
- 1 tablespoon canola oil
- 2 tablespoons chopped shallots
- 2 tablespoons brandy
- 1 cup beef broth
- 2 tablespoons Dijon mustard
- ⅛ teaspoon Worcestershire sauce
- ½ cup heavy cream, room temperature

In small bowl, mix together the peppercorns and red pepper flakes. Press peppercorn mixture into both sides of the steaks. Place on plate; cover and refrigerate for 2 to 6 hours. Bring steaks to room temperature before cooking.

In large skillet, heat oil over medium-high heat until hot but not smoking. Add medallions and sear on one side. Turn medallions, then add shallots to skillet and cook until steaks are seared on second side. Carefully add brandy. Allow to warm for a moment. Remove from heat and carefully ignite with long-handled match. When flames die out, transfer medallions to platter; set aside and keep warm.

Add broth, mustard and Worcestershire sauce to skillet. Heat to simmering over medium heat; cook for about 1 minute, stirring constantly. Add cream and heat to simmering. If the steaks are warm, serve immediately with the sauce ladled over the top of the steaks. If they have cooled slightly, add the steaks back to the skillet to heat through; serve immediately.

## Venison Parmigiana

*Serves: 6 * Prep Time: 10 minutes * Cooking Time: 25 minutes*

*Serve with a side of hot linguini, fresh romaine salad and garlic bread with "the works"!*

- ¼ cup all-purpose flour
- Salt and pepper
- 2 eggs
- ½ cup milk
- 3 cups seasoned bread crumbs
- ¼ teaspoon garlic powder
- 12 venison cutlets (3 to 4 oz. each), pounded as needed to even thickness
- ½ cup olive oil (approx.)
- 4 cups tomato sauce
- 1 lb. mozzarella cheese, shredded
- 1½ cups grated Parmesan cheese

Place flour in large plastic food-storage bag; add salt and pepper to taste and shake well to mix. In medium bowl, beat together eggs and milk. In large bowl, mix together bread crumbs and garlic powder.

Pat cutlets dry. Flour each cutlet, dip into egg mixture, then coat with bread crumb mixture; transfer to plate in a single layer as each is coated. Heat broiler. In large skillet, heat about ¼ inch of the oil over mediumhigh heat until hot but not smoking. Fry cutlets in small batches until just browned on both sides, adding additional oil as necessary. Transfer browned cutlets to paper towel-lined plate.

Spread a thick layer of tomato sauce on the bottom of a large rectangular baking dish (the dish needs to be large enough to hold all cutlets in a single layer; use 2 smaller dishes if necessary). Place browned cutlets on sauce in a single layer. Top each cutlet with about ¼ cup tomato sauce, some mozzarella cheese and 2 tablespoons Parmesan cheese. Place dish under broiler and broil until cheeses melt and bubble. Serve immediately.

## Western Style Bar-B-Que Venison Chops

*Serves: 6 * Prep Time: 30 minutes * Marinating Time: 1 to 4 hours * Cooking Time: 10 minutes or less*

*I was practicing shooting my five arrows for the day, when out of the corner of my eye I thought I saw a deer bolt across our food plot. I slowly put my bow down and glanced across the clearing, resting my gaze momentarily on each apple tree to see if there were any hungry customers munching away. Suddenly, another deer jumped out from the thick cover and darted across. I patiently watched these two young bucks run in and out of the woods, quickly grabbing apples and flicking their tails nervously. As I moved uphill to see what might be spooking them, I spotted a small black bear cub just down the hill. Not knowinf where the snow was, I retreated to the safety of my deck, just before the cub bawled out to the sow. Had it been deer season at the time, I probably would not have ever seen the bear cub, as the 5-pointer would not have gotten away from my arrow.*

*This leads me to a pointer for deer chops. If your chops are from a young deer, they will probably be so tender that they won't need much marinating; in fact, you could probably just sprinkle the trimmed chops with pepper and grill them. In the recipe below, use the shorter marinating time for young chops, just for a flavor boost. If your chops are from a more mature deer, use the longer marinating time, which will help tenderize the meat. Serve with a potato salad and grilled corn on the cob.*

- ½ cup white wine vinegar
- ¼ lemon, diced
- 1 teaspoon ground coriander seed
- ½ teaspoon cumin
- ¼ teaspoon cayenne pepper
- ⅛ teaspoon paprika
- Hot red pepper flakes and black pepper to taste
- 6 venison chops (6 oz. each), about ½ inch thick, well trimmed

To prepare the sauce: Combine all sauce ingredients in small nonaluminum saucepan. Simmer over medium-low heat for about 20 minutes. Let cool.

Place chops in glass pan and cover with cooled sauce. Cover and refrigerate for 1 to 4 hours.

When you're ready to cook, prepare grill for high heat; light coals or preheat gas grill (high heat is necessary to sear the chops while still maintaining medium-rare doneness). Remove chops from marinade. Place on grate and grill for 2 to 4 minutes on each side; the length of time will depend upon the thickness of the chops and desired doneness.

## Pan-Fried Venison with Creamy Peppercorn Sauce

*Serves: 8 * Prep Time: 10 minutes * Cooking Time: 30 minutes*

- ¾ cup white wine vinegar
- ¾ cup sauterne or sweet white wine
- 1 tablespoon whole black peppercorns
- 1 tablespoon dried whole green peppercorns*
- 1 tablespoon dried whole pink peppercorns*
- 2 cups heavy cream, room temperature

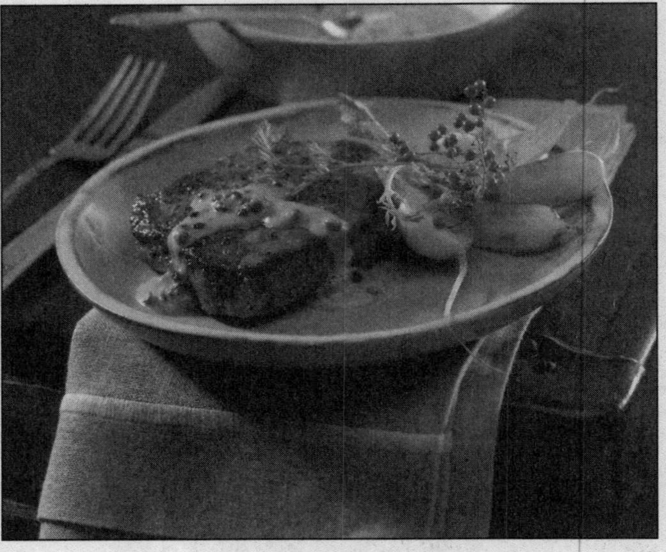

- 2 cups all-purpose flour
- 1 teaspoon salt
- 1 teaspoon pepper
- ¼ teaspoon garlic powder
- 3 lbs. venison steaks
- 2 tablespoons canola oil

In heavy nonstick saucepan, stir together vinegar, sauterne and peppercorns. Heat to boiling over medium-high heat. Boil until liquid is reduced to about half, about 10 minutes, stirring frequently. Reduce heat to medium, stir in cream and simmer until liquid is reduced to about 1¼ cups; stir frequently and remove pan from heat temporarily if sauce begins to boil over. Keep sauce warm over very low heat.

Place flour in large plastic food-storage bag; add salt, pepper and garlic powder and shake well to mix. Add steaks and toss to coat. In large, heavy skillet, heat oil over medium-high heat until hot but not smoking. Add steaks and cook for about 2 minutes on each side, or until desired doneness. Serve steaks with peppercorn sauce.

**Available at specialty foods shops and some supermarkets and also from Specialty World Foods. The green and pink peppercorns add color and contribute* *subtle flavors to the sauce; however, you may prepare the sauce using black peppercorns only.*

## Venison Steak Forestiere

*Serves: 8 * Prep Time: 10 minutes * Cooking Time: 15 minutes*

- 1½ cups all-purpose flour
- Salt and pepper
- 8 boneless venison steaks (4 to 6 oz. each), well trimmed
- 2 tablespoons canola oil
- 1 cup sliced mushrooms*
- ½ cup crumbled cooked bacon
- 1 tablespoon minced garlic
- 1 tablespoon chopped fresh parsley
- ½ cup red wine
- ¾ cup brown sauce or beef gravy

Place flour in large plastic food-storage bag; add salt and pepper to taste and shake well to mix. Pat steaks dry, and dredge in seasoned flour.

In large skillet, heat oil over medium-high heat until hot but not smoking. Add steaks, and cook for 2 to 3 minutes on each side. Transfer steaks to plate; set aside and keep warm.

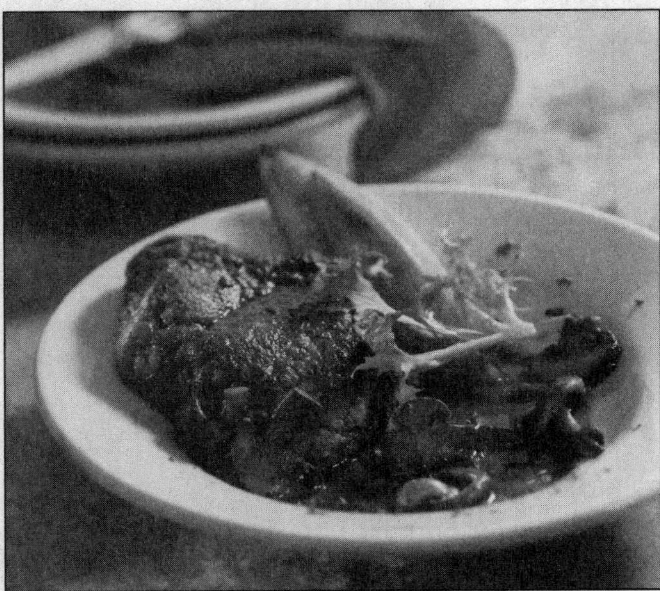

Add mushrooms, bacon, garlic and parsley to skillet; stir well. Add wine, stirring to loosen any browned bits. Add brown sauce and stir well. Return steaks to skillet; simmer for 5 minutes.

**To add flavor, try using half baby portobello mushrooms.*

## Venison Steak Fajitas

*Serves: 5 * Prep Time: 20 minutes * Cooking Time: 7 to 8 hours, largely unattended*

*When the summer days are getting longer, most of us want to spend our time outdoors on a bass pond rather than in the kitchen. This is one of my favorite dishes for times like that. You can start it in the slow cooker at noontime, or a little before, and you'll have a late, quick meal to enjoy while you discuss how "the big one" got away!*

- 2 lbs. boneless venison steak
- 2 limes, halved
- 1½ cups tomato juice
- 3 cloves garlic, minced
- 1 tablespoon minced fresh parsley
- 2 teaspoons chili powder
- 1 teaspoon crumbled dried oregano
- 1 teaspoon ground cumin
- ½ teaspoon ground coriander seed
- ½ teaspoon salt
- ¼ teaspoon pepper
- 1 medium onion, sliced
- 1 green bell pepper, sliced
- 1 red bell pepper, sliced
- 1 jalapeño pepper, thinly sliced
- 10 flour tortillas
- Accompaniments: Sour cream, chopped tomatoes, guacamole, salsa or grated cheddar cheese

Slice venison thinly across the grain. Place slices in medium bowl. Squeeze limes over venison slices, picking out any seeds. Toss to coat well. Place venison in slow cooker. Combine tomato juice, garlic, parsley, chili powder, oregano, cumin, coriander, salt and pepper; stir to mix well. Pour over venison. Cover and cook on LOW for 6 to 7 hours.

Add the onion, bell peppers and jalapeno. Re-cover and cook for 1 hour longer. Warm the tortillas in the microwave. With a slotted spoon, put about ½ cup of the venison mixture in each flour tortilla. Add one or more accompaniments as desired; roll up tortilla.

## Hunter's Venison Stroganoff

*Serves: 4 * Prep Time: 10 minutes * Cooking Time: 30 minutes*

*When time is short but it's just the right weather for a hearty meal, try this simple version of the classic main course. Serve it over egg noodles, to catch all of the savory sauce.*

- 1 to 1¼ lbs. boneless venison sirloin steak, cut into ¾-inch strips
- Salt and pepper
- 2 tablespoons vegetable or canola oil
- 1 lb. button or baby portobello mushrooms, sliced
- 1 large yellow onion, thinly sliced
- 1 tablespoon all-purpose flour
- 1 cup beef broth
- ½ cup dry red wine
- ¾ cup sour cream, room temperature
- 1½ teaspoons paprika

Sprinkle venison strips with salt and pepper to taste. In large nonstick skillet, heat oil over high heat. Add venison strips in batches and cook, stirring frequently, until browned on all sides. Use slotted spoon to transfer browned strips to large bowl after each batch. When all venison has been browned and removed from skillet, add mushrooms and onion to skillet. Saute until browned, about 12 minutes. Sprinkle flour into skillet, stirring constantly. Add broth and wine. Reduce heat to medium and simmer, stirring frequently, until sauce thickens and coats spoon, about 5 minutes. Reduce heat to low. Return venison and any accumulated juices to skillet. Mix in sour cream and paprika. Cook, stirring frequently, until heated through, about 3 minutes; do not boil or the sour cream may separate. Check for seasoning, and add salt and pepper as necessary.

## Grilled Elk Steak Florentine

*Serves: 4 * Prep Time: 10 minutes * Cooking Time: 15 minutes*

- 2 elk steaks (1½ lbs. each), about 1½ inches thick
- 2 tablespoons coarsely crushed black peppercorns
- 1 tablespoon plus 1½ teaspoons crumbled dried sage
- 1 tablespoon crumbled dried thyme
- 1 tablespoon crumbled dried rosemary

- 1½ teaspoons garlic powder
- 2 tablespoons sea salt
- ½ cup olive oil plus additional for brushing steaks
- 8 cloves garlic, thinly sliced
- 3 lbs. fresh spinach leaves
- 2 tablespoons lemon juice
- Salt and pepper
- Grated Parmesan cheese for garnish

Prepare grill for high heat; light coals or preheat gas grill. Trim steaks of all fat and connective tissue. Pat dry. In small bowl, combine crushed peppercorns, sage, thyme, rosemary, garlic powder and sea salt. Press mixture evenly into both sides of steaks. Brush steaks gently with oil. Place on grate directly over hot coals and sear both sides. Cook for 3 to 5 minutes on each side, or until internal temperature is about 125°F (rare). Transfer to plate; cover loosely with foil and let stand for 5 minutes.

In large skillet, heat ½ cup oil over high heat. Add sliced garlic and cook, stirring constantly, until golden. Add spinach to pan and cook, stirring constantly, until just limp, about 30 seconds. Remove from heat and season with lemon juice and salt and pepper to taste. Toss to coat well.

Divide spinach among 4 plates. Slice steaks into ¼-inchthick strips and arrange on plates. Sprinkle lightly with Parmesan cheese; serve immediately

## Thai Marinated Venison Ribbons

*Serves: 4 * Prep Time: 10 minutes * Marinating Time: 4 hours * Cooking Time: 15 minutes*

*Thank goodness for Chinese take-out! As our schedules become busier, ready-to-eat meals play a bigger role in our daily lives, and Chinese food is comfortingly similar at small take-out restaurants across the country. My experience with Chinese food began when I was still in grade school. Every Friday, Dad came home with a take-out Chinese meal. My sister and I loved to giggle over our favorite, the PuPu Platter. I can still envision Chrisi looking at me with her silly grin and snickering, "Please pass the PuPu."*

*As I look back on many marvelous years of Chinese food indulgence, I can appreciate its reliable convenience with my family. It's a comfort to know that all members of our household will vote "yes" when it comes to Chinese take-out as a last minute dinner decision. The best part, however, is hearing my twelve-year-old son snicker, "Mom, please pass the PuPu."*

*Here's one of my favorite Asian-style vension recipes. It's quick and delicious. Serve with a salad or marinated cucumbers. Good eating!*

**Marinade:**

- ½ cup fresh basil leaves, chopped
- ¼ cup reduced-sodium soy sauce
- 2 tablespoons crushed red pepper flakes
- 2 teaspoons sugar
- 2 teaspoons vinegar
- 1 teaspoon minced garlic
- 1 lb. boneless venison cutlets, well trimmed
- 2 tablespoons peanut oil (approx.)
- 2 cups water
- 1 cup no-salt beef broth
- 2 tablespoons reduced-sodium soy sauce
- 2 cups cooked, unseasoned ramen or cellophane noodles*
- Chopped green onions for garnish

In large zipper-style plastic bag, combine all marinade ingredients. Thinly slice venison diagonally across the grain into ¼ inch-wide strips (partially frozen meat is easier to slice). Add venison strips to bag with marinade. Seal bag well and shake until strips are thoroughly coated with marinade. Refrigerate for about 4 hours, turning bag occasionally.

Remove meat from marinade and place on paper towels to drain. Add 1 teaspoon of the oil to wok or large skillet. Heat over medium-high heat until very hot. Stir-fry venison in batches for 3 to 5 minutes per batch, transferring to warm platter as it is cooked; add additional oil as necessary for subsequent batches. When all venison has been cooked, return all to the wok. Add water, beef broth, soy sauce and pre-cooked noodles. Cook, stirring constantly, until entire mixture is heated through. Place on platter, garnish with green onions and serve immediately.

** Reserve ¼ cup of the cooking water and mix with cooked noodles to prevent them from sticking together.*

**Kate's Cooking Tips**

*It's good to note here that you don't need a wok to cook a stirfry meal. Any large skilletpreferably one that's coated with a non-stick finish-will do. I like to use peanut oil for stirfrying, as it imparts a slightly different flavor to the meat and has a higher smoking point than regular corn oil. Watch the temperature of the oil when you're adding meat to the pan; if the oil is too hot, the meat will clump together when you begin cooking it.*

*When using fresh garlic, place the cloves on a cutting board. Place the side of a chef's knife on top of the cloves. With the palm of one hand, whack the side of the knife to crush open the clove. The peel will come off easily, and the crushed clove is ready to be chopped or added whole to your dish.*

## Broccoli-Venison Stir-Fry

*Serves: 2 * Prep Time: 15 minutes * Cooking Time: 10 minutes*

- ½ lb. boneless venison, preferably rump or loin meat
- 1 tablespoon plus 1 teaspoon soy sauce, divided
- ½ cup peanut oil or vegetable oil, divided
- ¼ teaspoon pepper
- ½ cup no-salt beef broth
- ½ lb. fresh broccoli heads, cut into small flowerets
- ½ cup thinly sliced bok choy or celery
- ½ cup fresh chives, cut into ½-inch slices before measuring
- ¼ cup sliced water chestnuts
- ¼ cup canned baby corn ears
- Hot cooked white rice
- Fried Chinese noodles for garnish

Slice venison across the grain into very thin strips. In medium bowl, mix together 1 tablespoon of the soy sauce, 2 teaspoons of the oil and the pepper. Add venison strips and toss to coat.

In wok or large nonstick skillet, heat remaining oil over medium-high heat until hot but not smoking. Add venison strips, keeping them separated as you add them to prevent them from clumping together. Cook for 1 to 2 minutes, stirring constantly. With slotted spoon, transfer venison to paper towel-lined plate; set aside and keep warm.

Remove all but 2 tablespoons oil from wok; increase heat to high. Add remaining 1 teaspoon soy sauce, the beef broth and broccoli to wok. Cook for about 3 minutes, stirring frequently. Add bok choy, chives, water chestnuts and corn to wok; return drained venison to wok. Stir-fry for 2 minutes longer. Serve hot over a bed of white rice, with a decorative topping of fried Chinese noodles.

## Venison Steak Heroes

*Serves: 4 * Prep Time: 15 minutes * Cooking Time: 10 minutes*

- ¼ cup A-l Steak Sauce
- 1 tablespoon brown sugar
- 1 tablespoon soy sauce

- ½ teaspoon ground ginger
- 1 tablespoon peanut oil
- 1 lb. venison loin, cut into ½-inch strips
- 1 medium red bell pepper, thinly sliced
- 1 medium yellow bell pepper, thinly sliced
- 1 medium onion, thinly sliced
- 1 cup sliced fresh button mushrooms
- 2 cloves garlic, minced
- 4 hero rolls, split and toasted

In small saucepan, combine steak sauce, brown sugar, soy sauce and ginger. Heat over low heat, stirring constantly, until sugar dissolves. Remove from heat and set aside.

In wok or large nonstick skillet, heat oil over high heat until hot but not smoking. Add venison strips and stir-fry for about 1 minute. Add red and yellow peppers, onion, mushrooms and garlic. Stir-fry for 3 to 4 minutes. Stir in steak-sauce mixture. Cook for 5 minutes longer, stirring constantly. Spoon hot mixture onto split rolls.

## Venison and Vegetable Kabobs

*Serves: 4 * Prep Time: 20 minutes * Marinating Time: 4 to 6 hours * Cooking Time: 10 minutes or less*

**Meat Marinade:**

- ¾ cup olive oil
- ¾ cup red wine vinegar
- 1 tablespoon chopped fresh parsley
- 1 teaspoon cumin
- ⅛ teaspoon crumbled dried oregano, preferably Mexican
- Salt and pepper to taste
- 4 cloves garlic, chopped
- 1½ lbs. boneless venison loin or top round, well trimmed and cut into 1-inch cubes

**Vegetable Marinade:**

- ½ cup soy sauce
- ¼ cup sesame oil
- 2 tablespoons lemon juice
- 1 tablespoon shredded fresh gingerroot
- 5 cloves garlic, chopped
- 8 fresh button or small portobello mushrooms, cut into 1-inch chunks
- 1 large onion, cut into 1-inch chunks
- 1 red bell pepper, cut into 1-inch chunks
- 1 green bell pepper, cut into 1-inch chunks
- 1 yellow bell pepper, cut into 1-inch chunks

In large zipper-style plastic bag (or nonreactive bowl), combine all meat marinade ingredients. Add venison cubes. Seal bag well and shake until cubes are thoroughly coated with marinade. In another large zipper-style plastic bag, combine all vegetable marinade ingredients. Add mushrooms, onion and bell pepper chunks. Seal bag well and shake until vegetables are thoroughly coated with marinade. Refrigerate both bags for 4 to 6 hours, turning bags occasionally.

Bring venison and vegetables to room temperature prior to grilling. Prepare grill for high heat; light coals or preheat gas grill. Drain venison and vegetables, reserving venison marinade. Thread mushrooms, peppers, onions and venison onto metal skewers. Grill for 5 to 10 minutes, turning skewers and basting with the venison marinade several times.

## Chinese Venison Steak with Mushrooms

*Serves: 6 * Prep Time: 15 minutes * Marinating Time: 30 to 60 minutes * Cooking Time: 10 minutes or less*

- 1½ lbs. boneless venison steak, well trimmed
- 2 tablespoons soy sauce
- 2 tablespoons sherry
- 1 tablespoon Worcestershire sauce
- 2 teaspoons cornstarch
- 1 teaspoon sugar
- 1 teaspoon sesame oil
- ½ teaspoon pepper
- ½ cup peanut oil
- ½ lb. mushrooms, quartered
- 4 scallions, cut into ½-inch lengths
- 1 can (8 oz.) whole water chestnuts, drained
- 1 package (10 oz.) frozen snow peas, thawed
- 3 tablespoons water
- 2 tablespoons sesame seeds
- Hot cooked white rice

Cut steak into 1½-inch cubes. Pound cubes with meat mallet to flatten to about ¾ inch thick. In nonreactive bowl, combine soy sauce, sherry, Worcestershire sauce, cornstarch, sugar, sesame oil and pepper. Add flattened venison, stirring to coat. Cover and refrigerate for 30 to 60 minutes.

Remove venison from marinade; discard marinade. Let venison stand until room temperature.

Set a colander inside a pot or large bowl; set aside. In wok or large nonstick skillet, heat oil over high heat until hot but not smoking. Add venison and stir-fry for about 2 minutes (if using smaller skillet, cook venison in batches). Transfer venison to colander to drain.

Remove all but 2 tablespoons oil from wok. Add mushrooms and scallions; stir-fry for 2 minutes. Add water chestnuts and snow peas; stir-fry for 30 seconds longer. Return drained venison to wok and stir well. Add water and cook for 30 seconds longer. Sprinkle venison mixture with sesame seeds. Serve immediately with hot white rice.

## Gunnison Venison Goulash

*Serves: 4 to 6 ∗ Prep Time: 10 minutes ∗ Marinating Time: 8 hours ∗ Cooking Time: 1¾ hours*

*The mountains surrounding Crawford, Colorado harbor large numbers of elk. One year, Peter and I were hunting that area during early October when the rut was in full swing. We had summited one peak, which Peter had affectionately nicknamed "Zit-Zit Mountain" (due to its propensity to be struck by lightning), and were glassing the clearing below. My heart nearly skipped a beat when I spotted a dandy 5x5 elk just on the edge of the forest. It was grazing with a harem of four cows. Peter and I planned our route to get closer to the bull and lure it in with a few seductive cow calls.*

*Forty minutes later, we set up behind a large fallen tree and started with a few soft news. What happened next still sends chills down my spine. The big 5x5 lifted its head and answered with a bellowing bugle. In the middle of the bugle, from just to the elk's right, out stepped another bull, with a massive 6x5 rack. The pushing, shoving, grunting and fighting that ensured was awe-inspiring! When they finally broke, I got an opportunity to rest my gun and take one well-placed shot. The bullet from my .308 single-shot rifle put plenty of elk vension in our freezer that season. Here's one recipe that I used to take advantage of that bounty. The recipe can be doubled if you're serving a large group. Serve this with hot buttered noodles.*

**Marinade:**

- 3 cups dry red wine
- 2 medium onions, diced
- 4 cloves garlic, crushed
- ½ teaspoon whole black peppercorns
- ¼ teaspoon crumbled dried rosemary
- ¼ teaspoon crumbled dried thyme
- 2 lbs. boneless venison stew meat (shoulder), well trimmed and cut into 1-inch cubes
- Salt and pepper
- 3 tablespoons canola oil
- 1 tablespoon flour
- 1 carrot, diced
- ¼ teaspoon cinnamon
- ¼ teaspoon cloves
- ½ cup sour cream

Combine all marinade ingredients in large nonreactive saucepan and heat to boiling. Remove from heat and let cool. Place venison cubes in marinade. Cover and refrigerate for 8 hours or overnight, stirring occasionally.

Remove the venison from the marinade; reserve marinade. Pat venison dry, and season to taste with salt and pepper. In large Dutch oven, heat oil over medium-high heat until hot but not smoking. Add venison cubes and brown on all sides, cooking in batches if necessary. Transfer venison to bowl as it is browned; set aside.

Add flour and carrot to pan. Cook over medium heat, stirring constantly, until oil is absorbed into flour, 2 to 3 minutes. Stir in reserved marinade, cinnamon, cloves and browned venison.

Heat to boiling. Lower heat; cover and let simmer for about 1½ hours, or until venison is very tender. Remove venison from pan. Stir sour cream into pan juices and cook, stirring constantly, for about 5 minutes; don't let the mixture boil or the sour cream will curdle. Add salt and pepper to taste.

## Wild Game Lasagna Italiano

*Serves: 8 to 10 * Prep Time: 1¼ hours, mostly for sauce preparation * Cooking Time: 50 minutes*

*For those who love lasanga but prefer it without all the mozzarella cheese, this is a tasty alternative. This dish is based on a recipe from a long-time friend of Peter's who served us a delicious meal while we were fishing salmon in Alaska many years ago. It was prepared compliments of an Alaskan moose that had made its way into camp—through many feet of slow—the previous hunting season.*

- 1 quantity of Venison Bolognese Sauce
- 1 quantity of Bechamel Sauce
- 1 package (16 oz.) lasagna noodles
- 1¼ cups grated Parmesan cheese

Prepare sauces according to recipe directions. While sauces are simmering, cook lasagna according to package directions; drain well. Arrange drained lasagna noodles on wax paper to prevent them from sticking together.

Heat oven to 350°F. Pour a layer of Venison Bolognese Sauce into 13x9x2-inch baking dish. Top with a layer of lasagna noodles; they should touch but not overlap. Next, top with another layer of Bolognese Sauce. Follow with a thin layer of Bechamel Sauce. Sprinkle some of the Parmesan cheese over the Béchamel.

Repeat layering order until pan is almost full, ending with a layer of Parmesan cheese. Cover with foil and bake for about 30 minutes, or until bubbly. Remove foil and bake for 10 minutes longer to lightly brown the dish. Let stand for 10 minutes before serving.

This can be assembled a day ahead and refrigerated before baking. Cover with plastic wrap, then foil. Bring to room temperature, remove plastic wrap and re-cover with foil before baking.

## Venison Bolognese Sauce

*Serves: 4 * Prep Time: 5 minutes * Cooking Time: 1¼ hours*

*Serve over a bed of hot linguini, topped with freshly grated Parmesan cheese and red pepper flakes. A green salad and garlic bread go well on rhe side.*

- 2 onions, chopped
- 3 garlic cloves, minced
- 3 tablespoons olive oil
- 1 lb. ground venison
- 1 can (28 oz.) plum tomatoes, drained and chopped
- 1 can (6 oz.) tomato paste
- 1 teaspoon salt
- ½ teaspoon pepper
- ½ teaspoon sugar
- ½ teaspoon crumbled dried oregano
- 1 bay leaf, crumbled

In large skillet, cook onions and garlic in oil over medium heat until soft. Add venison and cook until meat is no longer pink, stirring to break up. Add tomatoes and tomato paste, and simmer for about 30 minutes. Add seasonings and cook for 30 minutes longer. Remove bay leaf before serving.

## Meatloaf Parmentier

*Serves: 6 to 8 * Prep Time: 15 minutes * Cooking Time: 1¼ hours*

*This is an easy meal to put together, because the potatoes roast in the same dish as the meattoaf. Pop in the Broccoli Casserole for the last hour the meatloaf bakes, and you've got the entire meal in the oven at once.*

- 2 lbs. ground venison
- ½ cup chopped onion
- ¼ cup minced green bell pepper
- 2 cloves garlic, minced
- 1 teaspoon salt
- ½ teaspoon cumin
- ¼ teaspoon pepper
- 2 eggs
- 3 tablespoons beef broth
- 2 tablespoons Worcestershire sauce
- 1 tablespoon green Tabasco sauce
- 2 lbs. tiny new potatoes, scrubbed but not peeled
- 2 teaspoons canola oil, optional

Heat oven to 350°F. In large bowl, mix together the venison, onion, green pepper, garlic, salt, cumin and pepper. In another bowl, beat together the eggs, broth, Worcestershire sauce and Tabasco. Pour egg mixture into meat mixture, and mix gently but thoroughly. Shape into loaf and place in roasting pan that has enough room for the potatoes as well.

Peel a narrow band around each of the potatoes; this prevents the skin from splitting during roasting. If you like crisp skins, place them around the meatloaf

with no further preparation. If you like softer skins, toss potatoes with oil to lightly coat them first. Bake meatloaf and potatoes for about 1 hour. When the meatloaf is done, transfer to serving platter and let stand for about 10 minutes. If the potatoes are not quite done yet, depending upon their size, put the pan back in the oven for another 10 minutes or so.

## Sicilian Venison Burgers

*Serves: 4 * Prep Time: 10 minutes * Cooking Time: 10 minutes*

*Those burgers are a little smaller than my other burger recipes because they are not stuffed. Here, the delicious accompaniments go on top.*

- 1¼ lbs. ground venison
- ⅓ cup fresh bread crumbs
- 2 oz. pitted black olives, finely chopped
- Salt and pepper
- 2 teaspoons canola oil*
- 2 teaspoons butter,* cut into 4 equal pieces
- 1 tablespoon olive oil
- 1 medium red onion, thinly sliced
- 1 clove garlic, minced

- 1 jar (10 oz.) artichoke hearts in oil, drained and chopped
- ¼ cup sun-dried tomato paste
- 1 teaspoon Italian herb blend
- 4 slices mozzarella cheese (1 oz. each)
- 4 club rolls, optional

In medium bowl, combine venison, bread crumbs, olives, and salt and pepper to taste. Mix gently but thoroughly, and shape into 4 flat patties (flat patties cook more evenly than rounded ones).

Heat broiler. In large skillet, heat canola oil over medium-high heat until hot but not smoking. Add patties and fry first side for about 3 minutes.

While first side is cooking, place 1 piece of the butter on top of each patty. Flip and cook the other side for about 3 minutes. While second side is cooking, heat olive oil in medium skillet over medium-high heat. Add onion and garlic and sauté until onion is soft. Add artichoke hearts and stir until they are warm.

Transfer patties to rack of broiler pan. Spread each patty with 1 tablespoon of the sun-dried tomato paste. Divide onion mixture into 4 even portions and spoon on top of patties. Sprinkle with herb blend. Place 1 cheese slice on top of each patty. Broil until cheese melts. Serve on club rolls, or sans bun.

**If you are using ground venison with some type of fat added, ignore the oil and butter suggestions as you will have enough from the mixture for the pan-frying*

## Grilled Moose Burgers

*Serves: 4 * Prep Time: 5 minutes **
*Cooking Time: 10 minutes or less*

*When I grill burgers, I like to use a long-handled, hinged grill basket that holds four burgers at once. These racks allow you to flip the burgers without breaking them or losing them between the grill slats.*

- 1½ lbs. ground moose or venison
- 8 slices bacon, cut in half
- 4 hamburger buns, split
- Salt and pepper
- Herbed Butter or Garlic Butter for serving

Prepare grill for medium-high heat; light coals or preheat gas grill. Shape the ground venison into 4 thick patties. Place 2 half-strips of bacon on each patty and place them, bacon-side down, in hinged grill basket. Place two more half-strips on each patty and close the basket.

Grill about 4 inches from coals until bacon is crisp and burgers are done to taste, 7 to 9 minutes per side. Remove from rack. Place on buns, season with salt and pepper and top with a pat of Herbed Butter or Garlic Butter.

## Grilled Stuffed Venison Burgers

*Serves: 4 * Prep Time: 5 minutes **
*Cooking Time: 15 to 20 minutes*

*Here's a fun recipe for burgers. I like to serve them with fresh Jersey tomatoes, sans bun.*

- 2 lbs. ground venison
- 1 teaspoon salt
- ¼ teaspoon pepper
- 1 small yellow onion, minced
- 2 tablespoons pickle relish
- 4 thin slices Cheddar cheese
- 2 teaspoons canola oil (approx.)

Prepare grill for medium-high heat; light coals or preheat gas grill. Season venison with salt and pepper. Mix gently but thoroughly, and shape into 8 flat patties. In small bowl, combine onion and relish. Divide onion mixture evenly among 4 of the patties, spreading out but keeping away from edges. Top each with 1 cheese slice, then with remaining patties. Seal edges well with wet fingers. Lightly brush each patty with canola oil; this will prevent them from sticking. Place in hinged grill basket and grill to desired doneness, 8 to 10 minutes per side.

## Savory Doe Burgers

*Serves: 4 * Prep Time: 5 minutes * Cooking Time: 15 to 20 minutes*

*Before beginning preparation of this recipe, bring all ingredients to cool room temperature. This will ensure even cooking of the burgers.*

- 2 lbs. ground venison
- 4 slices bacon, cooked and finely crumbled
- ½ teaspoon salt
- ¼ teaspoon pepper
- 4 oz. Roquefort or blue cheese, room temperature
- Heavy cream as needed (1 to 2 tablespoons)
- 2 teaspoons canola oil (approx.)

Prepare grill for medium-high heat; light coals or preheat gas grill.* In medium bowl, combine venison, bacon, salt and pepper. Mix gently but thoroughly, and shape into 4 patties.

In another small bowl, beat cheese until it reaches a smooth consistency, adding a little cream if need be. Split each patty almost in half, as though butterflying. Place ¼ of the cheese in the middle of each patty and fold back together. Seal edges well with wet fingers.

Lightly brush each patty with canola oil; this will prevent them from sticking. Place in hinged grill basket and grill to desired doneness, 8 to 10 minutes per side.

** If you prefer, you may pan-fry these burgers in a small amount of canola oil.*

## Venison Lasagna De Katarina

*Serves: 6 to 8 * Prep Time: 1 hour * Cooking Time: 1 hour*

*Anyone who has gone deer hunting with Italians knows that hunting is but a small part of the overall experience. My Italian deer-hunting husband, Pietro, introduced me to this facet of hunting early on in our relationship.*

*We were hunting small game with a few of his relatives. After only an hour or so of chasing rabbits, Cousin Anthony announced it was time for a break. In perfect synchronization, shotguns were unloaded and we headed back to the vehicles. As I rounded the back of one car, I detected a peculiar odor. Just then, Cousin Guido and Uncle Nunzio popped open the trunk, and to my utter surprise, they began to unpack a feast of Italian cheeses, frutti di mare (seafood salad), prosciutto, fried calamari, backed ziti, lasanga, pasta and meatballs, and shortribs and gravy. It was the longest and most delicious lunch I've had afield!*

*In the tradition of my family by marriage, here's a tasty vension dish that you can prepare and freeze ahead of time to take to camp.*

- 3 tablespoons olive oil
- ½ cup chopped onion
- 4 cloves garlic, minced
- 1 to 1½ lbs. ground venison
- 1 can (16 oz.) plum tomatoes, undrained
- 1 tablespoon crumbled dried basil
- 1 teaspoon crumbled dried oregano
- 1 teaspoon pepper
- ½ teaspoon salt
- ¾ lb. lasagna noodles
- ¾ lb. ricotta cheese
- ¾ lb. fresh spinach leaves, cut into bite-size bits
- ½ lb. shredded mozzarella cheese
- ½ cup grated Parmesan cheese

In large skillet, heat oil over medium heat. Add onion and garlic; cook until golden, stirring occasionally. Use slotted spoon to transfer onion and garlic to bowl; set aside. Add venison to skillet and cook until no longer pink, stirring to break up. Return onion and garlic to skillet.

Place tomatoes in food processor and pulse a few times to puree them; do not let them get foamy. Add to skillet with venison. Simmer for about 15 minutes over low heat. Add basil, oregano, pepper and salt; simmer for 20 minutes longer. While sauce is simmering, cook lasagna according to package directions; drain well. Arrange drained lasagna on wax paper to prevent them from sticking together. Heat oven to 350°F. Pour a thin layer of the venison mixture into 13x9x2-inch baking dish. Top with a layer of lasagna noodles; they should touch but not overlap. Spoon one-third of the ricotta cheese onto noodles and spread evenly. Scatter half of the spinach over the ricotta. Sprinkle with one-third of the mozzarella and one-quarter of the Parmesan cheeses.

For the second layer, top cheeses with another layer of lasagna noodles. Spread half of the remaining meat sauce over the noodles. Spoon half of the remaining ricotta cheese over the sauce. Top with half of the remaining mozzarella, and one-third of the remaining Parmesan.

For the third layer, top cheeses with another layer of lasagna noodles. Top with remaining ricotta cheese, then with remaining spinach. Sprinkle with the remaining mozzarella cheese and half of the remaining Parmesan cheese. Top with a final layer of lasagna noodles. Spread remaining meat sauce over the noodles, and sprinkle with remaining Parmesan cheese. Bake for 30 to 45 minutes, or until browned and bubbly. Let stand for 10 to 15 minutes before serving.

This can be assembled a day ahead and refrigerated before baking. Cover with plastic wrap, then foil. Bring to room temperature, remove plastic wrap and re-cover with foil before baking. You may also freeze the assembled lasagna; thaw and bring to room temperature, remove plastic wrap, recover with foil and bake.

## Venison Chili Tostadas

*Serves: 6 to 8 * Prep Time: 20 minutes * Cooking Time: 20 minutes*

*These are fabulous when served with a pitcher of Sangria and a side of Spanish rice.*

- 1 tablespoon canola oil, divided
- 1 small onion, chopped
- ¾ lb. ground venison
- 1½ teaspoons chili powder
- ½ teaspoon cumin
- ¼ teaspoon salt
- ⅛ teaspoon pepper
- ¼ cup water

- ¼ cup retried beans
- 4 flour tortillas (6 to 7 inches in diameter)
- ¼ cup shredded Monterey Jack or sharp cheddar cheese
- ¼ cup sour cream
- 1 cup shredded fresh spinach or lettuce
- 1 cup chopped tomatoes
- 1 red onion, thinly sliced and separated into rings

Heat oven to 375°F. In medium skillet, heat 1½ teaspoons of the oil over medium heat. Add onion and saute until translucent. Add venison and cook until meat is no longer pink, stirring to break up. Drain grease. Add chili powder, cumin, salt and pepper. Mix well and cook for 1 minute longer. Add water and cook until mixture is almost dry. Add beans and mix well. Remove from heat, set aside and keep warm.

Brush tortillas lightly with the remaining 1½ teaspoons oil. Place on baking sheet and bake until crisp and golden, 8 to 10 minutes. Remove from oven.

Re-warm venison mixture if necessary; it should be hot. Divide venison mixture evenly between tortillas, spreading it evenly. Sprinkle 1 tablespoon of cheese over each. Return tortillas to oven and bake until cheese melts, about 3 to 4 minutes. Transfer tostadas to individual serving plates.

Spread 1 tablespoon sour cream in the middle of each tostada. Sprinkle shredded spinach around outside of sour cream circle. Sprinkle chopped tomatoes on top of spinach and top with red onion rings. Serve immediately.

## Kate's Cooking Tips

*If you've never made cabbage rolls before, here's a tip for preparing the cabbage leaves. Cut the stem off a large head of cabbage. Cut out just enough of the core so the leaves begin to separate. Gently place the head in a large pot of boiling water. Peel the leaves off as they begin to loosen. When you've peeled off enough leaves, remove the head from the water. Place the peeled leaves back in the boiling water for no more than 2 minutes. Remove and rinse under very cold water to stop the cooking. Pat dry.*

## Venison-Stuffed Cabbage

*Serves: 4 * Prep Time: 10 minutes * Cooking Time: 1 hour*

*My mom used to prepare this for us using a combination of ground beef, pork and veal; she even found a good use for leftover rice with this dish. Over the years, I have prepared this with straight ground vension and even a mix of vension and ground pork. Either way, it is always a delicious, filling meal with an attractive presentation.*

- 1 lb. ground venison
- ¾ cup leftover cooked white rice
- 4 tablespoons minced onion
- 2 tablespoons chopped fresh parsley
- ¼ teaspoon salt
- 1/8 teaspoon cayenne pepper
- 1 clove garlic, minced
- 8 large cabbage leaves, par-blanched

- 4 teaspoons butter
- ¾ cup tomato juice, heated

Heat oven to 375°F. In medium bowl, combine venison, rice, onion, parsley, salt, cayenne and garlic; mix gently but thoroughly. Divide into 8 equal parts. Place 1 part at the base of each cabbage leaf and roll up, folding in the sides before the last turn. Secure with long wooden toothpicks.

Place rolls in buttered baking dish. Dot each roll with ½ teaspoon butter. Pour tomato juice around rolls. Cover and bake for about 50 minutes, basting with tomato juice several times; internal temperature must be above 140°F. Remove from oven and let stand for 10 minutes before serving.

## Venetian Venison Pizza Pie

*Serves: 4 * Prep Time: 10 minutes * Cooking Time: 15 minutes*

*A few years ago, Peter and I owned an Italian restaurant with a fine dining section in the back and a unique pizza area in the front. We introduced many new pizza toppings to the community. We served 24 different types of international pizza pies including Russian pizza (with vodka sauce and peas), Polish pizza (with Kielbasa and sauerkrant) and even the All-American Pie (with sliced franks and beans). They were a hit! One of the most popular pies was the Venetian Italian Pie. On it, we had Italian suasage and a saitied Italian vegetable known as braccoli rabe, a bitter version, of the more common broccoli. If you can't find it in your grocery store, you can substitute Chinese broccoli, which has a similar flavor. Try this version of our Italian Pizza Pie—with vension!*

- 1 to 2 tablespoons olive oil
- 1 clove garlic, minced
- ½ lb. broccoli rabe, trimmed
- Dough for 1 pizza crust
- ⅓ cup tomato sauce
- 1 cup shredded mozzarella cheese
- ¼ lb. venison garlic sausage or spicy venison sausage (remove casings if using links)
- 1 tablespoon grated Parmesan cheese

Heat oven to 450°F. In medium skillet, heat oil over medium-high heat. Add garlic and saute until golden. Add broccoli rabe and saute for 1 to 2 minutes. Transfer broccoli rabe to paper towel-lined plate; blotto remove excess oil. Chop coarsely.

Place dough on pizza pan or baking sheet, shaping to fill to edges. Spread tomato sauce over dough. Top with mozzarella cheese. Crumble sausage over the cheese. Arrange broccoli rabe evenly over all. Sprinkle with Parmesan cheese. Bake for 12 to 15 minutes.

## Venison Sausage

*Yield: 2¾ lbs. * Prep Time: 20 minutes * Cooking Time: 30 minutes*

- 2 lbs. venison meat, trimmed of all fat and connective tissue, cut into ½ x 3-inch pieces

- ¾ lb. unsalted pork fat, cut into ½ x 3-inch pieces
- 1 tablespoon brown sugar
- 2 teaspoons sea salt
- 1½ teaspoons crumbled dried sage
- ½ teaspoon black pepper
- ½ teaspoon hot red pepper flakes
- ½ teaspoon nutmeg
- ½ teaspoon cayenne pepper
- ¼ teaspoon crumbled dried rosemary
- ¼ teaspoon allspice

It will be easier to work with the fat and venison if they are well chilled. In large bowl, combine venison and fat cubes, tossing to mix. Chop or grind to coarse consistency. Return ground mixture to bowl. Add remaining ingredients. Mix with your hands until thoroughly combined.

Form sausage into patties, or use in bulk for pizza, casseroles, etc. Sausage should be kept refrigerated no longer than 3 days. If you make more than you will be using in that time, freeze bulk sausage or patties (layered with wax paper) immediately after chopping.

To prepare patties, pan-fry in nonstick skillet over medium heat until cooked completely through; if patties are frozen, thaw in refrigerator before cooking. *Note: When making sausage, everything must be as clean as possible. Wash your hands and equipment very carefully before you begin and again when you're finished. And because home-ground meat can harbor bacteria, wear clean plastic kitchen gloves if you have any abrasions or cuts.*

## Sausage and Peppers Skillet

*Serves: 4 * Prep Time: 15 minutes * Cooking Time: 30 minutes*

- 1 lb. spicy venison sausage links, cut into 1-inch chunks

- 1 tablespoon canola oil, if needed
- 1 medium yellow onion, cut into 1-inch chunks
- 1 large red bell pepper, cut into 1-inch chunks
- 1 large green bell pepper, cut into 1-inch chunks
- 1 lb. small new potatoes, cut into ¾ -inch cubes
- ¾ cup water
- ⅛ teaspoon pepper

In deep skillet, cook sausage over medium heat for about 5 minutes. Remove all but 2 tablespoons fat from skillet. If you have lean sausage and don't have 2 tablespoons fat remaining, add canola oil as needed and let it heat up before proceeding.

Add onion, red and green peppers, potatoes, water and pepper to skillet. Reduce heat to low; cover and simmer for 20 to 25 minutes or until potatoes are tender, stirring occasionally. *Note: For a special presentation, serve in roasted red peppers. Cut off stems of peppers and remove seeds. Place under broiler for 5 to 7 minutes to blacken peppers while vegetables are simmering.*

## New Year's Eve Rack of Venison Ribs

*Serves: 4 ∗ Prep Time: 45 minutes ∗ Cooking Time: 40 minutes*

*The winter holiday season is my favorite time to prepare wild game. At that time of year, I have a wide variety of vension to choose from and plenty of opportunities to prepare decorative and festive-looking wild-game dishes for family and friends.*

*My family's traditional meal for New Year's Eve was laden with all kinds of seafood—breaded, fried or swimming in aromatic tomato sauce. One year, however, I decided to experiment with a vension dish for the main course. Keeping with tradition, I prepared an appetizer dish with an assortment of fishes and let everyone wonder what I was going to present for the main dish.*

*While the vension was cooking in the oven, the piquant aroma permeated the house and I could see the anticipation growing—or was it that I heard stomachs growling!? Scrumptions is hardly the world for this mouth-watering dish, which was such a hit that we have made it an annual tradition since. I always serve this with the Rummied Sweet Potato Casserole; green peas with pearl onions add a splash of color.*

- 2 racks of venison ribs (about 8 ribs each)
- 4 cups cubed white bread (you might need a little more)
- 2 cups heavy cream (you might need a little more)
- 3 tablespoons Dijon mustard
- 2 tablespoons chopped fresh parsley
- 2 tablespoons snipped fresh chives
- 2 tablespoons chopped garlic
- 1 tablespoon prepared horseradish
- Salt and pepper

Heat oven to 350°F. "French" the ribs by trimming away the scant amount of meat that surrounds the tips of the rib bones. Trim and discard all fat from the ribs as well. Cover rib tips with foil to prevent burning. Combine bread cubes, cream, mustard, parsley, chives, garlic, horseradish, and salt and pepper to taste in food processor. Process until mixture is soft and smooth. It should be neither runny nor too firm; add a little additional bread or cream as necessary to adjust texture. Coat meat side of ribs with the mixture.* Place ribs in a single layer, coating-side up, in baking dish. Bake for 30 to 40 minutes, or until internal temperature reaches about 125°F. Remove foil from rib tips. Cut ribs into portions and serve with pan juices.

**Because venison is such lean meat, the coating must cover the meat side of the ribs completely to ensure that the heat does not dry out the meat. The coating will impart a delicious seasoning to the meat as well.*

## Baked Moose Ale Ribs

*Serves: 4 ∗ Prep Time: 10 minutes ∗ Marinating Time:24 hours ∗ Cooking Time: 2 to 2½ hours*

- 4 lbs. moose ribs
- Spicy Beer Marinade

Trim and discard all outer fat from ribs. Place ribs and marinade in large plastic container or large zipper-style plastic bag. Cover or seal, and refrig erate for 24 hours, turning ribs occasionally.

Heat oven to 275°F. Place ribs and sauce in shallow roasting pan or 9x13-inch baking dish (choose a pan that will hold ribs in single layer). Cover pan with foil and bake for 2 to 2½ hours, until the venison begins to fall off the bone.

# Part 7

# *Projects*

# Introduction

Bowhunters are, by nature, constant tinkerers. We're always fine-tuning our bows, reexamining the straightness of our arrows, the sharpness of our broadheads, the accuracy of our sights, the straight flights of our shots, and who knows what else. All this often extends beyond our archery tackle, however. Many of us like to get into the woodshop and build stuff—or, go out into the woods and construct things.

With this in mind, in this section we bring you seven projects for the off-season, all by the long-time *Woods 'N' Water* television host, Peter Fiduccia, and his constant hunting buddy, fellow woodworker, cousin Leo Somma. Here they show you how to build a reusable target, how to make a bow rack, how to build a five-star treestand, and much for. Want plans for many more projects? Then pick up a copy of their Skyhorse book, *Do-It-Yourself Projects for Bowhunters*. When the season is over and you're looking for things to do, I'll bet you'll turn to this book right away!

—Jay Cassell

# Skinning and Butchering Game Pole

**TOOLS**

Hand saw
Level
Tape measure
Hammer
Drill and 3/8" bit 12" long
Post hole digger
Shovel

We honestly can't take any credit for this project since we saw it at a major trade show and feel that it's a must have at any serious hunting camp. The brackets, pulley, rope, 900-pound winch, and game hanger come as a kit manufactured by Southern Outdoor Technologies, LLC. Refer to their Web site www.southernoutdoortechnologies.com for ordering information and pricing. You will also find several other products that may interest you.

We have the game pole set up directly outside our barn, but it can alsobe set up inside when the weather gets real bad since it is easily transportable. In any case, it makes skinning and butchering your deer or any big game a pleasure.

Dimensions: 13' high; 8' long; 4' wide

| CUTTING LIST | | | | |
|---|---|---|---|---|
| **Key** | **Part** | **Dimensions** | **Pcs.** | **Material** |
| A | Posts | 3 1/2" x 3 1/2" x 14' | 2 | Pressure-treated ACQ |
| B | Top rails | 1 1/2" x 5 1/2" x 8' | 2 | Pressure-treated ACQ or telephone pole |
| C | Braces | 2 1/2" x 3 1/2" x 8' | 2 | Douglas fir |

**Materials:** Hot-dipped galvanized nails, 12d, 16d; or lag bolts. Meat Pole Kit from Southern Outdoor Technologies, LLC. (www.southernoutdoortechnologies.com)

Note: Measurements reflect the actual thickness of dimension lumber.

**Directions:** Place a 4x4 post in one end of the bracket and another one in the other side. Mount them securely to the bracket using screws provides. Repeat for the other side.

Stand both assemblies upright spaced 8' apart. You will need help from your buddy. Have someone else place the two top rails in the upper portion of the bracket. Mount to the bracket using screws. Nail the two pieces together using 12d nails.

Provide additional support to the posts, by securing a brace on each side about 3' from the bottom. Secure using several 16d nails into the posts.

Mount the pulley and rope assembly.

If the game pole is placed outside, dig around the bottom of each post to make the unit level.

Lay out locations of post holes and set posts in place.

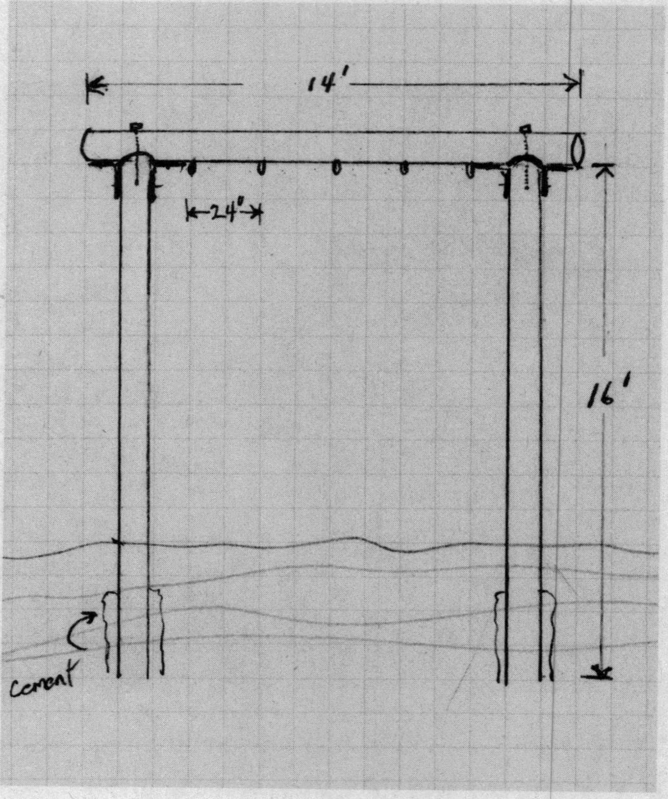

This is a simpler version of a game pole, using 8'x8' round poles.

# Premier Tree Stand

**TOOLS**

Chain saw, hand pruning saw, pole saw
Hand saw, circular saw, or jigsaw
Drill and drill bits
Screw gun and bits
Air-powered gun with 16d nails
Torpedo level
T-square
Socket wrench or open-end wrench set
Miter box
Staple gun and 1/2" staples

This stand was designed to be large and sturdy, which also makes it heavy. The platform is large and strong enough to accommodate two adults quite comfortably. The archer's premier stand allows you to invite either a beginning hunter or a non-hunting companion (a child, wife, spouse, or friend) with you to experience the excitement of your hunt, or anyone you'd like to accompany as they take their deer as well. In any case, the archer's premiere tree stand provides enough platform space for two to sit safely and comfortably during the hunt.

This stand incorporates a 3/8" threaded rod that is about 3 to 4 feet long that fits around at least two tree trunks and is then secured tightly with 3/8" nuts and washers. The stand must be attached to healthy, tall trees with a main trunk of sizeable diameter (at least 18 inches). We like to attach this stand to a group of oaks. It should be set in a group of trees (at least three or four) or one very large tree with a few good sized trunks growing from it. Although the rear platform measures 48" in width, the tree stand can be mounted to wider trees since the rear platform measures 72" wide.

This tree stand is one of our favorite designs because it is also intended to give you more height than many tree stands. The height of the platform is approximately 15 feet, when using 16-foot side rungs. Since 2x4s are not readily available in longer lengths, making the platform any higher is not possible unless you want to extend the side rungs by bolting two pieces together. However, we do not recommend that since doing this lessens the overall strength of the stand and makes it very cumbersome and heavy to move.

Although it is most definitely intended to be mounted in one spot as a longtime stand, with some time and effort it can be removed and relocated, if absolutely necessary, by removing the mounting bolts and rods used to secure it to the tree. Unlike smaller and lighter designs, however, this stand will require up to two or three strong people to move it to another location.

We try locating a fairly large group of trees so the base can be mounted to two separate limbs. This also requires you to find only a spot with one solid, good-sized tree trunk for setup.

For this stand and any other stand we build, we strongly recommend that it be constructed from pressure-treated ACQ wood, including all rails, steps, braces, and supports. If built from pressure-treated wood, this stand will withstand the weight of two adults and remain strong and durable over the years, as long as you also check it at least twice a year to make sure none of the components needs to be secured or replaced.

Dimensions: 14' high; 48" wide; 48" long; ladder steps 25" wide

| CUTTING LIST | | | | |
|---|---|---|---|---|
| **Key** | **Part** | **Dimensions** | **Pcs.** | **Material** |
| A | Ladder tree steps | 1 1/2" x 3 1/2" x 25" | 12 | Pressure-treated ACQ |
| B | Ladder side rails | 1 1/2" x 3 1/2" x 16' | 2 | Pressure-treated ACQ |
| C | Rear platform support | 1 1/2" x 5 1/2" x 72" | 1 | Pressure-treated ACQ |
| D | Front platform support | 1 1/2" x 5 1/2" x 36" | 1 | Pressure-treated ACQ |
| E | Side platform supports | 1 1/2" x 5 1/2" x 46" | 2 | Pressure-treated ACQ |
| F | Platform decking | 3/4" x 48" x 48" | 1 | Pressure-treated ACQ-plywood |
| G | Ladder/Platform supports | 1 1/2" x 3 1/2" x 62" | 2 | Pressure-treated ACQ |
| H | Ladder tree supports | 1 1/2" x 3 1/2" x 65" | 2 | Pressure-treated ACQ |
| I | Safety railing supports | 1 1/2" x 3 1/2" x 42" | 4 | Pressure-treated ACQ |
| J | Side railings | 1 1/2" x 3 1/2" x 49" | 2 | Pressure-treated ACQ |
| K | Front railing | 1 1/2" x 3 1/2" x 40" | 1 | Pressure-treated ACQ |
| L | Seat support | 1 1/2" x 3 1/2" x 48" | 1 | Pressure-treated ACQ |
| M | Seat platform | 3/4" x 16" x 48" | 1 | Exterior plywood |
| N | Seat brace | 1 1/2" x 3 1/2" x 16" | 1 | Pressure-treated ACQ |
| O | Optional deck supports | 1 1/2" x 5 1/2" x 45" | 2 | Pressure-treated ACQ |

**Directions:**

**Materials:** Hot-dipped galvanized nails, 16d, 10d; 1 1/2", 2 1/2", and 3" wood deck screws; 20d nails and/or hooks; 20' nylon rope; 3/8" x 6" carriage bolts, nuts, and washers; two 4-foot lengths of 3/8" threaded rod, washers, and nuts. Two wooden wedges (1 1/2" x 2" x 1/4"). Camouflage burlap, three pieces 48" x 48".

Note: Measurements reflect the actual thickness of dimension lumber.

**Construct the ladder.** (See Figures 1 and 2)

1. Cut the ladder steps (A) to size as shown in the cutting list, using a hand saw or circular saw.

2. Lay out the two ladder rails (B) on edge on a flat surface. Measure the distance between each step, and mark the edges of each side rail. The actual spread of the steps can be made to vary, depending on your size and comfort level. You will find that the older you get, the closer together you'll want to

the ladder steps. For this particular design, using steps that are 3 1/2" wide, the spread between steps was made at approximately 12-13", for a total of 12 steps.

3. Secure each step to the side rails by nailing one 16d nail in the center of the step to the rail on each side. If you have access to an air powered nail gun, I highly recommend its use. It will save you lots of time and energy as you are nailing the stand pieces together and to the trees.

4. Provide additional support to the steps by using 3" wood screws. Screw two screws on each side of each step and repeat for both side rails.

**Construct the platform.** (See Figure 3).

1. Cut the remaining pieces (C), (D), (E), (F), and (G) to size using a hand saw or circular saw as shown in the cutting list.

2. Lay out the two side platform supports (E) on edge on a flat surface approximately 48" apart. Place the rear platform support (C) at the ends of the side platform supports. Make sure that the ends overlap the side supports by approximately 16" on each side. Secure together by nailing a 16d nail into the ends of the side platform support. Provide additional support by screwing at least two 3" screws into each end.

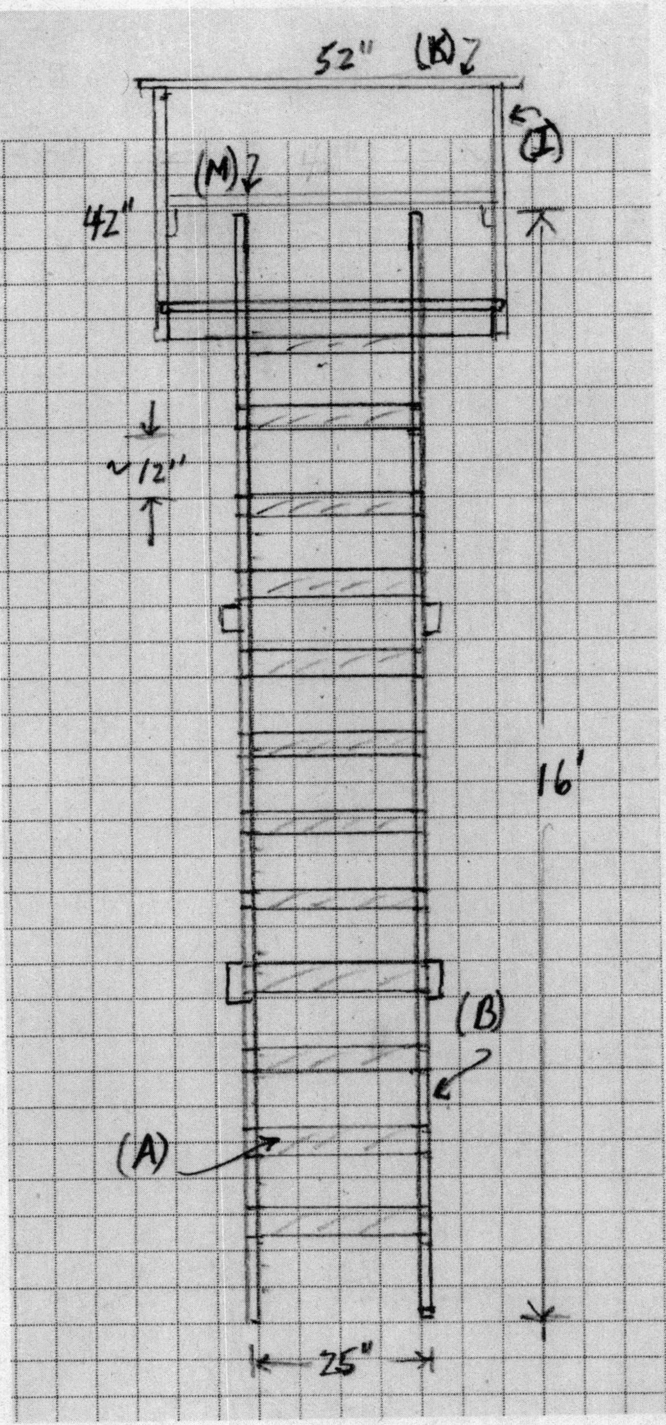


Figure 1 - Front View

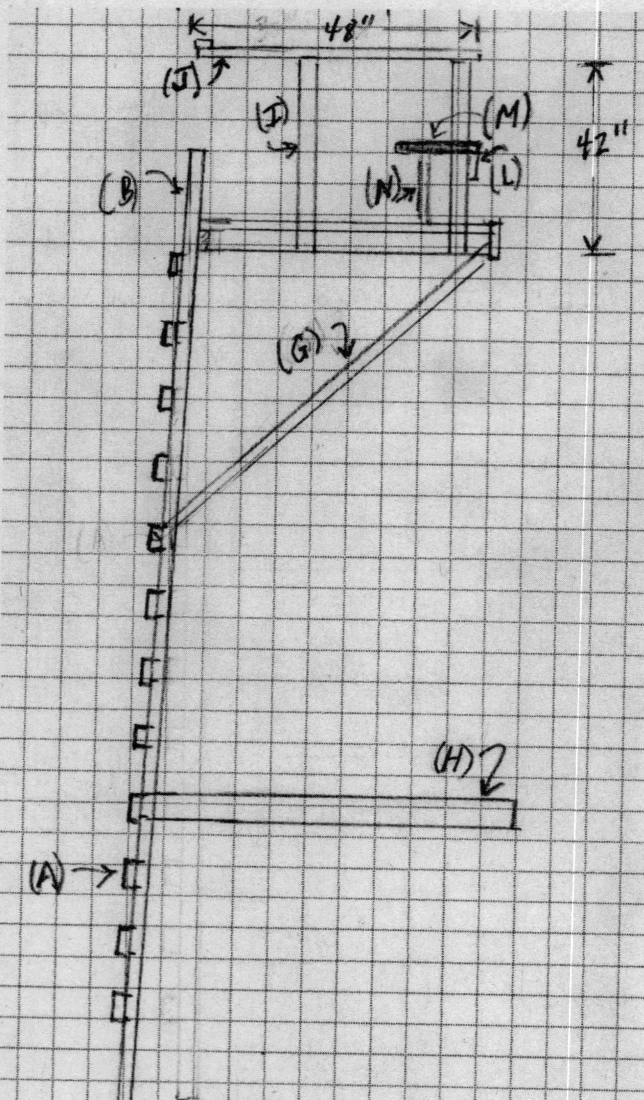

Figure 2 - Side View

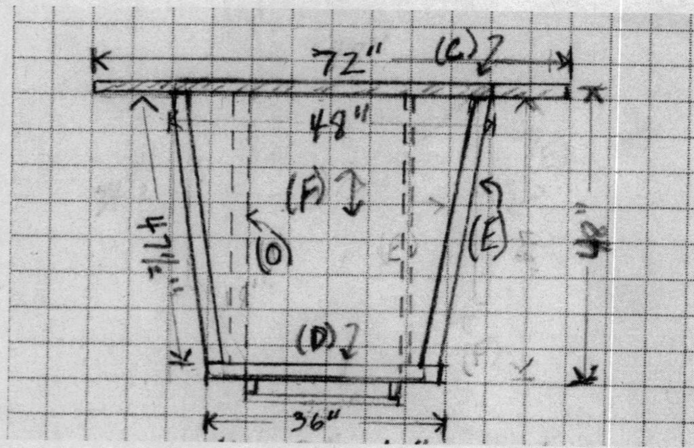

Figure 3 - Top View

3. Place the front platform support (D) at the front end of the side platform supports. Secure together by nailing a 1d nail from the front into the ends of the side platform support. Provide additional support by screwing at least two 3" screws into each end. (Author's note: The ends of the side platform supports can be cut at a slight angle to make for a closer fit against the rear and front platform supports.)

4. Lay the platform decking (F) on top of the finished platform support with the rear flush with the outside edge of the rear platform support. Mark the underside of the platform to match the support frame. Using a circular saw, jigsaw, or hand saw, cut out the finished shape of the platform. Place it back on the frame and secure the platform decking (F) to the side and rear platform supports using 1 1/2" nails or screws into the platform support frame edges.

5. As an added option, install two deck supports in the bottom side of the platform. Place them centered 24" apart. Secure them to the front and rear platform supports using 16d nails. Use 1 1/2" nails or screws and secure the platform into the two supports.

**Assemble the ladder to the platform.** (See Figures 2 and 3).

1. Lay out the platform on end on a flat surface. Place the assembled ladder on the front platform support, so that the ladder extends past the top of the platform by approximately 14". Temporarily support the other end so the ladder is at a slight angle with the platform. Position it so that it sits evenly between the front platform supports.

2. Drill two 3/8" holes through the ladder side rail through the front platform support about 2 1/2" apart. Repeat for the other side.

3. Secure the ladder to the platform with two 3/8" x 6" carriage bolts, nuts, and washers on each side. Slip a small wooden wedge (1 1/2" x 2" x 1/4") on each side where the bottom of the front platform support meets the ladder side rails. Tighten the nuts using a socket or open-end wrench.

4. Make sure that the ladder is at a slight angle to the platform.

5. Cut the ends of the platform angle supports (G) at 45-degree angles using a hand saw.

6. Place one of the supports against the inside of the rear bottom of the platform and the other end so it just overlaps the ladder side rail. Secure it in place by using at least three 2 1/2" wood screws at each location. Repeat for the other support.

**Mount the tree stand, safety railing, and seat.** (See Figures 2 and 3)

1. Pick out the location and trees you want to use for your tree stand. For this stand, we like to look for a grouping of trees with at least two solid main trunks side-by-side, which provides a sturdy footing for mounting the platform.

2. You will need at least three people to erect this stand and secure it against the tree. Have two people pick up the platform from both sides, with the bottom of the ladder on the ground. Start walking it up off the ground. The third person, on the opposite side of the trees, can pull up on a piece of rope tied to the rear platform support.

3. A fourth person could brace their feet on the bottom of the ladder to prevent it from slipping while grabbing and pulling up toward the tree by grabbing the steps. If a fourth person is not available, make sure that the bottom of the ladder is wedged up against the bottom of the tree base.

4. Now that the platform back edge is against the trees, level off the platform by moving the ladder out away from the tree trunk. Have one person lean against the front of the ladder, putting pressure on the platform against the tree trunk. If a rope was used to pull up from the backside of the trees, tie it around another tree to hold the platform in place temporarily.

5. Have one person carefully and slowly climb the ladder with a couple of 3" wood screws and a screw gun. Screw into the back of the rear platform support into the trees. For additional strength and support, use a four-foot length of 3/8" threaded rod on each end. Predrill two sets of 3/8" pilot holes on both sides of the rear platform support. The holes should be spaced at least 14" apart so they align slightly wider than both sides of the tree trunk. These holes will be used for the 3/8" threaded rods.

6. Bend the threaded rod into shape around the backside of the tree, placing both ends into the predrilled holes in the rear platform support. Place washers and nuts and tighten up the nuts until the platform is secured tightly to the trees. Repeat for the other side with another length of threaded rod.

7. Secure two of the safety railing supports (I) on one side of the side platform supports. Place the first one on the tree end and the second one at the front edge of the platform. Secure to the side platform supports using three 3" wood screws in each end. Repeat this for the other side.

8. Place one of the side railing (J) pieces on the top ends of the side railing supports (I). Secure in place by screwing two 3" wood screws into each end. Repeat this for the other side.

9. Place the front railing (K) on the front ends of the two side rails (J). Secure in place at both ends by screwing two 3" screws into the side rails.

10. There are a variety of seats that can be used for this type of tree stand. We have found that a bench seat mounted across the backside against the two trees works best and affords you the most

versatility. Secure the seat support (L) against the trees at 17" from the base of the platform. This piece can also be mounted between the rear side railing supports (I).

11. Place the seat platform (M) on top of the seat support (L). Secure it in place by screwing five 3" screws into the seat support.

12. Place the seat brace (N) in the middle of the seat platform in the front. Secure it to the seat by screwing two screws into the seat brace end. Secure the other end of the seat brace into the platform decking by toenailing 2" screws.

## APPLY THE FINISHING TOUCHES

1. For additional support, secure the ladder tree support (H) approximately 50" from the base of the tree stand. One end should be screwed into the side of the ladder side rail, and the other end into the tree using at least three 3" wood screws at each location. Repeat for the other side.

2. Using several different colors of exterior spray paint (brown, black, and green), paint the tree stand steps, platform, and railing so the tree stands blends in with the trees.

3. Use hooks or 20d nails, placing several of them at heights above the platform to hang your bow, gun, and other hunting equipment.

4. Measure and cut a piece of nylon cord and secure it to the top of the platform to be used to pull up your bow or gun safely from the ground. Never climb a tree stand while holding a bow or gun.

5. For additional concealment when in the tree, wrap the platform area with camouflage burlap. Simply staple it to the top side and front railing with a staple gun.

6. Using a chain saw, hand pruning saw, or pole saw, trim out any overhanging branches or limbs from around the tree stand location.

This is how we used the threaded 3/8" rods to attach the tree stand to the tree. We repeated the process with the tree stand and the other tree next to this one.

# Quick and Easy Tree Stand

When you find two trees spaced apart just like these two - it's easy to build your own simple tree stand. Here we are finishing the floor.

**TOOLS**

Chain saw, hand pruning saw, pole saw
Hand saw, circular saw
Cordless drill
Screw gun and bits
Air-powered gun with 16d nails
Torpedo level

Well, it doesn't get much easier than this tree stand design. True to its name, this one is quick and easy to set up. It requires a minimal amount of wood for the small platform and seat, and does not require any wood for the steps, since access to the platform is made through the use of screw-in steps or removable pegs. We have also shown how to build and mount a ladder with steps, for those of you who might feel more comfortable climbing a ladder rather than screw-in steps or pegs. It is so easy that Peter was able to build this one by himself (okay, not actually by himself—he needed the assistance from his amazing son Cody, and the director Katie).

We do not recommend this one for novice hunters, because the platform is small and offers very little protection in the fall. The seat is small, but large enough to be comfortable and a comfortable seat is what I would recommend that you have for this stand.

It can literally be built in less than two hours. Simply find a few tree spread apart by 3–4 feet and you are in business. We have built several of these on the farm, and tend to use them as scouter stands, erecting one of these in an area that we want to scout. If the area proves to be a good one, we tend to follow up by building one of our more solid designs.

We have provided three options for the steps. Simply use the screw-in steps, removable step bolts, or—if you are looking for more comfort and ease in climbing—construct and install the ladder as described.

The removable step bolts are a great choice when constructing a platform in an area where others may be able to hunt, and you don't want to make it too easy for someone else to climb into the stand. Step bolts are also good to use if you have several different platforms, where you don't want to provide permanent steps. Simply carry the step bolts in your fanny pack, use them to climb into the stand, and remove them as you descend the stand at the end of your hunt.

These step bolts are available from E-Z KUT Hunting Products (www.woodyhunting.com).

They are easily installed using Woody's Convertible Hand and Cordless Drill bit. The step bolts, hand drill, and bit come in a convenient case. We also strongly recommend the use of the E-Z UP Climbing System when drilling the holes, installing/removing the step bolts as you climb or descend the stand. This climbing belt can be worn either right- or left-handed. It is adjustable to fit anyone in your camp, whether they are thin or on the heavy side. It is by far the most comfortable, safest, and most adjustable climbing belt we have ever used. In fact, we keep several extra climbing belts at our camp for our guests. For insurance reasons and to assure the utmost in safety for our guests, we require them to use a climbing belt when climbing any of our stands. All hunters at our camp understand and follow our safety rules. E-Z UP Climbing System belts are highly recommended when setting up or removing portable platform tree stands, as well as when hunting.

Last but not least, this climbing belt makes a great deer drag belt. Simply fasten the belt around your waist, extend the rope to the desired length, and tie the end around the head of your deer or the end of your Game Sled. Now you can walk and drag your trophy to your vehicle or camp.

Once the stand is erected, prune the trees and branches. Besides the use of an extendable pole pruning saw, we recommend the use of the E-Z KUT Hunting Products heavy-duty ratchet pruner.

Dimensions: 15'high; 18" wide; 36" long

**CUTTING LIST**

| Key | Part | Dimensions | Pcs. | Material |
|---|---|---|---|---|
| A | Platform supports | 1 1/2" x 5 1/2" x 58" | 2 | Pressure-treated ACQ |
| B | Platform | 1 1/2" x 3 1/2" x 18" | 8–10 | Pressure-treated ACQ |
| C | Seat brace | 1 1/2" x 3 1/2" x 16" | 1 | Pressure-treated ACQ |
| D | Seat platform | 3/4" x 15" x 15" | 1 | Exterior plywood |
| E | Seat support | 1 1/2" x 3 1/2" x 17" | 1 | Pressure-treated ACQ |
| F | Ladder Tree Steps | 1 1/2" x 3 1/2" x 26" | 13 | Pressure-treated ACQ |
| G | Ladder side rails | 1 1/2" x 3 1/2" x 16' | 2 | Pressure-treated ACQ |
| H | Safety railing | 1 1/2" x 3 1/2" x 58" | 1 | Pressure-treated ACQ |

**Materials:** Hot-dipped galvanized nails, 16d, 1 1/2", 2 1/2"; wood deck screws, 3"; 20d nails and/or hooks; 20' nylon rope; 10–14 screw-in steps; 10–14 step bolts, available from E-Z KUT Hunting Products (www.woodyhunting.com).

Note: Measurements reflect the actual thickness of dimension lumber.

**Directions:**

Cut all pieces to the desired lengths as shown in the cutting list, or to the proper lengths depending on your chosen tree.

**Install screw-in steps, step bolts, or wooden ladder.**

1. Install screw-in steps. This is the easiest approach. If you prefer to use a ladder, skip this step and proceed to Step 3, below.

A. Depending on the desired height of the platform, screw the tree steps one at a time into the tree trunk. Space them approximately 12–14" apart or whatever makes it comfortable for you to climb.

B. When installing the screw-in steps, make sure that you use a safety belt.

C. To make screw-in steps a bit easier to install, I suggest that you use a cordless drill and predrill 1/4" holes, approximately 1" deep.

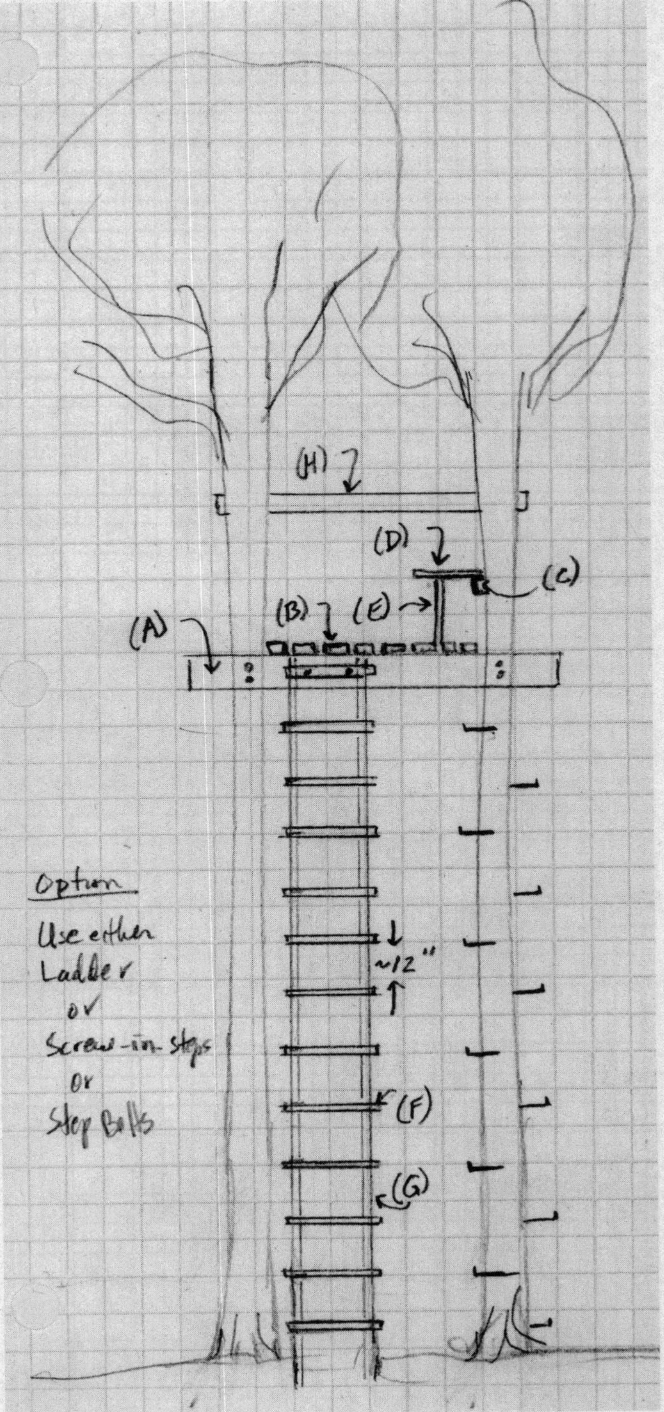


Figure 1 - Front View

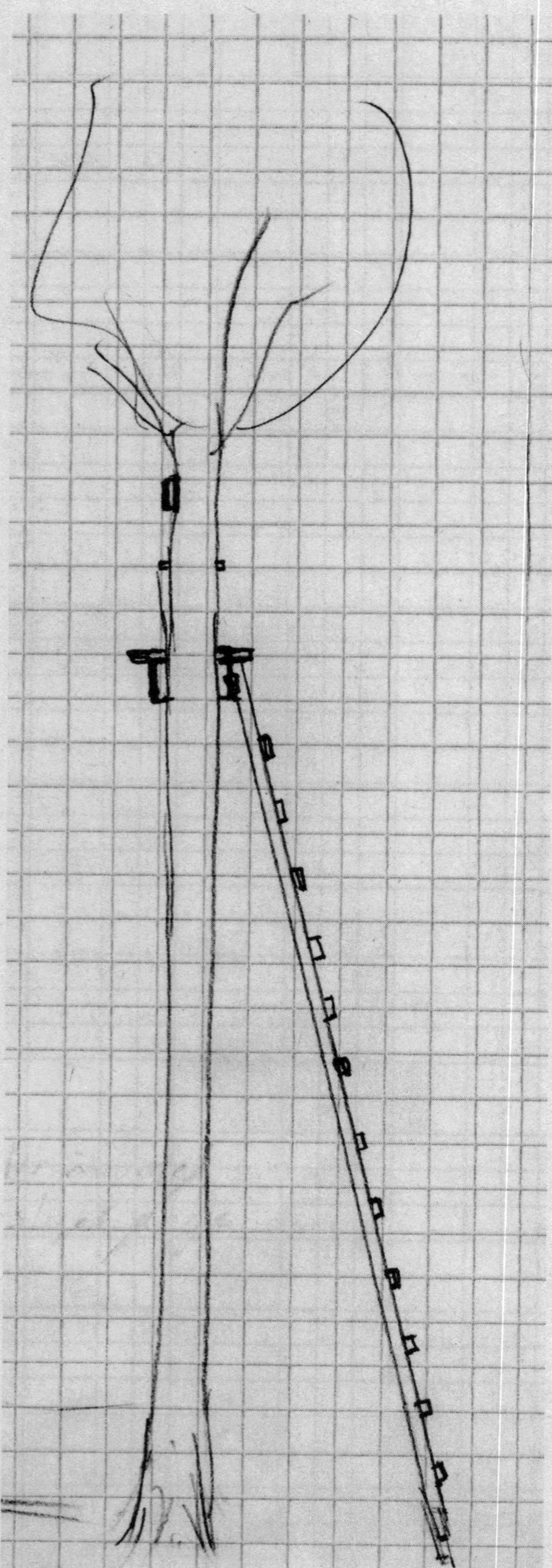

Figure 2 - Side View

2. Install step bolts. This approach is great when you want easy access to your stand and to deter others from using it. You install the pegs as you climb the stand, and remove them as you descend at the end of your hunt. The steps can be installed using a hand drill with a bit or a cordless power drill with bit.

A. Using the hand drill, place the heel of your left hand against the tree and grasp the hand drill by its collar with your thumb underneath and your first and middle fingers on the top of the collar. Angle the drill bit down slightly—this will prevent the step bolts from falling out.

B. Exert just enough inward pressure to start the drill; the drill bit is self-feeding and requires no inward pressure while drilling the hole. Don't try to change the bit's cutting angle; the self-feeding tip is very hard and may break off. If you're not happy with the angle or placement, remove the bit and start over at a different location.

C. When the bit reaches the proper depth, it will stop drilling. At that point, you will feel the last wood chip break; continue turning the drill a few more times, then grasp the drill by the handle with the bit between your first and middle fingers and pull the bit straight out; there is no need to turn the drill backwards. Pulling the bit out will pull out the wood chips. As you climb the tree, just leave the hand drill and bit in the last highest hole to free up both hands so you can raise up your safety belt, then step up to a higher Bolt Step.

3. Slide in your Woody Step Bolts.

Using the Convertible Cordless Drill Bit (these instructions are provided with kit):

A. Place the drill bit in the chuck of your cordless drill. Angle the bit downward slightly and exert slight inward pressure to start the bit cutting. Then just support the drill so the bit doesn't bind;

the bit is self-feeding and will pull itself into the tree that you are drilling.

B. When the bits stops cutting just run the drill for a few seconds then pull the drill bit out of the tree. Flick out the chips from the bit flutes before starting another hole. (Authors note: As you ascend the tree it is imperative that you use a safety climbing belt. We highly recommend the use of the E-Z UP Climbing Belt available from www.ezkutpruners.com.)

C. As you are ascending up the tree just leave the drill and the bit in the last highest hole to free up both hands so you can raise up your safety belt and step up higher on the step bolts.

D. Slide in your Woody Bolt Steps as you go up.

**Construct the ladder** (optional).

1. Cut the ladder steps (F) to size as shown in the cutting list, using a hand saw or circular saw.

2. Lay out the two ladder rails (G) on edge on a flat surface. Measure the distance between the steps and mark the edges of each side rail. The actual spread of the steps can vary, depending on your size and comfort level. You will find that the older you get, the closer you will want the steps to be. For this particular design, using steps that are 3 1/2" wide, the spread between each step was made at approximately 12" for a total of 12 steps.

3. Install the last step at the top on the back side of the side rails.

4. Secure each step to the side rails by nailing one 16d nail in the center of the step to the rail on each side. If you have access to an air-powered nail gun I highly recommend its use. It will save you lots of time and energy as you are nailing the pieces together and to the trees.

5. Provide additional support to the steps by using 3" wood screws. Screw two screws on each side of each step and repeat for both side rails.

**Construct the platform and install the ladder.** (Author's note: As you construct the platform, it is imperative that you use a safety climbing belt. We highly recommend the use of the E-Z UP Climbing Belt.)

1. Measure the distance between the outsides of the two trees at the location of the platform. For our tree stand, this distance was 48". Therefore the length of the platform supports (A) should be made 4–5" longer on each end, or in our case 58".

2. Position yourself up the tree, either on the tree steps or using an extension ladder. Get help from your partner to hold the platform in position as you mount it to the trees. When using the ladder, make sure that it is safely tied to the tree at the top step. Using two 16d nails, secure it to the tree. Use at least two 3" wood screws for additional support into the tree. For additional support, use one 3/8" x 5" lag bolt in each end and tighten using a ratchet or hand wrench. Repeat this for the other end into the other tree trunk. Using a torpedo level, make sure that the platform support is level.

3. If you have access to an air-powered nail gun, I highly recommend its use. It will save you lots of time and energy as you are nailing the pieces to the trees.

4. Repeat this same procedure making sure that both sides of the platform supports are at the same height. Place a board across the mounted support and use a torpedo level to align both sides.

5. Secure the platform (B) pieces one at a time by screwing two 3" wood screws into the platform supports at each side. They should overhand each side by 1–2".

6. Repeat Step 4 for each platform piece, spacing them apart by 1". For our tree stand, the inside distance between the two trees was 34", therefore we used eight pieces spaced approximately one 1" apart.

7. If a ladder was constructed, mount it to the stand. It can be mounted on either side of the platform. Secure it to the platform by using several 3" screws through the top back step into the base of the platform.

**Complete seat and safety railing**

1. Place the seat brace (C) against the side of the tree where you want the seat, approximately 17" from the bottom of the platform. Secure it to the tree by using three 3" screws into the tree.

2. Position the seat platform (D) on top of the seat brace (G) and secure it by drilling four 1 1/2" decking screws into the brace.

3. Place the seat support (E) in the middle of the front of the seat. Screw the seat bottom to the seat support by screwing two 2 1/2" screws in the top end of the seat support. Secure the bottom of the seat support to the bottom platform by using a 2 1/2" wood screw, and toenail it into the platform.

Note: Another option is to assemble the seat on the ground, hoist it up with a rope, and then install in to the tree and the platform as described above.

4. Place the safety railing (H) in place against the tree stumps approximately 40" from the base of the platform. Secure in place by using three screws into the tree on each side.

**APPLY FINISHING TOUCHES**

1. Using several different colors of exterior spray paint (brown, black, and green), paint the platform and seat so the tree stand blends in with the trees.

2. Place hooks or 20d nails at heights above the platform to hang your bow, gun, and other hunting equipment.

3. Measure and cut a piece of nylon cord and secure it to the top of the platform to be used to pull up your bow or gun safely.

4. Using a chain saw, hand pruning saw, or pole saw, trim out any overhanging branches or limbs from around the tree stand location. (Author's note: When hand pruning we highly recommend the use of an E-Z KUT Hunting Products heavy-duty ratchet pruner.)

# Wall-Hanging Bow Rack

**TOOLS**

Hand saw or table saw
Drill
Router
1/4" round router bit
1/4" shank 25/64" keyhole router bit
Jigsaw
Palm sander

How often have you come back from bowhunting to the deer camp or even your home and had to struggle to find a place to hang your bow on the porch, in the garage, or even inside the house or camp? If you're like me, finding a place to hang a bow safely and conveniently has proven to be both frustrating and difficult.

Many times I have gotten so annoyed looking for a place to put my bow out of harm's way between the morning and evening hunts that I wound up either putting it on my bed at deer camp or back in the bow case at home. Of course, that meant also taking my arrows out of the quiver and storing them separately as well.

When we bought our farm, we hung storage hooks on the back deck, and when we returned from a hunt we hung the bows from the hooks. While this worked, it always left the bows exposed to the elements. One day it was so windy that the bows swung from side to side as they hung there.

Leo stared at them as they drifted back and forth in the breeze. I could smell the odor of wood burning, as he concentrated on a solution to the problem at hand. Moments later he announced, "I've got it; I know what to build to solve this problem!" Without another word he was off to the shop. About two hours later we were hanging our unfinished "bow-holders" all over the place.

Some hung on the deck for use in calm weather, and some hung in the trophy room of our deer camp. That was several years ago and ever since we have never had to worry about where to place our bows when we return from a hunt.

The Wall-Hanging Bow Rack has become part of our bowhunting equipment. I even take one with me when I'm going bowhunting to tape an episode for our television show *Woods 'N' Water,* which is seen on The Sportsman Channel (visit our Web site for exact times and dates of our show, at www.woodsnwater.tv). I can hang it in my room or in a safe place out of the wind outside on the deck.

Keeping your bow safe from someone accidentally bumping into it, moving it, or just handling it, is paramount to keeping everything—especially your sights and rests—from being moved or broken.

The best parts about building this handy bow rack are that it is very simple to make, it can be hung anywhere without taking up much room, and once finished it looks nice as well. A tip from Leo is to make several of them so you'll have some extras for guests and to hang in different places for yourself as well. The one in the book is made from solid oak and finished with a stain and then protected with a varnish finish. Any type of wood will work just as well, however.

Dimensions: 7" high; 3 1/2" wide

| CUTTING LIST | | | | |
|---|---|---|---|---|
| **Key** | **Part** | **Dimensions** | **Pcs.** | **Material** |
| A | Wall rack | 3/4" x 3 1/2" x 7" | 1 | Oak |
| B | Dowels | 1/4" x 2 3/4" | 1 | Oak |

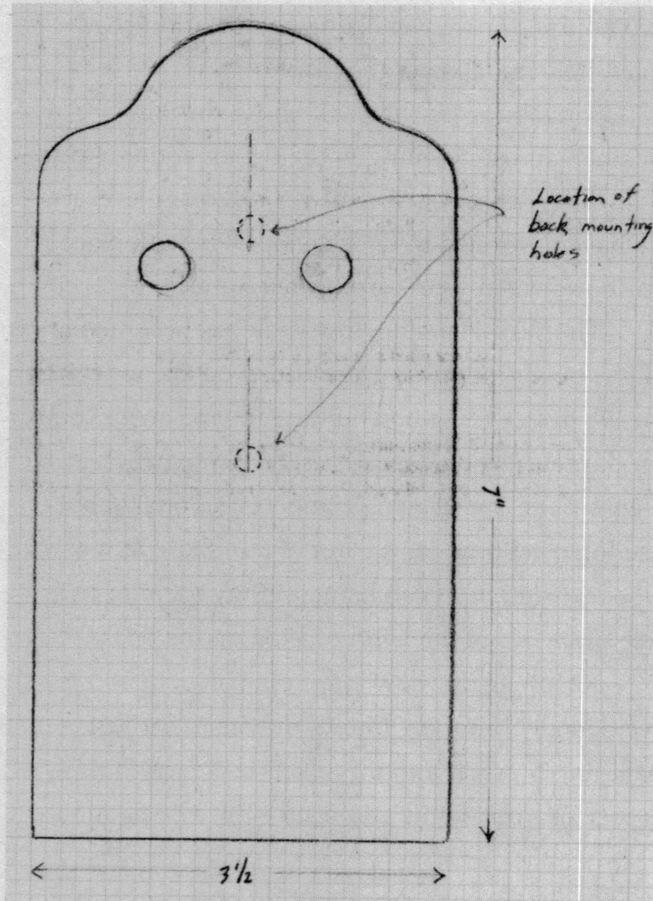

Figure 1 - Front View

**Materials:** Wood glue

Note: Measurements reflect the actual thickness of dimension lumber.

**Directions:**

Cut and shape the wall rack (A).

1. Cut the wall rack (A) to size as shown in Figure 1.

2. Finish off the front edge with a router using a 1/4" round router bit.

3. Drill 1/4" holes as shown through to the back.

4. Round off the tips of both dowels (B) by sanding the ends.

5. Place a little glue in the hole and tap the dowels into the hole so that the dowels lie even with the back.

6. Prior to mounting, holes need to be made in the back of the wall rack. Drill two 1/4" holes 1/4" deep at two locations in the back of the wall rack, approximately 2 1/2" apart along the center line of the rack. Use a keyhole bit on the router and go up 1" toward the top of each hole.

7. Cut a piece of green felt the same shape as the rack and glue it to the back.

## APPLY FINISHING TOUCHES

1. Finish-sand the rack using a sheet of sandpaper or a palm sander.

2. Apply a coat of stain, and then two coats of varnish. Allow drying time between coats.

## MOUNT THE WALL RACK

The wall rack can be mounted anywhere. Use anchors if there are no studs in the area, line up the back holes and install anchors. Use wood screws and slip the shelf back over the screw heads and push down. Use a level when placing the anchors or screws into the wall.

# Bowhunter's Reusable Practice Target

**TOOLS**

Hand saw or table saw
Hammer
Drill and 3/8" wood bit and metal bit
Screw gun
Square
Jigsaw
3/8" wrench

Believe it or not, I saw this practice stand at a friend's house almost ten years ago. When I was asked to write this book, this is one of the first projects I thought of adding to the table of contents. The reasons were simple: this practice stand is so practical; it can easily be moved, and you can use cardboard, Styrofoam, or simply place a pre-made target block in it.

As mentioned above, I first saw this stand at a friend's house. I can't take credit for this design; only for providing the step-by-step directions for making one similar to his.

John Bennete deserves credit for the design. A retired carpenter, John spends much of his time bowhunting, mostly in eastern Long Island-poor unlucky guy. All kidding aside, I am sure he spends the off-season using this practice stand to keep in shape.

Dimensions: 46" high; 33" wide; 22" deep

| CUTTING LIST | | | | |
|---|---|---|---|---|
| Key | Part | Dimensions | Pcs. | Material |
| A | Vertical Sides | 1 1/2" x 5 1/2" x 46" | 2 | ACQ |
| B | Shelf | 1 1/2" x 5 1/2" x 24" | 1 | ACQ |
| C | Bottom supports | 3/4" x 3 1/2" x 27" | 2 | ACQ plywood |
| D | Front stops | 3/4" x 3 1/2" x 22" | 2 | ACQ plywood |
| E | End supports | 3/4" x 12" x 22" | 2 | ACQ plywood |
| F | Shelf supports | 3/4" x 5 1/2" x 12" | 2 | ACQ plywood |

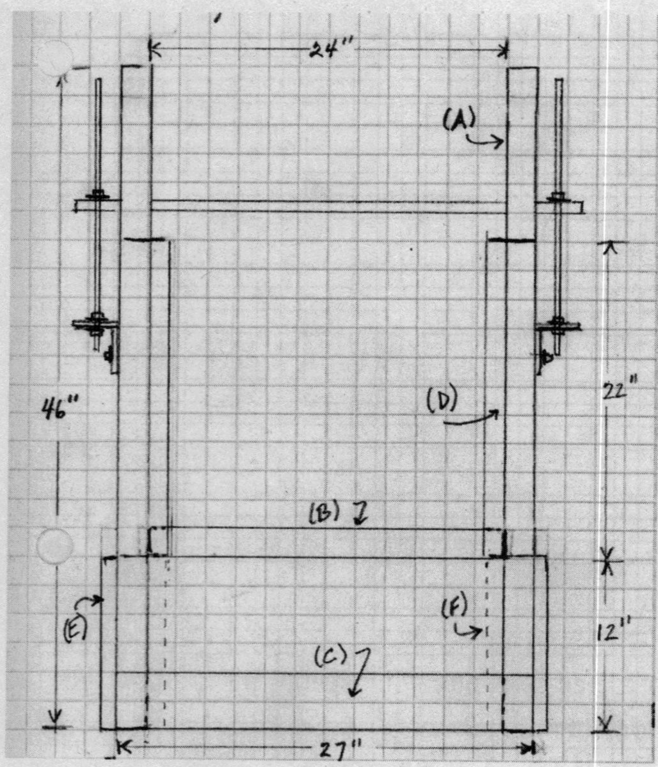


Figure 1 - Front View

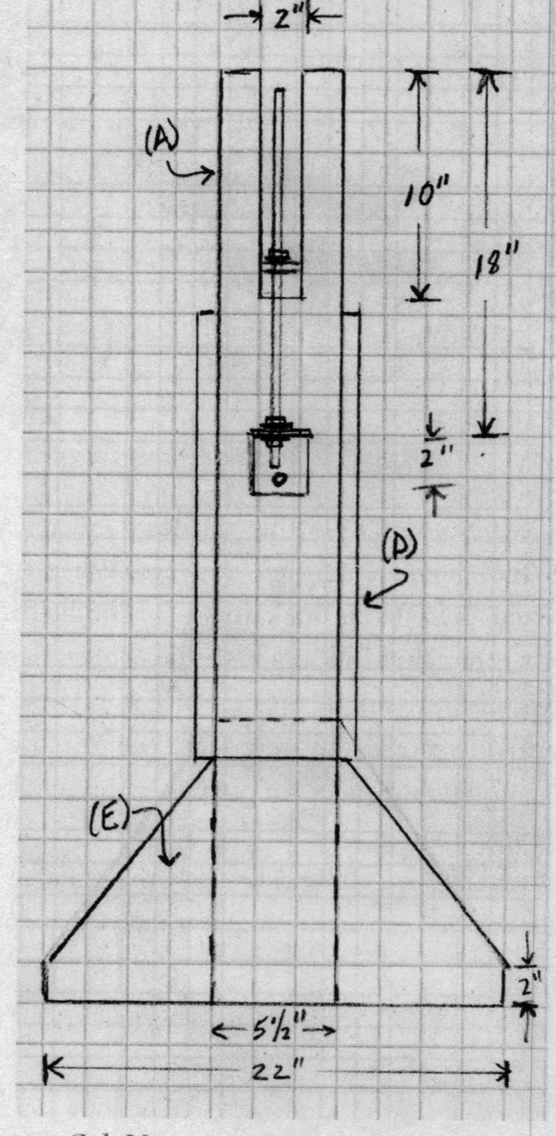


Figure 2 - Side View

**Materials:** Wood glue; 3" and 1 1/2" decking screws; 3/8" thick steel plate, 6" x 33"; two 3/8" galvanized threaded bolts 20" long, six 3/8" nuts and flat washers; two 3 x 3" L-brackets, 3" wide; two 3/8" x 3" carriage bolts, nuts, and washers.

Note: Measurements reflect the actual thickness of dimension lumber.

**Directions:**

Measure and cut all the pieces (A), (B), (C), (D), (E) and (F) as shown in cutting list. Use a hand saw, circular saw, or table saw.

1. Using a hand saw, jigsaw, or table saw, make the cutout in pieces (A), as shown in Figure 2.

2. Using a hand saw or jigsaw, cut the shape of pieces (E), as shown in Figure 2.

3. Have the cutout made, as shown in Figure 3, for the metal top plate. We recommend that you have this done at a steel and iron shop, including the drilling of a 3/8" hole at each end of the plate.

**Assemble the frame.**

1. Lay out the two vertical sides (A) on a flat surface approximately 24" apart. Place the shelf (B) 12" from the bottom. Secure in place by using wood glue and three 3" decking screws into the ends on each side.

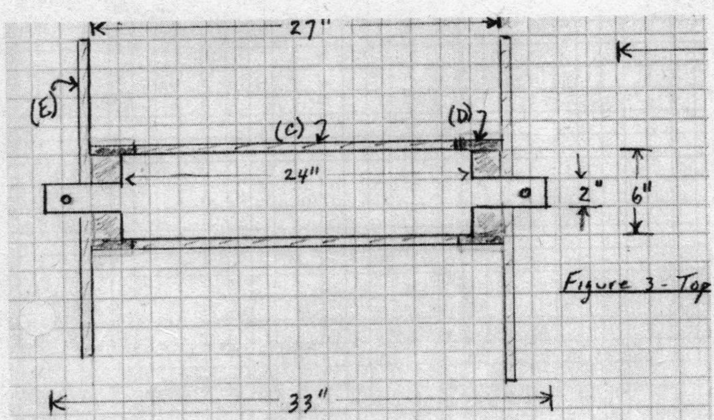


Figure 3 - Top View

2. Place the bottom supports (C) at the bottom of the vertical sides (A). Secure in place by using wood glue and two 1 1/2" decking screws at each of the four locations.

3. Place the end supports (E) on both sides and secure in place by using wood glue and five 1 1/2" decking screws.

4. Place the bottom shelf supports (F) under each shelf against the vertical sides. Secure in place using wood glue and six 1 1/2" decking screws on each side.

5. Place the front stops (D) against the front edge of the vertical sides (A). Secure in place using wood glue and six 1 1/2" decking screws on each side.

6. Using a drill and a 3/8" metal bit, drill two holes in the 3" x 3" brackets. One hole should be drilled in the middle of the top of the bracket, and the other in the middle of the bottom side of the bracket.

7. Using a drill with a 3/8" wood bit, drill a hole in the center of each vertical side (A), 20" down from the top (see Figure 2).

8. Mount the bracket on each side using a carriage bolt, nut, and washer. Tighten using a 3/8" open-end wrench.

9. Place a threaded rod in each of the brackets. Secure in place using a nut and washer on each side of the bracket, as shown in Figure 1.

10. Place the metal top plate in the cutout of the vertical sides so that the ends of the plate fit over the top ends of the threaded rods.

**Place the desired target material in the target.** The design of this target allows you to use layers of cardboard, Styrofoam, or a target block between the metal top plate and the bottom shelf. Cardboard is good if you're shooting target tips; Styrofoam works well if using broadheads, and either target tips or broadheads may work, depending on the type of target block used.

1. If you are using cardboard, cut the pieces so they fit between the two vertical sides. Make the cardboard at least 24" deep.

2. Layer the cardboard so that it fills in the space from the bottom shelf and the top metal plate. Using enough cardboard pieces, make sure that the

top metal plate sits a few inches higher than the bottom cutout in the vertical sides.

3. Using a 3/8" wrench, tighten down the nuts on both sides evenly until the cardboard is crushed as tightly as possible. The target is now ready to use. As you shoot arrows into the target, periodically tighten the nuts to keep the cardboard as tight as possible.

4. Repeat this same procedure using dense Styrofoam.

5. If neither cardboard nor Styrofoam is used, simply get a block target slightly smaller than the opening of this stand. Place it on the bottom shelf and tighten up on the nuts.

# Bow and Arrow Practice Stand

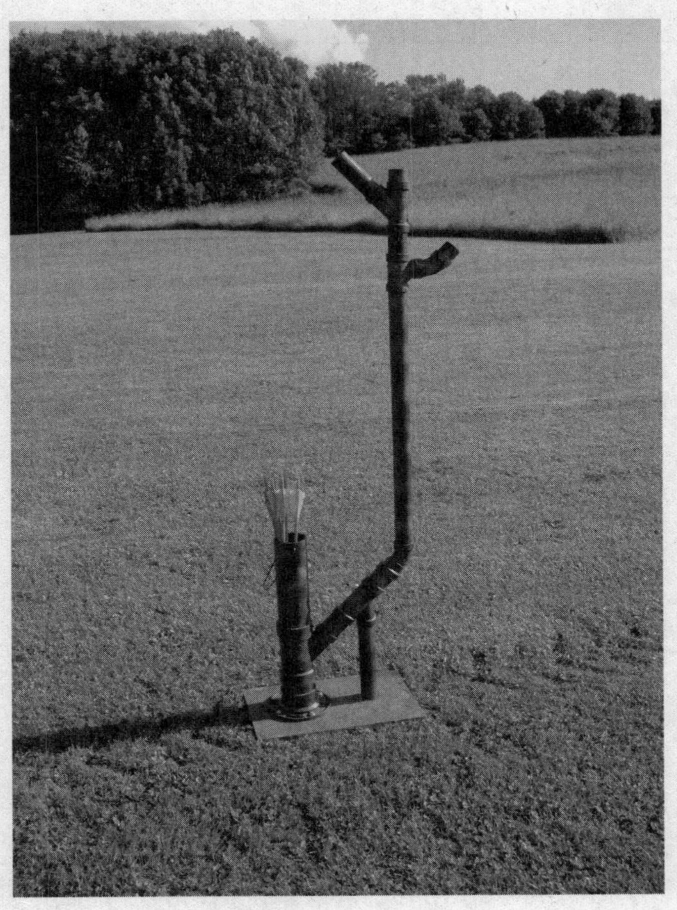

We built the archer's shed, the archer's target stand, and then found that something was missing. Since the shed and target are out in an open field, there is no place to hang our bows or store our arrows when target shooting. I can't tell you how many times, when laying my bow on the ground to retrieve my arrows from the target, that someone came quite close to stepping on my bow. Therefore, the need for a freestanding bow and arrow practice stand was born.

Another relatively easy project to make is this bow and arrow practice stand. It is made of standard PVC pipe and fittings. It holds a couple of bows and provides a convenient place to store practice arrows while target shooting. Both broadheads and target tip arrows can be stored. It is portable so place it anywhere you want, set up your target, and you are ready to go.

Dimensions: 65" high; 19" wide

**TOOLS**

Drill and 1/8" drill bit
PVC hand saw
Miter box
Needlenose pliers

| CUTTING LIST | | | | |
|---|---|---|---|---|
| **Key** | **Part** | **Dimensions** | **Pcs.** | **Material** |
| A | Toilet flange | 3" toilet flange | 1 | PVC |
| B | Nipple | 3" | 1 | PVC |
| D | Arrow holder | 3" x 12" | 1 | PVC |
| E | Nipples | 2" x 2" long | 2 | PVC |
| G | Support pipe | 1 1/2" x 8-10" long | 1 | PVC |
| J | Bow support | 1 1/2" x 30" long | 1 | PVC |
| M | Bow holder 1 | 1 1/2" x 2" long | 1 | PVC |
| N | Nipple | 1 1/2" x 3" long | 1 | PVC |
| P | Nipple | 1 1/2" x 2" long | 1 | PVC |
| Q | Bow holder 2 | 1 1/2" x 5" long | 1 | PVC |
| R | Bottom plate | 3/4" x 12" x 20" | 1 | Exterior-grade plywood |

**Materials:** 12" piece of wire hanger; brown, black, and green spray paint; PVC cement and assorted PVC fittings as follows: one 3" x 2" reducing Y (part C); one 2" x 1 1/2" reducing coupling (part H); two 1 1/2" straight 45-degree elbows (parts I and L); one 1 1/2" T-fitting part K); one 2" x 1 1/2" Y (parts F and O), three 1 1/2" plugs; three 3/4" long # 6 wood screws; small piece of foam about 3"diameter.

**Directions:**

Cut all the PVC nipples and other pieces (B through Q) to the specified lengths, as shown in the cutting list, using a PVC hand saw and miter box.

**Assemble the arrow holder and base.**

1. Place the toilet flange (A) on a flat surface. Using PVC cement on the bottom of the cut pipe and on the inside of the toilet flange, place the nipple (B) in the flange, twisting it slightly until flush with the bottom. Allow cement to dry for a few minutes.

2. Using PVC cement, place the 3" x 2" Y (C) on top of (B). Make sure that the Y is facing up.

3. Attach (D) into the top of (C).

4. Drill an 1/8" hole on each side at the top of PVC pipe (D) approximately 1" from the top.

5. Bend the piece of wire hanger to shape, as shown in Figure 1, and then place it in each of the holes. Using a pair of needlenose pliers, bend the tips of the wire on both sides inside of the pipe.

6. Screw down the toilet flange using 3/4" #6 wood screws to the bottom wood plate (R), as shown in Figure 1.

**Assemble the bow holder.**

1. Attach the nipple (E) into the Y portion of (C).

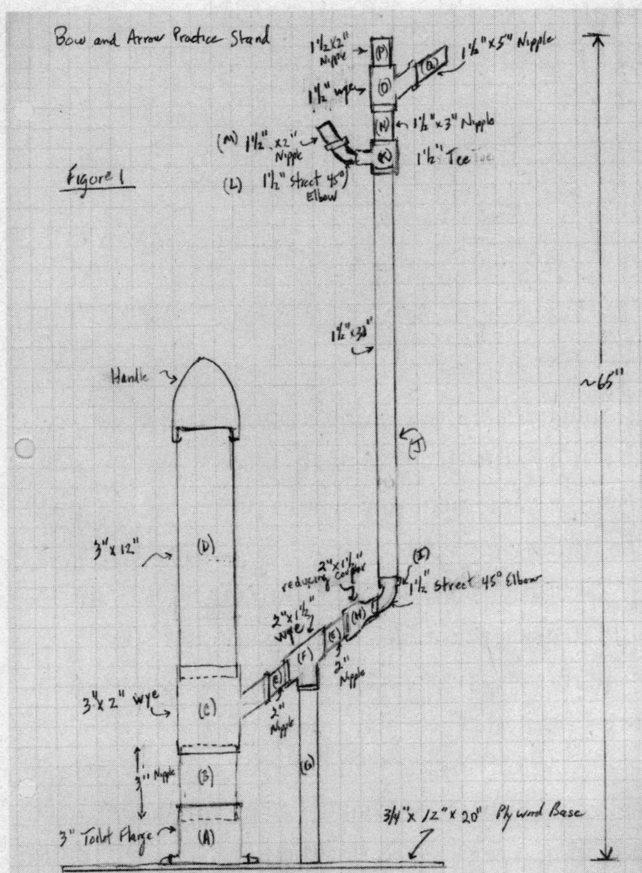


Figure 1 - Side View

2. Attach the 2" x 1 1/2" Y (F) into the other end of (E). Make sure that the bottom of the Y faces the bottom plate.

3. Attach another nipple (E) into the top portion of the Y (F).

4. Attach the 2" x 1 1/2" reducing coupling to (E).

5. Attach the 1 1/2" straight 45-degree elbow (I) into (H). Make sure that the top of the elbow faces up in a vertical position and is parallel to the arrow holder section.

6. Attach the bow support (J) into (I).

7. Attach the 1 1/2" T (K) onto (J).

8. Attach the 1 1/2" straight 45-degree elbow (L) into the side of the T (K). Make sure that the elbow is lined up in the vertical upright position.

9. Attach the bow holder 1 (M) into (L).

10. Attach the nipple (N) into top of (K).

11. Attach the 1 1/2" Y (O) into the top of (N). Make sure that the Y faces up and it is faced 180 degrees from the bottom bow holder (M).

12. Attach the nipple (P) into the top of (O).

13. Attach the bow holder 2 (Q) into (O).

14. Attach 1 1/2" plugs into the top pipe sections at locations (M), (P), and (Q).

## APPLY FINISHING TOUCHES

1. Using three different colors (black, brown, and green) spray paint the bow and arrow holder, creating a camouflage pattern. Wait at least 30 minutes between colors.

2. Place the small piece or foam in the bottom of the arrow holder to provide protection for the arrow tips.

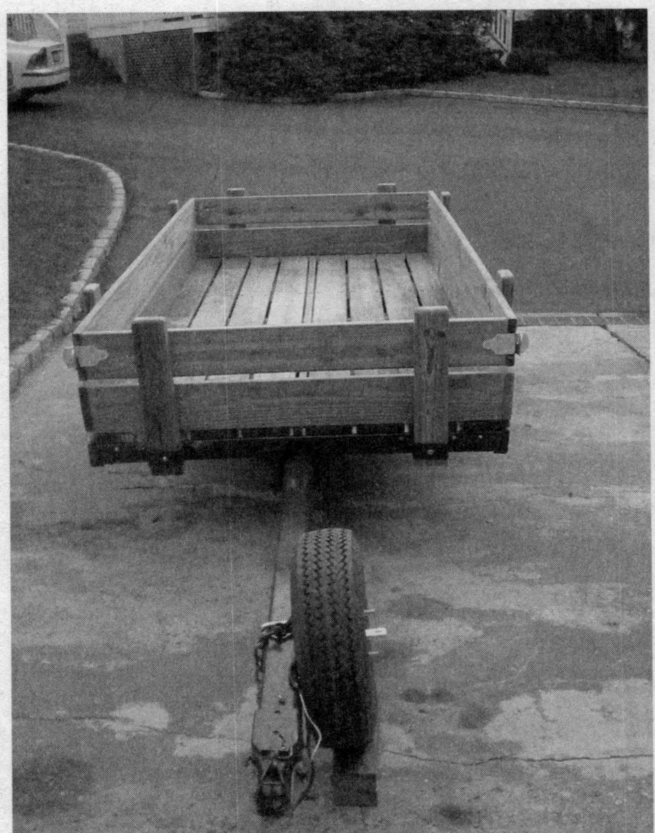

Archer's equipment trailer; take a spare tire wherever you go.

# How to Build a False Rub to Attract Bucks

Many years ago, I accidentally discovered how making a fake buck rub on a tree can attract both resident and transient bucks post-haste—especially during the big chase period.

It happened in early November of 1986, when I discovered the haunts of a solid 135-class 10-point buck. I was hunting on public ground, so other hunters were using the area as well. Every morning, two noisy bowhunters would tramp down the trail, talking and cracking limbs, as they walked to their respective stands. I could hear them coming from the moment they slammed the truck door until they passed my location.

One morning, they actually arrived earlier than I and one of them caught sight of me as I was leaving the main trail and moving into the woods. They must have thought that's where my stand was located. (Actually, I had stopped to pee.)

It was my third year as host of my television show, *Woods 'N' Water,* and I was viewed as something of a local celebrity at the time—which often meant added competition in the places I hunted. The two nodded and continued on their way, but not before mentioning that they had seen "some good bucks" in the area I was heading to. They had been planning on hunting that area, they said, but would go someplace else that day.

I knew they were fibbing because my spot was another 200 yards down the trail. The times they has been in the woods when I was, I'd heard them walk past me and continue along for at least 100 yards before I couldn't hear them anymore. I had to come up with a game plan that would prevent those guys from finding my spot.

That night, I fell asleep thinking about how I could distract them into hunting another spot long before they got near my stand. Then a light went on! Since I hunted off the left side of the trail, I would make a big rub on the right side, along with several smaller rubs that would make a rub line about 75 yards long. I decided to put the first rub right off the trail and at least 200 yards before the spot where I had entered the woods.

I made the rubs the next day during a time when I knew the two hunters had left the woods, and I must admit those rubs were impressive and realistic looking. The next morning, I waited along the trail hidden in some brush. As the duo came down the trail, I saw them stop and heard them get all excited about the first rub. When they spotted the second rub, which was about 30 yards from the first, one of them instantly took off in that direction. The other quickly walked back the way he'd come, and I suspect he set up not far away as well. I almost laughed out loud, and it took all my willpower to hold it in.

"What a freakin' genius I am," I whispered to myself, and then quickly made my way to my stand.

I didn't see the buck that morning, so about 10 a.m. I decided I'd go get some coffee and return to hunt around 1 p.m. I was walking down the trail when my heart skipped a beat. There on the trail were the bow hunters, resting. Attached to a deer drag was "my" 10-point buck!

The first knucklehead spoke to me—and I am paraphrasing here, but until this day I remember most of what he said:

"How the hell did a guy like you miss those rubs along the trail this morning? You're supposed to be a big deer hunter—you must have come in half asleep! We almost didn't go out this morning. I'm glad we did, though, because on the way in I spotted a really fresh rub off the trail that led to a rub line and I set up about 50 yards off the trail, figuring the buck that made them would show up again. About 9 a.m. this bad boy came walking in, freshening up each rub as he passed it. When he got to my rub, I drew back and let 'er fly."

The second knucklehead then chimed in, "Not a bad morning's hunt—huh?"

"No, not at all," I said. Then I congratulated Mr. Knucklehead and offered to help them drag the buck out—which, thankfully, they declined.

I continued cursing myself out with cuss words that hadn't been invented yet, asking myself one important question: "*Who's really the knucklehead, knucklehead?*"

On the drive home, (note: I didn't have the ambition to return to the area to go hunting that afternoon), it finally hit me. The false rubs had actually attracted that buck! "*You jerk,*" I thought. (I don't want to repeat what I really called myself.) "*You created an ass-kicking, buck-killing tactic that worked for the guys you were trying to deceive! How's that for turn-around-is-fair-play,*" I mused. Oh well, as the old adage goes, "payback is a bitch."

From that day on, I swore I would share each and every tactic I ever created, used, thought of, or read about with any and all deer hunters who cared to listen. Now, are you ready to learn how to use this mock-rub tactic to bag your next buck? You should be.

I have been using this tactic successfully since 1986. While, like other deer hunting strategies I use, it doesn't work every time, it works enough times to make it worthwhile.

## RUBS: VISUAL & OLFACTORY SIGNPOSTS

Let's take a serious look at what a rub actually means to a buck. Most hunters know a rub can indicate a buck's travel route. Let's say you're hunting near the top of a ridge and above you is the bedding area. Below you are feeding sources like corn or soybean fields, apple orchards, acorn crops, etc. While you are walking up to the ridge, you spot a rub facing you. If you walk beyond that rub, turn around, face down the ridge and look carefully about 30 to 50 yards to either side of the rub you first found, you will see more rubs facing you.

You have just discovered the morning and evening travel routes of a buck moving between his bedding and feeding areas. This may seem insignificant, but the sign helps hunters to set up a stand based on the time of day or evening that the buck is actually using one trail or the other. So you now can maximize your time afield by not hunting a spot that a buck will not be using that time of the day.

This is just a minor point when it comes to rubs. A rub is a very important social signpost to both the local bucks and, equally important, to transient bucks who enter areas outside their home turf. Rubs are used by ALL bucks that come from the same area to express their social status and current rutting condition.

A buck rub is a visual and olfactory sign post to other deer. By depositing several of his individual odors against the bark of the tree his is leaving a very specific mes sage. The combination of odors tell other deer exactly who the buck was, how long ago he visited the rub, how old he is and the status of his present rut condition is. Courtesy Ted Rose.

Despite what some hunters think, within a given herd there is not a single dominant buck. *Dominance* (in the true sense of the word) is not part of the white-tailed deer's behavior. The term is only used to hype products and get hunters to believe that certain deer scents, calls, and other gimmicks should be used if they want to kill a "dominant buck." This often leads some veteran hunters and a lot of novices down a path that distorts the real facts about whitetail behavior.

Real *dominance* is seen in the large cats and canines of Africa; wolves and coyotes of North America, and other animals that specifically delineate a territorial boundary. They use urine to warn others of their species not to trespass. If the area is infringed upon, the interloper will find itself in a fight for its very life.

Whitetails simply don't fight to the death when transient bucks enter their territory. Nor do they protect a specific area with urine to warn other bucks away. Therefore, dominance is not part of the white-tail's lifestyle—at least, not as it is hyped.

Every buck within a given herd knows his place in the pecking order long before the rut. While they are in velvet, bucks use body language to establish what step of the ladder each occupies in their world. That way, by the time the rut comes around they are able to avoid serious fights that could injure or possibly even kill them. It is very rare for bucks to kill each other unless the buck-to-doe population is seriously out of kilter and there are many more bucks than does. This simply doesn't happen often in the wild.

An individual buck uses a wide variety of visual, aural, and olfactory signs to communicate (and I use that word loosely) with other bucks and does in his territory, including his glands, saliva, urine, defecation, antlers, body language, vocalizations, body size and position in the pecking order. Each gland releases specific odors that "say" to another buck, "Hey I'm Joe. Any other buck smelling this rub (or scrape, urine, scat, etc.) will detect by these odors that I rank among the top of the pecking order."

Each and every buck that approaches an existing rub, or is ready to make a fresh rub, does the exact same things each time: he either approaches the existing rub or the tree he is about to make a rub on or stops about five feet from it.

Then the buck squats and urinates.

While urinating, the buck squats slightly further down, putting (I believe) added pressure on a gland in the penis called the *pre-pucial* gland. The secretions from the gland help to lubricate the penal sheath and release pheromones that tell other bucks and does the status of the buck's present rutting condition. This is an important part of the rubbing sequence.

Next, the buck approaches the rub or the tree he is about to rub and he sniffs it carefully several times before doing anything else.

The buck then licks the rub, or the back of the tree he is about to rub, several times in order to deposit scent from a gland called the *vomeronasal organ*, located in the roof of his mouth. This organ is used primarily to analyze the status of an estrus doe as her urine scent flows past it when the buck lip curls (called the *flehmen gesture*). It is also used to analyze the rut status of other bucks.

When making a rub, however, the buck is leaving scent from his vomeronasal organ to express his current rutting status. At the same time, he is leaving scent from his salivary glands. These glands contain enzymes that primarily aid in the digestion of foods. When saliva is deposited on a rub, the enzymes also let other bucks in his herd know exactly which buck left it and his exact rutting status. A buck will also leave saliva on overhanging branches above a scrape that he is making or one that he may be refreshing that was made by another buck. (Yes, bucks do use scrapes of other bucks and some does will, too). A buck will use the same saliva scent when making or refreshing a licking stick as well.

His next move will be to rub his forehead glands (located between the top of the eyes and the antlers) on the tree. These glands, which are most active during the rut, are vitally important when deer rub trees. Biologists have substantiated that there is a correlation between the buck's age, social status (his position in the pecking order), and these glands. They seem to be most pungent and active in mature, high-ranking bucks. (Note: I did not use the "D" word—*dominant*) The glands produce an oily substance that makes the hair around them dark and, in some cases, black. When the buck is rubbing a tree, the oil is transferred to the rub. It is also deposited on overhanging branches. Some experts believe that the scent from the forehead gland also helps to attract does to a buck's rub or scrape. I can tell you this for sure: I know when I make a fake rub and use real or synthetic forehead gland scent, I will often see does visit the rub.

I cannot overemphasize that all the scents a buck deposits on the rub, in a scrape, or on an overhanging branch help to announce his social status and current rut condition to other bucks within his herd and even to the "dreaded" transient buck.

If you are still unsure that making a mock rub will work, consider this point: Deer survive within their daily environment (especially during the hunting season) not through the power of intelligence, or accumulated learning abilities stored to memory. They survive entirely by their keen instinctive and olfactory abilities. Period. End of story. A deer comes to a call not because it understands anything else, but because its instinct tells it that the sound is coming from another deer. It investigates a decoy not because the brain says, "Hey, that is a deer I just have to check out," but rather because its instinct forces it to investigate it . . . if all else is right with its nose.

Deer react to visual stimulation much more than hunters like to believe, and will often be instinctively forced to investigate something when they really shouldn't. Therefore, a mock rub acts on this instinctive behavior. The buck is drawn to it because his instinct tells him that it is natural and should be immediately investigated. When a buck-be it a spike or trophy-class animal-sees a freshly made rub, it has no choice but to investigate it. All its natural instincts are telling it how to behave, as long as it doesn't pick up any danger signal (like human odor) while doing so.

Not many tactics work on so many of a deer's instincts at one time as a false rub does. The buck can see the highly visual object from quite a distance as he meanders through the area, and he instantly recognizes it as a signpost to deposit his scent and calling card in order to communicate his presence and status to other bucks. This fresh, new rub demands the buck's attention. Instinctively, he thinks it was made by another competitive buck—one that is, perhaps, still in the area making rubs and scrapes.

In addition, as I mentioned above, the rub will contain a combination of odors that the buck can detect from a distance as well—sometimes long before he even sees the rub. Again, these olfactory cues play on the buck's instincts to check the rub out as soon as possible.

By now you're saying, "Alright already—tell me how I make a false rub!" So, ok. Here we go:

The key to making a false rub is to find a natural rub that was made recently (earlier that season). Then go about 30 to 50 yards from it and select a tree that is similar in circumference and height to make your mock rub. Why? Well, that is going to take a bit of explaining. Your mock rub must look and smell natural to attract a buck—that is the fact of the matter. It must NOT suggest to a buck, no matter how large its antlers are, that the rub was made by a bigger, more aggressive buck within the area. (Please note: once again, I did not use the "D" word.)

As I have said, bucks establish the pecking order within their herd long before they shed the velvet from their antlers. They know who is sitting at the top of the social ladder and who is on the lowest rung. Pushing and shoving matches and even some more serious fighting only occur between rivals in the group that are closely matched in body weight, antler size, and age. Therefore, a two-and-a-half-year-old buck will seldom pick a fight with a four-and-a-half-year-old or older buck—especially one he knows from his group. Instinct tells him the fight is hopeless and he avoids the conflict instead of risking injury.

I often tell people at my seminars that if they want to use deer calls, they should NOT use them loudly or aggressively. It just isn't natural. Hunters who use calls that are sold as "dominant" or "aggressive" grunts, snort wheezes, or barks and roars are kidding themselves and are being sold a bunch of hype.

What? You don't agree? Then ask yourself these questions: In all the years that you have hunted, isn't it true that 99.999999 percent of the grunts you have heard are low, guttural sounds? Did you ever hear a roar, or a bark, or a loud, piercing grunt? I'm going to bet that you probably haven't. And for those of you who think you have, consider this: If such loud, aggressive barks, roars, and overly audible grunts were made by bucks, then all of us would be hearing them throughout the woods. However, we're not, are we? Instead, an overwhelming majority of the grunts detected by hunters are barely audible until the buck is close by. Even then, they can be so low-pitched that a hunter may miss them.

The fact is that a buck will avoid another aggressive buck about 95 percent of the time. Most potential "fights" are simply and quickly settled with aggressive displays of body language. If you want to be consistently successful when using deer calls, rattling antlers or decoys, don't try to be the biggest bad-boy on the block. Instead, make sounds that other bucks instinctively find attractive because they hear them as "beatable" opponents.

Still having trouble believing what I'm saying? Then follow this analogy: I grew up boxing. I boxed in the Police Athlete League (PAL) in the army and in more than my share of street fights in Brooklyn, New York. I can take care of myself when it comes to using my fists. But under normal conditions, I wouldn't fight with someone who is bigger, appears stronger, or displays more aggressive body language.

Why? Survival instinct dictates that I avoid the fight. So I show some sign to the larger, more aggressive opponent that I want to back off. I dart my eyes toward the ground or make some other physical gesture that indicates I'm looking for a way out of the fight. In other words, I acknowledge his strength and communicate that I'm not looking to get a butt whipping—a message I want to send quickly and clearly to my would-be opponent. If he doesn't back off, then my "fight or flight" response kicks in. In most cases when facing a larger, more physically fit opponent, people and animals will choose the latter.

A rub gives off signals in much the same way. Its mere presence (and odor) tells another buck about the potential size and status of the buck that made it. Therefore, when a buck sees a rub that is substantially larger than the surrounding rubs, he is immediately put off by its size and becomes instantly cautious. He will avoid it rather than approach it. Trust me on this point.

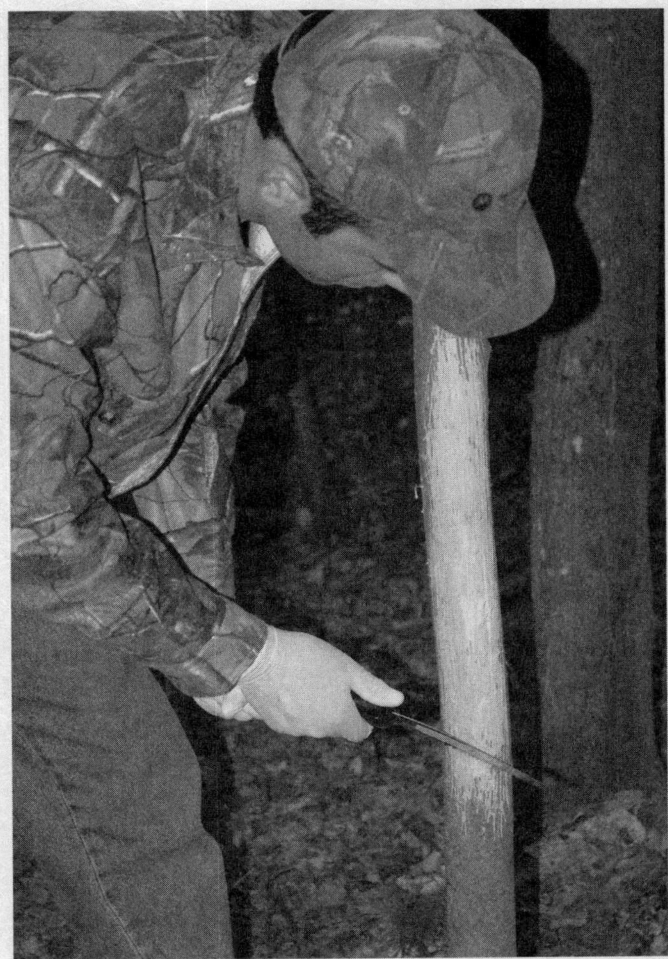

When creating mock-rub reduce human scent by wearing surgeon gloves and rubber boots. Make the fake rub within 30 yards of a natural rub. Allow the shavings to hang from the false rub.

Rubs on large diameter trees are often rubbed by several different bucks of different ages. The gouge mark at the top left suggests at least one buck had a full rack with long tines, one of which probably made the deep gouge.

To make a natural looking mock-rub—one that won't spook a deer's sense of smell or vision—you will need the following items:

- A bottle of pure buck urine
- A bottle of All-Season Deer Lure (a combination of hide and body odors of deer)
- A bottle of interdigital scent (although you will only use one single drop of it at the site of your mock rub)
- A bottle of forehead gland and tarsal scent (Buck Fever Synthetics makes a scent that combines both odors.)

You will also need a pair of thin latex gloves (like the ones doctors wear), and several large bore-cleaning patches (placed in a small plastic zip-top bag). Lastly, you will need a small, easy-to-carry tape measure, essential for helping you make your fake rub more realistic.

The soles of your boots (rubber or leather) should be clean and free of foreign odors. Wash them with non-scented soap the evening before making a mock rub and apply a drop of interdigital scent on each boot sole. Of course, your clothes and body should be as scent free as you can make them.

When you have located a natural rub, find another tree that is equal in circumference and height. Measure the natural rub from where it begins at the lower end of the tree to where it ends at the upper part. No matter what size it is, you should make your mock rub about three inches smaller. You don't want it to look like it was made by King-Kong, right? You want it to suggest it was made by a buck that is easily intimidated, which is the key to all calling, rattling and decoying tactics—yes?

Once you select a tree on which to make your mock-rub, use one small-to-average natural antler that has at least four tines on it. Begin to shred the bark with an aggressive up and down motion on the same side of the tree that the natural rub you found is showing. Make sure you don't remove any peeling bark. Let it hang or fall naturally while you are rubbing the antlers on the tree.

This process can be done with a small handsaw, as long as the saw's teeth are fine and not large. (A saw with large teeth will not scrape the bark away like a deer's antlers would, and the rub will look unnatural.) But I prefer to use a small natural shed antler (mine is probably 10 years old) because I feel it leaves a realistic look and still provides some type of bone scent on the rub as well.

Remember, do not rub all around the trunk of the tree—just one side. When you think your mock rub is finished, step back and see if it compares to the natural rub you are trying to duplicate. If so, go to the next step. (If not, get it right before going on.)

Take your antler (if you're using a saw to make the rub, you'll need a nail-punch to replace the tine of the antler) and press a single point of a tine into the trunk of the tree. Just create a small dent in a few places high and low within the rub and a few in the bark of the tree above the rub. This duplicates the penetration made by the tips of the tines on the rack of a buck (big or small) as he rubs a tree. As I have said about all my deer-hunting tactics, once you are committed to using the tactic, always make a concerted effort to create the ENTIRE illusion.

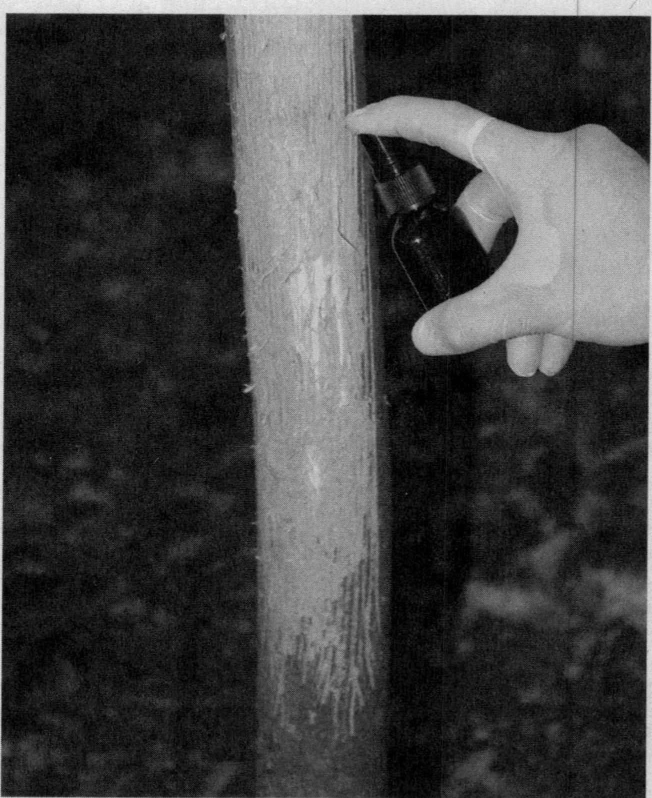

Add a tiny amount of forehead or preorbital scent on the tree. Then place a few drops of buck urine mixed with tarsal scent on the ground. By adding scent to your mock rub this will help "create the entire illusion."

Before doing anything else, measure the size of your rub and write it down on paper. Do not try to record the size to memory. I will explain why soon.

Now, take some forehead scent and place several drops onto a fresh bore-cleaning patch. Rub the patch and scent along the entire portion of the rub. Put a few drops of All-Season Deer Lure on another clean patch and dab it along the sides of the rub. At the base of the tree squirt several drops of pure buck urine and a SINGLE DROP of interdigital scent. Those of you who think more than one drop will work better will find out it won't—the hard way. (All deer avoid excess odors of interdigital.) Then put down a couple of drops of tarsal scent around the tree—two drops will do nicely; more won't.

Walk back from your mock rub about 10 yards and put down about 10 to 15 drops or a few good squirts worth of the straight buck urine on the forest floor. Make it spray in several directions, like a buck would—but not all over the place. A doe urinates in a single spot. A buck dangles while urinating. (You know what I mean. You don't always hit the bowl, do you?) "Create the entire illusion."

When you have completed your mock rub, waste no time in setting up your treestand or ground blind, and then wait. The first buck to happen through the area will see and smell the rub and he will have no freakin' choice but to instinctively head to it to check it out. Unless he catches wind of you, sees you or hears you, he will go toward the mock rub, stop, stare at it, smell the buck urine, and then urinate over it or close by it and move to the rub. He will go through all the traditional sniffing, licking, and rubbing motions to try and discover the buck that made the rub, and to let him know who made the new rub.

I want to be perfectly clear here. The tactic doesn't work all the time—but it does work often enough to be high on my list of strategies to use. My records also indicate the most successful dates for making false rubs are from October 31 through November 13. But I have had success with this tactic through the third week of November and, occasionally, during the post rut of December. Like all tactics, it has its moments of huge success and days of no response at all. You can use deer calls, like a soft grunt or an estrus doe blat, to bring a buck in to where he may see your mock rub. Rattling also works, but not as often as deer calls do.

But no matter what you decide to use: just an ambush, deer calls, rattling, or a combination, when this strategy works your heart will pound out of your chest, I promise you that!

After two or three days of not seeing a buck, it is time to reevaluate the spot. Here is where your tape measure comes in and the measurement you jotted down on paper. (You did jot it down, right?) After three days without anything happening, measure your rub. If it is the same length you made it—what was that number again? Wait, let me check my paper . . . oh 13 1/2 inches—and it is still that size, it is time to move on and try the tactic someplace else. It will eventually work.

If your 13 1/2-inch rub has turned into 15 1/2 inches, you will know without question that the rub was indeed visited—but just not when you were there. You can spend another day over it (I would hunt it from 10 a.m. to 2 p.m. if you have been hunting it in the mornings and evenings). If it doesn't produce then, move on to another location at least 200 yards away.

While this tactic has proven to work best by creating all the elements I mentioned above, you could improvise if need be. I have made mock rubs when I came across a really large, fresh rub and made them with nothing more than my handsaw and some buck urine, and I have had reasonable response.

So there you have it—one of my better and more successful strategies.

After making a mock rub, measure the exact length and write it down. The next time you hunt near the rub, measure it again. If it is larger, a buck visited your mock rub when you weren't there. A trail camera will provide the exact time the buck visited the rub— don't be surprised if it was between 10 am and 1 pm!

# Part 8

# *Contributors and Their Works*

All short stories, articles, recipes, and other works appearing in this compendium have been reprinted courtesy of the authors listed below. To buy any of their books, go to the websites indicated.

### Steve Bartylla (http://www.amazon.com/Steve-Bartylla)

Bowhunting Tactics That Deliver Trophies*

### Hal Blood (bigwoodsbucks.com)

Hunting Big Woods Bucks

### Monte Burch (monteburch.com)

Backyard Structures and How to Build Them
Black Bass Basics
Building Small Barns, Sheds & Shelters
Cleaning and Preparing Gamefish
Country Crafts and Skills
Denny Brauer's Jig Fishing Secrets
Field Dressing and Butchering Upland Birds,Waterfowl and Wild Turkeys
Lohman Guide to Calling & Decoying Waterfowl
Lohman Guide to Successful Turkey Calling
Making Native American Hunting, Fighting and Survival Tools
Mounting Your Deer Head at Home
Monte Burch's Pole Building Projects
Pocket Guide to Bowhunting Whitetail Deer*
Pocket Guide to Field Dressing, Butchering & Cooking Deer*
Pocket Guide to Old Time Catfish Techniques*
Pocket Guide to Seasonal Largemouth Bass Patterns*
Pocket Guide to Seasonal Walleye Tactic*s
Pocket Guide to Spring and Fall Turkey Hunting*
Solving Squirrel Problems
The Complete Guide to Sausage Making*
The Complete Jerky Book*
The Hunting and Fishing Camp Builder's Guide*
The Joy of Smoking and Salt Curing*
The Ultimate Guide to Growing Your Own Food*
The Ultimate Guide to Making Outdoor Gear and Accessories
The Ultimate Guide to Skinning and Tanning

### Jay Cassell (http://www.amazon.com/s/ref=ntt_athr_dp_sr_1?_encoding=UTF8&field-author=Jay%20Cassell&ie=UTF8&search-alias=books&sort=relevancerank)

North America's Greatest Big Game Lodges & Outfitters: More Than 250 Prime Destinations in the U.S. & Canada
North America's Greatest Whitetail Lodges & Outfitters: More Than 250 Prime Destinations in the U.S. & Canada (with Peter Fiduccia)
Shooter's Bible: The World's Bestselling Firearms Reference*
The Best Hunting Stories Ever Told*
The Gigantic Book of Hunting Stories*
The Little Red Book of Hunter's Wisdom (with Peter Fiduccia)*
The Quotable Hunter

The Ultimate Guide to Fishing Skills, Tactics, and Techniques *
The Ultimate Guide to Deer Hunting Skills, Tactics, and Techniques*
The Ultimate Guide to Hunting Skills, Tactics, and Techniques*
The Ultimate Guide to Self-Reliant Living

## Richard P. Combs (http://www.amazon.com/ Richard-Combs/e/B001KMGYQQ/ref=sr_ntt_srch_lnk_1?qid=1341340136&sr=1-1)

Canoeing and Kayaking Ohio's Streams: An Access Guide for Paddlers and Anglers

Guide to Advanced Turkey Hunting: How to Call and Decoy Even Wary Boss Gobblers into Range*

Turkey Hunting Tactics of the Pros: Expert Advice to Help You Get a Gobbler This Season

## Judd Cooney (http://www.juddcooney.com/)

Sensible Bowhunter

Advanced Scouting for Whitetails

Decoying Big Game: Successful Tactics for Luring Deer, Elk, Bears, and Other Animals into Range

How to Attract Whitetails

The Bowhunter's Field Manual

## Chris Dubbs and Dave Herberle (http://www.amazon.com/Chris-Dubbs)

Smoking Food: A Beginner's Guide*

## Fred Eichler ((http://www.amazon.com/Fred-Eichler)

Bowhunting Western Big Game*

## Kathy Etling (www.amazon.com/Kathy-Etling/e/ B001K8D1XE)

Bowhunting's Superbucks: How Some of the Biggest Bucks in North America Were Taken*

Cougar Attacks: Encounters of the Worst Kind

Denise Parker: A Teenage Archer's Quest for Olympic Glory

Hunting Bears: Black, Brown, Grizzly and Polar Bears

Hunting Superbucks: How to Find and Hunt Today's Trophy Mule and Whitetail Deer*

The Art of Whitetail Deception*

The Quotable Cowboy

The Ultimate Guide to Calling, Rattling, and Decoying Whitetails*

Thrill of the Chase

## J. Wayne Fears (http://www.jwaynefears.com/)

Backcountry Cooking

How to Build Your Dream Cabin in the Woods: The Ultimate Guide to Building and Maintaining a Backcountry Getaway*

Hunting Club Guide

Hunting North America's Big Bear: Grizzly, Brown, and Polar Bear Hunting Techniques and Adventures

Hunting Whitetails East & West (with Larry Weishuhn)

Scrape Hunting from A to Z

The Complete Book of Dutch Oven Cooking*

The Field & Stream Wilderness Cooking Handbook: How to Prepare, Cook, and Serve Backcountry Meals

The Pocket Outdoor Survival Guide: The Ultimate Guide for Short-Term Survival*

## Kate Fiduccia (www.amazon.com/Kate-Fiduccia/e/ B001K8AD58)

Cabin Cooking from Campfire to Cast-Iron Skillet

Cooking Wild in Kate's Camp

Cooking Wild in Kate's Kitchen: Venison

Grillin' and Chili'n: Eighty Easy Recipes for Venison to Sizzle, Smoke, and Simmer

The Jerky Bible

The Quotable Wine Lover

The Venison Cookbook: Venison Dishes from Fast to Fancy*

## Peter Fiduccia (http://www.woodsnwater.tv)

101 Deer Hunting Tips: Practical Advice from a Master Hunter

North America's Greatest Whitetail Lodges & Outfitters: More Than 250 Prime Destinations in the U.S. & Canada (with Jay Cassell)

The Little Red Book of Hunter's Wisdom (with Jay Cassell)

Whitetail Strategies: A No-Nonsense Approach to Successful Deer Hunting

Whitetail Strategies: The Ultimate Guide

Whitetail Strategies, Vol. II: Straightforward Tactics for Tracking, Calling, the Rut, and Much More

Shooter's Bible Guide to Planting Food Plots

Shooter's Bible Guide to Whitetail Strategies

Do-It-Yourself Projects for Bowhunters (with Lee Somma)

Little Red Book of Hunter's Wisdom (with Jay Cassell)

## Tom Indrebo (http://www.amazon.com/Tom-Indrebo/e/B002EID7K6)

Growing & Hunting Quality Bucks: A Hands-On Approach to Better Land and Deer Management*

## Dr. Todd A. Kuhn (http://www.amazon.com/ Shooters-Bible-Guide-Bowhunting-Todd/ dp/1620878127/ref=sr_1_1?s=books&ie=UTF8&qid=1404409989&sr=1-1)

The Shooter's Bible Guide to Bowhunting*

## Jeff Murray (http://www.amazon.com/Jeff-Murray/e/B001K8Z7UO/ref=sr_tc_2_0?qid=1404409535&sr=1-2-ent)

For Big Bucks Only

Moon Phase Deer Hunting

Moon Struck: Hunting Strategies that Revolve Around the Moon

## Rick Sapp (http://www.amazon.com/Rick-Sapp)

The Bowhunter's Digest*

The Complete Bowhunting Journal*

The Ultimate Guide to Traditional Archery*

The Gun Digest Book of Firearms, Fakes and Reproductions

The Gun Digest Book of Trap and Skeet Shooting

The Gun Digest Book of Sporting Clays

The Gun Digest Book of Green Shooting: A Practical Guide to Non-Toxic Hunting and Recreation

Reloading for Shotgunners

## Leo Somma (http://www.amazon.com/s/ref=dp_byline_sr_book_2?ie=UTF8&field-

## author=Leo+Somma&search-alias=books&text=Leo+Somma&sort=relevancerank)

25 Projects for Outdoorsmen: Quick and Easy Plans for the Deer Camp, Home, Woods, and Backyard

Do-It-Yourself Projects for Bowhunters

## John Trout, Jr. (www.amazon.com/John-Trout/e/ B001JP29BI)

Ambushing Trophy Whitetails: Tactical Systems for Big-Buck Success

Finding Wounded Deer

Hunting Rutting Bucks: Secrets for Tagging the Biggest Buck of Your Life

Solving Coyote Problems: How to Coexist with North America's Most Persistent Predator

The Complete Book of Wild Turkey Hunting

## John Weiss (http://www.amazon.com/John-Weiss/e/B001HMQ12Q)

Advanced Deerhunter's Bible

Planting Food Plots for Deer and Other Wildlife

Sure-Fire Whitetail Tactics

The Bass Angler's Almanac: More Than 750 Tips & Tactics

The Whitetail Deer Hunter's Almanac

The Ultimate Guide to Butchering Deer: A Step-by-Step Guide to Field Dressing, Skinning, Aging, and Butchering Deer*

Camp Florida: A Comprehensive Guide to Hundreds of Camps

Standard Catalog of Colt Firearms

Archery

*A Skyhorse publication

## ALSO AVAILABLE

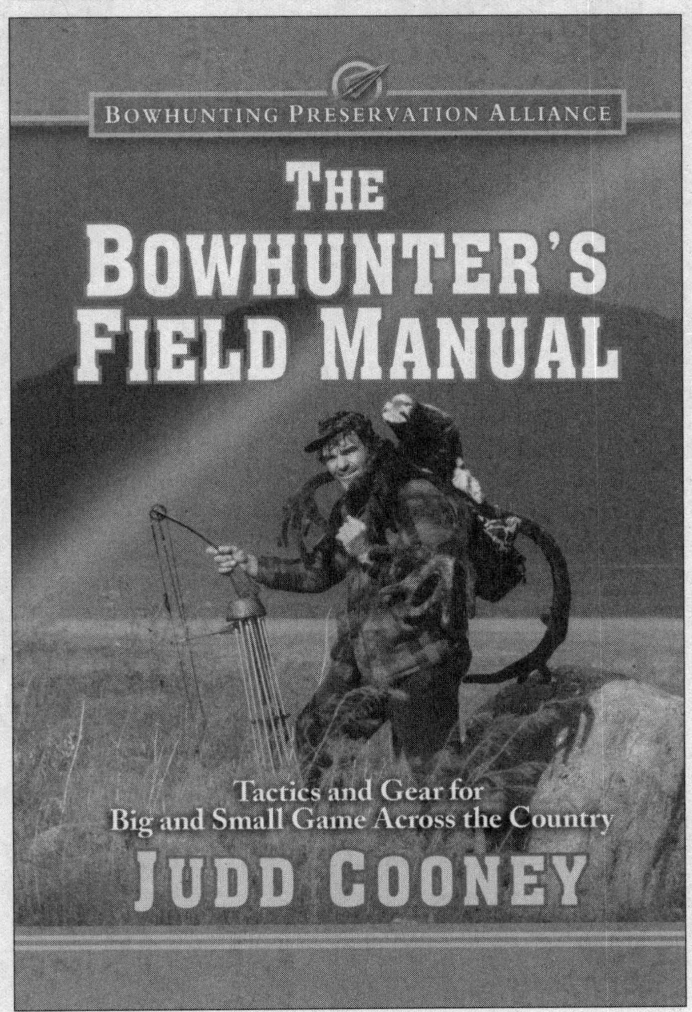


## The Bowhunter's Field Manual

*by Judd Cooney*

Drawing on his years of experience, Judd Cooney—one of America's most prominent outdoor writers and photographers—offers practical information on bowhunting big and small game across North America. With Cooney's own practical field experience of over fifty years, you'll find useful suggestions on gear, tatics, and much more.

With crisp, honest, understandable language, this invaluable reference will teach everything a bowhunter needs to know when he sets out. With the multitude of game that Cooney discusses, this guide is the ideal package. In the words of M. R. James, author of the book's foreword, it's "good reading and generous information offered by an outdoorsman who has lived the words he chooses to share."

$19.95 ISBN 978-1-62087-692-3

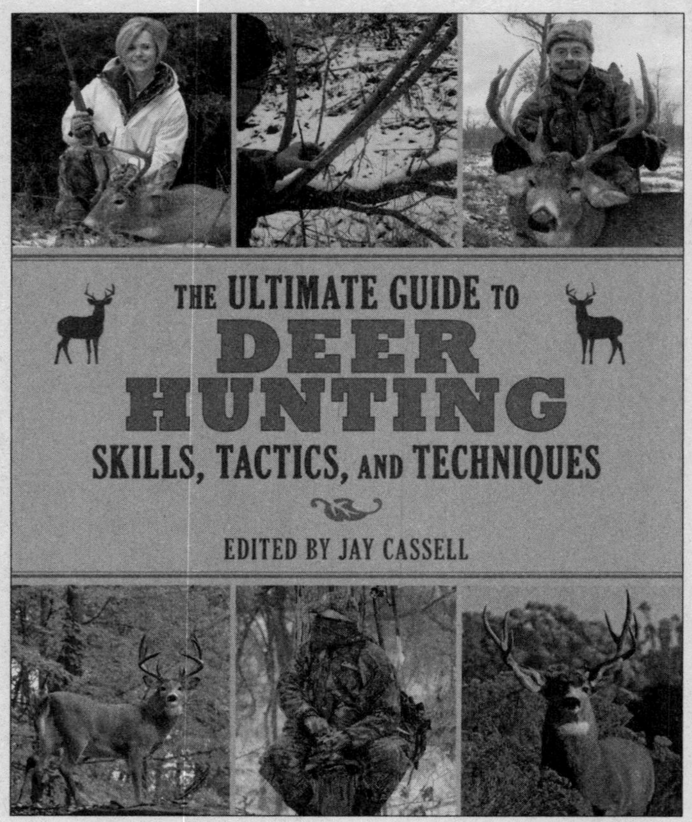


## The Ultimate Guide to Deer Hunting
**Skills, Tactics, and Techniques**

*Edited by Jay Cassell*

With hunting advice from a wide variety of experts, including Peter Fiduccia, Dave Henderson, J. Wayne Fears, John Weiss, and Monte Burch, *The Ultimate Guide to Deer Hunting Skills, Tactics, and Techniques* really drills down and examines every major tactic—from rattling to driving to stalking and more. Rifle hunting is the major focus in this compendium, but there is also a wealth of information on bowhunting and muzzleloader hunting.

As a bonus, there is also a chapter devoted entirely to venison recipes with step-by-step instructions for cooking stews, chili, roasts, steaks, burgers, and more.

$24.95 ISBN 978-1-62914-464-1

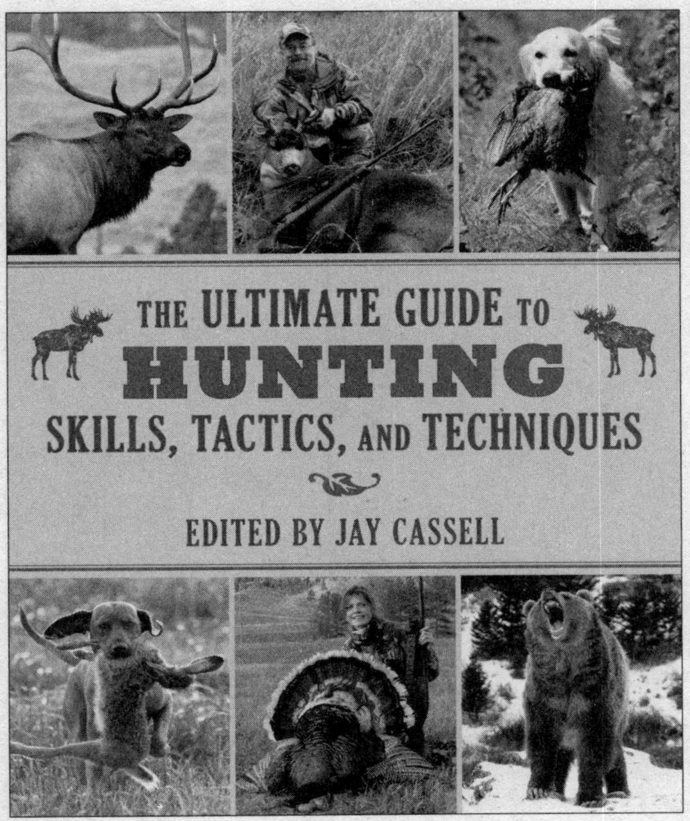


## The Ultimate Guide to Hunting

**Skills, Tactics, and Techniques**

*Edited by Jay Cassell*

With hunting advice from a wide variety of experts, including Peter Fiduccia, Dave Henderson, Hal Blood, Ron Spomer, Kathy Etling, Rick Sapp, and Rich Combs, *The Ultimate Guide to Hunting Skills, Tactics, and Techniques* profiles all of the major game species and reveals pro secrets on how to successfully hunt them. There is no collection of hunting knowledge available elsewhere to feature more tips, techniques, and tactics than this completely comprehensive compendium.

This book is the perfect gift for a longtime hunter who wants the widest selection of information available, or for the enthusiastic beginning hunter looking to learn as much as possible about the exhilarating sport. This is a must-have for every hunter's library.

$24.95 ISBN 978-1-61608-879-8

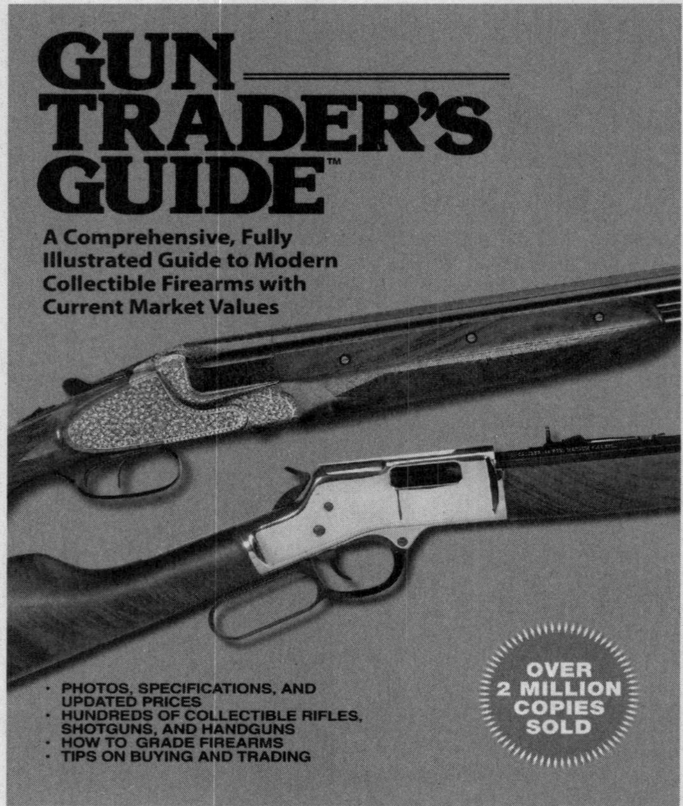


## Gun Trader's Guide
### 37th Edition

*Edited by Robert A. Sadowski*

The one-stop guide to buying collectible firearms, with more than two million copies sold!

If you are seeking a comprehensive reference for collectible gun values, the *Gun Trader's Guide* is the only book you need. For more than half a century, this guide has been the standard reference for collectors, curators, dealers, shooters, and gun enthusiasts. Updated annually, it remains the definitive source for making informed decisions on used firearms purchases.

This thirty-seventh edition boasts dozens of new entries. It also includes a complete index and a guide on how to properly and effectively use this book in order to find the market value for your collectible modern firearm. With new introductory materials that every gun collector and potential buyer should read, no matter what kind of modern firearm you own or collect, the *Gun Trader's Guide* should remain close at hand.

$29.99 ISBN 978-1-63450-459-1

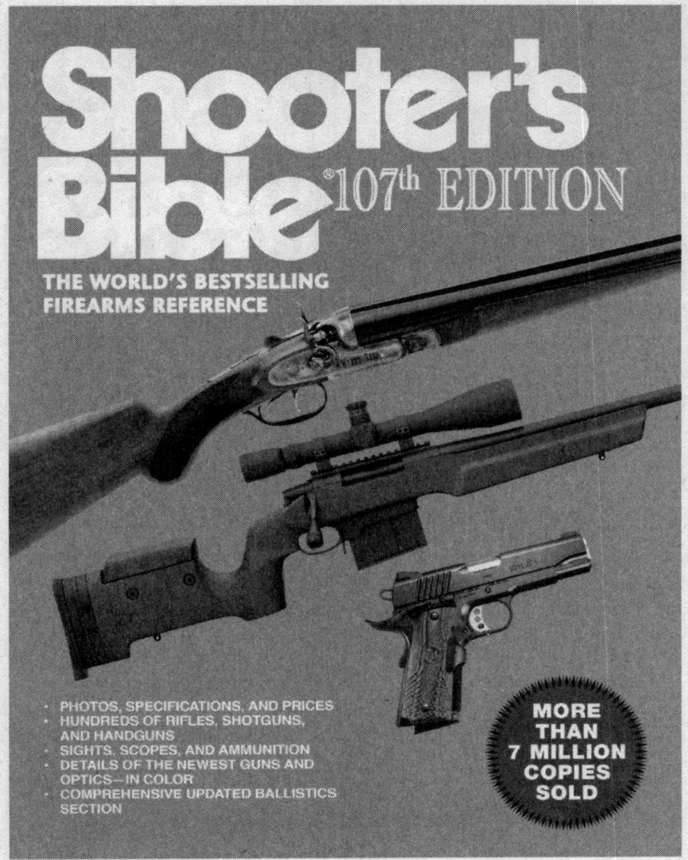


## Shooter's Bible
### 107th Edition
*Edited by Jay Cassell*

The world's bestselling firearms reference! Published annually for more than eighty years and with more than seven million copies sold, this is the must-have reference book for gun collectors and firearm enthusiasts of all ages.

The 107th edition also contains new and existing product sections on ammunition, optics, and accessories, plus updated handgun and rifle ballistic tables along with extensive charts of currently available bullets and projectiles for handloading.

With a timely feature on the newest products on the market, and complete with color and black-and-white photographs, the *Shooter's Bible* is an essential authority for any beginner or experienced hunter, firearm collector, or gun enthusiast.

$29.99 ISBN 978-1-63450-588-8

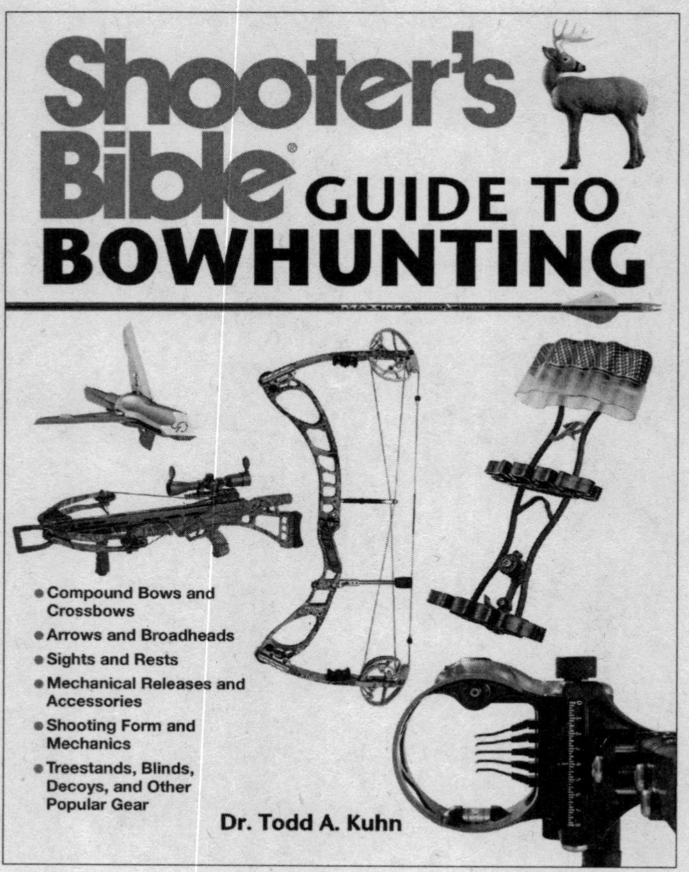


## Shooter's Bible

### Guide to Bowhunting

*by Dr. Todd A Kuhn*

From the most trusted name in guns and ammunition comes this ultimate reference on bowhunting. The *Shooter's Bible Guide to Bowhunting* offers everything you need to know about the sport and its gear, from its origin as a means of survival to modern hunting practices.

This exhaustive desk reference provides a never before seen look into the history and engineering of archery, theories and trends in game discipline, and, of course, an exhaustive catalog of archery equipment both new and traditional.

$19.95 ISBN 978-1-62087-812-5